Odoo 12 Development Cookbook
Third Edition

190+ unique recipes to build effective enterprise and business applications

Parth Gajjar
Alexandre Fayolle
Holger Brunn
Daniel Reis

Pack<t>

BIRMINGHAM - MUMBAI

Odoo 12 Development Cookbook
Third Edition

Commissioning Editor: Aaron Lazar
Acquisition Editor: Alok Dhuri
Content Development Editor: Digvijay Bagul
Technical Editor: Ashi Singh
Copy Editor: Safis Editing
Language Support Editors: Mary McGowan, Storm Mann
Project Coordinator: Prajakta Naik
Proofreader: Safis Editing
Indexer: Manju Arasan
Graphics: Tom Scaria
Production Coordinator: Deepika Naik

First published: April 2016
Second edition: January 2018
Third edition: April 2019

Production reference: 1270419

Published by Packt Publishing Ltd.
Livery Place
35 Livery Street
Birmingham
B3 2PB, UK.

ISBN 978-1-78961-892-1

www.packtpub.com

Mapt

mapt.io

Mapt is an online digital library that gives you full access to over 5,000 books and videos, as well as industry leading tools to help you plan your personal development and advance your career. For more information, please visit our website.

Why subscribe?

- Spend less time learning and more time coding with practical eBooks and Videos from over 4,000 industry professionals

- Improve your learning with Skill Plans built especially for you

- Get a free eBook or video every month

- Mapt is fully searchable

- Copy and paste, print, and bookmark content

Packt.com

Did you know that Packt offers eBook versions of every book published, with PDF and ePub files available? You can upgrade to the eBook version at www.packt.com and as a print book customer, you are entitled to a discount on the eBook copy. Get in touch with us at customercare@packtpub.com for more details.

At www.packt.com, you can also read a collection of free technical articles, sign up for a range of free newsletters, and receive exclusive discounts and offers on Packt books and eBooks.

Contributors

About the author

Parth Gajjar is Application Engineer at Odoo and has been working on Odoo for the past 6 years. For the past year and a half, Parth has been working as a code reviewer at Odoo India. During this time, he has worked in several departments of Odoo, including offshore, migration, and research and development. During his time in research and development, he has developed several key features in Odoo, including the marketing automation module Odoo mobile app (The hybrid JavaScript Part), mobile push notification, Less/CSS editor, Domain Selector widget, and the Qweb report engine prototype. He often gives technical training to Odoo partners. Also, he handes technical interviews at Odoo India.

> *I would like to thank my parents, brother, and wife for all of the support they have given throughout writing this book. I would like to thank again my parents for giving me the freedom and support to follow my ambitions throughout my childhood.*

Previous edition authors

Alexandre Fayolle started working with Linux and free software in the mid 1990s and quickly became interested in the Python programming language. In 2012, he joined Camptocamp to share his expertise on Python, PostgreSQL, and Linux with the team implementing Odoo. He currently manages projects for Camptocamp and is strongly involved in the Odoo Community Association. In his spare time, he likes to play jazz on the vibraphone.

Holger Brunn has been a fervent open source advocate since he came into contact with the open source market sometime in the nineties. He has programmed for ERP and similar systems in different positions since 2001. For the last 10 years, he has dedicated his time to TinyERP, which became OpenERP and evolved into Odoo. Currently, he works at Therp BV in the Netherlands as a developer and is an active member of the Odoo Community Association (OCA).

Daniel Reis has had a long career in the IT industry, mostly as a consultant implementing business applications in variety of sectors, and today works for Securitas, a multinational security services provider. He has been working with Odoo (formerly OpenERP) since 2010, is an active contributor to the Odoo Community Association projects, is currently a member of the board of the Odoo Community Association, and collaborates with ThinkOpen Solutions, a leading Portuguese Odoo integrator.

About the reviewers

Dharmang Soni has master's degree in Information Technology. He loves to do code and has worked with multiple technologies and frameworks, such as ASP.NET, Android (Java), PHP, iOS (Swift), and Odoo. He has more than 6 years' of experience in development of Odoo applications, websites, and mobile applications. He joined the Indian branch of Odoo S.A. (TinyERP Pvt. Ltd.) in 2012, starting his career at Odoo by developing the Odoo mobile framework for the Android. Later, he developed mobile applications for Android and iOS, currently used worldwide. Currently, he is working as an R&D developer at Odoo and works on IoT and the optimization of the screens for mobile.

> *I would like to thank my parents for their love, good advice, and continuous support. I would also like to thank all my friends that I met along the way who enriched my life, for motivating me and helping me progress.*

Kishan Gajjar has a degree in computer engineering. He loves programming and designing. He has expertise in various technologies, including Python, JavaScript, and CSS. He is an employee at the Indian branch of Odoo. He joined Odoo 2 years ago and currently works in the R&D department. At Odoo, he mostly works on website builders, themes, and the backend JavaScript framework.

> *To begin with, I'd like to thank my parents for allowing me to follow my ambitions throughout my childhood, and also my brother, who gives encouragement in his particular way. He has been my inspiration and motivation for me continuing to improve my knowledge and move my career forward.*

Packt is searching for authors like you

If you're interested in becoming an author for Packt, please visit `authors.packtpub.com` and apply today. We have worked with thousands of developers and tech professionals, just like you, to help them share their insight with the global tech community. You can make a general application, apply for a specific hot topic that we are recruiting an author for, or submit your own idea.

Table of Contents

Preface   1

Chapter 1: Installing the Odoo Development Environment   9
Introduction   9
Odoo ecosystem   10
Odoo editions   10
Git repositories   11
Runbot   11
Odoo app store   12
Odoo community association   13
Official Odoo help forum   13
Easy installation of Odoo from a source   13
Getting ready   14
How to do it...   14
How it works...   17
    Virtual environments   17
    PostgreSQL configuration   19
    Git configuration   20
    Downloading the Odoo source code   20
    Starting the instance   21
Managing Odoo environments using the start command   22
Getting ready   22
How to do it...   22
How it works...   23
There's more...   23
Managing Odoo server databases   23
Getting ready   24
How to do it...   24
    Accessing the database management interface   24
    Setting or changing the master password   24
    Creating a new database   26
    Duplicating a database   28
    Removing a database   28
    Backing up a database   29
    Restoring a database backup   30
How it works...   31
There's more...   32
Storing the instance configuration in a file   34
How to do it...   34
How it works...   35
Activating the Odoo developer tools   38

How to do it...   38
How it works...   39
Updating Odoo from source   40
Getting ready   40
How to do it...   40
How it works...   42
Chapter 2: Managing Odoo Server Instances   43
Introduction   43
Configuring the add-ons path   44
Getting ready   44
How to do it...   45
How it works...   45
There's more...   46
Updating the add-on modules list   47
Getting ready   47
How to do it...   47
How it works...   48
Standardizing your instance directory layout   49
How to do it...   49
How it works...   51
See also   52
There's more...   52
Installing and upgrading local add-on modules   53
Getting ready   53
How to do it...   54
From the web interface   54
From the command line   57
How it works...   58
Add-on installation   58
Add-on update   58
There's more...   60
Installing add-on modules from GitHub   60
Getting ready   61
How to do it...   61
How it works...   62
There's more...   62
Applying changes to add-ons   62
Getting ready   62
How to do it...   63
How it works...   63
See also   64
Applying and trying proposed pull requests   64
Getting ready   64
How to do it...   65
How it works...   65

There's more…   65
Chapter 3: Server Deployment   67
Introduction   67
Installing Odoo for production use   67
Getting ready   68
How to do it…   68
How it works…   70
There's more…   70
   Server dimensioning   71
   PostgreSQL tuning   71
   Source code version   73
   Backups   74
Adapting the configuration file for production   75
Getting ready   75
How to do it…   75
How it works…   77
There's more…   79
Setting up Odoo as a system service   80
Getting ready   80
How to do it…   80
How it works…   81
Configuring a reverse proxy and SSL with nginx and Let's Encrypt 81
Getting ready   81
How to do it…   82
How it works…   85
There's more…   87
See also   88
Using Docker to run Odoo   89
Getting ready   89
How to do it…   89
How it works…   90
   Running the Odoo image with a configuration file   90
   Running the Odoo image with custom add-ons   91
   Running multiple Odoo instances   91
There is more…   91
Running Odoo through docker-compose   92
Getting ready   92
How to do it…   92
How it works…   93
There's more…   94
Managing content delivery networks for websites   95
Getting ready   95
How to do it…   95
   Configuring the CDN provider   96

Configuring CDN at Odoo | 98
How it works... | 100
There's more... | 101

Chapter 4: Creating Odoo Add-On Modules | 103
Technical requirements | 103
Introduction | 104
What is an Odoo add-on module? | 104
Creating and installing a new add-on module | 105
Getting ready | 106
How to do it... | 106
How it works... | 107
Completing the add-on module manifest | 108
Getting ready | 108
How to do it... | 108
How it works... | 108
There's more... | 110
Organizing the add-on module file structure | 111
Getting ready | 111
How to do it... | 111
How it works... | 112
Adding models | 113
Getting ready | 114
How to do it... | 114
How it works... | 115
Adding menu items and views | 116
Getting ready | 116
How to do it... | 117
Accessing Odoo as a superuser | 119
How it works... | 120
Adding access security | 122
Getting ready | 122
How to do it... | 123
How it works... | 124
See also | 124
Using the scaffold command to create a module | 124
Getting ready | 125
How to do it... | 125
How it works... | 126

Chapter 5: Application Models | 127
Introduction | 127
Technical requirements | 128
Defining the model representation and order | 128
Getting ready | 128
How to do it... | 129

How it works...   130
There's more...   131
Adding data fields to a model   131
Getting ready   131
How to do it...   132
How it works...   133
There's more...   136
Using a float field with configurable precision   138
Getting ready   138
How to do it...   138
How it works...   140
Adding a monetary field to a model   140
Getting ready   140
How to do it...   140
How it works...   141
Adding relational fields to a model   142
Getting ready   142
How to do it...   142
How it works...   144
There's more...   145
Adding a hierarchy to a model   146
Getting ready   146
How to do it...   147
How it works...   148
There's more...   149
Adding constraint validations to a model   149
Getting ready   150
How to do it...   150
How it works...   151
There's more...   151
Adding computed fields to a model   152
Getting ready   152
How to do it...   152
How it works...   154
Exposing related fields stored in other models   155
Getting ready   155
How to do it...   156
How it works...   156
There's more...   157
Adding dynamic relations using reference fields   157
Getting ready   157
How to do it...   158
How it works...   158
Adding features to a model using inheritance   159
Getting ready   159

How to do it... 160
How it works... 160
There's more... 161
Using abstract models for reusable model features 161
Getting ready 162
How to do it... 162
How it works... 163
There's more... 163
Using delegation inheritance to copy features to another model 164
Getting ready 164
How to do it... 165
How it works... 165
There's more... 166

Chapter 6: Basic Server-Side Development 169
Introduction 169
Technical requirements 170
Defining model methods and using the API decorators 170
Getting ready 170
How to do it... 171
How it works... 172
There's more... 174
Reporting errors to the user 174
Getting ready 174
How to do it... 174
How it works... 175
There's more... 176
Obtaining an empty recordset for a different model 176
Getting ready 177
How to do it... 177
How it works... 177
See also 178
Creating new records 178
Getting ready 179
How to do it... 179
How it works... 180
There's more... 181
Updating values of recordset records 182
Getting ready 182
How to do it... 182
How it works... 183
There's more... 183
Searching for records 185
Getting ready 185

How to do it...   185
How it works...   186
There's more...   187
Combining recordsets   188
Getting ready   188
How to do it...   188
How it works...   188
Filtering recordsets   189
Getting ready   189
How to do it...   190
How it works...   190
There's more...   191
Traversing recordset relations   191
Getting ready   191
How to do it...   191
How it works...   192
There's more...   192
See also   193
Sorting recordsets   193
Getting ready   193
How to do it...   193
How it works...   194
There's more...   194
Extending the business logic defined in a model   194
Getting ready   195
How to do it...   196
How it works...   196
There's more...   197
Extending write() and create()   198
Getting ready   198
How to do it...   199
How it works...   199
There's more...   200
Customizing how records are searched   201
Getting ready   201
How to do it...   202
How it works...   202
There's more...   203
See also   204
Fetching data in groups with read_group()   204
Getting ready   204
How to do it...   205
How it works...   205

Chapter 7: Module Data   207

Introduction	207
Technical requirements	208
Using external IDs and namespaces	208
How to do it...	208
How it works...	209
There's more...	209
See also	210
Loading data using XML files	211
How to do it...	211
How it works...	212
There's more...	214
Using the noupdate and forcecreate flags	214
How to do it...	215
How it works...	215
There's more...	216
See also	216
Loading data using CSV files	216
How to do it...	217
How it works...	217
There's more...	218
Add-on updates and data migration	218
How to do it...	219
How it works...	220
There's more...	221
See also	221
Deleting records from XML files	222
Getting ready	222
How to do it...	222
How it works...	222
Invoking functions from XML files	223
How to do it...	223
How it works...	224
There's more...	224
Chapter 8: Debugging	227
Introduction	227
The auto-reload and --dev options	227
Getting ready	228
How to do it...	228
How it works...	228
Producing server logs to help debug methods	229
Getting ready	229
How to do it...	230
How it works...	231
There's more...	232

Using the Odoo shell to interactively call methods   232
Getting ready   233
How to do it...   233
How it works...   234
There's more...   235
Using the Python debugger to trace method execution   235
Getting ready   235
How to do it...   235
How it works...   237
There's more...   239
See also   240
Using the Odoo Community Association maintainer quality tools   240
Getting ready   240
How to do it...   241
How it works...   245
There's more...   246
    Using Pylint to check your code   246
    Using Flake8 to check your code   247
Understanding the debug mode options   248
How to do it...   248
How it works...   249

Chapter 9: Advanced Server-Side Development Techniques   253
Introduction   253
Technical requirements   253
Changing the user that performs an action   254
Getting ready   254
How to do it...   255
How it works...   256
There's more...   257
See also   257
Calling a method with a modified context   258
Getting ready   258
How to do it...   258
How it works...   259
There's more...   260
See also   260
Executing raw SQL queries   260
Getting ready   261
How to do it...   261
How it works...   262
There's more...   262
See also   263
Writing a wizard to guide the user   263

Getting ready	263
How to do it...	264
How it works...	265
There's more...	266
Using the context to compute default values	266
Wizards and code reuse	267
Redirecting the user	268
Defining onchange methods	**268**
Getting ready	269
How to do it...	269
How it works...	270
There's more...	270
Calling onchange methods on the server side	**272**
Getting ready	272
How to do it...	272
How it works...	273
There's more...	275
See also	275
Defining a model based on an SQL view	**275**
Getting ready	275
How to do it...	276
How it works...	277
There's more...	277
Adding custom settings options	**278**
Getting ready	278
How to do it...	278
How it works...	280
There's more...	281
Implementing init hooks	**282**
Getting ready	282
How to do it...	282
How it works...	283
Chapter 10: Backend Views	**285**
Introduction	**286**
Technical requirements	**286**
Adding a menu item and window action	**286**
How to do it...	287
How it works...	287
There's more...	289
See also	290
Having an action open a specific view	**291**
How to do it...	291
How it works...	293
ir.actions.act_window.view	293
There's more...	294

Adding content and widgets to a form view 294
How to do it... 294
How it works... 295
Form 295
Header 296
Button 296
Group 296
Field 297
Notebook and page 297
General attributes 298
Other tags 298
There's more... 299
See also 299
Adding buttons to forms 300
How to do it... 300
How it works... 300
There's more... 301
Passing parameters to forms and actions – Context 301
Getting ready 301
How to do it... 302
How it works... 302
There's more... 303
See also 304
Defining filters on record lists – Domain 305
How to do it... 305
How it works... 306
There's more... 307
Operators 307
Pitfalls of searching using domains 308
See also 308
Defining list views 309
How to do it... 309
How it works... 310
There's more... 310
Defining search views 311
How to do it... 311
How it works... 312
There's more... 314
See also 315
Changing existing views – view inheritance 315
How to do it... 316
How it works... 316
There's more... 318
Order of evaluation in view inheritance 318
See also 319
Defining document-style forms 320

How to do it...	320
How it works...	321
Dynamic form elements using attrs	**322**
How to do it...	322
How it works...	323
There's more...	323
Defining embedded views	**323**
How to do it...	323
How it works...	324
There's more...	324
Displaying attachments on the side of the form view	**324**
How to do it...	325
How it works...	326
There's more...	326
Defining kanban views	**327**
How to do it...	327
How it works...	328
There's more...	329
Showing kanban cards in columns according to their state	**329**
Getting ready	330
How to do it...	330
How it works...	330
There's more...	331
Defining calendar and gantt views	**331**
How to do it...	332
How it works...	332
There's more...	333
Gantt View	333
Defining graph and pivot views	**334**
Getting ready	334
How to do it...	334
How it works...	335
There's more...	335
Defining the cohort view	**336**
Getting ready	336
How to do it...	336
How it works...	337
Defining the dashboard view	**338**
Getting ready	338
How to do it...	338
How it works...	339
There's more....	339
Chapter 11: Access Security	**341**
Technical requirements	**341**

Creating security groups and assigning them to users 342
Getting ready 342
How to do it... 342
How it works... 344
There's more... 345
Adding security access to models 346
Getting ready 347
How to do it... 347
How it works... 348
There's more... 350
Limiting access to fields in models 350
How to do it... 351
How it works... 351
There's more... 352
Limiting record access using record rules 353
How to do it... 353
How it works... 354
There's more... 356
Using security groups to activate features 356
Getting ready 357
How to do it... 357
How it works... 360
There's more... 362
Accessing recordsets as a superuser 362
How to do it... 363
How it works... 364
There's more... 364
Hiding view elements and menus based on groups 365
Getting ready 365
How to do it... 365
How it works... 366

Chapter 12: Internationalization 367
Installing a language and configuring user preferences 367
Getting ready 368
How to do it... 368
How it works... 369
There's more... 370
Configuring language-related settings 371
Getting ready 371
How to do it... 372
How it works... 372
There's more... 373
Translating texts through the web client user interface 373
Getting ready 373

How to do it...	373
How it works...	375
There's more...	376
Exporting translation strings to a file	**376**
Getting ready	376
How to do it...	377
How it works...	378
There's more...	379
Using gettext tools to make translations easier	**380**
How to do it...	380
How it works...	381
There's more...	382
Importing translation files into Odoo	**382**
Getting ready	383
How to do it...	383
How it works...	384
Chapter 13: Automation, Workflows, and Printouts	**385**
Introduction	**385**
Technical requirements	**386**
Managing dynamic record stages	**386**
Getting ready	386
How to do it...	386
How it works...	389
There's more...	390
Managing kanban stages	**391**
Getting started	391
How to do it...	391
How it works...	393
There's more...	393
Adding a quick create form in a kanban card	**394**
Getting started	394
How to do it...	394
How it works...	395
Creating interactive kanban cards	**396**
Getting started	396
How to do it...	396
How it works...	399
Adding a progress bar in kanban views	**400**
Getting started	400
How to do it...	400
How it works...	401
Creating server actions	**402**
Getting ready	402
How to do it...	402

How it works...   404
There's more...   405
Using Python code server actions   405
Getting ready   406
How to do it...   406
How it works...   407
There's more...   408
Using automated actions on time conditions   408
Getting ready   409
How to do it...   409
How it works...   411
There's more...   412
Using automated actions on event conditions   413
Getting ready   413
How to do it...   413
How it works...   415
There's more...   416
Creating QWeb-based PDF reports   417
Getting ready   417
How to do it...   417
How it works...   419
There's more...   420

Chapter 14: Web Server Development   421
Introduction   421
Technical requirements   421
Making a path accessible from the network   422
Getting ready   422
How to do it...   422
How it works...   423
odoo.http.route   424
Return values   424
odoo.http.request   425
There's more...   426
See also   427
Restricting access to web accessible paths   427
Getting ready   427
How to do it...   427
How it works...   429
There's more...   429
Consuming parameters passed to your handlers   430
How to do it...   430
How it works...   431
There's more...   431
See also   432

Modifying an existing handler   432
  Getting ready   432
  How to do it...   433
  How it works...   434
  There's more...   435
  See also   435
Chapter 15: CMS Website Development   437
  Introduction   437
  Managing static assets   438
    What are asset bundles and different assets in Odoo?   438
    Custom assets   440
      How to do it...   440
      How it works...   441
    There's more...   441
  Extending CSS and JavaScript for the website   443
    Getting ready   443
    How to do it...   443
    How it works...   445
  Creating or modifying templates – QWeb   447
    Getting ready   448
    How to do it...   448
    How it works...   450
      Loops   450
      Dynamic attributes   451
      Fields   453
      Conditionals   454
      Setting variables   454
      Subtemplates   454
      Inline editing   455
    There's more...   456
    See also   456
  Managing dynamic routes   456
    Getting ready   457
    How to do it...   457
    How it works...   458
    There's more...   459
  Offering snippets to the user   460
    Getting ready   460
    How to do it...   460
    How it works...   463
    There's more...   465
  Getting input from users   466
    Getting ready   466
    How to do it...   467
    How it works...   469

There's more...   469
Managing Search Engine Optimization (SEO) options   470
Getting ready   470
How to do it...   471
How it works...   471
There's more...   472
Managing sitemaps for the website   472
Getting ready...   472
How to do it...   473
How it works...   474
Getting a visitor's country information   474
Getting ready...   474
How to do it...   475
How it works...   476
Tracking a marketing campaign   476
Getting ready   477
How to do it...   477
How it works...   478
Managing multiple websites   479
Getting ready   479
How to do it...   479
How it works...   481

Chapter 16: Web Client Development   483
Introduction   483
Technical requirements   484
Creating custom widgets   484
Getting ready   484
How to do it...   485
How it works...   488
There's more...   490
Using client-side QWeb templates   490
Getting ready   490
How to do it...   491
How it works...   492
There's more...   492
See also   493
Making RPC calls to the server   493
Getting ready   493
How to do it...   494
How it works...   495
There's more...   496
See also   496
Creating a new view   496
Getting ready   497

How to do it... 497
How it works... 504
There's more... 507
Debugging your client-side code 508
Getting ready 508
How to do it... 508
How it works... 510
There's more... 511
Improving onboarding with tour 511
Getting ready 511
How to do it... 511
How it works... 513
Mobile app JavaScript 513
Getting ready 513
How to do it... 514
How to works... 515
There's more... 515

Chapter 17: In-App Purchasing with Odoo 517
Introduction 517
Technical requirements 518
In-app purchase concepts 518
How it works... 518
The IAP service flow 519
There's more... 520
Registering an IAP service in Odoo 521
Getting ready 521
How to do it... 521
How it works... 525
Creating an IAP service module 526
Getting ready 527
How to do it... 527
How it works... 531
Authorizing and charging IAP credits 532
Getting ready 532
How to do it... 533
How it works... 535
There's more... 537
See also 538
Creating an IAP client module 538
Getting ready 538
How to do it... 539
How it works... 542
There's more... 543
Displaying offers when an account lacks credits 544

Getting ready   544
How to do it...   544
How it works...   547
There's more...   547

Chapter 18: Automated Test Cases   549
  Introduction   549
  Technical requirements   550
  Python test cases   551
    Getting ready   551
    How to do it...   551
    How it works...   552
    There's more...   553
  Running tagged Python test cases   553
    Getting ready   553
    How to do it...   554
    How it works...   554
    There's more...   555
  Setting up Headless Chrome for client-side test cases   556
    How to do it...   556
    How it works...   557
  Client-side QUnit test cases   557
    Getting ready   557
    How to do it...   558
    How it works...   560
    There's more...   561
  Adding tour test cases   562
    Getting ready   562
    How to do it...   562
    How it works...   564
  Running client-side test cases from the UI   565
    How to do it...   565
      Running QUnit test cases   566
      Running tours from the UI   567
    How it works...   568
  Debugging client-side test cases   568
    Getting ready   568
    How to do it...   568
    How it works...   569
  Generating videos/screenshots for failed test cases   570
    How to do it...   570
    How it works...   570

Chapter 19: Managing, Deploying, and Testing with Odoo.sh   573
  Introduction   573
  Technical requirements   574

Exploring some basic concepts of Odoo.sh   574
What is Odoo.sh?   575
Why was Odoo.sh introduced?   575
When should you use Odoo.sh?   576
What are the features of Odoo.sh?   576
Creating an Odoo.sh account   578
Getting ready   578
How to do it...   578
How it works...   580
There's more...   581
Adding and installing custom modules   581
Getting ready   582
How to do it...   582
How it works...   583
There's more...   584
Managing branches   584
Getting ready   585
How to do it...   585
     Creating the production branch   585
     Creating a development branch   586
     Creating a staging branch   588
     Merging new features in the production branch   589
How it works...   589
Accessing debugging options   590
How to do it...   590
     Branch history   591
     Mail catcher   591
     Web shell   592
     Code editor   594
     Logs   594
There's more...   595
Getting a backup of your instance   596
How to do it...   596
How it works...   596
Checking the status of your builds   597
How to do it...   597
How it works...   598
There's more...   598
All Odoo.sh options   599
Getting ready   599
How to do it...   599
     Project name   600
     Collaborators   600
     Public access   601
     Module installation   601
     Submodules   602

Database workers 603
Staging branches 603
There's more... 603
Database size 604
Odoo source code revisions 604

Chapter 20: Remote Procedure Calls in Odoo 605
Technical requirements 606
Logging in/connecting Odoo with XML-RPC 606
Getting ready 606
How to do it... 606
How it works... 607
There's more... 608
Searching/reading records through XML-RPC 609
Getting ready 609
How to do it... 609
How it works... 610
There's more... 611
Creating/updating/deleting records through XML-RPC 612
Getting ready 612
How to do it... 613
How it works... 614
There's more... 615
Calling methods through XML-RPC 616
Getting ready 616
How to do it... 616
How it works... 617
There's more... 618
Logging in/connecting Odoo with JSON-RPC 618
Getting ready 618
How to do it... 619
How it works... 620
There's more... 621
Fetching/searching records through JSON-RPC 621
Getting ready 622
How to do it... 622
How it works... 623
There's more... 624
Create/update/delete records through JSON-RPC 624
Getting ready 625
How to do it... 625
How it works... 626
There's more... 627
Calling methods through JSON-RPC 628
Getting ready 628
How to do it... 628

How it works...   629
The OCA odoorpc library   630
Getting ready   630
How to do it...   630
How it works...   632
There's more...   633
See also   633

Chapter 21: Performance Optimization   635
The prefetching pattern for the recordsets   635
How to do it...   635
How it works...   636
There's more...   638
The in-memory cache – ormcache   638
How to do it...   638
   ormcache   639
   ormcache_context   639
   ormcache_multi   640
How it works...   640
There's more...   641
Generating image thumbnails   641
How to do it...   642
How it works...   642
There's more...   643
Accessing grouped data   644
How to do it...   644
How it works...   645
There's more...   646
Creating or writing multiple records   646
How to do it...   647
How it works...   648
There's more...   648
Accessing records through database queries   648
How to do it...   649
How it works...   649
There's more...   650
Profiling Python code   651
How to do it...   651
How it works...   652
There's more...   653

Chapter 22: Point of Sale   655
Introduction   655
Technical requirements   656
Adding custom JavaScript/SCSS files   656
Getting ready   656

How to do it...   657
How it works...   658
There's more...   659
Adding an action button on the keyboard   659
Getting ready   659
How to do it...   659
How it works...   661
There's more...   662
Making RPC calls   663
Getting ready   663
How to do it...   663
How it works...   665
Modifying the POS screen UI   667
Getting ready   667
How to do it...   667
How it works...   668
Modifying existing business logic   669
Getting ready   670
How to do it...   670
How it works...   671
Modifying customer receipts   672
Getting ready   672
How to do it...   672
How it works...   674
There's more...   674

Chapter 23: Manage Emails in Odoo   675
Technical requirements   675
Configuring incoming and outgoing mail servers   676
Getting ready   676
How to do it...   676
Configuring the incoming mail server   677
Configuring the outgoing mail server   678
How it works...   679
There's more...   680
Managing chatter on documents   680
Getting ready   680
How to do it...   680
How it works...   682
There is more...   682
Managing activities on documents   683
Getting ready   683
How to do it...   683
How it works...   684
There's more...   685

Sending mail using the Jinja template   685
Getting ready   685
How to do it...   685
How it works...   688
There's more...   689
Sending mail using the QWeb template   689
Getting ready   690
How to do it...   690
How it works...   691
There's more...   693
Managing the mail alias   694
Getting ready   694
How to do it...   695
How it works...   696
There's more...   698
Logging user changes in chatter   698
Getting ready   698
How to do it...   698
How it works...   700

Chapter 24: IoT Box   701
Technical requirements   702
Flashing the IoT Box image for Raspberry Pi   702
Getting ready   702
How to do it...   702
How it works...   703
There's more...   705
Connecting the IoT Box with the network   705
Getting ready   705
How to do it...   705
How it works...   708
Adding the IoT Box to Odoo   708
Getting ready   708
How to do it...   709
    Connecting the IoT Box automatically   710
    Connecting the IoT Box manually   711
How it works...   713
There's more...   714
Loading drivers and listing connected devices   715
Getting ready   715
How to do it...   716
How it works...   718
Taking input from devices   718
Getting ready   719
How to do it...   719

How it works...   720
There is more...   721
Accessing the IoT Box through SSH   721
Getting ready   722
How it works...   722
How to do it...   722
There's more...   723
Configuring a point of sale   724
Getting ready   724
How to do it...   724
How it works...   725
There's more...   726

Other Book You May Enjoy   727
Index   729

Preface

Odoo is a suite of integrated business applications. Odoo comes with over 25 different business applications covering CRM, manufacturing, e-commerce, accounting, and more. In short, it is an all-in-one solution covering all of your business needs.

Odoo is great software for developers too. Thanks to Odoo's strong framework, developers can build powerful applications from scratch. The Odoo framework has a built-in extension mechanism. Odoo's built-in applications are also built with the same framework, and its extensibility helps developers to create extension modules to modify existing applications.

The scope of the Odoo framework is huge, and it is very hard for newcomers to follow its learning curve. *Odoo 12 Development Cookbook - Third Edition* provides step-by-step recipes that help you learn every aspect of the Odoo framework, including all of the latest features of version 12. Its unique problem-and-solution approach helps you to solve your day-to-day Odoo development issues.

Who this book is for

This book is suitable for both newcomers and experienced developers. If you have basic knowledge of the Python programming language, then this book will help you to easily gain expertise in the Odoo framework. If you are a developer who wants to develop a highly efficient business application with the Odoo framework, and wants practical examples with which to learn the Odoo framework, then this book is for you!

What this book covers

Chapter 1, *Installing the Odoo Development Environment*, starts with an introduction to the Odoo ecosystem. Here you will learn how to install and set up Odoo for the development environment. You will also learn how to activate developer tools.

Chapter 2, *Managing Odoo Server Instances*, is about installing and upgrading add-ons. It provides you with useful tips to organize custom add-ons downloaded from GitHub.

Chapter 3, *Server Deployment*, is about how to install and configure Odoo instances for production use. This chapter includes the NGINX reverse proxy, SSL configuration, the startup service, and basic Docker deployment. It also includes the configuration for the CDN of a website.

Chapter 4, *Creating Odoo Add-On Modules*, explains the structure of the Odoo add-on module and provides a step-by-step guide to create a simple Odoo module from scratch.

Chapter 5, *Application Models*, focuses on Odoo model structure, and explains all types of fields with their attributes. This chapter also includes different ways to inherit and extend existing models.

Chapter 6, *Basic Server-Side Development*, introduces the API of the Odoo framework, presenting the usage of CRUD methods and other commonly used methods. This chapter also explains how to write business logic in Odoo.

Chapter 7, *Module Data*, shows how to ship built-in data along with your add-on module. It also explains the basic steps to write migration functions.

Chapter 8, *Debugging*, provides different strategies for debugging Odoo code. This chapter includes the usage of developer options and Odoo shell.

Chapter 9, *Advanced Server-Side Development Techniques*, covers more advanced topics of the ORM framework. It is useful for developing wizards, SQL views, installation hooks, on-change methods, and more. This chapter also explains how to execute raw SQL queries in the database.

Chapter 10, *Backend Views*, teaches you how to create different UI views and how to invoke the business logic from the user interface. It covers the all of the usual views, such as the list, form, kanban, calendar, graph, search, and pivot, as well as newly introduced views, such as cohort and dashboard. This chapter also includes a recipe for modifying/inheriting existing views.

Chapter 11, *Access Security*, covers the security aspect of the Odoo framework. It shows how to control/restrict user access on the models by creating security groups, access control lists, and record level rules.

Chapter 12, *Internationalization*, shows how to translate the user interface for your add-on modules, and provides useful tricks for managing translation files.

Chapter 13, *Automation, Workflows, and Printouts*, illustrates the different tools and techniques available in Odoo to implement better business processes. It shows how to use server actions, automated actions, and time-based scheduled actions. This chapter also includes a recipe for creating PDF reports for your model.

Chapter 14, *Web Server Development*, covers the core of the Odoo web server. It shows how to create custom URL routes to serve data on a given URL, and also shows how to control access to these URLs.

Chapter 15, *CMS Website Development*, show how to manage a website with Odoo. It also shows how to create and modify beautiful web pages and QWeb templates. This chapter also includes how to create dynamic building blocks with options. It includes some dedicated recipes for managing SEO, user forms, UTM tracking, sitemaps, and fetching visitor location information. This chapter also highlights the latest concept of a multi-website in Odoo.

Chapter 16, *Web Client Development*, dives into the JavaScript part of the Odoo. It covers how to create a new field widget and make RPC calls to the server. This also includes how to create a brand new view from scratch. You will also learn how to create on-boarding tours.

Chapter 17, *In-App Purchasing with Odoo*, covers everything related to the latest concept of **In-App Purchasing (IAP)** in Odoo. In this chapter, you will learn how to create client and service modules for IAP. You will also learn how to create an IAP account and draw IAP credits from the end user.

Chapter 18, *Automated Test Cases*, covers how to write and execute automated test cases in Odoo, including server-side, client-side, and tour integration test cases. This chapter also has a recipe to set up chrome-headless to capture screenshots and videos to see failed client-side test cases.

Chapter 19, *Managing, Deploying, and Testing with Odoo.sh*, explains Odoo.sh, a PaaS platform for deploying Odoo instances that cover different aspects of the production, staging, and development branches. This also explains the different options of the platform.

Chapter 20, *Remote Procedure Calls in Odoo*, covers different ways to connect Odoo instances from external applications. This chapter teaches you how to connect and access the data from an Odoo instance through XML-RPC, JSON-RPC, and the odoorpc library.

Chapter 21, *Performance Optimization*, explains the different concepts and patterns used to gain performance improvements in Odoo. This chapter includes the concept of prefetching, ORM-cache, and profiling the code to detect performance issues.

Chapter 22, *Point of Sale*, covers customization in a point-of-sale application. This includes customization of the user interface, adding a new action button, modifying business flow, and extending customer recipes.

Chapter 23, *Manage Emails in Odoo*, explains how to manage email and chatter in Odoo. It starts with configuring mail servers and moves towards the mailing API of the Odoo framework. This chapter also covers the Jinja2 and QWeb mail templates, chatters on the form view , field logs, and activities.

Chapter 24, *IoT Box*, gives you the highlight of the latest hardware of IoT Box. This chapter covers how to configure, access, and debug IoT Box. It also includes a recipe to integrate IoT Box with your custom add-ons.

To get the most out of this book

This book is meant for developers who have basic knowledge of the Python programming language, as the Odoo backend runs on Python. In Odoo, data files are created with XML, so basic knowledge of XML is required.

This book also covers the backend JavaScript framework, point-of-sale applications, and the website builder, which requires basic knowledge JavaScript, jQuery, and Bootstrap 4.

The community edition of Odoo is open source and freely available, but a few features, including IoT, cohort, and dashboard, are available only in the Enterprise edition, so to follow along with that recipe, you will need the Enterprise edition.

To follow Chapter 24, *IoT Box*, you will require the Raspberry Pi 3 Model B+, which is available at https://www.raspberrypi.org/products/raspberry-pi-3-model-b-plus/.

Download the example code files

You can download the example code files for this book from your account at www.packtpub.com. If you purchased this book elsewhere, you can visit www.packtpub.com/support and register to have the files emailed directly to you.

You can download the code files by following these steps:

1. Log in or register at `www.packtpub.com`.
2. Select the **SUPPORT** tab.
3. Click on **Code Downloads & Errata**.
4. Enter the name of the book in the **Search** box and follow the onscreen instructions.

Once the file is downloaded, please make sure that you unzip or extract the folder using the latestversion of:

- WinRAR/7-Zip for Windows
- Zipeg/iZip/UnRarX for Mac
- 7-Zip/PeaZip for Linux

The code bundle for the book is also hosted on GitHub at `https://github.com/PacktPublishing/Odoo-12-Development-Cookbook-Third-Edition`. Note that, the code bundle has the **separate folder for each recipe**. We also have other code bundles from our rich catalog of books and videos available at `https://github.com/PacktPublishing/`. Check them out!

Download the color images

We also provide a PDF file that has color images of the screenshots/diagrams used in this book. You can download it here:
`http://www.packtpub.com/sites/default/files/downloads/9781789618921_ColorImages`.

Code in Action

Visit the following link to check out videos of the code being run: Place holder link

Conventions used

There are a number of text conventions used throughout this book.

`CodeInText`: Indicates code words in text, database table names, folder names, filenames, file extensions, pathnames, dummy URLs, user input, and Twitter handles. Here is an example: "Mount the downloaded `WebStorm-10*.dmg` disk image file as another disk in your system."

A block of code is set as follows:

```
{
    'name': "My library",
    'summary': "Manage books easily",
    'description': """Long description""",
    'author': "Your name",
    'website': "http://www.example.com",
    'category': 'Uncategorized',
    'version': '12.0.1',
    'depends': ['base'],
    'data': ['views.xml'],
    'demo': ['demo.xml'],
}
```

When we wish to draw your attention to a particular part of a code block, the relevant lines or items are set in bold:

```
from odoo import models, fields
class LibraryBook(models.Model):
    _name = 'library.book'
    name = fields.Char('Title', required=True)
    date_release = fields.Date('Release Date')
    author_ids = fields.Many2many(
        'res.partner',
        string='Authors'
    )
```

Any command-line input or output is written as follows:

```
$ sudo apt-get update
```

Bold: Indicates a new term, an important word, or words that you see onscreen. For example, words in menus or dialog boxes appear in the text like this. Here is an example: "Odoo has special support for **monetary** values related to a **currency**."

Warnings or important notes appear like this.

Tips and tricks appear like this.

Sections

In this book, you will find several headings that appear frequently (*Getting ready*, *How to do it...*, *How it works...*, *There's more...*, and *See also*).

To give clear instructions on how to complete a recipe, use these sections as follows:

Getting ready

This section tells you what to expect in the recipe and describes how to set up any software or any preliminary settings required for the recipe.

How to do it...

This section contains the steps required to follow the recipe.

How it works...

This section usually consists of a detailed explanation of what happened in the previous section.

There's more...

This section consists of additional information about the recipe in order to make you more knowledgeable about the recipe.

See also

This section provides helpful links to other useful information for the recipe.

Get in touch

Feedback from our readers is always welcome.

General feedback: Email feedback@packtpub.com and mention the book title in the subject of your message. If you have questions about any aspect of this book, please email us at questions@packtpub.com.

Errata: Although we have taken every care to ensure the accuracy of our content, mistakes do happen. If you have found a mistake in this book, we would be grateful if you would report this to us. Please visit www.packtpub.com/submit-errata, selecting your book, clicking on the Errata Submission Form link, and entering the details.

Piracy: If you come across any illegal copies of our works in any form on the internet, we would be grateful if you would provide us with the location address or website name. Please contact us at copyright@packtpub.com with a link to the material.

If you are interested in becoming an author: If there is a topic that you have expertise in and you are interested in either writing or contributing to a book, please visit authors.packtpub.com.

Reviews

Please leave a review. Once you have read and used this book, why not leave a review on the site that you purchased it from? Potential readers can then see and use your unbiased opinion to make purchase decisions, we at Packt can understand what you think about our products, and our authors can see your feedback on their book. Thank you!

For more information about Packt, please visit packtpub.com.

1
Installing the Odoo Development Environment

In this chapter, we will cover the following recipes:

- Odoo ecosystem
- Easy installation of Odoo from source
- Managing Odoo environments using the `start` command
- Managing Odoo server databases
- Storing the configuration instance in a file
- Activating Odoo developer tools
- Updating Odoo from source

Introduction

There are lots of ways to set up an Odoo development environment. This chapter proposes one of them; you will certainly find a number of other tutorials on the web explaining other approaches. Keep in mind that this chapter is about a development environment that has different requirements from a production environment. This will be covered in Chapter 3, *Server Deployment*.

If you are new to Odoo development, you must know about certain aspects of the Odoo ecosystem. The next section will give you a brief introduction to those aspects, and then we will move on to the installation of Odoo for development.

Odoo ecosystem

Odoo provides the developer with out-of-the-box modularity. Its powerful framework helps the developer to build projects very quickly. There are various characters in the Odoo ecosystem that you should be familiar with before starting your journey of becoming a successful Odoo developer.

Odoo editions

Odoo comes with two editions. The first is the **Community Edition,** which is open source, and the second is the **Enterprise Edition,** which has licensing fees. Unlike other software vendors, Odoo Enterprise Edition is just a bunch of advance applications that adds extra features/apps in the Community Edition. Basically, Enterprise Edition runs on top of the Community Edition. The Community Edition comes under the **Lesser General Public License v3.0 (LGPLv3)** license and comes with all of the basic **Enterprise resource planning** (ERP) applications, such as sale, **Customer Relationship Management** (CRM), invoicing, purchase, website builder, and so on. Alternatively, Enterprise Edition comes with the Odoo Enterprise Edition License, which is a proprietary license. Odoo Enterprise Edition comes with advanced features such as full accounting, studio, **Voice over Internet Protocol** (VoIP), mobile responsive design, e-sign, marketing automation, and delivery and banking integrations. Enterprise Edition also provides you with unlimited *bugfixes*. The following diagram shows that Enterprise Edition depends on the Community Edition, which is why you need Community Edition to use Enterprise Edition:

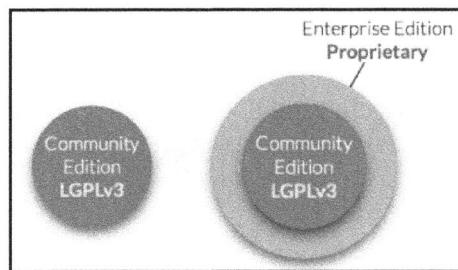

You can see a full comparison of both editions here: https://www.odoo.com/page/editions.

Odoo has the largest number of community developers, which is why you will find a large number of third-party apps (modules) on the app store. Most of the free apps use an **Affero General Public License version 3** (**AGPLv3**). You cannot use the proprietary license on your app if your application has dependencies on such apps. Apps with an Odoo proprietary license can be developed only on modules that have LGPL or other proprietary licenses.

Git repositories

The whole code base of Odoo is hosted on GitHub. You can post bugs/issues for stable versions here. You can also propose a new feature by submitting **Pull Requests** (**PR**). There are several repositories in Odoo; see the following table for more information:

Repositories	Purpose
https://github.com/odoo/odoo	This is the Community Edition of Odoo. It's available publicly.
https://github.com/odoo/enterprise	This is the Enterprise Edition of Odoo. It's **available to official Odoo partners only**.
https://github.com/odoo-dev/odoo	This is an Ongoing development repository. It's available publicly.

Every year, Odoo releases one major (**Long Term Support** (**LTS**)) version and a few minor versions. Minor versions are mostly used in Odoo's online SaaS service, meaning that Odoo SaaS users get early access to these features. Major version branches have names such as 12.0, 11.0, and 10.0, while minor version branches have names such as saas-12.1, saas-11.1, and saas-11.2 on GitHub. The `master` branch is under development and is subject to change at any time. Consequently, it is advisable not to use this for production, since it might break down your database.

Runbot

Runbot is Odoo's automated testing environment. This pulls the latest branches from Odoo's Git repositories and creates the builds for the last four commits. Here, you can test all stable and in-development branches. You can even play with the Enterprise Edition and its development branches.

Every build has a different background color, which indicates the status of the test cases. A green background color means that all of the test cases run successfully and you can test that branch, while a red background color means that some test cases have failed on this branch and some features might be broken on that build. You can view the logs for all test cases, which show exactly what happens during installation. Every build has two databases. The `all` database has all of the modules installed on it, while the `base` database only has base Odoo modules installed. Every build is installed with basic demo data, and therefore you can test it quickly without extra configurations.

> You can access runbot with from the following URL: `http://runbot.odoo.com/runbot`.

The following credentials can be used to access any runbot build:

- **Login ID:** admin **Password:** admin
- **Login ID:**demo **Password:** demo
- **Login ID:** portal **Password:** portal

> This is a public testing environment, so sometimes it is possible that other users are using/testing the same branch that you are testing.

Odoo app store

Odoo launched the app store a few years back, and this was an instant success. Right now, there are over 15,000 different apps hosted there. In the app store, you will find lots of free and paid applications for different versions. This includes specific solutions for different business verticals, such as education, food industries, and medicine. It also includes apps that extend/add new features to existing Odoo applications. The app store also provides numerous beautiful themes for the Odoo website builder. In Chapter 4, *Creating Odoo Add-On Modules*, we will look at how you can set pricing and currency for your custom module.

You can access the Odoo app store via the following URL: `https://www.odoo.com/apps`.

Odoo community association

Odoo Community Association (OCA) is a non-profit organization that develops/manages community-based Odoo modules. All OCA modules are open source and maintained by Odoo community members. Under the OCA's GitHub account, you will find multiple repositories for different Odoo applications. Apart from Odoo modules, it also contains various tools, a migration library, accounting localizations, and so on.

Here is the URL for OCA's official GitHub account: `https://github.com/OCA`.

Official Odoo help forum

Odoo has a very powerful framework, and tons of things can be achieved just by using/activating options or by following specific patterns. Consequently, if you run into some technical issues or if you are not sure about some complex cases, then you can post your query on Odoo's official help forum. Lots of developers are active on this forum, including some official Odoo employees.

You can search for or post your questions at the following URL: `https://help.odoo.com`.

Easy installation of Odoo from a source

For Odoo deployment, it is recommended to use a **GNU/Linux** environment. You may be more at ease using **Microsoft Windows** or **Mac OS X**, but the fact is that most Odoo developers use GNU/Linux, and you are much more likely to get support from the community for OS-level issues that occur on GNU/Linux than on Windows.

It is also recommended to develop using the same environment (the same distribution and the same version) as the one that will be used in production. This will avoid nasty surprises, such as discovering on the day of deployment that a library has a different version than expected with slightly different and incompatible behavior. If your workstation is using a different OS, a good approach is to set up a **Virtual Machine (VM)** on your workstation and install a GNU/Linux distribution in the VM.

To avoid copying files between the workstation where you are running your development environment and the VM that runs Odoo, you can configure a SAMBA share inside the VM and store the source code there. You can then mount the share on your workstation in order to edit the files easily.

This book assumes that you are running **Debian GNU/Linux** as its stable version (this is version 9, code name Stretch, at the time of writing). **Ubuntu** is another popular choice, and since it is built on top of Debian, most of the examples in this book should work without needing to be changed. Whatever Linux distribution you choose, you should have some notion of how to use it from the command line, and having knowledge about system administration will certainly not cause any harm.

Getting ready

We are assuming that you have Linux up and running and that you have an account with root access, either because you know the root password, or because sudo has been configured. In the following sections, we will use $ (whoami) whenever the login of your work user is required in a command line. This is a shell command that will substitute your login in the command you are typing.

Some operations will definitely be easier if you have a GitHub account. If you don't have one already, go to https://github.com and create one.

How to do it...

To install Odoo from a source, you need to follow these steps:

1. Run the following commands to install the main dependencies:

```
$ sudo apt-get update
$ sudo apt-get install -y git python3.5 postgresql nano
virtualenv xz-utils wget fontconfig libfreetype6 libx11-6
libxext6 libxrender1 xfonts-75dpi
```

Odoo v12 has moved from less to scss for stylesheet preprocessing. Consequently, if you are using <v12, then you need to install node-less node-clean-css in order to get the correct stylesheets.

---
[14]

2. Download and install `wkhtmltopdf`:

```
$ wget -O wkhtmltox.tar.xz \
https://github.com/wkhtmltopdf/wkhtmltopdf/releases/download/0
.12.4/wkhtmltox-0.12.4_linux-generic-amd64.tar.xz
$ tar xvf wkhtmltox.tar.xz
$ sudo mv wkhtmltox/lib/* /usr/local/lib/
$ sudo mv wkhtmltox/bin/* /usr/local/bin/
$ sudo mv wkhtmltox/share/man/man1 /usr/local/share/man/
```

3. Now, use the following code to install the build dependencies:

```
$ sudo apt-get install -y gcc python3.5-dev libxml2-dev \
libxslt1-dev libevent-dev libsasl2-dev libssl1.0-dev libldap2-
dev \
libpq-dev libpng-dev libjpeg-dev
```

4. Configure PostgreSQL:

```
$ sudo -u postgres createuser --createdb $(whoami)
$ createdb $(whoami)
```

5. Configure `git`:

```
$ git config --global user.name "Your Name"
$ git config --global user.email youremail@example.com
```

6. Clone the Odoo code base:

```
$ mkdir ~/odoo-dev
$ cd ~/odoo-dev
$ git clone -b 12.0 --single-branch\
https://github.com/odoo/odoo.git
$ cd odoo
```

7. Create an `odoo-12.0` virtual environment and activate it:

```
$ virtualenv -p python3 ~/odoo-12.0
$ source ~/odoo-12.0/bin/activate
```

8. Install the Python dependencies of Odoo in `virtualenv`:

```
$ pip3 install -r requirements.txt
```

9. Create and start your first Odoo instances:

```
$ createdb odoo-test
$ python3 odoo-bin -d odoo-test --addons-path=addons \
--db-filter=odoo-test$
```

10. Point your browser to `http://localhost:8069` and authenticate it by using the **admin** account and using `admin` as the password.

> You can download the example code files for this book from your account at `http://www.packtpub.com`. If you purchased this book elsewhere, you can visit `http://www.packtpub.com/support` and register to have the files emailed to you directly.
> You can download the code files by following these steps:
>
> 1. Log in or register on our website using your email address and password
> 2. Hover the mouse pointer over the **SUPPORT** tab at the top
> 3. Click on **Code Downloads and Errata**
> 4. Enter the title of this book in the search box
> 5. Select the book that you're looking to download the code files for
> 6. Choose where you purchased this book from in the drop-down menu
> 7. Click on **Code Download**
>
> You can also download the code files by clicking on the **Code Files** button on this book's web page on the *Packt Publishing* website. This page can be accessed by entering this book's title in the search box. Note that you need to be logged into your Packt account to do this.
>
> Once the file has been downloaded, ensure that you unzip or extract the folder using the latest version of the following tool:
>
> - WinRAR/7-Zip for Windows
> - Zipeg/iZip / UnRarX for Mac
> - 7-Zip/PeaZip for Linux

How it works...

Dependencies come from various sources. First, you have the core dependencies of Odoo, the Python interpreter, which is used to run the source code, and the PostgreSQL database server, which is used to store the instance data. Git is used for source code versioning and getting the source code of Odoo itself.

> Prior to 11.0, versions of Odoo ran with Python 2.7. Starting with Odoo 11.0, the minimum supported version of Python is 3.5. These two versions of Python are not compatible, so a module running on Python 2.7 (with Odoo 9.0 or 10.0, for instance) will require both porting to the specifics of Odoo 11.0 and porting to Python 3.

Since we will need to edit some files as `root` or as `postgres` (the PostgreSQL administrative user) on our server, we need to install a console-based text editor. We suggest `nano` for this as it is very simple to use, but feel free to choose any editor that you feel at ease with, as long as it works on the Console. For example, you can use `vim`, `e3`, or `emacs-nox`.

`Wkhtmltopdf` is a runtime dependency of Odoo that's used to produce PDF reports. The version that's required by Odoo 12.0 is 0.12.4, which is not included in the current GNU/Linux distributions. Fortunately for us, the maintainers of `wkhtmltopdf` provide pre-built packages for various distributions at `http://wkhtmltopdf.org/downloads.html`.

There are lots of other runtime dependencies that are Python modules, which we can install using `pip3` in a virtual environment. However, some of these Python modules can feature some dependencies on native C libraries, for which the Python bindings need to be compiled. Consequently, we install the development packages for these C libraries as well as the Python development package and a C compiler. Once these build dependencies are installed, we can use `pip3 install -r requirements.txt` (a file that comes from the Odoo source code distribution) to download, compile, and install the Python modules.

Virtual environments

Python **virtual environments**, or `virtualenv` for short, are isolated Python workspaces. These are very useful to Python developers because they allow different workspaces with different versions of various Python libraries to be installed, possibly on different Python interpreter versions.

You can create as many environments as you wish using the `virtualenv -p python3 path/to/newenv` command. This will create a `newenv` directory in the specified location, containing a `bin/` subdirectory and a `lib/python3.5` subdirectory. Don't forget `-p python3`, or you are likely to get a Python 2.7 virtual environment that won't be able to run Odoo 12.0.

In `bin/`, you will find several scripts:

- `activate`: This script is not executed and is sourced using the shell's built-in `source` command. This will activate the environment by adjusting the `PATH` environment variable to include the `bin/` directory of `virtualenv`. It also installs a shell function called `deactivate`, which you can run in order to exit `virtualenv`, and changes the shell prompt to let you know which `virtualenv` is currently activated.
- `pip3`: This is a special version of the `pip3` command that acts inside `virtualenv` only.
- `python3`: This is a wrapper around your system's Python interpreter, which uses the packages that have been installed in `virtualenv`.

> The shell built-in `source` command is also available as `.` (a single dot, followed by a space and the path to the file to source.) This means you can use `. ~/odoo-12.0/bin/activate` instead of `source ~/odoo-12.0/bin/activate`. The shortcut form is perfectly fine, but we will stick to the source in this book for the purpose of readability.

There are two main ways of using a `virtualenv`. You may `activate` it, as shown in this recipe (and call `deactivate` when you're done), or you may use the scripts in the `bin/` directory of the environment explicitly by calling them with their full path, in which case you don't need to `activate` the `virtualenv` script. This is mainly a matter of taste, so you should experiment and find out which style suits you better.

You may have executable Python scripts within the first line. This should look as follows:

```
#! /usr/bin/env python3
```

These will be easier to use with an activated `virtualenv` script.

This is the case with the `odoo-bin` script, which you can call in the following way:

```
$ ./odoo-bin -d odoo-test --addons-path=addons --db-filter=odoo-test
```

PostgreSQL configuration

On a GNU/Linux system, Odoo uses the `psycopg2` Python library to connect with a PostgreSQL database. Odoo works very well with the default values, which are used to access a PostgreSQL database with `psycopg2`. It uses the following default values:

- By default, `psycopg2` tries to connect to a database with the same username as the current user on local connections, which enables password-less authentication
- The local connection uses Unix domain sockets
- The database server listens on port `5432`

There is nothing special to do here, so we simply use the `postgres` administrative user to create a database user who shares our login name and gives it the right to create new databases. We then create a new database with the same name as the new user. This will be used as a default database when we use the `psql` command.

When on a development server, it is okay to give the PostgreSQL user more rights and use the `--superuser` command-line option rather than just `--createdb`. The net effect is that this user can then also create other users and globally manage the database instance. If you feel that `--superuser` is too much, you may still want to use `--createrole` in addition to `--createdb` when creating your database user. Avoid doing this on production servers as it will give additional leverage to an attacker exploiting a vulnerability in some part of the deployed code (refer to `Chapter 3, Server Deployment`).

If you want to use a database user with a different login, you will need to provide a password for the user. This is done by passing the `--pwprompt` flag on the command line when creating the user, in which case the command will prompt you for the password.

If the user has already been created and you want to set a password (or modify a forgotten password), you can use the following command:

```
$ psql -c "alter role $(whoami) with password 'newpassword'"
```

If this command fails with an error message saying that the database does not exist, it is because you did not create a database named after your login name in step 4 of this recipe. That's fine; just add the --dbname option with an existing database name, such as --dbname template1.

Git configuration

At some point in this book, you will need to use git commit. This will fail unless some basic configuration is performed; therefore, you need to provide Git with your name and email address. Git will remind you to do this with a nice error message, but you may as well do it now.

This is also something to keep in mind if you are using a service such as Travis for continuous integration, and your test scripts need to perform some git merges. You have to provide a dummy name and email for the merging to succeed.

Downloading the Odoo source code

Downloading the Odoo code base is done by performing a git clone operation; be patient, as this will take some time. The --branch 12.0 --single-branch options avoid downloading other branches and save a little time. The --depth option can also be used to avoid downloading the whole repository history, but the downside of that option is that you will not be able to explore that history when looking for issues.

Odoo developers also propose nightly builds, which are available as tarballs and distribution packages. The main advantage of using git clone is that you will be able to update your repository when new bug fixes are committed in the source tree. You will also be able to easily test any proposed fixes and track regressions so that you can make your bug reports more precise and helpful for developers.

Starting the instance

Now comes the moment you've been waiting for. To start our first instance, we first create a new empty database and then use the `odoo-bin` script with the following command-line arguments:

- `-d database_name`: Use this database by default.
- `--db-filter=database_name$`: Only try to connect to databases that match the supplied regular expression. One Odoo installation can serve multiple instances that live in separate databases, and this argument limits the available databases. The trailing `$` is important as the regular expression is used in match mode; this allows to to avoid selecting names starting with the specified string.
- `--addons-path=directory1,directory2,...`: This is a comma-separated list of directories in which Odoo will look for add-ons. This list is scanned at instance creation time to populate the list of available add-on modules in the instance.

If you are using a database user with a database login that is different from your Linux login, you need to pass the following additional arguments:

- `--db_host=localhost`: Use a TCP connection to the database server
- `--db_user=database_username`: Use the specified database login
- `--db_password=database_password`: This is the password for authenticating against the PostgreSQL server

To get an overview of all available options, use the `--help` argument. We will see more of the `odoo-bin` script later in this chapter, as well as in `Chapter 2`, *Managing Odoo Server Instances*.

When Odoo is started on an empty database, it will first create the database structure that's needed to support its operations. It will also scan the add-ons path to find the available add-on modules and insert some into the initial records in the database. This includes the **admin** user with the default `admin` password, which you will use for authentication.

Odoo includes an HTTP server. By default, it listens on all local network interfaces on TCP port `8069`, so pointing your web browser to `http://localhost:8069/` leads you to your newly created instance.

Managing Odoo environments using the start command

We will often want to use custom or community modules with our Odoo instance. Keeping them in a separate directory makes it easier to install upgrades to Odoo or troubleshoot issues from our custom modules. We just have to add that directory to the add-ons path and they will be available in our instance, just like the core modules are.

It is possible to think about this module directory as an Odoo environment. The Odoo `start` command makes it easy to organize Odoo instances as directories, each with its own modules.

Getting ready

For this recipe, we need to have already installed Odoo. We are assuming that it will be located at `~/odoo-dev/odoo`, and that `virtualenv` has been activated.

This means that the following command should successfully start an Odoo server:

```
$ ~/odoo-dev/odoo/odoo-bin
```

How to do it...

To create a work environment for your instance, you need to follow these steps:

1. Change to the directory where Odoo is:

   ```
   $ cd ~/odoo-dev
   ```

2. Choose a name for the environment and create a directory for it:

   ```
   $ mkdir my-odoo
   ```

3. Change to that directory and start an Odoo server instance for that environment:

   ```
   $ cd my-odoo/
   $ ../odoo/odoo-bin start
   ```

How it works...

The Odoo start command is a shortcut to start a server instance using the current directory. The directory name is automatically used as the database name (for the -d option), and the current directory is automatically added to the add-ons path (the --addons-path option), as long as it contains an Odoo add-on module. In the preceding recipe, you won't see the current directory in the add-ons path because it doesn't contain any modules yet.

> With the start command, if you are on the virtual environment, it will take the virtual environment name as the database instead of the directory that you are in. However, if you aren't in the virtual environment, this should work fine.

There's more...

By default, the current directory is used, but the --path option allows you to set a specific path that you can use instead. For example, this will work from any directory:

```
$ ~/odoo-dev/odoo/odoo-bin start --path=~/odoo-dev/my-odoo
```

The database to use can also be overridden using the usual -d option. In fact, all of the other usual odoo-bin command-line arguments will work, except --addons-path. For example, to set the server listening port, use the following command:

```
$ ../odoo/odoo-bin start -p 8080 -i base
```

As we can see, the Odoo start command can be a convenient way to quick-start Odoo instances with their own module directory.

Managing Odoo server databases

When working with Odoo, all of the data of your instance is stored in a PostgreSQL database. All of the standard database management tools you are used to are available, but Odoo also proposes a web interface for some common operations.

Getting ready

We are assuming that your work environment is set up and that you have an instance running. Do not start this using the `odoo-bin start` command that was shown in the previous recipe, as this configures the server with some options that interfere with multi-database management.

How to do it...

The Odoo database management interface provides tools to create, duplicate, remove, back up, and restore a database. There is also a way to change the master password, which is used to protect access to the database management interface.

Accessing the database management interface

To access the database, the following steps need to be performed:

1. Go to the login screen of your instance (if you are authenticated, log out).
2. Click on the **Manage Databases** link. This will navigate to `http://localhost:8069/web/database/manager` (you can also point your browser directly to that URL).

Setting or changing the master password

If you've set up your instance with default values and haven't modified it yet, as we will explain in the following section, the database management screen will display a warning, telling you that the **master password** hasn't been set and will advise you to set one with a direct link:

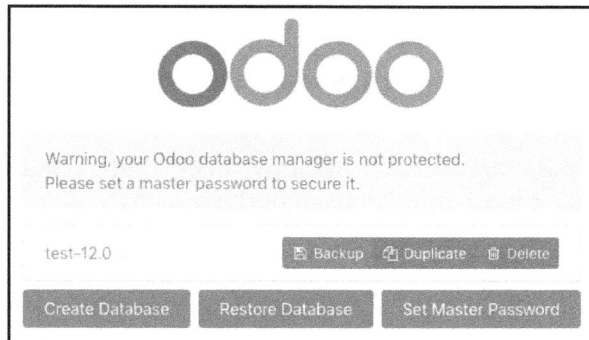

To set the master password, you need to perform the following steps:

1. Click on the **Set Master Password** button. You will get a dialog box asking you to provide the **New Master Password**:

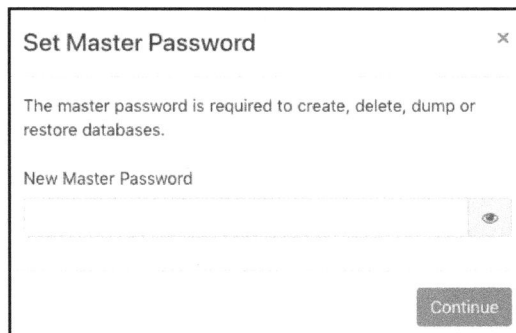

2. Type in a non-trivial new password and click on **Continue**

If the master password is already set, click on the **Set Master Password** button at the bottom of the screen to change it. In the displayed dialog box, type the previous master password and the new one and then click on **Continue**.

> The master password is the server configuration file under the `admin_password` key. If the server was started without specifying a configuration file, a new one will be generated in `~/.odoorc`. See the next recipe for more information about the configuration file.

Creating a new database

This dialog box can be used to create a new database instance that will be handled by the current Odoo server:

1. In the database management window, click on the **Create Database** button, which can be found at the bottom of the screen:

2. Fill in the form, as follows:
   - **Master Password**: This is the master password for this instance.
   - **Database Name**: Input the name of the database you wish to create.
   - **Password:** Type in the password you want to set for the admin user of the new instance.

- **Phone Number**: Set the phone number (optional).
- **Language**: Select the language you wish to be installed by default in the new database in the drop-down list.
- **Country**: Select the country of the main company in the drop-down list. Selecting this will automatically configure a few things, such as company currency.
- **Load demonstration data**: Check this box to obtain demonstration data. This is useful for running interactive tests or setting up a demonstration for a customer, but it should not be checked for a database that is designed to contain production data.

> If you wish to use the database to run the automated tests of the modules (refer to `Chapter 8`, *Debugging and Automated Testing*), you need to have the demonstration data, as the vast majority of the automated tests in Odoo depend on these records in order to run successfully.

3. Click on the **Continue** button and wait a while until the new database is initialized. You will then be redirected to the instance and connected as the administrator.

> **Troubleshooting**: If you are redirected to a login screen, this is probably because the `--db-filter` option was passed to Odoo and the new database name didn't match the new database name. Note that the `odoo-bin start` command does this silently, making only the current database available. To work around this, simply restart Odoo without the `start` command, as shown in the *Easy installation of Odoo from a source* recipe of this chapter. If you have a configuration file (refer to the *Storing the instance configuration in a file* recipe later in this chapter), then check that the `db_filter` option is unset or set to a value matching the new database name.

Duplicating a database

Often, you will have an existing database, and you will want to experiment with it to try a procedure or run a test, but without modifying the existing data. The solution here is simple: duplicate the database and run the test on the copy. Repeat this as many times as required:

1. In the database management screen, click on the **Duplicate Database** link next to the name of the database you wish to clone:

2. Fill in the form as follows:
   - **Master Password**: This is the master password of the Odoo server
   - **New Name**: The name you want to give to the copy

3. Click on the **Continue** button.
4. You can then click on the name of the newly created database in the database management screen to access the login screen for that database.

Removing a database

When you have finished your tests, you will want to clean up the duplicated databases. To do this, perform the following steps:

1. In the database management screen, click on the **Delete Database** link next to the name of the database you want to remove:

2. Fill in the form and enter the **Master Password**, which is the master password of the Odoo server.
3. Click on the **Delete** button.

Caution! Potential data loss!
If you selected the wrong database, and have no backup, there is no way to recover the lost data.

Backing up a database

For creating a backup, the following steps need to be performed:

1. In the database management screen, click on the **Backup Database** link next to the database you want to back up:

2. Fill in the form:
    - **Master Password**: This is the master password of the Odoo server.
    - **Backup Format**: Always use `zip` for a production database, as it is the only real full backup format. Only use the `pg_dump` format for a development database when you don't really care about the file store.

3. Click on the **Backup** button. The backup file will then be downloaded to your browser.

Restoring a database backup

If you need to restore a backup, this is what you need to do:

1. In the database management screen, click on the **Restore Database** button at the bottom of the screen:

Restore Database   ✕

Master Password

[   ]

File   [Browse...]   No file selected.

Database Name

[   ]

This database might have been moved or copied.

In order to avoid conflicts between databases, Odoo needs to know if this database was moved or copied.
If you don't know, answer "This database is a copy".

- ● This database is a copy
- ○ This database was moved

[Continue]

---

2. Fill in the form:
   - **Master Password**: This is the master password of the Odoo server.
   - **File**: This is a previously downloaded Odoo backup.
   - **Database Name**: Provide the name of the database in which the backup will be restored. The database must not exist on the server.
   - **This database might have been moved or copied**: Choose **This database was moved** if the original database was on another server or if it has been deleted from the current server. Otherwise, choose **This database is a copy**, which is the safe default option.
3. Click on the **Continue** button.

> It isn't possible to restore a database on top of itself. If you try to do this, you will get an error message (**Database restore error: Database already exists**). You need to remove the database first.

How it works...

These features, apart from the **Change master password** screen, run PostgreSQL administration commands on the server and report back through the web interface.

The master password is a very important piece of information that only lives in the Odoo server configuration file and is never stored in the database. There used to be a default value of `admin`, but using this value is a security liability, which is well-known. In Odoo v9 and later, this is identified as an *unset* master password, and you are urged to change it when accessing the database administration interface. Even if it is stored in the configuration file under the `admin_passwd` entry, this is not the same as the password of the `admin` user; these are two independent passwords. The master password is set for an Odoo server process, which itself can handle multiple database instances, each of which has an independent `admin` user with their own password.

Security considerations: Remember that we are considering a development environment in this chapter. The Odoo database management interface is something that needs to be secured when you are working on a production server, as it gives access to a lot of sensitive information, especially if the server hosts Odoo instances for several different clients. This will be covered in `Chapter 3`, *Server Deployment*.

To create a new database, Odoo uses the PostgreSQL `createdb` utility and calls the internal Odoo function to initialize the new database in the same way as when you start Odoo on an empty database.

To duplicate a database, Odoo uses the `--template` option of `createdb`, passing the original database as an argument. This essentially duplicates the structure of the template database in the new database using internal and optimized PostgreSQL routines, which is much faster than creating a backup and restoring it (especially when using the web interface, which requires downloading the backup file and uploading it again).

Backup and restore operations use the `pg_dump` and `pg_restore` utilities, respectively. When using the `zip` format, the backup will also include a copy of the file store that contains a copy of the documents when you configure Odoo to not keep these in the database, which is the default option in 12.0. Unless you change it, these files live in `~/.local/share/Odoo/filestore`.

If the backup gets large, downloading it may fail. This is either because the Odoo server itself is unable to handle the large file in memory or because the server is running behind a reverse proxy (refer to `Chapter 3`, *Server Deployment*) because there is a limit to the size of HTTP responses that were set in the proxy. Conversely, for the same reasons, you will likely experience issues with the database restore operation. When you start running into these issues, it is time to invest in a more robust external backup solution.

There's more...

Experienced Odoo developers generally don't use the database management interface and perform operations from the command line. To initialize a new database with demo data, for instance, the following one-liner can be used:

```
$ createdb testdb && odoo-bin -d testdb
```

The additional bonus of this command line is that you can request the installation of add-ons while you are using, for instance, `-i sale,purchase,stock` (more on this in `Chapter 2`, *Managing Odoo Server Instances*).

To duplicate a database, stop the server and run the following commands:

```
$ createdb -T dbname newdbname
$ cd ~/.local/share/Odoo/filestore # adapt if you have changed the
data_dir
$ cp -r dbname newdbname
$ cd -
```

Note that, in the context of development, the file store is often omitted.

> The use of `createdb -T` only works if there are no active sessions on the database, which means that you have to shut down your Odoo server before duplicating the database from the command line.

To remove an instance, run the following command:

```
$ dropdb dbname
$ rm -rf ~/.local/share/Odoo/filestore/dbname
```

To create a backup (assuming that the PostgreSQL server is running locally), use the following command:

```
$ pg_dump -Fc -f dbname.dump dbname
$ tar cjf dbname.tgz dbname.dump ~/.local/share/Odoo/filestore/dbname
```

To restore the backup, run the following command:

```
$ tar xf dbname.tgz
$ pg_restore -C -d dbname dbname.dump
```

> **Caution!**
> If your Odoo instance uses a different user to connect to the database, you need to pass `-U username` so that the correct user is the owner of the restored database.

Storing the instance configuration in a file

The `odoo-bin` script has dozens of options, and it is tedious to remember them, all as well as remembering to set them properly when starting the server. Fortunately, it is possible to store them all in a configuration file and to only specify by hand the ones you want to alter, for example, for development.

How to do it...

To generate a configuration file for your Odoo instance, run the following command:

```
$ ./odoo-bin --save --config myodoo.cfg --stop-after-init
```

You can add additional options, and their values will be saved in the generated file. All of the unset options will be saved with their default value set. To get a list of possible options, use the following command:

```
$ ./odoo-bin --help | less
```

This will provide you with some help about what the various options perform. To convert from the command-line form into the configuration form, use the long option name, remove the leading dashes, and convert the dashes in the middle into underscores:
`--without-demo` then becomes `without_demo`. This works for most options, but there are a few exceptions, which are listed in the following section.

Edit the `myodoo.cfg` file (use the table in the following section for some parameters you may want to change). Then, to start the server with the saved options, run the following command:

```
$ ./odoo-bin -c myodoo.cfg
```

The `--config` option is commonly abbreviated as `-c`.

How it works...

At startup, Odoo loads its configuration in three passes. First, a set of default values for all options is initialized from the source code, then the configuration is parsed, and any value that's defined in the file overrides the defaults. Finally, the command-line options are analyzed and their values override the configuration that was obtained from the previous pass.

As we mentioned earlier, the names of the configuration variables can be found from the names of the command-line options by removing the leading dashes and converting the middle dashes into underscores. There are a few exceptions to this, notably the following:

Command line	Configuration file
--db-filter	dbfilter
--no-http	http_enable = True/False
--database	db_name
--dev	dev_mode
--i18n-import/--i18n-export	Unavailable

Here's a list of options that are commonly set through the configuration file:

Option	Format	Usage
without_demo	Comma-separated list of module names, or all (to disable demo data for all modules), or False (to enable demo data for all modules)	This prevents module demo data from being loaded.
addons_path	Comma-separated list of paths	This is a list of directory names in which the server will look for add-ons (refer to Chapter 2, *Managing Odoo Server Instances*).
admin_passwd	Text	This is the master password (take a look at the preceding recipe).
data_dir	Path to a directory	This is a directory in which the server will store session information, add-ons downloaded from the internet, and documents if you enable the file store.

db_host	Hostname	This is the name of the server running the PostgreSQL server. Use `False` to use local Unix Domain sockets, and `localhost` to use TCP sockets locally.
db_user	Database user login	This is generally empty if `db_host` is `False`. This will be the name of the user used for connecting database.
db_password	Database user password	This is generally empty if `db_host` is `False` and when `db_user` has the same name as the user running the server. Read the main page of `pg_hba.conf` for more information on this.
db_name	Database name	This is used to set the database name on which some commands operate by default. This does not limit the databases on which the server will act. Refer to the following `dbfilter` option for this.
dbfilter	A regular expression	The expression should match the name of the databases that are considered by the server. If you run the website, it should match a single database, so it will look like `^databasename$`. More information on this can be found in Chapter 3, *Server Deployment*.
http_interface	IP address of a network interface	This defaults to `0.0.0.0`, which means that the server listens on all interfaces.
http_port longpolling_port	Port number	These are the ports on which the Odoo server will listen. You will need to specify both to run multiple Odoo servers on the same host; `longpolling_port` is only used if `workers` is not 0. `http_port` defaults to `8069` and `longpolling_port` default to `8072`.
logfile	Path to a file	The file in which Odoo will write its logs.

`log_level`	Log verbosity level	Specifies the level of logging. Accepted values (in increasing verbosity order) include `critical`, `error`, `warn`, `info`, `debug`, `debug_rpc`, `debug_rpc_answer`, `debug_sql`.
`workers`	Integer	The number of worker processes. Refer to Chapter 3, *Server Deployment*, for more information.
`list_db`	True/False	Set to True to disable listing of databases. See Chapter 3, *Server Deployment*, for more information.
`proxy_mode`	True/False	Activate reverse proxy WSGI wrappers. Only enable this when running behind a trusted web proxy!

The parsing of the configuration file by Odoo is now using the Python `ConfigParser` module. However, the implementation in Odoo 11.0 has changed, and it is no longer possible to use variable interpolation. So, if you are used to defining values for variables from the values of other variables using the `%(section.variable)s` notation, you will need to change your habits and revert to explicit values.

Some options are not used in config files, but they are widely used during development:

Options	Format	Usage
-i or --init	Comma-separated list of module names	It will install given modules by default while initializing the database.
-u or --update	Comma-separated list of module names	It will update given modules when you restart the server. It is mostly used when you modify source code or update the branch from git.
--dev	`all`, `reload`, `qweb`, `werkzeug`, `xml`	This enables developer mode and the auto-reload feature.

Activating the Odoo developer tools

When using Odoo as a developer, you need to know how to activate **developer mode** in the web interface so that you can access the technical settings menu and developer information. Enabling debug mode will expose several advance configuration options and fields. These options and fields are hidden in Odoo for better usability because they are not used on a daily basis.

How to do it...

To activate developer mode in the web interface, follow these steps:

1. Connect to your instance and authenticate as `admin`.
2. Go to the **Settings** menu.
3. Locate the **Share the love** card, which should be on the right-hand side of the screen:

4. Click on the **Activate the developer mode** link.
5. Wait for the UI to reload.

Alternative way: It is also possible to activate the developer mode by editing the URL. Before the # sign, insert `?debug`. For instance, if you are starting from `http://localhost:8069/web#menu_id=102&action=94`, then you need to change this to `http://localhost:8069/web?debug=#menu_id=102&action=94`. Furthermore, if you want debug mode with assets, then change the URL to `http://localhost:8069/web?debug=assets#menu_id=102&action=94`.

To exit developer mode, you can do either of the following:

- Edit the URL and remove that string
- Use the **Deactivate the developer mode** link displayed in the **Share the love** card when the developer mode is active

Lots of developers are using browser extensions to toggle debug mode. By using this, you can toggle debug mode quickly without accessing the settings menu. These extensions are available for Firefox and Chrome. Take a look at the given screenshot, it will help you to identify the plugin in the Chrome store:

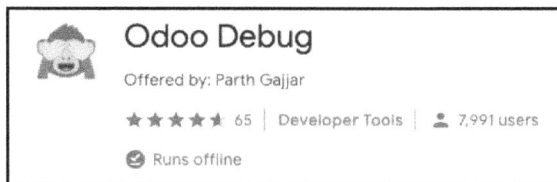

Odoo Debug

Offered by: Parth Gajjar

★ ★ ★ ★ ✦ 65 | Developer Tools | 👤 7,991 users

🔌 Runs offline

How it works...

In developer mode, two things happen:

- You get tooltips when hovering over a field in a form view or over a column in list view, providing technical information about the field (internal name, type, and so on)
- A drop-down menu with a **Bug** icon is displayed next to the user's menu in the top-right corner, giving access to technical information about the model being displayed, the various related view definitions, the workflow, custom filter management, and so on

There is a variant of the developer mode: the **Developer mode (with assets)**. This mode behaves like the normal developer mode, but additionally, the JavaScript and CSS code that's sent to the browser is not minified, which means that the web development tools of your browser are easy to use for debugging the JavaScript code (more on this in Chapter 15, *Web Client Development*).

Caution!

Test your add-ons both with and without developer mode, as the unminified versions of the JavaScript libraries can hide bugs that only bite you in the minified version.

Updating Odoo from source

In the first recipe, we saw how to install Odoo from source using the git repository. The main benefit of this setting is being able to update the source code of Odoo using git to get the latest bug fixes.

Getting ready

Stop any instance that's currently running with the Odoo source you are about to update, and then make a backup of all of the databases you care about in case something goes wrong. This is obviously something you need to do for production databases. Refer to the *Managing Odoo server databases* recipe of this chapter for further instructions.

Next, make a note of the current version of the source you are running. The best way to do this is by creating a lightweight tag using the following command:

```
$ cd ~/odoo-dev/odoo
$ git checkout 12.0
$ git tag 12.0-before-update-$(date --iso)
```

How to do it...

To update the source code of Odoo, use the following command:

```
$ git pull --ff-only origin 12.0
```

This will fetch the latest version of the source code that's committed to the current branch.

To update an instance running on this code, run the following command:

```
$ ./odoo-bin -c myodoo.cfg --stop-after-init -u base
```

-u is the shortcut notation for the --update option of odoo-bin.

If you don't have a database set in the configuration file, you will have to add the -d database_name option. This command is to be repeated for all of the instances that are running with this version of the source code.

If the update fails, don't panic, because you have backups:

1. Read the error message carefully and save it to a file, as it will be useful for making a bug report later.
2. If you cannot figure out what the problem is, restore the service and the Odoo source code to the previous version, which is known to work using the tag you set before updating the source version:

   ```
   $ git reset --hard 12.0-before-update-$(date --iso)
   ```

3. Drop the broken databases and restore them from the backups you made (refer to the *Managing Odoo server databases* recipe of this chapter for instructions).
4. Restart your instances and tell your users that the upgrade has been postponed.

Note that, in real life, this should never happen on a production database because you would have tested the upgrade beforehand on a copy of the database, fixed the issues, and only done the upgrade on the production server after ensuring that it runs flawlessly. However, you sometimes still get surprises, so even if you are really sure, make a backup.

How it works...

Updating the source code is done by ensuring that we are on the correct branch using `git checkout` and then fetching the new revisions using `git pull`. The `--ff-only` option will cause a failure if you have local commits that aren't present in the remote repository. If this happens and you want to keep your changes, you can use git pull (without `--ff-only`) to merge the remote changes with yours. If not, use `git reset --hard origin/12.0` to force the update, hence discarding your local modifications.

The update command uses the following options:

- `-c`: Specifies the configuration file
- `--stop-after-init`: Stops the instance when the update is over
- `-u base` or `--update base`: Requests the update of the `base` module

When updating a module, Odoo does the following:

- It updates the database structure for the models defined in the module for which the structure changes. For updates on the stable branch of Odoo, there should be no such changes, but this can happen for your own add-ons or third-party add-ons.
- It updates the database records that are stored in data files of the module, most notably, the views. It then recursively updates the installed modules that have declared a dependency on the module.

Since the `base` module is an implicit dependency of all Odoo modules, updating it will trigger an update of all of the installed modules in your instance. To update all installed modules, the `all` alias can be used instead of `base`.

2
Managing Odoo Server Instances

In this chapter, we will cover the following recipes:

- Configuring the add-ons path
- Updating the add-on modules list
- Standardizing your instance directory layout
- Installing and upgrading local add-on modules
- Installing add-on modules from GitHub
- Applying changes to add-ons
- Applying and trying proposed pull requests

Introduction

In `Chapter 1`, *Installing the Odoo Development Environment*, we looked at how to set up an Odoo instance using only the standard core add-ons that are shipped with the editor. This chapter focuses on adding non-core add-ons to an Odoo instance. In Odoo, you can load add-on from multiple directories. In addition, it is recommended that you load your third-party add-ons (for example, OCA modules) or your own custom add-ons from separate folders to avoid conflicts with Odoo core modules. Even Odoo Enterprise Edition is a type of add-on directory, and you need to load this just like a normal add-ons directory.

About the terminology – add-on versus module

In this book, we will use the term *add-on* or *add-on module* to refer to a Python package that respects the expected format to be installed in Odoo. The user interface often uses the words *app* or *module* for this, but we prefer keeping the term *module* for Python modules or packages that are not necessarily Odoo add-ons, and *app* for add-on modules that are properly defined as applications, meaning that they have an entry in the main menu of Odoo.

Configuring the add-ons path

With the help of the `addons_path` parameter, you can load your own add-on modules into Odoo. When Odoo initializes a new database, it will search for one of these directories that's been given in the `addons_path` configuration parameter. Odoo will search on these directories for the potential add-on module. Directories listed in `addons_path` are expected to contain subdirectories, each of which is an add-on module. After the initialization of the database, you will be able to install modules that are given in these directories.

Getting ready

This recipe assumes that you have an instance ready with a configuration file generated, as described in the *Storing the instance configuration in a file* recipe of `Chapter 1`, *Installing the Odoo Development Environment*. The source code of Odoo is available in `~/odoo-dev/odoo`, and the configuration file is in `~/odoo-dev/my-instance.cfg`.

How to do it...

To add the `~/odoo-dev/local-addons` directory to `addons_path` of the instance, follow these steps:

1. Edit the configuration file for your instance, that is, `~/odoo-dev/my-instance.cfg`.

2. Locate the line starting with `addons_path =`. By default, this should look like the following:

    ```
    >addons_path = ~/odoo-dev/odoo/odoo/addons,~/odoo-
    dev/odoo/add-ons
    ```

3. Modify the line by appending a comma, followed by the name of the directory you want to add to `addons_ path`, as shown in the following code:

    ```
    addons_path = ~/odoo-dev/odoo/odoo/addons,
    ~/odoo-dev/odoo/addons,~/odoo-dev/local-addons
    ```

4. Restart your instance:

    ```
    $ ~/odoo-dev/odoo/odoo-bin -c my-instance.cfg
    ```

How it works...

When Odoo is restarted, the configuration file is read. The value of the `addons_path` variable is expected to be a comma-separated list of directories. Relative paths are accepted, but they are relative to the current working directory and therefore should be avoided in the configuration file.

At this point, the new add-ons present in `~/odoo-dev/local-addons` are not available in the list of available add-on modules of the instance. For this, you need to perform an extra operation, as explained in the next recipe, *Updating the add-on modules list*.

There's more...

When you call the `odoo-bin` script for the first time to initialize a new database, you can pass the `--addons-path` command-line argument with a comma-separated list of directories. This will initialize the list of available add-on modules with all of the add-ons found in the supplied add-ons path. When you do this, you have to explicitly include the base add-ons directory (`odoo/odoo/addons`), as well as the core add-ons directory (`odoo/addons`).

A small difference with the preceding recipe is that the local add-ons must not be empty; they must contain at least one sub-directory, which has the minimal structure of an add-on module. In Chapter 4, *Creating Odoo Add-On Modules*, we will look at how to write your own modules. In the meantime, here's a quick hack to produce something that will make Odoo happy:

```
$ mkdir -p ~/odoo-dev/local-addons/dummy
$ touch ~/odoo-dev/local-addons/dummy/__init__.py
$ echo '{"name": "dummy", "installable": False}' > \
~/odoo-dev/local-addons/dummy/__manifest__.py
```

You can use the `--save` option to save the path to the configuration file:

```
$ odoo/odoo-bin -d mydatabase \
--add-ons-path="odoo/odoo/addons,odoo/addons,~/odoo-dev/local-addons" \
--save -c ~/odoo-dev/my-instance.cfg --stop-after-init
```

In this case, using relative paths is okay, since they will be converted into absolute paths in the configuration file.

> Since Odoo only checks directories in the add-ons path for the presence of add-ons when the path is set from the command line, not when the path is loaded from a configuration file, the dummy module is no longer necessary. You may, therefore, remove it (or keep it until you're sure that you won't need to create a new configuration file).

Updating the add-on modules list

As we said in the preceding recipe, when you add a directory to the add-ons path, just restarting the Odoo server is not enough to be able to install one of the new add-on modules. A specific action is required for Odoo to scan the add-ons path and update the list of available add-on modules.

Getting ready

Start your instance and connect to it using the Administrator account. After doing this, activate developer mode (if you don't know how to activate developer mode, refer to `Chapter 1`, *Installing the Odoo Development Environment*).

How to do it...

To update the list of available add-on modules in your instance, you need to perform the following steps:

1. Open the **Apps** menu.
2. Click on **Update Apps List**:

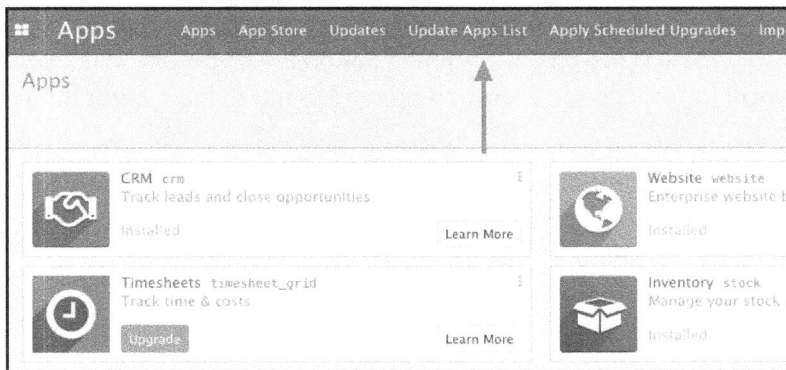

3. In the dialog, click on the **Update** button:

```
⋔  Module Update

Module Update Result

Click on Update below to start the process...


[ Update ]  Cancel
```

4. At the end of the update, you can click on the **Apps** entry to see the updated list of available add-on modules. You will need to remove the default filter on **Apps** in the search box to see all of them.

How it works...

When the **Update** button is clicked, Odoo will read the add-ons path configuration variable. For each directory in the list, it will look for immediate subdirectories containing an add-on manifest file, which is a file named __manifest__.py that's stored in the add-on module directory. Odoo reads the manifest, expecting to find a Python dictionary. Unless the manifest contains a key installable set to False, the add-on module metadata is recorded in the database. If the module was already present, the information is updated. If not, a new record is created. If a previously available add-on module is not found, the record is not deleted from the list.

> An update app list is only required if you added the new add-on path after initializing the database. If you add the new add-on path to the configuration file before initializing the database, then there will be no need to update the module list manually.

Standardizing your instance directory layout

We recommend that your development and production environments all use a similar directory layout. This standardization will prove helpful when you have to perform maintenance operations, and it will also ease your day-to-day work.

This recipe creates a directory structure that groups files with similar life cycles or similar purposes in standardized subdirectories. Feel free to alter this structure to suit your needs, but ensure that you have this documented somewhere.

How to do it...

To create the proposed instance layout, you need to perform the following steps:

1. Create one directory per instance:

   ```
   $ mkdir ~/odoo-dev/projectname
   $ cd ~/odoo-dev/projectname
   ```

2. Create a Python `virtualenv` in a subdirectory called `env/`:

   ```
   $ virtualenv -p python3 env
   ```

3. Create some subdirectories, as follows:

   ```
   $ mkdir src local bin filestore logs
   ```

   The functions of the subdirectories are as follows:

- `src/`: This contains the clone of Odoo itself, as well as the various third-party add-on projects (we have added Odoo source code to next step in this recipe)
- `local/`: This is used to save your instance-specific add-ons
- `bin/`: This includes various helper executable shell scripts
- `filestore/`: This is used as a file store
- `logs/` (optional): This is used to store the server log files

4. Clone Odoo and install the requirements (refer to `Chapter 1`, *Installing the Odoo Development Environment*, for details on this):

```
$ git clone https://github.com/odoo/odoo.git src/odoo
$ env/bin/pip3 install -r src/odoo/requirements.txt
```

5. Save the following shell script as `bin/odoo`:

```
#!/bin/sh
ROOT=$(dirname $0)/..
PYTHON=$ROOT/env/bin/python3
ODOO=$ROOT/src/odoo/odoo-bin
$PYTHON $ODOO -c $ROOT/projectname.cfg "$@"
exit $?
```

6. Make the script executable:

```
$ chmod +x bin/odoo
```

7. Create an empty dummy local module:

```
$ mkdir -p local/dummy
$ touch local/dummy/__init__.py
$ echo '{"name": "dummy", "installable": False}' >\
local/dummy/__manifest__.py
```

8. Generate a configuration file for your instance:

```
$ bin/odoo --stop-after-init --save \
  --addons-path src/odoo/odoo/addons,src/odoo/addons,local \
  --data-dir filestore
```

9. Add a `.gitignore` file, which is used to tell GitHub to exclude given directories so that Git will ignore these directories when you commit the code, for example, `filestore/`, `env/`, `logs/`, and `src/`:

```
# dotfiles, with exceptions:
.*
!.gitignore
# python compiled files
*.py[co]
# emacs backup files
*~
# not tracked subdirectories
/env/
/src/
/filestore/
/logs/
```

10. Create a Git repository for this instance and add the files you've added to Git:

```
$ git init
$ git add .
$ git commit -m "initial version of projectname"
```

How it works...

We generate a clean directory structure with clearly labeled directories and dedicated roles. We are using different directories to store the following:

- The code maintained by other people (in `src/`)
- The local-specific code
- `filestore` of the instance

By having one `virtualenv` environment per project, we are sure that the project's dependencies will not interfere with the dependencies of other projects that can be running a different version of Odoo or will use different third-party add-on modules, which need different versions of Python dependencies. This comes at the cost of a little disk space.

In a similar way, by using separate clones of Odoo and third-party add-on modules for our different projects, we are able to let each of these evolve independently and only install updates on the instances that need them, hence reducing the risk of introducing regressions.

The `bin/odoo` script allows us to run the server without having to remember the various paths or activate the `virtualenv`. This also sets the configuration file for us. You can add additional scripts in there to help you in your day-to-day work. For instance, you can add a script to check out the different third-party projects that you need to run your instance.

Regarding the configuration file, we have only showed the bare minimum options to set up here, but you can obviously set more, such as the database name, the database filter, or the port on which the project listens. Refer to Chapter 1, *Installing the Odoo Development Environment*, for more information on this topic.

Finally, by managing all of this in a Git repository, it becomes quite easy to replicate the setup on a different computer and share the development among a team.

Speedup tip

To ease project creation, you can create a template repository containing the empty structure, and fork that repository for each new project. This will save you from retyping the bin/odoo script, the .gitignore file, and any other template file you need (continuous integration configuration, README.md, ChangeLog, and so on).

See also

If you like this approach, we suggest trying out the *Using Docker to run Odoo* recipe in Chapter 3, *Server Deployment*.

There's more...

The development of complex modules requires various configuration options, which leads to updating the configuration file whenever you want to try any configuration option. Updating the configuration frequently can be a headache, and to avoid this, an alternative way is to pass all configuration options from the command line, as follows:

1. Activate virtualenv manually:

   ```
   $ source env/bin/activate
   ```

2. Go to the Odoo source directory:

   ```
   $ cd src/odoo
   ```

3. Run the server:

   ```
   ./odoo-bin --addons-path=addons,../../local -d test-12 -i
   account,sale,purchase --log-level=debug
   ```

In step 3, we passed a few configuration options directly from the command line. The first is --add-ons-path, which loads Odoo's core add-ons directory, adcons, and your add-ons directory, local, in which you will put your own add-ons modules. Option -d will use the test-12 database or create a new database if it isn't present. The -i option will install the account, sale, and purchase modules. Next, we passed the log-level option and increased the log level to debug so that it will display more information in the log.

> By using the command line, you can quickly change the configuration options. You can also see live logs in the Terminal. For all available options, see Chapter 1, *Installing the Odoo Development Environment*, or use the --help command to view a list of all options and the description of each option.

Installing and upgrading local add-on modules

The core of the functionality of Odoo comes from its add-on modules. You have a wealth of add-ons available as part of Odoo itself, as well as add-on modules that you can download from the app store or write yourself.

In this recipe, we will demonstrate how to install and upgrade add-on modules through the web interface and from the command line.

The main benefits of using the command line for these operations include being able to act on more than one add-on at a time and having a clear view of the server logs as the installation or update progresses, which is very useful when in development mode or when scripting the installation of an instance.

Getting ready

Make sure that you have a running Odoo instance with its database initialized and the add-ons path properly set. In this recipe, we will install/upgrade a few add-on modules.

How to do it...

There are two possible methods to install or update add-ons—you can use the web interface or the command line.

From the web interface

To install a new add-on module in your database using the web interface, follow these steps:

1. Connect to the instance using the **Administrator** account and open the **Apps** menu:

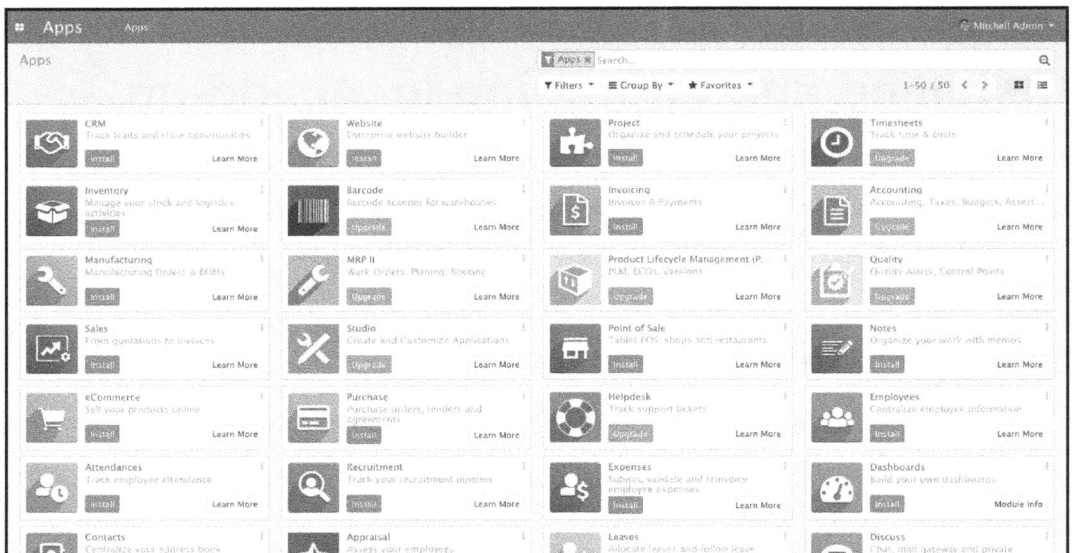

2. Use the search box to locate the add-on you want to install. Here are a few instructions to help you with this task:
   - Activate the **Not Installed** filter
   - If you're looking for a specific functionality add-on rather than a broad functionality add-on, remove the **Apps** filter
   - Type a part of the module name in the search box and use this as a **Module** filter
   - You may find that using the list view gives something more readable

3. Click on the **Install** button under the module name in the card.

Note that some Odoo add-on modules have external Python dependencies. If Python dependencies are not installed in your system, then Odoo will abort the installation and it will show the following dialog:

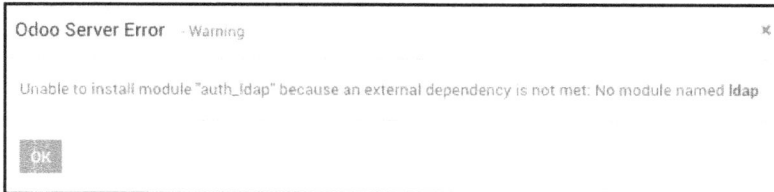

To fix this, just install the relevant Python dependencies on your system.

To update a pre-installed module in your database, use the following steps:

1. Connect to the instance using the **Administrator** account.
2. Open the **Apps** menu.
3. Click on **Apps**:

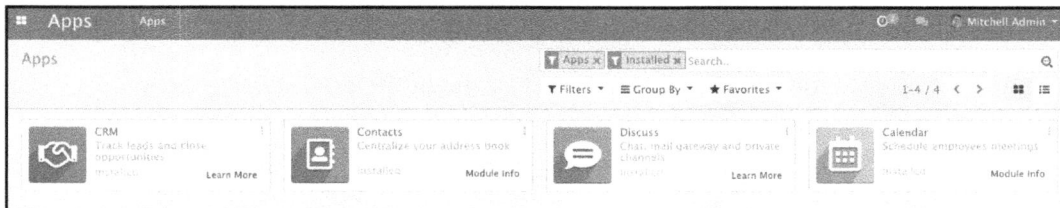

4. Use the search box to locate the add-on you want to install. Here are a few tips:
   - Activate the **Installed** filter.
   - If you're looking for a specific functionality add-on rather than a broad functionality add-on, remove the **Apps** filter.
   - Type a part of the add-on module name into the search box and then press *Enter* to use this as a **Module** filter. For example, type CRM and press *Enter* to search CRM apps
   - You may find that using the list view gives you something more readable.

5. Click on the three dots at the top right-corner of the card and click on the **Upgrade** option:

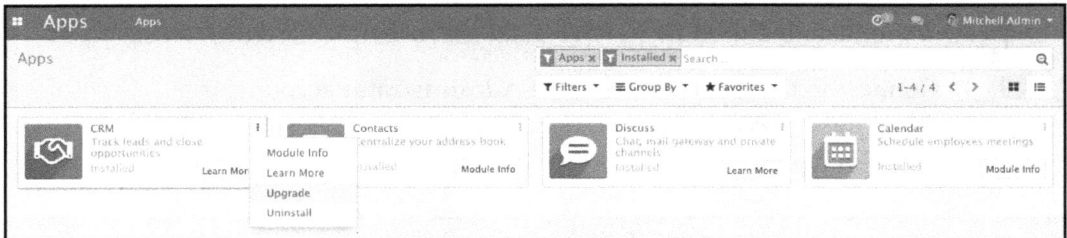

Activate developer mode to see the technical name of the module. See Chapter 1, *Installing the Odoo Development Environment,* if you don't know how to activate developer mode:

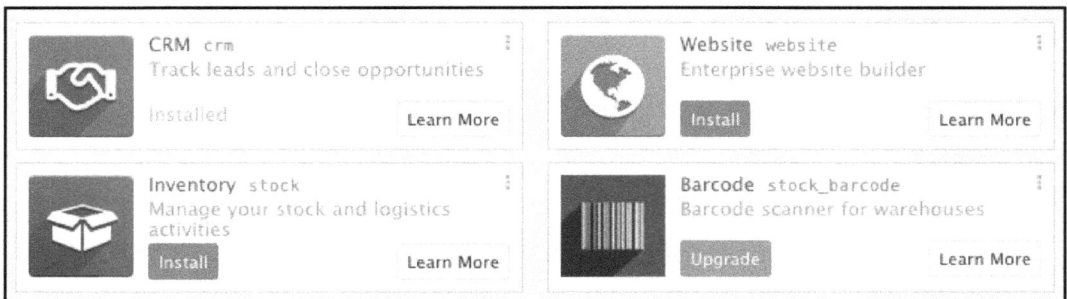

After activating developer mode, it will show the module's technical name in red. If you are using Odoo Community Edition, you will see some extra apps with the **Upgrade** button. Those apps are Odoo Enterprise Edition apps, and in order to install/use them, you need to purchase a licence.

From the command line

To install new add-ons in your database, follow these steps:

1. Find the names of the add-ons. This is the name of the directory containing the `__manifest__.py` file, without the leading path.
2. Stop the instance. If you are working on a production database, make a backup.
3. Run the following command:

```
$ odoo/odoo-bin -c instance.cfg -d dbname -i addon1,addon2 \
--stop-after-init
```

> You may omit `-d dbname` if this is set in your configuration file.

4. Restart the instance.

To update an already installed add-on module in your database, follow these steps:

1. Find the name of the add-on module to update; this is the name of the directory containing the `__manifest__.py` file, without the leading path.
2. Stop the instance. If you are working on a production database, make a backup.
3. Run the following command:

```
$ odoo/odoo-bin -c instance.cfg -d dbname -u addon1 \
--stop-after-init
```

> You may omit `-d dbname` if this is set in your configuration file.

4. Restart the instance.

How it works...

The add-on module installation and update are two closely-related processes, but there are some important differences, as highlighted in the following two sections.

Add-on installation

When you install an add-on, Odoo checks its list of available add-ons for an uninstalled add-on with the supplied name. It also checks for the dependencies of that add-on and, if there are any, it will recursively install them before installing the add-on.

The installation process of a single module consists of the following steps:

1. If there are any, run the add-on `preinit` hook.
2. Load the model definitions from the Python source code and update the database structure, if necessary (refer to `Chapter 5`, *Application Models*, for details).
3. Load the data files of the add-on and update the database contents, if necessary (refer to `Chapter 7`, *Module Data*, for details).
4. Install the add-on demo data if demo data has been enabled in the instance.
5. If there are any, run the add-on `postinit` hook.
6. Run a validation of the view definitions of the add-on.
7. If demo data is enabled and a test is enabled, run the tests of the add-on (refer to `Chapter 18`, *Automated Test Cases*, for details).
8. Update the module state in the database.
9. Update the translations in the database from the add-on's translations (refer to `Chapter 12`, *Internationalization*, for details).

> The `preinit` and `postinit` hooks are defined in the `__manifest__.py` file using the `pre_init_hook` and `post_init_hook` keys, respectively. These hooks are used to invoke Python functions before and after the installation of an add-on module. To learn more about `init` hooks, refer to `Chapter 4`, *Creating Odoo Modules*.

Add-on update

When you update an add-on, Odoo checks in its list of available add-on modules for an installed add-on with the given name. It also checks for the reverse dependencies of that add-on (these are the add-ons that depend on the updated add-on). If any, it will recursively update them, too.

The update process of a single add-on module consists of the following steps:

1. Run the add-on module's pre-migration steps, if any (refer to Chapter 7, *Module Data*, for details).
2. Load the model definitions from the Python source code and update the database structure if necessary (refer to Chapter 5, *Application Models*, for details).
3. Load the data files of the add-on and update the database's contents if necessary (refer to Chapter 7, *Module Data*, for details).
4. Update the add-on's demo data if demo data is enabled in the instance.
5. If your module has any migration methods, run the add-on post-migration steps (refer to Chapter 7, *Module Data*, for details).
6. Run a validation of the view definitions of the add-on.
7. If demo data is enabled and a test is enabled, run the tests of the add-on (refer to Chapter 18, *Automated Test Cases*, for details).
8. Update the module state in the database.
9. Update the translations in the database from the add-on's translations (refer to Chapter 12, *Internationalization*, for details).

> Note that updating an add-on module that is not installed does nothing at all. However, installing an add-on module that is already installed reinstalls the add-on, which can have some unintended effects with some data files that contain data that is supposed to be updated by the user and not updated during the normal module update process (refer to the *Using the noupdate and forcecreate flags* recipe in Chapter 7, *Module Data*). There is no risk of error from the user interface, but this can happen from the command line.

There's more...

Be careful with dependency handling. Consider an instance where you want to have the `sale`, `sale_stock`, and `sale_specific` add-ons installed, with `sale_specific` depending on `sale_stock`, and `sale_stock` depending on `sale`. To install all three, you only need to install `sale_specific`, as it will recursively install the `sale_stock` and `sale` dependencies. To update all three, you need to update `sale`, as this will recursively update the reverse dependencies, `sale_stock` and `sale_specific`.

Another tricky part with managing dependencies is when you add a dependency to an add-on that already has a version installed. Let's understand this by continuing with the previous example. Imagine that you add a dependency on `stock_dropshipping` in `sale_specific`. Updating the `sale_specific` add-on will not automatically install the new dependency, and neither will requesting the installation of `sale_specific`. In this situation, you can get very nasty error messages because the Python code of the add-on is not successfully loaded, but the data of the add-on and the models tables in the database are present. To solve this, you need to stop the instance and manually install the new dependency.

Installing add-on modules from GitHub

GitHub is a great source of third-party add-ons. A lot of Odoo partners use GitHub to share the add-ons they maintain internally, and the **Odoo Community Association** (**OCA**) collectively maintains several hundred add-ons on GitHub. Before you start writing your own add-on, ensure that you check that nothing already exists that you can use as is or as a starting point.

This recipe will show you how to clone the `partner-contact` project of the OCA from GitHub and make the add-on modules it contains available in your instance.

Getting ready

Suppose you want to change the way addresses are handled in your instance; your customer needs a third field in addition to Odoo's two fields (`street` and `street2`) to store addresses. You can certainly write your own add-on to add a field to `res.partner`, but the issue is a bit trickier than it seems if you want the address to be properly formatted on invoices. Fortunately, someone on a mailing list tells you about the `partner_address_street3` add-on, which is maintained by the OCA as part of the `partner-contact` project.

The paths that are used in this recipe reflect the layout that was proposed in the *Standardizing your instance directory layout* recipe.

How to do it...

To install `partner_address_street3`, follow these steps:

1. Go to your project's directory:

   ```
   $ cd ~/odoo-dev/my-odoo/src
   ```

2. Clone the `12.0` branch of the `partner-contact` project in the `src/` directory:

   ```
   $ git clone --branch 12.0 \
   https://github.com/OCA/partner-contact.git src/partner-contact
   ```

3. Change the add-ons path to include that directory and update the add-ons list of your instance (refer to the *Configuring the add-ons path* and *Updating the add-on modules list* recipes of this chapter). The `add-ons_path` line of `instance.cfg` should look like this:

   ```
   addons_path = ~/odoo-dev/my-odoo/src/odoo/odoo/addons, \
   ~/odoo-dev/my-odoo/src/odoo/addons, \
   ~/odoo-dev/my-odoo/src/, \
   ~/odoo-dev/local-addons
   ```

4. Install the `partner_address_street3` add-on (if you don't know how to install the module, take a look at the previous recipe, *Installing and upgrading local add-on modules*).

How it works...

All of the Odoo Community Association code repositories have their add-ons contained in separate subdirectories, which is coherent in accordance with what is expected by Odoo regarding the directories in the add-ons path. Consequently, just cloning the repository somewhere and adding that location in the add-ons path is enough.

There's more...

Some maintainers follow a different approach and have one add-on module per repository, living at the root of the repository. In that case, you need to create a new directory, which you will add to the add-ons path and clone all of the add-ons from the maintainer you need in this directory. Remember to update the add-on modules list each time you add a new repository clone.

Applying changes to add-ons

Most add-ons that are available on GitHub are subject to change and do not follow the rules that Odoo enforces for its stable release. They may receive bug fixes or enhancements, including issues or feature requests that you have submitted, and these changes may introduce database schema changes or updates in the data files and views. This recipe explains how to install the updated versions.

Getting ready

Suppose you reported an issue with `partner_address_street3` and received a notification that the issue was solved in the last revision of the `12.0` branch of the `partner-contact` project. In this case, you will want to update your instance with this latest version.

How to do it...

To apply a source modification to your add-on from GitHub, you need to perform the following steps:

1. Stop the instance using that add-on.
2. Make a backup if it is a production instance (refer to the *Manage Odoo server databases* recipe in `Chapter 1`, *Installing the Odoo Development Environment*).
3. Go to the directory where `partner-contact` was cloned:

   ```
   $ cd ~/odoo-dev/my-odoo/src/partner-contact
   ```

4. Create a local tag for the project so that you can revert to that version in case things break:

   ```
   $ git checkout 12.0
   $ git tag 12.0-before-update-$(date --iso)
   ```

5. Get the latest version of the source code:

   ```
   $ git pull --ff-only
   ```

6. Update the `partner_address_street3` add-on in your databases (refer to the *Installing and upgrading local add-on modules* recipe).
7. Restart the instance.

How it works...

Usually, the developer of the add-on module occasionally releases the newest version of the add-on. This update typically contains bug fixes and new features. Here, we will get a new version of the add-on and update it in our instances.

If `git pull --ff-only` fails, you can revert to the previous version using the following command:

```
$ git reset --hard 12.0-before-update-$(date --iso)
```

Then, you can try `git pull` (without `--ff-only`), which will cause a merge, but this means that you have local changes on the add-on.

See also

If the update step breaks, refer to the *Updating Odoo from Source* recipe in `Chapter 1`, *Installing the Odoo Development Environment*, for recovery instructions. Remember to always test an update on a copy of a database production first.

Applying and trying proposed pull requests

In the GitHub world, a **Pull Request (PR)** is a request that's made by a developer so that the maintainers of a project can include some new developments. Such a PR may contain a bug fix or a new feature. These requests are reviewed and tested before being pulled into the main branch.

This recipe explains how to apply a PR to your Odoo project in order to test an improvement or a bug fix.

Getting ready

As in the previous recipe, suppose you reported an issue with `partner_address_street3` and received a notification that the issue was solved in a pull request, which hasn't been merged in the 12.0 branch of the project. The developer asks you to validate the fix in PR #123. You need to update a test instance with this branch.

You should not try out such branches directly on a production database, so first create a test environment with a copy of the production database (refer to `Chapter 1`, *Installing the Odoo Development Environment*, and `Chapter 3`, *Server Deployment*).

How to do it...

To apply and try out a GitHub pull request for an add-on, you need to perform the following steps:

1. Stop the instance.
2. Go to the directory where `partner-contact` was cloned:

   ```
   $ cd ~/odoo-dev/my-odoo/src/partner-contact
   ```

3. Create a local tag for the project so that you can revert to that version in case things break:

   ```
   $ git checkout 12.0
   $ git tag 12.0-before-update-$(date --iso)
   ```

4. Pull the branch of the `pull` request. The easiest way to do this is by using the number of the PR, which should have been communicated to you by the developer. In our example, this is pull request number `123`:

   ```
   $ git pull origin pull/123/head
   ```

5. Update the `partner_address_street3` add-on module in your database and restart the instance (refer to the *Installing and upgrading local add-on modules* recipe if you don't know how to update the module).
6. Test the update—try to reproduce your issue, or try out the feature you wanted.

If this doesn't work, comment on the PR page of GitHub, explaining what you did and what didn't work so that the developer can update the PR.

If it works, say so on the PR page too; this is an essential part of the PR validation process, and it will speed up the merging in the main branch.

How it works...

We are using a GitHub feature that enables pull requests to be pulled by number using the `pull/nnnn/head` branch name, where `nnnn` is the number of the PR. The Git pull command will merge the remote branch in ours, applying the changes in our code base. After this, we update the add-on module, test it, and report back to the author of the change with regards to any failures or success.

There's more...

You can repeat step 4 of this recipe for different pull requests in the same repository if you want to test them simultaneously. If you are really happy with the result, you can create a branch to keep a reference to the result of the applied changes:

```
$ git checkout -b 12.0-custom
```

Using a different branch will help you remember that you are not using the version from GitHub, but a custom one.

> The `git branch` command can be used to list all of the local branches you have in your repository.

From then on, if you need to apply the latest revision of the 12.0 branch from GitHub, you will need to pull it without using `--ff-only`:

```
$ git pull origin 12.0
```

Server Deployment 3

In this chapter, we will cover the following recipes:

- Installing Odoo for production use
- Adapting the configuration file for production
- Setting-up Odoo as a system service
- Configuring a reverse proxy and SSL with nginx and Let's Encrypt
- Using Docker to run Odoo
- Running Odoo through docker-compose
- Managing content delivery networks for a website

Introduction

In `Chapter 1`, *Installing the Odoo Development Environment* (in the *Easy installation from source* recipe), as well as in `Chapter 2`, *Managing Odoo Server Instances* (in the *Standardizing your instance directory layout* recipe), we explored the setup of a development environment. The requirements for a production environment are slightly different to this. This chapter covers the specificity of the deployment of Odoo.

Installing Odoo for production use

Installing Odoo in the production phase is not very different from installing Odoo for development. While there are several possible approaches, this recipe proposes a setup that is similar to the development installation.

Getting ready

We expect you to have a development instance ready. In this recipe, we assume the following:

- The project of your instance is managed in the same way as suggested in `Chapter 2`, *Managing Odoo Server Instances*, in the *Standardize your instance directory layout* recipe. We will use `https://github.com/yourlogin/project.git`. This repository should contain the configuration file of the instance used during development, the specific add-ons of the instance, and any helper script that you may have created in the context of the project.

  Caution:
  If the configuration files of your project include security information, such as passwords, you should not push the project on a public service such as GitHub. Use an internal Git repository or a private GitHub project instead.

- The deployment server is running Debian Stretch (but it should work with little change on derived distributions, such as Ubuntu see `Chapter 1`, *Installing the Odoo Development Environment*, for more information on this).
- You have `root` access to the final server using `ssh` or `sudo`. If you don't, you will have to find a system administrator to assist you in the configuration of the deployment server.
- You know the final fully-qualified domain name under which the server will be accessed.

How to do it...

To install Odoo for production, you need to carry out the following steps:

1. As `root`, install and build the following dependencies:

```
# apt-get update
# apt-get install git python3.5 postgresql nano virtualenv \
      gcc python3.5-dev libxml2-dev libxslt1-dev \
      libevent-dev libsasl2-dev libldap2-dev libpq-dev \
      libpng-dev libjpeg-dev \
      xfonts-75dpi xfonts-base wget xz-utils
# wget -O wkhtmltox.tar.xz \
  https://github.com/wkhtmltopdf/wkhtmltopdf/releases/download/0
```

```
.12.4/wkhtmltox-0.12.4_linux-generic-amd64.tar.xz
# tar xvf wkhtmltox.tar.xz
# mv wkhtmltox/lib/* /usr/local/lib/
# mv wkhtmltox/bin/* /usr/local/bin/
# mv wkhtmltox/share/man/man1 /usr/local/share/man/
```

2. As `root`, create a user called `odoo`:

```
# adduser odoo
```

3. Configure the PostgreSQL database:

```
# sudo -u postgres createuser odoo
# sudo -u postgres createdb -O odoo odoo_project
```

4. As `odoo`, clone the project repository:

```
# su odoo
$ mkdir ~/odoo-prod
$ cd ~/odoo-prod
$ git clone https://github.com/yourlogin/project.git project
$ mkdir -p project/src
```

5. As the `odoo` user, clone the Odoo source code:

```
$ cd project/src
$ git clone -b 12.0 --single-branch
https://github.com/odoo/odoo.git odoo
```

6. Create `virtualenv` and install the dependencies:

```
$ virtualenv -p python3 ~/env-odoo-12.0
$ source ~/env-odoo-12.0/bin/activate
$ pip3 install -r odoo/requirements.txt
```

7. Clone all third-party add-on repositories in the `project/src` subdirectory:

```
$ git clone -b 12.0 https://github.com/OCA/partner-contact.git
```

8. Create the `~/odoo-prod/project/bin` directory:

```
$ mkdir ~/odoo-prod/project/bin
```

9. Create a script to easily start Odoo in the production environment in `~/odoo-prod/project/bin/start-odoo`:

```
#! /bin/sh
PYTHON=~env-odoo-12.0/bin/python3
```

```
ODOO=~odoo/odoo-prod/project/src/odoo/odoo-bin
CONF=~odoo/odoo-prod/project/production.conf
${PYTHON} ${ODOO} -c ${CONF} "$@"
```

10. Make the script executable:

```
$ chmod +x ~/odoo-prod/project/bin/start-odoo
```

11. As `root`, uninstall `gcc`:

```
# apt-get remove gcc
```

How it works...

Most of the recipe is identical to what is described in `Chapter 1`, *Installing the Odoo Development Environment*, but there are a few key differences.

We are using a dedicated system user with an Odoo login. This enables us to control who has access to the account, for example, by configuring the `sudo` or `ssh` authorized keys. It also allows us to give this user as few permissions as possible, in case the instance is compromised.

The database user linked to this account does not have any privileges – not even database creation. We create the database externally, just once. If the instance is compromised, an attacker won't be able to create additional databases on the server.

The Odoo script we are creating will be used in the *Setting-up Odoo as a system service* recipe later in this chapter. It uses the `production.conf` configuration file, which is explained in the next recipe, *Adapting the configuration file for production*.

We uninstall `gcc` at the end of the process so that if an attacker gains access, they will not be able to use this to recompile executables locally.

At the end of this recipe, your server will not be ready yet. You will need to refer to the *Adapting the configuration file for production, Setting-up Odoo as a system service,* and *Configuring a reverse proxy and SSL recipes*, which are included in this chapter.

There's more...

The following are a few more important points to consider when preparing the deployment of your instance.

Server dimensioning

What should you use for a server? Pretty much any physical server these days is more than enough to handle an average sized Odoo instance with about 20 simultaneous users. Since virtual machines typically have fewer resources provisioned, you will need to pay a little more attention to this if you are planning to run on a virtual machine. Here are a few key points to get you started. Obviously, they will need fine-tuning to match your use of Odoo.

A small Odoo instance needs at least 1 GB of RAM. Don't be shy with this the last thing you want to happen for your server to swap 2-4 GB is a good starting point. Give your server two CPU/cores at the very least. If you are running the PostgreSQL server on the same host, provision at least four CPU/cores and add 1 GB of RAM for the database. The additional CPU/cores will be used by the Odoo workers that are covered in the next recipe, *Adapting the configuration file for production*.

The source code of your instance will eat up 1-2 GB of hard disk if you are keeping the Git history, which we recommend in this recipe. The file store (`data_dir` in the configuration file) will grow as the instance is used, and the growth heavily depends on what you are doing in the instance. Start with 5 GB, which should give you plenty of time before getting full, and monitor the disk usage. If you are running the database on the same host, give plenty of disk space to the partition that will contain the database working files, starting at 50 GB.

You will also need space for the on-site backups, both of the databases, and the file store. A lot can depend on your back-up plan 200 GB is a good starting point.

PostgreSQL tuning

Discussing **PostgreSQL tuning** is beyond the scope of this book. You may want to checkout out *PostgreSQL 10 Admin Cookbook* or *PostgreSQL 10.0 High Performance*, both from Packt Publishing, for in-depth coverage of these topics.

The default configuration of PostgreSQL is generally very conservative and is meant to prevent the database server from hogging all the system resources. On production servers, you can safely increase some parameters in the `postgresql.conf` file to get better performance. Here are some settings for PostgreSQL 9.6 that you can use to get started:

```
max_connections = 80
shared_buffers = 256MB
effective_cache_size = 768MB
work_mem = 3276kB
```

```
maintenance_work_mem = 64MB
min_wal_size = 2GB
max_wal_size = 4GB
checkpoint_completion_target = 0.9
wal_buffers = 7864kB
default_statistics_target = 100
```

You will need to restart PostgreSQL after modifying these settings.

The pgtune utility can help in finding a more suitable configuration. An online version is available at http://pgtune.leopard.in.ua/:

Connect to the website and fill in the following form:

- **DB Version**: Use the database version you have installed (by default, `9.6` in Debian Stretch or 10.5 in Ubuntu 18.04).
- **OS Type**: `Linux`.
- **DB Type**: Choose `Online transaction processing system`, as Odoo instances are heavy users of transactions.
- **Total Memory (RAM)**: Put the amount of RAM you want to allocate to PostgreSQL this will be almost all of it if you are using a dedicated server (see more details about the dedicated database server in the next paragraph).
- **Number of CPUs (core)**: The value of this parameter will be the amount of CPU/core you want to allocate to PostgreSQL.
- **Number of Connections**: The max number of simultaneous queries your database server will accept.
- **Data Storage**: The type of data storage device. For example, SSD or HDD.

If your instance is heavily loaded, you will benefit from separating the database server and the Odoo server onto two different hosts. Don't use two virtual machines running on the same physical server if you reach this point use two physical servers with a high-speed network connection between both. In that case, you will need to ensure that the `pg_hba.conf` file on the database server host allows password-authenticated connections on the database from the Odoo server, and that the `postgresql.conf` file lets the PostgreSQL server listen in on the network interface connecting both servers.

Source code version

When cloning Odoo and the third-party dependencies, you may want to ensure that you are using the exact same revision as the one you had in development. There are several ways to do this:

- You can manually mark down the SHA1 version of the local revision in a file, record this in the project repository, and ensure that you are using the same revision on the production server.
- You can use tags or branches on forks of these repositories in your GitHub account.

- You can use `git submodule` to tie these revisions to the repository of your project (visit `https://git-scm.com/book/en/v2/Git-Tools-Submodules` for some documentation on this handy tool).

> **Why not use the Linux distribution packages provided by Odoo?**
> If you do this, you will get started much faster because a lot of things are handled for you by the packages. However, there are a few issues with using the packaged source. Most importantly, you cannot easily patch the source code of Odoo, which is easier if you run from the source. Granted, this is not something you have to do every day, but being able to use the standard development tools to achieve this, rather than manually applying and tracking patches on production servers, is a big help and a precious time gain.

Backups

This recipe does not cover **backups**. At the very least, you should have the `cron` task on the server running a daily backup. A simple and basic solution is to edit the `crontab` file as `root` by running `crontab -e` and adding the following lines:

```
@daily su postgres -c pg_dumpall | gzip >\
 /backups/postgresql-$(date +%u).dump.gz
@daily tar czf /backups/odoo-filestore-$(date +%u).tgz \
/home/odoo/odoo-prod/project/filestore
```

Don't forget to create the `/backups` directory. The backup files should not be stored on the same hard disk and, ideally, they would be mirrored on a server in a different physical location. Check these backups on a regular basis having backups that you can't restore when you need them is useless.

The proposed solution is to keep daily backups of the last seven days, which means you will lose one day of work if a problem arises. There are more advanced solutions available for PostgreSQL that allow point-in-time recovery. You can find more information about this in *PostgreSQL 9 Admin Cookbook*, by Packt Publishing. Similarly, there are many Linux tools, such as duplicity (`http://duplicity.nongnu.org/`), which you can use for file backups, allowing easy management.

Adapting the configuration file for production

In Chapter 1, *Installing the Odoo Development Environment*, we saw how to save the configuration of the instance in a file. We used the default values for lots of parameters, and, if you followed the *Standardize your instance directory layout* recipe in Chapter 2, *Managing Odoo Server Instances*, as well as the *Installing Odoo for production use* recipe for the production installation, you should now have that same configuration file in the production environment. This recipe shows how to derive a configuration file that is suitable for use in production.

Getting ready

We assume that you have installed Odoo on the production server with the *Install Odoo for production* recipe. We assume that you will be running PostgreSQL on the same server as Odoo.

You may want to install the pwgen utility to generate random passwords.

We will describe the steps here as if we are running them on the production server, but they can also be executed on your development server, since the new configuration file is added to the Git repository of the project that we use to deploy on the production server.

How to do it...

To adapt the configuration file for production, you need to follow these steps:

1. Create a new configuration file for production based on the development file:

   ```
   $ cd ~/odoo-prod/project
   $ cp development.conf production.conf
   ```

2. Edit the production configuration production.conf file.
3. Change addons_path to match the production base directory:

   ```
   addons_path = /home/odoo/odoo-prod/project/src/odoo/addons,
   /home/odoo/odoo-prod/project/src/odoo/odoo/addons,
   /home/odoo/odoo-prod/project/src/partner-contact
   ```

4. Change the data directory:

```
data_dir = /home/odoo/odoo-prod/project/filestore
```

5. Change the server log path to match the production base directory:

```
logfile = /home/odoo/odoo-prod/project/logs/odoo.log
```

6. Configure the log rotation:

```
logrotate = True
```

7. Configure the logging handlers:

```
log_level = warn
log_handler =
:WARNING,werkzeug:CRITICAL,odoo.service.server:INFO
```

8. Adapt the database connection parameters:

```
db_host = False
db_maxconn = 64
db_name = odoo-project
db_password = False
db_port = False
db_template = template1
db_user = False
```

9. Configure the database filter and disable the database listing:

```
dbfilter = odoo-project$
list_db = False
```

10. Change the master password using a random password generated with pwgen:

```
admin_password = use a random password
```

11. Configure Odoo to run with workers:

```
workers = 4
# limit_memory_hard: 4GB
limit_memory_hard = 4294967296
# limit_memory_soft: 640MB
limit_memory_soft = 671088640
limit_request = 8192
limit_time_cpu = 120
limit_time_real = 300
```

12. Only listen on the local network interface:

```
http_interface = 127.0.0.1
```

13. Save the file and add it to the Git repository:

```
$ git add production.conf
$ git commit -m "add production configuration file"
```

How it works...

Most of the parameters shown in this recipe are explained in the *Manage Odoo server instances* recipe in `Chapter 1`, *Installing the Odoo Development Environment*.

In *steps 3, 4 and 5*, we change the add-ons path and the log file. If you are developing in an environment with the same layout as the production environment, this is required, because Odoo expects absolute paths in the configuration file.

Step 6 enables log rotation. This will cause Odoo to configure the logging module to archive the server logs on a daily basis, and to keep the old logs for 30 days. This is useful on production servers to avoid logs eventually consuming all the available disk space.

Step 7 configures the logging level. The proposed setting is very conservative and will only log messages with at least the `WARNING` level, except for `werkzeug` (`CRITICAL`) and `odoo.service.server` (`INFO`). For more information on log filtering, refer to `Chapter 8`, *Debugging*, where you will find the *Producing server logs to help debug methods* recipe. Feel free to tune this to your taste.

Step 8 configures the database settings. This will work if you are running the PostgreSQL database server locally and have set it up as explained in the previous recipe. If you're running PostgreSQL on a different server, you will need to replace the `False` values with the appropriate connection settings for your database instance.

Step 9 restricts the database available to the instance by configuring a database filter. We also disable the database listing, which is not strictly necessary given that the regular expression we set in `dbfilter` can only match one single database. It is still a good thing to do though, in order to avoid displaying the list of databases to anyone, and to avoid users connecting to the wrong database.

Step 10 sets a nontrivial master password for the instance. The master password is used for database management through the user interface, and a few community add-ons also use it for extra security before performing actions that can lead to data loss. You really need to set this to a nontrivial value. We propose using the `pwgen` utility to generate a random password, but any other method is also valid.

Step 11 configures Odoo to work with **workers**. In this mode, Odoo will create a number of worker processes (in this example, 4) to handle HTTP requests. This has several advantages over the default configuration, in which request handling is performed in separate threads, which are as follows:

- Requests can be handled in parallel by making better use of multiple cores or CPUs on the server (Python threads are penalized by the existence of the **Global Interpreter Locks** (GIL) in the Python interpreter).
- It is possible to terminate one of the workers depending on resource consumption. The following table gives the various resource limits that can be configured:

Parameter	Suggested value	Description
limit_memory_hard	4294967296	This is the maximum amount of RAM a worker will be able to allocate. We recommend using 4 GB, as some processes launched by Odoo can allocate large amounts of RAM.
limit_memory_soft	671088640	If a worker ends up consuming more than this limit (640 MB in our setting), it will be terminated after it finishes processing the current request.
limit_request	8192	A worker will be terminated after having processed this many requests.
limit_time_cpu	120	This is the maximum amount of CPU time allowed to process a request.
limit_time_real	300	This is the maximum amount of wall-clock time allowed to process a request.

Step 12 configures the internal Odoo web server to only listen on the local interface. This means that the instance will not be reachable from other servers. This enables us to configure a **reverse proxy** on the same server to access the server and to force encrypted connections. Take a look at the *Configuring a reverse proxy and SSL* recipe later in this chapter.

> If you are not sure about the number of workers for your server setup, use the following formula to calculate number of workers for your system:
>
> ```
> No. of workers = (No. of CPU * 2) + 1
> ```
>
> Here, one worker can handle approximately six concurrent users.

There's more...

When running with workers, you may encounter some issues specific to this mode:

- If you get strange errors when running with workers, with `wkhtmltopdf` not working as intended (for example, prematurely exiting with a -11 or -6 status), then you likely have `limit_memory_hard` set to a value that is too low. Try raising it a bit, as the default value is notoriously too low.
- If you get timeout errors when performing long operations (this includes CSV imports and exports and add-on module installations), try increasing the `limit_time_cpu` and `limit_time_real` parameters, as there, too, the default value is quite low. If you have a reverse proxy, you may want to check its timeout limit too (too low a limit in the reverse proxy will not prevent the transactions from completing, but will display an error message in the user's browser, which can cause them to retry the import and unnecessarily put a load on the server).
- If your instance gets completely stuck when printing reports, try raising the number of workers. This can be a deadlock caused by `wkhtmltopdf` blocking up all the available workers while printing.

> In any case, always validate the setup before going to production, and remember to test printing reports when enabling workers.

Setting up Odoo as a system service

For a production instance, it is very important that the Odoo server gets started when the computer reboots. On current Linux systems, this is achieved through a `systemd` configuration. If your OS is not using `systemd`, you will have to check the documentation to obtain this result.

Getting ready

We assume that you followed the first two recipes to install and configure your Odoo instance especially the deployed source of Odoo, which is at `/home/odoo/odoo-prod/project/src/odoo/`, and the configuration file of the instance, which is at `/home/odoo/odoo-prod/project/production.conf`. The scripts also make use of the `start-odoo` script created in step nine of the *Install Odoo for production* recipe.

How to do it...

To configure `systemd` to start Odoo, you need to perform the following steps:

1. As root, create a file called `/lib/systemd/system/odoo.service` with the following contents:

```
[Unit]
Description=Odoo 12.0
After=postgresql.service
[Service]
Type=simple
User=odoo
Group=odoo
WorkingDirectory=/home/odoo/odoo-prod/project
ExecStart=/home/odoo/odoo-prod/project/bin/start-odoo
[Install]
WantedBy=multi-user.target
```

2. As `root`, register the service:

```
# systemctl enable odoo.service
```

3. As `root`, start the service:

```
# service odoo start
```

4. To stop the service, you can run the following:

```
# service odoo stop
```

How it works...

Systemd uses some configuration files or scripts to know which programs must run when the server boots. The configurations provided in the recipe will need small adaptations to match the paths of your instance.

> Don't forget to reboot your server and check that Odoo is properly started!

Configuring a reverse proxy and SSL with nginx and Let's Encrypt

When you access the Odoo server via HTTP protocol, all the information between the user's browsers and the Odoo server are exposed to the network, so it is necessary to use the HTTPS protocol that encrypts the exchanges. Odoo cannot do this natively, and it is necessary to configure a **reverse proxy** that will handle the encryption and decryption on behalf of the Odoo server. This recipe shows how to use nginx (http://nginx.net) for this. We will also show how to use **Let's Encrypt** (https://letsencrypt.org) to manage the certificate and renewal if your organisation does not have its own way of getting a signed **SSL certificate**.

Getting ready

You should know the public name of the server and should configure your DNS accordingly. In this recipe, we will use odoo.example.com as the name of our server. You will need to replace it with your domain.

Make sure that port 80 and 443 of the server are reachable from outside using the DNS name you will be using if you are getting the SSL certificate from Let's Encrypt.

How to do it...

In order to access your instance using HTTPS through NGINX, you need to follow these steps:

1. As `root`, install the Let's Encrypt client, `certbot`:

```
# apt-get update
# apt-get install software-properties-common
# add-apt-repository universe
# add-apt-repository ppa:certbot/certbot
# apt-get update
# apt-get install certbot python-certbot-nginx
```

2. As `root`, request a certificate from Let's Encrypt (don't forget to change the email and the address of the server):

```
# certbot certonly --standalone -n --agree-tos\
 -m youremail@example.com -d odoo.example.com
```

3. As `root`, install `nginx`:

```
# apt-get install nginx
```

4. Create a configuration file in `/etc/nginx/sites-available/odoo-ssl` and add an upstream reference as follows:

```
upstream odoo {
    server 127.0.0.1:8069;
}
upstream odoochat {
    server 127.0.0.1:8072;
}
```

5. In the same file, add the rewrite rule to redirect `http` into the `https` website:

```
server {
    listen 80;
    server_name odoo.example.com;
    rewrite ^(.*) https://$host$1 permanent;
}
```

6. In the same file, add the following `nginx` configuration to serve the Odoo instance over `https`:

```
server {
    listen 443;
    server_name odoo.example.com;
    proxy_read_timeout 720s;
    proxy_connect_timeout 720s;
    proxy_send_timeout 720s;

    # Place configuration of steps 7 to 12 here
}
```

7. Add the SSL configuration to the server block:

```
# SSL Configuration
ssl on;
ssl_certificate
/etc/letsencrypt/live/odoo.example.com/fullchain.pem;
ssl_certificate_key
/etc/letsencrypt/live/odoo.example.com/privkey.pem;
ssl_session_timeout 30m;
ssl_protocols TLSv1 TLSv1.1 TLSv1.2;
ssl_ciphers "ECDHE-ECDSA-AES256-GCM-SHA384:ECDHE-RSA-
AES256-GCM-SHA384:ECDHE-ECDSA-CHACHA20-POLY1305:ECDHE-RSA-
CHACHA20-POLY1305:ECDHE-ECDSA-AES256-SHA384:ECDHE-RSA-AES256-
SHA384";
ssl_prefer_server_ciphers on;
```

8. Add the log file configuration to the server block:

```
# Add log files
access_log /var/log/nginx/odoo.access.log;
error_log /var/log/nginx/odoo.error.log;
```

9. Enable `gzip` by adding the following configuration to the server block:

```
# enable gzip
gzip on;
gzip_types text/css text/scss text/plain text/xml
application/xml application/json application/javascript;
```

10. Add proxy headers configuration to the server block:

```
# Add Headers
proxy_set_header X-Forwarded-Host $host;
proxy_set_header X-Forwarded-For
$proxy_add_x_forwarded_for;
proxy_set_header X-Forwarded-Proto $scheme;
proxy_set_header X-Real-IP $remote_addr;
```

11. Add reverse proxy configuration to the server block:

```
# Manage longpolling on 8072 port
location /longpolling {
    proxy_pass http://odoochat;
}

# Redirect requests to odoo server on 8069
location / {
    proxy_redirect off;
    proxy_pass http://odoo;
}
```

12. Enable the static `cache` by adding the following configuration to the server block:

```
# Enable static cache
location ~* /web/static/ {
    proxy_cache_valid 200 60m;
    proxy_buffering on;
    expires 864000;
    proxy_pass http://odoo;
}
```

13. As `root`, link the configuration file in `/etc/nginx/sites-enabled/`:

```
# ln -s /etc/nginx/sites-available/odoo-ssl\
/etc/nginx/sites-enabled/odoo-ssl
```

14. As `root`, remove `/etc/nginx/sites-enabled/default`:

```
# rm /etc/nginx/sites-enabled/default
```

15. As `Odoo`, edit the production configuration file of the instance to enable `proxy_mode`:

    ```
    proxy_mode = True
    ```

16. As `root`, restart your `odoo` instance and `nginx`:

    ```
    # service odoo restart
    # service nginx restart
    ```

17. As `root`, create a cron `/etc/cron.d/letsencrypt` file to ensure that the certificate will get renewed with the following content:

    ```
    11 5 * * * certbot renew
    ```

How it works...

In *steps 1* and *2*, we installed `certbot` and generated the **SSL certificate** for the `odoo.example.com` website. The `certbot` program is a command-line utility that eases interacting with `letsencrypt.org` to generate a free SSL certificate. The complete documentation is available at `https://certbot.eff.org/docs/`. In this recipe, we used a subcommand, `certbot certonly <options>`, which will request a signed certificate from Let's Encrypt for the domains passed to the `-d` option. Use the `-m` option to specify your email address. The `--standalone` option asks `certbot` to set up a local temporary web server, which Let's Encrypt will attempt to contact to check that you control the domain for which you are requesting a certificate. It is, therefore, important that the command is run on the server that will be hosting Odoo, that the DNS is pointing to that server, and that no firewall is blocking port `80` and `443` on the server.

> This check is done by connecting to `http://<yourdomain>:80/.well-known/acme`. The `--standalone` mode of `certbot` creates a temporary web server listening on this port and able to answer the request, but this only works if no other process is listening on port `80` and if the external firewall is letting external connections on that port pass.

We are using nginx as a reverse HTTP proxy. Incoming HTTP and HTTPS connections are handled by nginx, which delegates the processing of the requests to the Odoo server. The Odoo server is configured to only listen on the local loopback interface (127.0.0.1) on port 8069 for normal requests (http_port) and port 8072 for long polling requests (longpolling_port). You may need to adapt the port numbers to your configuration:

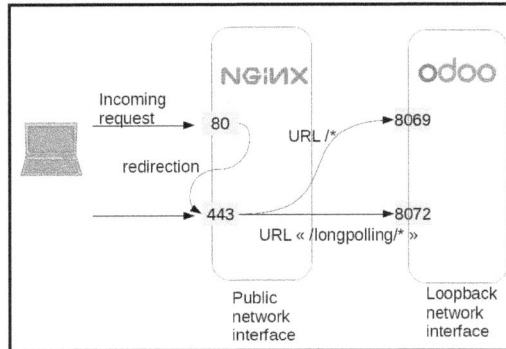

In *step 4*, we added the /etc/nginx/sites-available/odoo-ssl nginx configuration file. In this file, we added an upstream reference. This is the reference of your local server and we are going to use it in the next steps.

In *step 5*, we added server configuration to manage incoming connections on port 80 using the HTTP protocol. We don't want to serve our website on HTTP because the data is transferred in clear text, meaning that the passwords can be sniffed. Consequently, we add a URL and rewrite a rule in order to permanently redirect URLs to port 443 using the encrypted HTTPS protocol.

Steps 6-13 are bit more complex and the configurations are added to handle connections using the HTTPS protocol. Here are the details of different blocks of configurations:

- The configuration block in step six configures the server to handle the requests of the odoo.example.com domain on port 433.
- The configuration block in step seven configures the SSL protocol, the encryption key, and the certificate.
- The configuration block in step eight adds the log file's location. Whenever the request is served through Nginx, this file will be used to store logs.

- Step nine adds the `gzip` block, which is used to compress files. This plays an important role in reducing the page size.
- The configuration block in step 10 adds extra headers to provide more information with each request. These extra headers are used to provide more information to the Odoo server.
- *Step 11* adds the `location /` block, which defines the default processing of incoming requests they will be proxied to the Odoo server listening on port `8069`.
- *Step 11* also adds the `location /longpolling` block, which is used to handle queries made on URLs starting with `/longpolling`, which are then forwarded to Odoo on port `8072`. These connections are used by the bus add-on module to send notifications to the web client.
- *Step 12* adds the `location ~* /web/static/` block, which uses a regular expression to match the URLs of the static files of Odoo modules. These files are rarely updated, and so we ask nginx to cache them in order to lighten the load on the Odoo server.

In the last step, we used the `certbot renew` command, which checks for certificates pending renewal, and automatically renews them. By default, Let's Encrypt certificates have a validity of 90 days, which is quite short. Thanks to this utility, which we run on a daily basis, certificates that are about to expire are automatically renewed.

There's more...

This recipe focuses on the nginx configuration. You may be more familiar with other tools, such as the Apache web server and `mod_proxy`. In this case, you can, of course, use these to achieve a similar setup.

If you would rather not rely on Let's Encrypt and prefer using another **Certification Authority** (**CA**), you can use the following process:

1. Install `openssl`:

```
$ sudo apt-get install openssl
```

2. Generate the key for your server:

```
$ mkdir ~/sslkey
$ openssl genrsa -out ~/sslkey/server.key 2048
```

3. Generate a signing request:

```
$ openssl req -new -key ~/sslkey/server.key\
-out ~/sslkey/server.csr
```

4. The preceding command will ask you a series of questions about your company and your Odoo server's URL. Don't get these wrong, or your certificate will be unusable.

5. You will be able to send the `~/sslkey/server.csr` file to a **Certification Authority (CA)** of your choice. The CA will send you back a file called `server.crt`.

6. You will need to store the file in the `/etc/nginx/ssl/` directory, together with the `server.key` file generated in step two:

```
# mkdir -p /etc/nginx/ssl
# chown www-data /etc/nginx/ssl
# mv server.key server.crt /etc/nginx/ssl
# chmod 710 /etc/nginx/ssl
# chown root:www-data /etc/nginx/ssl/*
# chmod 640 /etc/nginx/ssl/*
```

7. Then, in the nginx `/etc/nginx/sites-available/odoo-443` configuration file provided in the recipe, rewrite the `ssl_certificate` and `ssl_certificate_key` lines, as follows:

```
ssl_certificate /etc/nginx/ssl/server.crt;
ssl_certificate_key /etc/nginx/ssl/server.key;
```

8. Finally, restart `nginx`.

See also

- For more information about the various nginx configuration options, see `http://nginx.org/en/docs/`.
- For a tutorial on the configuration of Apache2 as a reverse proxy and the use of a personal certification authority, take a look at `http://antiun.github.io/odoo-reverse-proxy-howto/`.

Using Docker to run Odoo

Docker is a project meant to make **Linux Containers** (**LXC**) easy to manage by providing high-level tools. These containers can be used to ease the distribution of applications and their dependencies. There is a whole ecosystem built around Docker, meant to ease the deployment and management of dockerized applications. Discussing the details is far beyond the scope of this recipe, and the interested reader may want to check *Learning Docker* by *Packt Publishing* for more in-depth explanations.

In this recipe, we will look at how to use an official Odoo Docker image to run a development or a production server.

Getting ready

We assume that Docker is installed both on your development station and on the production server. The instructions for installing Docker Community Edition for Debian GNU/Linux are on https://docs.docker.com/engine/installation/linux/docker-ce/debian/ (and the instructions for installing Docker for other platforms are close by). Alternatively, you can install docker in your Ubuntu server through the following command:

```
$ sudo apt-get install docker.io
```

How to do it...

Follow these steps to run Docker from the official Odoo image:

1. Set up the PostgreSQL server `docker` instance through the following command:

```
# docker run -d -e POSTGRES_USER=odoo -e
POSTGRES_PASSWORD=odoo -e POSTGRES_DB=postgres --name db
postgres:10
```

2. Run the PostgresSQL database through the following command:

```
# docker start db
```

3. Set up the Odoo `docker` instance through the following command:

```
# docker run -p 8069:8069 --name odoo --link db:db -t odoo
```

4. Run the `odoo` instance through the following command:

```
# docker start odoo
```

The preceding command will start the Odoo server on port `8069`. In your local machine, you will be able to access the `odoo` instance at `http://localhost: 8069`.

If you want to see the status of the running docker containers, then run the following command:

```
# docker ps
```

The `docker ps` command will display the output like this:

```
pga@pga:~$ sudo docker ps
CONTAINER ID    IMAGE          COMMAND                 CREATED         STATUS          PORTS                                    NAMES
34e4293ea70f    odoo           "/entrypoint.sh odoo"   13 hours ago    Up 13 hours     0.0.0.0:8069->8069/tcp, 8071/tcp         odoo
44afda3e8386    postgres:10    "docker-entrypoint.s…"  14 hours ago    Up 13 hours     5432/tcp                                 db
```

How it works...

Docker allows you to create system images and then ship them around to run them on other servers. Docker images are created by writing a Dockerfile, which describes how to add layers generally to a pre-existing Dockerfile. The Docker images are hosted at `https://hub.docker.com`, and, in this recipe, we have used official images of PostgreSQL and Odoo.

Before running the Odoo instance container, we need to set up a container for PostgreSQL. In the first step, we ran the Docker image for PostgreSQL 10. The command will search for the`PostgreSQL` Docker image. If it is not available in your system, Docker will download it. In the command, we passed the `--name db` option. Here, `db` will be the name of the PostgreSQL container. In *step 2*, we started the Docker container for PostgreSQL.

In *step 3*, we ran the Docker image for Odoo. This runs the Odoo instance on port `8069`. If you want to run the command with a different configuration, you can use different options. Here are some examples of how to run the Odoo instance with custom options discussed further.

Running the Odoo image with a configuration file

You can run the Odoo instance with your own configuration file. To do so, you will need to use the -v volume option. Here is the command to run the Odoo container with the configuration file at /path/to/config/odoo.conf:

```
# docker run -v /path/to/config.conf:/etc/odoo -p 8069:8069 --name
odoo --link db:db -t odoo
```

If you don't want to load the configuration file and you want to use configuration options with the command directly, then you can pass the option with -- in the command line, like this:

```
# docker run -p 8069:8069 --name odoo --link db:db -t odoo -- --db-
filter=test
```

Running the Odoo image with custom add-ons

By default, the Odoo container runs with the Community edition add-ons. If you want to run Odoo with your own add-on modules, you can do this by mounting your add-ons in the /mnt/extra-addons directory as follows:

```
$ docker run -v /path/to/my_addons:/mnt/extra-addons -p 8069:8069 --
name odoo --link db:db -t odoo
```

Running multiple Odoo instances

If you want to run multiple Odoo instances in a single server, then you can do this by changing the container name and exposing the port. Look at the following command, which will run two odoo containers with the names odoo1 and odoo2. These Odoo instances will run on port 8090 and 8091 respectively:

```
# docker run -p 8070:8069 --name odoo2 --link db:db -t odoo
# docker run -p 8071:8069 --name odoo3 --link db:db -t odoo
```

There is more...

If your server requirements are not satisfied with the official Odoo Docker image, then you can create your own Docker image with Dockerfile. Dockerfile of the official Odoo is available at https://github.com/odoo/docker. You can modify the Docker file and then build the Docker image with the docker build command.

Running Odoo through docker-compose

In the previous recipe, we ran the Odoo instance using two Docker containers, the PostgreSQL and Odoo containers. In this recipe, we will look at `docker-compose`. `docker-compose` is the tool used to manage the multi-container Docker application.

Getting ready

In order to set up Odoo with the `docker-compose` tool, you will need to install `docker-compose` in your system. Execute the following command in the Terminal to install `docker-compose` in your system:

```
$ sudo apt-get install docker-compose
```

How to do it...

Follow these commands to run the Odoo instance through `docker-compose`:

1. Add a new `docker-compose.yaml` file with the following content:

```
version: '2'
services:
  web:
    image: odoo:12.0
    depends_on:
      - db
    ports:
      - "8069:8069"
  db:
    image: postgres:10
    environment:
      - POSTGRES_DB=postgres
      - POSTGRES_PASSWORD=odoo
      - POSTGRES_USER=odoo
```

2. Execute the following command in the Terminal to run the Odoo instance:

```
# docker-compose up -d
```

The preceding command will start the Odoo server on port 8069. In your local machine, you will be able to access the Odoo instance at `http://localhost: 8069`. Use the `docker ps` command to see the running containers.

How it works...

`docker-compose` needs a YAML file to set up the services. In the YAML file, you will need to add the details of the services you want to deploy. After creating the YAML file, you can start all services in a single command.

In *step 1*, we created the YAML file for our services. To run the Odoo instance, we need two containers: one of the PostgreSQL database and one for Odoo itself. In the `services:` section we added two services. The first one is named `web`. This service is used to run the Odoo instance. In the service, you will need to specify the image name you want to containerize. So, in the `web` service, we have added `odoo:12.0` as an image.

The Odoo instance cannot run without a database. Consequently, we need to specify the dependencies via the `depends_on` key. Next, we specified the service for PostgreSQL. We gave the name `db` to this service. Note that this is the same service that we added in the dependencies of the `web` service.

In *step 2*, we used the `docker-compose` command to run the Odoo instance. The `docker-compose` command will run the two containers. You can see the details with the `docker ps` command. After running the command, you can access Odoo through `https://localhost:8069`.

If you want to use custom add-ons or your own configuration, you can do so by specifying volumes in the docker compose YAML file like this:

```
version: '2'
services:
  web:
    image: odoo:12.0
    depends_on:
      - db
    ports:
      - "8069:8069"
    volumes:
```

```
        - odoo-web-data:/var/lib/odoo
        - ./config:/etc/odoo
        - ./addons:/mnt/extra-addons
  db:
    image: postgres:10
    environment:
        - POSTGRES_DB=postgres
        - POSTGRES_PASSWORD=odoo
        - POSTGRES_USER=odoo
        - PGDATA=/var/lib/postgresql/data/pgdata
    volumes:
        - odoo-db-data:/var/lib/postgresql/data/pgdata
volumes:
  odoo-web-data:
  odoo-db-data:
```

The YAML file will run the Odoo instance with your custom add-ons and custom configuration. It also uses the volumes for the Odoo and PostgreSQL data directories.

There's more...

The way we set up the Docker image in this recipe is merely a starting point. You will probably want to tune a lot of parameters to ease the management of the instance and modify `Dockerfile` to allow you to run Odoo from your local sources, rather than requiring a rebuild each time you edit a module, all of which is far beyond the scope of this book.

Docker is a huge universe, and offers a wealth of options. You may want to publish your images on a Docker image repository and use Docker push and Docker pull to publish and retrieve the Docker images of your projects. You may also want to run a container management platform, such as `Rancher`, to run your images on a cluster of servers with load balancing. Alternatively, you can integrate the image building step with your continuous integration environment to publish snapshots of your developments for testing.

Managing content delivery networks for websites

Content delivery networks (**CDN**) are quite popular nowadays. CDNs helps to decrease the loading time of websites by serving static resources from the nearest server, geographically. Odoo has built-in options for configuring a CDN for a website app. In the following example, we will see how you can set up a CDN in Odoo.

Getting ready

We assume that your Odoo instance is up and running and you have installed the `website` app. If you don't know how to install an app in Odoo, please refer to the *Installing and upgrading local add-on modules* recipe from `Chapter 2`, *Managing Odoo Server Instances*.

There are several CDN providers available on the market, such as MaxCDN, KeyCDN, and CloudFlare. In the following example, we are going to use KeyCDN as our CDN provider. If you are using any other CDN provider, you will find the same kind of configuration options, because most CDN providers re running similar concepts, so you can use any pull-based CDN provider.

How to do it...

In order to set up a CDN for the Odoo website, you need to do two configurations:

- Configuration of the CDN provider
- Configuration of the CDN at Odoo

Configuring the CDN provider

Please follow these steps to configure the CDN provider. Here, we will use the KeyCDN account:

1. Log in to your KeyCDN account.
2. Click on the **Zones** Menu and add a new zone:

3. Set the following options to activate the CDN zone:
   - **Zone Name**: Any name to identify your zone
   - **Zone Status**: **active**
   - **Zone Type**: **Pull**
   - **Origin URL**: The URL on which your Odoo instance is running

4. Save the **pull** zone and copy **Zone URL** from the list. We will use this URL in the Odoo configuration in the next few steps:

Configuring CDN at Odoo

To configure a CDN in Odoo, log into your Odoo instance with the
`Administrator` account and follow these steps:

1. Activate the **Developer** mode, because the CDN configuration options are
   displayed only if you activated the **Developer** mode. Refer to the *Activating
   the Odoo developer tools* recipe from `Chapter 1`, *Installing the Odoo
   Development Environment*.
2. Open the **Configuration** menu of the website app and search for the
   Content Delivery Networks (CDN) option:

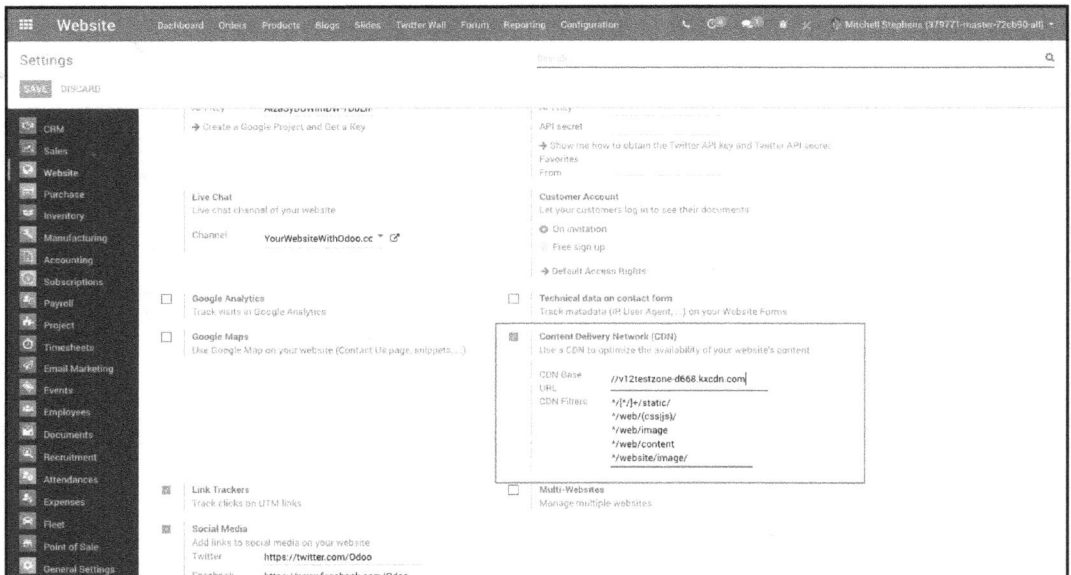

3. Set the following options in the website configuration and save the settings:
   - **CDN Base URL**: Set the URL provided by the CDN provider. In
     our example, we will use the `zone` URL we copied in step three
     the previous subsection.
   - **CDN Filters**: It is list of URL regex for website static resources.
     This rules used to identify the static resources which are going to
     served with CDN . Odoo will fill default values in this field, but
     if you are serving a static resource from any other URL, please
     add those URLs manually in a separate line.

To check whether the CDN integration is working well or not, follow this procedure:

1. Log out from Odoo and open the website publicly,
2. Open the browser developer tools and open the network tab.
3. Reload the page and check the static resources URL in the networking log. Static resources should be loaded via CDN URLs exactly like in the following screenshot:

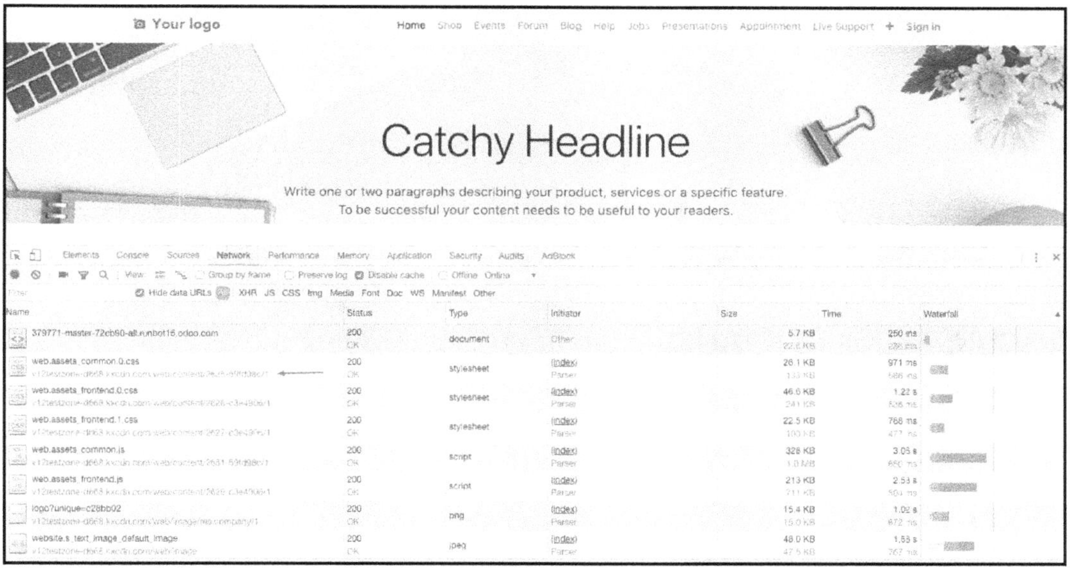

You might get **Cross-Origin Resource** errors, as shown in the following screenshot:

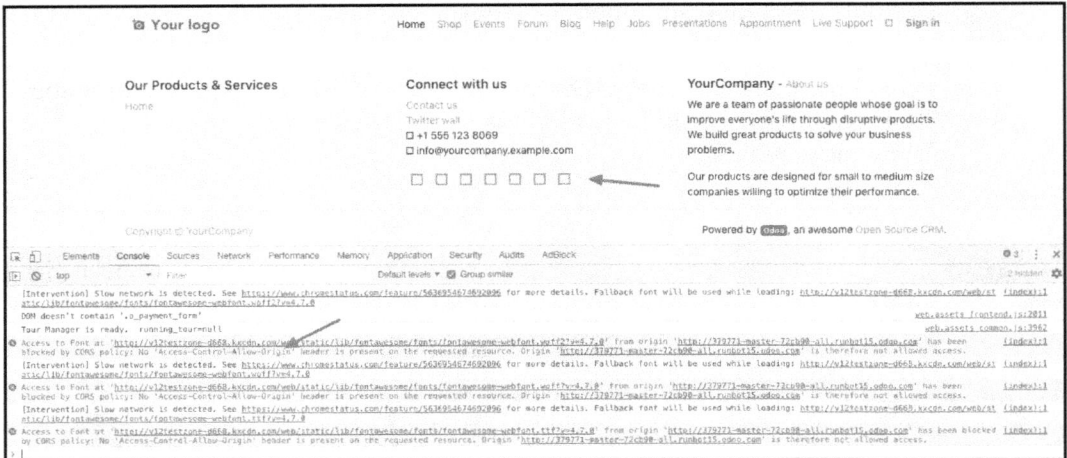

In order to fix these errors, you need to activate **CORS** from your CDN provider. In **keyCDN,** you will see the **CORS** option in advanced features, such as in the following screenshot:

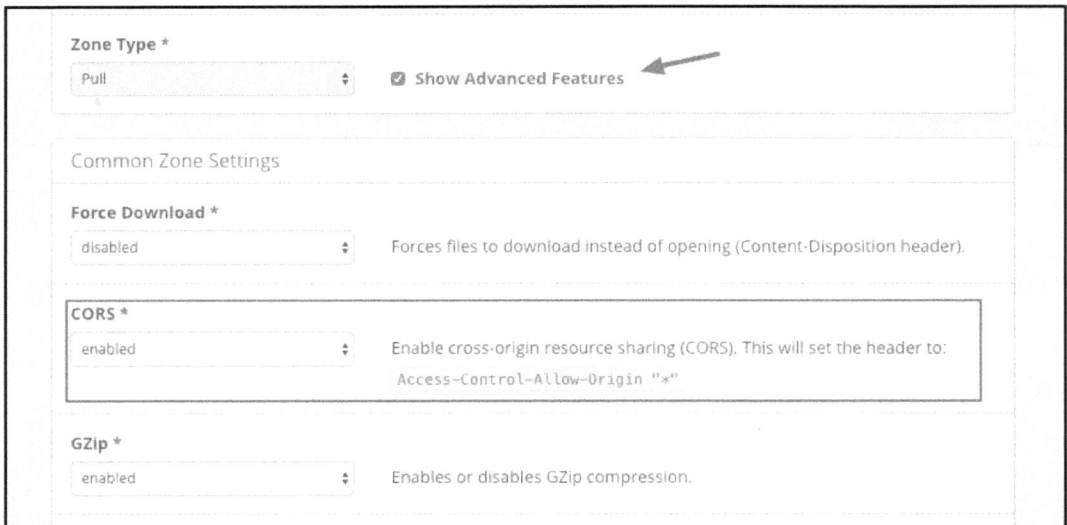

How it works...

When you activate a pull zone, KeyCDN will automatically fetch all the static resources from your website. It will cache these resources in various servers around the globe. In order to use these cached resources in your Odoo website, you need to load static resources through the URL given by CDN providers. In step five, we configured this URL for Odoo websites, so that after this step, Odoo will load the static resources CDN URL.

> In order to avoid issues for backend users, Odoo loads static resources through CDN URLs for public users only. Once you have logged in, Odoo will stop using CDN URLs and it will load static resources from the same origin.

There's more...

CDN providers, such as Cloudflare, are using DNS-based techniques to serve website content. If you want to configure CDN with Cloudflare, you need to configure a few more things. In order to do that, you need to serve a cached website through different domains/subdomains than your website domain. For example, odoo.com uses odoocdn.com to serve CDN resources. After that, you need to set this domain/subdomain as a **CDN Base URL** in Odoo configuration.

> **Warning**
> You need to be extra careful when serving the same website from different URLs, as it might change your sitemap.xml file if you submit this CDN domain for search engine indexing.

4
Creating Odoo Add-On Modules

In this chapter, we will cover the following recipes:

- Creating and installing a new add-on module
- Completing the add-on module manifest
- Organizing the add-on module file structure
- Adding models
- Adding menu items and views
- Adding Access Security
- Using the scaffold command to create a module

Technical requirements

For this chapter, you are expected to have Odoo installed and you are also expected to have followed the recipes in `Chapter 1`, *Installing the Odoo Development Environment*. You are also expected to be comfortable in discovering and installing extra add-on modules, as described in `Chapter 2`, *Managing Odoo Server Instances*. All the code used in this chapter can be downloaded from the following GitHub repository, at: `https://github.com/PacktPublishing/Odoo-12-Development-Cookbook-Third-Edition/tree/master/Chapter04`

Check out the following video to see the Code in Action: `http://bit.ly/2UGuw2f`

Introduction

Now that we have a development environment and know how to manage Odoo server instances and databases, you can learn how to create Odoo add-on modules.

Our main goal here is to understand how an add-on module is structured and the typical incremental workflow to add components to it. The various components that are mentioned in the recipe names of this chapter will be covered extensively in subsequent chapters.

What is an Odoo add-on module?

Except for the framework code, all of the code bases of Odoo are packed in the form of modules. These modules can be installed or uninstalled at any time from the database. There are two main purposes for these modules. Either you can add new apps/business logic, or you can modify an existing application. Put simply, in Odoo, everything starts and ends with modules.

Odoo is being used by companies of all sizes; each company has a different business flow and requirements. To deal with this issue, Odoo splits the features of the application into different modules. These modules can be loaded in the database on demand. Basically, the user can enable/disable these feature at any time. Consequently, the same software can be adjusted for different requirements. Check out the following screenshot of Odoo modules; the first module in the column is the main application and others are designed for adding extra features in that app. To get a modules list grouped by the apps category, go to the **Apps** menu and apply grouping on **Category**:

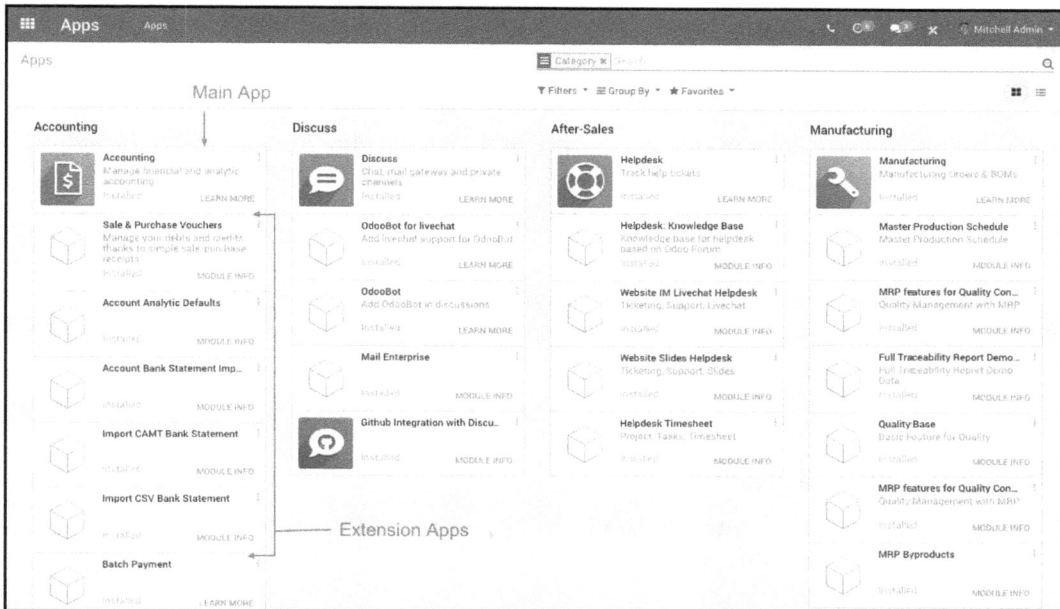

If you plan on developing the new application in Odoo, you should create boundaries for various features. This will be very helpful for dividing your application into different add-on modules. Now that you know the purpose of the add-on module in Odoo, we can start building our own add-on module.

Creating and installing a new add-on module

In this recipe, we will create a new module, make it available in our Odoo instance, and install it.

Getting ready

To begin, we will need an Odoo instance that's ready to use.

If you followed the *Easy installation of Odoo from source* recipe in `Chapter 1`, *Installing the Odoo Development Environment*, Odoo should be available at `~/odoo-dev/odoo`. For explanation purposes, we will assume this location for Odoo, although you can use any other location of your preference.

We will also need a location to add our own Odoo modules. For the purpose of this recipe, we will use a `local-addons` directory alongside the `odoo` directory, at `~/odoo-dev/local-addons`.

How to do it...

As an example for this chapter, we will create a small add-on module for managing a list of the books for the library.

The following steps will create and install a new add-on module:

1. Change the working directory in which we will work and create the add-ons directory where our custom module will be placed:

```
$ cd ~/odoo-dev
$ mkdir local-addons
```

2. Choose a technical name for the new module and create a directory with that name for the module. For our example, we will use `my_library`:

```
$ mkdir local-addons/my_library
```

> A module's *technical name* must be a valid Python identifier; it must begin with a letter, and only contain letters, numbers, and underscore characters. It is preferable that you only use lowercase letters in the module name.

3. Make the Python module importable by adding an `__init__.py` file:

```
$ touch local-addons/my_library/__init__.py
```

4. Add a minimal module manifest for Odoo to detect it as an add-on module. Create a `__manifest__.py` file with this line:

```
{'name': 'My Library'}
```

5. Start your Odoo instance, including our module directory, in the add-ons path:

```
$ odoo/odoo-bin --addons-path=odoo/addon/,local-addons/
```

If the `--save` option is added to the Odoo command, the add-ons path will be saved in the configuration file. The next time you start the server, if no add-ons path option is provided, this will be used.

6. Make the new module available in your Odoo instance; log in to Odoo using `admin`, enable the **Developer Mode** in the **About** box, and in the **Apps** top menu, select **Update Apps List**. Now, Odoo should know about our Odoo module.

7. Select the **Apps** menu at the top and, in the search bar in the top-right, delete the default **Apps filter** and search for `my_library`. Click on its **Install** button, and the installation will be concluded.

How it works...

An Odoo module is a directory that contains code files and other assets. The directory name that's used is the module's technical name. The `name` key in the module manifest is its title.

The `__manifest__.py` file is the module manifest. This contains a Python dictionary with module metadata like category, version, the modules it depends on, and a list of the data files that it will load. In this recipe, we used a minimal manifest file, but in real modules, we will need other important keys. These are discussed in the next recipe, *Completing the add-on module manifest*.

The module directory must be Python-importable, so it also needs to have an `__init__.py` file, even if it's empty. To load a module, the Odoo server will import it. This will cause the code in the `__init__.py` file to be executed, so it works as an entry point to run the module Python code. Due to this, it will usually contain import statements to load the module Python files and submodules.

Known modules can be installed directly from the command line using the `--init` or `-i` option. This list is initially set when you create a new database from the modules found on the add-ons path provided at that time. It can be updated in an existing database with the **Update Module List** menu.

Completing the add-on module manifest

The manifest is an important piece for Odoo modules. It contains important metadata about the add-on module and declares the data files that should be loaded.

Getting ready

We should have a module to work with, already containing a `__manifest__.py` manifest file. You may want to follow the previous recipe to provide such a module to work with.

How to do it...

We will add a manifest file and an icon to our add-on module:

1. To create a manifest file with the most relevant keys, edit the module's `__manifest__.py` file so that it looks like this:

    ```python
    {
        'name': "My library",
        'summary': "Manage books easily",
        'description': """Long description""",
        'author': "Your name",
        'website': "http://www.example.com",
        'category': 'Uncategorized',
        'version': '12.0.1',
        'depends': ['base'],
        'data': ['views.xml'],
        'demo': ['demo.xml'],
    }
    ```

2. To add an icon for the module, choose a PNG image to use and copy it to `static/description/icon.png`.

How it works...

The content in the manifest file is a regular Python dictionary, with keys and values. The example manifest we used contains the most relevant keys:

*   `name`: This is the title for the module.
*   `summary`: This is the subtitle with a one-line description.

- `description`: This is a long description written in plain text or **ReStructuredText (RST)** format. It is usually surrounded by triple quotes, and is used in Python to delimit multi-line texts. For an RST quick-start reference, visit
  `http://docutils.sourceforge.net/docs/user/rst/quickstart.html`.
- `author`: This is a string with the name of the authors. When there is more than one, it is common practice to use a comma to separate their names, but note that it should still be a string, not a Python list.
- `website`: This is a URL people should visit to learn more about the module or the authors.
- `category`: This is used to organize modules by areas of interest. The list of the standard category names available can be seen at `https://github.com/odoo/odoo/blob/12.0/odoo/addons/base/data/ir_module_category_data.xml`. However, it's also possible to define other new category names here.
- `version`: This is the module's version number. It can be used by the Odoo app store to detect newer versions for installed modules. If the version number does not begin with the Odoo target version (for example, `12.0`), it will be automatically added. Nevertheless, it will be more informative if you explicitly state the Odoo target version, for example, by using `12.0.1.0.0` or `12.0.1.0`, instead of `1.0.0` or `1.0`.
- `depends`: This is a list with the technical names of the modules it directly depends on. If your module is not depending on any other add-on module, then you should at least add a `base` module. Don't forget to include any module defining XML IDs, views, or models that are referenced by this module. That will ensure that they all load in the correct order, avoiding hard-to-debug errors.
- `data`: This is a list of relative paths for the data files to load during module installation or upgrade. The paths are relative to the module root directory. Usually, these are XML and CSV files, but it's also possible to have YAML data files. These are discussed in depth in `Chapter 7`, *Module Data*.
- `demo`: This is the list of relative paths to the files with demonstration data to load. These will only be loaded if the database was created with the **Demo Data** flag enabled.

The image that is used as the module icon is the PNG file at `static/description/icon.png`.

> **TIP**
>
> Odoo is expected to have significant changes between major versions, so modules that have been built for one major version are not likely to be compatible with the next version without conversion and migration work. Due to this, it's important to be sure about a module's Odoo target version before installing it.

There's more...

Instead of having the long description in the module manifest, it's possible to have a separate description file. Since version 8.0, it can be replaced by a README file, with either a .txt, .rst, or an .md (Markdown) extension. Otherwise, include a description/index.html file in the module.

This HTML description will override the description that's defined in the manifest file.

There are a few more keys that are frequently used:

- licence: The default value is LGPL-3. This identifier is used for licence under the module that is made available. Other licence possibilities include AGPL-3, Odoo Proprietary License v1.0 (mostly used in paid apps), and Other OSI Approved Licence.
- application: If this is True, the module is listed as an application. Usually, this is used for the central module of a functional area.
- auto_install: If this is True, it indicates that this is a *glue* module, which is automatically installed when all of its dependencies are installed.
- installable: If this is True (the default value), it indicates that the module is available for installation.
- external_dependencies: Some Odoo modules internally use Python/bin libraries. If your modules are using such libraries, you need to put them here. This will stop users from installing the module if the listed modules are not installed on the host machine.
- {pre_init, post_init, uninstall}_hook: This is a Python function hook that's called during installation/uninstallation. For a more detailed example, refer to Chapter 9, *Advanced Server-side Development Techniques*.

Organizing the add-on module file structure

An add-on module contains code files and other assets, such as XML files and images. For most of these files, we are free to choose where to place them inside the module directory.

However, Odoo uses some conventions on the module structure, so it is advisable to follow them.

Getting ready

We are expected to have an add-on module directory with only the `__init__.py` and `__manifest__.py` files. In this recipe, we assume this is `local-addons/my_library`.

How to do it...

To create the basic skeleton for the add-on module, perform the following steps:

1. Create the directories for code files:

```
$ cd local-addons/my_library
$ mkdir models
$ touch models/__init__.py
$ mkdir controllers
$ touch controllers/__init__.py
$ mkdir views
$ mkdir security
$ mkdir data
$ mkdir demo
$ mkdir i18n
```

2. Edit the module's top `__init__.py` file so that the code in the subdirectories is loaded:

```
from . import models
from . import controllers
```

This should get us started with a structure containing the most used directories, similar to this one:

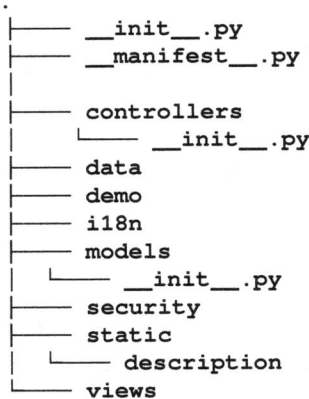

```
├──── __init__.py
├──── __manifest__.py
│
├──── controllers
│     └──── __init__.py
├──── data
├──── demo
├──── i18n
├──── models
│     └──── __init__.py
├──── security
├──── static
│     └──── description
└──── views
```

How it works...

To provide some context, an Odoo add-on module can have three types of files:

- The **Python code** is loaded by the `__init__.py` files, where the `.py` files and code subdirectories are imported. Subdirectories containing Python code, in turn, need their own `__init__.py`.
- **Data files** that are to be declared in the `data` and `demo` keys of the `__manifest__.py` module manifest in order to be loaded are usually XML and CSV files for the user interface, fixture data, and demonstration data. There can also be YAML files, which can include some procedural instructions that are run when the module is loaded, for instance, to generate or update records programmatically rather than statically in an XML file.
- **Web assets** such as JavaScript code and libraries, CSS, SASS, and QWeb/HTML templates. These files are used to build UI parts and manage user actions in those UI elements. These are declared through an XML file that's extending the master templates, which adds these assets to the web client or website pages.

The add-on files are to be organized into the following directories:

- models/ contains the backend code files, thus creating the models and their business logic. A file per model is recommended with the same name as the model, for example, library_book.py for the library.book model. These are addressed in depth in Chapter 5, *Application Models*.
- views/ contains the XML files for the user interface, with the actions, forms, lists, and so on. Like models, it is advised to have one file per model. Filenames for website templates are expected to end with the _template suffix. Backend views are explained in Chapter 10, *Backend Views*, and website views are addressed in Chapter 16, *CMS Website Development*.
- data/ contains other data files with module initial data. Data files are explained in Chapter 7, *Module Data*.
- demo/ contains data files with demonstration data, which is useful for tests, training, or module evaluation.
- i18n/ is where Odoo will look for the translation .pot and .po files. Refer to Chapter 12, *Internationalization*, for more detail. These files don't need to be mentioned in the manifest file.
- security/ contains the data files that define access control lists, which is usually a ir.model.access.csv file, and possibly an XML file to define access *groups and record rules* for row level security. Take a look at Chapter 11, *Access Security*, for more details on this.
- controllers/ contains the code files for the website controllers, and for modules providing that kind of feature. Web controllers are covered in Chapter 14, *Web Server Development*.
- static/ is where all web assets are expected to be placed. Unlike other directories, this directory name is not just a convention. The files inside this directory are public and can be accessed without user login. This directory mostly contains files like JavaScript, Style sheet, Images, and so on. They don't need to be mentioned in the module manifest, but will have to be referred to in the web template. This is discussed in detail in Chapter 16, *CMS Website Development*.

> **TIP**
>
> When adding new files to a module, don't forget to declare them either in the __manifest__.py (for data files) or __init__.py (for code files) file; otherwise, those files will be ignored and won't be loaded.

Adding models

Models define the data structures that will be used by our business applications. This recipe shows you how to add a basic model to a module.

In our example, we want to manage books for a library. To do this, we need to create a model to represent books. Each book will have a name and a list of authors.

Getting ready

We should have a module to work with. If you followed the first recipe in this chapter, *Creating and installing a new add-on module*, you will have an empty module called my_library. We will use that for our explanation.

How to do it...

To add a new Model, we need to add a Python file describing it and then upgrade the add-on module (or install it, if this was not already done). The paths that are used are relative to our add-on module's location (for example, ~/odoo-dev/local-addons/my_library/):

1. Add a Python file to the models/library_book.py module with the following code:

```
from odoo import models, fields class
LibraryBook(models.Model): _name = 'library.book' name =
fields.Char('Title', required=True) date_release =
fields.Date('Release Date')
 author_ids = fields.Many2many(
 'res.partner',
 string='Authors'
 )
```

2. Add a Python initialization file with code files to be loaded by the models/__init__.py module with the following code:

```
from . import library_book
```

3. Edit the module Python initialization file to have the models/ directory loaded by the module:

```
from . import models
```

4. Upgrade the Odoo module either from the command line or from the **Apps** menu in the user interface. If you look closely at the server log while upgrading the module, you should see the following line:

```
odoo.modules.registry: module my_library: creating or updating
database table
```

After this, the new `library.book` model should be available in our Odoo instance. There are two ways to check whether our model has been added to the database or not.

First, you can check it in the Odoo user interface. Activate the developer tools and open the menu at **Settings | Technical | Database Structure | Models**. Search for the `library.book` model here.

The second way is to check the table entry in your PostgreSQL database. You can search for the `library_book` table in the database. In the following code example, we used the `test-12.0` database. However, you can replace this with your database name:

```
$ psql test-12.0
test-12.0# \d library_book;
```

How it works...

Our first step was to create a Python file where our new module was created.

The Odoo framework has its own ORM framework. This ORM framework provides abstraction over the PostgreSQL database. By inheriting the Odoo Python class `Model`, we can create our own model (table). When a new model is defined, it is also added to a central model registry. This makes it easier for other modules to make modifications to it later.

Models have a few generic attributes prefixed with an underscore. The most important one is _name, which provides a unique internal identifier that will be used throughout the Odoo instance. The ORM framework will generate the database table based on this attribute. In our recipe, we used _name = 'library.book'. Based on this attribute, the ORM framework will create a new table called `library_book`. Note that the ORM framework will create a table name by replacing . with _ in the value of the _name attribute.

The model fields are defined as class attributes. We began by defining the `name` field of the `Char` type. It is convenient for models to have this field because, by default, it is used as the record description when referenced by other models.

We also used an example of a relational field, `author_ids`. This defines a many-to-many relation between `Library Books` and its partners. A book can have many authors and each author can have written many books.

There's much more to say about models, and they will be covered in depth in `Chapter 5`, *Application Models*.

Next, we must make our module aware of this new Python file. This is done by the `__init__.py` files. Since we placed the code inside the `models/` subdirectory, we need the previous `__init__` file to import that directory, which should in turn contain another `__init__` file, importing each of the code files there (just one, in our case).

Changes to Odoo models are activated by upgrading the module. The Odoo server will handle the translation of the `model` class into database structure changes.

Although no example is provided here, business logic can also be added to these Python files, either by adding new methods to the model's class, or by extending the existing methods, such as `create()` or `write()`. This is addressed in `Chapter 6`, *Basic Server-Side Development*.

Adding menu items and views

Once we have models for our data structure needs, we want a user interface so that our users can interact with them. This recipe builds on the `Library Book` model from the previous recipe and adds a menu item to display a user interface featuring list and form views.

Getting ready

The add-on module for implementing the `library.book` model, which was provided in the previous recipe, is needed. The paths that will be used are relative to our add-on module location (for example, `~/odoo-dev/local-addons/my_library/`).

How to do it...

To add a view, we will add an XML file with its definition to the module. Since it is a new model, we must also add a menu option for the user to be able to access it.

Be aware that the sequence of the following steps is relevant, since some of them use references to IDs that are defined in the preceding steps:

1. Create the XML file to add the data records describing the user interface views/library_book.xml:

```
<?xml version="1.0" encoding="utf-8"?>
<odoo>
  <!-- Data records go here -->
</odoo>
```

2. Add the new data file to the add-on module manifest, __manifest__.py, by adding it to views/library_book.xml:

```
{
    'name': "My Library",
    'summary': "Manage books easily",
    'depends': ['base'],
    'data': ['views/library_book.xml'],
}
```

3. Add the action that opens the views in the library_book.xml file:

```
<record id='library_book_action'
model='ir.actions.act_window'>
    <field name="name">Library Books</field>
    <field name="res_model">library.book</field>
    <field name="view_type">form</field>
    <field name="view_mode">tree,form</field>
</record>
```

4. Add the menu items to the library_book.xml file, making it visible to the users:

```
<menuitem name="My Library" id="library_base_menu" />
<menuitem name="Books" id="library_book_menu"
parent="library_base_menu" action="library_book_action"/>
```

5. Add a custom form view to the `library_book.xml` file:

```xml
<record id="library_book_view_form" model="ir.ui.view">
    <field name="name">Library Book Form</field>
    <field name="model">library.book</field>
    <field name="arch" type="xml">
        <form>
            <group>
                <group>
                    <field name="name"/>
                    <field name="author_ids"
widget="many2many_tags"/>
                </group>
                <group>
                    <field name="date_release"/>
                </group>
            </group>
        </form>
    </field>
</record>
```

6. Add a custom tree (list) view to the `library_book.xml` file:

```xml
<record id="library_book_view_tree" model="ir.ui.view">
    <field name="name">Library Book List</field>
    <field name="model">library.book</field>
    <field name="arch" type="xml">
        <tree>
            <field name="name"/>
            <field name="date_release"/>
        </tree>
    </field>
</record>
```

7. Add custom `Search` options to the `library_book.xml` file:

```xml
<record id="library_book_view_search" model="ir.ui.view">
    <field name="name">Library Book Search</field>
    <field name="model">library.book</field>
    <field name="arch" type="xml">
        <search>
            <field name="name"/>
            <field name="author_ids"/>
            <filter string="No Authors"
                    name="without_author"
                    domain="[('author_ids','=',False)]"/>
        </search>
    </field>
```

```
</record>
```

From version 12, `admin` user must gain proper access rights in order to access our model from the user interface. Odoo will not show your menus and views until you give proper access rights. In the next recipe, we will add access rights to our model, and only after that will you be able to see your menus and views from the `admin` user.

Accessing Odoo as a superuser

By converting the `admin` user into a `superuser`, you can bypass the access rights and therefore access menus and views without giving default access rights. To convert the `admin` user into a `superuser`, activate Developer Mode. After doing this, from the developer tool options, click on the **Become super user** option.

The following screenshot has been provided as a reference:

After becoming the `superuser`, your menu will have a striped background, as shown in the following screenshot:

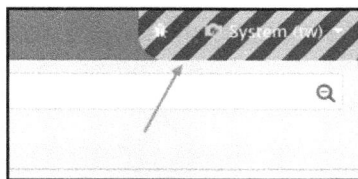

If you try and upgrade the module now, you should be able to see a new menu option (you might need to refresh your web browser). Clicking on the **Books** menu will open a list view for book models, as shown in the following screenshot:

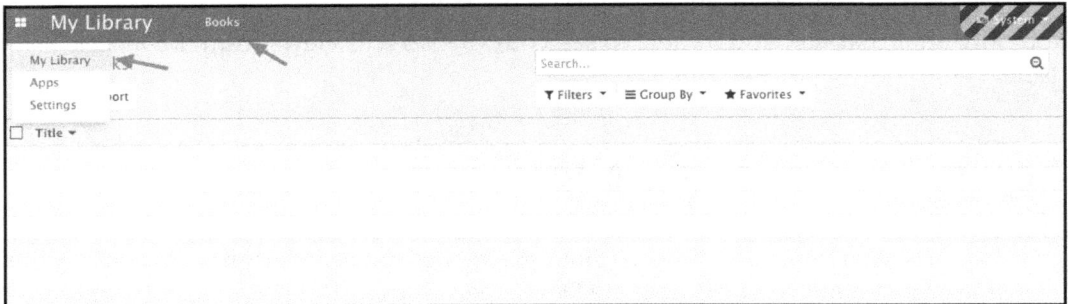

How it works...

At a low level, the user interface is defined by records stored in special models. The first two steps create an empty XML file to define the records to be loaded, and then add them to the module's list of data files to be installed.

Data files can be placed anywhere inside the module directory, but the convention is for the user interface to be defined inside a `views/` subdirectory. Usually, the name of these files is based on the name of the model. In our case, we are creating the user interface for the `library.book` model, so we created the `views/library_book.xml` file.

The next step is to define a window action to display the user interface in the main area of the web client. The action has a target model defined by `res_model`, and the `name` attribute is used to display the title to the user when the user opens the action. These are just the basic attributes. The window action supports additional attributes, giving much more control over how the views are rendered, such as what views are to be displayed, adding filters on the records that are available, or setting default values. These are discussed in detail in `Chapter 10`, *Backend Views*.

In general, data records are defined using a `<record>` tag, and we created a record for the `ir.actions.act_window` model in our example. This will create the window actions.

Similarly, menu items are stored in the `ir.ui.menu` model, and we can create these with the `<record>` tag. However, there is a shortcut tag called `<menuitem>` available in Odoo, so we used this in our example.

These are the menu item's main attributes:

- `name`: This is the menu item text to be displayed.
- `action`: This is the identifier of the action to be executed. We use the ID of the window action we created in the previous step.
- `sequence`: This is used to set the order in which the menu items of the same level are presented.
- `parent`: This is the identifier for the parent menu item. Our example menu item had no parent, meaning that it is to be displayed at the top of the menu.

At this point, we haven't defined any of the views in our module. However, if you upgrade your module at this stage, Odoo will automatically create them on the fly. Nevertheless, we will surely want to control how our views look, so, in the next two steps, a form and a tree view are created.

Both views are defined with a record on the `ir.ui.view` model. The attributes we used are as follows:

- `name`: This is a title identifying the view. In the source code of Odoo, you will find the XML ID repeated here, but if you want, you can add a more human readable title as a name.

  > If the `name` field is omitted, Odoo will generate one using the model name and the type of view. This is perfectly fine for the standard view of a new model. It is recommended to have a more explicit name when you are extending a view, as this will make your life easier when you are looking for a specific view in the user interface of Odoo.

- `model`: This is the internal identifier of the target model, as defined in its `_name` attribute.
- `arch`: This is the view architecture, where its structure is actually defined. This is where different types of views differ from each other.

Form views are defined with a top <form> element, and its canvas is a two-column grid. Inside the form, <group> elements are used to vertically compose fields. Two groups result in two columns with fields, which are added using the <field> element. Fields use a default widget according to their data type, but a specific widget can be used with the help of the widget attribute.

Tree views are simpler; they are defined with a top <tree> element that contains <field> elements for the columns to be displayed.

Finally, we added a Search view to expand the search option in the box at the top-right. Inside the <search> top-level tag, we can have the <field> and <filter> elements. Field elements are additional fields that can be searched from the input given in the search view. Filter elements are predefined filter conditions that can be activated with a click. These subjects are discussed in detail in Chapter 10, *Backend Views*.

Adding access security

When adding a new data model, you need to define who can create, read, update, and delete records. When creating a totally new application, this can involve defining new user groups. Consequently, if a user doesn't have these access rights, then Odoo will not display your menus and views. In the previous recipe, we accessed our menu by converting an admin user into a superuser. After completing this recipe, you will be access menus and views for our Library module directly as an admin user.

This recipe builds on the Library Book model from the previous recipes and defines a new security group of users to control who can access or modify the records of the books.

Getting ready

The add-on module that implements the library.book model, which was provided in the previous recipe, is needed because, in this recipe, we will add the security rules for it. The paths that are used are relative to our add-on module location (for example, ~/odoo-dev/local-addons/my_library/).

How to do it...

The security rules we want to add in this recipe are as follows:

- Everyone will be able to read library book records.
- A new group of users called **Librarians** will have the right to create, read, update, and delete book records.

To implement this, you need to perform the following steps:

1. Create a file called `security/groups.xml` with the following content:

```xml
<?xml version="1.0" encoding="utf-8"?>
<odoo>
  <record id="group_librarian" model="res.groups">
    <field name="name">Librarians</field>
    <field name="users" eval="[(4, ref('base.user_admin'))]"/>
  </record>
</odoo>
```

2. Add a file called `security/ir.model.access.csv` with the following content:

```
id,name,model_id:id,group_id:id,perm_read,perm_write,perm_crea
te,perm_unlink
acl_book,library.book default,model_library_book,,1,0,0,0
acl_book_librarian,library.book_librarian,model_library_book,g
roup_librarian,1,1,1,1
```

3. Add both files in the `data` entry of `__manifest__.py`:

```python
# ...
'data': [
    'security/groups.xml',
    'security/ir.model.access.csv',
    'views/library_book.xml'
],
# ...
```

The newly defined security rules will be in place once you update the add-on in your instance.

How it works...

We are providing two new data files that we add to the add-on module's manifest so that installing or updating the module will load them in the database:

- The `security/groups.xml` file defines a new security group by creating a `res.groups` record. We also gave rights of Librarians to the `admin` user by using its reference ID, `base.user_admin`, so that the admin user will have rights for the `library.book` model.
- The `ir.model.access.csv` file associates permissions on models with groups. The first line has an empty `group_id:id` column, which means that the rule applies to everyone. The last line gives all privileges to members of the group we just created.

> **TIP**
> The order of the files in the data section of the manifest is important; the file for creating the security groups must be loaded before the file listing the access rights, as the access right's definition depends on the existence of the groups. Since the views can be specific to a security group, we recommend putting the group's definition file in the list to be on the safer side.

See also

- This book has a chapter dedicated to security. For more information on security, refer to `Chapter 11`, *Access Security*.

Using the scaffold command to create a module

When creating a new Odoo module, there is some boilerplate code that needs to be set up. To help quick-start new modules, Odoo provides the `scaffold` command.

This recipe shows you how to create a new module using the `scaffold` command, which will put in place a skeleton of the file for directories to use.

Getting ready

We will create the new add-on module in a custom module directory, so we need Odoo installed and a directory for our custom modules. We will assume that Odoo is installed at ~/odoo-dev/odoo and that our custom modules will be placed in the ~/odoo-dev/local-addons directory.

How to do it...

We will use the scaffold command to create boilerplate code. Follow the given steps to create new a module using the scaffold command:

1. Change the working directory to where we will want our module to be. This can be whatever directory you choose, but it needs to be within an add-on path to be useful. Following the directory choices that we used in the previous recipe, it should be as follows:

   $ cd ~/odoo-dev/local-addons

2. Choose a technical name for the new module, and use the scaffold command to create it. For our example, we will choose my_module:

   $ ~/odoo-dev/odoo/odoo-bin scaffold my_module

3. Edit the __manifest__.py default module manifest provided and change the relevant values. You will surely want to at least change the module title in the name key.

This is what the generated add-on module should look like:

```
$ tree my_module
my_module/
├── __init__.py
├── __manifest__.py
├── controllers
│   ├── __init__.py
│   └── controllers.py
├── demo
│   └── demo.xml
├── models
│   ├── __init__.py
│   └── models.py
├── security
│   └── ir.model.access.csv
```

```
└──── views
    ├──── templates.xml
    └──── views.xml

5 directories, 10 files
```

You should now edit the various generated files and adapt them to the purpose of your new module.

How it works...

The `scaffold` command creates the skeleton for a new module based on a template.

By default, the new module is created in the current working directory, but we can provide a specific directory to create the module, passing it as an additional parameter.

Consider the following example:

```
$ ~/odoo-dev/odoo/odoo-bin scaffold my_module ~/odoo-dev/local-addons
```

A `default` template is used, but a `theme` template is also available for website theme authoring. To choose a specific template, the `-t` option can be used. We are also allowed to use a path for a directory with a template.

This means that we can use our own templates with the `scaffold` command. The built-in themes can be used as a guide, and they can be found in the `./odoo/cli/templates` Odoo subdirectory. To use our own template, we can use something like this:

```
$ ~/odoo-dev/odoo/odoo-bin scaffold -t path/to/template my_module
```

Application Models 5

In this chapter, we will cover the following recipes:

- Defining the model representation and order
- Adding data fields to a model
- Using a float field with configurable precision
- Adding a monetary field to a model
- Adding relational fields to a model
- Adding a hierarchy to a model
- Adding constraint validations to a model
- Adding computed fields to a model
- Exposing related fields stored in other models
- Adding dynamic relations using Reference fields
- Adding features to a model using inheritance
- Using abstract models for reusable model features
- Using delegation inheritance to copy features to another model

Introduction

The recipes in this chapter will make small additions to an existing add-on module. We will be using the module we created in the recipes in Chapter 4, *Creating Odoo Add-On Modules*.

Technical requirements

To follow the examples in this chapter, you should have the module that we created in Chapter 4, *Creating Odoo Add-On Modules,* and the module must be ready to use.

All the code used in this chapter can be downloaded from the GitHub repository at `https://github.com/PacktPublishing/Odoo-12-Development-Cookbook-Third-Edition/tree/master/Chapter05`.

Check out the following video to see the code in action: Place holder link

Defining the model representation and order

Models have structural attributes for defining their behavior. These are prefixed with an underscore. The most important model is _name, as this defines the internal global identifier. Odoo creates the database table with this _name attribute. For example, if you provide _name="`library.book`", then the Odoo ORM will create the `library_book` table in the database. This is why the _name attribute must be unique across Odoo.

There are two other attributes that we can use on a model: one to set the field that's used as a representation or title for the records, and another to set the order in which the records are presented.

Getting ready

This recipe assumes that you have an instance ready with `my_library`, as described in Chapter 4, *Creating Odoo Add-On Modules.*

How to do it...

The `my_library` instance should already contain a Python file called `models/library_book.py`, which defines a basic model. We will edit it to add a new class-level attribute after _name:

1. To add a user-friendly title to the model, add the following code:

```
_description = 'Library Book'
```

2. To sort the records first (from newer to older, and then by title), add the following code:

```
_order = 'date_release desc, name'
```

3. To use the `short_name` field as the record representation, add the following code:

```
_rec_name = 'short_name'
short_name = fields.Char('Short Title', required=True)
```

4. Add the `short_name` field in the form view so that it can display the new field in the view:

```
<field name="short_name"/>
```

When we're done, our `library_book.py` file should look as follows:

```python
from odoo import models, fields
class LibraryBook(models.Model):
    _name = 'library.book'
    _description = 'Library Book'
    _order = 'date_release desc, name'
    _rec_name = 'short_name'
    name = fields.Char('Title', required=True)
    short_name = fields.Char('Short Title', required=True)
    date_release = fields.Date('Release Date')
    author_ids = fields.Many2many('res.partner', string='Authors')
```

Your `<form>` view in the `library_book.xml` file will look as follows:

```xml
<form>
    <group>
        <group>
            <field name="name"/>
            <field name="author_ids" widget="many2many_tags"/>
        </group>
```

```
        <group>
            <field name="short_name"/>
            <field name="date_release"/>
        </group>
    </group>
</form>
```

We should then upgrade the module to activate these changes in Odoo.

How it works...

The first step adds a more user-friendly title to the model's definition. This is not mandatory, but can be used by some add-ons. For instance, it is used by the tracking feature in the `mail` add-on module for the notification text when a new record is created. For more details, refer to `Chapter 23`, *Managing Emails*.

By default, Odoo orders the records using the internal `id` value. However, this can be changed so that we can use the fields of our choice by providing an `_order` attribute with a string containing a comma-separated list of field names. A field name can be followed by the `desc` keyword to sort it in descending order.

Only fields stored in the database can be used. Non-stored computed fields can't be used to sort records.

> The syntax for the `_order` string is similar to SQL `ORDER BY` clauses, although it's stripped down. For instance, special clauses, such as `NULLS FIRST`, are not allowed.

Model records use a representation when they are referenced from other records. For example, a `user_id` field with the value 1 represents the **Administrator** user. When displayed in a form view, Odoo will display the username, rather than the database ID. By default, the `name` field is used. In fact, this is the default value for the `_rec_name` attribute, which is why it's convenient to have a `name` field in our models.

> If no `name` field exists in the model, a representation is generated with the model and record identifiers, similar to (`library.book`, `1`).

Since we have added a new field, `short_name`, to the model, the Odoo ORM will add a new column in the database table, but it won't display this field in the view. To do this, we need to add this field in the form view. In step 4, we added the `short_name` in the form view.

There's more...

Record representation is available in a magic `display_name` computed field, and has been automatically added to all models since version 8.0. Its values are generated using the `name_get()` model method, which was already in existence in the previous versions of Odoo.

The default implementation of `name_get()` uses the `_rec_name` attribute to find which field holds the data, which is used to generate the display name. If you want your own implementation for the display name, you can override the `name_get()` logic to generate a custom display name. The method must return a list of tuples with two elements: the ID of the record and the Unicode string representation for the record.

For example, to have the title and its release date in the representation, such as `Moby Dick (1851-10-18)`, we can define the following:

```
def name_get(self):
    result = []
    for record in self:
        rec_name = "%s (%s)" % (record.name, record.date_release)
        result.append((record.id, rec_name))
    return result
```

Adding data fields to a model

Models are meant to store data, and this data is structured in fields. Here, you will learn about the several types of data that can be stored in fields, and how to add them to a model.

Getting ready

This recipe assumes that you have an instance ready with the `my_library` add-on module available, as described in `Chapter 4`, *Creating Odoo Add-On Modules*.

How to do it...

The my_library add-on module should already have models/library_book.py,
defining a basic model. We will edit it to add new fields:

1. Use the minimal syntax to add fields to the Library Books model:

```python
from odoo import models, fields
class LibraryBook(models.Model):
    # ...
    short_name = fields.Char('Short Title')
    notes = fields.Text('Internal Notes')
    state = fields.Selection(
        [('draft', 'Not Available'),
         ('available', 'Available'),
         ('lost', 'Lost')],
        'State')
    description = fields.Html('Description')
    cover = fields.Binary('Book Cover')
    out_of_print = fields.Boolean('Out of Print?')
    date_release = fields.Date('Release Date')
    date_updated = fields.Datetime('Last Updated')
    pages = fields.Integer('Number of Pages')
    reader_rating = fields.Float(
        'Reader Average Rating',
        digits=(14, 4),  # Optional precision (total,
decimals),
    )
```

2. We have added new fields to the model. We still need to add these fields in
   the form view, in order to reflect these changes in the user interface. Refer
   to the following code to add fields in the form view:

```xml
<form>
    <group>
        <group>
            <field name="name"/>
            <field name="author_ids" widget="many2many_tags"/>
            <field name="state"/>
            <field name="pages"/>
            <field name="notes"/>
        </group>
        <group>
            <field name="short_name"/>
            <field name="date_release"/>
            <field name="date_updated"/>
            <field name="cover" widget="image" class="oe_avatar"/>
```

```
          <field name="reader_rating"/>
       </group>
    </group>
    <group>
       <field name="description"/>
    </group>
 </form>
```

Upgrading the module will make these changes effective in the Odoo model.

Take a look at the following samples of different fields. Here, we have used different attributes on various types in the fields. This will give you a better idea of field declaration:

```
short_name = fields.Char('Short Title',translate=True,
index=True)
state = fields.Selection(
    [('draft', 'Not Available'),
        ('available', 'Available'),
        ('lost', 'Lost')],
    'State', default="draft")
description = fields.Html('Description', sanitize=True,
strip_style=False)
pages = fields.Integer('Number of Pages',
        groups='base.group_user',
        states={'lost': [('readonly', True)]},
        help='Total book page count', company_dependent=False)
```

How it works...

Fields are added to models by defining an attribute in their Python classes. The non-relational field types that are available are as follows:

- Char is used for string values.
- Text is used for multiline string values.
- Selection is used for selection lists. This has a list of values and description pairs. The value that is selected is what gets stored in the database, and it can be a string or an integer. The description is automatically translatable.

> In fields of the Selection type, you can use integer keys, but you must be aware that Odoo interprets 0 as unset internally and will not display the description if the stored value is zero. This can happen, so you will need to take this into account.

- Html is similar to the text field, but is expected to store rich text in an HTML format.
- Binary fields store binary files, such as images or documents.
- Boolean stores True/False values.
- Date stores date values. They are stored in the database as dates. The ORM handles them in the form of Python date objects. The ORM handles dates in the form of strings in version prior to Odoo 12. The format that's used is defined in odoo.fields.DATE_FORMAT.
- Datetime is used for datetime values. They are stored in the database in a naive datetime, in UTC time. The ORM handles them in the form of Python datetime objects. The ORM handles datetime in the form of strings in the versions prior to Odoo 12. The format that's used is defined in odoo.fields.DATETIME_FORMAT.
- The Integer fields need no further explanation.
- The Float fields store numeric values. Their precision can optionally be defined with a total number of digits and decimal digit pairs.
- Monetary can store an amount in a certain currency. This will also be explained in the *Adding a monetary field* recipe of this chapter.

The first step in this recipe shows the minimal syntax to add to each field type. The field definitions can be expanded to add other optional attributes, as shown in step 2.

Here's an explanation for the field attributes that were used:

- string is the field's title, and it is used in UI view labels. It's optional; if it is not set, a label will be derived from the field name by adding a title case and replacing the underscores with spaces.
- translate, when set to True, makes the field translatable; it can hold a different value, depending on the user interface language.
- default is the default value. It can also be a function that is used to calculate the default value; for example, default=_compute_default, where _compute_default is a method that was defined on the model before the field definition.
- help is an explanation text that's displayed in the UI tooltips.
- groups makes the field available only to some security groups. It is a string containing a comma-separated list of XML IDs for security groups. This is addressed in more detail in Chapter 11, *Access Security*.

- `states` allows the user interface to dynamically set the value for the `readonly`, `required`, and `invisible` attributes, depending on the value of the `state` field. Therefore, it requires a `state` field to exist and be used in the form view (even if it is invisible). The name of the `state` attribute is hardcoded in Odoo and cannot be changed.
- `copy` flags whether the field value is copied when the record is duplicated. By default, it is `True` for non-relational and `Many2one` fields, and `False` for `One2many` and computed fields.
- `index`, when set to `True`, creates a database index for the field, which sometimes allows for faster searches. It replaces the deprecated `select=1` attribute.
- The `readonly` flag makes the field read-only by default in the user interface.
- The `required` flag makes the field mandatory by default in the user interface.
- The `sanitize` flag is used by HTML fields and strips its content from potentially insecure tags. Using this performs a global cleanup of the input. If you need finer control, there are a few more keywords you can use, which only work if `sanitize` is enabled:
  - `sanitize_tags=True`, to remove tags that are not part of a white list (this is the default)
  - `sanitize_attributes=True`, to remove attributes of the tags which are not part of a white list
  - `sanitize_style=True`, to remove style properties that are not part of a white list
  - `strip_style=True`, to remove all style elements
  - `strip_class=True`, to remove the class attributes

The various white lists that are mentioned here are defined in `odoo/tools/mail.py`.

- The `company_dependent` flag makes the field store different values per company. It replaces the deprecated `Property` field type.

Finally, we updated the form view according to the newly added fields in the model. We placed `<field>` tags in an arbitrary manner here, but you can place them anywhere you want. Form views are explained in more detail in `Chapter 10`, *Backend Views*.

There's more...

The `Selection` field also accepts a function reference as its `selection` attribute instead of a list. This allows for dynamically generated lists of options. You can find an example relating to this in the *Adding dynamic relations using Reference fields* recipe in this chapter, where a `selection` attribute is also used.

The `Date` and `Datetime` field objects expose a few utility methods that can be convenient.

For `Date`, we have the following:

- `fields.Date.to_date(string_value)` parses the string into a `date` object.
- `fields.Date.to_string(date_value)` represents the `Date` object as a string.
- `fields.Date.today()` returns the current day in a string format. This is appropriate to use for default values
- `fields.Date.context_today(record, timestamp)` returns the day of the `timestamp` (or the current day, if `timestamp` is omitted) in a string format, according to the time zone of the record's (or record set's) context.

For `Datetime`, we have the following:

- `fields.Datetime.to_datetime(string_value)` parses the string into a `datetime` object.
- `fields.Datetime.to_string(datetime_value)` represents the `datetime` object as a string.
- `fields.Datetime.now()` returns the current day and time in a string format. This is appropriate to use for default values.

- `fields.Datetime.context_timestamp(record, timestamp)` converts a `timestamp` naive `datetime` into a time zone aware `datetime` using the time zone in the context of the `record`. This is not suitable for default values, but can be used for instances when you're sending data to an external system.

Other than the basic fields, we also have relational fields: `Many2one`, `One2many`, and `Many2many`. These are explained in the *Adding relational fields to a model* recipe of this chapter.

It's also possible to have fields with automatically computed values, defining the computation function with the `compute` field attribute. This is explained in the *Adding computed fields to a Model* recipe.

A few fields are added by default in Odoo models, so we should not use these names for our fields. These are the `id` field, for the record's automatically generated identifier, and a few audit log fields, which are as follows:

- `create_date` is the record creation timestamp
- `create_uid` is the user who created the record
- `write_date` is the last recorded edit timestamp
- `write_uid` is the user who last edited the record

The automatic creation of these log fields can be disabled by setting the `_log_access=False` model attribute.

Another special column that can be added to a model is `active`. It must be a `Boolean` field, allowing users to mark records as inactive. Its definition is as follows:

```
active = fields.Boolean('Active', default=True)
```

By default, only records with `active` set to `True` are visible. To retrieve them, we need to use a domain filter with `[('active', '=', False)]`. Alternatively, if the `'active_test': False` value is added to the environment's context, the ORM will not filter out inactive records.

> **TIP**
>
> In some cases, you may not be able to modify the context to get both the active and the inactive records. In this case, you can use the `['|', ('active', '=', True), ('active', '=', False)]` domain.
>
> **Caution**: `[('active', 'in' (True, False))]` does not work as you might expect. Odoo is explicitly looking for an `('active', '=', False)` clause in the domain. It will default to restricting the search to active records only.

Using a float field with configurable precision

When using float fields, we may want to let the end user configure the precision that is to be used. The **Decimal Precision Configuration** module add-on provides this ability.

We will add a `Cost Price` field to the Library Book model, with a user-configurable number of digits.

Getting ready

We will reuse the `my_library` add-on module from `Chapter 4`, *Creating Odoo Add-On Modules*.

How to do it...

We need to install the `decimal_precision` module, add a `Usage` entry for our configuration, and then use it in the `model` field:

1. Ensure that the Decimal Accuracy module is installed; select **Apps** from the top menu, remove the default filter, search for the **Decimal Precision Configuration** app, and install it if it's not already installed:

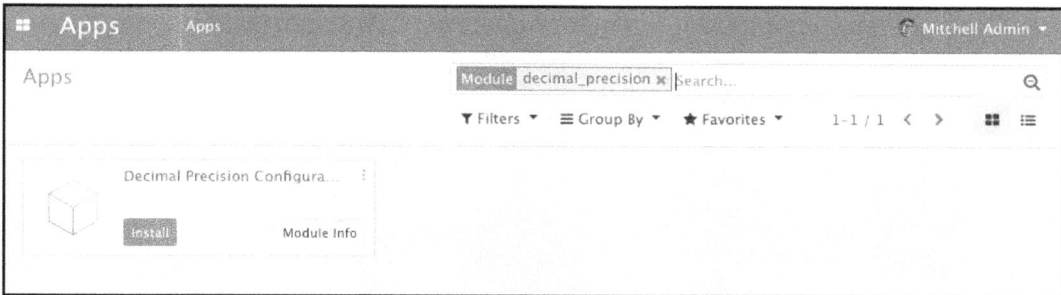

2. Activate **Developer Mode** from the link in the **Settings** menu (refer to the *Activating the Odoo developer tools* recipe in `Chapter 1`, *Installing the Odoo Development Environment*). This will enable the **Settings | Technical** menu.

3. Access the Decimal Precision configurations. To do this, open the **Settings** top menu and select **Technical | Database Structure | Decimal Accuracy**. We should see a list of the currently defined settings.

4. Add a new configuration, setting **Usage** to `Book Price` and choosing the **Digits** precision:

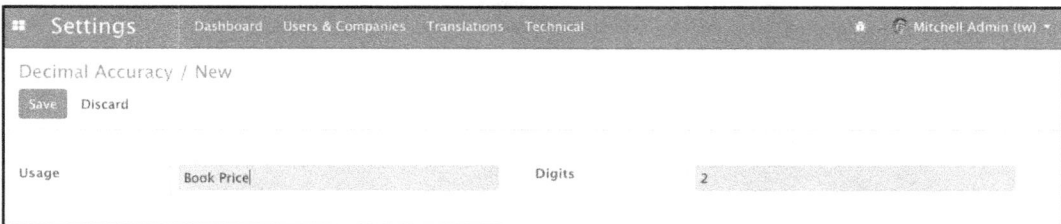

5. Add the new dependency to the `__manifest__.py` manifest file. It should look as follows:

```
{    'name': 'Chapter 05 code',
     'depends': ['base', 'decimal_precision'],
     'data': ['views/library_book.xml'] }
```

6. To add the `model` field using this decimal precision setting, edit the `models/library_book.py` file by adding the following code:

```
from odoo.addons import decimal_precision as dp
class LibraryBook(models.Model):
    cost_price = fields.Float(
        'Book Cost', dp.get_precision('Book Price'))
```

> Whenever you add new fields in models, you will need to add them into views in order to access them from the user interface. In the previous example, we added the `cost_price` field. To see this in the form view, you need to add it with `<field name="cost_price"/>`.

How it works...

The `get_precision()` function looks up the name in the Decimal Accuracy's **Usage** field and returns a tuple with 16-digit precision and the number of decimals that were defined in the configuration.

Using this function in the field definition, instead of having it hardcoded, allows the end user to configure it according to their needs.

Adding a monetary field to a model

Odoo has special support for **monetary** values related to a **currency**. Let's see how we can use this in a model.

Getting ready

We will reuse the `my_library` add-on module from Chapter 4, *Creating Odoo Add-On Modules*.

How to do it...

The monetary field needs a complementary currency field to store the currency for the amounts.

`my_library` already has `models/library_book.py`, which defines a basic model. We will edit this to add the required fields:

1. Add the field to store the currency that is to be used:

```
class LibraryBook(models.Model):
    # ...
    currency_id = fields.Many2one(
```

```
'res.currency', string='Currency')
```

2. Add the monetary field to store the amount:

```
class LibraryBook(models.Model):
    # ...
    retail_price = fields.Monetary(
        'Retail Price',
        # optional: currency_field='currency_id',
        )
```

Now, upgrade the add-on module, and the new fields should be available in the model. They won't be visible in views until they are added to them, but we can confirm their addition by inspecting the model fields in **Settings** | **Technical** | **Database Structure** | **Models**. After adding them into the form view, it will look as follows:

| Retail Price | $0.00 |
| Currency | USD |

How it works...

Monetary fields are similar to Float fields, but Odoo is able to represent them correctly in the user interface since it knows what their currency is through the second field.

This currency field is expected to be called `currency_id`, but we can use whatever field name we like as long as it is indicated using the `currency_field` optional parameter.

> **TIP**
>
> This is very useful when you need to maintain the amounts in different currencies in the same record, for example, if we want to include the currency of the sale order and the currency of the company. You can configure the two fields as `fields.Many2one(res.currency)` and use the first one for the first amount and the other one for the second amount.

You might like to know that the decimal precision for the amount is taken from the currency definition (the `decimal_precision` field of the `res.currency` model).

Adding relational fields to a model

Relations between Odoo models are represented by relational fields. There are three different types of **relations**:

- **many-to-one**, commonly abbreviated as **m2o**
- **one-to-many**, commonly abbreviated as **o2m**
- **many-to-many**, commonly abbreviated as **m2m**

Looking at the `Library Books` example, we can see that each book can only have one publisher, so we can have a many-to-one relation between books and publishers.

Each publisher, however, can have many books. So, the previous many-to-one relation implies a one-to-many reverse relation.

Finally, there are cases in which we can have a many-to-many relation. In our example, each book can have several (many) authors. Also, inversely, each author may have written many books. Looking at it from either side, this is a many-to-many relation.

Getting ready

We will reuse the `my_library` add-on module from Chapter 4, *Creating Odoo Add-On Modules*.

How to do it...

Odoo uses the Partner model, `res.partner`, to represent people, organizations, and addresses. We should use it for authors and publishers. We will edit the `models/library_book.py` file to add these fields:

1. Add the many-to-one field for the book's publisher to `Library Books`:

```
class LibraryBook(models.Model):
    # ...
    publisher_id = fields.Many2one(
        'res.partner', string='Publisher',
        # optional:
        ondelete='set null',
        context={},
        domain=[],
```

```
)
```

2. To add the one-to-many field for a publisher's books, we need to extend the partner model. For simplicity, we will add that to the same Python file:

```
class ResPartner(models.Model):
    _inherit = 'res.partner'
    published_book_ids = fields.One2many(
        'library.book', 'publisher_id',
        string='Published Books')
```

> The _inherit attribute we use here is for inheriting an existing model. This will be explained in the *Adding features to a model using inheritance* recipe later in this chapter.

3. We've already created the many-to-many relation between books and authors, but let's revisit it:

```
class LibraryBook(models.Model):
    # ...
    author_ids = fields.Many2many(
        'res.partner', string='Authors')
```

4. The same relation, but from authors to books, should be added to the partner model:

```
class ResPartner(models.Model):
    # ...
    authored_book_ids = fields.Many2many(
        'library.book',
        string='Authored Books',
        # relation='library_book_res_partner_rel'  # optional
        )
```

Now, upgrade the add-on module, and the new fields should be available in the model. They won't be visible in the views until they are added to them, but we can confirm their addition by inspecting the model fields in **Settings | Technical | Database Structure | Models**.

How it works...

Many-to-one fields add a column to the database table of the model, storing the database ID of the related record. At the database level, a foreign key constraint will also be created, ensuring that the stored IDs are a valid reference to a record in the related table. No database index is created for these relation fields, but this can be done by adding the `index=True` attribute.

We can see that there are four more attributes that we can use for many-to-one fields. The `ondelete` attribute determines what happens when the related record is deleted. For example, what happens to books when their publisher record is deleted? The default is `'set null'`, which sets an empty value on the field. It can also be `'restrict'`, which prevents the related record from being deleted, or `'cascade'`, which causes the linked record to also be deleted.

The last two (`context` and `domain`) are also valid for the other relational fields. These are mostly meaningful on the client-side, and, at the model level, they act as default values that will be used in the client side views:

- `context` adds variables to the client context when clicking through the field to the related record's view. We can, for example, use it to set default values for new records that are created through that view.
- `domain` is a search filter that's used to limit the list of related records that are available.

Both context and domain are explained in more detail in Chapter 10, *Backend Views*.

One-to-many fields are the reverse of many-to-one relations, and although they are added to models just like other fields, they have no actual representation in the database. Instead, they are programmatic shortcuts and enable views to represent these lists of related records.

Many-to-many relations don't add columns to the tables for the models, either. This type of relation is represented in the database using an intermediate relation table, with two columns to store the two related IDs. Adding a new relation between a book and an author creates a new record in the relation table with the ID of the book and the ID of the author.

Odoo automatically handles the creation of this relation table. The relation table name is, by default, built using the name of the two related models, alphabetically sorted, plus a `_rel` suffix. However, we can override this using the `relation` attribute.

A case to keep in mind is when the two table names are large enough for the automatically generated database identifiers to exceed the PostgreSQL limit of 63 characters. As a rule of thumb, if the names of the two related tables exceed 23 characters, you should use the `relation` attribute to set a shorter name. In the next section, we will go into more detail on this.

There's more...

The `Many2one` fields support an additional `auto_join` attribute. This is a flag that allows the ORM to use SQL joins on this field. Due to this, it bypasses the usual ORM control, such as user access control and record access rules. In specific cases, it can solve performance issues, but it is advised to avoid using it.

We have covered the shortest way to define the relational fields. Let's take a look at the attributes specific to this type of field.

The `One2many` field attributes are as follows:

- `comodel_name`: This is the target model identifier and is mandatory for all relational fields, but it can be defined position-wise, without the keyword
- `inverse_name`: This only applies to `One2many` and is the field name in the target model for the inverse `Many2one` relation
- `limit`: This applies to `One2many` and `Many2many`, and sets an optional limit on the number of records to read that are used at the user interface level

The `Many2many` field attributes are as follows:

- `comodel_name`: This is the same as it is for the `One2many` field
- `relation`: This is the name to use for the table supporting the relation, overriding the automatically defined name
- `column1`: This is the name for the `Many2one` field in the relational table linking to this model
- `column2`: This is the name for the `Many2one` field in the relational table linking to `comodel`

For `Many2many` relations, in most cases, the ORM will take care of the default values for these attributes. It is even capable of detecting inverse `Many2many` relations, detecting the already existing `relation` table, and appropriately inverting the `column1` and `column2` values.

However, there are two cases where we need to step in and provide our own values for these attributes. One is the case where we need more than one `Many2many` relations between the same two models. For this to be possible, we must provide ourselves with the `relation` table name for the second relation, which must be different from the first relation. The other case is when the database names of the related tables are long enough for the automatically generated relation name to exceed the 63-character PostgreSQL limit for database object names.

The relation table's automatic name is `<model1>_<model2>_rel`. However, this relation table also creates an index for its primary key with the following identifier:

```
<model1>_<model2>_rel_<model1>_id_<model2>_id_key
```

This primary key also needs to meet the 63-character limit. So, if the two table names combined exceed a total of 63 characters, you will probably have trouble meeting the limits and will need to manually set the `relation` attribute.

Adding a hierarchy to a model

Hierarchies are represented like a model having relation with the same model; each record has a parent record in the same model, and many child records. This can be achieved by simply using many-to-one relations between the model and itself.

However, Odoo also provides improved support for this type of field by using the **Nested set model** (https://en.wikipedia.org/wiki/Nested_set_model). When activated, queries using the `child_of` operator in their domain filters will run significantly faster.

Staying with the `Library Books` example, we will build a hierarchical category tree that can be used to categorize books.

Getting ready

We will reuse the `my_library` add-on module from `Chapter 4`, *Creating Odoo Add-On Modules*.

How to do it...

We will add a new Python file, `models/library_book_categ.py`, for the category tree, as follows:

1. To load the new Python code file, add the following line to `models/__init__.py`:

   ```
   from . import library_book_categ
   ```

2. To create the Book Category model with the parent and child relations, create the `models/library_book_categ.py` file with the following code:

   ```
   from odoo import models, fields, api
   class BookCategory(models.Model):
       _name = 'library.book.category'
       name = fields.Char('Category')
       parent_id = fields.Many2one(
           'library.book.category',
           string='Parent Category',
           ondelete='restrict',
           index=True)
       child_ids = fields.One2many(
           'library.book.category', 'parent_id',
           string='Child Categories')
   ```

3. To enable the special hierarchy support, also add the following code:

   ```
   _parent_store = True
   _parent_name = "parent_id" # optional if field is
   'parent_id'
   parent_path = fields.Char(index=True)
   ```

4. To add a check preventing looping relations, add the following line to the model:

   ```
   from odoo.exceptions import ValidationError
   ...
   @api.constrains('parent_id')
   def _check_hierarchy(self):
       if not self._check_recursion():
           raise models.ValidationError(
               'Error! You cannot create recursive
   categories.')
   ```

5. Now, we need to assign a category to a book. To do this, we will add a new `many2one` field in the `library.book` model:

```
category_id = fields.Many2one('library.book.category')
```

Finally, a module upgrade will make these changes effective.

> To display the `librart.book.category` model in the user interface, you will need to add menus, views, and security rules. For more details, refer to `Chapter 4`, *Creating Odoo Add-On Modules*. Alternatively, you can access all code from `https://github.com/PacktPublishing/Odoo-12-Development-Cookbook-Third-Edition`.

How it works...

Steps 1 and 2 create the new model with hierarchic relations. The `Many2one` relation adds a field to reference the parent record. For faster child record discovery, this field is indexed in the database using the `index=True` parameter. The `parent_id` field must have `ondelete` set to either `'cascade'` or `'restrict'`. At this point, we have all that is required to achieve a hierarchic structure, but there are a few more additions we can make to enhance it. The `One2many` relation does not add any additional fields to the database, but provides a shortcut to access all the records with this record as their parent.

In step 3, we activate the special support for the hierarchies. This is useful for high-read but low-write instructions, since it brings faster data browsing at the expense of costlier write operations. It is done by adding one helper field, `parent_path`, and setting the `model` attribute to `_parent_store=True`. When this attribute is enabled, the helper field will be used to store data in searches in the hierarchic tree. By default, it is assumed that the field for the record's parent is called `parent_id`, but a different name can also be used. In this case, the correct field name should be indicated using the additional model attribute `_parent_name`. The default is as follows:

```
_parent_name = 'parent_id'
```

Step 4 is advised in order to prevent cyclic dependencies in the hierarchy, which means having a record in both the ascending and descending trees. This is dangerous for programs that navigate through the tree, since they can get into an infinite loop. The `models.Model` provides a utility method for this (`_check_recursion`) that we have reused here.

Step 5 is to add the `category_id` field with the type `many2one` to the `libary.book` book, so that we can set a category on book records. It is just for completing our example.

There's more...

The technique shown here should be used for *static* hierarchies, which are read and queried often but are updated less frequently. Book categories are a good example, since the library will not be continuously creating new categories; however, readers will often be restricting their searches to a category and its child categories. The reason for this lies in the implementation of the Nested set model in the database, which requires an update of the `parent_path` column (and the related database indexes) for all records whenever a category is inserted, removed, or moved. This can be a very expensive operation, especially when multiple editions are being performed in parallel transactions.

> **TIP**
> If you are dealing with a very dynamic hierarchical structure, the standard `parent_id` and `child_ids` relations will often result in better performance by avoiding table-level locks.

Adding constraint validations to a model

Models can have validations preventing them from entering undesired conditions.

Two different types of constraints can be used:

- The ones checked at the database level
- The ones checked at the server level

Database-level constraints are limited to the constraints supported by PostgreSQL. The most commonly used ones are the `UNIQUE` constraints, but the `CHECK` and `EXCLUDE` constraints can also be used. If these are not enough for our needs, we can use Odoo server-level constraints written in Python code.

We will use the `Library Books` model that we created in `Chapter 4`, *Creating Odoo Add-On Modules,* and add a couple of constraints to it. We will add a database constraint that prevents duplicate book titles, and a Python model constraint that prevents release dates in the future.

Getting ready

In this recipe, we will add the constraints in `library.book` model. To do so we will use the `my_library` module from `Chapter 4`, *Creating Odoo Add-On Modules.*

We expect it to contain at least the following:

```
from odoo import models, fields
class LibraryBook(models.Model):
    _name = 'library.book'
    name = fields.Char('Title', required=True)
    date_release = fields.Date('Release Date')
```

How to do it...

We will edit the `LibraryBook` class in the `models/library_book.py` Python file:

1. To create the database constraint, add a `model` attribute:

```
class LibraryBook(models.Model):
    # ...
    _sql_constraints = [
        ('name_uniq',
         'UNIQUE (name)',
         'Book title must be unique.')
        ]
```

2. To create the Python code constraint, add a `model` method:

```
from odoo import api, models
from odoo.exceptions import ValidationError
class LibraryBook(models.Model):
    # ...
    @api.constrains('date_release')
    def _check_release_date(self):
    for record in self:
        if record.date_release and
                record.date_release > fields.Date.today():
            raise models.ValidationError(
```

```
'Release date must be in the past')
```

After these changes are made to the code file, an add-on module upgrade and a server restart are needed.

How it works...

The first step creates a database constraint on the model's table. It is enforced at the database level. The `_sql_constraints` model attribute accepts a list of constraints to create. Each constraint is defined by a three-element tuple; they are listed as follows:

- A suffix to use for the constraint identifier. In our example, we used `name_uniq`, and the resulting constraint name is `library_book_name_uniq`.
- The SQL to use in the PostgreSQL instruction to alter or create the database table.
- A message to report to the user when the constraint is violated.

As we mentioned earlier, other database table constraints can also be used. Note that column constraints, such as `NOT NULL`, can't be added this way. For more information on PostgreSQL constraints in general and table constraints in particular, take a look at `http://www.postgresql.org/docs/current/static/ddl-constraints.html`.

In the second step, we added a method to perform Python code validation. It is decorated with `@api.constrains`, meaning that it should be executed to run checks when one of the fields in the argument list is changed. If the check fails, a `ValidationError` exception will be raised.

There's more...

Normally, if you have complex validation constraints, you can use `@api.constrains`, but for simple cases, you can also use `_sql_constraints` with the `CHECK` option. Take a look at the following example. This prevents the user from adding books with no pages or a negative number of pages:

```
_sql_constraints = [
    ('positive_page', 'CHECK(pages>0)', 'No of pages must be positive')
]
```

Adding computed fields to a model

Sometimes, we need to have a field that has a value calculated or derived from other fields in the same record or in related records. A typical example is the total amount, which is calculated by multiplying a unit price by a quantity. In Odoo models, this can be achieved using computed fields.

To show you how computed fields work, we will add one to the `Library Books` model to calculate the days since the book's release date.

It is also possible to make computed fields editable and searchable. We will implement this in our example, as well.

Getting ready

We will reuse the `my_library` add-on module from `Chapter 4`, *Creating Odoo Add-On Modules*.

How to do it...

We will edit the `models/library_book.py` code file to add a new field and the methods supporting its logic:

1. Start by adding the new field to the `Library Books` model:

```
class LibraryBook(models.Model):
    # ...
    age_days = fields.Float(
        string='Days Since Release',
        compute='_compute_age',
        inverse='_inverse_age',
        search='_search_age',
        store=False,        # optional
        compute_sudo=False  # optional
    )
```

2. Next, add the method with the value computation logic:

```
# ...
from odoo import api  # if not already imported
# ...
class LibraryBook(models.Model):
    # ...
    @api.depends('date_release')
    def _compute_age(self):
        today = fields.Date.today()
        for book in self.filtered('date_release'):
            delta = today - book.date_release
            book.age_days = delta.days
```

3. To add the method and implement the logic to write on the computed field, use the following code:

```
from datetime import timedelta
# ...
class LibraryBook(models.Model):
    # ...
    def _inverse_age(self):
        today = fields.Date.today()
        for book in self.filtered('date_release'):
            d = today - timedelta(days=book.age_days)
            book.date_release = d
```

4. To implement the logic that will allow you to search in the computed field, use the following code:

```
from datetime import timedelta
class LibraryBook(models.Model):
    # ...
    def _search_age(self, operator, value):
        today = fields.Date.today()
        value_days = timedelta(days=value)
        value_date = today - value_days
        # convert the operator:
        # book with age > value have a date < value_date
        operator_map = {
            '>': '<', '>=': '<=',
            '<': '>', '<=': '>=',
        }
        new_op = operator_map.get(operator, operator)
        return [('date_release', new_op, value_date)]
```

An Odoo restart, followed by a module upgrade, is needed to correctly activate these new additions.

How it works...

The definition of a computed field is the same as that of a regular field, except that a `compute` attribute is added to specify the name of the method to use for its computation.

Their similarity can be deceptive, since computed fields are internally quite different from regular fields. Computed fields are dynamically calculated at runtime, and unless you specifically add that support yourself, they are not writable or searchable.

The computation function is dynamically calculated at runtime, but the ORM uses caching to avoid inefficiently recalculating it every time its value is accessed. So, it needs to know what other fields it depends on. It uses the `@depends` decorator to detect when its cached values should be invalidated and recalculated.

> Ensure that the `compute` function always sets a value on the computed field. Otherwise, an error will be raised. This can happen when you have `if` conditions in your code that sometimes fail to set a value on the computed field. This can be tricky to debug.

Write support can be added by implementing the `inverse` function. This uses the value assigned to the computed field to update the origin fields. Of course, this only makes sense for simpler calculations; nevertheless, there are still cases where it can be useful. In our example, we make it possible to set the book release date by editing the **Days Since Release** computed field. The `search` attribute is optional; if you don't want to make the compute field editable, you can skip it.

It is also possible to make a non-stored computed field searchable by setting the `search` attribute to the method name (similar to `compute` and `inverse`). Like `inverse`, `search` is also optional; if you don't want to make the compute field searchable, you can skip it.

However, this method is not expected to implement the actual search. Instead, it receives the operator and value used to search on the field as parameters, and is expected to return a domain with the replacement search conditions to use. In our example, we translate a search of the **Days Since Release** field into an equivalent search condition on the **Release Date** field.

The optional `store=True` flag stores the field in the database. In this case, after being computed, the field values are stored in the database, and from there on, they are retrieved like regular fields instead of being recomputed at runtime. Thanks to the `@api.depends` decorator, the ORM will know when these stored values need to be recomputed and updated. You can think of it as a persistent cache. It also has the advantage of making the field usable for search conditions, including sorting and grouping by operations, without the need to implement the `search` method.

The `compute_sudo=True` flag is to be used in cases in which the computations need to be done with elevated privileges. This might be the case when the computation needs to use data that may not be accessible to the end user.

> Be careful when using this, as it will bypass all security rules, including the company separation rules in a multi-company setup. Ensure that you double-check the domains you use in the computation for possible issues related to this.

Exposing related fields stored in other models

When reading data from the server, Odoo clients can only get values for the fields that are available in the model and being queried. Client-side code, unlike server-side code, can't use dot notation to access data in the related tables.

However, these fields can be made available there by adding them as related fields. We will do this to make the publisher's city available in the `Library Books` model.

Getting ready

We will reuse the `my_library` add-on module from `Chapter 4`, *Creating Odoo Add-On Modules*.

How to do it...

Edit the `models/library_book.py` file to add the new `related` field:

1. Ensure that we have a field for the book publisher:

```
class LibraryBook(models.Model):
    # ...
    publisher_id = fields.Many2one(
        'res.partner', string='Publisher')
```

2. Now, add the related field for the publisher's city:

```
# class LibraryBook(models.Model):
    # ...
    publisher_city = fields.Char(
        'Publisher City',
        related='publisher_id.city',
        readonly=True)
```

Finally, we need to upgrade the add-on module for the new fields to be available in the model.

How it works...

Related fields are just like regular fields, but they have an additional attribute, `related`, with a string for the separated chain of fields to traverse.

In our case, we access the publisher related record through `publisher_id`, and then read its `city` field. We can also have longer chains, such as `publisher_id.country_id.country_code`.

Note that in this recipe, we set the related field as `readonly`. If we don't do that, the field will be writable, and the user may change its value. This will have the effect of changing the value of the `city` field of the related publisher. While this can be a useful side effect, caution needs to be exercised; all the books that are published by the same publisher will have their `publisher_city` field updated, which may not be what the user expects.

There's more...

Related fields are, in fact, computed fields. They just provide a convenient shortcut syntax to read field values from related models. As a computed field, this means that the `store` attribute is also available. As a shortcut, they also have all the attributes from the referenced field, such as `name`, `translatable`, and `required`.

Additionally, they support a `related_sudo` flag similar to `compute_sudo`; when set to `True`, the field chain is traversed without checking the user access rights.

> **TIP**
>
> Using related fields in a `create()` method can affect performance, as the computation of these fields is delayed until the end of their creation. So, if you have a `One2many` relation, such as in `sale.order` and `sale.order.line` models, and you have a related field on the line model referring to a field on the order model, you should explicitly read the field on the order model during record creation, instead of using the related field shortcut, especially if there are a lot of lines.

Adding dynamic relations using reference fields

With relational fields, we need to decide the relation's target model (or comodel) beforehand. However, sometimes, we may need to leave that decision to the user and first choose the model we want and then the record we want to link to.

With Odoo, this can be achieved using Reference fields.

Getting ready

We will reuse the `my_library` add-on module from `Chapter 4`, *Creating Odoo Add-On Modules*.

How to do it...

Edit the `models/library_book.py` file to add the new related field:

1. First, we need to add a helper method to dynamically build a list of selectable target models:

```
from odoo import models, fields, api
class LibraryBook(models.Model):
    # ...
    @api.model
    def _referencable_models(self):
        models = self.env['ir.model'].search([
            ('field_id.name', '=', 'message_ids')])
        return [(x.model, x.name) for x in models]
```

2. Then, we need to add the Reference field and use the previous function to provide a list of selectable models:

```
ref_doc_id = fields.Reference(
    selection='_referencable_models',
    string='Reference Document')
```

Since we are changing the model's structure, a module upgrade is needed to activate these changes.

How it works...

Reference fields are similar to many-to-one fields, except that they allow the user to select the model to link to.

The target model is selectable from a list that's provided by the `selection` attribute. The `selection` attribute must be a list of two element tuples, where the first is the model's internal identifier, and the second is a text description for it.

Here's an example:

```
[('res.users', 'User'), ('res.partner', 'Partner')]
```

However, rather than providing a fixed list, we can use most common models. For simplicity, we are using all the models that have the messaging feature. Using the `_referencable_models` method, we provided a model list dynamically.

Our recipe started by providing a function to browse all the model records that can be referenced to dynamically build a list that will be provided to the `selection` attribute. Although both forms are allowed, we declared the function name inside quotes, instead of directly referencing the function without quotes. This is more flexible, and it allows for the referenced function to be defined only later in the code, for example, which is something that is not possible when using a direct reference.

The function needs the `@api.model` decorator because it operates on the model level, not on the recordset level.

> While this feature looks nice, it comes with a significant execution overhead. Displaying the Reference fields for a large number of records (for instance, in a list view) can create heavy database loads, as each value has to be looked up in a separate query. It is also unable to take advantage of database referential integrity, unlike regular relation fields.

Adding features to a model using inheritance

One of the most important Odoo features is the ability of module add-ons to extend features that are defined in other module add-ons without having to edit the code of the original feature. This might be to add fields or methods, modify the existing fields, or extend the existing methods to perform additional logic.

It is the most frequently used method of inheritance and is referred to by the official documentation as **traditional inheritance** or **classical inheritance**.

We will extend the built-in Partner model to add it to a computed field with the authored book count. This involves adding a field and a method to an existing model.

Getting ready

We will reuse the `my_library` add-on module from Chapter 4, *Creating Odoo Add-On Modules*.

How to do it...

We will be extending the built-in Partner model. We should do this in its own Python code file, but to keep the explanation as simple as possible, we will reuse the `models/library_book.py` code file:

1. First, we will ensure that the `authored_book_ids` inverse relation is in the Partner model and add the computed field:

```
class ResPartner(models.Model):
    _inherit = 'res.partner'
    _order = 'name'
    authored_book_ids = fields.Many2many(
        'library.book', string='Authored Books')
    count_books = fields.Integer( 'Number of Authored Books',
compute='_compute_count_books' )
```

2. Next, add the method that's needed to compute the book count:

```
# ...
from odoo import api  # if not already imported
# class ResPartner(models.Model):
    # ...
    @api.depends('authored_book_ids')
    def _compute_count_books(self):
        for r in self:
            r.count_books = len(r.authored_book_ids)
```

Finally, we need to upgrade the add-on module for the modifications to take effect.

How it works...

When a model class is defined with the `_inherit` attribute, it adds modifications to the inherited model, rather than replacing it.

This means that fields defined in the inheriting class are added or changed on the parent model. At the database layer, the ORM is adding fields on the same database table.

Fields are also incrementally modified. This means that if the field already exists in the superclass, only the attributes declared in the inherited class are modified; the other ones are kept as they are in the parent class.

Methods defined in the inheriting class replace methods in the parent class. If you don't invoke parent method with the `super` call, in that case the parent's version of the method will not be executed and we will lose the features. So, whenever you add a new logic by inheriting existing methods, you should include a statement with `super` to call its version in the parent class. This is discussed in more detail in `Chapter 6`, *Basic Server-Side Development*.

> This recipe will add new fields to the existing model. If you also want to add these new fields to existing views (the user interface), refer to the *Changing existing views – view inheritance* recipe in `Chapter 10`, *Backend Views*.

There's more...

With the `_inherit` traditional inheritance, it's also possible to copy the parent model's features to a completely new model. This is done by simply adding a `_name` class attribute with a different identifier. Here's an example:

```
class LibraryMember(models.Model):
    _inherit = 'res.partner'
    _name = 'library.member'
```

The new model has its own database table with its own data that's totally independent from the `res.partner` parent model. Since it still inherits from the Partner model, any later modifications to it will also affect the new model.

In the official documentation, this is called **prototype inheritance**, but in practice, it is seldom used. The reason for this is that delegation inheritance usually answers to that need in a more efficient way, without the need to duplicate data structures. For more information on this, you can refer to the *Using delegation inheritance to copy features to another model* recipe of `Chapter 5`, *Application Models*.

Using abstract models for reusable model features

Sometimes, there is a particular feature that we want to be able to add to several different models. Repeating the same code in different files is a bad programming practice; it would be better to implement it once and reuse it.

Abstract models allow us to create a generic model that implements some features that can then be inherited by regular models, in order to make that feature available.

As an example, we will implement a simple Archive feature. It adds the active field to the model (if it doesn't exist already) and makes an archive method available to toggle the active flag. This works because active is a magic field; if present in a model by default, the records with active=False will be filtered out from queries.

We will then add it to the Library Books model.

Getting ready

We will reuse the my_library add-on module from Chapter 4, *Creating Odoo Add-On Modules*.

How to do it...

The archive feature certainly deserves its own add-on module, or at least its own Python code file. However, to keep the explanation as simple as possible, we will cram it into the models/library_book.py file:

1. Add the abstract model for the archive feature. It must be defined in the Library Book model, where it will be used:

```
class BaseArchive(models.AbstractModel):
    _name = 'base.archive'
    active = fields.Boolean(default=True)

    def do_archive(self):
        for record in self:
            record.active = not record.active
```

2. Now, we will edit the Library Book model to inherit the Archive model:

```
class LibraryBook(models.Model):
    _name = 'library.book'
    _inherit = ['base.archive']
    # ...
```

An upgrade of the add-on module is needed for the changes to be activated.

How it works...

An abstract model is created by a class based on `models.AbstractModel`, instead of the usual `models.Model`. It has all the attributes and capabilities of regular models; the difference is that the ORM will not create an actual representation for it in the database. This means that it can't have any data stored in it. It only serves as a template for a reusable feature that is to be added to regular models.

Our Archive abstract model is quite simple; it just adds the `active` field and a method to toggle the value of the `active` flag, which we expect to be used later, via a button on the user interface.

When a model class is defined with the `_inherit` attribute, it inherits the attribute methods of those classes, and the attribute methods that are defined in the current class add modifications to those inherited features.

The mechanism at play here is the same as that of a regular model extension (as per the *Adding features to a model using inheritance* recipe). You may have noticed that `_inherit` uses a list of model identifiers instead of a string with one model identifier. In fact, `_inherit` can have both forms. Using the list form allows us to inherit from multiple (usually `Abstract`) classes. In this case, we are inheriting just one, so a text string would be fine. A list was used instead, for illustration purposes.

There's more...

A noteworthy built-in abstract model is `mail.thread`, which is provided by the `mail` (Discuss) add-on module. On models, it enables, the discussion features that power the message wall that's seen at the bottom of many forms.

Other than `AbstractModel`, a third model type is available: `models.TransientModel`. This has a database representation like `models.Model`, but the records that are created there are supposed to be temporary and regularly purged by a server-scheduled job. Other than that, Transient models work just like regular models.

The `models.TransientModel` is useful for more complex user interactions, known as **wizards**. The wizard is used to request inputs from the user. In Chapter 9, *Advanced Server-Side Development Techniques*, we explore how to use these for advanced user interaction.

Using delegation inheritance to copy features to another model

Traditional inheritance using `_inherit` performs in-place modification to extend the model's features.

However, there are cases where, rather than modifying an existing model, we want to create a new model based on an existing one to use the features it already has. This is done with Odoo's **delegation inheritance**, which uses the `_inherits` model attribute (note the additional s).

Traditional inheritance is quite different from the concept in object-oriented programming. Delegation inheritance, in turn, is similar, in that a new model can be created to include the features from a parent model. It also supports polymorphic inheritance, where we inherit from two or more other models.

We have a library with books. It's about time for our library to also have members. For a library member, we need all the identification and address data that's found in the Partner model, and we also want it to keep some information regarding the membership: a start date, a termination date, and a card number.

Adding those fields to the Partner model is not the best solution, since they will not be used for Partners that are not members. It would be great to extend the Partner model to a new model with some additional fields.

Getting ready

We will reuse the `my_library` add-on module from Chapter 4, *Creating Odoo Add-On Modules*.

How to do it...

The new Library Member model should be in its own Python code file, but to keep the explanation as simple as possible, we will reuse the `models/library_book.py` file:

1. Add the new model, inheriting from `res.partner`:

```
class LibraryMember(models.Model):
    _name = 'library.member'
    _inherits = {'res.partner': 'partner_id'}
    partner_id = fields.Many2one(
        'res.partner',
        ondelete='cascade')
```

2. Next, we will add the fields that are specific to Library Members:

```
# class LibraryMember(models.Model):
    # ...
    date_start = fields.Date('Member Since')
    date_end = fields.Date('Termination Date')
    member_number = fields.Char()
    date_of_birth = fields.Date('Date of birth')
```

Now, we should upgrade the add-on module to activate the changes.

How it works...

The `_inherits` model attribute sets the parent models that we want to inherit from. In this case, we just have one—`res.partner`. Its value is a key-value dictionary, where the keys are the inherited models and the values are the field names that were used to link to them. These are `Many2one` fields that we must also define in the model. In our example, `partner_id` is the field that will be used to link with the `Partner` parent model.

To better understand how this works, let's look at what happens on the database level when we create a new member:

- A new record is created in the `res_partner` table
- A new record is created in the `library_member` table
- The `partner_id` field of the `library_member` table is set to the `id` of the `res_partner` record that is created for it

The Member record is automatically linked to a new Partner record. It's just a many-to-one relation, but the delegation mechanism adds some magic so that the Partner's fields are seen as if they belong to the Member record, and a new Partner record is also automatically created with the new Member.

You might be interesting in knowing that this automatically created Partner record has nothing special about it. It's a regular Partner, and if you browse the Partner model, you will be able to find that record (without the additional Member data, of course). All Members are Partners, but only some Partners are also Members.

So, what happens if you delete a Partner record that is also a Member? You decide by choosing the `ondelete` value for the relation field. For `partner_id`, we used `cascade`. This means that deleting the Partner will also delete the corresponding Member. We could have used the more conservative setting, `restrict`, to forbid deleting the Partner while it has a linked Member. In this case, only deleting the Member will work.

It's important to note that delegation inheritance only works for fields, and not for methods. So, if the Partner model has a `do_something()` method, the Members model will not automatically inherit it.

There's more...

There is a shortcut for this inheritance delegation. Instead of creating an `_inherits` dictionary, you can use the `delegate=True` attribute in the `Many2one` field definition. This will work exactly like the `_inherits` option. The main advantage is that this is simpler. In the given example, we have performed the same inheritance delegation as in the previous one, but in this case, instead of creating an `_inherits` dictionary, we have used the `delegate=True` option on the `partner_id` field:

```
class LibraryMember(models.Model):
    _name = 'library.member'
    partner_id = fields.Many2one('res.partner', ondelete='cascade',
delegate=True)
    date_start = fields.Date('Member Since')
    date_end = fields.Date('Termination Date')
    member_number = fields.Char()
    date_of_birth = fields.Date('Date of birth')
```

A noteworthy case of delegation inheritance is the Users model, `res.users`. It inherits from Partners (`res.partner`). This means that some of the fields that you can see on the User are actually stored in the Partner model (notably, the `name` field). When a new User is created, we also get a new, automatically created Partner.

We should also mention that traditional inheritance with `_inherit` can also copy features into a new model, although in a less efficient way. This was discussed in the *Adding features to a model using inheritance* recipe.

6
Basic Server-Side Development

In this chapter, we will cover the following recipes:

- Defining model methods and using API decorators
- Reporting errors to the user
- Obtaining an empty recordset for a different model
- Creating new records
- Updating values of recordset records
- Searching for records
- Combining recordsets
- Filtering recordsets
- Traversing recordset relations
- Extending the business logic defined in a model
- Extending write() and create()
- Customizing how records are searched

Introduction

In Chapter 5, *Application Models*, we saw how to declare or extend business models in custom modules. The recipes in that chapter covered writing methods for computed fields, as well as methods to constrain the values of fields. This chapter focuses on the basics of server-side development in Odoo method definitions, recordset manipulation, and extending inherited methods.

Technical requirements

The technical requirements for this chapter include Odoo online platform.

All the code used in this chapter can be downloaded from the following GitHub repository, at: https://github.com/PacktPublishing/Odoo-12-Development-Cookbook-Third-Edition/tree/master/Chapter06

Check out the following video to see the Code in Action: http://bit.ly/2UH0VFR

Defining model methods and using the API decorators

The model classes that define custom data models declare fields for the data that's processed by the model. They can also define custom behavior by defining methods on the model class.

In this recipe, we will see how we can write a method that can be called by a button in the user interface, or by another piece of code in our application. This method will act on LibraryBooks and perform the required actions to change the state of a selection of books.

Getting ready

This recipe assumes that you have an instance ready, with the my_library add-on module available, as described in Chapter 4, *Creating Odoo Add-On Modules*. You will need to add a state field to the LibraryBook model, which is defined as follows:

```
from odoo import models, fields, api
class LibraryBook(models.Model):
    # [...]
    state = fields.Selection([
        ('draft', 'Unavailable'),
        ('available', 'Available'),
        ('borrowed', 'Borrowed'),
        ('lost', 'Lost')],
        'State', default="draft")
```

Refer to the *Adding models* recipe in `Chapter 4`, *Creating Odoo Add-On Modules,* for more information.

How to do it...

To define a method on Library Books to change the state of a selection of books, you need to add the following code to the model definition:

1. Add a helper method to check whether a state transition is allowed:

```
@api.model
def is_allowed_transition(self, old_state, new_state):
    allowed = [('draft', 'available'),
               ('available', 'borrowed'),
               ('borrowed', 'available'),
               ('available', 'lost'),
               ('borrowed', 'lost'),
               ('lost', 'available')]
    return (old_state, new_state) in allowed
```

2. Add a method to change the state of some books to a new state that is passed as an argument:

```
@api.multi
def change_state(self, new_state):
    for book in self:
        if book.is_allowed_transition(book.state, new_state):
            book.state = new_state
        else:
            continue
```

3. Add a method to change the book state by calling the `change_state` method:

```
@api.model
def make_available(self):
    self.change_state('available')

@api.model
def make_borrowed(self):
    self.change_state('borrowed')

@api.model
def make_lost(self):
    self.change_state('lost')
```

4. Add buttons in the `<form>` view. This will help us trigger these methods from the user interface:

```
<form>
...
    <button name="make_available" string="Make Available"
type="object"/>
    <button name="make_borrowed" string="Make Borrowed"
type="object"/>
    <button name="make_lost" string="Make Lost"
type="object"/>
...
</form>
```

Update or install the module to make these changes available.

How it works...

The code in this recipe defines a few methods. They are normal Python methods that have `self` as their first argument, and can have additional arguments as well. The methods are decorated with **decorators** from the `odoo.api` module.

> A number of these decorators were initially introduced in Odoo 9.0 to ensure that the conversion of calls is made using the **old** or **traditional** API to the **new** API. As of Odoo 10.0, the old API is no longer supported, but the decorators are a core part of the new API.

When writing a new method, you will generally use `@api.multi`. This decorator indicates that the method is meant to be executed on a recordset. In such methods, `self` is a recordset that can refer to an arbitrary number of database records (this includes empty recordsets), and the code will often loop over the records in `self` to do something on each individual record.

The `@api.model` decorator is similar, but it's used on methods for which only the model is important, not the contents of the recordset, which is not acted upon by the method. The concept is similar to Python's `@classmethod` decorator.

In *step 1*, we created the `is_allowed_transition()` method. The purpose of this method is to verify whether a transition from one state to another is valid or not. The tuples in the `allowed` list are the available transitions. For example, we don't want to allow a transition from `lost` to `borrow`, which is why we haven't put (`'lost, 'borrowed'`).

In *step 2*, we created the `change_state()` method. The purpose of this method is to change the status of the book. When this method is called, it changes the status of the book to the state given by the `new_state` parameter. It only changes the book status if the transition is allowed. We used a `for` loop here because we used the `@api.multi` decorator and it can handle multiple recordsets.

In *step 3*, we created the methods that change the state of the book by calling the `change_state()` method. In our case, this method will be triggered by the buttons that were added to the user interface.

In *step 4*, we added the `<button>` in `<form>` view. On a click of these buttons, the Odoo web client will invoke the Python function mentioned in the `name` attribute. Refer to the *Adding buttons to form* recipe in `Chapter 10`, *Backend Views*, to learn how to call such a method from the user interface.

When the user clicks on the button from the user interface, one of the methods from step 3 will be called. `self` is a (possibly empty) recordset that contains the records of the `library.book` model. After that, we call the `change_state()` method and pass the appropriate parameter based on the button that was clicked.

When `change_state()` is called, `self` is the same recordset of the `library.book` model. The body of the `change_state()` method loops over `self` to process each book in the recordset. Looping on `self` looks strange at first, but you will get used to this pattern very quickly.

Inside the loop, `change_state()` calls `is_allowed_transition()`. The call is made using the `book` local variable, but it can be made on any recordset for the `library.book` model, including, for example, `self`, since `is_allowed_transition()` is decorated with `@api.model`. If the transition is allowed, `change_state()` assigns the new state to the book by assigning a value to the attribute of the recordset. This is only valid on recordsets of a length of 1, which is guaranteed to be the case when iterating over `self`.

There's more...

You may encounter the @api.one decorator while reading source code. This decorator was **deprecated** because its behavior can be confusing at first glance. Also, if you are aware of @api.multi, you might think that this decorator allows the method to be called only on recordsets of a size of 1, but it does not. When it comes to the recordset length, @api.one is similar to @api.multi, but it does a for loop on the recordset outside the method and aggregates the returned value of each iteration of the loop in a list, which is returned to the caller.

Reporting errors to the user

During method execution, it is sometimes necessary to abort the processing because the action that's requested by the user isn't valid or an error condition has been met. This recipe shows you how to manage these cases by showing a helpful error message.

Getting ready

This recipe assumes that you have an instance ready, with the my_library add-on module available, as described in the previous recipe.

How to do it...

We will make a change in the change_state method from the previous recipe and display a helpful message when the user is trying to change the state that is not allowed by the is_allowed_transition method. Follow these steps to get started:

1. Add the following import at the beginning of the Python file:

```
from odoo.exceptions import UserError
from odoo.tools.translate import _
```

2. Modify the change_state method and raise a UserError exception from the else part:

```
@api.multi
def change_state(self, new_state):
    for book in self:
```

```
if book.is_allowed_transition(book.state, new_state):
    book.state = new_state
else:
    msg = _('Moving from %s to %s is not allowed') %
(book.state, new_state)
    raise UserError(msg)
```

How it works...

When an exception is raised in Python, it propagates up the call stack until it is processed. In Odoo, the RPC layer that answers the calls made by the web client catches all exceptions and, depending on the exception class, triggers different possible behaviors on the web client.

Any exception not defined in odoo.exceptions will be handled as an Internal Server Error (**HTTP status** 500) with the stack trace. A UserError will display an error message in the user interface. The code of the recipe raises UserError to ensure that the message is displayed in a user-friendly way. In all cases, the current database transaction is rolled back.

We are using a function with a strange name, _(), which is defined in odoo.tools.translate. This function is used to mark a string as translatable, and to retrieve the translated string at runtime, given the language of the end user that's found in the execution context. More information on this is available in Chapter 12, *Internationalization*.

> When using the _() function, ensure that you pass only strings with the interpolation placeholder, not the whole interpolated string. Example for, _('Warning: could not find %s') % value is correct, but _('Warning: could not find %s' % value) is incorrect because the first one will not find the string with the substituted value in the translation database.

There's more...

Sometimes, you are working on error-prone code, meaning that the operation you are performing may generate an error. Odoo will catch this error and display a traceback to the user. If you don't want to show a full error log to the user, you can cache the error and raise a custom exception with a meaningful message. In the given example, we are generating UserError from the try...cache block so that instead of showing a full error log, Odoo will now show a warning with a meaningful message:

```
def post_to_webservice(self, data):
    try:
        req = requests.post('http://my-test-service.com', data=data,
timeout=10)
        content = req.json()
    except IOError:
        error_msg = _("Something went wrong during data submission")
        raise UserError(error_msg)
    return content
```

There are a few more exception classes defined in odoo.exceptions, all deriving from the base legacy except_orm exception class. Most of them are only used internally, apart from the following:

- Warning: In Odoo 8.0, odoo.exceptions.Warning played the role of UserError in 9.0 and later. It is now deprecated because the name was deceptive (it is an error, not a warning) and it collided with the Python built-in Warning class. It is kept for backward compatibility only, and you should use UserError in your code.
- ValidationError: This exception is raised when a Python constraint on a field is not respected. In Chapter 5, *Application Models*, refer to the *Adding constraint validations to a model* recipe for more information.

Obtaining an empty recordset for a different model

When writing Odoo code, the methods of the current model are available through self. If you need to work on a different model, it is not possible to directly instantiate the class of that model; you need to get a recordset for that model to start working.

This recipe shows you how to get an empty recordset for any model that's registered in Odoo inside a model method.

Getting ready

This recipe will reuse the setup of the library example in the `my_library` add-on module.

We will write a small method in the `library.book` model and search for all `library.members`. To do this, we need to get an empty recordset for `library.members`.

How to do it...

To get a recordset for `library.members` in a method of `library.book`, you need to perform the following steps:

1. In the `LibraryBook` class, write a method called `get_all_library_members`:

```
class LibraryBook(models.Model):
    # ...
    @api.model def get_all_library_members(self):
        # ...
```

2. In the body of the method, use the following code:

```
library_member_model = self.env['library.member']
return library_member_model.search([])
```

How it works...

At startup, Odoo loads all the modules and combines the various classes that derive from `Model`, and also defines or extends the given model. These classes are stored in the Odoo **registry**, indexed by name. The `env` attribute of any recordset, available as `self.env`, is an instance of the `Environment` class defined in the `odoo.api` module.

This class plays a central role in Odoo development:

- It provides shortcut access to the registry by emulating a Python dictionary. If you know the name of the model you're looking for, `self.env[model_name]` will get you an empty recordset for that model. Moreover, the recordset will share the environment of `self`.
- It has a `cr` attribute, which is a database cursor you may use to pass raw SQL queries. Refer to the *Executing raw SQL queries* recipe in `Chapter 9`, *Advanced Server-Side Development Techniques*, for more on this.
- It has a `user` attribute, which is a reference to the current user performing the call. Take a look at `Chapter 9`, *Advanced Server-Side Development Techniques*, and the *Changing the user performing an action* recipe for more on this.
- It has a `context` attribute, which is a dictionary that contains the context of the call. This includes information about the language of the user, the timezone, the current selection of records, and much more. Refer to the *Calling a method with a modified context* recipe in `Chapter 9`, *Advanced Server-Side Development Techniques* for more on this.

The call to `search()` is explained in the *Searching for records* recipe later.

See also

The *Changing the user performing an action* and *Calling a method with a modified environment* recipes in `Chapter 9`, *Advanced Server-Side Development Techniques*, deal with modifying `self.env` at runtime.

Creating new records

A common requirement when writing business logic methods is creating new records. This recipe explains how to create records of the `library.book.category` model. For our example, we will add a method that will create dummy categories for the `library.book.category` model. To trigger this method, we will add a button to the form view.

Getting ready

You need to know the structure of the models for which you want to create a record, especially their names and types, as well as any constraints that exist on these fields (for example, whether some of them are mandatory). For this recipe, we will reuse the `my_library` module from Chapter 5, *Application Models*. Take a look at the following example to quickly recall the `library.book.category` model:

```
class BookCategory(models.Model):
    _name = 'library.book.category'

    name = fields.Char('Category')
    description = fields.Text('Description')
    parent_id = fields.Many2one(
        'library.book.category',
        string='Parent Category',
        ondelete='restrict',
        index=True
    )
    child_ids = fields.One2many(
        'library.book.category', 'parent_id',
        string='Child Categories')
```

How to do it...

To create a category with some child categories, you need to perform the following steps:

1. Create a method in the `library.book.category` model with the name `create_dummy_category`:

    ```
    def create_categories(self):
        ......
    ```

2. Inside the body of this method, prepare a dictionary of values for the fields of the first child category:

    ```
    categ1 = {
        'name': 'Child category 1',
        'description': 'Description for child 1'
    }
    ```

3. Prepare a dictionary of values for the fields of the second category:

```
categ2 = {
    'name': 'Child category 2',
    'description': 'Description for child 2'
}
```

4. Prepare a dictionary of values for the fields of the parent category:

```
parent_category_val = {
    'name': 'Parent category',
    'email': 'Description for parent category',
    'child_ids': [
        (0, 0, categ1),
        (0, 0, categ2),
    ]
}
```

5. Call the create() method to create the new records:

```
record =
self.env['library.book.category'].create(parent_category_v
al)
```

6. Add a button in the <form> view to trigger the create_categories
method from the user interface:

```
<button name="create_categories" string="Create
Categories" type="object"/>
```

How it works...

To create a new record for a model, we can call the create(values) method on any
recordset related to the model. This method returns a new recordset of a length of 1
and contains the new record, with the field values specified in the values dictionary.

In the dictionary, the keys give the name of the fields, and the corresponding values
correspond to the value of the field. Depending on the field type, you need to pass
different Python types for the values:

- Text field values are given with Python strings.
- Float and Integer field values are given using Python floats or integers.

- `Boolean` field values are given preferably using Python Booleans or integers.
- `Date` field values are given with the Python `datetime.date` object.
- `Datetime` field values are given with the Python `datetime.datetime` object.
- `Binary` field values are passed as a Base64 encoded string. The `base64` module from the Python standard library provides methods such as `encodebytes(bytestring)` to encode a string in Base64.
- `Many2one` field values are given with an integer, which has to be the database ID of the related record.
- `One2many` and `Many2many` fields use a special syntax. The value is a list that contains tuples of three elements, as follows:

Tuple	Effect
`(0, 0, dict_val)`	Creates a new record that will be related to the main record.
`(6, 0, id_list)`	Creates a relation between the record being created and existing records, whose IDs are in the Python list called `id_list`. Caution: When used on a `One2many` field, this will remove the records from any previous relation.

In this recipe, we create the dictionaries for two contacts in the company we want to create, and then we use these dictionaries in the `child_ids` entry of the dictionary for the company being created by using the `(0, 0, dict_val)` syntax we explained earlier.

When `create()` is called in step 5, three records are created:

- One for the parent book category, which is returned by `create`
- Two records for the child book category, which are available in `record.child_ids`

There's more...

If the model defined some **default values** for some fields, nothing special needs to be done; `create()` will take care of computing the default values for the fields that aren't present in the supplied dictionary.

From Odoo version 12, the `create()` method also supports the creation of records in a batch. **To create multiple records in a batch**, you need to pass a list of multiple values to the `create()` method, as shown in the following example:

```
categ1 = {
    'name': 'Category 1',
    'description': 'Description for Category 1'
}
categ2 = {
    'name': 'Category 2',
    'description': 'Description for Category 2'
}
multiple_records = self.env['library.book.category'].create([categ1,
categ2])
```

Updating values of recordset records

Business logic often requires us to update records by changing the values of some of their fields. This recipe shows you how to modify the `date` field of the partner as we go.

Getting ready

This recipe will use the same simplified `library.book` definition of the *Creating new records* recipe. You may refer to this simplified definition to find out about the fields.

We have the `date_updated` field in the `library.book` model. For illustration purposes, we will write on this field with the click of a button.

How to do it...

To update a book's `date_updated` field, you can write a new method called `change_update_date()`, which is defined as follows:

```
@api.multi
def change_update_date(self):
    self.ensure_one()
    self.date_updated = fields.Datetime.now()
```

Then, you can add a button in the book's `<form>` view in `xml`, as follows:

```
<button name="change_update_date" string="Update Date" type="object"/>
```

Restart the server and update the `my_library` module to see the changes. Upon clicking the **Update Date** button, `update_date` will be changed.

How it works...

The method starts by checking whether the book recordset that's passed as `self` contains exactly one record by calling `ensure_one()`. This method will raise an exception if this is not the case, and the processing will abort. This is needed, because we don't want to change the date of multiple records. If you want to update multiple values, you can remove `ensure_one()` and update the attribute using a loop on the recordset.

Finally, the method modifies the values of the attributes of the book record. It updates the `date_updated` field by the current time. Just by modifying the field attributes of the recordset, you can perform write operations.

There's more...

There are three options available if you want to write new values to the fields of records:

- Option one is the one that was explained in this recipe. It works in all contexts by assigning values directly to the attribute representing the field of the record. It isn't possible to assign a value to all recordset elements in one go, so you need to iterate on the recordset, unless you are certain that you are only handling a single record.
- Option two is to use the `update()` method by passing dictionary mapping field names to the values you want to set. This also only works for recordsets of a length of 1. It can save some typing when you need to update the values of **several fields at once** on the same record. Here's step two of the recipe, rewritten to use this option:

```
@api.multi
def change_update_date(self):
    self.ensure_one()
    self.update({
        'date_updated': fields.Datetime.now(),
```

```
          'another_field': 'value'
              ...
      })
```

- Option three is to call the `write()` method, passing a dictionary that maps the field names to the values you want to set. This method works for **recordsets of arbitrary size** and will update all records with the specified values in one single database operation when the two previous options perform one database call per record and per field. However, it has some limitations:

    - It does not work if the records are not yet present in the database. (Refer to the *Writing onchange methods* recipe in `Chapter 9`, *Advanced Server-Side Development Techniques*, for more information on this.)

    - It requires a special format when writing relational fields, similar to the one used by the `create()` method,. Check the following table for the format that's used to generate different values for the relational fields:

Tuple	Effect
`(0, 0, dict_val)`	This creates a new record that will be related to the main record.
`(1, id, dict_val)`	This updates the related record with the specified ID with the supplied values.
`(2, id)`	This removes the record with the specified ID from the related records and deletes it from the database.
`(3, id)`	This removes the record with the specified ID from the related records. The record is not deleted from the database.
`(4, id)`	This adds an existing record with the supplied ID to the list of related records.
`(5, )`	This removes all the related records, equivalent to calling `(3, id)` for each related `id`.
`(6, 0, id_list)`	This creates a relation between the record being updated and the existing record, whose IDs are in the Python list called `id_list`.

At the time of writing, the official documentation is outdated and mentions that the operation numbers 3, 4, 5, and 6 are not available on the One2many fields, which is no longer true. However, some of these may not work with One2many fields, depending on constraints on the models. For instance, if the reverse Many2one relation is required, then operation 3 will fail because it will result in an unset Many2one relation.

Searching for records

Searching for records is also a common operation in business logic methods. This recipe shows you how to find the book by name and category.

Getting ready

This recipe will use the same library.book definition as the *Creating new records* recipe did previously. We will write the code in a method called find_book(self).

How to do it...

To find the books, you need to perform the following steps:

1. Add the find_book method in the library.book model:

```
def find_book(self):
    . . .
```

2. Write the search domain for your criteria:

```
domain = [
    '|',
        '&', ('name', 'ilike', 'Book Name'),
            ('category_id.name', 'ilike', 'Category Name'),
        '&', ('name', 'ilike', 'Book Name 2'),
            ('category_id.name', 'ilike', 'Category Name 2')
]
```

3. Call the `search()` method with the domain, which will return the recordset:

```
books = self.search(domain)
```

How it works...

Step 1 defines the method.

Step 2 creates a search domain in a local variable. Often, you'll see this creation inline in the call to search, but with complex domains, it is good practice to define it separately.

For a full explanation of the *search domain* syntax, refer to the *Defining filters on record lists – Domain* recipe in `Chapter 10`, *Backend Views*.

Step 3 calls the `search()` method with the domain. The method returns a recordset that contains all the records that match the domain, which can then be further processed. In this recipe, we call the method with just the domain, but the following keyword arguments are also supported:

- `offset=N`: This is used to skip the N first records that match the query. This can be used along with `limit` to implement pagination or to reduce memory consumption when processing a very large number of records. It defaults to `0`.
- `limit=N`: This indicates that, at most, N records should be returned. By default, there is no limit.
- `order=sort_specification`: This is used to force the order on the returned recordset. By default, the order is given by the `_order` attribute of the model class.
- `count=boolean`: If `True`, this returns the number of records instead of the recordset. It defaults to `False`.

> **TIP**
>
> We recommend using the `search_count(domain)` method rather than `search(domain, count=True)`, as the name of the method conveys the behavior in a much clearer way; both will give the same result.

Sometimes, you need to search from another model so that searching on self will return a recordset of the current model. To search from another model, we need to get an empty recordset for the model. For example, let's say we want to search on the `res.partner` model because we want to search the contacts of the `res.partner` records. To do that, we would need to search on an empty recordset of the `res.partner` model. See the following code sample:

```
@api.multi
def find_partner(self):
    PartnerObj = self.env['res.partner']
    domain = [
        '&', ('name', 'ilike', 'Parth Gajjar'),
            ('company_id.name', '=', 'Odoo')
    ]
    partner = PartnerObj.search(domain)
```

There's more...

We said previously that the `search()` method returned all the records matching the domain. This is not actually completely true. The method ensures that only records that the user performing the search has access to are returned. Additionally, if the model has a `boolean` field called **active** and no term of the search domain specifies a condition on that field, then an implicit condition is added by search to only return `active=True` records. So, if you expect a search to return something but you only get empty recordsets, ensure that you check the value of the `active` field (if present) to check for **record rules**.

Refer to the *Calling a method with a different context* recipe in `Chapter 9`, *Advanced Server-Side Development Techniques*, for a way to not have the implicit `active = True` condition added. Take a look at the *Limiting record access using record rules* recipe in `Chapter 11`, *Access Security*, for more information about record-level access rules.

If, for some reason, you find yourself writing raw SQL queries to find record IDs, ensure that you use `self.env['record.model'].search([('id', 'in', tuple(ids))]).ids` after retrieving the IDs to ensure that security rules are applied. This is especially important in **multi-company** Odoo instances where the record rules are used to ensure proper discrimination between companies.

Combining recordsets

Sometimes, you will find that you have obtained recordsets that are not exactly what you need. This recipe shows various ways of combining them.

Getting ready

To use this recipe, you need to have two or more recordsets for the same model.

How to do it...

Follow these steps to perform common operations on recordsets:

1. To merge two recordsets into one while preserving their order, use the following operation:

   ```
   result = recordset1 + recordset2
   ```

2. To merge two recordsets into one while ensuring that there are no duplicates in the result, use the following operation:

   ```
   result = recordset1 | recordset2
   ```

3. To find the records that are common to two recordsets, use the following operation:

   ```
   result = recordset1 & recordset2
   ```

How it works...

The class for recordsets implements various Python operator redefinitions, which are used here. Here's a summary table of the most useful Python operators that can be used on recordsets:

Operator	Action performed
R1 + R2	This returns a new recordset containing the records from R1, followed by the records from R2. This can generate duplicate records in the recordset.
R1 - R2	This returns a new recordset consisting of the records from R1 that are not in R2. The order is preserved.

Operator	Action performed
R1 & R2	This returns a new recordset with all the records that belong to both R1 and R2 (intersection of recordsets). The order is *not* preserved here.
R1 | R2	This returns a new recordset with the records belonging to either R1 or R2 (union of recordsets). The order is *not* preserved, but there are no duplicates.
R1 == R2	True if both recordsets contain the same records.
R1 <= R2 R1 in R2	True if all records in R1 are also in R2. Both syntaxes are equivalent.
R1 >= R2 R2 in R1	True if all records in R2 are also in R1. Both syntaxes are equivalent.
R1 != R2	True if R1 and R2 do not contain the same records.

There are also in-place operators, +=, -=, &=, and |=, which modify the left-hand side operand instead of creating a new recordset. These are very useful when updating a record's One2many or Many2many fields. Refer to the *Updating values of recordset records* recipe for an example of this.

Filtering recordsets

In some cases, you already have a recordset, but only you need to operate on certain records. You can, of course, iterate on the recordset, checking for the condition on each iteration and acting depending on the result of the check. It can be easier, and in some cases, more efficient, to construct a new recordset containing only the interesting records and calling a single operation on that recordset.

This recipe shows you how to use the filter() method to extract recordsets from another one.

Getting ready

We will reuse the simplified library.book model that was shown in the *Creating new records* recipe. This recipe defines a method to extract books that have multiple authors from a supplied recordset.

How to do it...

To extract records that have multiple authors from a recordset, you need to perform the following steps:

1. Define the method to accept the original recordset:

```
@api.model
def books_with_multiple_authors(self, all_books):
```

2. Define an inner predicate function:

```
def predicate(book):
    if len(book.author_ids) > 1:
        return True
    return False
```

3. Call `filter()`, as follows:

```
return all_books.filter(predicate)
```

How it works...

The implementation of the `filter()` method creates an empty recordset in which all the records for which the predicate function evaluates to `True` are added. The new recordset is finally returned. The order of records in the original recordset is preserved.

The preceding recipe used a named internal function. For such simple predicates, you will often find an anonymous lambda function being used:

```
@api.model
def books_with_multiple_authors(self, all_books):
    return all_books.filter(lambda b: len(b.author_ids) > 1)
```

Actually, you need to filter a recordset based on the fact that the value of a field is *truthy* in the Python sense (non-empty strings, non-zero numbers, non-empty containers, and so on). So, if you want to filter records that have a category set, you can pass the field name to filter like this: `all_books.filter('category_id')`.

There's more...

Keep in mind that `filter()` operates in memory. If you are trying to optimize the performance of a method on the critical path, you may want to use a search domain or even move to SQL, at the cost of readability.

Traversing recordset relations

When working with a recordset of a length of `1`, various fields are available as record attributes. Relational attributes (`One2many`, `Many2one`, and `Many2many`) are also available with values that are recordsets too. As an example, let's say we want to access the name of the category from the recordset of the `library.book` model. You can access the category name by traversing through the `category_id many2one` field, as follows: `book.category_id.name`. However, when working with recordsets with more than one record, the attributes cannot be used.

This recipe shows you how to use the `mapped()` method to traverse recordset relations; we will write a method to retrieve the names of authors from the recordset of books, passed as an argument.

Getting ready

We will reuse the `library.book` model that was shown in the *Creating new records* recipe of this chapter.

How to do it...

To get the name of authors from the book recordset, you need to perform the following steps:

1. Define a method called `get_author_names()`:

```
@api.model
def get_author_names(self, books):
```

2. Call `mapped()` to get the email addresses of the contacts of the partner:

```
return books.mapped('author_ids.name')
```

How it works...

Step 1 is just defining the method. In step 2 , we call the `mapped(path)` method to traverse the fields of the recordset; `path` is a string that contains field names separated by dots. For each field in the path, `mapped()` produces a new recordset that contains all the records related by this field to all elements in the current recordset. It then applies the next element in the path on that new recordset. If the last field in the path is a relational field, `mapped()` will return a recordset; otherwise, a Python list is returned.

The `mapped()` method has two useful properties:

- If the path is a single scalar field name, then the returned list is in the same order as the processed recordset
- If the path contains a relational field, then the order is not preserved, but duplicates are removed from the result

> This second property is very useful in a method that's decorated with `@api.multi`, where you want to perform an operation on all the records that are pointed to by a `Many2many` field for all the records in `self`, but you need to ensure that the action is performed only once (even if two records of `self` share the same target record).

There's more...

When using `mapped()`, keep in mind that it operates in memory inside the Odoo server by repeatedly traversing relations and therefore making SQL queries, which may not be efficient. However, the code is terse and expressive. If you are trying to optimize a method on the critical path of the performance of your instance, you may want to rewrite the call to `mapped()` and express it as a `search()` with the appropriate domain, or even move to SQL (at the cost of readability).

The `mapped()` method can also be called with a function as an argument. In this case, it returns a list containing the result of the function that's applied to each record of `self`, or the union of the recordsets that's returned by the function, if the function returns a recordset.

See also

- The *Searching for records* recipe of this chapter
- The *Executing raw SQL queries* recipe in `Chapter 9`, *Advanced Server-Side Development Techniques*

Sorting recordsets

When you fetch a recordset with the `search()` method, you can pass an optional argument order to get a recordset that's in a particular order. This is useful if you already have a recordset from a previous bit of code and you want to sort it. It may also be useful if you use a set operation to combine two recordsets, for example, which would cause the order to be lost.

This recipe shows you how to use the `sorted()` method to sort an existing recordset. We will sort books by release date.

Getting ready

We will reuse the `library.book` model that was shown in the *Creating new records* recipe of this chapter.

How to do it...

You need to perform the following steps to get the sorted recordset of books based on `release_date`:

1. Define a method called `sort_books_by_date()`:

```
@api.model
def sort_books_by_date(self, books):
```

2. Call `sort()` to get the email addresses of the contacts of the partner:

```
return books.sorted(key='release_date')
```

How it works...

Step 1 is just defining the method. In step 2, we call the `sorted()` method in the recordset of books. Internally, the `sorted()` method will fetch the data of the field that's passed as the key argument. Then, by using Python's native sorted method, it returns a sorted recordset.

It also has one optional argument, `reverse=True`, which returns a recordset in reverse order. `reverse` is used as follows:

```
books.sorted(key='release_date', reverse=True)
```

There's more...

The `sorted()` method will sort the records in a recordset. Called without arguments, the `_order` attribute of the model will be used. Otherwise, a function can be passed to compute a comparison key in the same way as the Python built-in sorted (sequence, key) function.

> When the default `_order` parameter of the model is used, the sorting is delegated to the database, and a new `SELECT` function is performed to get the order. Otherwise, the sorting is performed by Odoo. Depending on what is being manipulated, and depending on the size of the recordsets, there might be some important performance differences.

Extending the business logic defined in a model

It is a very common practice to divide application features into different modules. By doing so, you can enable/disable features by installing/uninstalling the application. It then becomes necessary to customize the behavior of some methods that were defined in the original model. Sometimes, you want to add a new fields to an existing model. This is a very easy task in Odoo, and one of the most powerful features of the underlying framework.

We will demonstrate this by extending a method that creates records to add a new field in the created records.

Getting ready

For this recipe, we will continue to use the `my_library` module from the last recipe. Make sure that you have the `library.book.categroy` model in the `my_library` module.

For this recipe, we will create a new module called `my_library_return`, which depends on the `my_library` module. In this module, we will manage return dates for the borrowed book. We will also automatically calculate the return date based on the category.

In the *Adding features to a Model using inheritance* recipe in `Chapter 5`, *Application Models*, we saw how to add a field in the existing model. In this module, extend the `library.book` model, as follows:

```
class LibraryBook(models.Model):
    _inherit = 'library.book'

    date_return = fields.Date('Date to return')
```

Then, extend the `library.book.category` model, as follows:

```
class LibraryBookCategory(models.Model):
    _inherit = 'library.book.category'

    max_borrow_days = fields.Integer(
        'Maximum borrow days',
        help="For how many days book can be borrowed",
        default=10)
```

To add this field in views, you need to follow the *Changing existing views – view inheritance* recipe from `chapter 10`, *Backend Views*. You can find a full example of the code at `https://github.com/PacktPublishing/Odoo-12-Development-Cookbook-Third-Edition`.

How to do it...

To extend the business logic in the `library.book` model, you need to perform the following steps:

1. From `my_module_return`, we want to set `date_return` in the books record when we change the book status to `Borrowed`. For this, we will override the `make_borrowed` method from the `my_module_return` module:

```
def make_borrowed(self):
    day_to_borrow = self.category_id.max_borrow_days or 10
    self.date_return = fields.Date.today() +
timedelta(days=day_to_borrow)
    return super(LibraryBook, self).make_borrowed()
```

2. We also want to reset the `date_return` when the book is returned and available to borrow, so we will override the `make_available` method to reset the date:

```
def make_available(self):
    self.date_return = False
    return super(LibraryBook, self).make_available()
```

How it works...

Steps 1 and 2 carry out the extension of the business logic. We define a model that extends `library.books` and redefines the `make_borrowed()` and `make_available()` methods. In the last line of both methods, the result that was implemented by the parent class is returned:

```
return super(LibraryBook, self).make_borrowed()
```

In the case of Odoo models, the parent class is not what you'd expect by looking at the Python class definition. The framework has dynamically generated a class hierarchy for our recordset, and the parent class is the definition of the model from the modules that we depend on. So, the call to `super()` brings back the implementation of `library.book` from `my_module`. In this implementation, `make_borrowed()` changes the state of book to `Borrowed`. So, calling super will invoke the parent method and it will set the book state to `Borrowed`.

There's more...

In this recipe, we choose to extend the default implementation of the methods. In the `make_boorrow()` and `make_available()` methods, we modified the returned result *before* the `super()` call. Note that, when you call `super()`, it will execute the default implementation. It is also possible to perform some actions *after* the `super()` call. Of course, we can also do both at the same time.

However, it is more difficult to change the behavior of the middle of a method. To do this, we will need to refactor the code so that we can extract an extension point to a separate method and override this new method in the extension module.

> You may be tempted to completely rewrite a method. Always be very cautious when doing so; if you do not call the `super()` implementation of your method, you are breaking the extension mechanism and potentially breaking the add-ons that extend the method, meaning that the extension methods will never be called. Unless you are working in a controlled environment in which you know exactly which add-ons are installed and you've checked that you are not breaking them, avoid doing this. Also, if you have to, ensure that you document what you are doing in a very visible way.

What can you do before and after calling the original implementation of the method? There are lots of things, including (but not limited to) the following:

- Modifying the arguments that are passed to the original implementation (before)
- Modifying the context that is passed to the original implementation (before)
- Modifying the result that is returned by the original implementation (after)
- Calling another method (before and after)
- Creating records (before and after)
- Raising a `UserError` to cancel the execution in forbidden cases (before and after)
- Splitting `self` in smaller recordsets, and calling the original implementation on each of the subsets in a different way (before)

Extending write() and create()

The *Extending the business logic defined in a Model* recipe from this chapter showed us how to extend methods that are defined on a model class. If you think about it, methods that are defined on the parent class of the model are also part of the model. This means that all the base methods that defined on `models.Model` (actually, on `models.BaseModel`, which is the parent class of `models.Model`) are also available and can be extended.

This recipe shows you how to extend `create()` and `write()` to control access to some fields of the records.

Getting ready

We will extend on the library example from the `my_library` add-on module in `Chapter 4`, *Creating Odoo Add-On Modules*.

Add a `manager_remarks` field to the `library.book` model. We only want members of the `Library Managers` group to be able to write to that field:

```
from odoo import models, api, exceptions
class LibraryBook(models.Model):
    _name = 'library.book'
    manager_remarks = fields.Text('Manager Remarks')
```

Add the `manager_remarks` field in the `<form>` of the `view/library_book.xml` file to access this field from the user interface:

```
<field name="manager_remarks"/>
```

Modify the `security/ir.model.access.csv` file to give write access to library users:

```
id,name,model_id:id,group_id:id,perm_read,perm_write,perm_create,perm_
unlink
acl_book_user,library.book_default,model_library_book,base.group_user,
1,1,0,0
acl_book_librarian,library.book_librarian,model_library_book,group_lib
rarian,1,1,1,1
```

How to do it...

To prevent users who are not members of the **Librarian** group from modifying the value of `manager_remarks`, you need to perform the following steps:

1. Extend the `create()` method, as follows:

```
@api.model
def create(self, values):
    if not self.user_has_groups('my_library.acl_book_librarian'):
        if 'manager_remarks' in values:
            raise UserError(
                'You are not allowed to modify '
                'manager_remarks'
            )
    return super(LibraryBook, self).create(values)
```

2. Extend the `write()` method, as follows:

```
@api.multi
def write(self, values):
    if not self.user_has_groups('my_library.acl_book_librarian'):
        if 'manager_remarks' in values:
            raise UserError(
                'You are not allowed to modify '
                'manager_remarks'
            )
    return super(LibraryBook, self).write(values)
```

How it works...

Step 1 redefines the `create()` method. Before calling the base implementation of `create()`, our method uses the `user_has_groups()` method to check whether the user belongs to the `my_library.group_librarian` group (this is the XML ID of the group). If this is not the case and a value is passed for `manager_remarks`, a `UserError` exception is raised, preventing the creation of the record. This check is performed before the base implementation is called.

Step 2 does the same thing for the `write()` method; before writing, we check the group and the presence of the field in the values to write and raise a `UserError` if there is a problem.

Having the field set to read-only in the web client does not prevent RPC calls from writing it. This is why we extend `create()` and `write()`.

To test this implementation, you can log in as a demo user or revoke librarian access from the current user.

There's more...

When extending `write()`, note that, before calling the `super()` implementation of `write()`, `self` is still unmodified. You can use this to compare the current values of the fields to the ones in the values dictionary.

In this recipe, we chose to raise an exception, but we could have also chosen to remove the offending field from the values dictionary and silently skipped updating that field in the record:

```
@api.multi
def write(self, values):
    if not self.user_has_groups( 'my_library.group_librarian'):
        if 'manager_remarks' in values:
            del values['manager_remarks']
    return super(LibraryBook, self).write(values)
```

After calling `super().write()`, if you want to perform additional actions, you have to be wary of anything that can cause another call to `write()`, or you will create an infinite recursion loop. The workaround is to put a marker in the context that will be checked to break the recursion:

```
class MyModel(models.Model):
    @api.multi
    def write(self, values):
        sup = super(MyModel, self).write(values)
        if self.env.context.get('MyModelLoopBreaker'):
            return
        self = self.with_context(MyModelLoopBreaker=True)
        self.compute_things() # can cause calls to writes
        return sup
```

Customizing how records are searched

The *Defining the Model representation and order* recipe in `Chapter 4`, *Creating Odoo Add-On Modules*, introduced the `name_get()` method, which is used to compute a representation of the record in various places, including in the widget that's used to display `Many2one` relations in the web client.

This recipe will show you how to search for a book in the `Many2one` widget by title, author, or ISBN by redefining `name_search`.

Getting ready

For this recipe, we will use the following model definition:

```
class LibraryBook(models.Model):
    _name = 'library.book'
    name = fields.Char('Title')
    isbn = fields.Char('ISBN')
    author_ids = fields.Many2many('res.partner', 'Authors')

    @api.multi
    def name_get(self):
        result = []
        for book in self:
            authors = book.author_ids.mapped('name')
            name = '%s (%s)' % (book.name, ', '.join(authors))
            result.append((book.id, name))
            return result
```

When using this model, a book in a `Many2one` widget is displayed as **Book Title (Author1, Author2...)**. Users expect to be able to type in an author's name and find the list filtered according to this name, but this will not work since the default implementation of `name_search` only uses the attribute referred to by the `_rec_name` attribute of the model class, which in our case is `'name'`. We also want to allow filtering by ISBN number.

How to do it...

To be able to search for a `library.book` either by the book's title, one of the authors, or the ISBN number, you need to define the `_name_search()` method in the `LibraryBook` class, as follows:

```
@api.model
def _name_search(self, name='', args=None, operator='ilike',
                 limit=100, name_get_uid=None):
    args = [] if args is None else args.copy()
    if not(name == '' and operator == 'ilike'):
        args += ['|', '|',
                 ('name', operator, name),
                 ('isbn', operator, name),
                 ('author_ids.name', operator, name)
                 ]
    return super(LibraryBook, self)._name_search(
        name=name, args=args, operator=operator,
        limit=limit, name_get_uid=name_get_uid)
```

Add the `old_editions Many2one` field in the `library.book` model to test the `_name_search` implementation:

```
old_edition = fields.Many2one('library.book', string='Old Edition')
```

Add the following field to the user interface:

```
<field name="old_edition" />
```

Restart and update the module to reflect these changes. You can invoke the `_name_search` method by searching in the `old_edition Many2one` field.

How it works...

The default implementation of `name_search()` actually only calls the `_name_search()` method, which does the real job. This `_name_search()` method has an additional argument, `name_get_uid`, which is used in some corner cases such as if you want to compute the results using `sudo()` or with a different user.

We pass most of the arguments that we receive unchanged to the `super()` implementation of the method:

- `name` is a string that contains the value the user has typed so far.
- `args` is either `None` or a search domain that's used as a prefilter for the possible records. (It can come from the domain parameter of the `Many2one` relation, for instance.)
- `operator` is a string containing the match operator. Generally, you will have `'ilike'` or `'='`.
- `limit` is the maximum number of rows to retrieve.
- `name_get_uid` can be used to specify a different user when calling `name_get()` to compute the strings to display in the widget.

Our implementation of the method does the following:

1. It generates a new empty list if `args` is `None`, and makes a copy of `args` otherwise. We make a copy to avoid our modifications to the list having side effects on the caller.
2. Then, we check whether `name` is not an empty string or whether `operator` is not `'ilike'`. This is to avoid generating a dumb domain, `[('name', ilike, '')]`, that doesn't filter anything. In this case, we jump straight to the `super()` call implementation.
3. If we have a `name`, or if the `operator` is not `'ilike'`, then we add some filtering criteria to `args`. In our case, we add clauses that will search for the supplied name in the title of the books, in their ISBN, or in the author's names.
4. Finally, we call the `super()` implementation with the modified domain in `args` and force the `name` to `''` and the `operator` to `ilike`. We do this to force the default implementation of `_name_search()` to not alter the domain it receives, and so the one we specified will be used.

There's more...

We mentioned in the introduction that this method is used in the `Many2one` widget. For completeness, it is also used in the following parts of Odoo:

- When using the `in` operator on the `One2many` and `Many2many` fields in the domain

- To search for records in the `many2many_tags` widget
- To search for records in the CSV file import

See also

The *Defining the Model Representation and Order* recipe in `Chapter 4`, *Creating Odoo Add-On Modules*, demonstrates how to define the `name_get()` method, which is used to create a text representation of a record.

The *Defining filters on record lists – Domain* recipe in `Chapter 10`, *Backend Views*, provides more information about search domain syntax.

Fetching data in groups with read_group()

In the previous recipes, we saw how we can search and fetch data from the database. But sometimes, you want results by aggregating records, such as *the average cost for last month's sales order*. In this case, you can use the `read_group()` method to get the aggregate result.

Getting ready

In this recipe, we will use the `my_library` add-on module from `Chapter 4`, *Creating Odoo Add-On Modules*.

Modify the `library.book` model, as shown in the following model definition:

```
class LibraryBook(models.Model):
    _name = 'library.book'

    name = fields.Char('Title', required=True)
    date_release = fields.Date('Release Date')
    pages = fields.Integer('Number of Pages')
    cost_price = fields.Float('Book Cost')
    category_id = fields.Many2one('library.book.category')
    author_ids = fields.Many2many('res.partner', string='Authors')
```

Add the `library.book.category` model. For simplicity, we will just add it to the same `library_book.py` file:

```
class BookCategory(models.Model):
    _name = 'library.book.category'

    name = fields.Char('Category')
    description = fields.Text('Description')
```

We will be using the `library.book` model and getting an average cost price per category.

How to do it...

To extract grouped results, we will add the `_get_average_cost` method, which will use the `read_group()` method to fetch the data in a group:

```
@api.model
def _get_average_cost(self):
    grouped_result = self.read_group(
        [('cost_price', "!=", False)], # Domain
        ['category_id', 'cost_price:avg'], # Fields to access
        ['category_id'] # group_by
        )
    return grouped_result
```

To test this implementation, you need to add a button in the user interface that triggers this method.

How it works...

The `read_group()` method internally uses the SQL group by and aggregate functions to fetch the data. The most common arguments that are passed to the `read_group()` method are as follows:

- domain: This is used to filter records for grouping. For more information on the domain, refer to the *Searching views* recipe of `Chapter 10`, *Backend Views*.

- `fields`: This passes the names of fields you want to fetch with the grouped data. Possible values for this argument are as follows:
  - **field name**: You can pass the field name into the `fields` argument, but if you are using this option, then you must pass this field name to the `groupby` parameter too; otherwise, it will generate an error.
  - `field_name:agg`: You can pass the field name with the aggregate function. For example, in `cost_price:avg`, avg is a SQL aggregate function. A list of PostgreSQL aggregate functions can be found here: `https://www.postgresql.org/docs/current/static/functions-aggregate.html`.
  - `name:agg(field_name)`: This is the same as the previous one, but, with this syntax, you can give column aliases, such as `average_price:avg(cost_price)`.
- `groupby`: This argument accepts a list of field descriptions. Records will be grouped based on these fields. For the date and datetime column, you can pass `groupby_function` to apply date grouping based on different time durations, such as `date_release:month`. This will apply grouping based on months.

`read_group()` also supports some optional arguments, as follows:

- `offset`: This indicates an optional number of records to skip.
- `limit`: This indicates an optional maximum number of records to return.
- `orderby`: If this option is passed, the result will be sorted based on the given fields.
- `lazy`: This accepts boolean values and by default it is `True`. If true is passed, the results are only grouped by the first groupby and the remaining groupbys are put in the __context key. If `false`, all the groupbys are done in one call.

> **Performance tip:** `read_group()` is a lot faster than reading and processing values from a recordset. So, for KPIs or graphs, you should always use `read_group()`.

7
Module Data

In this chapter, we will cover the following recipes:

- Using external IDs and namespaces
- Loading data using XML files
- Using the `noupdate` and `forcecreate` flags
- Loading data using CSV files
- Add-on updates and data migration
- Deleting records from XML files
- Invoking functions from XML files

In order to avoid repeating a lot of code, we'll make use of the models that were defined in Chapter 5, *Application Models*. To follow these examples, make sure you grab the code for the `my_library` module from `Chapter05/r6_hierarchy_model/my_library`.

Introduction

In this chapter, we'll look at how add-on modules can provide data at installation time. This is useful for providing default values and adding metadata, such as view descriptions, menus, or actions. Another important usage is providing demonstration data, which is loaded when the database is created with the **Load demonstration data** checkbox checked.

Technical requirements

The technical requirements for this chapter include the online Odoo platform.

All the code that's used in this chapter can be downloaded from the following GitHub repository, at https://github.com/PacktPublishing/Odoo-12-Development-Cookbook-Third-Edition/tree/master/Chapter07.

Check out the following video to see the Code in Action:

Place holder link

Using external IDs and namespaces

So far in this book, we have used XML IDs in areas such as views, menus, and actions. However, we haven't seen what an XML ID actually is. This recipe will give you a deeper understanding.

How to do it...

We will write in the already-existing records to demonstrate how to use cross-module references:

1. Add a data file to your module manifest:

```
'data': [
    'data/data.xml',
],
```

2. Change the name of the main company:

```
<record id="base.main_company" model="res.company">
    <field name="name">Packt publishing</field>
</record>
```

3. Set the main company's partner as a publisher:

```
<record id="book_cookbook" model="library.book">
    <field name="publisher_id" ref="base.main_partner" />
</record>
```

Upon installation of this module, the company will be renamed and the book from the next recipe will be assigned to our partner. On subsequent updates of our module, only the publisher will be assigned, but the company's name will be left untouched.

How it works...

An XML ID is a string that refers to a record in the database. The IDs themselves are records of the `ir.model.data` model. This model's rows contain the modules that declare the XML ID, the identifier string, the referred model, and the referred ID. Every time we write to an XML ID, Odoo checks whether the string is namespaced (that is, whether it contains exactly one dot), and, if not, it adds the current module name as a namespace. Then, it looks up whether there is already a record in `ir.model.data` with the specified name. If so, an UPDATE statement for the listed fields is executed; if not, a CREATE statement is executed. This is how you can provide partial data when a record already exists, as we did earlier.

> A widespread application for partial data, apart from changing records defined by other modules, is using a shortcut element to create a record in a convenient way and writing a `field` on this record, which is not supported by the shortcut element:
> ```
> <act_window id="my_action" name="My action"
> model="res.partner" />
> <record id="my_action" model="ir.actions.act_window">
> <field name="auto_search" eval="False" />
> </record>
> ```

The `ref` function, as used in the *Loading data using XML files* recipe of this chapter, also adds the current module as a namespace if appropriate, but raises an error if the resulting XML ID does not exist already. This also applies to the `id` attribute if it is not namespaced already.

There's more...

You will probably need to access records with an XML ID from your code sooner or later. Use the `self.env.ref()` function in these cases. This returns a browse record of the referenced record. Note that here, you always have to pass the full XML ID. Here's an example of a full XML ID: `<module_name>.<record_id>`. You can see the XML ID of any record from the user interface. For that, you need to activate developer mode in Odoo.

Refer to `Chapter 1`, *Installing the Odoo Development Environment,* to activate developer mode in Odoo. After activating the developer mode, open the **Form View** of the record for which you want to find out the XML ID. You will see a bug icon in the top bar. From that menu, click on the **View Metadata** option. See the following screenshot for reference:

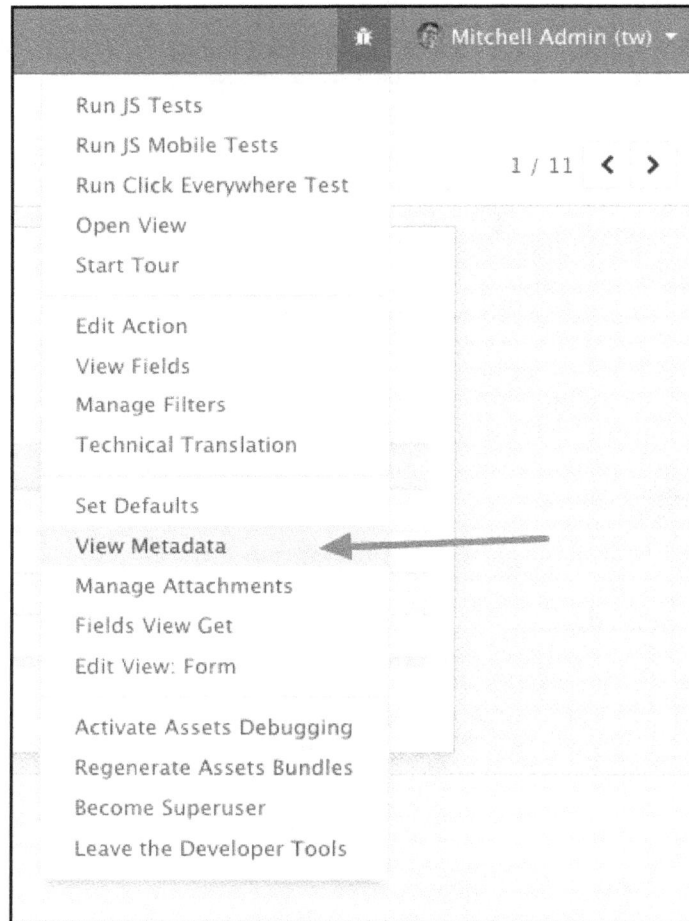

See also

Consult the *Using the noupdate and forcecreate flags* recipe of this chapter to find out why the company's name is changed only upon installation of the module.

Loading data using XML files

Using the data model in `Chapter 5`, *Application Models*, we'll add a book and an author as demonstration data. We'll also add a well-known publisher as normal data in our module.

How to do it...

Create two XML files and link them in your `__manifest__.py` file:

1. Add a file called `data/demo.xml` to your manifest, in the demo section:

```
'demo': [
    'data/demo.xml',
],
```

2. Add the following content to this file:

```xml
<odoo>
    <record id="author_pga" model="res.partner">
        <field name="name">Parth Gajjar</field>
    </record>
    <record id="author_af" model="res.partner">
        <field name="name">Alexandre Fayolle</field>
    </record>
    <record id="author_dr" model="res.partner">
        <field name="name">Daniel Reis</field>
    </record>
    <record id="author_hb" model="res.partner">
        <field name="name">Holger Brunn</field>
    </record>
    <record id="book_cookbook" model="library.book">
        <field name="name">Odoo Cookbook</field>
        <field name="short_name">cookbook</field>
        <field name="date_release">2016-03-01</field>
        <field name="author_ids"
                eval="[(6, 0, [ref('author_af'),
ref('author_dr'),
                                ref('author_hb')])]"
                                                        />
        <field name="publisher_id" ref="res_partner_packt" />
    </record>
</odoo>
```

3. Add a file called `data/data.xml` to your manifest, in the data section:

```
'data': [
    'data/data.xml',
    ...
],
```

4. Add the following XML content to `data/data.xml` file:

```
<odoo>
    <record id="res_partner_packt" model="res.partner">
        <field name="name">Packt Publishing</field>
        <field name="city">Birmingham</field>
        <field name="country_id" ref="base.uk" />
    </record>
</odoo>
```

When you update your module now, you'll see the publisher we created, and, if your database has demo data enabled, as pointed out in `Chapter 2`, *Creating Odoo Modules*, you'll also find this book and its authors.

How it works...

The demo data is technically the same as the normal data. The only difference is that the first is pulled by the `demo` key in the manifest, and the latter by the `data` key. To create a record, use the `<record>` element, which has the mandatory `id` and `model` attributes. For the `id` attribute, consult the *Using external IDs and namespaces* recipe; the `model` attribute refers to a model's `_name` property. Then, use the `<field>` element to fill the columns in the database, as defined by the model you named. The model also decides which fields are mandatory to fill and also possibly defines the default values. In this case, you don't need to give those fields a value explicitly. In step 2, the `<field>` element can contain a value as simple text in the case of scalar values. If you need to pass the content of a file (for setting an image, for example), use the `file` attribute on the `<field>` element and pass the file's name relative to the add-ons path.

For setting up references, there are two possibilities. The simplest is using the `ref` attribute, which works for `many2one` fields and just contains the XML ID of the record to be referenced. For `one2many` and `many2many` fields, we need to use the `eval` attribute. This is a general-purpose attribute that can be used to evaluate Python code to use as the field's value; think of `strftime('%Y-01-01')` as an example to populate a `date` field. `X2many` fields expect to be populated by a list of three tuples, where the first value of the tuple determines the operation to be carried out. Within an `eval` attribute, we have access to a function called `ref`, which returns the database ID of an XML ID given as a string. This allows us to refer to a record without knowing its concrete ID, which is probably different in different databases, as shown here:

- `(2, id, False)`: This deletes the linked record with `id` from the database. The third element of the tuple is ignored.
- `(3, id, False)`: This detaches the record with `id`, from the `one2many` field. Note that this operation does not delete the record—it just leaves the existing record as it is. The last element of the tuple is also ignored.
- `(4, id, False)`: This adds a link to the existing record `id` and the last element of the tuple is ignored. This should be what you use most of the time, usually accompanied by the `ref` function to get the database ID of a record known by its XML ID.
- `(5, False, False)`: This cuts all links, but keeps the linked records intact.
- `(6, False, [id, ...])`: This clears out currently-referenced records to replace them with the ones mentioned in the list of IDs. The second element of the tuple is ignored.

> Note that order matters in data files and that records within data files can only refer to records defined in data files earlier in the list. This is why you should always check whether your module installs in an empty database, because during development, you often add records all over the place, which works because the records defined afterwards are already in the database from an earlier update. Demo data is always loaded after the files from the data key, which is why the reference in this example works.

There's more...

While you can do basically anything with the record element, there are shortcut elements that make it more convenient for the developer to create certain kinds of records. These include **menu item**, **template**, or **act window**. Refer to Chapter 10, *Backend Views*, and Chapter 16, *CMS Website Development*, for information about these.

A field element can also contain the function element, which calls a function defined on a model to provide a field's value. Refer to the *Invoking functions from XML files* recipe for an application in which we simply call a function to directly write to the database, circumventing the loading mechanism.

The preceding list misses entries for 0 and 1, because these are not very useful when loading the data. They are entered, as follows, for the sake of completeness:

- (0, False, {'key': value}): This creates a new record of the referenced model, with its fields filled from the dictionary at position three. The second element of the tuple is ignored. As these records don't have an XML ID and are evaluated every time the module is updated, leading to double entries, it's better to avoid this. Instead, create the record in its own record element, and link it as explained in *How it works* section of this recipe.
- (1, id, {'key': value}): This can be used to write on an existing linked record. For the same reasons that we mentioned earlier, you should avoid this syntax in your XML files.

These syntaxes are the same as the ones we explained in the *Creating new records* and *Updating values of records* recipes in Chapter 6, *Basic Server-side Development*.

Using the noupdate and forcecreate flags

Most add-on modules have different types of data. Some data simply needs to exist for the module to work properly, other data shouldn't be changed by the user, and most data can be changed as the user wants and is only provided as a convenience. This recipe will detail how to address the different types. First, we'll write a field in an already-existing record, and then we'll create a record that is supposed to be recreated during a module update.

How to do it...

We can enforce different behaviors from Odoo when loading data by setting certain attributes on the enclosing `<odoo>` element or the `<record>` element itself:

1. Add a publisher that will be created at installation time, but not updated on subsequent updates. However, if the user deletes it, it will be recreated:

```
<odoo noupdate="1">
    <record id="res_partner_packt" model="res.partner">
        <field name="name">Packt publishing</field>
        <field name="city">Birmingham</field>
        <field name="country_id" ref="base.uk"/>
    </record>
</odoo>
```

2. Add a book category that is not changed during add-on updates and not recreated if the user deletes it:

```
<odoo noupdate="1">
    <record id="book_category_all"
model="library.book.category"
            forcecreate="false">
        <field name="name">All books</field>
    </record>
</odoo>
```

How it works...

The `<odoo>` element can have a `noupdate` attribute, which is propagated to the `ir.model.data` records that are created when reading the enclosed data records for the first time, thus ending up as a column in this table.

When Odoo installs an add-on (called `init` mode), all records are written whether `noupdate` is `true` or `false`. When you update an add-on (called the `update` mode), the existing XML IDs are checked to see whether they have the `noupdate` flag set, and if so, elements that try to write to this XML ID are ignored. This is not the case if the record in question was deleted by the user, which is why you can force not recreating `noupdate` records in the `update` mode by setting the `forcecreate` flag on the record to `false`.

In legacy add-ons (prior to and including version 8.0), you'll often find an <openerp> element enclosing a <data> element, which contains the <record> and other elements. This is still possible, but deprecated. By now, <odoo>, <openerp>, and <data> have exactly the same semantics; they are meant as a bracket to enclose XML data.

There's more...

If you want to load the records even with the noupdate flag, you can run the Odoo server with the --init=your_addon or -i your_addon parameter. This will force Odoo to reload your records. This will also cause deleted records to be recreated. Note that this can cause double records and related installation errors if a module circumvents the XML ID mechanism, for example, by creating records in Python code called by the <function> tag.

With this code, you can circumvent any noupdate flag, but first make sure that this is really what you want. Another option for solving the scenario presented here is to write a migration script, as outlined in the *Add-on updates and data migration* recipe.

See also

Odoo also uses XML IDs to keep track of which data is to be deleted after an add-on update. If a record has an XML ID from the module's namespace before the update, but the XML ID is not reinstated during the update, the record and its XML ID will be deleted from the database because they're considered obsolete. For a more in-depth discussion of this mechanism, refer to the *Add-on updates and data migration* recipe.

Loading data using CSV files

While you can do everything you need to with XML files, this format is not the most convenient when you need to provide larger amounts of data, especially given that many people are more comfortable preprocessing data in Calc or other spreadsheet software. Another advantage of the CSV format is that it is what you get when you use the standard export function. In this recipe, we'll take a look at importing table-like data.

How to do it...

Traditionally, **access-control lists** (**ACLs** – refer to `Chapter 11`, *Access Security*) are a type of data that is loaded through CSV files:

1. Add `security/ir.model.access.csv` to your data files:

   ```
   'data': [
       ...
       'security/ir.model.access.csv',
   ],
   ```

2. Add an ACL for our books in this file (we already have a few records from the *Adding access security* recipe from `Chapter 4`, *Creating Odoo Add-On Modules*):

   ```
   id,name,model_id:id,group_id:id,perm_read,perm_write,perm_crea
   te,perm_unlink
   acl_library_book_user,ACL for
   books,model_library_book,base.group_user,1,0,0,0
   ```

We now have an ACL that permits normal users to read book records, but does not allow them to edit, create, or delete them.

How it works...

You simply drop all your data files in your manifest's **data** list. Odoo will use the file extension to decide which type of file it is. A specialty of CSV files is that their file name must match the name of the model to be imported, in our case, `ir.model.access`. The first line needs to be a header with column names that match the model's field names exactly.

For scalar values, you can use a quoted (if necessary, because the string contains quotes or commas itself) or an unquoted string.

When writing `many2one` fields with a CSV file, Odoo first tries to interpret the column value as XML ID. If there's no dot, Odoo adds the current module name as a namespace, and looks up the result in `ir.model.data`. If this fails, the model's `name_search` function is called with the column's value as a parameter, and the first result returned wins. If this also fails, the line is considered invalid and Odoo raises an error.

Note that data read from CSV files is always `noupdate=False`, and there's no convenient way around this. This means that subsequent updates of your add-on will always overwrite possible changes made by the user.
If you need to load huge amounts of data and `noupdate` is a problem for you, load a CSV file from an init hook.

There's more...

Importing the `one2many` and `many2many` fields with CSV files is possible, but a bit tricky. In general, you're better off creating the records separately and setting up the relation with an XML file afterwards, or working with a second CSV file that sets up the relationship.

If you really need to create related records within the same file, order your columns so that all scalar fields are to the left and the fields of the linked model are to the right, with a column header consisting of the linking field's name and the linked model's field, separated by a colon:

```
"id","name","model_id:id","perm_read","perm_read", "group_id:name"
"access_library_book_user","ACL for books","model_library_book",1,
"my group"
```

This will create a group called `my group`; you can write more fields in the group record by adding columns to the right. If you need to link multiple records, repeat the line and change the right-hand side columns as appropriate. Given that Odoo fills empty columns with the previous line's value, you don't need to copy all the data—you can simply add a line with empty values saved for the fields of the linked model you want to fill.

For x2m fields, just list the XML IDs of the records to be linked.

Add-on updates and data migration

The data model you choose when writing an add-on module might turn out to have some weaknesses, so you may need to adjust it during the life cycle of your add-on module. In order to allow that without a lot of hacks, Odoo supports versioning in add-on modules and running migrations if necessary.

How to do it...

We assume that in an earlier version of our module, the `date_release` field was a character field, where people wrote whatever they saw fit as the date. We now realize that we need this field for comparisons and aggregations, which is why we want to change its type to `Date`. Odoo does a great job at type conversions, but, in this case, we're on our own, which is why we need to provide instructions as to how to transform a database with the previous version of our module installed on a database where the current version can run:

1. Bump the version in your `__manifest__.py` file:

```
'version': '12.0.1.0.1',
```

2. Provide the pre-migration code in `migrations/12.0.1.0.1/pre-migrate.py`:

```
def migrate(cr, version):
    cr.execute('ALTER TABLE library_book RENAME COLUMN date_release
                                                           TO
    date_release_char')
```

3. Provide the post-migration code in `migrations/12.0.1.0.1/post-migrate.py`:

```
from odoo import fields
from datetime import date

def migrate(cr, version):
    cr.execute('SELECT id, date_release_char FROM
    library_book')
    for record_id, old_date in cr.fetchall():
        # check if the field happens to be set in Odoo's
    internal
        # format
        new_date = None
        try:
            new_date = fields.Date.to_date(old_date)
        except ValueError:
            if len(old_date) == 4 and old_date.isdigit():
                # probably a year
                new_date = date(int(old_date), 1, 1)
            else:
                # try some separators, play with
    day/month/year
```

```
                              # order ...
                              pass
                    if new_date:
                            cr.execute('UPDATE library_book SET
        date_release=%s',
                                    (new_date,))
```

Without this code, Odoo would have renamed the old `date_release` column to `date_release_moved` and created a new one, because there's no automatic conversion from character fields to date fields. From the point of view of the user, the data in `date_release` will simply be gone.

How it works...

The first crucial point is that you increase the version number of your add-on, as migrations run only between different versions. During every update, Odoo writes the version number from the manifest at the time of the update into the `ir_module_module` table. The version number is prefixed with Odoo's major and minor versions if the version number has three or fewer components. In the preceding example, we explicitly named Odoo's major and minor version, which is good practice, but a value of `1.0.1` would have had the same effect, because, internally, Odoo prefixes short version numbers for add-ons with its own major and minor version number. Generally, using the long notation is a good idea because you can see at a glance which version of Odoo an add-on is meant for.

The two migration files are just code files that don't need to be registered anywhere. When updating an add-on, Odoo compares the add-on's version, as noted in `ir_module_module`, with the version in the add-on's manifest. If the manifest's version is higher (after adding Odoo's major and minor version), this add-on's `migrations` folder will be searched to see whether it contains folders with the version(s) in-between, up to, and including the version that is currently updated.

Then, within the folders found, Odoo searches for Python files whose names start with `pre-`, loads them, and expects them to define a function called `migrate`, which has two parameters. This function is called with a database cursor as the first argument and the currently-installed version as the second argument. This happens before Odoo even looks at the rest of the code the add-on defines, so you can assume that nothing changes in your database layout compared to the previous version.

After all the `pre-migrate` functions run successfully, Odoo loads the models and the data declared in the add-on, which can cause changes in the database layout. Given that we renamed `date_release` in `pre-migrate.py`, Odoo will just create a new column with that name, but with the correct data type.

After that, with the same search algorithm, the `post-migrate` files will be searched and executed if found. In our case, we need to look at every value to see whether we can make something usable out of it; otherwise, we keep the data as NULL. Don't write scripts that iterate over a whole table if not absolutely necessary; in this case, we would have written a very big, unreadable SQL switch.

> **TIP**
> If you simply want to rename a column, you don't need a migration script. In this case, you can set the `oldname` parameter of the field in question to the field's original column name; Odoo then takes care of the renaming itself.

There's more...

In both the pre- and post-migration steps, you only have access to a cursor, which is not very convenient if you're used to Odoo environments. It can lead to unexpected results to use models at this stage, because in the pre-migration step, the add-on's models are not yet loaded and also, in the post-migration step, the models defined by add-ons that depend on the current add-on are not yet loaded either. However, if this is not a problem for you, either because you want to use a model that your add-on doesn't touch or a model for which you know that this issue is not a problem, you can create the environment you're used to by writing the following:

```
from odoo import api, SUPERUSER_ID

def migrate(cr, version):
    env = api.Environment(cr, SUPERUSER_ID, {})
    # env holds all currently loaded models
```

See also

When writing migration scripts, you'll often be confronted with repetitive tasks, such as checking whether a column or table exists, renaming things, or mapping some old values to new values. It's frustrating and error-prone to reinvent the wheel here; consider using `https://github.com/OCA/openupgradelib` if you can afford the extra dependency.

Deleting records from XML files

In the previous recipes, we saw how we can create or update records from the XML file. Sometimes, from the dependent module, you want to delete the previously created records. This can be done with the `<delete>` tag.

Getting ready

In this recipe, we will add some categories from the XML file and then delete them. In real situations, you will create this record from another module. But for simplicity, we will just add some categories in the same XML file, as follows:

```
<record id="book_category_to_delete" model="library.book.category">
    <field name="name">Test Category</field>
</record>
<record id="book_category_not_delete" model="library.book.category">
    <field name="name">Test Category 2</field>
</record>
```

How to do it...

There are two ways to delete records from the XML file:

- With the XML ID of previously created records:

  ```
  <delete model="library.book.category"
  id="book_category_to_delete"/>
  ```

- With the search domain:

  ```
  <delete model="library.book.category" search="[('name',
  'ilike', 'Test')]"/>
  ```

How it works...

You will need to use the `<delete>` tag. To delete a record from a model, you need to provide the name of the model in the `model` attribute. This is a compulsory attribute.

In the first method, you need to provide the XML ID of the records that were previously created from another module's data files. During the installation of the module, Odoo will try to find the record. If the record is found for the given XML ID, it will delete the record, otherwise it will raise an error. You can delete only the records that are created from the XML files (or records that have XML IDs).

In the second method, you need to pass the domain in the `domain` attribute. During the installation of the module, Odoo will search the records by this domain. If records are found, it deletes them. This option will not raise an error if no records match the given domain. Use this option with extreme caution, because it might delete your user's data since the search option deletes all the records that match the domain.

> <delete> is rarely used in Odoo as it is dangerous. If you are not careful with this, you might break the system. Avoid it if possible.

Invoking functions from XML files

You can create all type of records from XML files, but sometimes it is difficult to generate data that includes some business logic. You might want to modify records when a user installs a dependent module in production. For example, let's say you want to create a module to display books online. The `my_library` module already has an image-cover field. Imagine that, in the new module, you implemented logic to reduce the size of the image and stored it in the new thumbnail field. Now, when the user installs this module, they might already have books and images. It is not possible to generate thumbnails from the <record> tags in the XML file. In this case, you can invoke the model method through the <function> tag.

How to do it...

For this recipe, we will use the code from the previous recipe. As an example, we will increase the existing book price by $10 USD. Note that you might using another currency based on company configurations.

Follow these steps to invoke the Python method from the XML file:

1. Add the _update_book_price() method in the library.book model:

```
@api.model
def _update_book_price(self):
    all_books = self.search([])
    for book in all_books:
        book.cost_price += 10
```

2. Add <function> in the data XML file:

```
<function model="library.book" name="_update_book_price"/>
```

How it works...

In the first step, we added the _update_book_price() method, which searches for all books and increases the price by $10 USD. We started the method name with _ as this is considered private by ORM and cannot be invoked through RPC.

In the second step, we used the <function> tag with two attributes:

- model: The model name in which the method is declared
- name : The name of the method you want to invoke

When you install this module, _update_book_price() will be called and the price of books will be increased by $10.

> Always put this function with the noupdate options. Otherwise, it will be invoked every time you update your module.

There's more...

With <function>, it is also possible to send parameters to the functions. Let's say you only want to increase the price of books in a particular category and you want to send that amount as a parameter.

For that, you need to create a method that accepts the category as a parameter, as
follows:

```
@api.model
def update_book_price(self, category, amount_to_increase):
    category_books = self.search([('category_id', '=',
category.id)])
    for book in category_books:
        book.cost_price += amount_to_increase
```

To pass the category and amount as a parameter, you need to use the eval attribute,
as follows:

```
<function model="library.book"
    name="update_book_price"
    eval="(ref('category_xml_id'), 20)"/>
```

When you install the module, it will increase the price of the books of the given
category by $20.

8
Debugging

In this chapter, we will cover the following recipes:

- The auto-reload and --dev options
- Producing server logs to help debug methods
- Using the Odoo shell to interactively call methods
- Using the Python debugger to trace method execution
- Using the Odoo Community Association maintainer quality tools
- Understanding the debug mode options

Introduction

In `Chapter 6`, *Basic Server-Side Development*, we saw how to write model methods to implement the logic of our module. However, we may get stuck when we encounter complex problems. Odoo provides you with some debugging tools that can help you to find the root cause of various issues. In this chapter, we will look at this debugging tool in detail.

The auto-reload and --dev options

In the previous chapters, we saw how to add a model, fields, and views. Whenever we make changes to Python files, we need to restart the server in order to apply those changes. If we make changes in XML files, we need to restart the server and update the module to reflect those changes in the user interface. If you are developing a large application, this can be time-consuming and frustrating. Odoo provides some command-line `--dev` options to overcome these issues. In this recipe, we will see how to use these options.

Getting ready

Install `watchdog` in your developer environment with the following command in the shell. Without `watchdog`, the auto-reload feature will not work:

```
$ pip3 install watchdog
```

How to do it...

To enable the `dev` option, you need to use `--dev=value` from the command line. Possible values for this option are `all`, `reload`, `pudb|wdb|ipdb|pdb`, `qweb`, `werkzeug`, and `xml`. Take a look at the following example for more information:

```
$ odoo/odoo-bin -c ~/odoo-dev/my-instance.cfg --dev=all
```

If you want to enable only a few options, you can use comma-separated values, as follows:

```
$ odoo/odoo-bin -c ~/odoo-dev/my-instance.cfg --dev=reload,qweb
```

How it works...

Check the following list for all `--dev` options and their purposes:

- `reload`: Whenever you make changes in Python, you need to restart the server to reflect those changes in Odoo. The `--dev=reload` option will reload the Odoo server automatically when you make changes in any Python file. This feature will not work if you haven't installed the Python `watchdog` package.
- `qweb`: You can create dynamic website pages in Odoo using QWeb templates. In `Chapter 15`, *CMS Website Development*, we will see how to develop a web page with the QWeb template. You can debug issues in the QWeb template with the `t-debug` attribute. The `t-debug` options will only work if you enable the `dev` mode with `--dev=qweb`.
- `werkzeug`: Odoo uses `werkzeug` to handle HTTP requests. Internally, Odoo will catch all exceptions generated by `werkzeug`. If you use `--dev=werkzeug`, werkzeug's interactive debugger will be displayed on the web page when the exception is generated.

- `xml`: Whenever you make changes in the view structure, you need to reload the server and update the module to apply those changes. With the `--dev=xml` option, you just need to reload Odoo from the browser; there is no need to restart the server or update the module.
- `pudb|wdb|ipdb|pdb`: You can use the **Python debugger** (**PDB**) to get more information about the errors. When you use the `--dev=pdb` option, it will activate the PDB whenever an exception is genarated in Odoo. Odoo supports four Python debuggers: `pudb`, `wdb`, `ipdb`, and `pdb`.

- `all`: If you use `--dev=all`, all of the preceding options will be enabled.

> If you have made changes to the database structure, such as if you have added new fields, the `--dev=reload` option will not reflect these in the database schema. You need to update the module manually; it only works for Python business logic.
>
> If you add a new view or menu, the `--dev=xml` option will not reflect this in the user interface. You need to update the module manually. This is very helpful when you are designing the structure of the view or the website page.

Producing server logs to help debug methods

Server logs are useful when trying to figure out what has been happening at runtime before a crash. They can also be added to provide additional information when debugging is an issue. This recipe shows you how to add logging to an existing method.

Getting ready

We will add some logging statements to the following method, which saves the stock levels of products to a file:

```
from os.path import join
from odoo import models, api, exceptions
EXPORTS_DIR = '/srv/exports'

class ProductProduct(models.Model):
```

```
_inherit = 'product.product'
@api.model
def export_stock_level(self, stock_location):
    products = self.with_context(
        location=stock_location.id
    ).search([])
    products = products.filtered('qty_available')
    fname = join(EXPORTS_DIR, 'stock_level.txt')
    try:
        with open(fname, 'w') as fobj:
            for prod in products:
                fobj.write('%s\t%f\n' % (prod.name,
                                         prod.qty_available))
    except IOError:
        raise exceptions.UserError('unable to save file')
```

How to do it...

In order to get some logs when this method is being executed, perform the following steps:

1. At the beginning of the code, import the `logging` module:

   ```
   import logging
   ```

2. Before the definition of the model class, get a logger for the module:

   ```
   _logger = logging.getLogger(__name__)
   ```

3. Modify the code of the `export_stock_level()` method, as follows:

   ```
   @api.model
   def export_stock_level(self, stock_location):
       _logger.info('export stock level for %s',
                    stock_location.name)
       products = self.with_context(
           location=stock_location.id).search([])
       products = products.filtered('qty_available')
       _logger.debug('%d products in the location',
                     len(products))
       fname = join(EXPORTS_DIR, 'stock_level.txt')
       try:
           with open(fname, 'w') as fobj:
               for prod in products:
                   fobj.write('%s\t%f\n' % (
                       prod.name, prod.qty_available))
   ```

```
except IOError:
    _logger.exception(
        'Error while writing to %s in %s',
        'stock_level.txt', EXPORTS_DIR)
    raise exceptions.UserError('unable to save file')
```

How it works...

Step 1 imports the `logging` module from the Python standard library. Odoo uses this module to manage its logs.

Step 2 sets up a logger for the Python module. We use the common idiom __name__ in Odoo as an automatic variable for the name of the logger and to call the logger by `_logger`.

> The __name__ variable is set automatically by the Python interpreter at module-import time, and its value is the full name of the module. Since Odoo does a little trick with the imports, the add-on modules are seen by Python as belonging to the `odoo.addons` Python package. So, if the code of the recipe is in `my_library/models/book.py`, the __name__ will be `odoo.addons.my_library.models.book`.

By doing this, we get two benefits:

- The global logging configuration set on the `odoo` logger is applied to our logger because of the hierarchical structure of loggers in the `logging` module.
- The logs will be prefixed with the full module path, which is a great help when trying to find where a given log line is produced.

Step 3 uses the logger to produce log messages. The available methods for this are (by increasing log level) `debug`, `info`, `warning`, `error`, and `critical`. All these methods accept a message in which you can have % substitutions and additional arguments to be inserted into the message. You should not do the % substitution yourself; the logging module is smart enough to perform this operation if the log has to be produced. If you are running with a log level of `INFO`, then `DEBUG` logs will avoid substitutions that will consume CPU in the long run.

Another useful method shown in this recipe is `_logger.exception()`, which can be used in an exception handler. The message will be logged with a level of `ERROR`, and the stack trace is also printed in the application log.

There's more...

You can control the **logging level** of the application from the command line or from the configuration file. There are two main ways of doing this:

- To control the log level globally, you can use the `--log-level` command-line options. Refer to `Chapter 1`, *Managing Odoo Server Instances,* for more information.
- To set the log level for a given logger, you can use `--log-handler=prefix:level`. In this case, the prefix is a piece of the path of the logger name, and the level is `DEBUG`, `INFO`, `WARNING`, `ERROR`, or `CRITICAL`. If you omit the prefix, you set the default level for all loggers. For instance, to set the logging level of `my_library` loggers to `DEBUG` and keep the default log level for the other add-ons, you can start Odoo as follows:

```
$ python odoo.py --log-handler=odoo.addons.my_library:DEBUG
```

It is possible to specify `--log-handler` multiple times on the command line. You can also configure the **log handler** in the configuration file of your Odoo instance. In that case, you can use a comma-separated list of `prefix:level` pairs. For example, the following line is the same configuration for a minimal logging output as before. We maintain the most important messages and the error messages by default, except for messages produced by `werkzeug`, for which we only want critical messages, and `odoo.service.server`, for which we keep info-level messages, including server startup notifications:

```
log_handler = :ERROR,werkzeug:CRITICAL,odoo.service.server:INFO
```

Using the Odoo shell to interactively call methods

The Odoo web interface is meant for end users, although the developer mode unlocks a number of powerful features. However, testing and debugging through the web interface is not the easiest way to do things, as you need to manually prepare the data, navigate in the menus to perform actions, and so on. The Odoo shell is a **command-line interface**, which you can use to issue calls. This recipe shows how to start the Odoo shell and perform actions such as calling a method inside the shell.

Getting ready

We will reuse the same code as in the previous recipe to produce server logs to help debug methods. This allows the `product.product` model to add a new method. We will assume that you have an instance with the add-on installed and available. In this recipe, we expect that you have an Odoo configuration file for this instance called `project.conf`.

How to do it...

In order to call the `export_stock_level()` method from the Odoo shell, you need to perform the following steps:

1. Start the Odoo shell and specify your project configuration file:

   ```
   $ ./odoo-bin shell -c project.conf --log-level=error
   ```

2. Check for error messages and read the information text that's displayed before the usual Python command-line prompt:

   ```
   env: <odoo.api.Environment object at 0x10e3277f0>
   odoo: <module 'odoo' from
   '/home/parth/community/odoo/__init__.py'>
   openerp: <module 'odoo' from
   '/home/parth/community/odoo/__init__.py'>
   self: res.users(1,)
   Python 3.6.5 (default, Apr 25 2018, 14:23:58)
   [GCC 9.3.0] on linux
   Type "help", "copyright", "credits" or "license" for more
   information.
   >>>
   ```

3. Get a recordset for `product.product`:

   ```
   >>> product = env['product.product']
   ```

4. Get the main stock location record:

   ```
   >>> location_stock = env.ref('stock.stock_location_stock')
   ```

5. Call the `export_stock_level()` method:

   ```
   >>> product.export_stock_level(location_stock)
   ```

6. Commit the transaction before exiting:

```
>>> env.cr.commit()
```

7. Exit the shell by pressing *Ctrl + D*.

How it works...

Step 1 uses `odoo-bin shell` to start the Odoo shell. All the usual command-line arguments are available. We use `-c` to specify a project configuration file and `--log-level` to reduce the verbosity of the logs. When debugging, you may want to have a logging level of `DEBUG` for some specific add-ons.

Before providing you with a Python command-line prompt, the `odoo-bin shell` starts an Odoo instance that does not listen on the network and initializes some global variables, which are mentioned in the output:

- `env` is an environment that's connected to the database and specified on the command line or in the configuration file.
- `odoo` is the `odoo` package that's imported for you. You get access to all the Python modules within that package to do what you want.
- `openerp` is an alias for the `odoo` package for backwards-compatibility.
- `self` is a recordset of `res.users` that contains a single record for the Odoo superuser (Administrator), which is linked to the `env` environment.

Steps 3 and *4* use `env` to get an empty recordset and find a record by the XML ID. *Step 5* calls the method on the `product.product` recordset. These operations are identical to what you would use inside a method, with the small difference that we use `env` and not `self.env` (although we can have both, as they are identical). Take a look at Chapter 6, *Basic Server-Side Development*, for more information on what is available.

Step 6 commits the database transaction. This is not strictly necessary here because we did not modify any record in the database, but if we had done so and wanted these changes to persist, this is necessary; when you use Odoo through the web interface, each RPC call runs in its own database transaction, and Odoo manages these for you. When running in shell mode, this no longer happens and you have to call `env.cr.commit()` or `env.cr.rollback()` yourself. Otherwise, when you exit the shell, any transaction in progress is automatically rolled back. When testing, this is fine, but if you use the shell, for example, to script the configuration of an instance, don't forget to commit your work!

There's more...

In shell mode, by default, Odoo opens Python's REPL shell interface. You can use the REPL of your choice using the `--shell-interface` option. The supported REPLs are `ipython`, `ptpython`, `bpython`, and `python`:

```
$ ./odoo-bin shell -c project.conf  --shell-interface=ptpython
```

Using the Python debugger to trace method execution

Sometimes, application logs are not enough to figure out what is going wrong. Fortunately, we also have the Python debugger. This recipe shows us how to insert a breakpoint in a method and trace the execution by hand.

Getting ready

We will reuse the `export_stock_level()` method that was shown in the *Using the Odoo shell to interactively call methods* recipe of this chapter. Ensure that you have a copy at hand.

How to do it...

To trace the execution of `export_stock_level()` with `pdb`, perform the following steps:

1. Edit the code of the method, and insert the line highlighted here:

```
def export_stock_level(self, stock_location):
    import pdb; pdb.set_trace()
    products = self.with_context( location=stock_location.id
).search([])
    fname = join(EXPORTS_DIR, 'stock_level.txt')
    try:
        with open(fname, 'w') as fobj:
            for prod in products.filtered('qty_available'):
                fobj.write('%s\t%f\n' % (prod.name,
prod.qty_available))
    except IOError:
        raise exceptions.UserError('unable to save file')
```

2. Run the method. We will use the Odoo shell, as explained in the *Using the Odoo shell to interactively call methods* recipe:

```
$ ./odoo-bin shell -c project.cfg --log-level=error
[...]
>>> product = env['product.product']
>>> location_stock = env.ref('stock.stock_location_stock')
>>> product.export_stock_level(location_stock)
> /home/cookbook/stock_level/models.py(18)export_stock_level()
-> products = self.with_context(
(Pdb)
```

3. At the (Pdb) prompt, issue the args command (the shortcut of which is a) to get the values of the arguments that were passed to the method:

```
(Pdb) a
self = product.product()
stock_location = stock.location(14,)
```

4. Enter the list command to check where in the code you are standing:

```
(Pdb) list
 13             @api.model
 14             def export_stock_level(self, stock_location):
 15             _logger.info('export stock level for %s',
 16                         stock_location.name)
 17             import pdb; pdb.set_trace()
 18 ->          products = self.with_context(
 19             location=stock_location.id).search([])
 20             products = products.filtered('qty_available')
 21             _logger.debug('%d products in the location',
 22                         len(products))
 23             fname = join(EXPORTS_DIR, 'stock_level.txt')
(Pdb)
```

5. Enter the next command three times to walk through the first lines of the method. You may also use n, which is a shortcut:

```
(Pdb) next
> /home/cookbook/stock_level/models.py(19)export_stock_level()
-> location=stock_location.id).search([])
(Pdb) n
> /home/cookbook/stock_level/models.py(20)export_stock_level()
-> products = products.filtered('qty_available')
(Pdb) n
> /home/cookbook/stock_level/models.py(21)export_stock_level()
-> _logger.debug('%d products in the location',
(Pdb) n
```

```
> /home/cookbook/stock_level/models.py(22)export_stock_level()
-> len(products))
(Pdb) n
> /home/cookbook/stock_level/models.py(23)export_stock_level()
-> fname = join(EXPORTS_DIR, 'stock_level.txt')
(Pdb) n
> /home/cookbook/stock_level/models.py(24)export_stock_level()
-> try:
```

6. Use the p command to display the values of the products and fname variables:

```
(Pdb) p products
product.product(32, 14, 17, 19, 21, 22, 23, 29, 34, 33, 26,
27, 42)
(Pdb) p fname
'/srv/exports/stock_level.txt'
```

7. Change the value of fname to point to the /tmp directory:

```
(Pdb) !fname = '/tmp/stock_level.txt'
```

8. Use the return (shortcut: r) command to execute the current function:

```
(Pdb) return
--Return--
>
/home/cookbook/stock_level/models.py(26)export_stock_level()->
None
-> for product in products:
```

9. Use the cont (shortcut: c) command to resume the execution of the program:

```
(Pdb) c
>>>
```

How it works...

In *step 1*, we hardcoded a breakpoint in the source code of the method by calling the set_trace() method of the pdb module from the Python standard library. When this method is executed, the normal flow of the program stops, and you get a (Pdb) prompt in which you can enter pdb commands.

Step 2 calls the `stock_level_export()` method using shell mode. It is also possible to restart the server normally and use the web interface to generate a call to the method you need to trace by clicking on the appropriate elements of the user interface.

When you need to manually step through some code using the Python debugger, here are a few tips that will make your life easier:

- Reduce the logging level to avoid having too many log lines, which pollutes the output of the debugger. Starting at the ERROR level is generally fine. You may want to enable some specific loggers with a higher verbosity, which you can do using the `--log-handler` command-line option (refer to the *Producing server logs to help debug methods* recipe).
- Run the server with `--workers=0` to avoid any multiprocessing issues that can cause the same breakpoint to be reached twice in two different processes.
- Run the server with `--max-cron-threads=0` to disable the processing of the `ir.cron` periodic tasks, which may otherwise trigger while you are stepping through the method, which produces unwanted logs and side effects.

Steps 3 to *8* use several `pdb` commands to step through the execution of the method. Here's a summary of the main commands of `pdb`. Most of these are also available using the first letter as a shortcut. We indicate this here by having the optional letters between parentheses:

- `h(elp)`: This displays help about the `pdb` commands.
- `a(rgs)`: This shows the value of the arguments of the current function/methods.
- `l(ist)`: This displays the source code being executed in chunks of 11 lines, initially centered on the current line. Successive calls will move further in the source code file. Optionally, you can pass two integers at the start and end, which specify the region to display.
- `p`: This prints a variable.
- `pp`: This pretty-prints a variable (useful with lists and dictionaries).
- `w(here)`: This shows the call stack, with the current line at the bottom and the Python interpreter at the top.
- `u(p)`: This moves up one level in the call stack.
- `d(own)`: This moves down one level in the call stack.
- `n(ext)`: This executes the current line of code and then stops.

- `s(tep)`: This is to step inside the execution of a method call.
- `r(eturn)`: This resumes the execution of the current method until it returns.
- `c(ont(inue))`: This resumes the execution of the program until the next breakpoint is hit.
- `b(reak) <args>`: This creates a new breakpoint and displays its identifier; `args` can be one of the following:
    - `<empty>`: This lists all breakpoints.
    - `line_number`: This breaks at the specified line in the current file.
    - `filename:line_number`: This breaks at the specified line of the specified file (which is searched for in the directories of `sys.path`).
    - `function_name`: This breaks at the first line of the specified function.
- `tbreak <args>`: This is similar to break, but the breakpoint will be canceled after it has been reached, so successive execution of the line won't trigger it twice.
- `disable bp_id`: This disables a breakpoint by ID.
- `enable bl_id`: This enables a disabled breakpoint by ID.
- `j(ump) lineno`: The next line to execute will be the one specified. This can be used to rerun or skip some lines.
- `(!) statement`: This executes a Python statement. The `!` character can be omitted if the command does not look like a `pdb` command. For instance, you need it if you want to set the value of a variable named `a`, because `a` is the shortcut for the `args` command.

There's more...

In the recipe, we inserted a `pdb.set_trace()` statement to break into `pdb` for debugging. We can also start `pdb` directly from within the Odoo shell, which is very useful when you cannot easily modify the code of the project using `pdb.runcall()`. This function takes a method as the first argument and the arguments to pass to the function as the next arguments. So, inside the Odoo shell, you do this:

```
>>> import pdb
>>> product = env['product.product']
```

```
>>> location_stock = env.ref('stock.stock_location_stock')
>>> pdb.runcall(product.export_stock_level, location_stock)
> /home/cookbook/stock_level/models.py(16)export_stock_level()
-> products = self.with_context(
(Pdb)
```

In this recipe, we focused on the Python debugger from the Python standard library, pdb. It is very useful to know about this tool because it is guaranteed to be available on any Python distribution. There are other Python debuggers available, such as ipdb (https://pypi.python.org/pypi/ipdb) and pudb (https://pypi.python.org/pypi/pudb), which can be used as drop-in replacements for pdb. They share the same API, and most of the commands that you saw in this recipe were unchanged. Also, of course, if you develop for Odoo using a Python IDE, you will have access to a debugger that was integrated with it.

See also

If you want to learn more about the pdb debugger, refer to the full documentation of pdb at https://docs.python.org/3.5/library/pdb.html.

Using the Odoo Community Association maintainer quality tools

The **Odoo Community Association** (OCA) manages a large number of Odoo projects using the GitHub infrastructure. The association projects use Travis CI for continuous integration. This recipe shows you how to use the maintainer QA tools developed by the community in your own GitHub repositories.

Getting ready

To use this recipe, you need to have a public GitHub repository with your modules. At the time of writing, the OCA tools expect that this repository contains several add-ons in subdirectories.

How to do it...

To integrate the OCA `maintainer-quality-tools` with your repository, you need to perform the following steps:

1. Connect to `https://travis-ci.org/`:

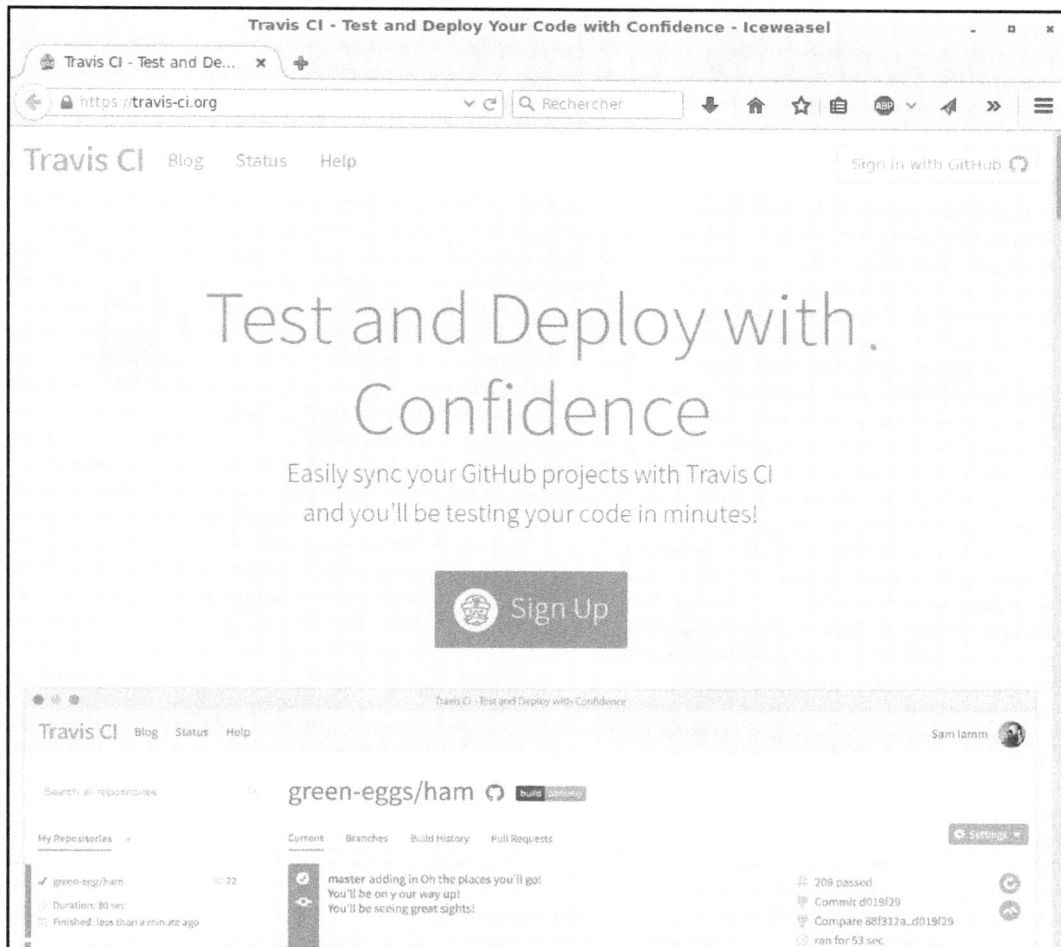

2. To sign in, choose **Sign in with GitHub**.

3. Click on your name in the top-right corner to access your profile settings, as shown in the following screenshot:

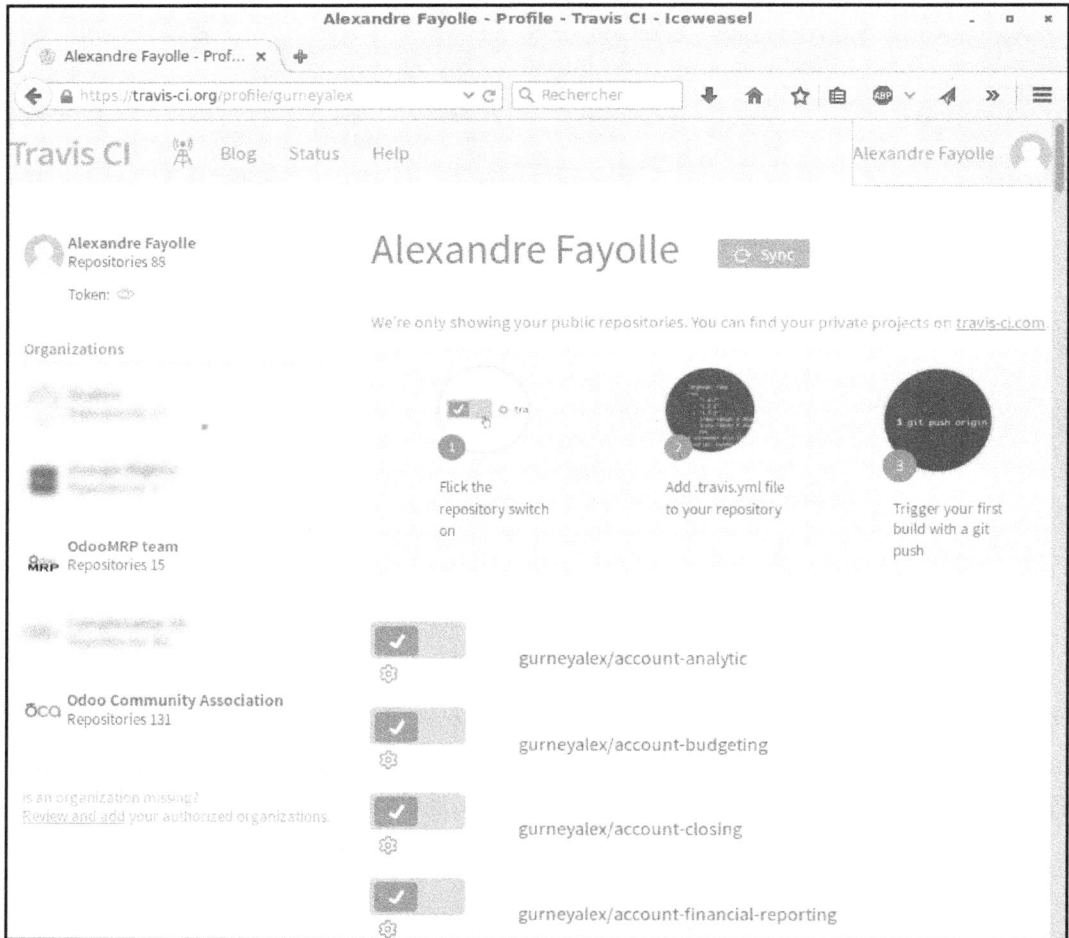

4. Click on the **Sync** button to load information about your public repositories in Travis. This might take a couple of minutes depending on how many repositories you have.

5. For all the repositories on which you want to use **Travis**, toggle the grey cross so that it displays a green checkmark.

6. You can click on the cogwheel to access each of the settings of each repository, but the default settings are okay too.

7. Inside a local clone of your repository, create a file called `.travis.yml` with the following content:

```
language: python
sudo: false
cache:
  apt: true
  directories:
    - $HOME/.cache/pip
python:
  - "3.5"
addons:
  apt:
    packages:
      - expect-dev  # provides unbuffer utility
      - python-lxml  # because pip installation is slow
      - python-simplejson
      - python-serial
      - python-yaml
virtualenv:
  system_site_packages: true
env:
  global:
    - VERSION="12.0" TESTS="0" LINT_CHECK="0"
  matrix:
    - LINT_CHECK="1"
    - TESTS="1" ODOO_REPO="odoo/odoo"
    - TESTS="1" ODOO_REPO="OCA/OCB"
install:
  - git clone --depth=1
https://github.com/OCA/maintainer-quality-tools.git
${HOME}/maintainer-quality-tools
  - export PATH=${HOME}/maintainer-quality-
tools/travis:${PATH}
  - travis_install_nightly
script:
  - travis_run_tests
after_success:
  - travis_after_tests_success
```

8. Commit the file and push it to GitHub:

```
$ git add .travis.yml
$ git commit -m "add travis configuration"
$ git push origin
```

9. Go to your `travis-ci.org` page and click on your project's name. You should see a first build in progress. If your code follows the OCA coding standard, it may even be green on the first run:

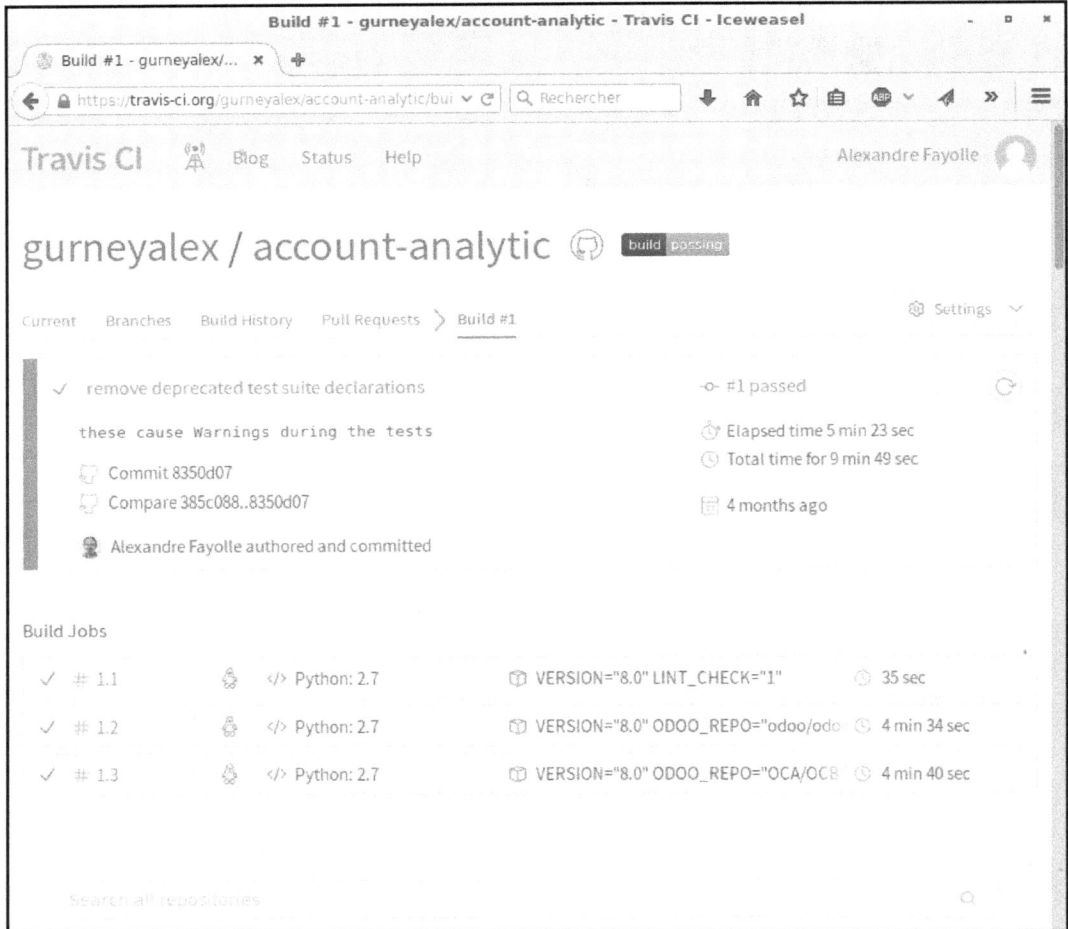

How it works...

When you enable the Travis CI on a repository, Travis registers a hook on GitHub. By default, the hook will trigger a Travis CI build for each push to a branch of the repository and for each pull request. Pull requests are built on a temporary merge to ensure that the merged branches pass the tests.

The Travis CI configuration file proposed here is fairly advanced and very close to the one found in the `sample_files` subdirectory of the maintainer-quality-tools project, which you can find at `https://github.com/OCA/maintainer-quality-tools` (we removed the `transifex` configuration that's used to manage module translations). Here's an explanation of the customized sections in the file:

- `addons`: This has nothing to do with Odoo add-on modules. It's used to ask Travis to install some Ubuntu packages using distribution packages in the testing environment. This saves us from installing Python packages, such as `python-lxml`, from source, which takes a lot of time.
- `env`: This section defines environment variables and the build matrix. The maintainer quality tools use these environment variables to know what to test, and will run each `env` line in a separate test run:
    - `VERSION`: This is the Odoo version to test against.
    - `LINT_CHECK`: Use 0 for a build with no `flake8` or `Pylint` tests, and 1 otherwise. In the matrix, we set the first build to perform the lint check, as this is fast and we want rapid feedback if the coding standards are not met or if the linter finds errors.
    - `TESTS`: Use 0 for a build in which the module tests are not run, otherwise use 1.
    - `ODOO_REPO`: This is the GitHub repository for Odoo to test against when `TESTS` is 1. In the recipe, we set up a build against both the official `https://github.com/odoo/odoo` repository and the community backports repository, `https://github.com/OCA/OCB`. If unset, only the official repository is used.
- `install`: This section downloads `maintainer-quality-tools` in the build environment and calls the `travis_install_nightly` utility, which will set up Odoo in Travis.

- `script`: This section calls `travis_run_tests` from `maintainer-quality-tools`. This script is in charge of checking the environment variables from the build matrix and performing the appropriate actions.
- `after_success`: After the tests in the `script` section have run successfully, the `travis_after_test_success` script is run. In the context of this recipe, this script will check the test coverage of the modules using `https://coveralls.io` and produce a report in the build.

There's more...

Maybe you are not interested in the whole setup, which is heavily dependent on the Travis CI, and you would like some lighter tools to help you in your day-to-day work. The good news is that some of the tools behind the setup shown in this recipe can be used individually, especially the **static code-checkers**, Pylint and Flake8.

Using Pylint to check your code

Pylint (`https://www.pylint.org/`) is a static code-checker for Python. There is a very interesting project called `pylint-odoo`, which provides a Pylint plugin to perform Odoo-specific checks. To install it, run the following command, preferably in a virtual environment:

```
$ pip3 install --upgrade --pre pylint-odoo
```

When this is done, you can check your add-on module with the following command:

```
$ pylint --load-plugins=pylint_odoo -rn -e epylint
<path_to_the_addon_directory>
```

This will produce the following output:

```
********** Module my_module
C: 1, 0: Missing ./README.rst file. Template here:
https://github.com/OCA/maintainer-tools/blob/master/template/module/RE
ADME.rst (missing-readme)
************* Module my_module.__manifest__
C: 2, 0: Missing author required "Odoo Community Association (OCA)" in
manifest file (manifest-required-author)
C: 2, 0: Deprecated key "description" in manifest file (manifest-
deprecated-key)
************* Module my_module.models.library_book
W: 14,12: The attribute string is redundant. String parameter equal to
name of variable (attribute-string-redundant)
```

The README file of the module (which can be found at `https://github.com/OCA/pylint-odoo/blob/master/README.rst`) will give you an up-to-date list of checks that have been performed by the tool. Then, you can use Pylint's command-line options to tune the output. For instance, if you are not interested in the *missing author* check, which is specific to the Odoo Community Association, you can remove the check by checking the message ID in the README file (in this case, this is `C8101`) and passing it to the `-d` or `--disable` command-line option, as follows:

```
$ pylint --load-plugin=pylint_odoo -rn -e epylint -d C8101 \
<path_to_the_addon_directory>
```

It is possible to store the command-line options you pass to Pylint in a configuration file to make your day-to-day work easier.

Using Flake8 to check your code

Flake8 (`http://flake8.pycqa.org/`) is another popular tool you can use to verify that your code is correctly formatted. Programming text editors and IDEs that support development generally offer a way to run flake8 as you type, highlighting portions of code that do not match with the flake8 rules.

To install `flake8`, run the following command:

```
$ pip install flake8
```

Here's a `flake8` configuration file that was used for the Odoo Community Association development:

```
[flake8]
# E123,E133,E226,E241,E242 are ignored by default by pep8 and flake8
# F811 is legal in odoo 8 when we implement 2 interfaces for a method
# F999 pylint support this case with expected tests
ignore = E123,E133,E226,E241,E242,F811,F601
max-line-length = 79
exclude = __unported__,__init__.py
```

Save this in a file called `.flake8` at the root of your project, and you should then be able to run the following:

```
$ flake8 <path_to_file_or_directory>
```

Better yet, set up your editor to check your code as you type!

Understanding the debug mode options

In Chapter 1, *Installing the Odoo Development Environment*, we saw how to enable debug/developer options in Odoo. These options are very helpful in debugging and reveal some further technical information. In this chapter, we will look at these options in detail.

How to do it...

Check the *Activating the Odoo developer tools* recipe of Chapter 1, *Installing the Odoo Development Environment*, and activate developer mode. After activating developer mode, you will see a drop-down menu with a bug icon in the top bar, as shown here:

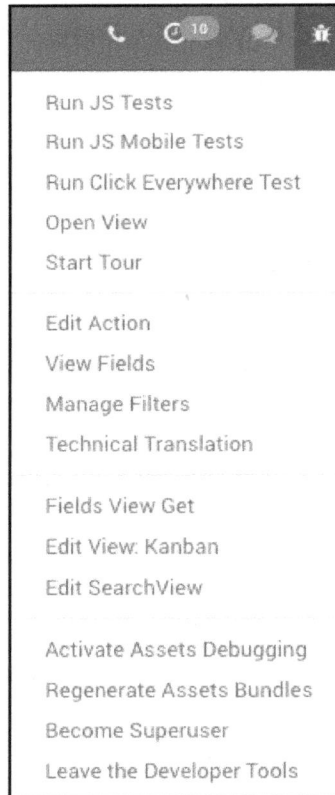

In this menu, you will see various options. Give them a go to see them in action. The next section will explain these options in more detail.

How it works...

Let's learn more about the options in the following points:

- **Run JS Tests**: This option will redirect you to the JavaScript QUnit test case page, as shown in the following screenshot. It will start running all test cases one by one. Here, you can see the progress and the status of the test cases. In Chapter 18, *Automated Test Cases*, we will see how can we create our own QUnit JavaScript test cases:

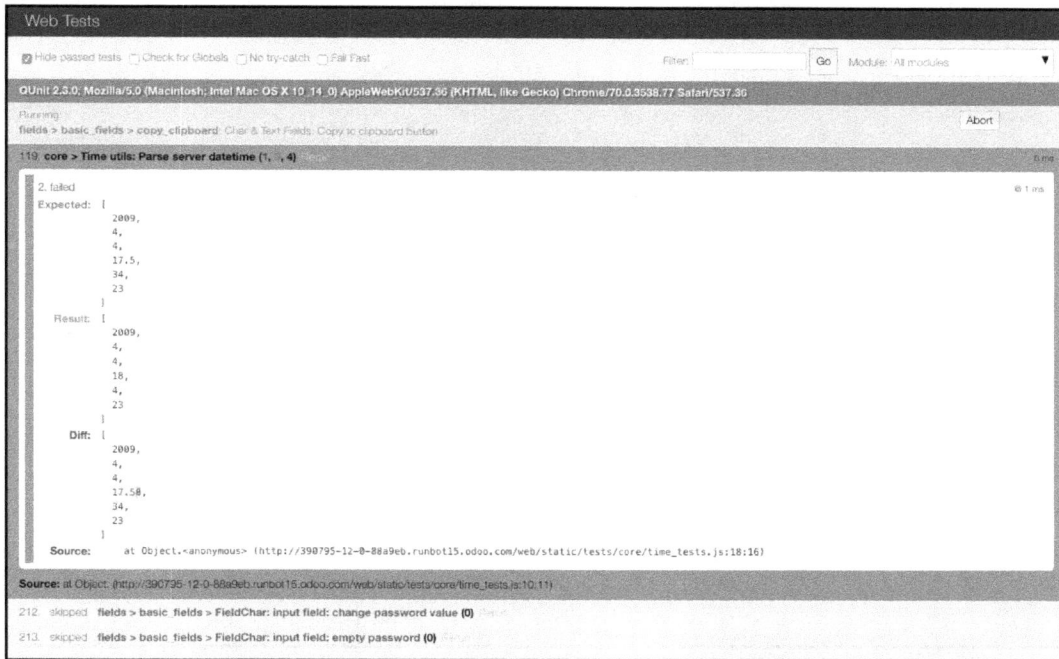

- **Run JS Mobile Tests**: Similar to the preceding option, but this one runs a QUnit test case for a mobile environment.
- **Run Click Anywhere Tests**: This option will start clicking on all menus one by one. It will click in all the views and search filters. If something is broken or there is any regression, it will show the tracebacks. To stop this test, you will need to reload the page.

- **Open View**: This option will open a list of all available views. By selecting any of them, you can open that view without defining any menus or actions.
- **Start Tour**: Odoo uses tours to improve the on-boarding of new users. It also uses tours for automated testing. We will create a custom onpboarding tour in `Chapter 16`, *Web Client Development*. This option will open a dialog box with a list of all tours, as shown in the following screenshot. By clicking on the play button next to a tour, Odoo will automatically perform all the steps of the tour:

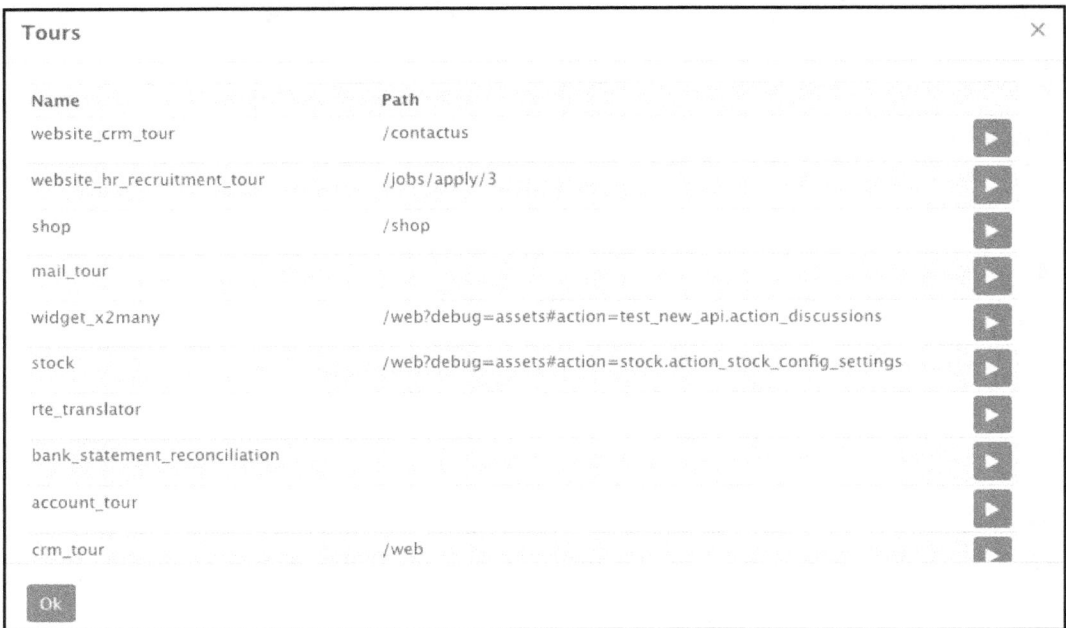

- **Edit Action**: In the *Adding menu items and views* recipe of `Chapter 4`, *Creating Odoo Add-On Modules*, we added a menu item and an action to open views in Odoo. Details of these actions are also stored in the database as a record. This option will open the record details of the action we open to display the current view.
- **View Fields**: This option will help you when you want to see the details of fields from the user interface. It will show a list of fields for the current model. For example, if you open a tree or form view for a `library.book` model, this option will show a list of fields for the `library.book` model.

- **Manage Filters**: In Odoo, users can create custom filters from the search view. This option will open a list of custom filters for the current model. Here, you can modify the custom filters.

- **Technical Translations**: This option will open a list of translated terms for the current model. You can modify the technical translation terms for your model from here. You can refer to `Chapter 12`, *Internationalization,* to learn more about translations.

- **Fields View Get**: You can extend and modify an existing view from other add-on modules. In some applications, these views are inherited by several add-on modules. Because of this, it is very difficult to get a clear idea of the whole view definition. With this option, you will get the final view definition after applying all view inheritance. Internally, it uses the `fields_view_get()` method.

- **Edit View: <view type>**: This option will open the dialog with the `ir.ui.view` record of the current view. This option is dynamic and it will show an option based on the view that is currently open. This means that if you open the **Kanban View**, you will get an **Edit View: Kanban** option, and if you open the **Form View**, you will get an **Edit View: Form** option.

> You can modify the view definition from the **Edit View** option. This updated definition will be applicable on the current DB and these changes will be removed when you update the module. It's therefore better to modify views from modules.

- **Edit Search View**: This option is the same as the preceding one, but it will open the `ir.ui.view` record of the current model's search view.

- **Activate Assets Debugging**: Odoo provide two types of developer mode: *Developer mode* and *Developer mode with assets*. With this option, you can switch from *Developer* mode to *Developer mode with assets* mode. Check the *Activating the Odoo developer tools* recipe of `Chapter 1`, *Installing the Odoo Development Environment,* for more details.

- **Regenerate Assets Bundles**: Odoo manages all CSS and JavaScript through assets bundles. This option deletes the old JavaScript and CSS assets and generates new ones. This option is helpful when you are getting issues because of asset caching. We will learn more about assets bundles in `Chapter 12`, *CMS Website Development.*

- **Become Super User**: This is a new option in version 12. By activating this option, you switch to a super user. You can access the records even if you don't have access rights. This option is not available for all users; it is only available for users who have **Administration: settings** access rights. After activating this mode, you will see a striped top menu, as shown here:

- **Leave Developer Tools:** This option allows you to leave developer mode.

9
Advanced Server-Side Development Techniques

In this chapter, we will look at the following recipes:

- Changing the user that performs an action
- Calling a method with a modified context
- Executing raw SQL queries
- Writing a wizard to guide the user
- Defining `onchange` methods
- Calling `onchange` methods on the server side
- Defining a model based on an SQL view
- Adding custom settings options
- Implementing init hooks

Introduction

In `Chapter 6`, *Basic Server-side Development*, you saw how to write methods on a model class, how to extend methods from inherited models, and how to work with recordsets. This chapter will deal with more advanced topics, such as working with the environment of a recordset and working with `onchange` methods.

Technical requirements

The technical requirements for this chapter include the Odoo online platform.

All the code used in this chapter can be downloaded from the GitHub repository at `https://github.com/PacktPublishing/Odoo-12-Development-Cookbook-Third-Edition/tree/master/Chapter09`.

Check out the following video to see the code in action: `http://bit.ly/2UEP4bj`

Changing the user that performs an action

When writing business logic code, you may have to perform some actions with a different security context. A typical case is performing an action with the rights of the Administrator, who bypasses security checks.

This recipe will show you how to let normal users modify the phone number of a company by using `sudo()`.

Getting ready

For a an easier to understand, we will add a new model to manage the book ratings. We will add a new model called `library.book.rent`. You can refer to the following definition to add this model:

```python
class LibraryBookRent(models.Model):
    _name = 'library.book.rent'

    book_id = fields.Many2one('library.book', 'Book', required=True)
    borrower_id = fields.Many2one('res.partner', 'Borrower',
required=True)
    state = fields.Selection([('ongoing', 'Ongoing'), ('returned',
'Returned')],
                              'State', default='ongoing',
required=True)
    book_id = fields.Many2one('library.book', 'Book', required=True)
    rent_date = fields.Date(default=fields.Date.today)
    return_date = fields.Date()
```

You will need to add a form view, an action, and a menu item to see this new model from the user interface. You will also need to add security rules for the librarian, so they can issue the book for rent. Please refer to `Chapter 4`, *Creating Odoo Modules*, if you don't know how to add these things.

Alternatively, you can use the ready-made initial module from our GitHub code examples to save time. This module will be available in the `Chapter09/r0_initial_module` folder. The GitHub code examples are available at `https://github.com/PacktPublishing/Odoo-12-Development-Cookbook-Third-Edition`.

How to do it...

If you have tested the module, you will find that only users who have librarian access rights can mark a book as borrowed. Non-librarian users cannot borrow a book by themselves; they need to ask a librarian user. Suppose that we want to add a new feature so that non-librarian users can borrow books by themselves. We will do this without giving them the access rights for the `library.book.rent` model.

In order to let normal users borrow books, you need to perform the following steps:

1. Add the `book_rent()` method in the `library.book` model:

   ```
   class LibraryBook(models.Model):
       _name = 'library.book'
       ...
       def book_rent(self):
   ```

2. In the method, ensure that we are acting on a single record:

   ```
   self.ensure_one()
   ```

3. Raise a warning if a book is not available to borrow:

   ```
   if self.state != 'available':
       raise UserError(_('Book is not available for
   renting'))
   ```

4. Get the empty recordset of `library.book.rent` as a superuser:

   ```
   rent_as_superuser = self.env['library.book.rent'].sudo()
   ```

5. Create a new book borrow record with the appropriate values:

   ```
   rent_as_superuser.create({
       'book_id': self.id,
       'borrower_id': self.env.user.partner_id.id,
   })
   ```

6. To trigger this method from the user interface, add the button to the book's form view:

```
<button name="book_rent"
        string="Rent this book"
        type="object"
        class="btn-primary"/>
```

Restart the server and update `my_library` to apply the given changes. After the update, you will see a **Rent this book** button on the book form view. When you click on that, a new rent record will be created. This will also work for non-librarian users. You can test this by accessing Odoo as a demo user.

How it works...

In *step 4*, we used `sudo()`. This method returns a new recordset with a new **environment** in which the user is not the same as the one in `self`. When called without an argument, `sudo()` will link the Odoo **superuser**, the Administrator, to the environment. All method calls through this sudo recordset are made with the new environment, and therefore, with superuser privileges. To get a better idea of this, remove `.sudo()` from the method and then click on the **Rent this book** button. It will raise an *Access Error* and the user will no longer have access to the model. Put simply, `sudo()` will bypass all security rules.

If you need a specific user, you can pass a recordset containing either that user or the database `id` of the user. The following snippet allows you to search books that are visible, using the `public` user:

```
public_user = self.env.ref('base.public_user')
public_book = self.env['library.book'].sudo(public_user)
```

> When you use `sudo()`, there is no traceability of actions, such as to who created or updated a record. In our recipe, the author of the last modification of the company will be the Administrator, not the user who originally called `create`.
> The community add-on, `base_suspend_security`, found at `https://github.com/OCA/server-backend/`, can be used to work around this limitation.

There's more...

When using `sudo()` without an argument, you set the user of the context to the Odoo superuser. This superuser bypasses all the security rules of Odoo, both the *access-control lists* and the *record rules*. By default, this user also has a `company_id` field set to the main company of the instance (the one with an ID of 1). This can be problematic in a *multi-company* instance:

- If you are not careful, new records created in this environment will be linked to the company of the superuser.
- If you are not careful, records searched in this environment may be linked to any company present in the database, which means that you may be leaking information to the real user; worse, you may be silently corrupting the database by linking records that belong to different companies.

> When using `sudo()`, always double-check to ensure that your calls to `search()` don't rely on the standard record rules to filter the results, and ensure that your calls to `create()` don't rely on default values that are computed using some of the current user's fields, such as `company_id`.

Using `sudo()` also involves creating a new `Environment` instance. This environment will have an initially-empty recordset cache, and that cache will evolve independently from the cache of `self.env`. This can cause spurious database queries. In any case, you should avoid creating a new environment inside loops and try to move these environment creations to the outermost possible scope.

See also

Check out these references for more information:

- If you want to learn more about the environments, refer to the *Obtaining an empty recordset for a model* recipe in Chapter 6, *Basic Server-side Development*.
- For more information about access-control lists and record rules, check out Chapter 11, *Access Security*.

Calling a method with a modified context

The context is part of the environment of a recordset. It is used to pass information such as the time zone and the language of the user from the user interface, as well as the contextual parameters specified in the actions. A number of methods in the standard add-ons use the context to adapt their behavior to these values. It is sometimes necessary to modify the context on a recordset to get the desired results from a method call or the desired value for a computed field.

This recipe will show how to get different output from the same method with the help of the context.

Getting ready

For this recipe, we will use the `my_library` module from the previous recipe. On the form view of the `library.book.rent` model, we will add a button to mark the book as lost, in case a normal user loses a book. Note that we already have the same button in the form view of the book, but here, we will have a slightly different behavior to understand the use of contexts in Odoo.

How to do it...

In order to add a button, you need to perform the following steps:

1. Update the definition of the `state` field to have a `lost` state:

```
state = fields.Selection([('ongoing', 'Ongoing'),
                          ('returned', 'Returned'), ('lost',
'Lost')],
                         'State', default='ongoing',
required=True)
```

2. Add a **Mark as lost** button in the form view of `library.book.rent`:

```
<button name="book_lost" string="Lost the Book"
states="ongoing" type="object"/>
```

3. Add the `book_lost()` method in the `library.book.rent` model:

```
def book_lost(self):
    ...
```

4. In the method, make sure that we are acting on a single record, and then change the state:

```
self.ensure_one()
self.state = 'lost'
```

5. Add the following code in the method to change the context of the environment and call the method to change the book's state to `lost`:

```
book_with_different_context =
self.book_id.with_context(avoid_deactivate=True)
book_with_different_context.make_lost()
```

6. Update the `make_lost()` method of the `library.book` model to have a different behavior:

```
def make_lost(self):
    self.ensure_one()
    self.state = 'lost'
    if not self.env.context.get('avoid_deactivate'):
        self.active = False
```

How it works...

Step 5 calls `self.book_id.with_context()` with some keyword arguments. This returns a new version of `book_id` (which is a `library.book` recordset) with the keys added to the current context. We are adding one key here, `avoid_deactivate=True`, but you can add multiple keys if you want.

In *step 6*, we checked whether the context has a positive value for the `avoid_deactivate` key. We avoid deactivating books, so the librarian can see them even if they are lost.

This is just a simple example of a context, but you can use it anywhere in the ORM, based on your requirements.

There's more...

It is also possible to pass a dictionary to `with_context()`. In this case, the dictionary is used as the new context, which overwrites the current one. So, *step 5* can also be written as follows:

```
new_context = self.env.context.copy()
new_context.update({'avoid_deactivate': True})
book_with_different_context = self.book_id.with_context(new_context)
book_with_different_context.make_lost()
```

Using `with_context()` involves creating a new `Environment` instance. This environment will have an initially-empty recordset cache, which will evolve independently of the cache of `self.env`. This can cause spurious database queries. In any case, you should avoid creating new environments inside loops and try to move these environment creations to the outermost-possible scope.

See also

Refer given the recipes to learn more about context in Odoo:

- The *Obtaining an empty recordset for a model* recipe in `Chapter 6`, *Basic Server-side Development*, explains what the environment is.
- The *Passing parameters to forms and actions – context* recipe in `Chapter 10`, *Backend Views*, explains how to modify the context in action definitions.
- The *Search for records* recipe in `Chapter 6`, *Basic Server-side Development*, explains active records.

Executing raw SQL queries

Most of the time, you can perform the operations you want by using the `search()` method. However, sometimes, you need more; either you cannot express what you want using the domain syntax (for which some operations are tricky, if not downright impossible), or your query requires several calls to `search()`, which ends up being inefficient.

This recipe shows you how to use raw SQL queries to get the average number of days a user borrows a particular book.

Getting ready

For this recipe, we will use the `my_library` module from the previous recipe. For simplicity, we will just print the results in a log, but in real scenarios, you will need to use the query result in your business logic. In `Chapter 10`, *Backend Views*, we will display the result of this query in the user interface.

How to do it...

To get the information about the average number of days a user keeps a particular book, you need to perform the following steps:

1. Add the `average_book_occupation()` method to `library.book`:

   ```
   def average_book_occupation(self):
       ...
   ```

2. In the method, write the following SQL query:

   ```
   sql_query = """
       SELECT
           lb.name,
           avg((EXTRACT(epoch from age(return_date, rent_date)) /
   86400))::int
       FROM
           library_book_rent AS lbr
       JOIN
           library_book as lb ON lb.id = lbr.book_id
       WHERE lbr.state = 'returned'
       GROUP BY lb.name;"""
   ```

3. Execute the query:

   ```
   self.env.cr.execute(sql_query)
   ```

4. Fetch the result and log it:

   ```
   result = self.env.cr.fetchall()
   logger.info("Average book occupation: %s", result)
   ```

5. Add a button in the form view of the `library.book` mode to trigger our method:

   ```
   <button name="average_book_occupation" string="Log Average
   Occ." type="object" />
   ```

Don't forgot to import `logging` in this file. Then, restart and update the `my_library` module.

How it works...

In *step 2*, we declare an SQL `SELECT` query. This will return the average number of days a user holds a particular book. If you run this query in the PostgreSQL CLI, you will get a result based on your book data:

```
+------------------------------------+-------+
| name                               | avg   |
|------------------------------------+-------|
| Odoo 12 Development Cookbook        | 33    |
| PostgreSQL 10 Administration Cookbook | 81 |
+------------------------------------+-------+
```

Step 3 calls the `execute()` method on the database cursor stored in `self.env.cr`. This sends the query to PostgreSQL and executes it.

Step 5 uses the `fetchall()` method of the cursor to retrieve a list of rows selected by the query. This method returns a list of rows. In my case, this is `[('Odoo 12 Development Cookbook', 33), ('PostgreSQL 10 Administration Cookbook', 81)]`. From the form of the query we execute, we know that each row will have exactly two values, the first being `name` and the other being the average number of days a user holds a particular book. Then, we simply logged it.

There's more...

The object in `self.env.cr` is a thin wrapper around a `psycopg2` cursor. The following methods are the ones that you will want to use most of the time:

- `execute(query, params)`: This executes the SQL `query` with the parameters marked as `%s` in the query substituted with the values in `params`, which is a tuple.

Warning: Never do the substitution yourself, as this can make the code vulnerable to SQL injections.

- `fetchone()`: This returns one row from the database, wrapped in a tuple (even if there is only one column selected by the query)
- `fetchall()`: This returns all the rows from the database as a list of tuples
- `fetchalldict()`: This returns all the rows from the database as a list of dictionaries mapping column names to values

Be very careful when dealing with raw SQL queries:

- You are bypassing all the security of the application. Ensure that you call `search([('id', 'in', tuple(ids)])` with any list of `ids` you are retrieving to filter out records to which the user has no access.
- Any modifications you are making are bypassing the constraints set by the add-on modules, except the `NOT NULL`, `UNIQUE`, and `FOREIGN KEY` constraints, which are enforced at the database level. This is also the case for any computed field recomputation triggers, so you may end up corrupting the database.

See also

- For access-rights management, refer to `Chapter 11`, *Access Security*.

Writing a wizard to guide the user

In the *Using abstract models for reusable model features* recipe in `Chapter 5`, *Application Models*, the `models.TransientModel` base class was introduced. This class shares a lot with normal `Models`, except that the records of transient models are periodically cleaned up in the database; hence, the name transient. These are used to create wizards, or dialog boxes, which are filled in the user interface by the users and are generally used to perform actions on the persistent records of the database.

Getting ready

For this recipe, we will use the `my_library` module from the previous recipe. This recipe will add a new wizard. With this wizard, librarians will be able to issue multiple books at a time.

How to do it...

Follow given steps to add a new wizard for creating book rent records:

1. Add a new transient model to the module, with the following definition:

```
class LibraryRentWizard(models.TransientModel):
    _name = 'library.rent.wizard'

    borrower_id = fields.Many2one('res.partner',
string='Borrower')
    book_ids = fields.Many2many('library.book',
string='Books')
```

2. Add the callback method that performs the action on the transient model. Add the following code to the `LibraryRentWizard` class:

```
def add_book_rents(self):
    rentModel = self.env['library.book.rent']
    for wiz in self:
        for book in wiz.book_ids:
            rentModel.create({
                'borrower_id': wiz.borrower_id.id,
                'book_id': book.id
            })
```

3. Create a form view for the model. Add the following view definition to the module views:

```
<record id='library_rent_wizard_form' model='ir.ui.view'>
    <field name='name'>library rent wizard form
view</field>
    <field name='model'>library.rent.wizard</field>
    <field name='arch' type='xml'>
        <form string="Borrow books">
            <sheet>
                <group>
                    <field name='borrower_id'/>
                </group>
                <group>
                    <field name='book_ids'/>
                </group>
            </sheet>
            <footer>
                <button string='Rent' type='object'
                        name='record_book_rents'
                        class='btn-primary'/>
                <button string='Cancel' class='btn-
```

```
            default' special='cancel'/>
                  </footer>
              </form>
         </field>
      </record>
```

4. Create an action and a menu entry to display the wizard. Add the following declarations to the module menu file:

```
<act_window id="action_wizard_rent_books"
            name="Give on Rent"
            res_model="library.rent.wizard"
            view_mode="form" target="new" />
<menuitem id="menu_wizard_rent_books"
          parent="library_base_menu"
          action="action_wizard_rent_books"
          sequence="20" />
```

How it works...

Step 1 defines a new model. It is no different from other models, apart from the base class, which is `TransientModel` instead of `Model`. Both `TransientModel` and `Model` share a common base class, called `BaseModel`, and if you check the source code of Odoo, you will see that 99% of the work is in `BaseModel`, and that both `Model` and `TransientModel` are almost empty.

The only things that change for the `TransientModel` records are as follows:

- Records are periodically removed from the database, so the tables for transient models don't grow in size over time.
- You cannot define access rules on `TransientModel`. Anyone is allowed to create a record, but only the user who created a record can read and use it.
- You must not define `One2many` fields on a `TransientModel` that refers to a normal model, as this will add a column on the persistent model that links to transient data. Use `Many2many` relations in this case. You can, of course, define `Many2one` and `One2many` fields for relations between transient models.

We define two fields in the model: one to store the member borrowing the books, and one to store the list of books being borrowed. We can add other scalar fields, to record a scheduled return date, for instance.

Step 2 adds the code to the wizard class that will be called when the button defined in *step 3* is clicked on. This code reads the values from the wizard and creates `library.book.rent` records for each book.

Step 3 defines a view for our wizard. Refer to the *Document-style forms* recipe in `Chapter 10`, *Backend Views*, for details. The important point here is the button in the footer; the type attribute is set to `'object'`, which means that when the user clicks on the button, the method with the name specified by the name attribute of the button will be called.

Step 4 ensures that we have an entry point for our wizard in the menu of the application. We use `target='new'` in the action, so that the form view is displayed as a dialog box over the current form. Refer to the *Adding a menu item and window action* recipe in `Chapter 10`, *Backend Views*, for details.

There's more...

Here are a few tips to enhance your wizards.

Using the context to compute default values

The wizard we are presenting requires the user to fill in the name of the member in the form. There is a feature of the web client that we can use to save some typing. When an action is executed, the **context** is updated with some values that can be used by wizards:

Key	Value
`active_model`	This is the name of the model related to the action. This is generally the model being displayed onscreen.
`active_id`	This indicates that a single record is active and provides the ID of that record.
`active_ids`	If several records are selected, this will be a list with the IDs. This happens when several items are selected in a tree view when the action is triggered. In a form view, you get `[active_id]`.
`active_domain`	This is an additional domain on which the wizard will operate.

These values can be used to compute the default values of the model, or even directly in the method called by the button. To improve on the example in this recipe, if we had a button displayed on the form view of a `res.partner` model to launch the wizard, the context of the creation of the wizard would contain `{'active_model': 'res.partner', 'active_id': <partner id>}`. In that case, you could define the `member_id` field to get a default value computed by the following method:

```
def _default_member(self):
    if self.context.get('active_model') == 'res.partner':
        return self.context.get('active_id', False)
```

Wizards and code reuse

In *step 2*, we could have removed the `for` loop in the wizard, and by assuming that `len(self)` will be 1, we can add `self.ensure_one()` at the beginning of the method, as follows:

```
def add_book_rents(self):
    self.ensure_one()
    rentModel = self.env['library.book.rent']
    for book in self.book_ids:
        rentModel.create({
            'borrower_id': self.borrower_id.id,
            'book_id': book.id
        })
```

Adding `self.ensure_one()` at beginning of the method will ensure that the number of records in the `self` is only one. An error will be raised if there is more than one records in the `self`.

We recommend using the version in the recipe, though, because this allows us to reuse the wizard from other parts of the code by creating records for the wizard, putting them in a single recordset (refer to the *Combining recordsets* recipe in `Chapter 6`, *Basic Server-side Development*, to see how to do this), and then calling `add_book_rents()` on the recordset. Here, the code is trivial, and you don't really need to jump through all those hoops to record that some books have been borrowed by different members. However, in an Odoo instance, some operations are much more complex, and it is always nice to have a wizard available that does the right thing. When using these wizards, ensure that you check the source code for any possible use of the `active_model/active_id/active_ids` keys from the context. If this is the case, you need to pass a custom context (refer to the *Calling a method with a modified context* recipe).

Redirecting the user

The method in *step 2* does not return anything. This will cause the wizard dialog to be closed after the action is performed. Another possibility is to have the method return a dictionary with the fields of `ir.action`. In this case, the web client will process the action as if a menu entry had been clicked on by the user. The `get_formview_action()` method defined on the `BaseModel` class can be used to achieve this. For instance, if we wanted to display the form view of the member who has just borrowed the books, we could have written the following:

```
def add_book_rents(self):
    rentModel = self.env['library.book.rent']
    for wiz in self:
        for book in wiz.book_ids:
            rentModel.create({
                'borrower_id': wiz.borrower_id.id,
                'book_id': book.id
            })
    members = self.mapped('borrower_id')
    action = members.get_formview_action()
    if len(borrowers.ids) > 1:
        action['domain'] = [('id', 'in', tuple(members.ids))]
        action['view_mode'] = 'tree,form'
    return action
```

This builds a list of members who have borrowed books from this wizard (in practice, there will only be one such member when the wizard is called from the user interface) and creates a dynamic action, which displays the members with the specified IDs.

The *redirecting the user* technique can be used to create a wizard which have several steps to be performed one after the other. Each step in the wizard can use the values of the previous steps. By providing a **Next** button that calls a method defined on the wizard which update some fields on the wizard, and return an action that will redisplay the same updated wizard and get ready for the next step.

Defining onchange methods

When writing Odoo models, it is often the case that some fields are interrelated. We looked at how to specify constraints between fields in the *Adding constraint validations to a model* recipe in `Chapter 5`, *Application Models*. This recipe illustrates a slightly different concept. Here, `onchange` methods are called when a field is modified in the user interface to update the values of other fields of the record in the web client, usually in a form view.

We will illustrate this by providing a wizard similar to the one defined in the *Writing a wizard to guide the user* recipe, but that can be used to record book returns. When a member is set in the wizard, the list of books is updated to the books that are currently borrowed by the member. While we are demonstrating `onchange` methods on a `TransientModel`, these features are also available on normal `Models`.

Getting ready

For this recipe, we will use the `my_library` module from the *Writing a wizard to guide the user* recipe of this chapter. We will create a wizard to return a borrowed book. We will add an `onchange` method, which will auto fill books when a librarian selects a member field.

You will also want to prepare your work by defining the following transient model for the wizard:

```
class LibraryReturnWizard(models.TransientModel):
    _name = 'library.return.wizard'    borrower_id =
fields.Many2one('res.partner', string='Member')
    book_ids = fields.Many2many('library.book', string='Books')

    def books_returns(self):
        loan = self.env['library.book.rent']
        for rec in self:
            loans = loan.search(
                [('state', '=', 'ongoing'),
                 ('book_id', 'in', rec.book_ids.ids),
                 ('borrower_id', '=', rec.borrower_id.id)]
            )
            for loan in loans:
                loan.book_return()
```

Finally, you will need to define a view, an action, and a menu entry for the wizard. These steps will be left as an exercise for you to carry out.

How to do it...

To automatically populate the list of books to return when the user is changed, you need to add an `onchange` method in the `LibraryReturnsWizard` step, with the following definition:

```
@api.onchange('borrower_id')
def onchange_member(self):
```

```
rentModel = self.env['library.book.rent']
books_on_rent = rentModel.search(
    [('state', '=', 'ongoing'),
     ('borrower_id', '=', self.borrower_id.id)]
)
self.book_ids = books_on_rent.mapped('book_id')
```

How it works...

An `onchange` method uses the `@api.onchange` decorator, which is passed the names of the fields that change and will thus trigger the call to the method. In our case, we say that whenever `borrower_id` is modified in the user interface, the method must be called.

In the body of the method, we search the books currently borrowed by the member, and we use an attribute assignment to update the `book_ids` attribute of the wizard.

> The `@api.onchange` decorator takes care of modifying the view sent to the web client to add an `on_change` attribute to the field. This was a manual operation in the old API.

There's more...

The basic use of `onchange` methods is to compute new values for fields when some other fields are changed in the user interface, as we've seen in the recipe.

Inside the body of the method, you get access to the fields displayed in the current view of the record, but not necessarily all the fields of the model. This is because `onchange` methods can be called while the record is being created in the user interface before it is stored in the database! Inside an `onchange` method, `self` is in a special state, denoted by the fact that `self.id` is not an integer, but an instance of `odoo.models.NewId`. Therefore, you must not make any changes to the database in an `onchange` method, because the user may end up canceling the creation of the record, which will not roll back any changes made by the `onchange` method during the process of editing. To check for this, you can use `self.env.in_onchange()` and `self.env.in_draft()`; the former returns `True` if the current context of execution is an `onchange` method, and the latter returns `True` if `self` is not yet committed to the database.

Additionally, onchange methods can return a Python dictionary. This dictionary can have the following keys:

- warning: The value must be another dictionary with the title and message keys containing the title and the content of a dialog box, respectively, which will be displayed when the onchange method is run. This is useful for drawing the attention of the user to inconsistencies or to potential problems.
- domain: The value must be another dictionary that maps field names to domains. This is useful when you want to change the domain of a One2many field, depending on the value of another field.

For instance, suppose that we have a fixed value set for expected_return_date in our library.book.rent model, and we want to display a warning when a member has some books that are late. We also want to restrict the choice of books to the ones currently borrowed by the user. We can rewrite the onchange method, as follows:

```
@api.onchange('member_id')
def onchange_member(self):
        rentModel = self.env['library.book.rent']
    books_on_rent = rentModel.search(
        [('state', '=', 'ongoing'),
         ('borrower_id', '=', self.borrower_id.id)]
    )
    self.book_ids = books_on_rent.mapped('book_id')
    result = {
        'domain': {'book_ids': [
                    ('id', 'in', self.book_ids.ids)]
                }
    }
    late_domain = [
        ('id', 'in', books_on_rent.ids),
        ('expected_return_date', '<', fields.Date.today())
    ]
    late_books = loans.search(late_domain)
    if late_books:
        message = ('Warn the member that the following '
                    'books are late:\n')
        titles = late_books.mapped('book_id.name')
        result['warning'] = {
            'title': 'Late books',
            'message': message + '\n'.join(titles)
        }
    return result
```

Calling onchange methods on the server side

The *Creating new records* and *Updating the values of a recordset record* recipes in `Chapter` 6, *Basic Server-side Development*, mentioned that these operations did not call the `onchange` methods automatically. Yet, in a number of cases, it is important that these operations are called, because they update important fields in the created or updated record. Of course, you can do the required computation yourself, but this is not always possible, as the `onchange` method can be added or modified by a third-party add-on module installed on the instance that you don't know about.

This recipe explains how to call the `onchange` methods on a record by manually invoking the `onchange` method before creating a record.

Getting ready

In the *Changing the user that performs an action* recipe, we added a **Rent this book** button so non-librarian users can borrow books by themselves. We now want to do the same for returning the books, but instead of writing the logic for returning the book, we will just use the book return wizard that we created in the *Defining onchange methods* recipe.

How to do it...

In this recipe, we will manually create a record of the `library.return.wizard` model. We want the `onchange` method to compute the returned books for us. To do this, you need to perform the following steps:

1. Create the `return_this_books` method in the `library.book` model:

```
@api.multi
def return_all_books(self):
    self.ensure_one()
```

2. Get an empty recordset for `library.return.wizard`:

```
wizard = self.env['library.return.wizard']
```

3. Prepare the values to create a new `wizard` record. Here, we will use a current user's partner ID as the `borrower_id`, but if you want to put this button on the `res.parnter` model, you can use `self.id`:

```
values = {
        'borrower_id': self.env.user.partner_id.id,
    }
```

4. Retrieve the `onchange` specifications for the `wizard`:

```
specs = wizard._onchange_spec()
```

5. Get the results of the `onchange` method:

```
updates = wizard.onchange(values, ['borrower_id'], specs)
```

6. Merge these results with the values of the new `wizard`:

```
value = updates.get('value', {})
for name, val in value.items():
    if isinstance(val, tuple):
        value[name] = val[0]
values.update(value)
```

7. Create the `wizard`:

```
wiz = wizard.create(values)
return wiz.sudo().books_returns()
```

How it works...

For an explanation of *step 1* to *step 3*, refer to the *Creating new records* recipe in `Chapter 6`, *Basic Server-side Development*.

Step 4 calls the `_onchange_spec` method on the model, passing no argument. This method will retrieve the updates that are triggered by the modification of the other field. It does this by examining the form view of the model (remember that `onchange` methods are normally called by the web client).

Step 5 calls the `onchange(values, field_name, field_onchange)` method of the model, with three arguments:

- `values`: The list of values we want to set on the record. You need to provide a value for all the fields you expect to be modified by the `onchange` method. In the recipe, we set `book_ids` to `False` for this reason.
- `field_name`: A list of fields for which we want to trigger the `onchange` methods. You can pass an empty list, and ORM will use the fields defined in `values`. However, you will often want to specify this list manually to control the order of evaluation, in case different fields can update a common field.
- `field_onchange`: The `onchange` specifications that were computed in *step 4*. This method finds out which `onchange` methods must be called, and in what order, and it returns a dictionary, which can contain the following keys:
  - `value`: This is a dictionary of newly-computed field values. This dictionary only features keys that are in the `values` parameter passed to `onchange()`. Note that the `Many2one` fields are mapped to a tuple that contains `(id, display_name)` as an optimization for the web client.
  - `warning`: This is a dictionary that contains a warning message that the web client will display to the user.
  - `domain`: This is a dictionary that maps field names to new validity domains.

Generally, when manually playing with `onchange` methods, we only care about what is in `value`.

Step 6 updates our initial values dictionary with the values computed by `onchange`. We process the values that correspond to the `Many2one` fields to only keep the `id`. To do this, we take advantage of the fact that these fields are only those whose values are returned as a tuple.

Finally *Step 7* creates the record.

There's more...

If you need to call an `onchange` method after modifying a field, the code is the same. You just need to get a dictionary for the values of the record, which can be obtained by using `values = dict(record._cache)` after modifying the field.

See also

If you want to know more about creating and updating records, refer to the *Creating new records* and *Updating the values of recordset records* recipes in `Chapter 6`, *Basic Server-side Development*.

Defining a model based on an SQL view

When working on the design of an add-on module, we model the data in classes that are then mapped to database tables by Odoo. We apply some well-known design principles, such as separation of concerns and data normalization. However, at later stages of the module design, it can be useful to aggregate data from several models in a single table, and to maybe perform some operations on them on the way, especially for reporting or producing dashboards. To make this easier, and to make use of the full power of the underlying PostgreSQL database engine in Odoo, it is possible to define a read-only model backed by a PostgreSQL view, rather than a table.

In this recipe, we will reuse the rent model from the *Writing a wizard to guide the user* recipe in this chapter, and we will create a new model to make it easier to gather statistics about books and authors.

Getting ready

For this recipe, we will use the `my_library` module from the previous recipe. We will create a new model called `library.book.rent.statistics` to hold the statistics data.

How to do it...

To create a new model backed by a PostgreSQL view, follow these instructions:

1. Create a new model with the _auto class attribute set to False:

```
class LibraryBookRentStatistics(models.Model):
    _name = 'library.book.rent.statistics'
    _auto = False
```

2. Declare the fields you want to see in the model, setting them as readonly:

```
    book_id = fields.Many2one('library.book', 'Book',
readonly=True)
    rent_count = fields.Integer(string="Times borrowed",
readonly=True)
    average_occupation = fields.Integer(string="Average
Occupation (DAYS)",
                            readonly=True)
```

3. Define the init() method to create the view:

```
    @api.model_cr
    def init(self):
        tools.drop_view_if_exists(self.env.cr, self._table)
        query = """
        CREATE OR REPLACE VIEW library_book_rent_statistics AS
(
        SELECT
                min(lbr.id) as id,
                lbr.book_id as book_id,
                count(lbr.id) as rent_count,
                avg((EXTRACT(epoch from age(return_date,
rent_date)) / 86400))::int as average_occupation

            FROM
                library_book_rent AS lbr
            JOIN
                library_book as lb ON lb.id = lbr.book_id
            WHERE lbr.state = 'returned'
            GROUP BY lbr.book_id
        );
        """
        self.env.cr.execute(query)
```

4. You can now define Views for the new model. A pivot view is especially useful to explore the data (refer to `Chapter 10`, *Backend Views*).

5. Don't forget to define some access rules for the new model (take a look at `Chapter 11`, *Access Security*).

How it works...

Normally, Odoo will create a new table for the model you are defining by using the field definitions for the columns. Actually, this is because in the `BaseModel` class, the `_auto` attribute defaults to `True`. In *step 1*, by positioning this class attribute to `False`, we tell Odoo that we will manage this by ourselves.

In *step 2*, we define some fields that will be used by Odoo to generate a table. We take care to flag them as `readonly=True`, so that the Views do not enable modifications that you will not be able to save, since PostgreSQL Views are read-only.

Step 3 defines the `init()` method. This method normally does nothing; it is called after `_auto_init()` (which is responsible for the table creation when `_auto = True`, but does nothing otherwise), and we use it to create a new SQL view (or to update the existing view in the case of a module upgrade). The view creation query must create a view with column names that match the field names of the Model.

> It is a common mistake, in this case, to forget to rename the columns in the view definition query, and this will cause an error message when Odoo cannot find the column.

Note that we also need to provide an **Integer column** called **ID** that contains unique values.

There's more...

It is also possible to have some computed and related fields on such models. The only restriction is that the fields cannot be stored (and therefore, you cannot use them to group records or to search). However, in the preceding example, we could have made the editor of the book available by adding a column, defined as follows:

```
publisher_id = fields.Many2one('res.partner',
related='book_id.publisher_id', readonly=True)
```

If you need to group by publisher, you need to store the field by adding it in the view definition, rather than using a related field.

Adding custom settings options

In Odoo, you can provide optional features through the Settings options. The user can enable or disable this option at any time. We will illustrate how to create settings options in this recipe.

Getting ready

In previous recipes, we have added buttons so that non-librarian users can borrow and return books. This is not the case for every library, however, so we will create a settings option to enable and disable this feature. We will do this by hiding these buttons. In this recipe, we will use the same `my_library` module from the previous recipe.

How to do it...

In order to create custom settings options, follow these steps:

1. Add a new group in the `my_library/security/groups.xml` file:

```
<record id="group_self_borrow" model="res.groups">
    <field name="name">Self borrow</field>
    <field name="users" eval="[(4, ref('base.user_admin'))]"/>
</record>
```

2. Add a new field by inheriting the `res.config.settings` model:

```
class ResConfigSettings(models.TransientModel):
    _inherit = 'res.config.settings'

    group_self_borrow = fields.Boolean(string="Self borrow",
implied_group='my_library.group_self_borrow')
```

3. Add this field in the existing `settings` view with `xpath` (for more details, refer to `Chapter 10`, *Backend Views*):

```
<record id="res_config_settings_view_form" model="ir.ui.view">
    <field
name="name">res.config.settings.view.form.inherit.library</fie
ld>
    <field name="model">res.config.settings</field>
    <field name="priority" eval="5"/>
    <field name="inherit_id"
ref="base.res_config_settings_view_form"/>
    <field name="arch" type="xml">
        <xpath expr="//div[hasclass('settings')]"
position="inside">
            <div class="app_settings_block"
                data-string="Library" string="Library" data-
key="my_library"
                groups="my_library.group_librarian">
            <h2>Library</h2>
            <div class="row mt16 o_settings_container">
                <div class="col-12 col-lg-6 o_setting_box"
id="library">
                    <div class="o_setting_left_pane">
                        <field name="group_self_borrow"/>
                    </div>
                    <div class="o_setting_right_pane">
                        <label for="group_self_borrow"/>
                        <div class="text-muted">
                            Allow users to borrow and
return books by themself
                        </div>
                    </div>
                </div>
            </div>
        </div>
    </xpath>
    </field>
</record>
```

4. Add some actions and a menu for the `Settings`:

```
<record id="library_config_settings_action"
model="ir.actions.act_window">
    <field name="name">Settings</field>
    <field name="type">ir.actions.act_window</field>
    <field name="res_model">res.config.settings</field>
    <field name="view_id"
ref="res_config_settings_view_form"/>
```

```
        <field name="view_mode">form</field>
        <field name="target">inline</field>
        <field name="context">{'module' : 'my_library'}</field>
    </record>

    <menuitem name="Settings"
        id="library_book_setting_menu"
        parent="library_base_menu"
        action="library_config_settings_action"
        sequence="50"/>
```

5. Modify the buttons in the book's form view and add a
   my_library.group_self_borrow group:

```
    <button name="book_rent"
        string="Rent this book"
        type="object" class="btn-primary"
        groups="my_library.group_self_borrow"/>
    <button
        name="return_all_books"
        string="Return all book"
        type="object" class="btn-primary"
        groups="my_library.group_self_borrow"/>
```

Restart the server and update the my_library module to apply the changes.

How it works...

In Odoo, all settings options are added in the res.config.settings model.
res.config.settings is a transient model. In *step 1*, we created a new security
group. We will use this group to create the hide and show buttons.

In *step 2*, we added a new Boolean field in the res.config.settings model by
inheriting it. We added an implied_group attribute with the value of
my_library.group_self_borrow. This group will be assigned to all odoo users
when the admin enables or disables options with the Boolean field.

Odoo settings use a form view to display settings options on a user interface. All of these options are added in a single form view with the external ID, `base.res_config_settings_view_form`. In *step 3*, we added our option in the user interface by inheriting this setting form view. We used `xpath` to add our `setting` option. In `Chapter 10`, *Backend Views*, we will see this in detail. In the form definition, you will find that the attribute data-key value of this option will be your module name. This is only needed when you are adding a whole new tab in **Settings**. Otherwise, you can just add your option in the **Settings** tab of the existing module with `xpath`.

In *step 4*, we added an action and a menu to access the configuration options from the user interface. You will need to pass the `{'module' : 'my_library'}` context from the action to open the **Settings** tab of the `my_library` module by default when the menu is clicked.

In *step 5*, we added `my_library.group_self_borrow` groups to the buttons. Because of this group, the **Borrow** and **Return** buttons will be hidden or shown, based on the settings options.

After this, you will see a separate **Settings** tab for the library, and, in the tab, you will see a `Boolean` field to enable or disable the self-borrowing option. When you enable or disable this option, in the background, Odoo will apply or remove the `implied_group` to or from all `odoo` users. Because we added the groups on buttons, the buttons will be displayed if the user has groups and will be hidden if the user doesn't have groups. In `Chapter 11`, *Access Security,* we will look at security groups in detail.

There's more...

There are a few other ways to manage the settings options. One of them is to separate features in the new module and install or uninstall them through options. To do this, you will need to add a `Boolean` field with the name of the module prefixed with `module_`. If, for example, we create a new module called `my_library_extras`, you will need to add a `Boolean` field, as follows:

```
module_my_library_extras = fields.Boolean(string='Library Extra
Features')
```

When you enable or disable this option, `odoo` will install or uninstall the `my_libarary_extras` module.

Implementing init hooks

In `Chapter 7`, *Module Data*, you saw how to add, update, and delete records from XML or CSV files. Sometimes, however, the business case is complex and it can't be solved using data files. In such cases, you can use the `init` hook from the manifest file to perform the operations you want.

Getting ready

We will use the same `my_library` module from the previous recipe. For simplicity, in this recipe, we will just create some book records through `post_init_hook`.

How to do it...

In order to add the `post_init_hook`, follow these steps:

1. Register the hook in the `__manifest__`.py file with the `post_init_hook` key:

   ```
   ...
   'post_init_hook': 'add_book_hook',
   ...
   ```

2. Add the `add_book_hook()` method in the `__init__`.py file:

   ```
   from odoo import api, fields, SUPERUSER_ID

   def add_book_hook(cr, registry):
       env = api.Environment(cr, SUPERUSER_ID, {})
       book_data1 = {'name': 'Book 1', 'date_release':
   fields.Date.today()}
       book_data2 = {'name': 'Book 2', 'date_release':
   fields.Date.today()}
       env['library.book'].create([book_data1, book_data2])
   ```

How it works...

In the first step, we registered `post_init_hook` in the manifest file with the `add_book_hook` value. This means that after the installation of the module, Odoo will look for the `add_book_hook` method in `__init__.py`. If found, if it's will call the method with the database cursor and registry.

In *step 2*, we declared the `add_book_hook()` method, which will be called after the module is installed. We created two records from this method. In real situations, you can write complex business logic here.

In the example, we looked at `post_init_hook`, but Odoo supports two more hooks:

- `pre_init_hook`: This hook will be invoked when you start installing a module. It is the opposite of `post_init_hook`; it will be invoked before installing the current module.
- `uninstall_hook`: This hook will be invoked when you uninstall the module. This is mostly used when your module needs a garbage-collection mechanism.

10
Backend Views

In this chapter, we will cover the following recipe:

- Adding a menu item and window actions
- Having an action open a specific view
- Adding content and widgets to a form view
- Adding buttons to forms
- Passing parameters to forms and actions – Context
- Defining filters on record lists – Domain
- Defining list views
- Defining search views
- Displaying attachments on the side of the form view
- Changing existing views – view inheritance
- Defining document-style forms
- Dynamic form elements using attrs
- Defining embedded views
- Defining kanban views
- Showing kanban cards in columns according to their state
- Defining calendar and gantt views
- Defining graph and pivot views
- Defining the cohort view
- Defining the dashboard view

Throughout this chapter, we will assume that you have a database with the base add-on installed and an empty Odoo add-on module where you can add XML code from the recipes to a data file referenced in the add-on's manifest. Refer to `Chapter 4`, *Creating Odoo Add-On Modules*, for more information on how to activate changes in your add-on.

Introduction

This chapter covers all the UI elements that users are confronted with when they use anything other than the website part of Odoo. Historically, this was all of OpenERP, so in an Odoo context, the user interface is often just referred to as the web client. To be more specific, we will call this the **backend**, as opposed to the website frontend.

Technical requirements

The technical requirements for this chapter include an online Odoo platform.

All of the code used in this chapter can be downloaded from the following GitHub repository, at `https://github.com/PacktPublishing/Odoo-12-Development-Cookbook-Third-Edition/tree/master/Chapter10`.

Check out the following video to see the Code in Action:

Place holder link

Adding a menu item and window action

The most obvious way to make a new feature available to users is by adding a menu item. When you click on a menu item, something happens. This recipe walks you through how to define that something.

We will create a top-level menu and its sub-menu, which will open a list of all customers.

This can also be done using the web user interface, through the settings menu, but we prefer to use XML data files since this is what we'll have to use when creating our add-on modules.

How to do it...

In an XML data file of our add-on module, perform the following steps:

1. Define an action to be executed:

```
<act_window id="action_all_customers"
    name="All customers"
    res_model="res.partner"
    view_mode="tree,form"
    domain="[('customer', '=', True)]"
    context="{'default_customer': True}" />
```

2. Create the top-level menu, which will be as follows:

```
<menuitem id="menu_custom_top_level"
    name="My App menu"
    web_icon="my_module,static/description/icon.png"/>
```

3. Refer to our action in the menu:

```
<menuitem id="menu_all_customers"
    parent="menu_custom_top_level"
    action="action_all_customers"
    sequence="10"/>
```

If we now upgrade the module, we will see a top-level menu that opens a sub-menu. Clicking on that menu item will open a list of all customers.

How it works...

The first XML element, `act_window`, declares a window action to display a list view with all the customers. We used the most important attributes:

- `name`: To be used as the title for views opened by the action.
- `res_model`: This is the model to be used. We are using `res.partner`, where Odoo stores all the partners and addresses, including customers.
- `view_mode`: This lists the view types to make available. It is a comma separated values of type of views. The default value is `list, form`, which makes list and form views available. If you just want to show calendar and form view then the value of `view_mode` will be `calendar, form`. Other possible view choices are *kanban, graph, pivot, calendar, cohort,* and *dashboard*. You will learn more about these views in forthcoming recipes.

- `domain`: This is optional and allows you to set a filter on the records to be made available in the views. In this case, we want to limit the partners to only those who are customers. We will see all of these view in more detail in the *Defining filters on record lists – Domain* recipe of this chapter.

- `context`: This can set values made available to the opened views, affecting their behavior. In our example, on new records, we want the customer flag's default value to be `True`. This will be covered in more depth in *Passing parameters to forms and actions – Context* recipe of this chapter.

- `limit`: This sets the default amount of records that can be seen on list views. It defaults to `80`.

> **TIP**
>
> In legacy code, you'll find the view mode *tree* quite often. This was the internal name of list views up to and including Odoo 11. Version 12 still accepts this value, but treats it as if you had written *list*.

Next, we create the menu item hierarchy from the top-level menu to the clickable end menu item. The most important attributes for the `menuitem` element are as follows:

- `name`: This is used as the text the menu items display. If your menu item links to an action, you can leave this out, because the action's name will be used in that case.

- `parent` (`parent_id` if using the `record` element): This is the XML ID that references the parent menu item. Items with no parents are top-level menus.

- `action`: This is the XML ID that references the action to be called.

- `sequence`: This is used to order the sibling menu items.

- `groups` (`groups_id` with the `record` tag): This is an optional list of user groups that can access the menu item. If empty, it will be available to all users.

- `web_icon`: This option only works on the top-level menu. It will display an icon of your application in the Enterprise edition.

Window actions automatically determine the view to be used by looking up views for the target model with the intended type (`form`, `tree`, and so on) and picking the one with the lowest sequence number.

act_window and menuitem are convenient shortcut XML tags that hide what you're actually doing. If you don't want to use the shortcut XML tags then you can create a record of the ir.actions.act_window and ir.ui.menu models via the <record> tag . For example, if you want to load act_window with <record>, you can do so as follows:

```
<record id='action_all_customers' model='ir.actions.act_window'>
    <field name="name">All customers</field>
    <field name="res_model">res.partner</field>
    <field name="view_mode">tree,form</field>
    <field name="domain">[('customer', '=', True)]</field>
    <field name="context">{'default_customer': True}</field>
    <field name="limit">20</field>
</record>
```

In the same way, you can create a menuitem through <record>.

Be aware that names used with the menuitem shortcut may not map to the field names that are used when using a record element – parent should be parent_id and groups should be groups_id.

To build the menu, the web client reads all the records from ir.ui.menu and infers their hierarchy from the parent_id field. Menus are also filtered based on user permissions to models and groups assigned to menus and actions. When a user clicks on a menu item, its action is executed.

There's more...

Window actions also support a target attribute to specify how the view is to be presented. The possible choices are as follows:

- **current**: This is the default and opens the view in the web client main content area.
- **new**: This opens the view in a popup.
- **inline**: Like current, but opens a form in edit mode and disables the **Action** menu.
- **fullscreen**: The action will cover the whole browser window, so this will overlay the menus too. Sometimes, this is called tablet mode.
- **main:** Like current, but also clears out the breadcrumbs.

The window action's `view_type` attribute is mostly obsolete by now. The alternative to the default form is **tree**, which causes grouped lists to render a hierarchical tree. Don't confuse this attribute with the `view_mode` attribute that's used and explained in the *How it works* section of this recipe, which actually decides which types of views are used.

There are also some additional attributes available for window actions that are not supported by the `act_window` shortcut tag. To use them, we must use the `record` element with the following fields:

- `res_id`: If opening a form, you can have it open a specific record by setting its ID here. This can be useful for multi-step wizards, or in cases when you have to view or edit a specific record frequently.
- `search_view_id`: This specifies a specific search view to use for tree and graph views.
- `auto_search`: This is `True` by default. Set this to `False` if searching for your object is very time- and/or resource-consuming. This way, the user can review the search parameters and press **Search** when satisfied. With the default value, the search is triggered immediately when the action is opened.

Keep in mind that the menu in the top-left (or the apps icon in the enterprise version) and the menu in the bar at the top are both made up of menu items. The only difference is that the items in the menu in the top-left don't have any parent menus, while the ones on the top bar have the respective menu item from the top bar as a parent. In the left bar, the hierarchical structure is more obvious.

Also bear in mind that for design reasons, the first-level menus will open the dropdown menu if your second-level menu has child menus. In any case, Odoo will open the first menu item's action based on the sequence of child menu items.

See also

Refer to the following to learn more about menus and views:

- You'll find a more detailed discussion of the XML ID reference mechanism in Chapter 7, *Module Data*. For now, just keep in mind that you can set references this way and, importantly, that order matters. If the preceding tags were inverted, the add-on that contains this XML code wouldn't install, because the `menuitem` would refer to an unknown `action`.

This can be a pitfall when you add new data files and new elements during your development process, because then the order in which you add those files and elements does not necessarily reflect the order in which they will be loaded in an empty database. Always check, before deployment, whether your add-on installs in an empty database without errors.

- The `ir.actions.act_window` action type is the most common action type, but a menu can refer to any type of action. Technically, it is the same if you link to a client action, a server action, or any other model defined in the `ir.actions.*` namespace. It just differs in what the backend makes out of the action.
- If you need just a tiny bit more flexibility in the concrete action to be called, look into server actions that return a window action. If you need complete flexibility, take a look at the client actions (`ir.actions.client`), which allow you to have a completely custom user interface. However, only do this as a last resort as you lose a lot of Odoo's convenient helpers when using them.

Having an action open a specific view

Window actions automatically determine the view to be used if none is given, but sometimes, we want an action to open a specific view.

We will create a basic form view for the `res.partner` model, and then we will create a new window action specifically open that form view.

How to do it...

1. Define the `partner` minimal tree and form view:

```
<record id="view_all_customers_tree" model="ir.ui.view">
    <field name="name">All customers</field>
    <field name="model">res.partner</field>
    <field name="arch" type="xml">
        <tree>
            <field name="name" />
        </tree>
    </field>
</record>
```

```
<record id="view_all_customers_form" model="ir.ui.view">
    <field name="name">All customers</field>
    <field name="model">res.partner</field>
    <field name="arch" type="xml">
        <form>
            <group>
                <field name="name" />
            </group>
        </form>
    </field>
</record>
```

2. Update the action from the *Adding a menu item and window action* recipe to use a new form view:

```
<record id="action_all_customers_tree"
model="ir.actions.act_window.view">
    <field name="act_window_id" ref="action_all_customers"
/>
    <field name="view_id" ref="view_all_customers_tree" />
    <field name="view_mode">tree</field>
    <field name="sequence" eval="2"/>
</record>

<record id="action_all_customers_form"
model="ir.actions.act_window.view">
    <field name="act_window_id" ref="action_all_customers"
/>
    <field name="view_id" ref="view_all_customers_form" />
    <field name="view_mode">form</field>
    <field name="sequence" eval="2"/>
</record>
```

Now, if you open your menu and click on a partner in the list, you should see the very minimal form and tree that we just defined.

How it works...

This time, we used the generic XML code for any type of record, that is, the `record` element with the required `id` and `model` attributes. The `id` attribute on the `record` element is an arbitrary string that must be unique for your add-on. The `model` attribute refers to the name of the model you want to create. Given that we want to create a view, we need to create a record of the `ir.ui.view` model. Within this element, you set fields as defined in the model you chose through the `model` attribute. For `ir.ui.view`, the crucial fields are `model` and `arch`. The `model` field contains the model you want to define a view for, while the `arch` field contains the definition of the view itself. We'll come to its contents in a short while.

The `name` field, while not strictly necessary, is helpful when debugging problems with views, so set it to a string that tells you what this view is intended to do. This field's content is not shown to the user, so you can fill in any technical hints that you deem sensible. If you set nothing here, you'll get a default name that contains the model name and view type .

ir.actions.act_window.view

The second record we defined works in tandem with `act_window`, which we defined earlier in the *Adding a menu item and window action* recipe. We already know that by setting the `view_id` field there, we can select which view is used for the first view mode. However, given that we set the `view_mode` field to the `tree, form` view, the `view_id` would have to pick a tree view, but we want to set the form view, which comes second here.

If you find yourself in a situation like this, use the `ir.actions.act_window.view` model, which gives you fine-grained control over which views to load for which view type. The first two fields defined here are examples of the generic way to refer to other objects; you keep the element's body empty but add an attribute called `ref`, which contains the XML ID of the object you want to reference. So, what happens here is that we refer to our action from the previous recipe in the `act_window_id` field, and refer to the view we just created in the `view_id` field. Then, though not strictly necessary, we add a sequence number to position this view assignment relative to the other view assignments, for the same action. This is only relevant if you assign views for different view modes by creating multiple `ir.actions.act_window.view` records.

> Once you define the `ir.actions.act_window.view` records, they take precedence over what you filled in the action's `view_mode` field. So, with the preceding records, you won't see a list at all, but only a form. You should add another `ir.actions.act_window.view` record that points to a list view for the `res.partner` model.

There's more...

As we saw in the *Adding a menu item and window action* recipe, we can replace `act_window` with `<record>`. If you want to use a custom view, you can follow the given syntax:

```
<record id='action_all_customers'
model='ir.actions.act_window'>
    <field name="name">All customers</field>
    <field name="res_model">res.partner</field>
    <field name="view_mode">tree,form</field>
    <field name="domain">[('customer', '=', True)]</field>
    <field name="context">{'default_customer': True,
      'tree_view_ref': 'my_module.view_all_customers_tree'.
      'form_view_ref': 'my_module.view_all_customers_form'
    }</field>
    <field name="limit">20</field>
</record>
```

Adding content and widgets to a form view

The preceding recipe showed how to pick a specific view for an action. Now, we'll demonstrate how to make the form view more useful. In this recipe, we will use the form view that we defined earlier in the *Having an action open a specific view* recipe.

How to do it...

1. Define the basic structure of the form view:

```
<record id="form_all_customers" model="ir.ui.view">
    <field name="name">All customers</field>
```

```
<field name="model">res.partner</field>
<field name="arch" type="xml">
    <form>
        <!--form content goes here -->
    </form>
</field>
</record>
```

2. To add a head bar, which is usually used for action buttons and stage pipeline, add this inside the form:

```
<header>
<button type="object" name="open_commercial_entity"
        string="Open commercial partner"
class="btn-primary" />
</header>
```

3. Add fields to the form, using `group` tags to organize them visually:

```
<group string="Content" name="my_content">
    <field name="name" />
    <field name="category_id" widget="many2many_tags" />
</group>
```

Now, the form should display a top bar with a button and two vertically-aligned fields.

How it works...

We'll look at the `arch` field of the `ir.ui.view` model first. First, note that views are defined in XML, so you need to pass the `type="xml"` attribute for the arch field, otherwise the parser will be confused. It is also mandatory that your view definition contains well-formed XML, otherwise you'll get in trouble when loading this snippet.

We'll now walk through the tags that we used previously and summarize the others that are available.

Form

When you define a form view, it is mandatory that the first element within the `arch` field is a `form` element. This fact is used internally to derive the record's `type` field, which is why you're not supposed to set this field. You'll see this a lot in legacy code, though.

The `form` element can have two legacy attributes itself, which are `string` and `version`. In previous versions of Odoo, these were used to decide on the title you saw in the breadcrumb and to differentiate between the forms written in pre-7.0 style and afterwards, but both can now be considered obsolete. The title in the breadcrumb is now inferred from the model's `name_get` function, while the version is assumed to be 7.0 or later.

In addition to the following elements, you can use arbitrary HTML within the form tag. The algorithm is that every element unknown to Odoo is considered plain HTML and simply passed through to the browser. Be careful with that, as the HTML you fill in can interact with the HTML code the Odoo elements generate, which might distort the rendering.

Header

This element is a container for elements that should be shown in a form's header, which is rendered as a white bar. Usually, as in this example, you place action buttons here. Alternatively, if your model has a state field, you could opt for a status bar.

Button

The `button` element is used to allow the user to trigger an action. Refer to the *Adding buttons to forms* recipe for details.

Group

The `<group>` element is Odoo's main element, which is used for organizing content. Fields placed within a `<group>` element are rendered with their title, and all fields within the same group are aligned so that there's also a visual indicator that they belong together. You can also nest `<group>` elements; this causes Odoo to render the contained fields in adjacent columns.

In general, you should use the `<group>` mechanism to display all of your fields in the from view and only revert to the other elements, like `<notebook>`, `<label>`, `<newline>`, and more when necessary.

If you assign the `string` attribute on a group, its content will be rendered as a heading for the group.

You should develop the habit of assigning a `name` to every logical group of fields, too. This name is not visible to the user, but is very helpful when we override views in the following recipes. Keep the name unique within the form definition to avoid confusion about which group you refer to. Don't use the `string` attribute for this, because the value of the string will change eventually because of translations.

Field

In order to actually show and manipulate data, your form view should contain some `field` elements. These have one mandatory attribute, called `name`, which refers to the field's name in the model. Earlier, we offered the user the ability to edit the partner's name and categories. If we only want to show one of these, without the user being able to edit the field, we set the `readonly` attribute to `1` or `True`. This attribute may actually contain a small subset of Python code, so `readonly="2>1"` will make the field read-only too. This also applies to the `invisible` attribute, for which you use to have a value that is read from the database, but not shown to the user. Later, we'll take a look at which situations this can be used in.

You must have noticed the `widget` attribute on the categories field. This defines how the data in the field is supposed to be presented to the user. Every type of field has a standard widget, so you don't have to explicitly choose a widget. However, several types provide multiple ways of representation, in which case you might opt for something other than the default. As a complete list of available widgets would exceed the scope of this recipe, consult Odoo's source code to try them out. Take a look at `Chapter 15`, *Web Client Development*, for details on how to make your own.

Notebook and page

If your model has too many fields, then you can use the `<notebook>` and `<page>` tags to create tabs. Each `<page>` in the `<notebook>` tag will create a new tab, and content inside the page will be the tab content. The following example, it will create 2 tabs with 3 fields in each tab:

```
<notebook>
    <page string="Tab 1">
        <field name="field1"/>
        <field name="field2"/>
        <field name="field3"/>
    </page>
    <page string="Tab 2">
        <field name="field4"/>
```

```
            <field name="field5"/>
            <field name="field6"/>
        </page>
    </notebook>
```

The `string` attribute in the `<page>` tag will be the name of the tab. You can only use `<page>` tags in the `<notebook>` tag, but in the `<page>` tag, you can use any other elements.

General attributes

On most elements (this includes `group`, `field`, and `button`), you can set the `attrs` and `groups` attributes. While `attrs` is discussed in the *Dynamic form elements using attrs* recipe, the `groups` attribute gives you the possibility to show some elements only to members of certain groups. Simply put, the group's full XML ID (separated by commas for multiple groups) is the attribute, and the element will be hidden for everyone who is not a member of at least one of the groups mentioned.

Other tags

There are situations in which you might want to deviate from the strict layout groups prescribed. For example, if you want the `name` field of a record to be rendered as a heading, the field's label will interfere with the appearance. In this case, don't put your field into a `group` element, but instead into a plain HTML `h1` element. Then, before the `h1` element, put a `label` element with the `for` attribute set to your `field` name:

```
<label for="name" />
<h1><field name="name" /></h1>
```

This will be rendered with the field's content as a big heading, but the field's name written in a smaller type, above the big heading. This is basically what the standard partner form does.

If you need a line break within a group, use the `newline` element. It's always empty:

```
<newline />
```

Another useful element is `footer`. When you open a form as a popup, this is a good place to put the action buttons. It will be rendered as a separate bar too, analogous to the `header` element.

> **TIP**
> Don't address XML nodes with their `string` attribute (or any other translated attribute, for that matter), as your view overrides will break for other languages because views are translated before inheritance is applied.

There's more...

Since form views are basically HTML with some extensions, Odoo also makes extensive use of CSS classes. Two very useful ones are `oe_read_only` and `oe_edit_only`. These cause elements with these classes applied to be visible only in read/view mode or in edit mode. To have the label visible only in edit mode, use the following:

```
<label for="name" class="oe_edit_only" />
```

Another very useful class is `oe_inline`, which you can use on fields to make them render as an inline element, to avoid causing unwanted line breaks. Use this class when you embed a field into text or other markup tags.

Further more, the `form` element can have the `create`, `edit`, and `delete` attributes. If you set one of these to `false`, the corresponding action won't be available for this form. Without this being explicitly set, the availability of the action is inferred from the user's permissions. Note that this is purely for straightening the UI; don't use this for security.

See also

The widgets and views already offer a lot of functionality, but sooner or later, you will have requirements that cannot be fulfilled with the exiting widgets and views. Refer to the following recipes to create your own views and widgets:

- To define your own widgets, refer to the *Creating custom widgets* recipe of `Chapter 16`, *Web Client Development*
- Refer to the *Creating a new view* recipe of `Chapter 16`, *Web Client Development*, to create your own view

Adding buttons to forms

We added a button in the previous form view, but there are quite a few different types of buttons that we can use. This recipe will add another button. It will also put the following code in the recipe's header element.

How to do it...

Add a button that refers to an action:

```
<button type="action"
  name="%(base.action_partner_category_form)d"
  string="Open partner categories" />
```

How it works...

The button's type attribute determines the semantics of the other fields, so we'll first take a look at the possible values:

- action: This makes the button call an action as defined in the ir.actions.* namespace. The name attribute needs to contain the action's database ID, which you can conveniently have Odoo look up with a Python format string that contains the XML ID of the action in question.
- object: This calls a method of the current model. The name attribute contains the function's name. The function should have the @api.multi signature and will act on the currently-viewed record.

The string attribute is used to assign the text the user sees.

> There used to be a third value, workflow, which sent a signal to the by now deprecated and removed workflow engine. If you come across this when migrating code from older versions, you'll probably have to replace it with a method call.

There's more...

Use the `btn-primary` CSS classes to render a button that is highlighted and `btn-default` to render a normal button. This is commonly used for cancel buttons in wizards or to offer secondary actions in a visually unobtrusive way. Setting the `oe_link` class causes the button to look like a link.

A call with a button of the **object** type can return a dictionary that describes an action, which will then be executed on the client side. This way, you can implement multiscreen wizards or just open another record. Note that clicking on a button always causes the client to issue a `write` or `create` call before running the method.

You can also have content within the `button` tag by replacing the `string` attribute. This is commonly used in button boxes, as described in the *Document style forms* recipe.

Passing parameters to forms and actions – Context

Internally, every method in Odoo has access to a dictionary, called **context**, that is propagated from every action to the methods involved in delivering that action. The UI also has access to it, and it can be modified in various ways by setting values in the context. In this recipe, we'll explore some of the applications of this mechanism by toying with the language, default values, and implicit filters.

Getting ready

While not strictly necessary, this recipe will be more fun if you install the French language, if you haven't got this already. Consult `Chapter 12`, *Internationalization*, for how to do it. If you have a French database, change **fr_FR** to some other language; **en_US** will do for English. Also, click on the **Active** button (changing to **Archive** when you hover it) on one of your customers in order to archive it and verify that this partner doesn't show up any more in the list.

How to do it...

1. Create a new action, very similar to the one from the *Adding a menu item and window action* recipe:

```
<act_window id="action_all_customers_fr" name="Tous les
clients" res_model="res.partner" domain="[('customer', '=',
True)]" context="{'lang': 'fr_FR', 'default_lang': 'fr_FR',
 'active_test': False}" />
```

2. Add a menu that calls this action. This is left as an exercise for the reader.

When you open this menu, the views will show up in French, and if you create a new partner, they will have French as their pre-selected language. A less obvious difference is that you will also see the deactivated partner records.

How it works...

The context dictionary is populated from several sources. First, some values from the current user's record (`lang` and `tz`, for the user's language and the user's timezone) are read. Then, we have some add-ons that add keys for their own purposes. Further more, the UI adds keys about which model and which record we're busy with at the moment (`active_id`, `active_ids`, `active_model`). Also, as seen in the *Having an action open a specific view* recipe, we can add our own keys in actions. These are merged together and passed to the underlying server functions, and also to the client-side UI.

So, by setting the `lang` context key, we force the display language to be French. You will note that this doesn't change the whole UI language, which is because only the list view that we open lies within the scope of this context. The rest of the UI was loaded already with another context that contained the user's original language. However, if you open a record in this list view, it will be presented in French too, and if you open a linked record on the form or press a button that executes an action, the language will be propagated too.

By setting `default_lang`, we set a default value for every record created within the scope of this context. The general pattern is `default_$fieldname: my_default_value`, which enables you to set default values for newly created partners, in this case. Given that our menu is about customers, it might have made sense to also set `default_customer: True` to have the **Customer** field checked by default. However, this is a model-wide default for `res.partner`, so this wouldn't have changed anything. For scalar fields, the syntax for this is as you would write it in Python code: `string` fields go in quotes, `number` fields as they are, and `Boolean` fields are either `True` or `False`. For relational fields, the syntax is slightly more complicated; refer to `Chapter 7`, *Module Data*, to learn how to write them. Note that the default values set in the context override the default values set in the model definition, so you can have different default values in different situations.

The last key is `active_test`, which has very special semantics. For every model that has a field called `active`, Odoo automatically filters out records where this field is `False`. This is why the partner where you unchecked this field disappeared from the list. By setting this key, we can suppress this behavior.

> This is useful for the UI in its own right, but even more useful in your Python code when you need to ensure that an operation is applied to all the records, not just the active ones.

There's more...

When defining a context, you have access to some variables, the most important one being `uid`, which evaluates to the current user's ID. You'll need this to set default filters (refer to the next recipe, *Defining filters on record lists – Domain*). Further more, you have access to the `context_today` function and the `current_date` variable, where the first is a `date` object that represents the current date, as seen from the user's time zone, and the latter is the current date as seen in UTC, formatted as YYYY-MM-DD. To set a default value for a `date` field to the current date, use `current_date` and, for default filters, use `context_today()`.

Further more, you can do some date calculations with a subset of Python's `datetime`, `time`, and `relativedelta` classes.

Most of the domains are evaluated on the client side. The server-side domain evaluation is restricted for security reasons. When client-side evaluation was introduced, the best option in order to not break the whole system was to implement a part of Python in JavaScript. There is a small JavaScript Python interpreter built into Odoo that works well for simple expressions, and that is usually enough.

Beware of use of the context variable in the `<act_window />` shortcut. These are evaluated at installation time, which is nearly never what you want. If you need variables in your context, use the `<record />` syntax.

We can add buttons in the same way as we added context keys in our action. This causes the function or action the button calls to be run in the context given.

Most form element attributes that are evaluated as Python also have access to the context dictionary. The `invisible` and `readonly` attributes are examples of these. So, in cases where you want an element to show up in a form some times, but not at other times, set the `invisible` attribute to `context.get('my_key')`. For actions that lead to a case in which the field is supposed to be invisible, set the context key to `my_key: True`. This strategy enables you to adapt your form without having to rewrite it for different occasions.

You can also set a context on relational fields, which influences how the field is loaded. By setting the `form_view_ref` or `tree_view_ref` keys to the full XML ID of a view, you can select a specific view for this field. This is necessary when you have multiple views of the same type for the same object. Without this key, you get the view with the lowest sequence number, which might not always be desirable.

See also

- The context is also used to set a default search filter. You can learn more about the default search filter in the *Defining search views* recipe of this chapter.

Defining filters on record lists – Domain

We've already seen the first example of a domain in the first action, which was
`[('customer', '=', True)]`. Often, you need to display a subset of all available
records from an action, or to allow only a subset of possible records to be the target of
a `many2one` relation. The way to describe these filters in Odoo is by using domains.
This recipe illustrates how to use a domain to display a selection of partners.

How to do it...

To display a subset of partners from your action, you need to perform the following
steps:

1. Add an action for non-French speaking customers:

```
<record id="action_my_customers"
model="ir.actions.act_window">
    <field name="name">All my customers who don't speak
French</field>
    <field name="res_model">res.partner</field>
    <field name="domain">
        [('customer', '=', True), ('user_id', '=', uid),
('lang', '!=', 'fr_FR')]
    </field>
</record>
```

2. Add an action for customers who are customers or suppliers:

```
<record id="action_customers_or_suppliers"
        model="ir.actions.act_window">
    <field name="name">Customers or suppliers</field>
    <field name="res_model">res.partner</field>
    <field name="domain">['|', ('customer', '=', True),
                             ('supplier', '=',
True)]</field>
</record>
```

3. Add menus that call these actions. This is left as an exercise for the reader.

How it works...

The simplest form of a domain is a list of three tuples that contain a field name of the model in question as a `string` in the first element, an operator as a `string` in the second element, and the value the field is to be checked against as the third element. This is what we did in the first action, and this is interpreted as, *All those conditions have to apply to the records we're interested in*. This is actually a shortcut, because the domains know the two prefix operators – & and | –, where & is the default. So, in normalized form, the first domain will be written as follows:

```
['&', '&', ('customer', '=', True), ('user_id', '=', uid), ('lang',
'!=', 'fr_FR')]
```

While they can be a bit hard to read for bigger expressions, the advantage of prefix operators is that their scope is rigidly defined, which saves you from having to worry about operator precedence and brackets. It's always two expressions: the first & applies to '&', ('customer', '=', True), ('user_id', '=', uid) as the first operand and ('lang', '!=', 'fr_FR') as the second. Then, the second & applies to ('customer', '=', True) as the first operand and ('user_id', '=', uid) as the second.

In the second action, we have to write out the full form because we need the | operator.

There is also a ! operator for negation, but, given logical equivalences and negated comparison operators such as != and not in, it is not really necessary. Note that this is a unary prefix operator, so it only applies to the following expression in the domain and not to everything that follows.

Note that the right operand doesn't need to be a fixed value when you write a domain for a window action or other client-side domains. You can use the same minimal Python as described earlier in the *Passing parameters to forms and actions – Context* recipe, so you can write filters such as *changed last week* or *my partners*.

There's more...

The preceding domains work only on fields of the model itself, while we often need to filter based on properties of linked records. To do this, you can use the notation that's also used in `@api.depends` definitions or related fields: create a dotted path from the current model to the model you want to filter for. To search partners that have a salesperson who is a member of a group starting with the letter G, you would use the `[('user_id.groups_id.name', '=like', 'G%')]` domain. The path can be long, so you only have to be sure that there are relation fields between the current model and the model you want to filter for.

Operators

The following table lists the available operators and their semantics:

Operator (equivalent)	Semantics
`=, !=, <>`	The first one is for an exact match, the second one is for not equal, and the last one is the deprecated notation of not equal.
`in, not in`	This checks whether the value is one of the values named in a list in the right operand. It is given as a Python list: `[('uid', 'in', [1, 2, 3])]` or `[('uid', 'not in', [1, 2, 3])]`.
`<, <=`	Greater than, greater or equal.
`>, >=`	Less than, less or equal.
`like, not like`	Checks whether the right operand is contained (substring) in the value.
`ilike, not ilike`	The same as the preceding one, but case-insensitive.
`=like, =ilike`	You can search for patterns here: `%` matches any string and `_` matches one character. This is the equivalent of PostgreSQL's `like`.
`child_of`	For models with a `parent_id` field, this searches for children of the right operand. The right operand is included in the results.
`=?`	Evaluates to `true` if the right operand is `false`; otherwise, it behaves like "=". This is useful when you generate domains programmatically and want to filter by a value if one is set, but ignore the value otherwise.

Pitfalls of searching using domains

This all works fine for traditional fields, but a notorious problem is searching for the value of a non-stored function field. People often omit the search function. This is simple enough to fix by providing the search function in your own code, as described in Chapter 5, *Application Models*.

Another issue that might baffle developers is Odoo's behavior when searching through `one2many` or `many2many` fields with a negative operator. Imagine that you have a partner with the A tag and you search for `[('category_id.name', '!=', 'B')]`. Your partner shows up in the result and this is what you expected, but if you add the B tag to this partner, it still shows up in your results, because for the search algorithm, it is enough that there is one linked record (A in this case) that does not fulfill the criterion. Now, if you remove the A tag so that B is the only tag, the partner will be filtered out. If you also remove the B tag so that the partner has no tags, it is still filtered out, because conditions on the linked records presuppose the existence of this record. In other situations, though, this is the behavior you want, so it is not really an option to change the standard behavior. If you need a different behavior here, provide a search function that interprets the negation the way you need.

> People often forget that they are writing XML files when it comes to domains. You need to escape the less than operator. Searching for records that have been created before the current day will have to be written as `[('create_date', '&lt;', current_date)]` in XML.

See also

If you ever need to manipulate a domain you didn't create programmatically, use the utility functions provided in `odoo.osv.expression`. The `is_leaf`, `normalize_domain`, `AND`, and `OR` functions will allow you to combine domains exactly the way that Odoo does. Don't do this yourself, because there are many corner cases that you have to take into account, and it's likely that you'll overlook one.

For the standard application of domains, see the *Search views* recipe.

Defining list views

After having spent quite some time on the form view, we'll now take a quick look at how to define list views. Internally, these are called tree views in some places and list views in others, but given that there is another construction within the Odoo view framework called tree, we'll stick to the wording **list** here.

How to do it...

1. Define your list view:

```
<record id="tree_all_customers" model="ir.ui.view">
    <field name="model">res.partner</field>
    <field name="arch" type="xml">
        <tree decoration-bf="customer"
                decoration-danger="supplier"
                decoration-warning="customer and supplier">
            <field name="name" />
            <field name="customer" invisible="1" />
            <field name="supplier" invisible="1" />
        </tree>
    </field>
</record>
```

2. Register a tree view in the action we created in the *Adding a menu item and window action* recipe of this chapter:

```
<record id="action_all_customers_tree"
        model="ir.actions.act_window.view">
    <field name="act_window_id" ref="action_all_customers" />
    <field name="view_id" ref="tree_all_customers" />
    <field name="view_mode">tree</field>
    <field name="sequence">5</field>
</record>
```

How it works...

You already know most of what happens here. We define a view, of the `tree` type this time, and attach it to our action with an `ir.actions.act_window.view` element. So, the only thing left to discuss is the `tree` element and its semantics. With a list, you don't have many design choices, so the only valid children of this element are the `field` and `button` elements. These follow the same semantics as earlier, except that there are fewer choices to make regarding widgets; the only really interesting choices are `progressbar`, `many2onebutton`, and `handle`. The first two behave like their form namesakes. `handle` is specific to list views. It is meant for integer fields and renders a drag handle that the user can use to drag a row to a different position in the list, thereby updating the field's value. This is useful for sequence or priority fields.

What is new here are the decoration attributes (*) in the `tree` element. This contains rules as to which font and/or color is chosen for the row, given in the form of `decoration-$name="Python code"`. All matches turn into the corresponding CSS class, so the previous view renders partners that are both suppliers and customers in brown, customers in a bold font, and suppliers in red. In your Python code, you can only use the fields you named in the view definition, which is why we have to pull the `customer` and `supplier` fields too. We made these invisible because we only need the data and don't want to bother our users with the two extra columns. The possible classes are `decoration-bf` (bold), `decoration-it` (italic), and the semantic bootstrap classes, `decoration-danger`, `decoration-info`, `decoration-muted`, `decoration-primary`, `decoration-success`, and `decoration-warning`.

There's more...

For numeric fields, you can add a `sum` attribute that causes this column to be summed up with the text you set in the attribute as a tooltip. Less common are the `avg`, `min`, and `max` attributes that display the average, minimum, and maximum, respectively. Note that these four only work on the records that are currently visible, so you might want to adjust the action's `limit` (covered earlier in the *Adding a menu item and window action* recipe) in order for the user to see all the records immediately.

A very interesting attribute for the `tree` element is `editable`. If you set this to **top** or **bottom**, the list behaves entirely differently. Without it, clicking on a row opens a form view for the row. With it, clicking on a row makes it editable inline, with the visible fields rendered as form fields. This is particularly useful in embedded list views, which are discussed later in the *Defining embedded views* recipe of this chapter. The choice of top or bottom relates to whether new lines will be added to the top or bottom of the list.

By default, records are ordered according to the `_order` property of the displayed model. The user can change the ordering by clicking on a column header, but you can also set a different initial order by setting the `default_order` property in the tree element. The syntax is the same as in `_order`.

> Ordering is often a source of frustration for new developers. As Odoo lets PostgreSQL do the work here, you can only order by fields that PostgreSQL knows about and also only the fields that live in the same database table. So, if you want to order by a function or a related field, ensure that you set `store=True`. If you need to order by a field inherited from another model, declare a stored related field.

The `create`, `edit`, and `delete` attributes of the `tree` element work the same as for the `form` element we described earlier in the *Adding content and widgets to a form view* recipe of this chapter. They also determine the available controls if the `editable` attribute is set.

Defining search views

When opening your list view, you'll notice the search field to the upper-right. If you type something there, you get suggestions about what to search for, and there is also a set of predefined filters to choose from. This recipe will walk you through how to define these suggestions and options.

How to do it...

1. Define your search view:

```
<record id="search_all_customers" model="ir.ui.view">
    <field name="model">res.partner</field>
    <field name="arch" type="xml">
```

```
            <search>
              <field name="name" />
              <field name="category_id"
                     filter_domain="[('category_id', 'child_of',
    self)]" />
              <field name="bank_ids" widget="many2one" />
              <filter name="suppliers" string="Suppliers"
                     domain="[('supplier', '=', True)]" />
              <group expand="0" string="Group By">
                  <filter string="Country" name="country"
                         context="{'group_by':'country_id'}"/>
              </group>
            </search>
        </field>
    </record>
```

2. Tell your action to use it:

```
<record id="action_all_customers"
model="ir.actions.act_window">
    <field name="name">All customers</field>
    <field name="res_model">res.partner</field>
    <field name="domain">[('customer', '=', True)]</field>
    <field name="search_view_id" ref="search_all_customers" />
</record>
```

When you type something in to the search bar now, you'll be offered the ability to search for this term in the name, categories, and bank account fields. If your term happens to be a substring of a bank account number in your system, you'll even be offered to search exactly for this bank account.

How it works...

In the case of name, we simply listed the field as the one to be offered to the user to search for. We left the semantics at the default, which is a substring search for character fields.

For categories, we do something more interesting. By default, your search term is applied to a many2many field triggers, name_search, which would be a substring search in the category names in this case. However, depending on your category structure, it can be very convenient to search for partners who have the category you're interested in or a child of it. Think about a main category, *Newsletter subscribers*, with the subcategories, *Weekly newsletter, Monthly newsletter*, and a couple of other newsletter types. Searching for *newsletter subscribers* with the preceding search view definition will give you everyone who is subscribed to any of those newsletters in one go, which is a lot more convenient than searching for every single type and combining the results.

The filter_domain attribute can contain an arbitrary domain, so you're neither restricted to searching for the same field you named in the name attribute, nor to using only one term. The self variable is what the user filled in, and also the only variable that you can use here.

Here's a more elaborate example from the default search view for partners:

```
<field name="name"
        filter_domain="[
            '|', '|',
            ('display_name', 'ilike', self),
            ('ref', '=', self),
            ('email', 'ilike', self)]"/>
```

This means that the user doesn't have to think about what to search for. All they need to do is type in some letters, press *Enter*, and, with a bit of luck, one of the fields mentioned contains the string we're looking for.

For the bank_ids field, we used another trick. The type of field not only decides the default way of searching for the user's input, but it also defines the way in which Odoo presents the suggestions. Also, given that many2one fields are the only ones that offer auto-completion, we force Odoo to do that, even though bank_ids is a one2many field, by setting the widget attribute. Without this, we will have to search in this field, without completion suggestions. The same applies to many2many fields. Note that every field with a many2one widget set will trigger a search on its model for every one of the user's keystrokes; don't use too many of them.

You should also put the most-used fields on the top, because the first field is what is searched if the user just types something and presses *Enter*. The search bar can also be used with the keyboard; select a suggestion by pressing the down arrow, and open the completion suggestion of a `many2one` by pressing the right arrow. If you educate your users in this and pay attention to a sensible ordering of fields in the search view, this will be much more efficient than typing something first, grabbing the mouse, and selecting an option.

The `filter` element creates a button that adds the content of the filter's `domain` attribute to the search domain. You should add a logical internal `name` and a `string` attribute to describe the filter to your users.

The `<group>` tag is used to provide grouping option under **Group by** button. In this recipe we have added option to group record based on `country_id` field.

There's more...

You can group the filters with the `group` tag, which causes them to be rendered slightly closer together than the other filters, but this has semantic implications, too. If you put multiple filters in the same group and activate more than one of them, their domains will be combined with the | operator, while filters and fields not in the same group are combined with the & operator. Sometimes, you might want disjunction for your filters, which is where they filter for mutually exclusive sets, in which case selecting both of them will always lead to an empty result set. Within the same group, you can achieve the same effect with the `separator` element.

Note that if the user fills in multiple queries for the same field, they will be combined with | too, so you don't need to worry about that.

Apart from `field`, the `filter` element can have a `context` attribute, whose content will be merged with the current context and eventually other context attributes in the search view. This is essential for views that support grouping (refer to the *Defining kanban view* and *Defining graph view* recipes), because the resulting context determines the field(s) to be grouped with the `group_by` key. We'll look into the details of grouping in the appropriate recipes, but the context has other uses, too. For example, you can write a function field that returns different values depending on the context, and then you can change the values by activating a filter.

The search view itself also responds to context keys. In a very similar way to default values when creating records, you can pass default values for a search view through the context. If we had set a context of `{'search_default_suppliers': 1}` in our previous action, the suppliers filter would have been preselected in the search view. This works only if the filter has a name, though, which is why you should always set it. To set defaults for fields in the search view, use `search_default_$fieldname`.

Further more, the `field` and `filter` elements can have a groups property with the same semantics as in the form views in order to make the element only visible to certain groups.

See also

For further details about manipulating the context, see the *Passing parameters to forms and actions – Context* recipe.

Users who speak languages with heavy use of diacritical marks will probably want to have Odoo search for **e**, **è**, **é**, and **ê** when filling in the **e** character. This is a configuration of the PostgreSQL server, called unaccent, which Odoo has special support for, but is outside the scope of this book. Refer to `https://www.postgresql.org/docs/10/unaccent.html` for more information about unaccents.

Changing existing views – view inheritance

So far, we have ignored the existing views and declared completely new ones. While this is didactically sensible, you'll rarely be in situations in which you want to define a new view for an existing model. Instead, you'll want to slightly modify the existing views, be it to simply have them show a field you added to the model in your addon, or to customize them according to your needs or your customers' needs.

In this recipe, we'll change the default partner form to show the record's last modification date and also make the mobile field searchable by modifying the search view. Then, we'll change the position of one column in the partners' list view.

How to do it...

1. Inject the field in to the default form view:

```
<record id="view_partner_form" model="ir.ui.view">
    <field name="model">res.partner</field>
    <field name="inherit_id" ref="base.view_partner_form" />
    <field name="arch" type="xml">
        <field name="website" position="after">
            <field name="write_date" />
        </field>
    </field>
</record>
```

2. Add the field to the default search view:

```
<record id="view_res_partner_filter" model="ir.ui.view">
    <field name="model">res.partner</field>
    <field name="inherit_id"
ref="base.view_res_partner_filter" />
    <field name="arch" type="xml">
        <xpath expr="." position="inside">
            <field name="mobile" />
        </xpath>
    </field>
</record>
```

3. Add the field to the default list view:

```
<record id="view_partner_tree" model="ir.ui.view">
    <field name="model">res.partner</field>
    <field name="inherit_id" ref="base.view_partner_tree" />
    <field name="arch" type="xml">
        <field name="email" position="after">
            <field name="phone" position="move"/>
        </field>
    </field>
</record>
```

After updating your module, you should see the **Last updated on** extra field beneath the website field on the partner form. When you type something into the search box, it should suggest that you search for the partners on the mobile field, and in the partner's list view, you will see that the order of the phone number and email has changed.

How it works...

The crucial field here is, as you've probably guessed, `inherit_id`. You need to pass it the XML ID of the view you want to modify (inherit from). The `arch` field contains instructions on how to modify the existing XML nodes within the view you're inheriting from. You should actually think of the whole process as simple XML processing, because all the semantic parts only come a lot later.

The most canonical instruction within the `arch` field of an inherited view is the `field` element, which has the required attributes, `name` and `position`. As you can have every field only once on a form, the name already uniquely identifies a field. With the `position` attribute, we can place whatever we put within the field element, either `before`, `inside`, or `after` the field we named. The default is **inside**, but for readability, you should always name the position you require. Remember that we're not talking semantics here; this is about the position in the XML tree relative to the field we have named. How this will be rendered afterwards is a completely different matter.

Step 2 demonstrates a different approach. The `xpath` element selects the first element that matches the XPath expression named in the `expr` attribute. Here, the `position` attribute tells the processor where to put the contents of the `xpath` element.

Step 3 shows how you can change the position of an element. This option was introduced in version 12 and it is rarely used. In our example, we moved the `phone` field to come after the `email` field with the `position=move` option.

XPath might look somewhat scary, but is a very efficient means of selecting the node you need to work on. Take the time to look through some simple expressions; it's worth it. You'll likely stumble upon the term **context node**, to which some expressions are relative. In Odoo's view inheritance, this is always the root element of the view you're inheriting from.

For all the other elements found in the `arch` field of an inheriting view, the processor looks for the first element with the same node name and matching attributes (with the attribute position excluded, as this is part of the instruction). Use this only in cases where it is very unlikely that this combination is not unique, such as a group element combined with a `name` attribute.

> Note that you can have as many instruction elements within the `arch` field as you need. We only used one per inherited view because there's nothing else we want to change currently.

There's more...

The position attribute has two other possible values: `replace` and `attributes`. Using `replace` causes the selected element to be replaced with the content of the instruction element. Consequently, if you don't have any content, the selected element can simply be removed. The preceding list or form view would cause the email field to be removed:

```
<field name="email" position="replace" />
```

> **Warning:**
> Removing fields can cause other inheriting views to break and several other undesirable side effects, so avoid that if possible. If you really need to remove fields, do so in a view that comes late in the order of evaluation (refer to the next section, *Order of evaluation in view inheritance* for more information).

`attributes` have a very different semantic from the preceding examples. The processor expects the element to contain the `attribute` elements with a `name` attribute. These elements will then be used to set attributes on the selected element. If you want to heed the earlier warning, you should set the `invisible` attribute to 1 for the email field:

```
<field name="email" position="attributes">
    <attribute name="invisible">1</attribute>
</field>
```

An `attribute` node can have `add` and `remove` attributes, which in turn should contain the value to be removed from or added to the space separated list. This is very useful for the `class` attribute, where you'd add a class (instead of overwriting the whole attribute) by using the following:

```
<field name="email" position="attributes">
    <attribute name="class" add="oe_inline" />
</field>
```

Order of evaluation in view inheritance

As we have only one parent view and one inheriting view currently, we don't run into any problems with conflicting view overrides. When you have installed a couple of modules, you'll find a lot of overrides for the partner form. This is fine as long as they change different things in a view, but there are occasions where it is important to understand how overriding works in order to avoid conflicts.

Direct descendants of a view are evaluated in ascending order of their `priority` field, so views with a lower priority are applied first. Every step of inheritance is applied to the result of the first, so if a view with priority 3 changes a field and another one with priority 5 removes it, this is fine. This does not work, however, if the priorities are reversed.

You can also inherit from a view that is an inheriting view itself. In this case, the second-level inheriting view is applied to the result of the view it inherits from. So, if you have four views, A, B, C, and D, where A is a standalone form, B and C inherit from A, and D inherits from B, the order of evaluation is A, B, D, C. Use this to enforce an order without having to rely on priorities; this is safer in general. If an inheriting view adds a field and you need to apply changes to this field, inherit from the inheriting view and not from the standalone one.

> This kind of inheritance always works on the complete XML tree from the original view, with modifications from the previous inheriting views applied.

See also

The following points provide information on some advance tricks that are used to tweak the behavior of view inheritance:

- For inheriting views, a very useful and not very well-known field is `groups_id`. This field causes the inheritance to take place only if the user requesting the parent view is a member of one of the groups mentioned there. This can save you a lot of work when adapting the user interface for different levels of access, because with inheritance, you can have more complex operations than just showing or not showing the elements based on group membership, as is possible with the `groups` attribute on form elements.
- You can, for example, remove elements if the user is a member of a group (which is the inverse of what the `groups` attribute does). You can also carry out some elaborate tricks, such as adding attributes based on group membership; think about simple things such as making a field read-only for certain groups, or more interesting concepts such as using different widgets for different groups.

- What was described in this recipe has the mode field of the original view set to primary, while the inheriting views have mode extension, which is the default. We'll look into the case that the mode of an inheriting view is set to primary later, where the rules are slightly different.

Defining document-style forms

In this recipe, we'll review some design guidelines in order to present a uniform user experience.

How to do it...

1. Start your form with a header element:

```
<header>
    <button type="object" name="open_commercial_entity"
        string="Open commercial partner"
        class="btn-primary" />
</header>
```

2. Add a sheet element for content:

```
<sheet>
```

3. Put in the stat button, which will be used to archive the record:

```
<div class="oe_button_box" name="button_box">
    <button name="toggle_active"
        type="object" class="oe_stat_button"
        icon="fa-archive">
            <field name="active" widget="boolean_button"
                options="{'terminology': 'archive'}"/>
    </button>
</div>
```

4. Add some prominent field(s):

```
<div class="oe_left oe_title">
    <label for="name" />
    <h1>
        <field name="name" />
    </h1>
</div>
```

5. Add your content, You can use a notebook if there are a lot of fields:

```
<group>
    <field name="category_id" widget="many2many_tags" />
    <field name="email"/>
    <field name="mobile"/>
</group>
```

6. After the sheet, add the `chatter` widget (if applicable):

```
</sheet>
<div class="oe_chatter">
    <field name="message_follower_ids"
widget="mail_followers"/>
    <field name="activity_ids" widget="mail_activity"/>
    <field name="message_ids" widget="mail_thread"/>
</div>
```

How it works...

The header should contain buttons that execute actions on the object that the user currently sees. Use the `btn-primary` class to make buttons visually stand out (in purple at the time of writing), which is a good way to guide the user regarding which is the most logical action to execute at the moment. Try to have all the highlighted buttons to the left of the non-highlighted buttons and hide the buttons that are not relevant in the current state (if applicable). If the model has a state, show it in the header using the `statusbar` widget. This will be rendered as right-aligned in the header.

The sheet element is rendered as a stylized sheet, and the most important fields should be the first thing the user sees when looking at it. Use the `oe_title` and `oe_left` classes to have them rendered in a prominent place (floating left with slightly adjusted font sizes at the time of writing).

If there are other records of interest concerning the record the user currently sees (such as the partner's invoices on a partner form), put them in an element with the `oe_right` and `oe_button_box` classes; this aligns the buttons in it to the right. On the buttons themselves, use the `oe_stat_button` class to enforce a uniform rendering of the buttons. It's also customary to assign an icon class from the font awesome icons for the `icon` attribute. You can learn more about font awesome at `https://fontawesome.com/v4.7.0/icons/`.

You can use the `oe_chatter` class and Chatter widgets to get default chatter at the bottom of the form view. For this, you need to use the `mail.thread` mixin. We will see this in detail in `Chapter 23`, *Manage emails in Odoo*.

> Even if you don't like this layout, stick to the element and class names described here, and adjust what you need with CSS and possibly JavaScript. This will make the user interface more compatible with existing addons and allow you to integrate better with core addons.

Dynamic form elements using attrs

So far, we have only looked into changing forms depending on the user's groups (the `groups` attribute on elements and the `groups_id` field on inherited views), but nothing more. This recipe will show you how to modify the form view based on the value of the fields in it.

How to do it...

1. Define an attribute called `attrs` on a form element:

```
<field name="parent_id"
 attrs="{
 'invisible': [('is_company', '=', True)],
 'required': [('is_company', '=', False)]
 }" />
```

2. Ensure that all the fields you refer to are available in your form:

```
<field name="is_company" invisible="True" />
```

This will make the `parent_id` field invisible if the partner is a company, and required if it's not a company.

How it works...

The `attrs` attribute contains a dictionary with `invisible`, `required`, and `readonly` keys (all of which are optional). The values are domains that may refer to the fields that exist on the form (and really only those, so there are no dotted paths), and the whole dictionary is evaluated according to the rules for client-side Python, as described earlier in the *Passing parameters to forms and actions – Context* recipe of this chapter. So, for example, you can access the context in the right-hand operand.

There's more...

While this mechanism is quite straightforward for scalar fields, it's less obvious how to handle `one2many` and `many2many` fields. In fact, in standard Odoo, you can't do much with those fields within an `attrs` attribute. However, if you only need to check whether such a field is empty, use `[[6, False, []]]` as your right-hand operand.

Defining embedded views

When you show a `one2many` or a `many2many` field on a form, you don't have much control over how it is rendered if you haven't used one of the specialized widgets. Also, in the case of the `many2one` fields, it is sometimes desirable to be able to influence the way the linked record is opened. In this recipe, we'll look at how to define private views for those fields.

How to do it...

1. Define your field as usual, but don't close the tag:

```
<field name="child_ids">
```

2. Write the view definition(s) into the tag:

```
<tree>
    <field name="name" />
    <field name="email" />
    <field name="phone" />
</tree>
<form>
    <group>
```

```
            <field name="name" />
            <field name="function" />
        </group>
    </form>
```

3. Close the tag:

```
</field>
```

How it works...

When Odoo loads a form view, it first checks if the `relational` type fields have embedded views in the field, as outlined previously. Those embedded views can have the exact same elements as the views we defined before. Only if Odoo doesn't find an embedded view of some type does it use the model's default view of this type.

There's more...

While embedded views might seem like a great feature, they complicate view inheritance a lot. For example, as soon as embedded views are involved, field names are not guaranteed to be unique, and you'll usually have to use some elaborate XPaths to select elements within an embedded view.

So, in general, you should better define standalone views and use the `form_view_ref` and `tree_view_ref` keys, as described earlier in the *Having an action open a specific view* recipe of this chapter.

Displaying attachments on the side of the form view

In some applications, such as invoicing, you need to fill data based on a document. To ease the data-filling process, a new feature was added to Odoo version 12 to display the document on the side of the form view.

In this recipe, we will learn how to display the form view and the document side by side:

This feature is only meant for large displays (>1534px), so if you have a small viewport, this feature will be hidden.

Internally, this feature uses some responsive utilities, so this feature only works in **enterprise edition**. However you can still use this code in your module. Odoo will automatically handle this, so if the module is installed in the enterprise edition, it will show the document, while in the community edition, it will hide everything without any side-effects.

How to do it...

We will enable this feature to modify a form view for the `res.partner` model, as follows:

```
<record id="view_all_customers_form" model="ir.ui.view">
    <field name="name">All customers</field>
    <field name="model">res.partner</field>
    <field name="arch" type="xml">
        <form>
            <sheet>
                <group>
                    <field name="name" />
                    <field name="email"/>
                </group>
            </sheet>
```

```
            <div class="o_attachment_preview"
                options="{types: ['image', 'pdf'], 'order': 'desc'}"
/>
            <div class="oe_chatter">
                <field name="message_follower_ids"
widget="mail_followers"/>
                <field name="activity_ids" widget="mail_activity"/>
                <field name="message_ids" widget="mail_thread"/>
            </div>
        </form>
    </field>
</record>
```

How it works...

This feature only works if your model has inherited the mail.thread model. To show the document on the side of any form view, you will need to add an empty <div> with the o_attachment_preview class before the chatter elements. That's it, the documents attached in the chatter will be displayed on the side of the form view.

By default, the pdf and image type documents will be displayed in ascending order by date. You can change this behavior by providing extra options, which include the following:

- type: You need to pass the list of document types you want to allow. Only two values are possible: pdf and image. For example, if you want to display only pdf type images, you can pass {'type': ['pdf']}.
- order: Possible values are asc and desc. These allow you to show documents in ascending order or descending order of the document creation date.

There's more...

In most cases, you want to display documents on the side of the initial state of any record. If you want to hide the attachment preview based on domain, you can use attrs on the <div> tag to hide the preview.

Take a look at the following example; it will hide the PDF preview if the value of the state field is not draft:

```
<div class="o_attachment_preview"
    attrs="{'invisible': [('state', '!=', 'draft')]/>
```

Defining kanban views

So far, we have presented you with a list of records that can be opened to show a form. While those lists are efficient when presenting a lot of information, they tend to be slightly boring, given the lack of design possibilities. In this recipe, we'll take a look at kanban views, which allow us to present lists of records in a more appealing way.

How to do it...

1. Define a view of the `kanban` type:

```
<record id="view_all_customers_kanban" model="ir.ui.view">
    <field name="model">res.partner</field>
    <field name="arch" type="xml">
        <kanban>
```

2. List the fields you'll use in your view:

```
<field name="name" />
<field name="supplier" />
<field name="customer" />
```

3. Implement a design:

```
<templates>
    <t t-name="kanban-box">
        <div class="oe_kanban_card">
            <a type="open">
                <field name="name" />
            </a>
                <t t-if="record.supplier.raw_value or
                        record.customer.raw_value">
                    is
                    <t t-if="record.customer.raw_value">
                        a customer
                    </t>
                    <t t-if="record.customer.raw_value and
                            record.supplier.raw_value">
                        and
                    </t>
                    <t t-if="record.supplier.raw_value">
                        a supplier
                    </t>
                </t>
```

```
                </div>
            </t>
        </templates>
```

4. Close all the tags:

```
            </kanban>
        </field>
    </record>
```

5. Add this view to one of your actions. This is left as an exercise for the reader. You will find a full working example in the GitHub example files: https://github.com/PacktPublishing/Odoo-12-Development-Cookbook-Third-Edition.

How it works...

We need to give a list of fields to load in *step 2* in order to be able to access them later. The content of the `templates` element must be a single `t` element with the `t-name` attribute set to `kanban-box`.

What you write inside this element will be repeated for each record, with special semantics for `t` elements and `t-*` attributes. For details about that, refer to the *Using client-side QWeb templates* recipe from `Chapter 15`, *Web Client Development*, because technically kanban views are just an application of QWeb templates.

There are a few modifications that are particular to kanban views. You have access to the `read_only_mode`, `record`, and `widget` variables during evaluation. Fields can be accessed using `record.fieldname`, which is an object with the `value` and `raw_value` properties, where `value` is the field's value that has been formatted in a way that is presentable to the user, and `raw_value` is the field's value as it comes from the database.

> `Many2many` fields make an exception here. You'll only get an ID list through the `record` variable. For a user-readable representation, you must use the `field` element.

Note the `type` attribute of the link at the top of the template. This attribute makes Odoo generate a link that opens the record in view mode (**open**) or edit mode (**edit**), or it deletes the record (**delete**). The `type` attribute can also be **object** or **action**, which will render links that call a function of the model or an action. In both cases, you need to supplement the attributes for buttons in form views, as outlined in the *Adding buttons to forms* recipe of this chapter. Instead of the `a` element, you can also use the `button` element; the `type` attribute has the same semantics there.

There's more...

There are a few more helper functions worth mentioning. If you need to generate a pseudo-random color for an element, use the `kanban_color(some_variable)` function, which will return a CSS class that sets the `background` and `color` properties. This is usually used in the `t-att-class` elements.

If you want to display an image stored in a binary field, use `kanban_image(modelname, fieldname, record.id.raw_value)`, which returns a data URI if you included the field in your fields list and the field is set, a placeholder if the field is not set, or a URL that makes Odoo stream the field's contents if you didn't include the field in your fields list. Do not include the field in the fields list if you need to display a lot of records simultaneously or you expect very big images. Usually, you'd use this in a `t-att-src` attribute of an `img` element.

> Doing design in kanban views can be a bit annoying. What often works better is generating HTML using a function field of the HTML type, and generating this HTML from a Qweb view. This way, you're still doing QWeb, but on the server side, which is a lot more convenient when you need to work on a lot of data.

Showing kanban cards in columns according to their state

This recipe shows you how to set up a kanban view where the user can drag and drop a record from one column to the other, thereby pushing the record in question into another state.

Getting ready

From now on, we'll make use of the project module here, as this defines models that lend themselves better to date- and state-based views than those defined in the base module. So, before proceeding, add `project` to the dependencies list of your add-on.

How to do it...

1. Define a kanban view for the tasks:

```xml
<record id="kanban_tasks" model="ir.ui.view">
    <field name="name">project.task.kanban</field>
    <field name="model">project.task</field>
    <field name="sequence">20</field>
    <field name="arch" type="xml">
        <kanban default_group_by="stage_id">
            <field name="stage_id" />
            <field name="name" />
            <templates>
                <t t-name="kanban-box">
                    <div class="oe_kanban_card
oe_kanban_global_click">
                        <field name="name" />
                    </div>
                </t>
            </templates>
        </kanban>
    </field>
</record>
```

2. Add a menu and an action using this view. This is left as an exercise for the reader.

How it works...

Kanban views support grouping, which allows you to display records that have a group field in common in the same column. This is commonly used for a `state` or `stage_id` field, because it allows the user to change this field's value for a record by simply dragging it into another column. Set the `default_group_by` attribute on the `kanban` element to the name of the field you want to group by in order to make use of this functionality.

To control the behavior of kanban grouping, there are a few options available in Odoo:

- `group_create`: This option is used to hide or show the **Add a new column** option in grouped kanban. The default value is `true`.
- `group_delete`: This option enables or disables the **Column delete** option in the kanban group context menu. The default value is `true`.
- `group_edit`: This option enables or disables the **Column edit** option in the kanban group context menu. The default value is `true`.
- `archivable`: This option enables or disables the option to archive and restore the records from the kanban group context menu. This only works if the `active` Boolean field is present in your model.
- `quick_create`: With this option, you can create records directly from the kanban view.
- `quick_create_view`: By default, the `quick_create` option displays only the name field in kanban. But with the `quick_create_view` option, you can give the reference of the minimal form view to display it in kanban.
- `on_create`: If you don't want to use `quick_create` when creating a new record and you don't want to redirect the user to the form view either, you can give the reference of the wizard so it will open the wizard on a click of the **Create** button.

There's more...

If not defined in the dedicated attribute, any search filter can add grouping by setting a context key named `group_by` to the field name(s) to group by.

Defining calendar and gantt views

This recipe walks you through how to display and edit information about dates and duration in your records in a visual way.

How to do it...

Follow these steps to add a calendar view for the `project.task` model:

1. Define a `calendar` view:

```xml
<record id="view_project_task_calendar" model="ir.ui.view">
    <field name="model">project.task</field>
    <field name="arch" type="xml">
        <calendar date_start="date_start" date_stop="date_end"
color="project_id">
            <field name="name" />
            <field name="user_id" />
        </calendar>
    </field>
</record>
```

2. Add menus and actions using this view. This is left as an exercise for the reader.

How it works...

The calendar view needs to be passed the field names in the `date_start` and `date_stop` attributes to indicate which fields to look at when building the visual representation. Only use fields with the `Datetime` or `Date` type, other types of fields will not work and will instead generate an error. While `date_start` is required, you can leave out `date_stop` and set the `date_delay` attribute instead, which is expected to be a `Float` field that represents the duration in hours.

The calendar view allows you to give records that have the same value in a field the same (arbitrarily-assigned) color. To use this functionality, set the `color` attribute to the name of the field you need. In our example, we can see at a glance which tasks belong to the same project, because we assigned `project_id` as the field to determine the color groups.

The fields you name in the calendar element's body are shown within the block that represents the time interval covered, separated by commas.

There's more...

The calendar view has some other helpful attributes. If you want to open calendar entries in a popup instead of the standard form view, set `event_open_popup` to 1. By default, you create a new entry by just filling in some text, which internally calls the model's `name_create` function to actually create the record. If you want to disable this behavior, set `quick_add` to 0.

If your model covers a whole day, set `all_day` to a field's name that is `true` if the record covers the whole day, and `false` otherwise.

Gantt View

Gantt view is part of the enterprise version, so it will not work if you are using the Odoo community edition. If you want to use it in the community edition, you can use a similar module `web_timeline` from the `web` repository of the OCA. This module introduces a view that can be used if you want a gantt-style representation.

To use the `gantt` view in your module, you need to add the `web_gantt` dependency in the manifest file. `web_gantt` is available in the enterprise edition. If you are using the enterprise edition, you can add the `gantt` view as follows:

```
<record id="view_project_task_calendar" model="ir.ui.view">
    <field name="model">project.task.gantt</field>
    <field name="model">project.task</field>
    <field name="arch" type="xml">
        <gantt date_start="date_assign"
            date_stop="date_deadline"
            default_group_by="user_id">
        </gantt>
    </field>
</record>
```

In the enterprise `gantt` view, you can use the following options:

- `date_start`: The value of this option will be the name of the date or the `datetime` field that holds the start date for the `gantt` record.
- `date_stop`: The value of this option will be the name of the date or the `datetime` field that holds the end date for the `gantt` record.

- `date_delay`: If you don't want to use `date_stop`, you can use this option. This will be used to calculate the duration of the `gantt` record.
- `duration_unit`: The value of this option will be one of the following: minute, hour (default), day, week, month, or year.
- `default_group_by`: This is the name of the field by which `gantt` records are grouped.

Defining graph and pivot views

In this recipe, we'll take a look at Odoo's business intelligence views. These are read-only views that are meant to present data.

Getting ready

We're still making use of the project module here. You can configure a graph and pivot views to get different statistics. For our example, we will focus on the assigned user. We will generate a graph and pivot view to see the users of the tasks per user. By the way, the end user can generate statistics of their choice by modifying the view options.

How to do it...

1. Define a graph view using bars:

```
<record id="view_project_tasks_graph" model="ir.ui.view">
    <field name="model">project.task</field>
    <field name="arch" type="xml">
        <graph type="bar">
            <field name="user_id"/>
            <field name="stage_id"/>
        </graph>
    </field>
</record>
```

2. Define a pivot view:

```
<record id="view_project_tasks_pivot" model="ir.ui.view">
    <field name="model">project.task</field>
    <field name="arch" type="xml">
        <pivot>
```

```
            <field name="user_id" type="row"/>
            <field name="project_id" type="col"/>
            <field name="stage_id" type="col"/>
        </pivot>
    </field>
</record>
```

3. Add menus and actions using this view. This is left as an exercise for the reader.

If everything went well, you should see graphs that show how many tasks are assigned to which user and the state of those tasks.

How it works...

The `type` attribute on a `graph` element determines the initial mode of a graph view. Possible values are `bar`, `line`, and `chart`, but `bar` is the default. The graph view is highly interactive, so the user can switch between the different modes and also add and remove fields. Pivot views have their own root element, `pivot`.

The `field` elements tell Odoo what to display on which axis. For all graph modes, you need at least one field with the `row` type and one with the `measure` type to see anything useful. Fields of the `row` type determine the grouping, while those of the `measure` type stand for the value(s) to be shown. Line graphs only support one field of each type, while charts and bars handle two group fields with one measure nicely. The pivot view supports an arbitrary amount of `group` and `measure` fields. Nothing will break if you switch to a mode that doesn't support the amount of groups and measures you defined; some fields will just be ignored and the result might not be as interesting as it could be.

There's more...

For all graph types, `Datetime` fields are tricky to group, because you'll rarely encounter the same field value here. So, if you have a `Datetime` field of `row` type, also specify the `interval` attribute with one of the following values: `day`, `week`, `month`, `quarter`, or `year`. This will cause the grouping to take place in the given interval.

The pivot table also supports grouping in columns. Use the `col` type for the fields you want to have there.

> Grouping, like sorting, relies heavily on PostgreSQL. So, here also, the rule applies that a field must live in the database and in the current table in order to be usable.
>
> It is a common practice to define database views that collect all the data you need and define a model on top of this view in order to have all the necessary fields available.
>
> Depending on the complexity of your view and the grouping, building the graph can be quite an expensive exercise. Consider setting the `auto_search` attribute to `False` in these cases, so that the user can first adjust all the parameters and only then trigger a search.

Defining the cohort view

For the cohort analysis of records, the new cohort view was added in Odoo version 12. The cohort view is used to find out the life cycle of a record over a particular time span. With the cohort view, you can see the churn and retention rate of any object for a particular time.

Getting ready

The cohort view is part of the **Odoo enterprise edition** so you can not use it with only the community edition. If you are using the enterprise edition, you need to add `web_cohort` in the manifest file of your module. For our example, we will create a view to see the cohort analysis for tasks.

How to do it...

Follow these steps to add the `cohort` view for the `project.task` model:

1. Define a `cohort` view:

```
<record id="view_project_tasks_graph" model="ir.ui.view">
    <field name="name">project task cohort</field>
    <field name="model">project.task</field>
```

```
<field name="arch" type="xml">
    <cohort date_start="date_start"
        date_stop="date_deadline"
        interval="month"
        string="Task Cohort" />
</field>
</record>
```

2. Add menus and actions using this view. This is left as an exercise for the reader.

How it works...

To create a cohort view, you need to provide `date_start` and `date_stop`. These will be used in the view to determine the time span of any record. For example, if you are managing the subscription of a service, the start date of the subscription will be `date_start` and the date when the subscription is going to expire will be `date_stop`.

By default, the cohort view will be displayed in retention mode by intervals of a month. You can use the given options to get different behaviors in the cohort view:

- `mode`: You can use cohort with two modes: retention (default) or churn. Retention mode starts with 100% and decreases with time, while churn mode starts at 0% and increases with time.
- `timeline`: This option accepts two values: forward (default) or backward. In most cases, you need to use the forwards timeline. But if the `date_start` is in the future, you will need to use the backwards timeline. An example of when we would use the backwards timeline would be for the registration of an event attendee where the event date is in the future and the registration date is in the past.
- `interval`: By default, the cohort is grouped by month, but you can change this in the interval options. Other than months, cohort also supports day, week, and year intervals.
- `measure`: Just like graph and pivot, measure is used to display the aggregated value of a given field. If no option is given, cohort will display the count of records.

Defining the dashboard view

A new view called dashboard was introduced with Odoo version 12. This is used to display multiple views and the various business KPIs in a single screen.

Getting ready

The dashboard view is part of the **Odoo enterprise edition** so you can't use it with community edition. If you are using the enterprise edition, you need to add dependency of the `web_dashboard` in the manifest file of your module.

In our example, we will display a few KPIs and a few existing views. We will display the graph and the pivot view in the same screen, so follow the *Defining graph and pivot views* recipe, if you haven't created the pivot and graph views. We will use the ID of these views in the dashboard view.

How to do it...

1. Define a dashboard view:

```
<record id="view_project_tasks_dashboard" model="ir.ui.view">
    <field name="name">project task dashbaord</field>
    <field name="model">project.task</field>
    <field name="arch" type="xml">
        <dashboard>
            <view ref="my_project.view_project_tasks_graph"
                type="graph" />
            <group>
                <aggregate name="all_task"
                    string="Total Tasks"
                    group_operator="count"
                    field="id" measure="__count__"/>
                <aggregate name="progress_task"
                    string="In Progress Tasks"
                    domain="[('stage_id.name', 'ilike', 'In
Progress')]"
                    group_operator="count"
                    field="id" measure="__count__"/>
                <aggregate name="done_task"
                    string="Completed Tasks"
                    domain="[('stage_id.name', 'ilike',
'Done')]"
                    group_operator="count" field="id"
```

```
                    measure="__count__"/>
                <formula name="price_average"
                    string="Overall Progress"
                    value="record.done_task / record.all_task"
                    widget="percentage"/>
            </group>
            <view ref="my_project.view_project_tasks_pivot"
                type="pivot"/>
        </dashboard>
    </field>
</record>
```

2. Add menus and actions using this view. This is left as an exercise for the reader.

How it works...

With dashboard view, you can display KPIs with `aggregate` and `formula`. You can display multiple views on the same screen. If you look at the definition of the view, you will see that we have added two views: graph at the beginning and pivot at the end. To display the views, you just need to use the `<view>` tag with the XML reference and the type of view.

We have displayed various KIPs, including the total tasks, the tasks in progress, and the completed tasks, with the `<aggregate>` tag. This tag will display the aggregated result for the records of the current domain in the search view. In the `<aggregate>` tag, you can use the optional domain attribute to display aggregates for a particular set of records. By default, the aggregate function displays the count of records, but you can provide a SQL aggregate function using a `group_operator` attribute, such as `avg` or `max`.

Sometimes, it is not possible to display the KPI with `<aggregate>`; it needs some extra computation. With the help of `<formula>`, you can define the formula for any KPI. In our example, we have displayed the progress of all tasks and we have used the optional attribute widget to display the value as a percentage.

There's more....

Another useful element is the `<widget>` tag. With this, you can display data with the UI of your choice. In `Chapter 16`, *Web Client Development*, we will look at how to create a custom widget.

11
Access Security

In this chapter, we will see how to carry out the following recipes:

- Creating security groups and assigning them to users
- Adding security access to models
- Limiting access to fields in models
- Limiting record access using record rules
- Using security groups to activate features
- Accessing recordsets as a superuser
- Hiding view elements and menus based on groups

In order to concisely get the point across, the recipes in this chapter make small additions to an existing module.

Technical requirements

The technical requirements for this chapter include using the module that we created by following the recipes in Chapter 4, *Creating Odoo Add-On Modules*. To follow the examples here, you should have that module created and ready to use.

All the code that's used in this chapter can be downloaded from the following GitHub repository, at https://github.com/PacktPublishing/Odoo-12-Development-Cookbook-Third-Edition/tree/master/Chapter11.

Check out the following video to see the Code in Action:

Place holder link

Creating security groups and assigning them to users

Security access in Odoo is configured through security groups: permissions are given to groups and then groups are assigned to users. Each functional area has base security groups provided by a central application.

When add-on modules extend an existing *application*, they should add permissions to the corresponding groups, as shown in the *Adding security access to models* recipe later.

When add-on modules add a new functional area not yet covered by an existing central *application*, they should add the corresponding security groups. Usually, we should have at least *user* and *manager* roles.

Taking the Library example we introduced in `Chapter 4`, *Creating Odoo Add-On Modules*, it doesn't fit neatly in any of the Odoo core apps, so we will add security groups for it.

Getting ready

This recipe assumes that you have an Odoo instance ready, with the `my_module` available, as described in `Chapter 4`, *Creating Odoo Add-On Modules*.

How to do it...

To add new access security groups to a module, perform the following steps:

1. Ensure that the `__manifest__.py` add-on module manifest has the `category` key defined:

   ```
   'category': 'Library',
   ```

2. Add the new `security/groups.xml` file to the manifest `data` key:

   ```
   'data': [
       'security/groups.xml',
       'views/library_book.xml',
   ],
   ```

3. Add the new XML file for the data records at `security/library_security.xml`, starting with an empty structure:

```
<?xml version="1.0" encoding="utf-8"?>
<odoo>
    <!--  Data records go here -->
</odoo>
```

4. Add the `record` tags for the two new groups inside the data XML element:

```
<record id="group_library_user" model="res.groups">
    <field name="name">User</field>
    <field name="category_id"
ref="base.module_category_library"/>
    <field name="implied_ids" eval="[(4,
ref('base.group_user'))]"/>
</record>

<record id="group_library_librarian" model="res.groups">
    <field name="name">Librarians</field>
    <field name="category_id"
ref="base.module_category_library"/>
    <field name="implied_ids" eval="[(4,
ref('group_library_user'))]"/>
    <field name="users" eval="[(4, ref('base.user_admin'))]"/>
</record>
```

If we upgrade the add-on module, these two records will be loaded. In order to see these groups in the UI, you need to activate developer mode. You'll then be able to see them through the **Settings|Users|Groups** menu option.

> In Odoo v12, the default security for newly added models works differently to previous models. In v12, if you are adding a new model, the admin user doesn't get access rights for that model. This means that the menus and views that have been added for that model are not visible to the admin user. In order to display it, you need to add access rules for that model, which is coming in the *Adding security access to models* recipe. By the way, you can access newly added models through the superuser; to learn more about it, please refer to the *Accessing Odoo as a superuser* recipe from `Chapter 4`, *Creating Odoo Add-On Modules.*

How it works...

Add-on modules are organized in to functional areas, or major *applications*, such as *Accounting and Finance*, *Sales*, or *Human Resources*. These are defined by the `category` key in the manifest file.

If a category name does not exist yet, it will be automatically created. For convenience, a `base.module_category_<category_name_in_manifest>` XML ID will also be generated for the new category name in lowercase letters, replacing the spaces with underscores. This is useful to relate security groups with application categories.

In our example, we used the **Library** category name, and it generated a `base.module_category_library` XML identifier.

By convention, data files that contain security-related elements should be placed inside a `security` subdirectory.

You also need to register security files in a manifest file. The order in which files are declared in the `data` key of the module manifest is important, since you can't use a reference of security groups in other views or ACL files before the group has been defined. It's best to place the security data file at the top of the list before the ACL files and the other user interface data files.

In our example, we created groups with the `<record>` tag, which will create a record of the `res.groups` model. The most important columns of the `res.group` model are as follows:

- `name`: This is the group's display name.
- `category_id`: This is a reference to the application category and is used to organize the groups in the user's form.
- `implied_ids`: These are other groups to inherit permissions from.
- `users`: This is the list of users that belong to this group. In new add-on modules, we usually want the admin user to belong to the application's manager group.

The first security group uses `implied_ids` as the `base.group_user` group. This is the Employee user group, and is the basic security group all the backend users are expected to share.

The second security group sets a value on the `users` field to assign it to the administrator user, which has the `base.user_admin` XML ID.

Users that belong to a security group will automatically belong to its implied groups. If you assign a *Librarians* group to any user, that user will also be included in the *User* group because the *Librarians* group has the *User* group in its `implied_ids` column.

Also, access permissions granted by security groups are cumulative. A user has permission if any of the groups they belong to (directly or implied) grants that permission.

Some security groups are shown in the user form as a selection box instead of individual check boxes. This happens when the involved groups are in the same application category and are linearly interrelated through `implied_ids`. For example, Group *A* has implied Group *B*, and Group *B* has implied Group *C*. If a group is not related with any other groups through `implied_ids`, instead of a selection box, you will see a checkbox.

Note that the relations defined in the preceding fields also have reverse relations that can be edited in the related models, such as security groups and users.

Setting values on reference fields, such as `category_id` and `implied_ids`, is done using the related records' XML IDs and some special syntax. This syntax is explained in detail in `Chapter 7`, *Module Data*.

There's more...

The special `base.group_no_one` security group called **Extra Rights** is also noteworthy. In previous Odoo versions, it was used for advanced features hidden by default, and only made visible when the `Technical Features` flag was activated. From version 9.0, this has changed, and the features are visible as long as `Developer Mode` is activated.

Access permissions granted by security groups are cumulative only. There is no way to deny access given by a group. This means that a manually created group to customize permissions should inherit from the closest group with fewer permissions than those intended (if any), and then add all the remaining permissions needed.

Groups also have these additional fields available:

- Menus (the `menu_access` field): These are the menu items the group has access to
- Views (the `view_access` field): These are the UI views the group has access to
- Access rights (the `model_access` field): This is the access it has on models, detailed in the *Adding security access to models* recipe
- Rules (the `rule_groups` field): These are the record-level access rules that apply to the group, as detailed in the *Limiting record access using record rules* recipe
- Notes (the `comment` field): This is a description or comment text for the group

Adding security access to models

It's common for add-on modules to add new models. For example, in Chapter 4, *Creating Odoo Add-On Modules*, we added a new Library Books model. It is easy to miss the creation of security access for new models during development, and you might find it hard to see menus and views that have created, because, from Odoo version 12, admin users don't get default access rights to new models. In order to see views and menus for the new model, you have to need to add security **Access-Control Lists (ACLs)**.

However, models with no ACLs will trigger a warning log message on loading, informing the user about the missing ACL definitions:

```
WARNING The model library.book has no access rules, consider adding
one example, access_library_book, access_library_book,
model_library_book, base.group_user,1,0,0,0
```

You can also access newly added models through a superuser, as this bypasses all security rules. To learn more about this, please refer to the *Accessing Odoo as a superuser* recipe from Chapter 4, *Creating Odoo Add-On Modules*. The superuser feature is only available for administrator users. So, for new models to be usable by non-admin users, we need to define their access control lists so that Odoo knows how it should access them and what operations each user group should be allowed to perform.

Getting ready

We will take the module we created in `Chapter 4`, *Creating Odoo Add-On Modules,* and add the missing ACLs to it.

How to do it...

`my_library` should already contain the `models/library_book.py` Python file that creates the `library.book` model. We will now add a data file that describes this model's security access control by performing the following steps:

1. Edit the `__manifest__.py` file to declare a new data file:

    ```
    data: [
        # ...Security Groups
        'security/ir.model.access.csv',
        # ...Other data files
    ]
    ```

2. Add a new `security/ir.model.access.csv` file to the module with the following lines:

    ```
    id,name,model_id:id,group_id:id,perm_read,perm_write,perm_crea
    te,perm_unlink
    acl_book,library.book_default,model_library_book,base_group_us
    er,1,0,0,0
    acl_book_librarian,library.book_librarian,model_library_book,g
    roup_library_librarian,1,1,1,1
    ```

We should then upgrade the module to have these ACL records added to our Odoo database. More importantly, if we sign into a demonstration database using the **demo** user, we should be able to access the **Library** menu option without any security errors.

How it works...

Security Access-Control Lists are stored in the core `ir.model.access` model. We just need to add the records that describe the intended access rights for each user group.

Any type of data file would do, but the common practice is to use a CSV file. The file can be placed anywhere inside the add-on module directory, but the convention is to have all the security-related files inside a `security` subdirectory.

The first step in our recipe adds this new data file to the manifest. The second step adds the files that describe the security access-control rules. The CSV file must be named after the model where the records will be loaded, so the name used is not just a convention and is mandatory; refer to `Chapter 7`, *Module Data,* for details.

If the module also creates new security groups, its data file should be declared in the manifest before the ACLs' data files, since you may want to use them for the ACLs. They must already be created when the ACL file is processed.

The columns in the CSV file are as follows:

- `id`: This is the XML ID internal identifier for this rule. Any unique name inside the module will do, but the convention is to use `access_<model>_<group>`.
- `name`: This is a title for the access rule. It is a common practice to use a `access.<model>.<group>` name.
- `model_id:id`: This is the XML ID for the model. Odoo automatically assigns this kind of ID to models with a `model_<name>` format, using the model's `_name` with underscores instead of dots. If the model was created in a different add-on module, a fully-qualified XML ID that includes the module name is needed.
- `group_id:id`: This is the XML ID for the user group. If left empty, it applies to all users. The base module provides some basic groups, such as `base.group_user` for all employees and `base.group_system` for the administration user. Other apps can add their own user groups.
- `perm_read`: Members of the preceding group can read the model records. It accepts two values: 0 or 1. Use 0 to restrict the read access on the model and 1 to provide read access.

- `perm_write`: Members of the preceding group can update the model records. It accepts two values: 0 or 1. Use 0 to restrict write access on the model and 1 to provide write access.
- `perm_create`: Members of the preceding group can add new records of this model. It accepts two values: 0 or 1. Use 0 to restrict create access on the model and 1 to provide create access.
- `perm_unlink`: Members of the preceding group can delete records of this model. It accepts two values: 0 or 1. Use 0 to restrict unlink access on the model and 1 to provide unlink access.

The CSV file we used adds read-only access to the **Employees | Employee** standard security group and full write access to the **Administration | Settings** group.

The **Employee** user group, `base.group_user`, is particularly important because the user groups that are added by the Odoo standard apps inherit from it. This means that if we need a new model to be accessible by all the backend users, regardless of the specific apps they work with, we should add that permission to the **Employee** group.

The resulting ACLs can be viewed from the GUI in debug mode by navigating to **Settings | Technical | Security | Access Controls List**, as shown in the following screenshot:

Some people find it easier to use this user interface to define ACLs and then use the export feature to produce a CSV file.

There's more...

It would make sense for us to give this permission to the Library user and the Librarian groups defined in the *Creating security groups and assigning them to users* recipe. If you followed that recipe, it's a good exercise to then follow this one, adapting the group identifiers to the Library ones.

It's important to note that access lists provided by add-on modules should not be directly customized, since they will be reloaded on the next module upgrade, destroying any customization that could have been done from the GUI.

To customize ACLs, two approaches can be used. One is to create new security groups that inherit from the one provided by the module and add additional permissions on it, but this only allows us to add permissions, not to remove them. A more flexible approach would be to uncheck the **Active** flag on the particular ACL lines to disable them. The active field is not visible by default, so we need to edit the tree view to add the `<field name="active" />` column. We can also add new ACL lines for additional or replacement permissions. On a module upgrade, the deactivated ACLs won't be reactivated and the added ACL lines won't be affected.

It's also worth noting that ACLs only apply to regular models and don't need to be defined for *Abstract* or *Transient* models. If defined, these will be disregarded, and a warning message will be triggered in the server log.

Limiting access to fields in models

In some cases, we may need more fine-grained access control, and we may also need to limit access to specific fields in a model.

It is possible for a field to be accessible only by specific security groups, using the `groups` attribute. We will show you how to add a field with limited access to the Library Books model.

How to do it...

To add a field with access limited to specific security groups, perform the following steps:

1. Edit the model file to add the field:

```
is_public =
fields.Boolean(groups='my_library.group_library_librarian'
)
private_notes =
fields.Text(groups='my_library.group_library_librarian')
```

2. Edit the view in the XML file to add the field:

```
<field name="is_public" />
<field name="private_notes" />
```

That's it. Now, upgrade the add-on module for the changes in the model to take place. If you sign in with a user with no system configuration access, such as demo in a database with demonstration data, the Library Books form won't display the field.

How it works...

Fields with the groups attribute are specially handled to check whether the user belongs to any of the security groups indicated in the attribute. If a user doesn't belong to a particular group, Odoo will remove the field from the UI and restrict ORM operations on that field.

Note that this security is not superficial. The field is not only hidden in the user interface, but is also made unavailable to the user in the other ORM operations, such as read and write. This is also true for XML-RPC or JSON-RPC calls.

Be careful when using these fields in business logic, or in on-change UI events (@api.onchange methods); they can raise errors for users with no access to the field. One workaround for this is to use privilege elevation, such as the sudo() model method or the compute_sudo field attribute for computed fields.

The `groups` value is a string that contains a comma-separated list of valid XML IDs for security groups. The simplest way to find the XML ID for a particular group is to activate the developer mode and navigate to the group's form, at **Settings | Users | Groups**, and then access the **View Metadata** option from the debug menu, as shown in the following screenshot:

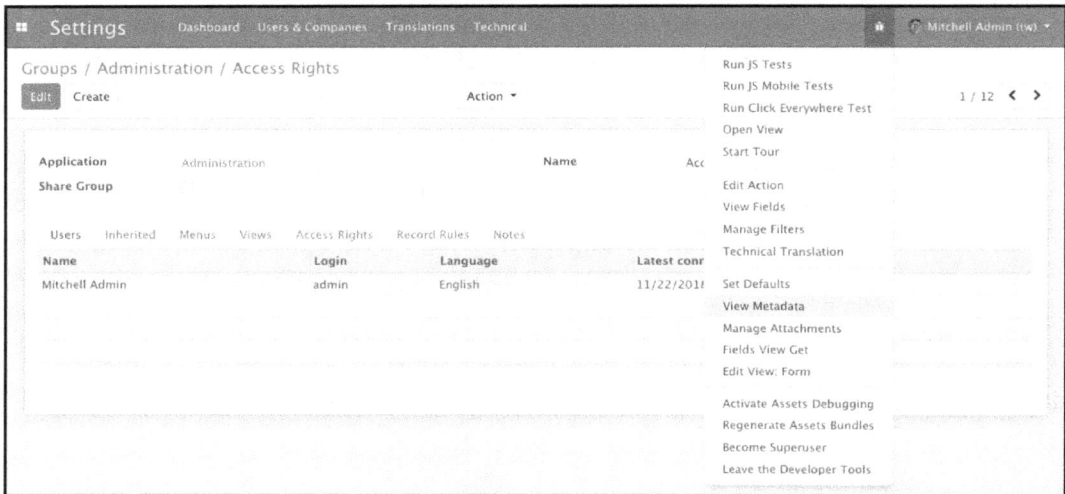

There's more...

In some cases, we need a field to be available or unavailable, depending on particular conditions, such as the values in a field, for example, `stage_id` or `state`. This is usually handled at the view level using attributes such as `states` or `attrs` to dynamically display or hide the field according to certain conditions. Refer to `Chapter 10`, *Backend Views*, for a detailed description.

Note that these techniques work at the user-interface level only and don't provide actual access security. To do this, you should add checks in the business logic layer. Either add model methods decorated with `@constrains`, implementing the specific validations intended, or extend the `create`, `write`, or `unlink` methods to add validation logic. You can get further insights on how to do this in `Chapter 6`, *Basic Server-Side Business Logic*.

Limiting record access using record rules

A common need for an application is to be able to limit which records are available to each user on a specific model.

This is achieved using record rules. A record rule is a domain filter expression defined on a model that will then be added on every data query made by the affected users.

As an example, we will add a record rule on the Library Books model so that users in the Employee group will only have access to the public books.

This recipe assumes that you have an instance ready, with `my_library` available, as described in `Chapter 4`, *Creating Odoo Add-On Modules*.

How to do it...

Record rules are added using a data XML file. To do this, perform the following steps:

1. Ensure that the `security/library_security.xml` file is referenced by the manifest `data` key:

```
'data': [
    'security/library_security.xml',
    # ...
],
```

2. We should have a `security/library_security.xml` data file, with a `<odoo>` section that creates the security group:

```
<odoo noupdate="1">
    <record model="ir.rule" id="library_book_user_rule">
        <field name="name">Library: see only own
books</field>
        <field name="model_id" ref="model_library_book"/>
        <field name="groups" eval="[(4,
ref('my_library.group_library_user'))]"/>
        <field name="domain_force">
            [('is_public', '=', True)]
        </field>
    </record>
    <record model="ir.rule" id="library_book_all_rule">
        <field name="name">Library: see all books</field>
        <field name="model_id" ref="model_library_book"/>
```

```
            <field name="groups"
                    eval="[(4,
    ref('my_library.group_library_librarian'))]"/>
            <field name="domain_force">[(1, '=', 1)]</field>
        </record>
    </odoo>
```

Upgrading the add-on module will load the record rules in the Odoo instance. If you are using demo data, you can test it through the default demo user to give library user rights to the demo user. If you are not using demo data, you can create a new user with library user rights.

How it works...

Record rules are just data records that are loaded in the ir.rule core model. While the file adding them can be anywhere in the module, the convention is for it to be in the security subdirectory. It is common to have a single XML file with both security groups and record rules.

Unlike groups, in the standard modules, the record rules are loaded in an odoo section with the noupdate="1" attribute. With this, those records will not be reloaded on a module upgrade, meaning that manual customization on them is safe and will survive later upgrades.

To stay consistent with the official modules, we should also have our record rules inside a <odoo noupdate="1"> section.

Record rules can be seen from the GUI at the **Settings | Technical | Security | Record Rules** menu option, as shown in the following screenshot:

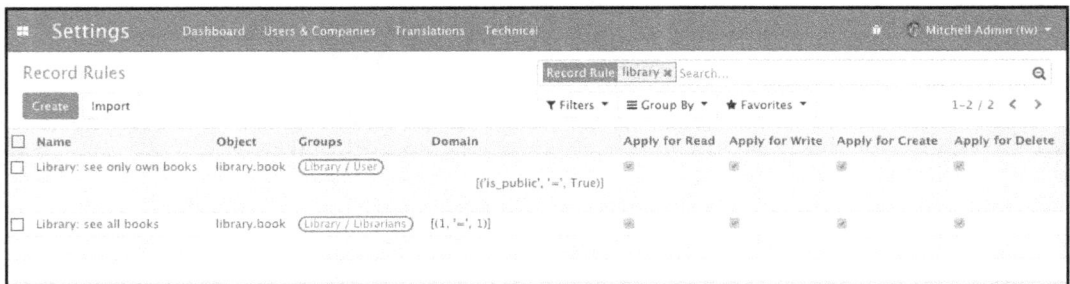

The following are the most important record rule fields that were used in this example:

- **Name** (name): A descriptive title for the rule.
- **Object** (model_id): A reference to the model the rule applies to.
- **Groups** (groups): The security groups that the rule applies to. If no security group is specified, the rule is considered *global* and is applied in a different way (continue with this recipe to learn more about the groups).
- Domain (domain): A domain expression which is used to filter the records. The rule is only going to applied on these filtered records.

The first record rule we created was for the *Library User* security group. It uses the [('is_public', '=', True)] domain expression to select only the books that are available publicly. Thus, users with the *Library User* security group will only be able to see the public books.

The domain expressions used in the record rules run on the server side using ORM objects. Due to this, dot notation can be used on the fields on the left-hand side (the first tuple element). For example, the [('country_id.code', '=', 'IN')] domain expression will only show records that have the country of *India*.

As record rules are mostly based on the current user, you can use the user recordset in the right-hand side (the third tuple element) of the domain. So, if you want to show the records for the company of the current user, you can use the [('conpany_id', '=', user.company_id.id)] domain. Alternatively, if you want to show the records that are created by the current user, you can use the [('user_id', '=', user.id)] domain.

We want the *Librarian* security group to be able to see all the books, independent of whether they are public or private. Since it inherits the *Library User* group, unless we do something about it, it will also be able to see only the public books.

The non-global record rules are joined together using the OR logical operator; each rule adds access and never removes the access. For the Librarian to have access to all the books, we can add to it a record rule to add access for all books, as follows: [('is_public', 'in', [True, False])].

We chose to do it differently here and instead use the `[(1, '=', 1)]` special rule to unconditionally give access to all book records. While this may seem redundant, remember that otherwise, the Library user rule can be customized in a way that will keep some books out of reach to the Settings user. The domain is special because the first element of a domain tuple must be a field name; this exact case is one of two cases where that is not true. The special domain of `[(1, '=', 0)]` is never true, but also not very useful in the case of record rules, because this type of rule is used to restrict access to all of the records. The same thing is also possible with access lists.

> Record rules are ignored if you activated SUPERUSER. When testing your record rules, ensure that you use another user for that.

There's more...

When a record rule is not assigned to any security group, it is marked as **global** and is handled differently from the other rules.

Global record rules have a stronger effect than group-level record rules, and set access restrictions that those can't override. Technically, they are joined with an AND operator. In standard modules, they are used to implement multi-company security access so that each user can see only their company's data.

In summary, regular non-global record rules are joined together with an OR operator; they are added together, and a record is accessible if any of the rules grant that access. Global record rules then add restrictions to the access given by regular record rules, using an AND operator. Restrictions added by global record rules can't be overridden by regular record rules.

Using security groups to activate features

Security groups can restrict some features so that they are accessible only to users that belong to these groups. Security groups can also inherit other groups, so they also grant their permissions.

These two features combined are used to implement a usability feature in Odoo: feature toggling. Security groups can also be used as a way to enable or disable features for some or all the users in an Odoo instance.

This recipe shows how to add options to configuration settings and showcases the two methods to enable additional features, making them visible using security groups or adding them by installing an additional module.

For the first case, we will make the book-release dates an optional additional feature and for the second, as an example, we will provide an option to install the Notes module.

Getting ready

This recipe uses the my_library, which was described in Chapter 4, *Creating Odoo Add-On Modules*. We will need security groups to work with, so you also need to have followed the *Adding security access to models* recipe from this chapter.

In this recipe, some identifiers need to refer to the add-on module's technical name. We will assume that this is my_library. In case you are using a different name, replace my_library with the actual technical name of your add-on module.

How to do it...

To add the configuration options, follow the given steps:

1. To add the needed dependency and the new XML data files, edit the __manifest__.py file like this and check that it depends on base_setup:

```python
{   'name': 'Cookbook code',
    'category': 'Library',
    'depends': ['base_setup'],
    'data': [
        'security/ir.model.access.csv',
        'security/groups.xml',
        'views/library_book.xml',
        'views/res_config_settings.xml',
    ],
}
```

2. To add the new security group that's used for feature activation, edit the
   `security/library_book.xml` file and add the following record to it:

```
<record id="group_release_dates" model="res.groups">
    <field name="name">Library: release date
feature</field>
    <field name="category_id"
ref="base.module_category_hidden" />
</record>
```

3. To make the book-release date visible only when this option is enabled, edit
   the field definition in the `models/library_book.py` file:

```
class LibraryBook(models.Model):
    # ...
    date_release = fields.Date(
        'Release Date',
        groups='my_library.group_release_dates',
    )
```

4. Edit the `models/__init__.py` file to add a new Python file for the
   configuration settings model:

```
from . import library_book
from . import res_config_settings
```

5. To extend the core configuration wizard by adding new options to it, add
   the `models/res_config_settings.py` file with this code:

```
from odoo import models, fields

class ConfigSettings(models.TransientModel):
    _inherit = 'res.config.settings'
    group_release_dates = fields.Boolean(
        "Manage book release dates",
        group='base.group_user',
        implied_group='my_library.group_release_dates',
    )
    module_note = fields.Boolean("Install Notes app")
```

6. To make the options available in the UI, add
   `views/res_config_settings.xml`, which extends the form view:

```
<?xml version="1.0" encoding="utf-8"?>
<odoo>
    <record id="view_general_config_library"
model="ir.ui.view">
```

```
        <field name="name">Configuration: add Library
options</field>
        <field name="model">res.config.settings</field>
        <field name="inherit_id"
ref="base_setup.res_config_settings_view_form" />
        <field name="arch" type="xml">
            <div id="business_documents" position="before">
                <h2>Library</h2>
                <div class="row mt16 o_settings_container">
                    <!-- Release Dates option -->
                    <div class="col-12 col-lg-6
o_setting_box">
                        <div class="o_setting_left_pane">
                            <field name="group_release_dates"
class="oe_inline"/>
                        </div>
                        <div class="o_setting_right_pane">
                            <label for="group_release_dates"/>
                            <div class="text-muted">
                                Enable relase date feature on
books
                            </div>
                        </div>
                    </div>
                    <!-- Release Dates option -->
                    <div class="col-12 col-lg-6
o_setting_box">
                        <div class="o_setting_left_pane">
                            <field name="module_note"
class="oe_inline"/>
                        </div>
                        <div class="o_setting_right_pane">
                            <label for="module_note"/>
                            <div class="text-muted">
                                Install note module
                            </div>
                        </div>
                    </div>
                </div>
            </div>
        </field>
    </record>
</odoo>
```

After upgrading the add-on module, the two new configuration options should be available at **Settings | General Settings**. The screen should look like this:

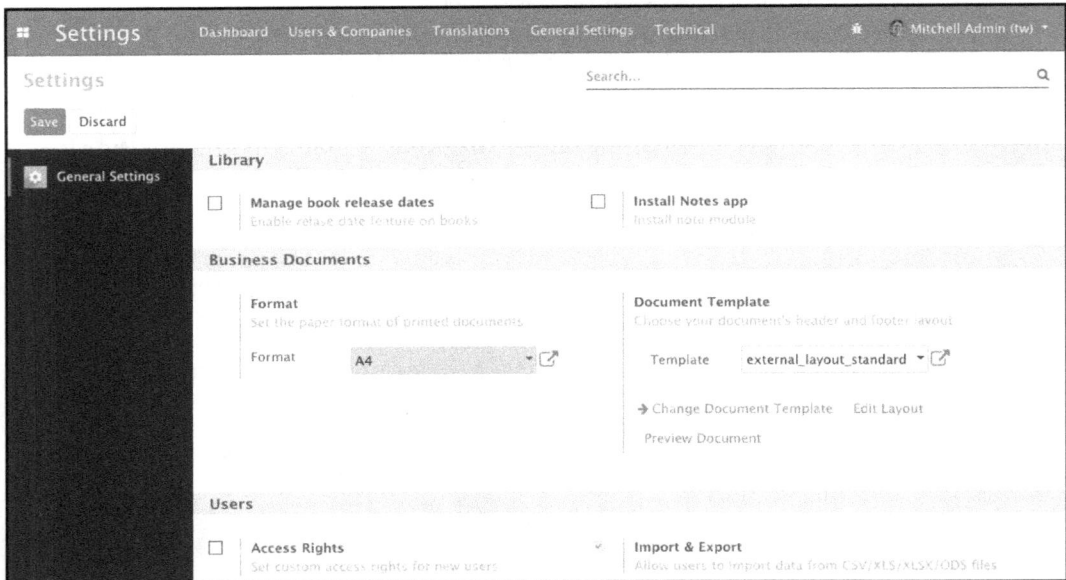

How it works...

The core `base` module provides the `res.config.settings` model, providing the business logic behind the option activation option. The `base_setup` add-on module uses the `res.config.settings` model to provide several basic configuration options to make available in a new database. It also makes the **Settings | General Settings** menu available.

The `base_setup` module adapts `res.config.settings` to a central management dashboard, so we need to extend it to add our own configuration settings.

If we decide to create a specific settings form for the Library app, we can still inherit from the `res.config.settings` model with a different `_name`, and then for the new model, provide the menu option and form view for just those settings. We already saw this method in the *Adding your own settings options* recipe of `Chapter 9`, *Advanced Server-Side Development Techniques*.

We used two different methods to activate the features: one by enabling a security group and making the feature visible to the user, and the other by installing an add-on module that provides the feature. The logic to handle both these cases is provided by the base `res.config.settings` model.

The first recipe step adds the `base_setup` add-on module to the dependencies, since it provides extensions to the `res.config.settings` model we want to use. It also adds an additional XML data file that we will need to add the new options to the **General Settings** form.

In the second step, we create a new security group, **Library: release date feature**. The feature to activate should be visible only for that group so it will be hidden until the group is enabled.

In our example, we want the book release date to be available only when the corresponding configuration option is enabled. To achieve this, we use the `groups` attribute on the field so that it is made available only for this security group. We did this at the model level so that it is automatically applied to all the UI views where the field is used.

Finally, we extend the `res.config.settings` model to add the new options. Each option is a `Boolean` field, and its name must begin either by `group_` or `module_`, according to what we want it to do.

The `group_` option field should have an `implied_group` attribute and should be a string that contains a comma-separated list of XML IDs for the security groups to activate when it is enabled. The XML IDs must be in a form that is complete, with the module name, dot, and identifier name, such as `module_name.identifier`.

We can also provide a `group` attribute to specify for which security groups the feature will be enabled. It will be enabled for all the Employee-based groups if no groups are defined. Thus, the related groups won't apply to portal security groups, since these don't inherit on the Employee base security group, like the other regular security groups.

The mechanism behind the activation is quite simple: it adds the security group in the `group` attribute to the `implied_group`, thus making the related feature visible to the corresponding users.

The `module_` option field does not require any additional attributes. The remaining part of the field name identifies the module to be installed when activating the option. In our example, `module_note` will install the note module.

Unchecking the box will uninstall the module without warning, which can cause data loss (models or fields and module data will be removed as a consequence). To avoid unchecking the box by accident, the `secure_uninstall` community module (from `https://github.com/OCA/server-tools`) prompts the user for a password before uninstalling the add-on module.

The last step of this recipe adds the to the **General Settings** form view, just before the **Business documents** group, which has `id="business_documents"`. We used this `id` for the view inheritance. It creates its own `div` with the module name as the ID, which is good practice because then other modules that extend `my_library` can easily add their own configuration items to this `div`.

There's more...

Configuration settings can also have fields named with the `default_` prefix. When one of these has a value, the ORM will set it as a global default. The settings field should have a `default_model` attribute to identify the model affected, and the field name after the `default_` prefix identifies the model's field that will have the default value set.

Additionally, fields with none of the three prefixes mentioned can be used for other settings, but you will need to implement the logic to populate their values, using the `get_default_` name prefixed methods, and to act when their values are edited, using the `set_` name prefixed methods.

For those who would like to go deeper into the details of the configuration settings, the best documentation is in Odoo's source code in `./odoo/addons/base/models/res_config.py`, which is extensively commented on with all the details explained.

Accessing recordsets as a superuser

In the previous recipes, we saw security techniques, such as access rules, security groups, and record rules. With these techniques, you can avoid unauthorized access. Sometimes, however, you have complex business cases in which you want to access or modify records, even if the user doesn't have access to them. For example, let's say the public user doesn't have access to the leads records, but by submitting the website form, the user can generate leads records in the backend.

Using `sudo()`, you can access recordsets as a superuser. We already saw `sudo()` in the *Changing the user that performs an action* recipe of `Chapter 9`, *Advanced Server-Side Development Techniques*. Here, we will see that even if you have given ACL rules or have added a security group on the field, you can still get access through `sudo()`.

How to do it...

We will use the same `my_library` module from the previous recipe. We already have an ALC rule that gives read-only read to the normal user. We will add a new field with security groups so that only the librarian has access to it. After that, we will modify the field value by the normal user. Follow these steps to achieve this:

1. Add the new field in the `library.book` model:

```
report_missing = fields.Text(
    string="Book is missing",
    groups='my_library.group_library_librarian')
```

2. Add the field in the form view:

```
<field name="report_missing"/>
```

3. Add the `report_missing_book()` method in the `library.book` model:

```
def report_missing_book(self):
    self.ensure_one()
    message = "Book is missing (Reported by: %s)" %
self.env.user.name
    self.sudo().write({
        'report_missing': message
    })
```

4. Add the button in the form view to trigger this method from the user interface:

```
<button name="report_missing_book"
    string="Report Missing Book"
    type="object"/>
```

Restart the server and update the module to apply these changes.

How it works...

In *steps 1* and *2*, we added a new field called report_missing in the model and form view. Note that we put the my_library.group_library_librarian group on the field in Python, so this field is only accessible by the Librarian user.

In the next step, we added the report_missing_book() method, in the body of which we updated the value of the report_missing field. Note that we used sudo() before calling the write method.

Finally, we added a button in the form view to trigger the method from the user interface.

To test this implementation, you need to log in with the non-librarian user. If you have loaded the database with demonstration data, you can log in with the demo user and then click on the **Missing book report** button in the form view of the book. Upon clicking that button, the report_missing_book() method will be called, and this will write the message in the report_missing field, even if the user doesn't have proper rights. You can check the value of the field through the admin user because this field will be hidden in the demo user.

On a click of the **Report Missing Book** button, we will get the recordset of the current book in the report_missing_book() method as an argument, self. Before writing the values in the book recordset, we used self.sudo(). This will return the same recordset but with a different environment. This recordset will have the environment from the superuser, and it will bypass all access rules and record rules. Because of that, the non-librarian user will be able to write in the book record. Even the model's logging field, write_uid, will have the value of the superuser.

There's more...

You need to be extra careful when you use sudo() because it bypasses all the access rights. In a multi-company environment, it can create issues if you don't use it properly. If you want to access the record set as another user, you can pass the ID of that user in sudo, such as self.sudo(uid). This will return a recordset with the environment of that user. This way, it will not bypass all access rules and record rules, but you can perform all the actions that are allowed to that user.

Hiding view elements and menus based on groups

In the previous recipes, we've seen how you we hide fields from some users with group arguments in the Python field definition. There is another way to hide fields in the user interface: by adding security groups on the XML tags in the view definition. You can also use security groups on menus to hide them from a particular user.

Getting ready

For this recipe, we will reuse the `my_library` add-on module from the previous recipe. In the previous recipe, we added a button in the `<header>` tag. We will hide that whole header from a few users by adding a groups attribute to it.

Add the model, the views, and the menus for the `book.category` model. We will hide the category menus from a user. Refer to `Chapter 5`, *Application Models*, to see how to add model views and menus.

How to do it...

Follow given steps to hide elements based in security groups:

1. Add a groups attribute on `<header>` to hide it from other users:

   ```
   ...
   <header groups="my_library.group_library_user">
   ...
   ```

2. Add the groups attribute on the `<menuitem>` book category to display it only for librarian users:

   ```
   <menuitem name="Book Categories"
       id="library_book_category_menu"
       parent="library_base_menu"
       action="library_book_category_action"
       groups="my_library.group_library_librarian"/>
   ```

Restart the server and update the module to apply the changes.

How it works...

In the first step, we added `groups="my_library.group_library_user"` on the `<header>` tag. This means that the whole header part will only be visible to library users and librarians. Normal backend users who don't have `group_library_user` will not see the header part.

In *step 2*, we added the `groups="my_library.group_library_librarian"` attribute on `menuitem`. This means that this menu is only visible to librarian users.

You can use the groups attribute almost everywhere, including `<field>`, `<notebook>`, `<group>`, `<menuitems>`, or any tag from the view architecture. Odoo will hide those elements if the user doesn't have that group. You can use the same group attributes in web pages and QWeb reports, which will be covered in `Chapter 13`, *Automation, Workflows, and Printouts,* and `Chapter 15`, *CMS Website Development.*

As we saw in the *Accessing recordsets as a superuser* recipe of this chapter, we can hide fields from some users using the groups argument in the Python field definition. Note that there is a big difference between security groups on fields and Python security groups in views. Security groups in Python provide real security; unauthorized users can't even access the fields through ORM or through RPC calls. However, the groups in views are just for improving usability. Fields hidden through groups in the XML file are still accessible through RPC or ORM.

12
Internationalization

In this chapter, we will cover the following recipes:

- Installing a language and configuring user preferences
- Configuring language-related settings
- Translating texts through a web client user interface
- Exporting translation strings to a file
- Using gettext tools to make translations easier
- Importing translation files into Odoo

Many of these actions can be done either from the web client user interface or from the command line. Wherever possible, we will show you how to use both of these options.

Installing a language and configuring user preferences

Odoo is localization-ready, meaning that it supports several languages and locale settings, such as date and number formats.

When first installed, only the default English language is available. To have other languages and locales available to users, we need to install them.

Getting ready

We need to have developer mode activated. If it's not, activate it as indicated in the *Activating the Odoo developer tools* recipe from Chapter 1, *Installing the Odoo Development Environment*.

How to do it...

To install a new language in an Odoo instance, follow these steps:

1. Select the **Settings | Translations | Load a Translation** menu option. In the resulting dialog box, select the language to install from the list of available languages. If **Website** is installed, you will also be given the option to pick the websites where the language is available:

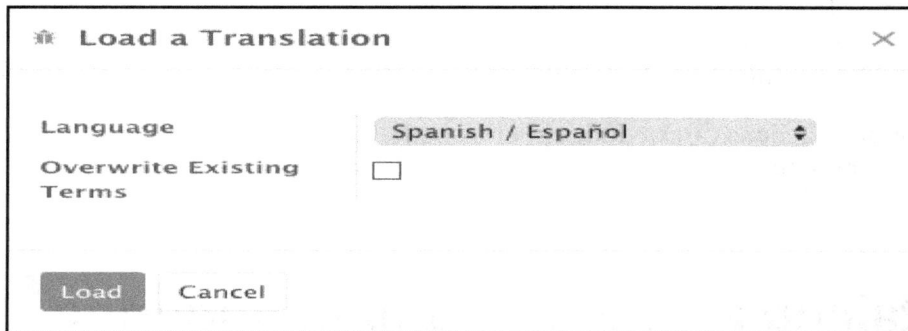

2. Now, click on the **Load** button and the language will be installed:

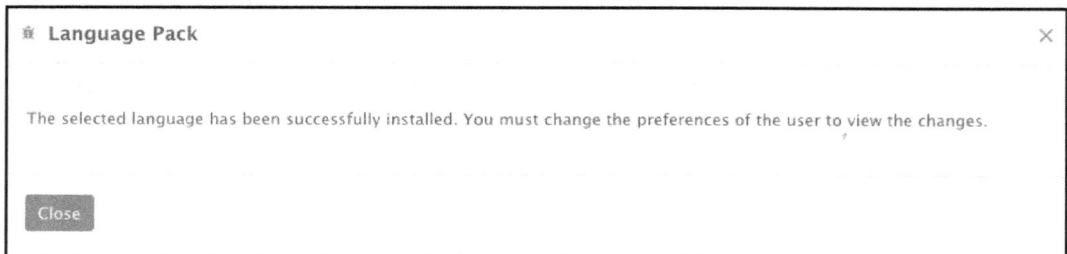

3. New languages can also be installed from the command line. The equivalent command for the preceding steps is as follows:

```
$ ./odoo-bin -d mydb --load-language=es_ES
```

4. To set the language used by a user, go to **Settings | Users & Companies | Users** and, in the **Preferences** tab of the **User** form, set the **Language** field value. While you're at it, you can use this opportunity to set the user's **Timezone**:

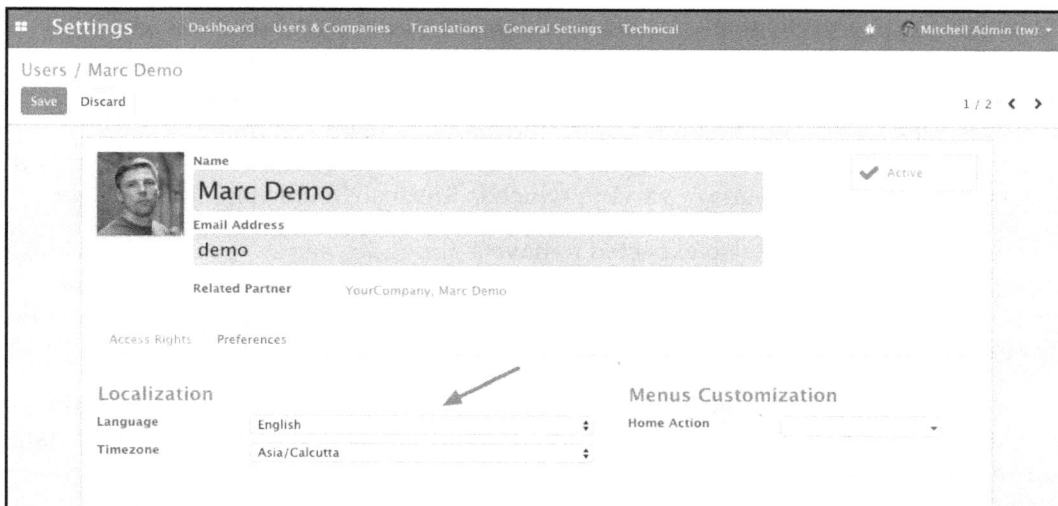

Users can also set these configurations themselves through the **Preferences** menu option. This is available when they click on the username at the top-right of the web client window.

How it works...

Users can have their own language and time zone preferences. The former is used to translate user interface text into the chosen language and apply local conventions for float and monetary fields.

Before a language is made available for the user to select, it must be installed with the **Load a Translation** feature. The list of available languages can be seen with the **Settings | Translations | Languages** menu option. The ones with the active flag set are installed.

Each Odoo add-on module is responsible for providing its own translation resources that should be placed inside an `i18n` subdirectory. Each language's data should be in a `.po` file. In our example, for the Spanish language, the translation data is loaded from the `es_ES.po` data file.

Odoo also supports the notion of **base language**. For example, if we have an `es.po` file for Spanish and an `es_MX.po` file for Mexican Spanish, then `es.po` is detected as the base language for `es_MX.po`. When the Mexican Spanish language is installed, both data files are loaded; first the one for the base language and then the specific language. Thus, the specific language translation file only needs to contain the strings that are specific to the language variant, which is Mexican Spanish in our example.

The `i18n` subdirectory is also expected to have a `<module_name>.pot` file, providing a template for translations and containing all the translatable strings. The *Exporting translation strings to a file* recipe of this chapter explains how to export the translatable strings to generate this file.

When an additional language is installed, the corresponding resources are loaded from all installed add-on modules and stored in the **Translated Terms** model. Its data can be viewed (and edited) within the **Settings | Translations | Application Terms | Translated Terms** menu option (note that this menu is only visible in developer mode).

Translation files for the installed languages are also loaded when a new add-on module is installed or an existing add-on module is upgraded.

There's more...

Translation files can be reloaded without upgrading the add-on modules by repeating the **Load a Translation** action. This can be used if you have updated translation files and don't want to go through the trouble of upgrading the modules (and all their dependencies).

If the **Overwrite Existing Terms** checkbox is left empty, only the newly translated strings are loaded. Thus, the changed translated strings won't be loaded. Check the box if you want the already existing translations to also be loaded and overwrite the currently loaded translations. Note that this can potentially be problematic if someone changes the translations manually through the interface.

The previous checkbox exists because we can edit specific translations by going to the **Settings | Translations | Application Terms | Translated Terms** menu item, or by using the **Technical Translation** shortcut option in the **Debug** menu. Translations that are added or modified in this way won't be overwritten unless the language is reloaded with the **Overwrite Existing Terms** checkbox enabled.

It can be useful to know that add-on modules can also have an i18n_extra subdirectory with extra translations. First, the .po files in the i18n subdirectory are downloaded. Then, Odoo ORM downloads files for the base language and, after that, for the language variant. Following this, the .po files in the i18n_extra subdirectory are downloaded, first for the base language and then for the language variant. The last string translation that's loaded is the one that prevails.

Configuring language-related settings

Languages and their variations (such as es_MX for Mexican Spanish) also provide locale settings, such as date and number formats.

They come with appropriate defaults, so as long as the user is using the correct language, the locale settings should be the correct ones.

However, you might still want to modify a language's settings. For example, you might prefer to have the user interface in the default English, but want to change the American default date and number formats to match your requirements.

Getting ready

We will need to have developer mode activated. If it's not already activated, activate it as pointed out in the *Activating the Odoo developer tools* recipe from Chapter 1, *Installing the Odoo Development Environment*.

How to do it...

To modify a language's locale settings, follow these steps:

1. To check the installed languages and their configurations, select the **Settings | Translations | Languages** menu option. Clicking on one of the installed languages will open a form with the corresponding settings:

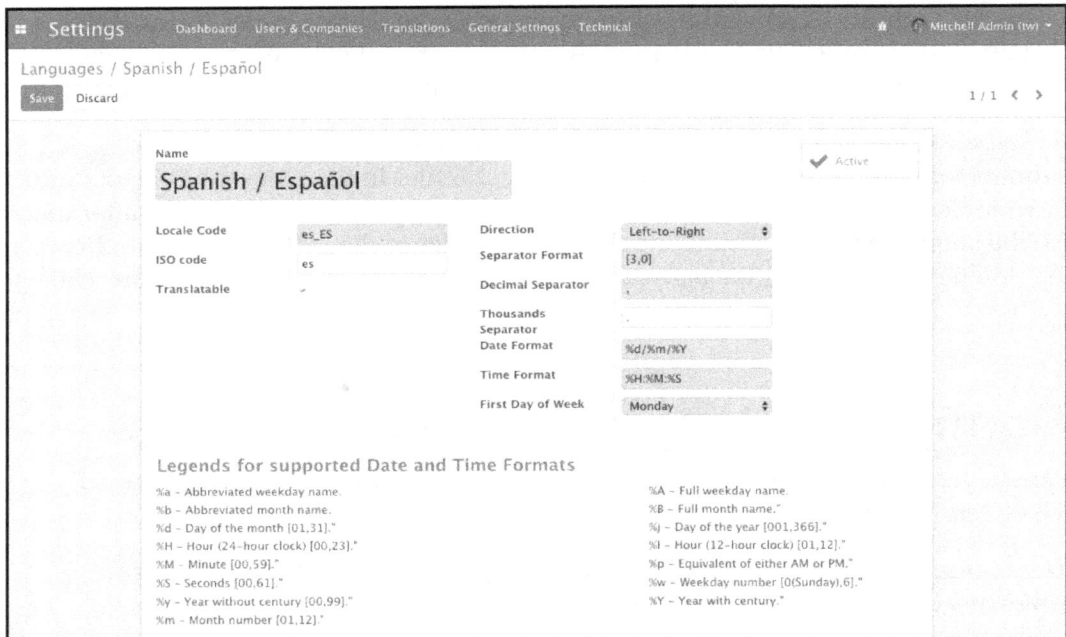

2. Edit the language settings. To change the date to the ISO format, change the **Date Format** to %Y-%m-%d. To change the number format to use a comma as a decimal separator, modify the **Decimal Separator** and **Thousands Separator** fields accordingly.

How it works...

When signing in and creating a new Odoo user session, the user language is checked in the user preferences and set in the lang context key. This is then used to format the output appropriately—the source texts are translated into the user language, and the dates and numbers are formatted according to the language's current locale settings.

There's more...

Server-side processes are able to modify the context in which actions are run. For example, to get a record set where the dates are formatted according to the American English format, independent of the current user's language preference, you can do the following:

```
en_records = self.with_context(lang='en_US').search([])
```

For more details, refer to the *Calling a method with a modified context* recipe from `Chapter 10`, *Advanced Server-Side Development Techniques*.

Translating texts through the web client user interface

The simplest way to translate is to use the translation feature provided by the web client. These translation strings are stored in the database and can later be exported to a `.po` file, either to be included in an add-on module or just to later be imported back manually.

Text fields can have translatable content, meaning that their value will depend on the current user's language. We will also see how to set the language-dependent values on these fields.

Getting ready

We will need to have developer mode activated. If it's not, activate it as pointed out in *Activating the Odoo developer tools* recipe in `Chapter 1`, *Installing the Odoo Development Environment*.

How to do it...

We will demonstrate how to translate terms through the web client using the **User Groups** feature as an example:

1. Navigate to the screen you want to translate. As an example, we will open the Groups view via the **Settings | Users & Companies | Groups** menu item.

2. In the top menu bar, click on the **Debug** menu icon and select the **Technical Translation** option:

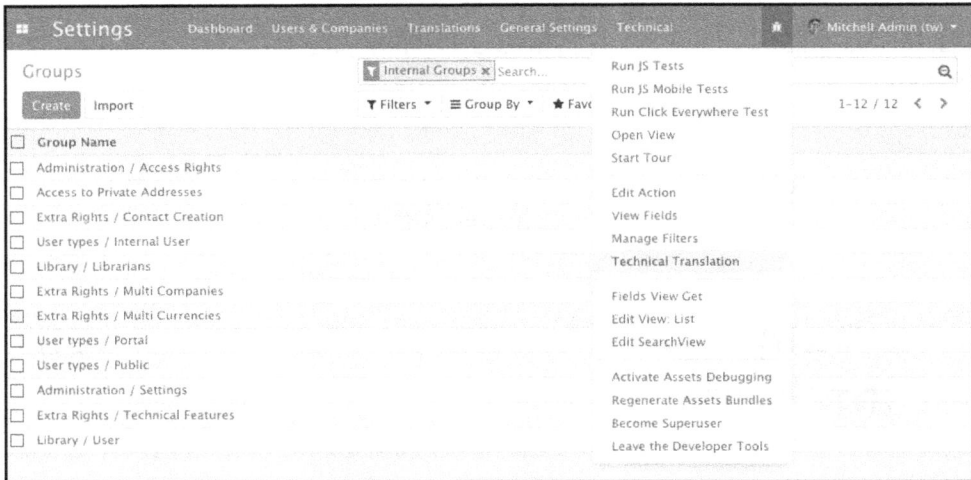

3. A list of the available translation terms for that view will be shown. Edit the **Translation Value** in a line to change (or add) its translation text. If you are looking for a particular source string, use the listed filters to narrow down the displayed text:

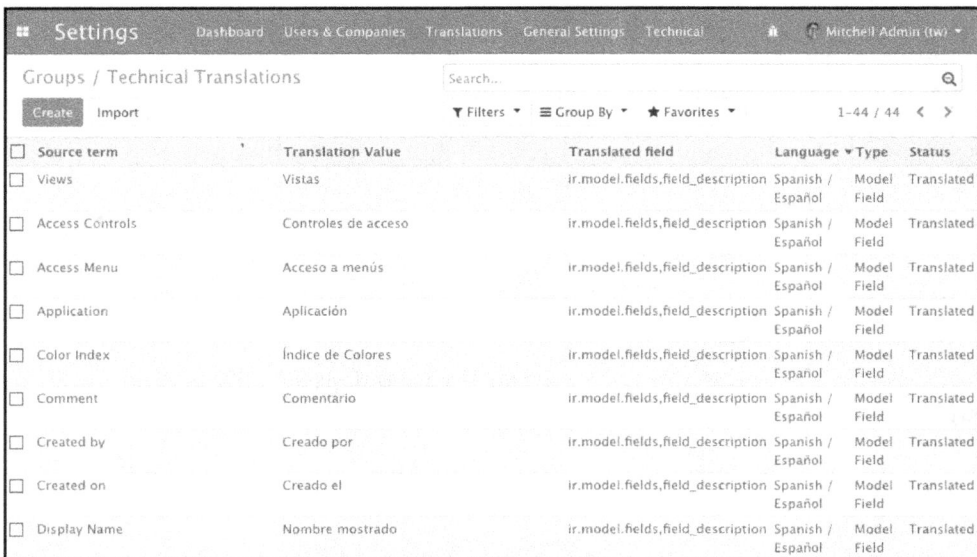

The **Group Name** is a translatable field. Let's translate a record's value to the several languages installed.

4. Navigate to the **User Groups** menu option once more, open one of the group records in the form view, and click on **Edit**:

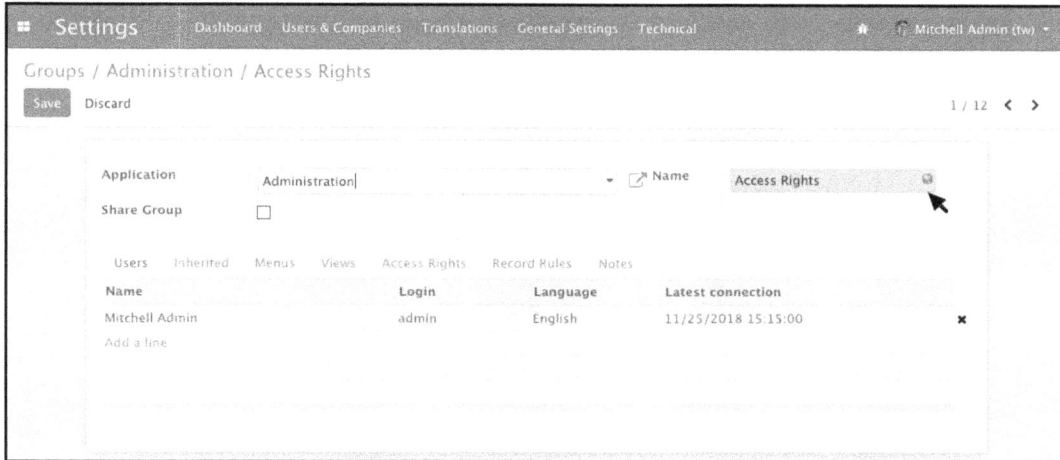

5. Note that the **Name** field has a special icon in the far right. This indicates that it is a translatable field. Clicking on the icon opens a **Translate** list with the different installed languages. This allows us to set the translation for each of those languages.

How it works...

Translated terms are stored in the database table for the ir.translation model. The **Technical Translation** option in the **Debug** menu provides quick access to those terms, in context with the currently selected view.

Similarly, model fields with translatable content will feature an icon to access the list of the installed languages and to set the appropriate value for each language.

Alternatively, the translation terms can be accessed from the **Settings** top menu using the **Translations | Application Terms | Translated Terms** menu option. Here, we can see all the terms that are available for our instance. We should use data filters to locate the terms we might be interested in.

There's more...

Alongside the **Translated Terms** menu option, we can also find the **Generate Missing Terms** option. Selecting this will display a dialog window to provide the desired language, and then launch a process to extract translatable strings from the installed add-on modules and add any new ones to the **Translated Terms** table. It is equivalent to performing the **Export Translation** steps, as described in the *Exporting translation strings to a file* recipe of this chapter.

This can be useful after changing some models or views. By doing this, the new strings will added so that we can translate them.

It can also be used to populate the strings from the en_US default language. We can then make use of the translation terms to replace the original English text with new ones that are better for the end user's specific business vocabulary.

> When editing a QWeb view in a language other than the main website language, you'll notice that you can only change strings. This is because, for other languages, you actually only add translations to the text content of nodes using Odoo's internationalization mechanism.

Exporting translation strings to a file

Translation strings can be exported with or without the translated texts for a selected language. This can either be to include i18n data in a module, or to later perform translations with a text editor or perhaps with a specialized tool.

We will demonstrate how to do this using the standard mail module, so feel free to replace mail with your own module.

Getting ready

We will need to have developer mode activated. If it's not already activated, activate it as demonstrated in the *Activating the Odoo developer tools* recipe in Chapter 1, *Installing the Odoo Development Environment*.

How to do it...

To export the translation terms for the `mail` add-on module, follow these steps:

1. In the web client user interface, from the **Settings** top menu, select the **Translations ᴵ Import/Export ᴵ Export Translation** menu option.

2. In the **Export Translations** dialog box, choose the language translation to export, the file format, and the modules to export. To export a translation template file, select **New Language (Empty translation template)** from the **Language** selection list. It's recommended to use the `.po` format and to export only one add-on module at a time—the **Discuss** module (`mail` is the technical name for the Discuss app) in our example:

3. Once the export process is complete, a new window will be displayed, with a link to download the file and some additional advice.

4. To export a translation template file for the `mail` add-on module from the Odoo command-line interface, enter the following command:

```
$ ./odoo-bin -d mydb --i18n-export=mail.po --modules=mail
$ mv mail.po ./addons/mail/i18n/mail.pot
```

5. To export the translation template file for a language—`es_ES` for Spanish, for example—from the Odoo command-line interface, enter the following command:

```
$ ./odoo-bin -d mydb --i18n-export=es_ES.po --modules=mail
   --language=es_ES
$ mv es_ES.po ./addons/mail/i18n
```

How it works...

The **Export Translation** feature does two things: extracts the translatable strings from the target modules, adding the new ones in the `ir.translation` model, and then creates a file with the translation terms. This can be done both from the web client and the command-line interface.

When exporting from the web client, we can choose to either export an empty translation template, that is, a file with the strings to translate along with empty translations, or export a language, resulting in a file with the strings to translate, along with the translation for the selected language.

The file formats that are available are CSV, PO, and TGZ. The TGZ file format exports a compressed file that contains a `<name>/i18n/` directory structure with the PO or POT file.

The CSV format can be useful for performing translations using a spreadsheet, but the format to use in the add-on modules is PO files. These are expected to be placed inside the `i18n` subdirectory. They are then automatically loaded once the corresponding language is installed. When exporting these PO files, we should export only one module at a time. The PO file is also a popular format supported by translation tools, such as Poedit.

Translations can also be exported directly from the command line, using the `--i18n-export` option. This recipe shows how to extract both the template files and the translated language files.

In *step 4* of this recipe, we exported a template file. The `--i18n-export` option expects the path and the file name to export. Bear in mind that the file extension is required to be either CSV, PO, or TGZ. This option requires the `-d` option, which specifies the database to use. The `--modules` option is also needed to indicate the add-on modules to export. Note that the `--stop-after-init` option is not needed, since the export command automatically returns to the command line when finished.

This exports a template file. The Odoo module expects this exported template in the `i18n` folder with the `.pot` extension. When working on a module, after the export operation, we usually want to move the exported PO file to the module's `i18n` directory with a `<module>.pot` name.

In *step 5*, the `--language` option was also used. With it, instead of an empty translation file, the translated terms for the selected language were also exported. One use case for this is to perform some translations through the web client user interface using the **Technical Translation** feature, and then export and include them in the module.

There's more...

Text strings in view and model definitions are automatically extracted for translation. For models, the `_description` attribute, the field names (the `string` attribute), help text, and selection field options are extracted, as well as the user texts for model constraints (`_constraints` and `_sql_constraints`).

Text strings to translate inside Python or JavaScript code can't be automatically detected, so the code should identify those strings, wrapping them inside the underscore function.

In a module Python file, we should ensure that it is imported with the following:

```
from odoo import _
```

It can then be used wherever a translatable text is used with something like this:

```
_('Hello World')
```

For strings that use additional context information, we should use Python string interpolation, as shown here:

```
_('Hello %s') % 'World'
```

Note that the interpolation should go outside the translation function. For example, `_("Hello %s" % 'World')` is wrong. String interpolations should also be preferred to string concatenation so that each interface text is just one translation string.

> Be careful with the `Selection` fields! If you pass an explicit list of values to the field definition, the displayed strings are automatically flagged for translation. On the other hand, if you pass a method that returns the list of values, the display strings must be explicitly marked for translation.

Regarding manual translation work, any text file editor will do, but using an editor that specifically supports the PO file syntax makes the work easier by reducing the risk of formatting errors. Such editors include those listed here:

- **POEDIT**: https://poedit.net/
- **Emacs (PO-mode)**:
  https://www.gnu.org/software/gettext/manual/html_node/PO-Mode.html
- **Lokalize**: http://i18n.kde.org/tools
- **Gtranslator**: https://wiki.gnome.org/Apps/Gtranslator

Using gettext tools to make translations easier

The PO file format is part of the `gettext` internationalization and localization system that's commonly used in Unix-like systems. This system includes tools to ease the translation work.

This recipe demonstrates how to use these tools to help translate our add-on modules. We want to use it on a custom module, so the `my_library` we created in Chapter 4, *Creating Odoo Add-On Modules*, is a good candidate. However, feel free to replace it with some other custom module you have at hand, replacing the recipe's `my_library` references as appropriate.

How to do it...

To manage translations from the command line, assuming that your Odoo installation is at `~/odoo-work/odoo`, follow these steps:

1. Create a compendium of translation terms for the target language, for example, Spanish. If we name our compendium file `odoo_es.po`, we should write the following code:

```
$ cd ~/odoo-work/odoo  # Use the path to your Odoo
installation
$ find ./ -name es_ES.po | xargs msgcat --use-first |
msgattrib
    -- translated  --no-fuzzy \ -o ./odoo_es.po
```

2. Export the translation template file for the add-on module from the Odoo command-line interface and place it in the module's expected location:

```
$ ./odoo-bin -d mydb --i18n-export=my_module.po --
modules=my_module
$ mv my_module.po ./addons/my_module/i18n/my_module.pot
```

3. If no translation file is available yet for the target language, create the PO translation file, reusing the terms that have been already found and translated in the compendium:

```
$ msgmerge --compendium ./odoo_es.po -o
./addons/my_module/i18n/es_ES.po \
/dev/null ./addons/my_module/i18n/my_module.pot
```

4. If a translation file exists, add the translations that can be found in the compendium:

```
$ mv ./addons/my_module/i18n/es_ES.po /tmp/my_module_es_old.po
$ msgmerge --compendium ./odoo_es.po -
o./addons/my_module/i18n/es_ES.po
    \ /tmp/my_module_es_old.po
./addons/my_module/i18n/my_module.pot
$ rm /tmp/my_module_es_old.po
```

5. To take a peek at the untranslated terms in a PO file, use this:

```
$ msgattrib --untranslated ./addons/my_module/i18n/es_ES.po
```

6. Use your favorite editor to complete the translation.

How it works...

Step 1 uses commands from the `gettext` toolbox to create a translation compendium for the chosen language—Spanish, in our case. It works by finding all the `es_ES.po` files in the Odoo code base, and passing them to the `msgcat` command. We use the `--use-first` flag to avoid conflicting translations (there are a few in the Odoo code base). The result is passed to the `msgattrib` filter. We use the `--translated` option to filter out the untranslated entries and the `--no-fuzzy` option to remove fuzzy translations. We then save the result in `odoo_es.po`.

Step 2 of the preceding section calls `odoo.py` with the `--i18n-export` option. You need to specify a database on the command line, even if one is specified in the configuration file and the `--modules` option, with a comma-separated list of modules to export the translation.

> In the `gettext` world, fuzzy translations are those created automatically by the `msgmerge` command (or other tools) using a proximity match on the source string. We want to avoid these in the compendium.

Step 3 creates a new translation file by using existing translated values found in the compendium. The `msgmerge` command is used with the `--compendium` option to find the `msgid` lines in the compendium files, matching those in the translation template file generated in *step 2*. The result is saved in the `es_ES.po` file.

If you have a preexisting `.po` file for your add-on with translations you would like to preserve, you should rename it and replace the `/dev/null` argument with this file. The renaming procedure is required to avoid using the same file for input and output.

There's more...

This recipe only skims the surface of the rich tools that are available with the GNU `gettext` toolbox. Full coverage is well beyond the scope of this book. If you are interested, the GNU `gettext` documentation contains a wealth of precious information about PO file manipulation, and is available at
`http://www.gnu.org/software/gettext/manual/gettext.html`.

Importing translation files into Odoo

The usual practice to load translations is by placing PO files inside the module's `i18n` subdirectory. Whenever the add-on module is installed or upgraded, the translation files are loaded and the new translated strings are added.

However, there may be cases where we want to directly import a translation file. In this recipe, we will see how to load a translation file, either from the web client or from the command line.

Getting ready

We need to have **Developer Mode** activated. If it's not activated already, activate it as demonstrated in the *Activating the Odoo developer tools* recipe from `Chapter 1`, *Installing the Odoo Development Environment*. We will also need a translation `po` file, which we are going import in this recipe, for example, the `myfile.po` file.

How to do it...

To import the translation terms, follow these steps:

1. In the web client user interface, from the **Settings** top menu, select the **Translations|Import/Export|Import Translation** menu option.
2. In the **Import Translations** dialog box, fill out the language name and the language code, and select the file to import. Finally, click on the **Import** button to perform the action:

3. To import a translation file from the Odoo command-line interface, we must place it inside the server add-ons path and then perform the import:

```
$ mv myfile.po ./addons/
$ ./odoo.py -d mydb --i18n-import="myfile.po" --lang=es_ES
```

How it works...

Import Translation takes a PO or CSV file and loads the translation strings into the `ir.translation` table.

The web client feature asks for the language name, but this is not used in the import process. It also has an overwrite option. If selected, it forces all the translation strings to be imported, even the ones that already exist, overwriting them in the process.

On the command line, the import can be done using the `--i18n-import` option. It must be provided with the path to the file, relative to an add-ons' path directory; `-d` and `--language` (or `-l`) are mandatory. Overwriting can also be achieved by adding the `--i18n-overwrite` option to the command. Note that we didn't use the `--stop-after-init` option here. It is not needed, since the import action stops the server when it finishes.

Automation, Workflows, and Printouts

13

In this chapter, we will cover the following recipes:

- Managing dynamic record stages
- Managing kanban stages
- Adding a quick create form in a kanban card
- Creating interactive kanban cards
- Adding a progress bar on kanban columns
- Using automated actions on time conditions
- Using automated actions on event conditions
- Creating QWeb-based PDF reports

Introduction

Business applications are expected not only to store records but also to manage business workflows. Some objects, such as leads or project tasks, have a lot of records that run in parallel. Having too many records for an object makes it harder to see a clear picture of the business. Odoo has several techniques that can deal with this problem. In this chapter, we will look at how we can set the business workflow with dynamic stages and kanban groups. This will help the user to get an idea about how their business is running.

We will also look at techniques such as server actions and automated actions that can be used by power users or functional consultants to add simpler process automation without the need to create custom add-ons. Finally, we will create QWeb-based PDF reports to print out.

Technical requirements

The technical requirements for this chapter include an online Odoo platform.

All the code used in this chapter can be downloaded from the following GitHub repository, at: `https://github.com/PacktPublishing/Odoo-12-Development-Cookbook-Third-Edition/tree/master/Chapter13`.

Check out the following video to see the Code in Action:

`http://bit.ly/2UICAzA`

Managing dynamic record stages

In `my_library`, we have a `state` field to indicate the current status of the book rent record. This `state` field is limited to the statuses `ongoing` or `returned` and it is not possible to add a new state to the business process. To avoid this, we can use the `many2one` field to give flexibility to designing the kanban workflow of the user's choice.

Getting ready

For this recipe, we will be using the `my_library` module from Chapter 9, *Advanced Server-Side Development Techniques*. That module manages books and their categories. It also records book loans. We added an initial module, `Chapter13/r0_initial_module/my_library`, in the GitHub repository for this book to help you get started: `https://github.com/PacktPublishing/Odoo-12-Development-Cookbook-Third-Edition`.

How to do it...

Follow these simple steps to add stages to the `library.book.rent` module:

1. Add a new model called `library.rent.stage`, as follows:

```
class LibraryRentStage(models.Model):
    _name = 'library.rent.stage'
    _order = 'sequence,name'

    name = fields.Char()
```

```
sequence = fields.Integer()
fold = fields.Boolean()
book_state = fields.Selection(
    [('available', 'Available'),
     ('borrowed', 'Borrowed'),
     ('lost', 'Lost')],
    'State', default="available")
```

2. Add access rights for this new module in the
security/ir.model.access.csv file, as follows:

```
acl_book_rent_stage,library.book_rent_stage_default,model_libr
ary_rent_stage,,1,0,0,0
acl_book_rent_librarian_stage,library.book_rent_stage_libraria
n,model_library_rent_stage,group_librarian,1,1,1,1
```

3. Remove the state field from the library.book.rent model and replace
it with a new stage_id field which is a many2one field and its methods, as
shown in the following example:

```
@api.model
def _default_rent_stage(self):
    Stage = self.env['library.rent.stage']
    return Stage.search([], limit=1)

stage_id = fields.Many2one(
    'library.rent.stage',
    default=_default_rent_stage
)
```

4. Replace the state field in the form view with the stage_id field, as
shown in the following example:

```
<header>
    <field name="stage_id" widget="statusbar"
            options="{'clickable': '1', 'fold_field': 'fold'}"/>
</header>
```

5. Replace the state field in the tree view and replace it with the stage_id
field, as follows:

```
<tree>
    <field name="book_id"/>
    <field name="borrower_id"/>
    <field name="stage_id"/>
</tree>
```

6. Add some initial stages from the `data/library_stage.xml` file. Don't forget to add this file in the manifest, as shown in the following example:

```xml
<?xml version="1.0" encoding="utf-8"?>
<odoo noupdate="1">
    <record id="stage_draft" model="library.rent.stage">
        <field name="name">Draft</field>
        <field name="sequence">1</field>
        <field name="book_state">available</field>
    </record>
    <record id="stage_rent" model="library.rent.stage">
        <field name="name">On rent</field>
        <field name="sequence">5</field>
        <field name="book_state">borrowed</field>
    </record>
    <record id="stage_due" model="library.rent.stage">
        <field name="name">Due</field>
        <field name="sequence">15</field>
        <field name="book_state">borrowed</field>
    </record>
    <record id="stage_returned" model="library.rent.stage">
        <field name="name">Completed</field>
        <field name="sequence">25</field>
        <field name="book_state">available</field>
    </record>
    <record id="stage_lost" model="library.rent.stage">
        <field name="name">Lost</field>
        <field name="sequence">35</field>
        <field name="fold" eval="True"/>
        <field name="book_state">lost</field>
    </record>
</odoo>
```

After installing the module, you will see stages in the form view, as shown in the following screenshot:

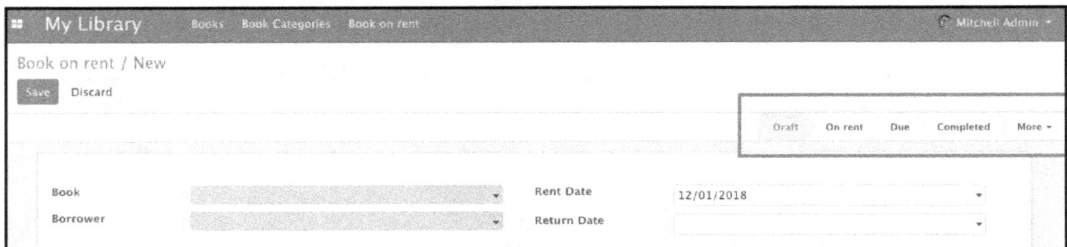

How it works...

As we want to manage the record stages dynamically, we need to create a new model. In step 1, we created a new model called `library.rent.stage` to store the dynamic stages. In this model, we added a few fields. One of these was the `sequence` field, which is used to determine the order of the stages. We also added the Boolean field `fold`, which is used to collapse the stages and put them in a drop-down list. This is very helpful when your business process has lots of stages because it means that you can hide insignificant stages in the drop-down menu by setting this field. We have added a `book_state` field to map the dynamic stage to the `state` of the book. We will use this field in the upcoming section.

The `fold` field is also used in kanban views to display folded kanban columns. Usually, **Work in Progress** items are expected to be in the **Unfolded** stage, and terminated items that are either **Done** or **Cancelled** should be in the **Folded** stage.

> By default, `fold` is the name field that is used to hold the value of the stage fold. You can change this, however, by adding the class attribute `_fold_name = 'is_fold'`.

In step 2, we added the basic access right rules for the new model.

In step 3, we added the `stage_id` many2one field in the `library.book.rent` model. While creating a new loan record, we wanted to set the default stage value to `Draft`. To accomplish this, we added a `_default_rent_stage()` method. This method will fetch the record of the `library.rent.stage` model with the lowest sequence number so, while creating a new record, the stage with the lowest sequence will be displayed as active in the form view.

In step 4, we added the `stage_id` field in form view. By adding the `clickable` option, we made the status bar clickable. We also added an option for the fold field which will allow us to display insignificant stages in the drop-down menu.

In step 5, we added `stage_id` in the tree view.

In step 6, we added the default data for the stages. The user will see these basic stages after installing our module. If you want to learn more about XML data syntax, refer to the *Loading data using XML files* recipe in `Chapter 7`, *Module Data*.

With this implementation, the user can define new stages on the fly. You will need to add views and menus for `library.rent.stage` so you can add new stages from the user interface. Refer to `Chapter 10`, *Backend View* if you don't know how to add views and menus.

If you don't want to do this, the kanban view provides inbuilt features for adding, removing, or modifying stages from the kanban view itself, which is coming up in the next recipe.

There's more...

Notice that we have the `state` field on the `library.book` model. This field is used to represent the status of the book, or, in other words, whether it is available or not. We have added a `book_state` field to map the state of the book with the dynamic stages.

In order to reflect the book state from the stage, we need to override the create and write methods in the `library.book.rent` model, as follows:

```
@api.model
def create(self, vals):
    rent = super(LibraryBookRent, self).create(vals)
    if rent.stage_id.book_state:
        rent.book_id.state = rent.stage_id.book_state
    return rent

@api.multi
def write(self, vals):
    rent = super(LibraryBookRent, self).write(vals)
    if self.stage_id.book_state:
        self.book_id.state = self.stage_id.book_state
    return rent
```

After this, whenever the user changes the stage of any loan record, it will be reflected in the book record.

Managing kanban stages

The kanban board is a simple method to manage workflows. It is organized in columns, each corresponding to stages, and the work items progress from left to right until they are finished. The kanban view, with the stages, provides flexibility because it allows users to choose their own workflows. It provides a full overview of the records in the single screen.

Getting started

For this recipe, we will be using the `my_library` module from the previous recipe. We will add kanban for the `libary.book.rent` model and we will group kanban cards by stage.

How to do it...

Follow the steps below to enable workflows, like kanban for the book rent model.

1. Add a kanban view for `libary.book.rent`, as follows:

```xml
<record id="library_book_rent_view_kanban" model="ir.ui.view">
    <field name="name">Rent Kanban</field>
    <field name="model">library.book.rent</field>
    <field name="arch" type="xml">
        <kanban default_group_by="stage_id">
            <field name="stage_id" />
            <templates>
                <t t-name="kanban-box">
                    <div class="oe_kanban_global_click">
                        <div class="oe_kanban_content">
                            <div class="oe_kanban_card">
                                <div>
                                    <i class="fa fa-user"/>
                                    <b>
                                        <field name="borrower_id" />
                                    </b>
                                </div>
                                <div class="text-muted">
                                    <i class="fa fa-book"/>
                                    <field name="book_id" />
                                </div>
                            </div>
```

```
                        </div>
                      </div>
                    </t>
                 </templates>
              </kanban>
            </field>
         </record>
```

2. Add kanban in the `library_book_rent_action` action, as follows:

```
...
<field name="view_mode">kanban,tree,form</field>
...
```

3. Add the `_group_expand_stages()` method and the `group_expand` attribute in the `stage_id` field, as follows:

```
@api.model
def _group_expand_stages(self, stages, domain, order):
    return stages.search([], order=order)

stage_id = fields.Many2one(
    'library.rent.stage',
    default=_default_rent_stage,
    group_expand='_group_expand_stages'
)
```

Restart the server and update the module to apply the changes. This will enable a kanban board, as shown in the following image:

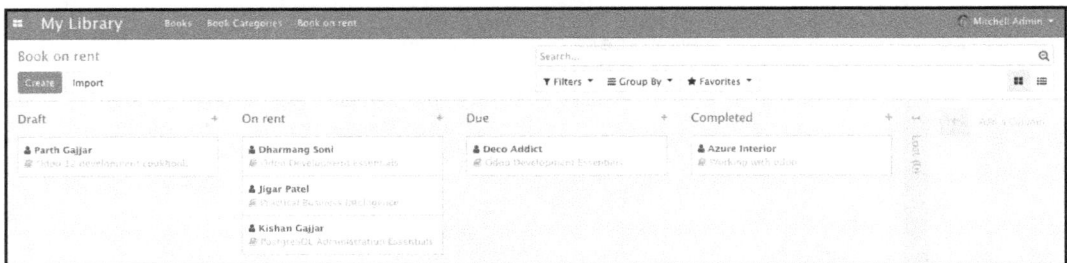

How it works...

In step 1, we added a kanban view for the `library.book.rent` model. Note that we have used `stage_id` as the default group for kanban, so, when the user opens kanban, the kanban cards will be grouped by stage. To find out more about kanban, please refer to `Chapter 10`, *Backend Views*.

In step 2, we added the kanban keyword in the existing action.

In step 3, we added the `group_expand` attribute in the `stage_id` field. We also added a new `_group_expand_stages()` method. `group_expand` changes the behavior of the field grouping. By default, field grouping shows the stages that are being used. For example, if there is no rent record that has the `lost` stage, the grouping will not return that stage, so kanban will not display the `lost` column. But, in our case, we want to display all of the stages, regardless of whether or not they are being used.

The `_group_expand_stages()` function is used to return all the records for the stages. Because of this, the kanban view will display all the stages and you will be able to use workflows by dragging and dropping them.

There's more...

If you play with the kanban board created in this recipe, you will find lots of different features. Some of these are mentioned, as follows:

- You can create a new stage by clicking on the add new column option. The `group_create` option can be used to disable the add column option from the kanban board.
- You can arrange columns in a different order by dragging them by their headers. This will update the sequence field of the `library.rent.stage` model.
- You can `edit` or `delete` columns with the gear icon on the header of a kanban column. The `group_edit` and `group_delete` options can be used to disable this feature.
- The stages that have a true value in the `fold` field will collapse and the column will be displayed like a slim bar. If you click on this, it will expand and display the kanban cards.

- If the model has the Boolean field `active`, it will display the option to archive and unarchive records in the kanban column. The `archivable` option can be used to disable this feature.
- The plus icon on the kanban column can be used to create records directly from the kanban view. The `quick_create` option can be used to disable this feature. For the moment, this feature will not work in our example. This will be solved in the next recipe.

Adding a quick create form in a kanban card

Grouped kanban views provide the quick create feature, which allows us to generate records directly from the kanban view. The plus icon on the column will display an editable kanban card on the column, using which you can create the record. In this recipe, we will see how you can design a quick create kanban form of your choice.

Getting started

For this recipe, we will be using the `my_library` module from the previous recipe. We will use the quick create option in kanban for the `library.book.rent` model.

How to do it...

Follow the steps below to add a custom quick create form for kanban.

1. Create a new minimal form view for the `library.book.rent` model, as follows:

```
<record id="library_book_rent_view_form_minimal"
model="ir.ui.view">
    <field name="name">Library Rent Form</field>
    <field name="model">library.book.rent</field>
    <field name="arch" type="xml">
        <form>
            <group>
                <field name="book_id" domain="[('state', '=',
'available')]"/>
                <field name="borrower_id"/>
            </group>
```

```
        </form>
      </field>
   </record>
```

2. Add quick create options on the `<kanban>` tag, as follows:

```
<kanban default_group_by="stage_id"
quick_create_view="my_library.library_book_rent_view_form_mini
mal"
        on_create="quick_create">
```

Restart the server and update the module to apply the changes. Then, click on the plus icon in the column. This will enable kanban forms, as shown in the following image:

How it works...

In order to create a custom quick create option, we need to create a minimal form view. We did this in *step 1*. We added two required fields, because creating a record without these would generate an error.

In *step 2*, we added this new form view into the kanban view. Using the `quick_create_view` option, you can map the custom form view to the kanban view. We also added one extra option—`on_create="quick_create"`. This option will display a quick create form in the first column when you click on the **Create** button in the control panel. Without this option, the **Create** button will open a form view in editable mode.

You can disable the quick create feature by adding `quick_create="false"` on the kanban tag.

> The `quick_create_view` option was added in Odoo version 12. In previous versions, the quick create option only displayed the name field. If you have some other required fields, you need to override `name_create()` to set other values. You can set default values to the required field if you don't want to override the `name_create()` method.

Creating interactive kanban cards

Kanban cards support all HTML tags, which means you can design them however you like. Odoo provides some built-in ways to make kanban cards more interactive. In this recipe, we will add color options, the star widget, and many2many tags on the kanban card.

Getting started

For this recipe, we will be using the `my_library` module from the previous recipe.

How to do it...

Follow the steps below to create an attractive kanban card.

1. Add a new model to manage the tags for the `library.book.rent` model, as follows:

```
class LibraryRentTags(models.Model):
    _name = 'library.rent.tag'
```

```
name = fields.Char()
color = fields.Integer()
```

2. Add basic access rights for the `library.rent.tag` model, as follows:

```
acl_book_rent_tags,library.book_rent_tags_default,model_librar
y_rent_tag,,1,0,0,0
acl_book_rent_librarian_tags,library.book_rent_tags_librarian,
model_library_rent_tag,group_librarian,1,1,1,1
```

3. Add new fields in the `library.book.rent` model, as follows:

```
color = fields.Integer()
popularity = fields.Selection([
    ('no', 'No Demand'),
    ('low', 'Low Demand'),
    ('medium', 'Average Demand'),
    ('high', 'High Demand')], default="no")
tag_ids = fields.Many2many('library.rent.tag')
```

4. Add fields in the form view, as follows:

```
<field name="popularity" widget="priority"/>
<field name="tag_ids" widget="many2many_tags"
    options="{'color_field': 'color', 'no_create_edit':
True}"/>
```

5. Update the kanban view to display colors, tags, and priorities, as shown in the following example:

```
<kanban default_group_by="stage_id" on_create="quick_create"
quick_create_view="my_library.library_book_rent_view_form_mini
mal">
    <field name="stage_id" />
    <field name="color" />
    <templates>
        <t t-name="kanban-box">
            <div t-attf-
class="#{kanban_color(record.color.raw_value)}
oe_kanban_global_click">
                <div class="o_dropdown_kanban dropdown">
                    <a class="dropdown-toggle o-no-caret btn"
role="button" data-toggle="dropdown">
                        <span class="fa fa-ellipsis-v"/>
                    </a>
                    <div class="dropdown-menu" role="menu">
                        <t t-if="widget.editable">
                            <a role="menuitem" type="edit"
```

```
                 class="dropdown-item">Edit</a>
                              </t>
                              <t t-if="widget.deletable">
                                  <a role="menuitem" type="delete"
class="dropdown-item">Delete</a>
                              </t>
                              <ul class="oe_kanban_colorpicker"
data-field="color"/>
                          </div>
                      </div>
                      <div class="oe_kanban_content">
                          <div class="oe_kanban_card
oe_kanban_global_click">
                              <div>
                                  <i class="fa fa-user"/>
                                  <b>
                                      <field name="borrower_id" />
                                  </b>
                              </div>
                              <div class="text-muted">
                                  <i class="fa fa-book"/>
                                  <field name="book_id" />
                              </div>
                              <span
class="oe_kanban_list_many2many">
                                  <field name="tag_ids"
widget="many2many_tags" options="{'color_field': 'color'}"/>
                              </span>
                              <div>
                                  <field name="popularity"
widget="priority"/>
                              </div>
                          </div>
                      </div>
                  </div>
          </t>
      </templates>
</kanban>
```

The code in bold should be added to the existing kanban view.

Restart the server and update the module to apply the changes. Then, click on the plus icon on the column. It will display kanban, as shown in the following figure:

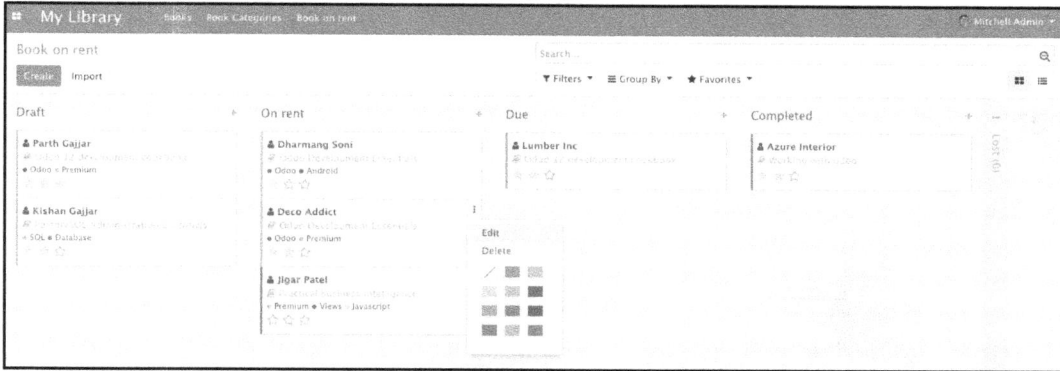

How it works...

In the first two steps, we added new model and security rules for tags. In the third step, we added a few fields in the rent model.

In step 4, we added those fields in the form view. Note that we used the `priority` widget on the `popularity` field, which displays the selection field with star icons. In the `tag_ids` field, we used the `many2many_tags` widget, which displays the many2many field in the form of tags. The `color_field` option is passed to enable the color feature on tags. The value of this option will be the field name where the color index is stored. The `no_create_edit` option will disable the feature of creating new tags via the form view.

In step 5, we improved lots of things. On the kanban card, we added `t-attf-class="#{kanban_color(record.color.raw_value)}`. This will be used to display the color of the kanban card. It uses the value of the color field and generates a class based on that value. For example, if a kanban record has the value 2 in the color field, it will add `kanban_color_2` in the class. After that, we added a drop-down menu to add options such as **Edit**, **Delete**, and the kanban color picker. The edit and delete options are only displayed if the user has proper access rights.

Finally, we added tags and priority to the kanban card. After adding all of this, the kanban card will look like the following screenshot:

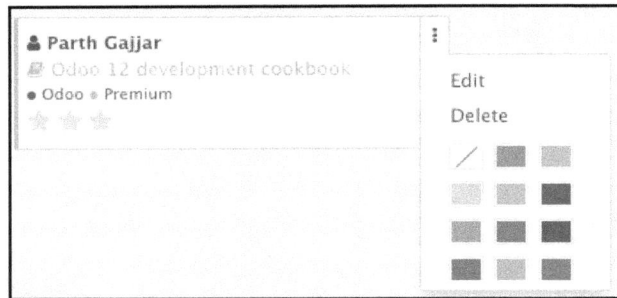

With this card design, you will able to set popularity stars and colors directly from the kanban card.

Adding a progress bar in kanban views

Sometimes, you have tons of records in columns and it is very difficult to get a clear picture of the particular stage. The progress bar can be used to display the status of any column. In this recipe, we will display the progress bar on kanban, based on the field named `popularity`.

Getting started

For this recipe, we will be using the `my_library` module from the previous recipe.

How to do it...

In order to add a progress bar in the kanban columns, you will need to add a progress bar tag in the kanban view definition, as follows:

```
<progressbar
    field="popularity"
    colors='{"low": "success", "medium": "warning", "high":
"danger"}'/>
```

Note that kanban column progress bars were introduced in Odoo version 11. Versions prior to that will not display column progress bars.

Restart the server and update the module to apply the changes. Then, click on the plus icon in the column. This will display the progress bar on the kanban columns, as shown in the following image:

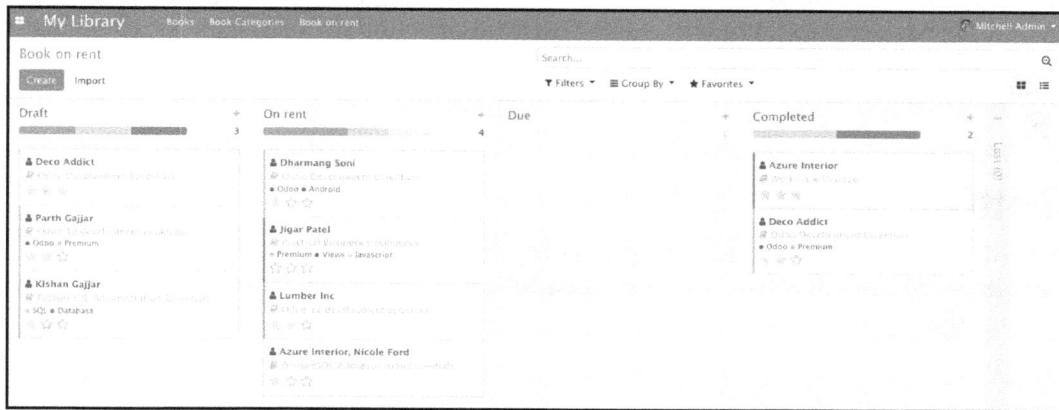

How it works...

Progress bars on kanban columns are displayed based on the values of the field. Progress bars support four colors, so you cannot display more than four states. The available colors are green (success), blue (information), red (danger), and yellow (warning). Then, you need to map colors to the field states. In our example, we mapped three states of the priority field because we didn't want any progress bars for the books that are not in demand.

By default, progress bars show a count of the records on the side. You can see the total of a particular state by clicking on it in the progress bar. Clicking on the progress bar will also highlight the cards for that state. Instead of the count of records, you can also display the sum of the integer or float field. To do this, you need to add the `sum_field` attribute with the field value, such as `sum_field="field_name"`.

Creating server actions

Server actions underpin the Odoo automation tools. They allow us to describe the actions to perform. These actions are then available to be called by event triggers, or to be triggered automatically when certain time conditions are met.

The simplest case is to let the end user perform an action on a document by selecting it from the **More** button. We will create this kind of action for project tasks, to **Set as Priority** by starring the currently selected task and setting a deadline on it for three days from now.

Getting ready

We will need an Odoo instance with the Project app installed. We will also need the **Developer Mode** activated. If it's not already activated, activate it in the Odoo Settings dashboard.

How to do it...

To create a server action and use it from the **More** menu, follow these steps:

1. On the **Settings** top menu, select the **Technical | Actions | Server Actions** menu item, and click on the **Create** button at the top of the record list, as shown in the following screenshot:

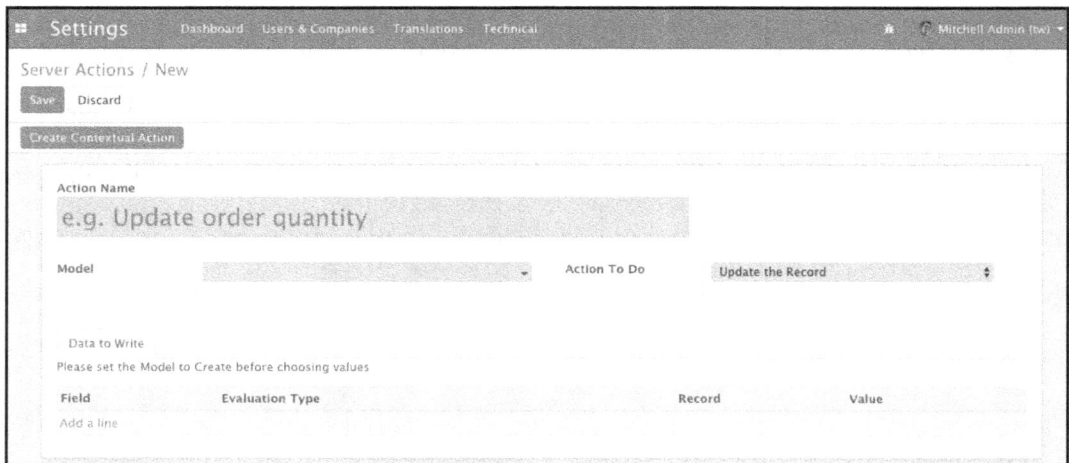

2. Fill out the server action form with these values:
   - **Action Name**: **Set as Priority**
   - **Base Model**: **Task**
   - **Action To Do**: **Update the Record**

3. In the server action, under the **Data to write** tab, add the following lines:
   - As the first value, we will enter the following parameters:
     - **Field**: `Deadline`
     - **Evaluation Type**: `Python expression`
     - **Value**: `datetime.date.today() + datetime.timedelta(days=3)`
   - As the second value, we will enter the following parameters:
     - **Field**: `Priority`
     - **Evaluation Type**: `Value`
     - **Value**: `1`

The following screenshot shows the entered values:

4. Save the server action and click on the **Create contextual action** button in the top left to make it available in the project task's **More** button.

5. To try it out, go to the **Project** top menu, select the **Search | Tasks** menu item, and open a random task. By clicking on the **More** button, we should see the **Set as Priority** option as shown in the following image. Selecting this will star the task and change the deadline date to three days from now:

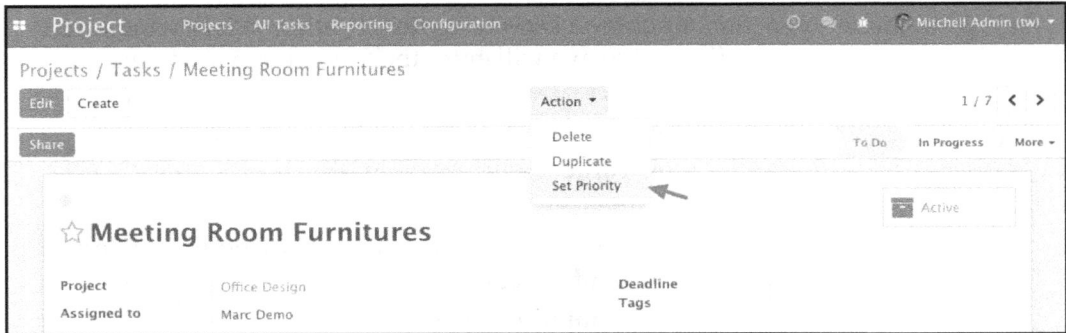

How it works...

Server actions work on a model, so one of the first things to do is to pick the **Base Model** we want to work with. In our example, we used project tasks.

Next, we should select the type of action to perform. There are a few options available:

- **Execute Python Code** allows you to write arbitrary code to execute, when none of the other options are flexible enough for what we need.
- **Create a new Record** allows you to create a new record on the current model, or on another model.
- **Update the Record** allows you to set values on the current record, or on another record.
- **Send Email** allows you to choose an email template. It will be used to send out an email when the action is triggered.
- **Execute several actions** can be used to trigger a client or window action, just like when a menu item is clicked on.
- **Add Followers** allows users or channels to subscribe to the record.
- **Create Next Activity** allows you create a new activity. This will be displayed in the chatter.

For our example, we used **Update the Record** to set some values on the current record. We set the **Priority** to 1 to star the task, and set a value on the **Deadline** field. This one is more interesting, because the value to use is evaluated from a Python expression. Our example makes use of the datetime Python module (https://docs.python.org/2/library/datetime.html) to compute the date three days from today.

Arbitrary Python expressions can be used there, as well as in several of the other action types available. For security reasons, the code is checked by the safe_eval function implemented in the odoo/tools/safe_eval.py file. This means that some Python operations may not be allowed, but this rarely proves to be a problem.

There's more...

The Python code is evaluated in a restricted context, where the following objects are available to use:

- env: This is a reference for the Environment object, just like self.env in a class method.
- model: This is a reference to the model class the server action acts upon. In our example, it is equivalent to self.env['project.task].
- Warning: This is a reference to openerp.exceptions.Warning, allowing for validations that block unintended actions. It can be used as raise Warning('Message!').
- record or records: This provides references to the current record or records, allowing you to access their field values and methods.
- log: This is a function to log messages in the ir.logging model, allowing for database-side logging-on actions.
- datetime, dateutil, and time: These provide access to the Python libraries.

Using Python code server actions

Server actions have several types available, but executing arbitrary Python code is the most flexible. Used wisely, it empowers the users with the capability to implement advanced business rules from the user interface, without the need to create specific add-on modules to install that code.

We will demonstrate using this type of server action by implementing a server action that sends reminder notifications to the followers of a project task.

Getting ready

We will need an Odoo instance with the Project app installed.

How to do it...

To create a Python code server action, follow these steps:

1. Create a new server action. In the **Settings** menu, select the **Technical | Actions | Server Actions** menu item, and click on the **Create** button at the top of the record list.
2. Fill out the **Server Action** form with the following values:
   - **Action Name: Send Reminder**
   - **Base Model: Task**
   - **Action To Do: Execute Python Code**

3. In the **Python code** text area, remove the default text and replace it with the following code:

```
if not record.date_deadline:
    raise Warning('Task has no deadline!')
delta = record.date_deadline - datetime.date.today()
days = delta.days
if days==0:
    msg = 'Task is due today.'
elif days < 0:
    msg = 'Task is %d day(s) late.' % abs(days)
else:
    msg = 'Task will be due in %d day(s).' % days
record.message_post(body=msg, subject='Reminder',
subtype='mt_comment')
```

The following screenshot shows the entered values:

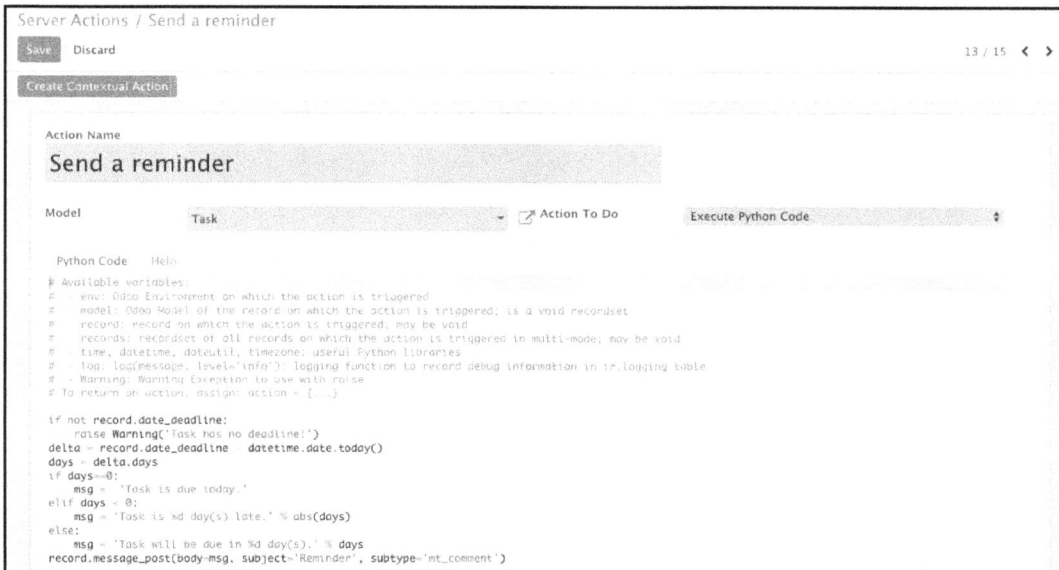

4. Save the **Server Action** and click on **Create Contextual Action** in the top-right to make it available in the project task's **More** button.
5. Now, click on the **Project** top menu and select the **Search | Tasks** menu item. Pick a random task, set a deadline date on it, and then try the **Send Reminder** option in the **More** button.

How it works...

The *Creating server actions* recipe of this chapter provides a detailed explanation of how to create a server action in general. For this particular type of action, we need to pick the **Execute Python Code** option and then write the code to run the text area.

The code can have multiple lines, as is the case in our recipe, and it runs in a context that has references to objects such as the current record object or the session user. The references available are described in the *Creating server actions* recipe.

The code we used computes the number of days from the current date until the deadline date and uses that to prepare an appropriate notification message. The last line does the actual posting of the message in the task's message wall. The subtype='mt_comment' argument is needed for email notifications to be sent to the followers, just like when we use the **New Message** button. If no subtype is given, mt_note is used as a default, posting an internal note without notification, as if we had used the **Log an internal note** button. Refer to Chapter 23, *Manage Emails in Odoo*, to learn more about mailing in Odoo.

There's more...

Python code server actions are a powerful and flexible resource, but they do have some limitations compared to the custom add-on modules.

Because the Python code is evaluated at runtime, if an error occurs, the stack trace is not as informative and can be harder to debug. It is also not possible to insert a break point in the code of a server action using the techniques shown in Chapter 8, *Debugging*, so debugging needs to be done using logging statements. Another concern is that, when trying to track down the cause of behavior in the module code, you may not find anything relevant. In this case, it's probably caused by a server action.

When carrying out a more intensive use of server actions, the interactions can be quite complex, so it is advisable to plan properly and keep them organized.

Using automated actions on time conditions

Automated actions can be used to automatically trigger actions based on time conditions. We can use them to automatically perform some operations on records that meet certain criteria and time conditions.

As an example, we can trigger a reminder notification for project tasks one day before their deadline, if they have one. Let's see how this can be done.

Getting ready

To follow this recipe, we will need to have both the **Project Management** app (which has the technical name `project`) and the **Automated Action Rules** add-on (which has the technical name `base_automation`) already installed, and have the **Developer Mode** activated. We will also need the server action created in the *Using Python code server actions* recipe of this chapter.

How to do it...

To create an automated action with a timed condition on tasks, follow these steps:

1. In the **Settings** menu, select the **Technical|Automation|Automated Actions** menu item, and click on the **Create** button.
2. Fill out the basic information on the **Automated Actions** form:
   - **Rule Name**: **Send notification near deadline**
   - **Related Document Model**: **Task**
   - Select **Based on Time Condition** in the **Trigger Condition** field
   - In **Action To Do**, select **Execute several actions**

3. To set the record criteria, click on the **Edit Domain** button in the **Apply on** section. In the pop-up dialog, set a valid domain expression in the code editor,
   `["&",["date_deadline","!=",False],["stage_id.fold","=",Fal se]]`, and click on the **Save** button. When changing to another field, the information on the number of records meeting the criteria is updated, and displays **Record(s)** buttons. By clicking on the records button, we can check the records list of the records meeting the domain expression.
4. To set the time condition on the **Trigger Date**, select the field to use, which is **Deadline**, and set the **Delay After Trigger Date** to **-1 Days**.

5. On the **Actions** tab, under **Server actions to run**, click on **Add an item** and pick **Send Reminder** from the list that should have been created previously. If not, we can still create the server action to run using the **Create** button, as shown in the following screenshot:

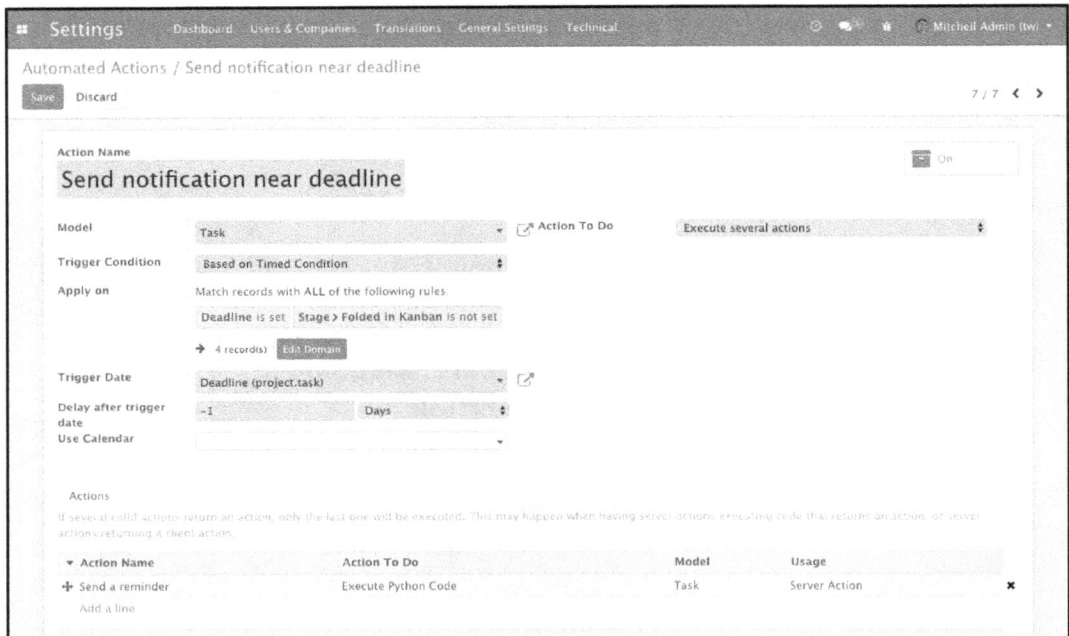

6. Click on **Save** to save the automated action.
7. Perform the following steps to try it out:
    1. Go to the **Project** menu, go to **Search | Tasks**, and set a deadline on a task with the date in the past.
    2. Go to the **Settings** menu, click on the **Technical | Automation | Scheduled Actions** menu item, find the **Base Action Rule: Check and execute** action in the list, open its form view, and press on the **Run Manually** button in the top-left. This forces timed automated actions to be checked now. This is shown in the following screenshot. Note that this should work on a newly created demo database, but might not work this way in an existing database:

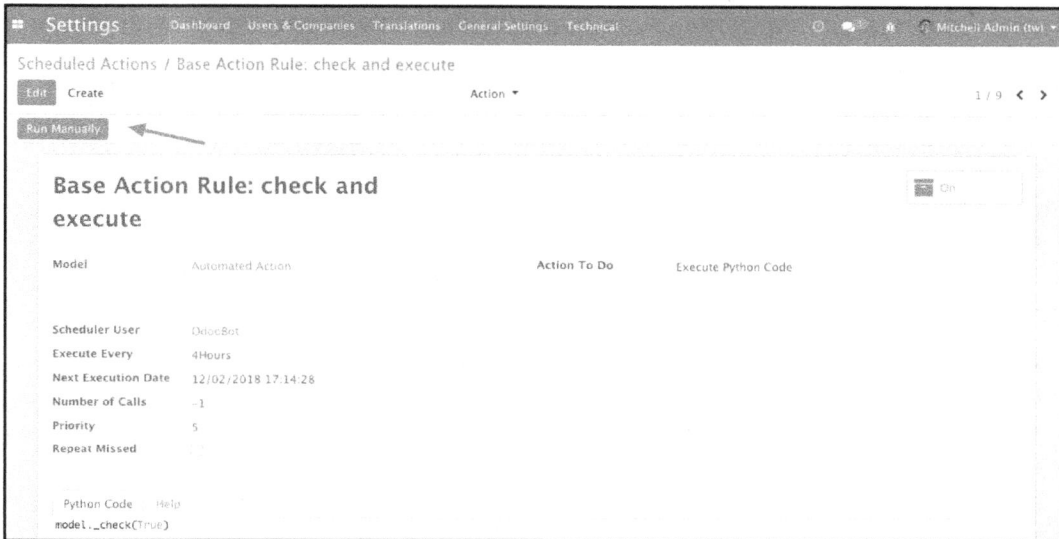

3. Again, go to the **Project** menu and open the same task you previously set a deadline date on. Check the message board; you should see the notification generated by the server action triggered by our automated action.

How it works...

Automated actions act on a model, and can be triggered either by events or by time conditions. The first steps are to set the **Model** and **When to Run** values.

Both methods can use a filter to narrow down the records that are eligible to perform the action on. We can use a domain expression for this. You can find further information about writing domain expressions in Chapter 10, *Backend Views*. Alternatively, you can create and save a filter on project tasks, using the user interface features, and then copy the automatically generated domain expression, selecting it from the **Set selection based on a search filter** list.

The domain expression we used selects all the records with a non-empty **Deadline** date, in a stage where the **Fold** flag is not checked. Stages without the **Fold** flag are considered to be work in progress. This way, we avoid triggering notifications on tasks that are in the **Done**, **Canceled**, or **Closed** stages.

Then, we should define the time condition—the date field to use and when the action should be triggered. The time period can be in minutes, hours, days, or months, and the number of periods can be positive, for time after the date, or negative, for time before the date. When using a time period in days, we can provide a **Resource Calendar** that defines the working days and that can be used by the day count.

These actions are checked by the **Check Action Rules** scheduled job. Note that, by default, this is run every four hours. This is appropriate for actions that work on a day or month scale, but, if you need actions that work on smaller timescales, you need to change the running interval to a smaller value.

Actions will be triggered for records that meet all the criteria and whose triggering date condition (the field date plus the interval) is after the last action execution. This is to avoid repeatedly triggering the same action. Also, this is why manually running the preceding action will work in a database in which the scheduled action has not yet been triggered, but why it might not work immediately in a database where it was already run by the scheduler.

Once an automated action is triggered, the **Actions** tab tells you what should happen. This might be a list of server actions that do things such as changing values on the record, posting notifications, or sending out emails.

There's more...

These types of automated actions are triggered once a certain time condition is reached. This is not the same as regularly repeating an action while a condition is still true. For example, an automated action will not be capable of posting a reminder for every day after the deadline has been exceeded.

This type of action can, instead, be performed by **Scheduled Actions**, which are stored in the `ir.cron` model. However, scheduled actions do not support server actions; they can only call an existing method of a model object. So, to implement a custom action, we need to write an add-on module, adding the underlying Python method.

For reference, the technical name for the **Automated Actions** model is `base.action.rule`.

Using automated actions on event conditions

Business applications provide systems with records for business operations, but are also expected to support dynamic business rules which are specific to the organization's use cases.

Carving these rules into custom add-on modules can be inflexible and out of the reach of functional users. Automated actions triggered by event conditions can bridge this gap and provide a powerful tool to automate or enforce the organization's procedures. As an example, we will enforce a validation on project tasks so that only the project manager can change **Tasks** to the **Done** stage.

Getting ready

To follow this recipe, you will need to have the Project Management app already installed. We also need to have the **Developer Mode** activated. If it's not activated already, activate it in the Odoo **About** dialog.

How to do it...

To create an automated action with an event condition on tasks, follow these steps:

1. In the **Settings** menu, select the **Technical | Automation | Automated Actions** menu item, and click on the **Create** button
2. Fill out the basic information in the **Automated Actions** form:
    - **Rule Name**: Validate Closing Tasks
    - **Related Document Model**: Task
    - **Conditions tab | When to Run**: On Update
    - **Action To Do**: Execute several actions

3. The `on update` rules allow you to set two record filters, before and after the update operation:
    - On the **Before Update Filter** field, click on the **Edit domain** button, set a valid domain expression—`[('stage_id.name', '!=', 'Done')]`—in the code editor, and save.
    - On the **Apply on** field, click on the **Edit domain** button, set the `[('stage_id.name', '=', 'Done')]` domain in the code editor, and save, as shown in the following screenshot:

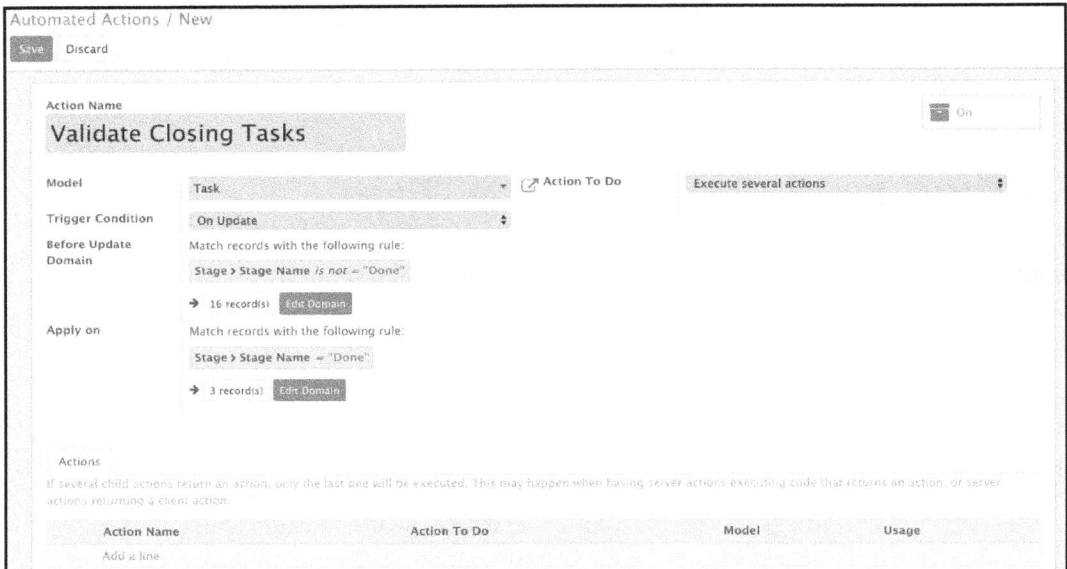

4. In the **Actions** tab, click on **Add an item**. In the list dialog, click on the **Create** button to create a new server action.

5. Fill out the server action form with the following values and then click on the **Save** button:
    - **Action Name**: Validate closing tasks
    - **Base Model**: Task
    - **Action To Do**: Execute Python code
    - **Python Code**: Enter the following code:

```
if user != record.project_id.user_id:
    raise Warning('Only the Project Manager can close
Tasks')
```

- The following screenshot shows the entered values:

```
Add: Child Actions                                                        ×

 Create Contextual Action

 Action Name
 Validate Closing tasks

 Model                    Task                ▾    [⇗ Action To Do    Execute Python Code    ⬍

 Python Code    Help
 # Available variables:
 #   - env: Odoo Environment on which the action is triggered
 #   - model: Odoo Model of the record on which the action is triggered; is a void recordset
 #   - record: record on which the action is triggered; may be void
 #   - records: recordset of all records on which the action is triggered in multi-mode; may be void
 #   - time, datetime, dateutil, timezone: useful Python libraries
 #   - log: log(message, level='info'): logging function to record debug information in ir.logging table
 #   - Warning: Warning Exception to use with raise
 # To return an action, assign: action = {...}

 if user != record.project_id.user_id:
     raise Warning('Only the Project Manager can close Tasks')

 Save & Close    Save & New    Discard
```

6. Click on **Save & Close** to save the automated action and try it out:
   1. On a database with demo data and logged in as Administrator, go to the **Project** menu and click on the **E-Learning Integration** project to open the kanban view of the tasks.
   2. Then, try dragging one of the tasks into the **Done** stage column. Since this project's manager is the Demo user and we are working with the Administrator user, our automated action should be triggered, and our warning message should block the change.

How it works...

We start by giving a name to our automated actions and setting the model it should work with. For the type of action we require we should choose **On Update**, but the **On Creation**, **On Creation & Update**, **On Deletion**, and **Based On Form Modification** options are also possible.

Next, we define the filters to determine when our action should be triggered. The **On Update** actions allow us to define two filters—one to check before and the other after the changes are made to the record. This can be used to express transitions—to detect when a record changes from state A to state B. In our example, we want to trigger the action when a not-done task changes to the `Done` stage. The **On Update** action is the only one that allows for these two filters; the other action types only allow for one filter.

> It is important to note that our example condition will only work correctly for English language users. This is because the **Stage Name** is a translatable field that can have different values for different languages. So, the filters on the translatable fields should be avoided or used with care.

Finally, we create and add one (or more) server actions with whatever we want to be done when the automated action is triggered. In this case, we chose to demonstrate how to implement custom validation, making use of a Python code server action that used the `Warning` exception to block the user's changes.

There's more...

In `Chapter 6`, *Basic Server-Side Development*, we saw how to redefine the `write()` methods of a model to perform actions on record updates. Automated actions on record updates provide another way to achieve this, with some benefits and drawbacks.

Among the benefits, it is easy to define an action triggered by the update of a stored computed field, which is tricky to do in pure code. It is also possible to define filters on records and have different rules for different records, or for records matching different conditions that can be expressed with search domains.

However, automated actions can have disadvantages when compared to Python business logic code inside modules. With poor planning, the flexibility provided can lead to complex interactions that are difficult to maintain and debug. Also, the before-and-after write filter operations bring some overhead, which can be an issue if you are performing sensitive actions.

Creating QWeb-based PDF reports

When communicating with the outside world, it is often necessary to produce a PDF document from a record in the database. Odoo uses the same template language as that used for form views, QWeb.

In this recipe, we will create a QWeb report to print information about a book that is currently being borrowed by a partner. This recipe will reuse the models presented in the *Adding a progress bar in kanban views* recipe from earlier on in this chapter.

Getting ready

If you haven't done so already, install `wkhtmltopdf` as described in Chapter 1, *Installing the Odoo Development Environment*; otherwise, you won't get shiny PDFs as a result of your efforts.

Also, double-check that the configuration parameter `web.base.url` (or alternatively, `report.url`) is a URL that is accessible from your Odoo instance; otherwise, the report will take a long time to generate and the result will look strange.

How to do it...

1. In this recipe, we add a report on `res.partner`, which prints a list of books the partner borrowed. We need to add a `one2many` field on the partner model with relation to the model `library.book.rent`, as shown in the following example:

```
class ResPartner(models.Model):
    _inherit = 'res.partner'

    rent_ids = fields.One2many('library.book.rent',
'borrower_id')
```

2. Define a view for your report in `reports/book_rent_templates.xml`, as follows:

```
<?xml version="1.0" encoding="utf-8"?>
<odoo>
<template id="book_rents_template">
    <t t-call="web.html_container">
        <t t-foreach="docs" t-as="doc">
```

```
                    <t t-call="web.internal_layout">
                        <div class="page">
                            <h1>Book Rent for <t t-
esc="doc.name"/></h1>
                            <table class="table table-condensed">
                                <thead>
                                    <tr>
                                        <th>Title</th>
                                        <th>Expected return date</th>
                                    </tr>
                                </thead>
                                <tbody>
                                    <tr t-foreach="doc.rent_ids" t-
as="rent" >
                                        <td><t t-
esc="rent.book_id.name" /></td>
                                        <td><t t-
esc="rent.return_date" /></td>
                                    </tr>
                                </tbody>
                            </table>
                        </div>
                    </t>
                </t>
            </t>
        </template>
    </odoo>
```

3. Use this view in a report tag in `reports/book_loan_report.xml`, as shown in the following example:

```
<?xml version="1.0" encoding="utf-8"?>
<odoo>
    <report id="report_book_rent"
        name="my_library.book_rents_template"
        model="res.partner"
        string="Book Rents"
        report_type="qweb-pdf" />
</odoo>
```

4. Add both files in the manifest of the add-on and add `contacts` in `depends`, so you can open the form view of the partner, as shown in the following example:

```
...
    'depends': ['base', 'contacts'],
    'data': [
        'views/library_book.xml',
```

```
                'views/library_member.xml',
                ...
                'reports/book_loan_report.xml',
                'reports/book_loan_report_template.xml',
        ],
    ...
```

Now, when opening the partner form view, or when selecting partners in the list view, you should be offered the option to print the book loans in a drop-down menu, as shown in the following image:

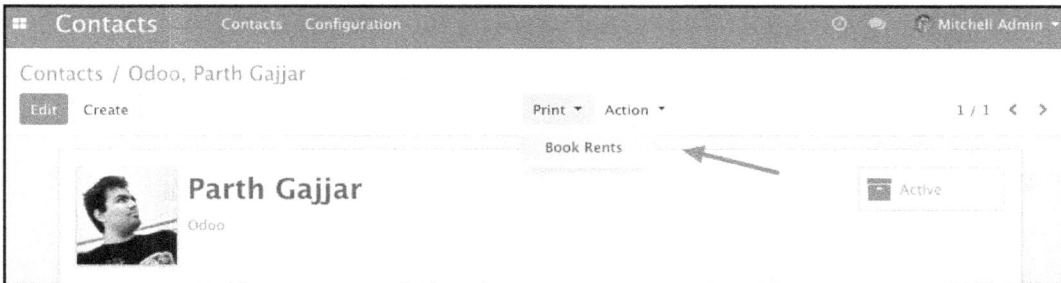

How it works...

In step 1, we defined the structure of the report using the QWeb template language. Instead of using the `record` syntax as we did earlier, we used the `template` element here. This is entirely for convenience; QWeb reports are just views like all the others. The reason for using this element is that the `arch` field of QWeb views has to follow quite strict rules, and the `template` element generates an `arch` content that fulfills these rules.

Don't worry about the syntax within the `template` element now. This topic will be addressed extensively in the *QWeb* recipe in `Chapter 16`, *Web Client Development*.

In step 2, we declared the report in another XML file. The `report` element is another shortcut for an action of the `ir.actions.report.xml` type. The crucial part here is that you set the `name` field to the complete XML ID (that is, `modulename.record_id`) of the template you defined, or the report generation will fail. The `model` attribute determines which type of record the report operates, and the `string` attribute is the name shown to the user in the print menu.

By setting `report_type` to `qweb-pdf`, we requested that the HTML generated by our view is run through `wkhtmltopdf` in order to deliver a PDF to the user. In some cases, you may want to use `qweb-html` to render the HTML within the browser.

There's more...

There are some marker classes in a report's HTML that are crucial for the layout. Ensure that you wrap all your content in an element with the class `page` set. If you forget that, you'll see nothing at all. To add a header or footer to your record, use the `header` or `footer` class.

Also, remember that this is HTML, so make use of CSS attributes such as `page-break-before`, `page-break-after`, and `page-break-inside`.

You'll have noted that all of our template body is wrapped in two elements with the `t-call` attribute set. We'll examine the mechanics of this attribute later in Chapter 15, *CMS Website Development*, but it is crucial that you do the same in your reports. These elements take care that the HTML generates links to all the necessary CSS files and contains some other data that is needed for the report generation. While `web.html_container` doesn't really have an alternative, the second `t-call` can be `web.external_layout`. The difference is that the external layout already comes with a header and footer displaying the company logo, the company's name, and some other information you expect from a company's external communication, while the internal layout just gives you a header with pagination, the print date, and the company's name. For the sake of consistency, always use one of the two.

Note that `web.internal_layout`, `web.external_layout`, `web.external_layout_header`, and `web.external_layout_footer` (the last two are called by the external layout) are just views by themselves, and you already know how to change them by inheritance. To inherit with the template element, use the `inherit_id` attribute.

In the previous versions of Odoo, these templates were defined in the `report` module, not `web`. When porting a module to Odoo 11, don't forget to change the identifiers in your calls to `t-call`.

Web Server Development

14

In this chapter, we'll cover the following topics:

- Making a path accessible from the network
- Restricting access to web accessible paths
- Consuming parameters passed to your handlers
- Modifying an existing handler

Introduction

We'll introduce the basics of the web server part of Odoo in this chapter. Note that this will cover the fundamental pieces. For high-level functionality, you should refer to Chapter 15, *CMS Website Development*.

All of Odoo's web request handling is driven by the Python library `werkzeug` (`http://werkzeug.pocoo.org`). While the complexity of `werkzeug` is mostly hidden by Odoo's convenient wrappers, it is an interesting read to see how things work under the hood.

Technical requirements

The technical requirements for this chapter include the online Odoo platform.

All the code used in this chapter can be downloaded from the GitHub repository at `https://github.com/PacktPublishing/Odoo-12-Development-Cookbook-Third-Edition/tree/master/Chapter14`.

Check out the following video to see the Code in Action: `http://bit.ly/2UDsr7n`

Making a path accessible from the network

In this recipe, we'll look at how to make a URL of the
`http://yourserver/path1/path2` form accessible to users. This can be either a
web page or a path returning arbitrary data to be consumed by other programs. In the
latter case, you would usually use the JSON format to consume parameters and to
offer your data.

Getting ready

We'll make use of the `library.book` model, which we looked at in Chapter 5,
Application Models; so, in case you haven't done so yet, grab its code, so that you will
be able to follow the examples.

We want to allow any user to query the full list of books. Furthermore, we want to
provide the same information to programs through a JSON request.

How to do it...

We'll need to add controllers, which go into a folder called `controllers` by
convention:

1. Add a `controllers/main.py` file with the HTML version of our page, as
   follows:

```python
from odoo import http
from odoo.http import request

class Main(http.Controller):
    @http.route('/my_library/books', type='http', auth='none')
    def books(self):
        books = request.env['library.book'].sudo().search([])
        html_result = '<html><body><ul>'
        for book in books:
            html_result += "<li> %s </li>" % book.name
        html_result += '</ul></body></html>'
        return html_result
```

2. Add a function to serve the same information in the JSON format, as shown in the following example:

```
@http.route('/my_library/books/json', type='json',
auth='none')
    def books_json(self):
        records =
request.env['library.book'].sudo().search([])
        return records.read(['name'])
```

3. Add the `controllers/__init__.py` file, as follows:

```
from . import main
```

4. Import the `controllers` to your `my_library/__init__.py` file, as follows:

```
from . import controllers
```

After restarting your server, you can visit `/my_library/books` in your browser and get presented with a flat list of book names. To test the JSON-RPC part, you'll have to craft a JSON request. A simple way to do that would be by using the following command to receive the output on the command-line:

```
curl -i -X POST -H "Content-Type: application/json" -d "{}"
localhost:8069/my_library/books/json
```

If you get **404** errors at this point, you probably have more than one database available on your instance. In that case, it's impossible for Odoo to determine which database is meant to serve the request.

Use the `--db-filter='^yourdatabasename$'` parameter to force Odoo to use the exact database you installed the module in. The path should now be accessible.

How it works...

The two crucial parts here are that our controller is derived from `odoo.http.Controller`, and that the methods we use to serve content are decorated with `odoo.http.route`. Inheriting from `odoo.http.Controller` registers the controller with Odoo's routing system in a similar way to how the models are registered, by inheriting from `odoo.models.Model`. Also, `Controller` has a metaclass that takes care of this.

In general, paths handled by your add-on should start with your add-on's name, to avoid name clashes. Of course, if you extend some of the add-on's functionality, you'll use this add-on's name.

odoo.http.route

The `route` decorator allows us to tell Odoo that a method should be web accessible in the first place, and the first parameter determines on which path it is accessible. Instead of a string, you can also pass a list of strings, in case you use the same function to serve multiple paths.

The `type` argument defaults to `http` and determines what type of request is to be served. While strictly speaking, JSON is HTTP, declaring the second function as `type='json'` makes life a lot easier, because Odoo then handles type conversions for us.

Don't worry about the `auth` parameter for now; it will be addressed in the *Restricting access to web accessible paths* recipe in this chapter.

Return values

Odoo's treatment of the functions' return values is determined by the `type` argument of the `route` decorator. For `type='http'`, we usually want to deliver some HTML, so the first function simply returns a string containing it. An alternative is to use `request.make_response()`, which gives you control over the headers to send in the response. So, to indicate when our page was last updated, we might change the last line in `books()` to the following code:

```
return request.make_response(
  html_result, [
    ('Last-modified', email.utils.formatdate(
      (
        fields.Datetime.from_string(
        request.env['library.book'].sudo()
        .search([], order='write_date desc', limit=1)
        .write_date) -
        datetime.datetime(1970, 1, 1)
      ).total_seconds(),
      usegmt=True)),
  ])
```

This code sends a `Last-modified` header along with the HTML we generated, telling the browser when the list was modified for the last time. We can extract this information from the `write_date` field of the `library.book` model.

In order for the preceding snippet to work, you'll have to add some imports on the top of the file, as follows:

```
import email
import datetime
from odoo import fields
```

You can also create a `Response` object of `werkzeug` manually and return that, but there's little to gain for the effort.

> Generating HTML manually is nice for demonstration purposes, but you should never do this in production code. Always use templates, as demonstrated in the *Creating or modifying templates – QWeb* recipe in `Chapter 16`, *Web Client Development*, and return them by calling `request.render()`.
>
> This will give you localization for free and will make your code better by separating business logic from the presentation layer. Also, templates provide you with functions to escape data before outputting HTML. The preceding code is vulnerable to cross-site scripting attacks (if a user manages to slip a `script` tag into the book name, for example).

For a JSON request, simply return the data structure you want to hand over to the client; Odoo takes care of serialization. For this to work, you should restrict yourself to data types that are JSON serializable, which are roughly dictionaries, lists, strings, floats, and integers.

odoo.http.request

The `request` object is a static object referring to the currently handled request, which contains everything you need in order to take action. The most important aspect here is the `request.env` property, which contains an `Environment` object that is just the same as `self.env` for models. This environment is bound to the current user, which is not in the preceding example, because we used `auth='none'`. The lack of a user is also why we have to `sudo()` all our calls to model methods in the example code.

If you're used to web development, you'll expect session handling, which is perfectly correct. Use `request.session` for an `OpenERPSession` object (which is quite a thin wrapper around the `Session` object of `werkzeug`), and `request.session.sid` to access the session ID. To store session values, just treat `request.session` as a dictionary, as shown in the following example:

```
request.session['hello'] = 'world'
request.session.get('hello')
```

> Note that storing data in the session is no different from using global variables. Onlu use it if you must. This is usually the case for multi-request actions, such as a checkout in the `website_sale` module. In this case, `tiy sgiykd` handles all functionality concerning sessions in your controllers, never in your models.

There's more...

The `route` decorator can have some extra parameters, in order to customize its behavior further. By default, all HTTP methods are allowed, and Odoo intermingles the parameters passed. Using the `methods` parameter, you can pass a list of methods to accept, which would usually be one of either `['GET']` or `['POST']`.

To allow cross-origin requests (browsers block AJAX and some other types of requests to domains other than where the script was loaded from, for security and privacy reasons), set the `cors` parameter to `*` to allow requests from all origins, or a URI to restrict requests to ones originating from this URI. If this parameter is unset, which is the default, the `Access-Control-Allow-Origin` header is not set, leaving you with the browser's standard behavior. In our example, we might want to set it on `/my_module/books/json`, in order to allow scripts pulled from other websites to access the list of books.

By default, Odoo protects certain types of requests from an attack known as cross-site request forgery, by passing a token along on every request. If you want to turn that off, set the `csrf` parameter to `False`, but note that this is a bad idea, in general.

See also

Refer to the following points to learn more about the HTTP routes:

- If you host multiple Odoo databases on the same instance then different database might running on different domains. In that case you can use `--db-filter` options or you can use the `dbfilter_from_header` module from `https://github.com/OCA/server-tools`, which helps you filter database based on domain. This module was not migrated to version 12 at the time of writing this book, but by the time of publication, it probably will have been.
- To see how using templates makes modularity possible, check out the *Modifying an existing handler* recipe later in the chapter.

Restricting access to web accessible paths

We'll explore the three authentication mechanisms Odoo provides for routes in this recipe. We'll define routes with different authentication mechanisms, in order to show their differences.

Getting ready

As we extend the code from the previous recipe, we'll also depend on the `library.book` model of `Chapter 5`, *Application Models*, so you should get its code in order to proceed.

How to do it...

Define the handlers in `controllers/main.py`:

1. Add a path that shows all the books, as shown in the following example:

```
@http.route('/my_library/all-books', type='http',
auth='none')
    def all_books(self):
        books = request.env['library.book'].sudo().search([])
        html_result = '<html><body><ul>'
```

```
        for book in books:
            html_result += "<li> %s </li>" % book.name
        html_result += '</ul></body></html>'
        return html_result
```

2. Add a path that shows all the books and indicates which was written by the current user, if any. This is shown in the following example:

```
    @http.route('/my_library/all-books/mark-mine',
type='http', auth='public')
    def all_books_mark_mine(self):
        books = request.env['library.book'].sudo().search([])
        html_result = '<html><body><ul>'
        for book in books:
            if request.env.user.partner_id.id in
book.author_ids.ids:
                html_result += "<li> <b>%s</b> </li>" %
book.name
            else:
                html_result += "<li> %s </li>" % book.name
        html_result += '</ul></body></html>'
        return html_result
```

3. Add a path that shows the current user's books, as follows:

```
    @http.route('/my_library/all-books/mine', type='http',
auth='user')
    def all_books_mine(self):
        books = request.env['library.book'].search([
            ('author_ids', 'in',
request.env.user.partner_id.ids),
            ])
        html_result = '<html><body><ul>'
        for book in books:
            html_result += "<li> %s </li>" % book.name
        html_result += '</ul></body></html>'
        return html_result
```

With this code, the /my_library/all-books and /my_library/all-books/mark-mine paths look the same for unauthenticated users, while a logged in user sees their books in a bold font on the latter path. The /my_library/all-books/mine path is not accessible at all for unauthenticated users. If you try to access it without being authenticated, you'll be redirected to the login screen in order to do so.

How it works...

The difference between authentication methods is basically what you can expect from the content of `request.env.user`.

For `auth='none'`, the user record is always empty, even if an authenticated user is accessing the path. Use this if you want to serve content that has no dependencies on users, or if you want to provide database agnostic functionality in a server-wide module.

The `auth='public'` value sets the user record to a special user with XML ID `base.public_user` for unauthenticated users, and to the user's record for authenticated ones. This is the right choice if you want to offer functionality to both unauthenticated and authenticated users, while the authenticated ones get some extras, as demonstrated in the preceding code.

Use `auth='user'` to ensure that only authenticated users have access to what you've got to offer. With this method, you can be sure that `request.env.user` points to an existing user.

There's more...

The magic of authentication methods happens in the `ir.http` model from the base add-on. For whatever value you pass to the `auth` parameter in your route, Odoo searches for a function called `_auth_method_<yourvalue>` on this model, so you can easily customize it by inheriting it and declaring a method that takes care of your authentication method of choice.

As an example, we will provide an authentication method called `base_group_user`, which will only authorize the user, if currently logged in user is part of the group `base.group_user`, as shown in the following example:

```python
from odoo import exceptions, http, models
from odoo.http import request

class IrHttp(models.Model):
    _inherit = 'ir.http'

    def _auth_method_base_group_user(self):
        self._auth_method_user()
        if not request.env.user.has_group('base.group_user'):
            raise exceptions.AccessDenied()
```

Now you can say `auth='base_group_user'` in your decorator, and be sure that users running this route's handler are members of the group. With a little trickery, you can extend this to `auth='groups(xmlid1,...)'`; its implementation is left as an exercise to the reader, but is included in the GitHub repository example code at `Chapter14/r2_paths_auth/my_library/models/sample_auth_http.py`.

Consuming parameters passed to your handlers

It's nice to be able to show content, but it's better to show content as a result of user input. This recipe will demonstrate the different ways to receive this input and react to it. As in the previous recipes, we'll make use of the `library.book` model.

How to do it...

First, we'll add a route that expects a traditional parameter with a book's ID to show some details about it. Then, we'll do the same, but we'll incorporate our parameter into the path itself:

1. Add a path that expects a book's ID as a parameter, as shown in the following example:

```
@http.route('/my_library/book_details', type='http',
auth='none')
    def book_details(self, book_id):
        record =
request.env['library.book'].sudo().browse(int(book_id))
        return u'<html><body><h1>%s</h1>Authors: %s' % (
            record.name,
            u', '.join(record.author_ids.mapped('name')) or
'none',
            )
```

2. Add a path where we can pass the book's ID in the path, as follows:

```
@http.route("/my_library/book_details/<model('library.book'):b
ook>",
            type='http', auth='none')
    def book_details_in_path(self, book):
        return self.book_details(book.id)
```

If you point your browser to /my_module/book_details?book_id=1, you should see a detailed page of the book with ID 1. If this doesn't exist, you'll receive an error page.

The second handler allows you to go to /my_module/book_details/1 and view the same page.

How it works...

By default, Odoo (actually, werkzeug) intermingles the GET and POST parameters and passes them as keyword arguments to your handler. So, by simply declaring your function as expecting a parameter called book_id, you introduce this parameter as either GET (the parameter in the URL) or POST (usually passed by <form> element with your handler as the action attribute). Given that we didn't add a default value for this parameter, the runtime will raise an error if you try to access this path without setting the parameter.

The second example makes use of the fact that in a werkzeug environment, most paths are virtual, anyway. So, we can simply define our path as containing some input. In this case, we say we expect the ID of a library.book as the last component of the path. The name after the colon is the name of a keyword argument. Our function will be called with this parameter passed as a keyword argument. Here, Odoo takes care of looking up this ID and delivering a browse record, which, of course, only works if the user accessing this path has appropriate permissions. Given that book is a browse record, we can simply recycle the first example's function by passing book.id as a book_id parameter, to give out the same content.

There's more...

Defining parameters within the path is a functionality delivered by werkzeug, called **converters**. The model converter is added by Odoo, which also defines the converter models that accept a comma-separated list of IDs and pass a recordset containing those IDs to your handler.

The beauty of converters is that the runtime coerces parameters to the expected type, while you're on your own with normal keyword parameters. These are delivered as strings, and you have to take care of the necessary type conversions yourself, as seen in the first example.

Built-in `werkzeug` converters include `int`, `float`, and `string`, but also more intricate, ones such as `path`, `any`, or `uuid`. You can look up their semantics at `http://werkzeug.pocoo.org/docs/0.11/routing/#builtin-converters`.

See also

If you want to learn more about the HTTP routes, refer to the following points:

- Odoo's custom converters are defined in `ir_http.py` in the base module and registered in the `_get_converters` class method of `ir.http`. As an exercise, you can create your own converter, which allows you to visit the `/my_library/book_details/Odoo+cookbook` page to receive the details of this book (if you added it to your library earlier).
- If you want to learn more about the form submission on the route, refer to the *Getting input from users* recipe from `Chapter 15`, *CMS Website Development*.

Modifying an existing handler

When you install the website module, the `/website/info` path displays some information about your Odoo instance. In this recipe, we will override this in order to change this information page's layout, and to also change what is displayed.

Getting ready

Install the `website` module and inspect the `/website/info` path. In this recipe, we will update the`/website/info` route to provide more information.

How to do it...

We'll have to adapt the existing template and override the existing handler. We can do this as follows:

1. Override the qweb template in a file called `views/templates.xml`, as follows:

```xml
<?xml version="1.0" encoding="UTF-8"?>
<odoo>
  <template id="show_website_info"
            inherit_id="website.show_website_info">
    <xpath expr="//dl[@t-foreach='apps']" position="replace">
      <table class="table">
        <tr t-foreach="apps" t-as="app">
          <th>
            <a t-att-href="app.website">
            <t t-esc="app.name" /></a>
          </th>
          <td><t t-esc="app.summary" /></td>
        </tr>
      </table>
    </xpath>
  </template>
</odoo>
```

2. Override the handler in a file called `controllers/main.py`, as shown in the following example:

```python
from odoo import http
from odoo.addons.website.controllers.main import Website

class WebsiteInfo(Website):
    @http.route()
    def website_info(self):
        result = super(WebsiteInfo, self).website_info()
        result.qcontext['apps'] =
result.qcontext['apps'].filtered(
            lambda x: x.name != 'website'
        )
        return result
```

Now, when visiting the info page, we'll only see a filtered list of installed applications in a table, as opposed to the original definition list.

How it works...

In the first step, we overrode an existing QWeb template. In order to find out which one it is, you'll have to consult the code of the original handler. Usually, this will end up with something similar to the following line, which tells you that you need to override `template.name`:

```
return request.render('template.name', values)
```

In our case, the handler used a template called `website_info`, but this one was immediately extended by another template called `website.show_website_info`, so it's more convenient to override this one. Here, we replaced the definition list showing installed apps with a table. For details on how QWeb inheritance works, consult `Chapter 16`, *Web Client Development*.

In order to override the handler method, we must identify the class that defines the handler, which is `odoo.addons.website.controllers.main.Website`, in this case. We need to import the class to be able to inherit from it. Now, we can override the method and change the data passed to the response. Note that what the overridden handler returns here is a `Response` object and not a string of HTML like the previous recipes did, for the sake of brevity. This object contains a reference to the template to be used and the values accessible to the template, but it is only evaluated at the very end of the request.

In general, there are three ways to change an existing handler:

- If it uses a QWeb template, the simplest way to change it is to override the template. This is the right choice for layout changes and small logic changes.
- QWeb templates get a context passed, which is available in the response as the `qcontext` member. This is usually a dictionary where you can add or remove values to suit your needs. In the preceding example, we filtered the list of apps to the website only.
- If the handler receives parameters, you can also preprocess those, in order to have the overridden handler behave in the way you want.

There's more...

As seen in the preceding section, inheritance with controllers works slightly differently than model inheritance; you actually need a reference to the base class and to use Python inheritance on it.

Don't forget to decorate your new handler with the `@http.route` decorator; Odoo uses it as a marker, for which methods are exposed to the network layer. If you omit the decorator, you actually make the handler's path inaccessible.

The `@http.route` decorator itself behaves similarly to field declarations: every value you don't set will be derived from the decorator of the function you're overriding, so we don't have to repeat values we don't want to change.

After receiving a `response` object from the function you override, you can do a lot more than just change the QWeb context:

- You can add or remove HTTP headers by manipulating `response.headers`
- If you want to render an entirely different template, you can overwrite `response.template`
- To detect whether a response is based on QWeb in the first place, query `response.is_qweb`
- The resulting HTML code is available by calling `response.render()`

See also

- Details on QWeb templates will be explained in `Chapter 16`, *Web Client Development*.

CMS Website Development **15**

In this chapter, we will cover the following recipes:

- Managing static assets
- Extending CSS and JavaScript for the website
- Creating or modifying templates – QWeb
- Managing dynamic routes
- Offering snippets to the user
- Get input from website users
- Managing **Search Engine Optimization (SEO)** options
- Managing site maps for websites
- Getting a visitor's country information
- Tracking a marketing campaign
- Managing multiple websites

Introduction

Odoo comes with a fully-featured **content management system (CMS)**. With drag and drop features, your end user can design a page in a few minutes, but it is not so simple to develop a new feature or building block in the Odoo CMS system. This chapter will give you a step-by-step guide to developing features in an Odoo CMS system.

All of the Odoo CMS features are implemented by the `website` and `web_editor` module. If you want to learn how CMS is working under the hood, take a look at both modules. You may find

Managing static assets

Modern websites contain lots of JavaScript and CSS files. When the page is loaded in the browser, these static files make a separate request to the server. The higher the number of requests, the lower the website speed. To avoid this issue, most websites serve the static assets by combining multiple files. There are several tools on the market to manage these sort of things, but Odoo has its own implementation for managing static assets.

What are asset bundles and different assets in Odoo?

In Odoo, static asset management is not as simple as it is in other apps. Odoo has a lot of different applications and code bases. Different Odoo applications have different purposes and UIs. These apps do not share common code, so there are some cases in which we want to load some assets, but not all of them. It is not a good practice to load unnecessary static assets in the page. To avoid loading extra assets in all applications, Odoo uses different asset bundles for the different code bases.

Here are the different asset bundles used in Odoo:

- `web.assets_common`: This asset bundle includes all basic utilities common to all applications, like JQurey, Underscore.js, FontAwesome, and so on. This asset bundle is used in the frontend (website), backend, point of sale, reports, and so on. This common asset is loaded almost everywhere in Odoo. It also contains the `boot.js` file, which is used for the Odoo module system.
- `web.assets_backend`: This asset bundle is used in the backend of Odoo (the ERP part). It contains all of the code related to the web client, views, field widgets, action manager, and so on.

- `web.assets_frontend`: This asset bundle is used in the frontend of Odoo (the website part). It contains all the code related to website-side applications, like e-commerce, blogs, online events, forums, live chat, and so on. Note that this asset bundle does not contain code related to website editing and the drag and drop feature (the website builder). The reason behind this is that we don't want to load editor assets for the public use of the website.

- `web_editor.assets_editor` and `web_editor.summernote`: This asset bundle contains code related to website editing snippets option and the drag and drop feature (the website builder). It is loaded in the website only if the user has the website editor access right. It is also used in the mass mailing designer.

- `web.report_assets_common`: QWeb reports are just PDF files generated from the HTML. This asset is loaded in the report layout.

> There are some other asset bundles used for specific applications: `point_of_sale.assets`, `survey.survey_assets`, `mass_mailing.layout`, and `website_slides.slide_embed_assets`.

Odoo manages its static assets through the `AssetsBundle` class, which is located at `/odoo/addons/base/models/assetsbundle.py`. The AssetBundle not only combines multiple files; it is also packed with more features. Here is the list of features it provides:

- It combines multiple JavaScript and CSS files.

- It minifies the JavaScript and CSS files by removing comments, extra spaces, and carriage returns from the file content. Removing this extra data will reduce the size of static assets and improve the page speed.

- It has built-in support for CSS preprocessors, like SASS and LESS. This means you can add SCSS and LESS files, and they will automatically be compiled and will get added to the bundle.

- It automatically splits the style sheet assets file if it reaches the `4095` rule limit.

Custom assets

As we have seen, Odoo has different assets for different code bases. To get the proper result, you will need to choose the right asset bundle in which to place your custom JavaScript and CSS files. For example, if you are designing a website, you need to put your file in `web.assets_frontend`. In the next recipe, you will see how you can include custom CSS/JavaScript in an existing asset bundle. Although it is rare, sometimes, you need to create a whole new asset bundle. You can create your own asset bundle, as we will describe in the following section.

How to do it...

Follow these steps to create a custom assets bundle:

1. Create the QWeb template and add your JavaScript, CSS, or SCSS files there, as follows:

```
<template id="my_custom_assets" name="My Custom Assets">
    <link rel="stylesheet" type="text/scss"
          href="/my_module/static/src/scss/my_scss.scss"/>
    <link rel="stylesheet" type="text/css"
          href="/my_module/static/src/scss/my_css.css"/>
    <script type="text/JavaScript"
src="/my_module/static/src/js/widgets/my_JavaScript.js"/>
</template>
```

2. Use `t-call-assets` in the QWeb template where you want to load this bundle, as follows:

```
<template id="some_page">
...
<head>
    <t t-call-assets="my_module.my_custom_assets" t-
js="false"/>
    <t t-call-assets="my_module.my_custom_assets" t-
css="false"/>
</head>
...
```

How it works...

In step 1, we have created the new QWeb template with the external ID `my_custom_assets`. In this template, you will need to list all of your CSS, SCSS, and JavaScript files. First, Odoo will compile the SCSS files into CSS, then, Odoo will combine all CSS and JavaScript files into an individual CSS and JavaScript file.

After declaring the assets, you need to load them into the QWeb template (web page). In step 2, we have loaded the CSS and JavaScript assets in the template. The `t-css` and `t-js` attributes are only used to load style sheets or scripts.

> In most website development, you will need to add your JavaScript and CSS files in existing assets bundles. Adding a new assets bundle is very rare. It is only required when you want to develop pages/apps without Odoo CMS features. In the next recipe, you will learn about adding custom CSS/JavaScript in an existing asset bundle.

There's more...

The following are a few things you need to know if you are working with assets in Odoo.

Debugging JavaScript can be very hard in Odoo because AssetBundle merges multiple JavaScript files into a single one, and also minifies them. By enabling developer mode with assets, you can skip assets bundling, and the page will load static assets separately so that you can debug easily.

Combined assets are generated once and stored in the `ir.attachment` model. After that, it is served from the attachment. If you want to regenerate assets, you can do it from the debug options, as shown in the following screenshot:

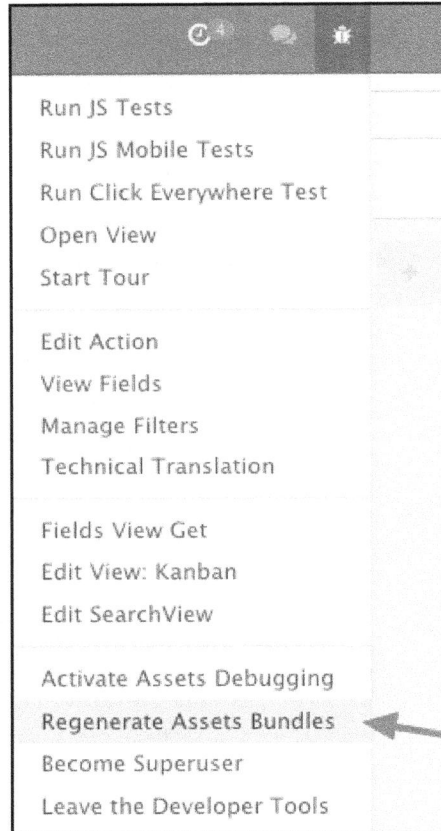

> **TIP**
> As you know, Odoo will generate the asset only once. This behavior can be a headache during development, as it requires a frequent server restart. To overcome this issue, you can use `dev=xml` in the command line, which will load assets directly, so there will be no need for a server restart.

Extending CSS and JavaScript for the website

In this recipe, we'll cover how to add custom style sheets and JavaScript to the website.

Getting ready

We will be using the `my_library` module from Chapter 4, *Creating Odoo Add-on Modules* for this recipe. We will add CSS, SCSS, and JavaScript files, which will modify the website. As we are modifying the website, we will need to add `website` in the dependency. Modify manifests like this:

```
...
    'depends': ['base', 'website'],
...
```

How to do it...

Override the main website template to inject your code, as follows:

1. Add a file called `views/templates.xml` and add an empty view override, as follows (don't forget to list the file in `__manifest__.py`):

```xml
<odoo>
    <template id="assets_frontend"
            inherit_id="web.assets_frontend">
        <xpath expr="." position="inside">
            <!-- points 2 & 3 go here /-->
        </xpath>
    </template>
</odoo>
```

2. Add the reference of the CSS and SCSS file, as follows:

```xml
<link href="/my_library/static/src/css/my_library.css"
rel="stylesheet" type="text/css"/>
<link href="/my_library/static/src/scss/my_library.scss"
rel="stylesheet" type="text/scss"/>
```

3. Add a reference to your JavaScript file, as follows:

```
<script src="/my_library/static/src/js/my_library.js"
type="text/JavaScript" />
```

4. Add some CSS code to `static/src/css/my_library.css`, as follows:

```
body main {
    background: #b9ced8;
}
```

5. Add some SCSS code to `static/src/scss/my_library.scss`, as follows:

```
$my-bg-color: #1C2529;
$my-text-color: #D3F4FF;

nav.navbar {
    background-color: $my-bg-color !important;
    .navbar-nav .nav-link span{
        color: darken($my-text-color, 15);
        font-weight: 600;
    }
}

footer.o_footer {
    background-color: $my-bg-color !important;
    color: $my-text-color;
}
```

6. Add some JavaScript code to `static/src/js/my_library.js` as follows:

```
odoo.define('my_library', function (require) {
    var core = require('web.core');

    alert(core._t('Hello world'));
    return {
        // if you created functionality to export, add it here
    }
});
```

After updating your module, you should see that Odoo websites have custom colors in the menu, body, and footer, and a somewhat annoying **Hello world** popup on each page load, as shown in the following screenshot:

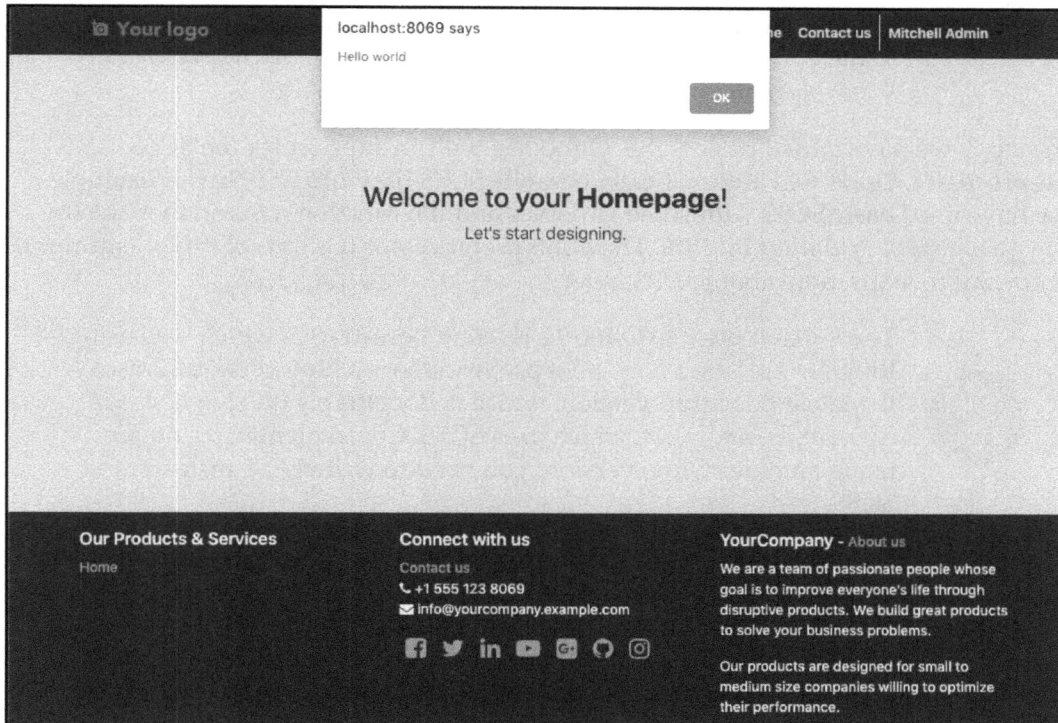

How it works...

At the base of Odoo's CMS lies an XML templating engine called QWeb, which will be discussed in detail in the next recipe. Asset bundles are just created with the templates. In steps 1, 2, and 3, we have listed our style sheets and JavaScript file in the `web.assets_frontend` by extending it. We have chosen `web.assets_frontend` because we want to update the website. These assets are loaded in every website page.

In step 4, we have added CSS, which sets the body background color of the website.

> For CSS/SCSS files, sometimes, order matters. So, if you need to override a style defined in another add-on, you'll have to take care that your file is loaded after the original file you want to modify. This can be done by either adjusting your view's priority field or directly inheriting from the add-on's view that injects the reference to the CSS file. For details, refer to the *Changing the existing views – View inheritance* recipe in `Chapter 10`, *Backend Views*.

In step 5, we have added basic SCSS. Odoo has built-in support for the SCSS preprocessor. Odoo will automatically compile SCSS files into CSS. In our example, we have used basic SCSS with some variables and the function `darken` to make the `$my-text-color` darker by 15%. The SCSS preprocessor has tons of other features; if you want to learn more about SCSS, refer to `http://sass-lang.com/`.

> The version prior to Odoo 12 is using Bootstrap 3, which was using LESS (`http://lesscss.org`) preprocessors. Odoo version 12 uses the latest Bootstrap version, which is Bootstrap 4 (`https://getbootstrap.com/`), which uses SCSS. Consequently, if you are using an older Odoo version, you need to write LESS instead of SCSS.

In step 6, we have added basic JavaScript, which just shows the `alert` message when the page is loaded. To avoid ordering issues with JavaScript, Odoo uses a mechanism very similar to RequireJS (`http://requirejs.org`). In our JavaScript file, we called `odoo.define()`, which needs two arguments, the namespace you want to define and a function that contains the actual implementation. If you export a lot of logically different parts of functionality, define them in different functions, with your add-on's name prepended and separated by dots to avoid naming conflicts in the future. This is what the `web` module does, which defines, among others, `web.core` and `web.data`.

With the second argument, the definition function receives only one parameter, `require`, which is a function you can use to obtain references to JavaScript namespaces defined in other modules or in the core. Use this for all interactions with Odoo, and never rely on the global `odoo` object.

Your own function can then return an object pointing to the references you want to make available for other add-ons, or nothing, if there are no such references. If you have returned some references from your function, you can use them in another function, as shown in the following example:

```
odoo.define('my_module', function (require) {
    var test = {
        key1: 'value1',
        key2: 'value2'
    };
    var square = function(number) {
        return 2*2;
    };
    return {
        test: test,
        square: square
    }
});

// In another file
odoo.define('another_module', function (require) {
    var my_module = require('my_module');

    console.log(my_module.test.key1);
    console.log('square of 5 is', my_module.square(5));

});
```

> The require mechanism discussed here was introduced for Odoo 9.0. In older versions, add-ons dealing with JavaScript need to define a function with the same name as the add-on in the openerp namespace. This function receives a reference to the currently-loaded instance as a parameter, from which API functions are to be accessed. So, in order to upgrade the existing code, change this to an odoo.define clause and import the necessary objects through require.

Creating or modifying templates – QWeb

We'll add website capabilities to the my_library add-on developed in Chapter 5, *Application Models*. What we're interested in is allowing users to browse through the library and, if they are logged in with the appropriate permissions, enable them to edit book details right from the website interface.

Getting ready

For this recipe, we will be using the `library.book` model of the add-on module `my_library` from `Chapter 4`, *Creating Odoo Modules*. For convenience, this recipe's code contains a copy of it.

How to do it...

We'll need to define the following couple of controllers and views:

1. Add a minimal template in `views/templates.xml`, as follows:

```xml
<?xml version="1.0" encoding="utf-8"?>
<odoo>

<template id="books">
    <t t-call="website.layout">
        <!-- Add page elements here -->
    </t>
</template>

</odoo>
```

2. Inside the `website.layout`, add the droppable element with the `oe_structure` class, as follows:

```xml
<div class="oe_structure">
    <section class="pt32 pb32 bg-secondary oe_custom_bg">
        <div class="container text-center">
            <h1> Editable text and supports drag and drop.</h1>
        </div>
    </section>
</div>
```

3. Append the code block into `website.layout` to display the books' information, as follows:

```xml
<div class="container">
    <t t-foreach="books" t-as="book">
        <div t-attf-class="card mt24 #{'bg-light' if book_odd else ''}">
            <div class="card-body">
                <h3 t-field="book.name"/>
                <t t-if="book.date_release">
```

```
                    <div t-field="book.date_release"
    class="text-muted"/>
                    </t>
                    <b class="mt8"> Authors </b>
                    <ul>
                        <li t-foreach="book.author_ids" t-
    as="author">
                            <span t-esc="author.name" />
                        </li>
                    </ul>
                </div>
            </div>
        </t>
    </div>
```

4. Append a non-editable element into `website.layout`, as follows:

```
<section class="container mt16" contenteditable="False">
    This is a non-editable text after the list of books.
</section>
```

5. Add a controller that serves the list of books in `controllers/main.py`, as follows:

```
from odoo import http
from odoo.http import request

class Main(http.Controller):
    @http.route('/books', type='http', auth="user",
website=True)
    def library_books(self):
        return request.render(
            'my_library.books', {
                'books':
request.env['library.book'].search([]),
            })
```

Open the `http://your-server-url:8069/books` URL in a browser and you will be able to see a list of books, with authors. With this code, a user can see a list of books and their details. Given the appropriate permissions, users will also be able to change the book details and a couple of other texts.

How it works...

First, we created a template called `books` that is used to generate the HTML necessary to display a list of books. All of the code is wrapped in a t element with the `t-call` attribute set, which makes Odoo render the page with the `website.layout` template and insert our content inside the template. `website.layout` includes all of the required utilities, like Bootstrap, jQuery, FontAwesome, and so on. These utilities are used for designing the web page. By default, it includes all necessary assets, like Bootstrap, jQuery, FontAwesome, and so on. The `website.layout` also includes the default header, footer, snippets, and page editing functionalities. This way, we get a full Odoo web page with the menus, footer, and page editing features, without having to repeat the code in all pages. If you don't use `t-call="website.layout"`, you will not get the default header, footers, and website editing features.

Inside `website.layout`, we have added HTML with some QWeb template attributes to display a list of books. Now, we will look at different QWeb attributes and their usage. In this template, you will be able to access parameters passed from the controller in `main.py`.

Loops

For working on recordsets or iterable data types, you need a construct to loop through lists. In the QWeb template, this can be done with the `t-foreach` element. Iteration can happen in a t element, in which case its contents are repeated for every member of the iterable that was passed in the `t-foreach` attribute, as follows:

```
<t t-foreach="[1, 2, 3, 4, 5]" t-as="num">
    <p><t t-esc="num"/></p>
</t>
```

This will be rendered as follows:

```
<p>1</p>
<p>2</p>
<p>3</p>
<p>4</p>
<p>5</p>
```

You can also place the `t-foreach` and `t-as` attributes in some arbitrary element, at which point this element and its contents will be repeated for every item in the iterable. Take a look at the following code block. This will generate exactly the same result as the previous example:

```
<p t-foreach="[1, 2, 3, 4, 5]" t-as="num">
    <t t-esc="num"/>
</p>
```

In our example, take a look at the inside of the `t-call` element, where the actual content generation happens. The template expects to be rendered with a context that has a variable called `books` set that iterates through it in the `t-foreach` element. The `t-as` attribute is mandatory and will be used as the name of the iterator variable, to use it for accessing the iterated data. While the most common use for this construction is to iterate over recordsets, you can use it on any Python object that is iterable.

Within `t-foreach` loops, you've got access to a couple of **extra variables**, whose names are derived from the accompanying `t-as` attribute. As it is `book` in the preceding example, we have access to the `book_odd` variable that contains the value `True` for odd indices while iterating, and `False` for even ones. In this example, we used this to be able to have alternating background colors in our cards.

The following are other available variables:

- `book_index`, which returns the current (zero-based) index in the iteration.
- `book_first` and `book_last`, which are `True` if this is the first or last iteration, respectively.
- `book_value`, which would contain the item's value if the book variable we iterate over were a dictionary; in this case, `book` would iterate through the dictionary's keys.
- `book_size`, which is the size of the collection (if available).
- `book_even` and `book_odd` get true values, based on the iteration index.
- `book_parity` contains the `even` value for even indices while iterating, and `odd` for odd ones.

> The given examples are based on our example. In your case, you need to replace `book` with the value placed at the `t-as` attribute.

Dynamic attributes

QWeb template can set attribute values dynamically. This can be done in the following three ways.

The first way is through t-att-$attr_name. At the time of template rendering, an attribute, $attr_name, is created; its value can be any valid Python expression. This is computed with the current context and the result is set as the value of the attribute, like this:

```
<div t-att-total="10 + 5 + 5"/>
```

It will be rendered like this:

```
<div total="20"></div>
```

The second way is through t-attf-$attr_name. This is the same as the previous option. The only difference is that only strings between {{ ..}} and #{..} are evaluated. This is helpful when values are mixed with the strings. It is mostly used to evaluate classes, like in this example:

```
<t t-foreach="['info', 'danger', 'warning']" t-as="color">
    <div t-attf-class="alert alert-#{color}">
        Simple bootstrap alert
    </div>
</t>
```

It will be rendered like this:

```
<div class="alert alert-info">
    Simple bootstrap alert
</div>
<div class="alert alert-danger">
    Simple bootstrap alert
</div>
<div class="alert alert-warning">
    Simple bootstrap alert
</div>
```

The third way is through the t-att=mapping option. This option accepts the dictionary after the template rendering the dictionary's data is converted into attributes and values. Take a look at the following example:

```
<div t-att="{'id': 'my_el_id', 'class': 'alert alert-danger'}"/>
```

After rendering this template, it will be converted into the following:

```
<div id="my_el_id" class="alert alert-danger"/>
```

In our example, we have used `t-attf-class` to get a dynamic background based on index values.

Fields

The `h3` and `div` tags use the `t-field` attribute. The value of the `t-field` attribute must be used with the recordset having a length of one, this allows the user to change the content of the web page when the user opens the website in edit mode. When you save the page, updated values will be stored in the database. Of course, this is subject to a permission check and is only allowed if the current user has write permissions on the displayed record. With an optional `t-options` attribute, you can give a dictionary option to be passed to the field renderer, including the widget to be used. Currently, there is not a vast amount of widgets for the backend, so the choices are a bit limited here. For example, if you want to display an image from the binary field, then you can use the image widget like this:

```
<span t-field="author.image_small" t-options="{'widget': 'image'}"/>
```

`t-field` has some limitations. It only works on recordsets and it cannot work on the `<t>` element. For this, you need to use some HTML elements, like `<span>` or `<div>`. There is an alternative of the `t-field` attribute, which is `t-esc`. The `t-esc` attribute is not limited to recordsets; it can also be used on any data types, but it is not editable in a website.

Another difference between `t-esc` and `t-field` is that `t-field` shows values based on the user's language, while `t-esc` shows raw values from the database. For example, for users who configured the English language in their preferences and set the `datetime` field as used with `t-field`, then the result will be rendered in the `12/15/2018 17:12:13` format. In contrast, if the `t-esc` attribute is used, then the result will in a rendered format, like this: `2018-12-15 16:12:13`.

Conditionals

Note that the division showing the publication date is wrapped by a t element with the t-if attribute set. This attribute is evaluated as Python code, and the element is only rendered if the result is a truthy value. In the following example, we only show the div class if there is actually a publication date set. However, in complex cases, you can use t-elif and t-else as in the following example:

```
<div t-if="state == 'new'">
    Text will be added of state is new.
</div>
<div t-elif="state == 'progress'">
    Text will be added of state is progress.
</div>
<div t-else="">
    Text will be added for all other stages.
</div>
```

Setting variables

The QWeb template is also capable of defining the variable in the template itself. After defining the template, you can use the variable in the subsequent template. You can set the variable like this:

```
<t t-set="my_var" t-value="5 + 1"/>
<t t-esc="my_var"/>
```

Subtemplates

If you are developing a big application, managing large templates can be difficult. The QWeb template supports subtemplates, so you can divide large templates into smaller subtemplates and you can reuse them in multiple templates. For subtemplates, you can use a t-call attribute, like in this example:

```
<template id="first_template">
    <div> Test Template </div>
</template>

<template id="second_template">
    <t t-call="first_template"/>
</template>
```

Inline editing

The user will be able to modify records directly from the website in edit mode. The data loaded with the `t-field` node will be editable by default. If the user changes the value in such a node and saves the page, the values will also be updated in the backend. Don't worry; in order to update the record, a user will need `write` permissions on the record. Note that `t-field` only works on a recordset. To display other types of data, you can use `t-esc`. This works exactly like `t-field`, but the only difference is that `t-esc` is not editable and can be used with any type of data.

If you want to enable snippet drag and drop support on the page, you can use the `oe_structure` class. In our example, we have added this at the top of the template. Using `oe_structure` will enable editing and snippet drag and drop support.

If you want to disable the website editing feature on some block, then you can use the `contenteditable=False` attribute. This makes an element read-only. In step 1, we have used this attribute in the last `<section>` tag.

> Note that editing a view through the website editor sets the `noupdate` flag on this view. This means that subsequent code changes will never make it into your customer's database. In order to also get the ease of use of inline editing and the possibility of updating your HTML code in subsequent releases, create one view that contains the semantic HTML elements and a second one that injects editable elements. Then, only the latter view will be `noupdate`, and you can still change the former.

For the other CSS classes used here, consult Bootstrap's documentation, as linked in this recipe's *See also* section.

In step 2, we have declared the route to render the template. If you noticed, we have used the `website=True` parameter in `route()`, which will pass some extra context in the template, like menus, user language, company, and so on. This will be used in `website.layout` to render the menus and footers. The `website=True` parameter also enables multilanguage support in a website. It also displays exceptions in a better way.

At the function end, we returned the result by rendering the template; we then passed the recordset of all books that are being used in the template. For more information about updating existing routes, refer to the *Modifying an existing handler* recipe in `Chapter 14`, *Web Server Development*.

There's more...

To modify existing templates, you can use the `inherit_id` attribute on the template and then use an `xpath` element like the view inheritance. For example, we want to display the count of authors near the `Authors` label by inheriting the `books` template. We can do this in the following way:

```
<template id="books_ids_inh" inherit_id="my_library.books">
    <xpath expr="//div[@class='card-body']/b" position="replace">
        <b class="mt8"> Authors (<t t-esc="len(book.author_ids)"/>)
</b>
    </xpath>
</template>
```

Inheritance works exactly like views, because internally, QWeb templates are a normal view with the type `qweb`. The `template` element is a shorthand for a `record` element that sets some properties on the record for you. While there's never a reason to not use the convenience of the `template` element, you should know what happens under the hood: the element creates a record of the `ir.ui.view` model with the `qweb` type. Then, depending on the `template` element's `name` and `inherit_id` attributes, the `inherit_id` field on the view record will be set.

See also

Refer to the following points to design QWeb templates effectively:

- Odoo, as a whole, makes extensive use of Bootstrap (http://getbootstrap.com), which you should use to get adaptive designs without much effort.
- For details on view inheritance, take a look at the *Changing the existing views – View inheritance* recipe in `Chapter 10`, *Backend Views*.
- For a more in-depth discussion of controllers, refer to the *Make a path accessible from the network* and *Restrict access to web accessible paths* recipes in `Chapter 14`, *Web Server Development*.

Managing dynamic routes

In website development projects, it is often the case that we need to create pages with dynamic URLs. For example, in e-commerce, each product has a detailed page with a different URL. In this recipe, we will create a web page to display the book details.

Getting ready

We will be using the `my_library` module from the previous recipe. To make a book detail page attractive, we will need to add a few new fields. Please add the following two new fields in the `library.book` model and form a view, like this:

```python
class LibraryBook(models.Model):
    _name = 'library.book'

    name = fields.Char('Title', required=True)
    date_release = fields.Date('Release Date')
    author_ids = fields.Many2many('res.partner', string='Authors')
    image = fields.Binary(attachment=True)
    html_description = fields.Html()
```

How to do it...

Follow these steps to generate a details page for books:

1. Add a new route for book details in `main.py`, as follows:

    1.  ```python
        @http.route('/books/<model("library.book"):book>',
            type='http', auth="user", website=True)
        def library_book_detail(self, book):
            return request.render(
                'my_library.book_detail', {
                    'book': book,
                })
        ```

2. Add a new template for book details in `templates.xml`, as follows:

    1.  ```xml
        <template id="book_detail" name="Books Detail">
            <t t-call="website.layout">
                <div class="container">
                    <div class="row mt16">
                        <div class="col-5">
                            <span t-field="book.image" t-options="{
                                'widget': 'image',
                                'class': 'mx-auto d-block img-
        thumbnail'}"/>
                        </div>
                        <div class="offset-1 col-6">
                            <h1 t-field="book.name"/>
                            <t t-if="book.date_release">
        ```

```
                                    <div t-field="book.date_release"
                                    class="text-muted"/>
                        </t>
                        <b class="mt8"> Authors </b>
                        <ul>
                            <li t-foreach="book.author_ids" t-
as="author">
                                    <span t-esc="author.name" />
                            </li>
                        </ul>
                    </div>
                </div>
            </div>
            <div t-field="book.html_description"/>
        </t>
</template>
```

2. Add a button in the book list template, as follows. This button will redirect to the book details web page:

   1. ...
   ```
   <div t-attf-class="card mt24 #{'bg-light' if book_odd else
   ''}">
       <div class="card-body">
           <h3 t-field="book.name"/>
           <t t-if="book.date_release">
               <div t-field="book.date_release" class="text-
   muted"/>
           </t>
           <b class="mt8"> Authors </b>
           <ul>
               <li t-foreach="book.author_ids" t-as="author">
                   <span t-esc="author.name" />
               </li>
           </ul>
           <a t-attf-href="/books/#{book.id}" class="btn btn-
   primary btn-sm">
               <i class="fa fa-book"/> Book Detail
           </a>
       </div>
   </div>
   ...
   ```

How it works...

In the first step, we created a dynamic route for the book details page. In this route, we have added `<model("library.book"):book>`. This accepts URLs with integers, like `/books/1`. Odoo considers this integer as the ID of the `library.book` model, and when this URL is accessed, Odoo fetches a recordset and passes it to the function as the argument. So, when `/books/1` is accessed from the browser, the `book` parameter in the function `library_book_detail()` will have a recordset of the `library.book` model with the ID `1`. We passed this `book` recordset and rendered a new template called `my_library.book_detail`.

In the second step, we created a new QWeb template called `book_detail` to render a book details page. This is simple and is created using the Bootstrap structure. If you check, we have added `html_description` in the detail page. The field `html_description` has a field type of HTML, so you can store the HTML data in the field. Odoo automatically adds the snippet drag and drop support to the HTML types of fields. So, now we are able to use snippets in the book details page. The snippets dropped in the HTML fields are stored in a book's records, so you can design different content for different books.

In the last step, we added a link with the anchor tag so that a visitor can be redirected to the book details page.

There's more...

Odoo uses `werkzeug` to handle HTTP requests. Odoo added a thin wrapper around `werkzeug` to easily handle routes. You saw the `<model("library.book"):book>` route in the last example. This is Odoo's own implementation, but it also supports all features from the `werkzeug` routing. Consequently, you can use routing like this:

- `/page/<int:page>` accepts integer values
- `/page/<any(about, help):page_name>` accepts selected values
- `/pages/<page>` accepts strings
- `/pages/<category>/<int:page>` accepts multiple values

There are lots of variations available for the routes, which you can read about at `http://werkzeug.pocoo.org/docs/0.14/routing/`.

Offering snippets to the user

The website designer offers building blocks in website edit mode, which can be dragged on the page. This recipe will cover how to offer your own blocks, called snippets, internally.

Getting ready

For this recipe, we will be using the `my_library` module from the previous recipe.

How to do it...

A snippet is actually just a QWeb view that gets injected in the **Insert blocks** bar, which is defined by a QWeb view itself. Follow these steps:

1. Add a file called `views/snippets.xml`, as follows:

```xml
<?xml version="1.0" encoding="UTF-8"?>
<odoo>

<!-- Assets for JS file added step 4 -->
<template id="assets_frontend"
inherit_id="web.assets_frontend">
    <xpath expr="." position="inside">
        <script src="/my_library/static/src/js/snippets.js"
type="text/JavaScript" />
    </xpath>
</template>

<!-- Step 2 and 3 comes here -->
</odoo>
```

2. Add a template for your snippet, as follows:

```xml
<template id="book_snippet">
    <section class="book_list">
        <div class="container">
            <h2>Latest books</h2>
            <table class="table book_snippet">
                <tr>
                    <th>Name</th>
                    <th>Release date</th>
                </tr>
            </table>
```

```
        </div>
    </section>
</template>
```

3. Inherit the snippet template and append the snippet and options, as follows:

```
<template id="book_snippets_options"
inherit_id="website.snippets">
    <xpath
expr="//div[@id='snippet_feature']/div[hasclass('o_panel_body'
)]" position="inside">
        <t t-snippet="my_library.book_snippet"
            t-
thumbnail="/my_library/static/description/icon.png"/>
    </xpath>
    <xpath expr="//div[@id='snippet_options']"
position="inside">
            <!-- add snippet options here -->
    </xpath>
</template>
```

4. Add the snippet options in the inherited snippet template, as follows:

```
<div data-js="book_count" data-selector="section.book_list">
    <div class="dropdown-submenu">
        <a tabindex="-2" href="#" class="dropdown-item">
            <i class="fa fa-book"/> Number of books
        </a>
        <div class="dropdown-menu" role="menu">
            <a href="#" class="dropdown-item" data-select-
count="3"> 3 </a>
            <a href="#" class="dropdown-item" data-select-
count="5"> 5 </a>
            <a href="#" class="dropdown-item" data-select-
count="10"> 10 </a>
            <a href="#" class="dropdown-item" data-select-
count="15"> 15 </a>
        </div>
    </div>
</div>

<div data-selector=".book_snippet">
    <div class="dropdown-submenu">
        <a tabindex="-2" href="#" class="dropdown-item">
            <i class="fa fa-columns"/> Table Style
        </a>
        <div class="dropdown-menu" role="menu">
```

```
                <a href="#" class="dropdown-item" data-toggle-
        class="table-bordered">
                    Bordered
                </a>
                <a href="#" class="dropdown-item" data-toggle-
        class="table-dark">
                    Dark
                </a>
                <a href="#" class="dropdown-item" data-toggle-
        class="table-striped">
                    Striped
                </a>
            </div>
        </div>
    </div>
```

5. Add the new file, /my_library/static/src/js/snippets.js, and add JavaScript code to populate our snippet, as follows:

```
odoo.define('my_library.snippets', function (require) {
    "use strict";
    var rpc = require('web.rpc');
    var Animation =
require('website.content.snippets.animation');
    var options = require('web_editor.snippets.options');

    // Add snippet option and animation JavaScript here

});
```

6. Add an option as follows to decide how many books we want to display in the snippet:

```
options.registry.book_count = options.Class.extend({
    selectCount: function (previewMode, value, $opt) {
        var table = this.$target.find('table');
        var oldClass = table.attr('class');
        var newTable = $('<table><tr><th>Name</th><th>Release
date</th></tr></table>');
        newTable.attr('class', oldClass);
        newTable.attr('data-rows', value);
        table.replaceWith(newTable);
        this._refreshAnimations();
    }
});
```

7. Add an animation to fetch book data and display it in the page, as follows:

```
Animation.registry.book_snippet = Animation.Class.extend({
    selector: '.book_snippet',
    start: function () {
        var self = this;
        var rows = this.$el.data().rows || 5;
        this.$el.find('td').parents('tr').remove();
        rpc.query({
            model: 'library.book', method: 'search_read',
            domain: [], fields: ['name', 'date_release'],
            orderBy: [{name: 'date_release', asc: false}],
            limit: rows,
        }).then(function (data) {
            _.each(data, function (book) {
                self.$el.append(
                    $('<tr />').append(
                        $('<td />').text(book.name),
                        $('<td />').text(book.date_release)
                    ));
            });
        });
    },
});
```

After updating the module, you will be offered a new snippet called **Latest books**, which has an option to change the number of recently added books. We have also added the option to change the table design, which can be displayed when you click on the table.

How it works...

In the first step, we added a new XML file, `snipptes.xml`, and added a JS file in the assets. Snippets are just QWeb templates without `website.layout`.

In the second step, we created the `book_snippet` template for the book. In general, it's a good idea to use **section** elements and Bootstrap classes, because for them, Odoo's editor offers edit, background, and resize controls out of the box. In our snippet body, we have just added a title and a table with the header. We want to display the latest books, in our case. The list of latest books is not fixed, and the list gets changed every time new books are published. Consequently, we want to insert the book details into the table on the fly. In the next few steps, we will add JavaScript to fetch the list of the latest books and add these to the table.

In the third step, we have inherited the `website.snippet` template to add our snippet and its options. The first `xpath` adds our `book_snippet` in the feature snippet section. To add the snippet, you need to use the `t-snippet` attribute. You also need to add the `t-thumbnail` attribute, which will be the URL of the thumbnail image for the snippet. The `position` attribute is used determines in which section the snippet will shows up. Our choice was `//div[@id='snippet_feature']/div[@class='o_panel_body']`, which places it in the features section. With the `snippet_structure`, `snippet_content`, and `snippet_effect` IDs, you can place your snippet in the other respective sections.

In the second `xpath`, we have added options for the snippet. Two options are added in this `xpath` through step 4. The first option is for selecting the number of books to be displayed in the table. Snippet options come in various types. In this example, we have used the custom option with `data-js="book_count"`. When you use the `data-js` option, you need to register it in `options.registry` with the value of the attribute. When the user changes the option, it will call the function in the registered option and you need to then set options values on the element. These values are used by the rendering function (the Odoo animation framework) when the page is reloaded.

You can check this in step 6, where we have added options like `options.registry.book_count`. In the function body, we get a snippet element in the `this.$target`, and the rest of the things in the function body are written with the basic JQuery syntax.

We have also added one more snippet option in step 4, which is used to change the table style. For this option, we have used the `data-toggle-class` attribute. When the user clicks on the option with the attribute `data-toggle-class`, Odoo will toggle a class given in the attribute value. No JavaScript code is needed for this type of option. One more type of option called `data-select-class`, is available in Odoo, which enables only one class at a time. We haven't used this in our example, but you can test it.

If you noticed, the `data-selector` attribute contains a JQuery selector for determining which element of the option is to be shown. In the example, the first option list is shown when the whole container is selected, while the second one, about the table style, is shown when the table is selected.

In steps 6 and 7, we have added `book_snippet` in the `Animation.registry`, which will fetch the book data from the database and append table rows in the snippet body. It uses the snippet animation framework to execute code every time the snippet is loaded. We use this to query the current list of books to be presented to the user. The key property here is the `selector` that's defined, which instructs the framework to run our class when there's an element matching the selector. Internally, we used the `data-rows` option, which is added from `options.registry.book_count` to determine how many rows need to be displayed.

The example given in our recipe is used for creating dynamic snippets. If you don't have a requirement for the dynamic snippet and you just want to add static content, then you can directly add everything in the snippet. There is no need for adding JavaScript for static snippets.

> In the preceding example, we have created a dynamic snippet. If you don't have a requirement for the dynamic snippet and you just want to add static content, then you can directly add everything in the snippet. In such cases, there will be no need for extra JavaScript.

There's more...

In such cases, there will be no need for extra JavaScript. Odoo's editor offers lots of options and control out of the box, and they are more than enough for static snippets. You will find all existing snippets and options at `website/views/snippets.xml`.

Snippet options also support `data-exclude`, `data-drop-near`, and `data-drop-in` attributes, which determine where the snippet can be placed when dragging it out of the snippet bar. These are also JQuery selectors, and in step 3 of this recipe, we haven't used them, because we allow for putting the snippet basically anywhere that content can go.

Getting input from users

In website development, often, you need to create forms to take input from the website users (visitors). In this recipe, we will create an HTML form in the page to report issues related to the books.

Getting ready

For this recipe, we will be using the `my_library` module from the previous recipe. We will need a new model to store issues submitted by users.

So, before starting this recipe, modify the previous code. Add a field in the `library.book` model and new `book.issues` model, as follows:

```
class LibraryBook(models.Model):
    _name = 'library.book'

    name = fields.Char('Title', required=True)
    date_release = fields.Date('Release Date')
    author_ids = fields.Many2many('res.partner', string='Authors')
    image = fields.Binary(attachment=True)
    html_description = fields.Html()
    book_issue_id = fields.One2many('book.issue', 'book_id')


class LibraryBookIssues(models.Model):
    _name = 'book.issue'

    book_id = fields.Many2one('library.book', required=True)
    submitted_by = fields.Many2one('res.users')
    isuue_description = fields.Text()
```

Add a `book_issues_id` field in the book form view, as follows:

```
...
<group string="Book Issues">
    <field name="book_issue_id" nolabel="1">
        <tree>
            <field name="create_date"/>
            <field name="submitted_by"/>
            <field name="isuue_description"/>
        </tree>
    </field>
</group>
...
```

Add access rights for the new `book.issue` model in the `ir.model.access.csv` file, as follows:

```
acl_book_issues,library.book_issue,model_book_issue,group_librarian,1,
1,1,1
```

We have added a new model for the book issues, and now, we will add a new template with an HTML form.

How to do it...

Follow these steps to create a new route and template page for the issue page:

1. Add a new route in `main.py`, as follows:

```
@http.route('/books/submit_issues', type='http', auth="user",
website=True)
def books_issues(self, **post):
    if post.get('book_id'):
        book_id = int(post.get('book_id'))
        issue_description = post.get('issue_description')
        request.env['book.issue'].sudo().create({
            'book_id': book_id,
            'issue_description': issue_description,
            'submitted_by': request.env.user.id
        })
        return
request.redirect('/books/submit_issues?submitted=1')

    return request.render('my_library.books_issue_form', {
        'books': request.env['library.book'].search([]),
        'submitted': post.get('submitted', False)
    })
```

2. Add a template with an HTML form in it, as follows:

```
<template id="books_issue_form" name="Book Issues Form">
    <t t-call="website.layout">
        <div class="container mt32">
            <!-- add the page elements here -->
        </div>
    </t>
</template>
```

3. Add the conditional header for the page, as follows:

```
<t t-if="submitted">
    <h3 class="alert alert-success mt16 mb16">
        <i class="fa fa-thumbs-up"/>
        Book submitted successfully
    </h3>
    <h1> Report the another book issue </h1>
</t>
<t t-else="">
    <h1> Report the book issue </h1>
</t>
```

4. Add`<form>` to submit the issues as follows:

```
<div class="row mt16">
    <div class="col-6">
        <form method="post">
            <input type="hidden" name="csrf_token"
                    t-att-value="request.csrf_token()"/>
            <div class="form-group">
                <label>Select Book</label>
                <select class="form-control" name="book_id">
                    <t t-foreach="books" t-as="book">
                        <option t-att-value="book.id">
                            <t t-esc="book.name"/>
                        </option>
                    </t>
                </select>
            </div>
            <div class="form-group">
                <label>Issue Description</label>
                <textarea name="issue_description"
                        class="form-control"
                        placeholder="e.g. pages are missing"/>
            </div>
            <button type="submit" class="btn btn-primary">
                Submit
            </button>
        </form>
    </div>
</div>
```

Update the module and open the /books/submit_issues URL. From this page, you will be able to submit the issues for the book. After submission, you can check them into the respective book form view in the backend.

How it works...

In step 1 of this recipe, we created a route to submit book issues. The `**post` argument in the function will accept all query parameters in the URL. You will also get the submitted form data in the `**post` argument. In our example, we have used the same controller to display the pages and submit the issue. If we find data in the post, we will create a new issue in the `book.issue` model and then redirect the user to the issue page with the submitted query parameters, so the user can see that the acknowledgment issue is submitted and can therefore submit another issue if he/she wants.

Note that we have used `sudo()` to create a book issue record because a normal user (visitor) does not have access rights to create the new book issue record. This is despite it being necessary to create the book issue record if a user has submitted an issue from a web page. This is a practical example of the usage of `sudo()`.

In step 2, we have created the template for the issue page. In step 3, we have added the conditional headers. The success header will be displayed after submitting an issue.

In step 4, we have added the `<form>` with three fields: `csrf_token`, book selection, and issue description. The last two fields are used to get input from the website user. However, `csrf_token` is used to avoid a **Cross-Site Request Forgery (CSRF)** attack. If you don't use it in the form, the user won't be able to submit the form. When you submit the form, you will get the submitted data as the `**post` parameter in the `books_issues()` method of step 1.

> In some cases, if you want to disable `csrf` validation, you can use
> `csrf=False` in the route, like this:
> ```
> @http.route('/url', type='http',auth="user",
> website=True, csrf=False )
> ```

There's more...

If you want, you can use separate routes page and for the post data, which you can do by adding `action` in the form as follows:

```
...
<form action="/my_url" method="post">
...
```

Additionally, you can restrict the `get` requests by adding the `method` parameter in the route like this:

```
@http.route('/my_url', type='http', method='POST' auth="user",
website=True)
```

Managing Search Engine Optimization (SEO) options

Odoo provides built-in support of SEO for the templates (pages). However, some templates are used in multiple URLs. For example, in an online shop, product pages are rendered with the same template and different product data. For these kinds of cases, we want separate SEO options for each URL.

Getting ready

For this recipe, we will be using the `my_library` module from the previous recipe. We will store separate SEO data for each book details page. Before developing this recipe, you should test the SEO options in the different book pages. You can get an SEO dialog from the **Promote** drop-down menu on the top, as shown in the following image:

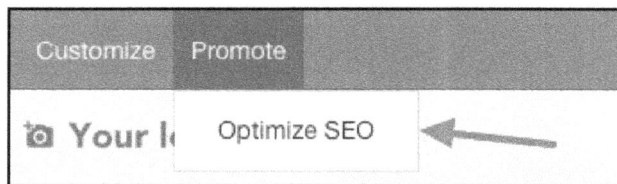

If you test SEO options in different book details pages, you will notice that changing the SEO data in one book page will reflect on all book pages. We will fix this issue in this recipe.

How to do it...

To manage separate SEO options for each book, follow these steps:

1. Inherit the SEO metadata `mixin` in the `library.book` model, as follows:

    1. ...
    ```python
    class LibraryBook(models.Model):
        _name = 'library.book'
        _inherit = ['website.seo.metadata']

        name = fields.Char('Title', required=True)
        date_release = fields.Date('Release Date')
    ...
    ```

2. Pass the book object in the book details route as a `main_object`, as follows:

    1. ...
    ```python
    @http.route('/books/<model("library.book"):book>',
    type='http', auth="user", website=True)
    def library_book_detail(self, book):
        return request.render(
            'my_library.book_detail', {
                'book': book,
                'main_object': book
            })
    ...
    ```

Update the module and change the SEO on the different book page. It can be changed through the **Optimize SEO** option. Now, you will be able to manage separate SEO details per book.

How it works...

To enable SEO on each record of the model, you will need to inherit the `website.seo.metadata` mixin in your model. This will add a few fields and methods in the `library.book` model. These fields and methods will be used from the website to store separate data for each book.

> If you want to see fields and methods for the SEO mixin, search for the `website.seo.metadata` model in the `/addons/website/models/website.py` file.

All SEO related code is written in the `website.layout` and it gets all the SEO meta information from the recordset passed as `main_object`. Consequently, in step 2, we have passed a book object with the `main_object` key, so the website layout will get all SEO information from the book. If you don't pass the `main_object` from the controller, then the template recordset will be passed as `main_object`, and that's why you were getting the same SEO data in all books.

There's more...

Odoo v12 added support for the metatags for the Open Graph and Twitter share. If you want to add your custom meta tags in the page, you can override `_default_website_meta()` after adding the SEO mixin.

Managing sitemaps for the website

A website's site maps are crucial for any website. The search engine will use website sitemaps to index the pages of the website. In this recipe, we will add book details pages to the sitemap.

Getting ready...

For this recipe, we will be using the `my_library` module from the previous recipe. If you want to check the current sitemap in Odoo, open `<your_odoo_server_url>/sitemap.xml` in your browser. This will not have the book's URL in it.

How to do it...

Follow these steps to add a book's page to `sitemap.xml`:

1. Import the given methods in `main.py`, as follows:

   1.
      ```
      from odoo.addons.http_routing.models.ir_http import slug
      from odoo.addons.website.models.ir_http import sitemap_qs2dom
      ```

2. Add the `sitemap_books` method in the `main.py`, as follows:

   1.
      ```
      class Main(http.Controller):
          ...
          def sitemap_books(env, rule, qs):
              Books = env['library.book']
              dom = sitemap_qs2dom(qs, '/books', Books._rec_name)
              for f in Books.search(dom):
                  loc = '/books/%s' % slug(f)
                  if not qs or qs.lower() in loc:
                      yield {'loc': loc}
          ...
      ```

2. Add the `sitemap_books` function reference in a book's detail routes as follows:

   1.
      ```
      ...
      @http.route('/books/<model("library.book"):book>',
      type='http', auth="user", website=True,
      sitemap=sitemap_books)
          def library_book_detail(self, book):
          ...
      ```

Update the module to apply the changes. The `sitemap.xml` file is generated and stored in attachments. Then, it is regenerated every few hours. To see our changes, you will need to remove the sitemap file from the attachment. To do this, visit **Settings | Technical | Database Structure | Attachments,** search for the sitemap, and delete the file. Now, access the `/sitemap.xml` URL in a browser, and you will see the book's pages in the sitemap.

How it works...

In the first step, we have imported a few required functions. The `slug` is used to generate a clean, user-friendly URL, based on a record name. The `sitemap_qs2dom` is used to generate a domain based on route and query strings.

In step 2, we have created a Python generator function `sitemap_books()`. This function will be called whenever a sitemap is generated. During the call, it will receive three arguments—the `env` Odoo environment, the `rule` route rule, and the `qs` query string. In the function, we have generated a domain with `sitemap_qs2dom`. Then, we used the generated domain to search the book records, which are used to generate the location through the `slug()` method. With slug, you will get a user-friendly URL, like `/books/odoo-12-development-cookbook-1` instead of `books/1`.

In step 3, we have passed the `sitemap_books()` function reference to the route with a keyword sitemap.

Getting a visitor's country information

The Odoo CMS has built-in support for the GeoIP. In the live environment, you can track a visitor's country based on IP. In this recipe, we will get the country of the visitor based on the visitor's IP address.

Getting ready...

For this recipe, we will be using the `my_library` module from the previous recipe. In this recipe, we will hide some books on the web page based on the visitor's country. You will need to download the GeoIP database for this recipe. After that, you will need to pass the database location from the `cli` option, like this:

```
./odoo-bin -c config_file --geoip-db=location_of_geoip_DB
```

How to do it...

Follow these steps to restrict books based on country:

1. Add the `restrict_country_ids` m2m field in the `library.book` model, as follows:

```
class LibraryBook(models.Model):
    _name = 'library.book'
    _inherit = ['website.seo.metadata']

    ...

    restrict_country_ids = fields.Many2many('res.country')
    ...
```

2. Add a `restrict_country_ids` field in the form view of the `library.books` model, as follows:

```
...
<group>
    <field name="date_release"/>
    <field name="restrict_country_ids"
widget="many2many_tags"/>
</group>
...
```

3. Update the `/books` controller to restrict books based on country, as follows:

```
@http.route('/books', type='http', auth="user", website=True)
def library_books(self):
    country_id = False
    country_code = request.session.geoip and
request.session.geoip.get('country_code') or False
    if country_code:
        country_ids =
request.env['res.country'].sudo().search([('code', '=',
country_code)])
        if country_ids:
            country_id = country_ids[0].id
    domain = ['|', ('restrict_country_ids', '=', False),
('restrict_country_ids', 'not in', [country_id])]
    return request.render(
        'my_library.books', {
            'books':
request.env['library.book'].search(domain),
        })
```

Update the module to apply the changes. Add your country in the restricted country field of the book, and access /book. This will not show restricted books in the list.

> **Warning**: This recipe does not work with the local server. It will require a hosted server, because in the local machine, you will get the local IP, which is not related to any country.
>
> You will also need to configure nginx properly.

How it works...

In the first step, we have added a new restricted_country_ids many2many type field in the library.book model. We will hide the book if the website visitor is from the restricted country.

In step 2, we have just added a restricted_country_ids field in the book's form view. If GeoIP and NGINX are configured properly, Odoo will add GeoIP information at request.session.geoip, and then you can get the country code from that.

In the third step, we have fetched the country code from the GeoIP, followed by the recordset of the country, based on the country_code. After getting a visitor's country information, we filtered books with domains based on a restricted country.

> If you don't have a real server and you want to test this anyway, you can add a default country code in the controller, like this:
> country_code = request.session.geoip and
> request.session.geoip.get('country_code') or 'IN'

Tracking a marketing campaign

In any business or service, it is really important to be familiar with the **Return on Investment (ROI)**. The ROI is used to evaluate the efficiency of an investment. Investments in ads can be tracked through **Urchin Tracking Module (UTM)** codes. A UTM code is a small string that you can add to a URL. This UTM code will help you to track campaigns, sources, and media.

Getting ready

For this recipe, we will be using the my_library module from the previous recipe. Odoo has built-in support for UTMs. With our library application, we don't have any practical case where UTMs can be used. However, in this recipe, we will add UTM in the issues generated from the /books/submit_issues from my_library.

How to do it...

Follow these steps to link UTMs in a book issue generated from the web page on the /books/submit_issues URL:

1. Add a utm module in the depends section of manifest.py, as follows:

```
'depends': ['base', 'website', 'utm'],
```

2. Inherit utm.mixin in the book.issue model, as follows:

```
class LibraryBookIssues(models.Model):
    _name = 'book.issue'
    _inherit = ['utm.mixin']

    book_id = fields.Many2one('library.book', required=True)
    submitted_by = fields.Many2one('res.users')
    issue_description = fields.Text()
```

3. Add a campaign_id field in the tree view of the book_issue_ids field, as follows:

```
...
<group string="Book Issues">
    <field name="book_issue_ids" nolabel="1">
        <tree name="Book isuues">
            <field name="create_date"/>
            <field name="submitted_by"/>
            <field name="issue_description"/>
            <field name="campaign_id"/>
        </tree>
    </field>
</group>
...
```

Update the module to apply the changes. To test the UTM, you need to perform the following steps:

- In Odoo, UTM is processed based on cookies, and some browsers do not support cookies in the localhost, so if you are testing it with the localhost, access the instance with `http://127.0.0.1:8069`.
- By default, UTM tracking is blocked for salespeople. Consequently, to test the UTM feature, you need to log in with a portal user.
- Now, open the URL like this `http://127.0.0.1:8069/books/submit_issues?utm_campaign=sale`.
- Submit the book issue and check the book issue in the backend. This will display the campaign in the book's form view.

How it works...

In the first step, we have inherited the `utm.mixin` in the `book.issue` model. This will add the following fields to the `book.issue` model:

- `campaign_id`: The `Many2one` field with the `utm.campaign` model. This is used to track different campaigns, such as the *Summer and Christmas Special*.
- `source_id`: The `Many2one` field with the `utm.source` model. This is used to track different sources, like search engines and other domains.
- `medium_id`: The `Many2one` field with the `utm.medium` model. This is used to track different media, like postcards, emails, or banner ads.

To track the campaign, medium, and source, you need to share a URL in the marketing media like this:
`your_url?utm_campaign=campaign_name&utm_medium=medium_name&utm_source=source_name`

If a visitor visits your website from any marketing media, then the `campaign_id`, `source_id`, and `medium_id` fields are automatically filled when records are created on the website page.

In our example, we have just tracked `campaign_id`, but you can also add `source_id` and `medium_id`.

Note: In our test example, we have used `campaign_id=sale`. `sale` is the name of the record in the model `utm.campaign`. By default, the `utm` module adds a few records of the campaign, medium, and source. The record `sale` is one of them. If you want to create a new campaign, medium, and source, you can do this by visiting the `Link Tracker > UTMs` menu in developer mode.

Managing multiple websites

In v12, Odoo added support for multiple websites. This means that the same Odoo instance can be run on multiple domains, as well as when displaying different records.

Getting ready

For this recipe, we will be using the `my_library` module from the previous recipe. In this recipe, we will hide the books based on the website.

How to do it...

Follow these steps to make the online website-multi website compatible:

1. Add `website.multi.mixin` in the `library.book` model, as follows:

```
class LibraryBook(models.Model):
    _name = 'library.book'
    _inherit = ['website.seo.metadata', 'website.multi.mixin']
...
```

2. Add `website_id` in the book form view, as follows:

```
...
<group>
    <field name="author_ids" widget="many2many_tags"/>
    <field name="website_id"/>
</group>
...
```

3. Modify the domain in the `/books` controller, as follows:

```
@http.route('/books', type='http', auth="user", website=True)
def library_books(self, **post):
    ...
    domain = ['|', ('restrict_country_ids', '=', False),
('restrict_country_ids', 'not in', [country_id])]
    domain += request.website.website_domain()
    return request.render(
        'my_library.books', {
            'books':
request.env['library.book'].search(domain),
        })
    ...
```

4. Import `werkzeug` and modify a book details controller to restrict book access from another website, as follows:

```
import werkzeug
...
@http.route('/books/<model("library.book"):book>',
type='http', auth="user", website=True, sitemap=sitemap_books)
def library_book_detail(self, book, **post):
    if not book.can_access_from_current_website():
        raise werkzeug.exceptions.NotFound()
    return request.render(
        'my_library.book_detail', {
            'book': book,
            'main_object': book
        })
    ...
```

Update the module to apply the changes. To test this module, set different websites in some books. Now, open the `/books` URL and check the list of books. After this, change the website and check the list of books. For testing, you can change the website from the website switcher drop-down menu. Refer to the following screenshot to do that:

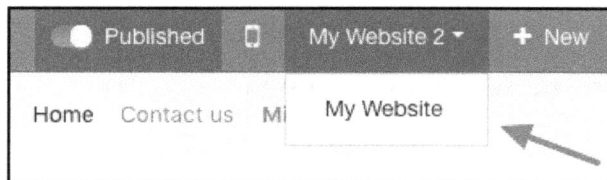

You can also try to access the book details directly from the URL, like /books/1. If a book is not from that website, it will show as **404**.

How it works...

In the first step, we have added website.multi.mixin. This mixin adds a basic utility to handle multiple websites in the model. This mixin adds the website_id field in the model. This field is used to determine which website a record is meant for.

In step 2, we have added the website_id field in the form view of the book, so the books will be filtered based on the website.
In step 3, we have modified the domain used to find a list of books. request.website.website_domain() will return the domain that filters out the books that are not from the website.

> Notice that there are records that do not have any website_id set. Such records will be displayed on all websites. This means that if you don't have a website_id field on a particular book, then that book will be displayed on all websites.

Then, we added the domain in the web search, as follows:

- In step 4, we have restricted book access. If the book is not meant for the current website, then we will raise a not found error. The method can_access_from_current_website() will return the value True if a book record is meant for the currently active website, and False if a book record is meant for another website.
- If you checked, we have added **post in both controllers. This is because without it, **post /books and /books/<model:library.book:book> will not accept a query parameter. It will also generate an error while switching the website from the website switcher, so we added it. Normally, it is a good practice to add **post in every controller so that it can handle query parameters.

Web Client Development **16**

In this chapter, we will cover the following recipes:

- Creating custom widgets
- Using client-side QWeb templates
- Making RPC calls to the server
- Creating a new view
- Debugging your client-side code
- Improving onboarding with tour
- Mobile app JavaScript

Introduction

Odoo's web client, or backend, is where employees spend most of their time. In Chapter 10, *Backend Views*, you saw how to use the existing possibilities that backends offer. Here, we'll take a look at how to extend and customize those possibilities. The web module contains everything related to the user interface in Odoo.

All of the code in this chapter will depend on the web module. As you know, Odoo has two different editions (Enterprise and Community). Community uses the web module for user interfaces, while the Enterprise version uses an extended version of the Community web module, which is the web_enterprise module.

The Enterprise version provides some extra features over the Community web, such as mobile compatibility, searchable menus, material design, and so on. We'll work on the Community edition here. Don't worry—the modules developed in Community work perfectly in the Enterprise edition because, internally web_enterprise depends on the Community web module and just adds some features to it.

In this chapter, you will learn how to create new field widgets to get input from the users. We will also be creating a new view from scratch. After reading this chapter, you will be able to create your own UI elements in the Odoo backend.

> **Note:** Odoo's user interface heavily depends on JavaScript. Throughout this chapter, we will assume you have basic knowledge of JavaScript, jQuery, Underscore.js, and SCSS.

Technical requirements

The technical requirements for this chapter include the online Odoo platform.

All the code used in this chapter can be downloaded from the GitHub repository at `https://github.com/PacktPublishing/Odoo-12-Development-Cookbook-Third-Edition/tree/master/Chapter16`.

Check out the following video to see the Code in Action:

`http://bit.ly/2UDXqQI`

Creating custom widgets

As you saw in `Chapter 10`, *Backend Views*, we can use widgets to display certain data in different formats. For example, we used `widget='image'` to display a binary field as an image. To demonstrate how to create your own widget, we'll write one widget that lets the user choose an `integer` field, but we will display it differently. Instead of an input box, we will display a color picker, so that we can select a color number.

Getting ready

For this recipe, we will be using the `my_library` module from `Chapter 4`, *Creating Odoo Add-On Modules*. In this recipe, we are going to add a new field widget that needs dependency of the `web` module. Make sure that you have added the dependency on `web` in the manifest file, like this:

```
...
'depends': ['base', 'web'],
...
```

How to do it...

We'll add a JavaScript file that contains our widget's logic, and an SCSS file to do some styling. Then, we will add one integer field on the books form to use our new widget. Follow these steps to add a new field widget:

1. Add a `static/src/js/field_widget.js` file. For the syntax that's used here, refer to the *Extending CSS and JavaScript for the website* recipe from `Chapter 15`, *CMS Website Development*:

```
odoo.define('my_field_widget', function (require) {
"use strict";

var AbstractField = require('web.AbstractField');
var fieldRegistry = require('web.field_registry');
```

2. Create your widget by extending `AbstractField`:

```
var colorField = AbstractField.extend({
```

3. Set the CSS class, root element tag, and supported field types for the widget:

```
className: 'o_int_colorpicker',
tagName: 'span',
supportedFieldTypes: ['integer'],
```

4. Capture some JavaScript events:

```
events: {
    'click .o_color_pill': 'clickPill',
},
```

5. Override `init` to do some initialization:

```
init: function () {
    this.totalColors = 10;
    this._super.apply(this, arguments);
},
```

6. Override `_renderEdit` and `_renderReadonly` to set up the DOM elements:

```
_renderEdit: function () {
    this.$el.empty();
    for (var i = 0; i < this.totalColors; i++ ) {
        var className = "o_color_pill o_color_" + i;
```

```
                    if (this.value === i ) {
                        className += ' active';
                    }
                    this.$el.append($('<span>', {
                        'class': className,
                        'data-val': i,
                    }));
                }
            },
            _renderReadonly: function () {
                var className = "o_color_pill active readonly o_color_" +
    this.value;
                this.$el.append($('<span>', {
                    'class': className,
                }));
            },
```

7. Define the handlers we referred to earlier:

```
        clickPill: function (ev) {
            var $target = $(ev.currentTarget);
            var data = $target.data();
            this._setValue(data.val.toString());
        }

    });       // closing AbstractField
```

8. Don't forget to register your widget:

```
    fieldRegistry.add('int_color', colorField);
```

9. Make it available for other add-ons:

```
return {
    colorField: colorField,
};
}); // closing 'my_field_widget' namespace
```

10. Add some SCSS in `static/src/scss/field_widget.scss`:

```
    .o_int_colorpicker {
        .o_color_pill {
            display: inline-block;
            height: 25px;
            width: 25px;
            margin: 4px;
            border-radius: 25px;
            position: relative;
```

```scss
@for $size from 1 through length($o-colors) {
    &.o_color_#{$size - 1} {
        background-color: nth($o-colors, $size);
        &:not(.readonly):hover {
            transform: scale(1.2);
            transition: 0.3s;
            cursor: pointer;
        }
        &.active:after{
            content: "\f00c";
            display: inline-block;
            font: normal normal normal 14px/1 FontAwesome;
            font-size: inherit;
            color: #fff;
            position: absolute;
            padding: 4px;
            font-size: 16px;
        }
    }
}
```

11. Register both files in the backend assets in `views/templates.xml`:

```xml
<?xml version="1.0" encoding="UTF-8"?>
<odoo>
    <template id="assets_end" inherit_id="web.assets_backend">
        <xpath expr="." position="inside">
            <script
src="/my_field_widget/static/src/js/field_widget.js"
                    type="text/javascript" />
            <link
href="/my_field_widget/static/src/scss/field_widget.scss"
                    rel="stylesheet" type="text/scss" />
        </xpath>
    </template>
</odoo>
```

12. Finally, add the color `integer` field in the `library.book` model:

```
color = fields.Integer()
```

13. Add the color field in the book's form view, and also add `widget="int_color"`:

```
...
<group>
```

```
        <field name="date_release"/>
        <field name="color" widget="int_color"/>
</group>
    . . .
```

Update the module to apply the changes. After the update, open the book's form view and you will see the color picker, as shown in the following screenshot:

How it works...

So that you can understand our example, let's go over the *life cycle of the widget* by looking at its components:

- `init()`: This is the widget constructor. It is used for initialization purposes. When the widget is initialized, this method is called first.
- `willStart()`: This method is called when the widget is initialized and in the process of being appended in the DOM. It is used to initialize asynchronous data into the widget. It is also supposed to return a deferred object, which can be obtained simply from a `super()` call. We will use this method in the subsequent recipe.
- `start()`: This method is called after the widget has completed the rendering but is not yet added in the DOM. It is very useful for a post rendering job and is supposed to return a deferred object. You can access a rendered element in `this.$el`.
- `destroy()`: This method is called when the widget is destroyed. It is mostly used for basic cleanup operations, like event unbinding.

> **TIP**
> The fundamental base class for widgets is `Widget` (defined by `web.Widget`). If you want to dig further into this, you can study it at `/addons/web/static/src/js/core/widget.js`.

In step 1, we imported `AbstractField` and `fieldRegistry`.

In step 2, we created `colorField` by extending `AbstractField`. Through this, our `colorField` will get all the properties and methods from the `AbstractField`.

In step 3, we added three properties—`className` is used to define the class for the root element of the widget, `tagName` is used for the root element type, and `supportedFieldTypes` is used for deciding which type of fields are supported by this widget. In our case, we want to create a widget for the integer type field.

In step 4, we mapped the events of our widget. Usually, the key is a combination of the event name and the optional CSS selector. The event and CSS selector are separated by a space, and the value will be the name of the widget method. So, when the event is performed, the assigned method is called automatically. In this recipe, when a user clicks on the color pill, we want to set the integer value in the field. To manage click events, we have added a CSS selector and the method name in the `events` key.

In step 5, we have overridden the init method and set the value of the `this.totalColors` attribute. We will use this variable to decide on the number of color pills. We want to display ten color pills, so we assigned the value of `10`.

In step 6, we added two methods—`_renderEdit` and `_renderReadonly`. As their names suggest, `_renderEdit` was called when the widget was in edit mode, and `_renderReadonly` was called when the widget was in read-only mode. In the edit method, we added a few `<span>` tags, with each representing a separate color in the widget. Upon clicking the `<span>` tag, we will set the value in the field. We added them into `this.$el`. Here, `$el` is the root element of the widget, and it will be added in the form view. In read-only mode, we just want to display the active color, so we added a single pill via the `_renderReadonly()` method. For now, we have added pills in a hardcoded way, but in the next recipe, we will use a JavaScript Qweb template to render the pills. Note that in the edit method, we used the `totalColors` property, which was set from the `init()` method.

In step 7, we added the `clickPill` handler method to manage pill clicks. To set the field value, we used the `_setValue` method. This method is added from the `AbstractField` class. When you set the field value, the Odoo framework will rerender the widget and call the `_renderEdit` method again, so that you can render the widget with the updated values.

In step 8, after we've defined our new widget, it's crucial to register it with the form widget registry, which lives in `web.field_registry`. Note that all view types look at this registry, so if you want to create another way of displaying a field in a list view, you can also add your widget here and set the widget attribute on the field in the view definition.

Finally, we exported our widget class so that other add-ons can extend it or inherit from it. Then, we added a new integer field called `color` in the `library.book` model. We also added the same field in the form view with the `widget="int_color"` attribute. This will display our widget in the form, instead of the default integer widget.

There's more...

The `web.mixins` namespace defines a couple of very helpful `mixin` classes that you should not miss out on when developing form widgets. You already used these mixins in this recipe. The `AbstractField` is created by inheriting from the `Widget` class, and the `Widget` class inherits two mixins. The first one is `EventDispatcherMixin`, which offers a simple interface for attaching event handlers and triggering them. The second one is `ServicesMixin`, which provides functions for RPC calls and actions.

> When you want to override a method, always study the base class to see what the function is supposed to return. A very common cause of bugs is forgetting to return the super user's deferred object, which causes trouble with asynchronous operations.

Widgets are responsible for validation. Use the `isValid` function to implement your customization of this aspect.

Using client-side QWeb templates

Just as it's a bad habit to programmatically create HTML code in JavaScript, you should only create the minimum amount of DOM elements in your client-side JavaScript code. Fortunately, there's a templating engine available for the client side, too, and even more fortunately, the client-side templating engine has the same syntax as the server-side templates.

Getting ready

For this recipe, we will be using the `my_library` module from the previous recipe. We will make this more modular by moving the DOM element creation to QWeb.

How to do it...

We need to add the QWeb definition in the manifest and change the JavaScript code so that we can use it. Follow these steps to get started:

1. Import `web.core` and extract the `qweb` reference into a variable, as shown in the following code:

```
odoo.define('my_field_widget', function (require) {
"use strict";

var AbstractField = require('web.AbstractField');
var fieldRegistry = require('web.field_registry');
var core = require('web.core');

var qweb = core.qweb;
...
```

2. Change the `_renderEdit` function to simply render the element (inherited from `widget`):

```
_renderEdit: function () {
    this.$el.empty();
    var pills = qweb.render('FieldColorPills', {widget:
this});
    this.$el.append(pills);
},
```

3. Add the template file to `static/src/xml/qweb_template.xml`:

```
<?xml version="1.0" encoding="UTF-8"?>
<templates>
    <t t-name="FieldColorPills">
        <t t-foreach="widget.totalColors" t-as='pill_no'>
            <span t-attf-class="o_color_pill o_color_#{pill_no}
#{widget.value === pill_no and 'active' or ''}"
                t-att-data-val="pill_no"/>
        </t>
    </t>
</templates>
```

4. Register the QWeb file in your manifest:

```
"qweb": [
        'static/src/xml/qweb_template.xml',
    ],
```

Now, with other add-ons, it is much easier to change the HTML code our widget uses, because they can simply override it with the usual QWeb patterns.

How it works...

As there is already a comprehensive discussion on the basics of QWeb in the *Creating or modifying templates – QWeb* recipe from `Chapter 15`, *CMS Website Development*, we'll focus on what is different here. First of all, you need to realize that we're dealing with the JavaScript QWeb implementation, as opposed to the Python implementation on the server side. This means that you don't have access to browsing records or the environment; you only have access to the parameters you have passed from the `qweb.render` function.

In our case, we have passed the current object via the `widget` key. This means that you should have all the intelligence in the widget's JavaScript code and have your template only access properties, or possibly functions. Given that we can access all the properties that are available on the widget, we can simply check the value in the template by checking the `totalColors` property.

As client-side QWeb has nothing to do with QWeb views, there's a different mechanism to make those templates known to the web client—add them via the `qweb` key to your add-on's manifest in a list of filenames relative to the add-on's root.

There's more...

The reason for going to the effort of using QWeb here was extensibility, and this is the second big difference between client-side and server-side Qweb. On the client side, you can't use XPath expressions; you need to use jQuery selectors and operations. If, for example, we want to add user icons in our widget from another module, we'll use the following code to have an icon in each pill:

```
<t t-extend="FieldColorPills">
    <t t-jquery="span" t-operation="prepend">
        <i class="fa fa-user" />
    </t>
</t>
```

If we also gave a `t-name` attribute here, we'd have made a copy of the original template and left that one untouched. Other possible values for the `t-operation` attribute are `append`, `before`, `after`, `inner`, and `replace`, which causes the content of the `t` element to either be appended to the content of the matched element via `append`, put before or after the matched element via `before` or `after`, replace the content of the matched element via `inner`, or replace the complete element via `replace`. There's also `t-operation='attributes'`, which allows you to set an attribute on the matched element, following the same rules as server-side QWeb.

Another difference is that the names in client-side QWeb are not namespaced by the module name, so you have to choose names for your templates that are probably unique over all add-ons you install, which is why developers tend to choose rather long names.

See also

If you want to learn more about the Qweb templates, refer to the following points:

- The client-side QWeb engine has less convenient error messages and handling than other parts of Odoo. A small error often means that nothing happens, and it's hard for beginners to continue from there.
- Fortunately, there are some debug statements for client-side QWeb templates that will be described later in this chapter, in the *Debugging your client-side code* recipe.

Making RPC calls to the server

Sooner or later, your widget will need to look up some data from the server. In this recipe, we will add a tooltip on the color pill. When the user hovers their cursor over the color pill element, the tooltip will show the number of books related to that color. We will make an RPC call to the server to fetch a book count of the data associated with that particular color.

Getting ready

For this recipe, we will be using the `my_library` module from the previous recipe.

How to do it...

Perform the following steps to make an RPC call to the server and display the result in a tooltip:

1. Add the `willStart` method and set `colorGroupData` in the RPC call:

```
willStart: function () {
    var self = this;
    this.colorGroupData = {};
    var colorDataDef = this._rpc({
        model: this.model,
        method: 'read_group',
        domain: [],
        fields: ['color'],
        groupBy: ['color'],
    }).then(function (result) {
        _.each(result, function (r) {
            self.colorGroupData[r.color] = r.color_count;
        });
    });
    return $.when(this._super.apply(this, arguments),
colorDataDef);
},
```

2. Update `_renderEdit` and set up a bootstrap `tooltip` on `pills`:

```
_renderEdit: function () {
    this.$el.empty();
    var pills = qweb.render('FieldColorPills', {widget: this});
    this.$el.append(pills);
    this.$el.find('[data-toggle="tooltip"]').tooltip();
},
```

3. Update the `FieldColorPills` template and add the `tooltip` data:

```
<t t-name="FieldColorPills">
    <t t-foreach="widget.totalColors" t-as='pill_no'>
        <span t-attf-class="o_color_pill o_color_#{pill_no}
#{widget.value === pill_no and 'active' or ''}"
        t-att-data-val="pill_no"
        data-toggle="tooltip"
        data-placement="top"
        t-attf-title="This color is used in
#{widget.colorGroupData[pill_no] or 0 } books."
        />
    </t>
</t>
```

Update the module to apply the changes. After the update, you will be able to see a tooltip on the pills, as shown in the following screenshot:

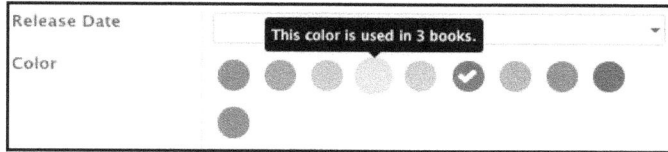

How it works...

The `willStart` function is called before rendering, and, more importantly, it returns a deferred object that must be resolved before the rendering starts. So, in a case like ours, where we need to run an asynchronous action before rendering can occur, this is the right function to do this.

When dealing with data access, we rely on the `_rpc` function provided by the `ServicesMixin` class, as we explained earlier. This function allows you to call any public function on models such as `search`, `read`, `write`, or, in this case, `read_group`.

In step 1, we made an RPC call and invoked the `read_group` method on the current model, which is `library.book`, in our case. We grouped data based on the `color` field, so that the RPC call will return book data that was grouped by `color` and add an aggregate in the `color_count` key. We also mapped the `color_count` and `color` index in the `colorGroupData` so that we could use it in the QWeb template. In the last line of the function, we resolved `willStart` with super and our RPC call using `$.when`. Because of this, rendering only occurs after the values are fetched and after whatever asynchronous action super was busy with has finished, too.

Step 2 is nothing special. We just initialized the bootstrap tooltip.

In step 3, we used `colorGroupData` to set the attributes that are needed to display the tooltip. In the `willStart` method, we assigned a color map via `this.colorGroupData`, so that you can access them in the QWeb template via `widget.colorGroupData`. This is because we passed the widget reference; this is the `qweb.render` method.

> **TIP**
>
> You can use _rpc anywhere in the widget. Note that it is an asynchronous call, and you need to manage a deferred object properly to get the desired result.

There's more...

The AbstractField class comes with a couple of interesting properties, one of which we just used. In our example, we used the this.model property, which holds the name of the current model (for example, library.book). Another property is this.field, which contains roughly the output of the model's fields_get() function for the field the widget is displaying. This will give all the information related to the current field. For example, for x2x fields, the fields_get() function gives you information about the co-model or the domain. You can also use this to query the field's string, size, or whatever other property you can set on the field during model definition.

Another helpful property is nodeOptions, which contains data passed via the options attribute in the <form> view definition. This is already JSON parsed, so you can access it like any object. For more information on such properties, dig further into the abstract_field.js file.

See also

Refer to the following documentation if you have issues managing asynchronous operations:

- Odoo's RPC relies on jQuery's deferred objects, so it is an asynchronous function. You should learn about deferred objects to completely understand RPC calls in JavaScript. You can learn more about deferred objects from jQuery's documentation, at https://api.jquery.com/jQuery.Deferred.

Creating a new view

As you saw in Chapter 10, *Backend Views*, there are different kinds of views, like form, list, kanban, and so on. In this recipe, we will create a brand new view. This view will display the list of authors, along with their books.

Getting ready

For this recipe, we will be using the my_library module from the previous recipe. Note that views are very complex structures, and each existing view has a different purpose and implementation. The purpose of this recipe is to make you aware of the MVC pattern view and how to create simple views. In this recipe, we will create a view called m2m_group, the purpose of which is to display records in groups. To divide records into different groups, the view will use the many2many field data. In the my_library module, we have the author_ids field. Here, we will group books based on authors and display them in cards.

In addition, we will add a new button to the control panel. With the help of this button, you will be able to add a new record of the book. We will also add a button on the author's card, so that we can redirect users to another view.

How to do it...

Follow these steps to add a new view called m2m_group:

1. Add a new view type in ir.ui.view:

```
class View(models.Model):
    _inherit = 'ir.ui.view'

    type = fields.Selection(selection_add=[('m2m_group', 'M2m
Group')])
```

2. Add a new view mode in ir.actions.act_window.view:

```
class ActWindowView(models.Model):
    _inherit = 'ir.actions.act_window.view'

    view_mode = fields.Selection(selection_add=[('m2m_group',
'M2m group')])
```

3. Add a new method by inheriting from the base model. This method will be called from the JavaScript model (see step 4 for more details):

```
class Base(models.AbstractModel):
    _inherit = 'base'

    @api.model
    def get_m2m_group_data(self, domain, m2m_field):
        records = self.search(domain)
```

```
result_dict = {}
for record in records:
    for m2m_record in record[m2m_field]:
        if m2m_record.id not in result_dict:
            result_dict[m2m_record.id] = {
                'name': m2m_record.display_name,
                'children': [],
                'model': m2m_record._name
            }
    result_dict[m2m_record.id]['children'].append({
            'name': record.display_name,
            'id': record.id,
        })
return result_dict
```

4. Add a new file called `/static/src/js/m2m_group_model.js`, and add
the following content to it:

```
odoo.define('m2m_group.Model', function (require) {
    'use strict';

    var AbstractModel = require('web.AbstractModel');

    var M2mGroupModel = AbstractModel.extend({
        get: function () {
            return this.data;
        },
        load: function (params) {
            this.modelName = params.modelName;
            this.domain = params.domain;
            this.m2m_field = params.m2m_field;
            return this._fetchData();
        },
        reload: function (handle, params) {
            if ('domain' in params) {
                this.domain = params.domain;
            }
            return this._fetchData();
        },
        _fetchData: function () {
            var self = this;
            return this._rpc({
                model: this.modelName,
                method: 'get_m2m_group_data',
                kwargs: {
                    domain: this.domain,
                    m2m_field: this.m2m_field
                }
```

```
            }).then(function (result) {
                self.data = result;
            });
        },
    });

    return M2mGroupModel;

});
```

5. Add a new file called `/static/src/js/m2m_group_controller.js`, and add the following content to it:

```
odoo.define('m2m_group.Controller', function (require) {
    'use strict';

    var AbstractController =
require('web.AbstractController');
    var core = require('web.core');
    var qweb = core.qweb;

    var M2mGroupController = AbstractController.extend({
        custom_events: _.extend({},
AbstractController.prototype.custom_events, {
            'btn_clicked': '_onBtnClicked',
        }),
        renderButtons: function ($node) {
            if ($node) {
                this.$buttons =
$(qweb.render('ViewM2mGroup.buttons'));
                this.$buttons.appendTo($node);
                this.$buttons.on('click', 'button',
this._onAddButtonClick.bind(this));
            }
        },
        _onBtnClicked: function (ev) {
            this.do_action({
                type: 'ir.actions.act_window',
                name: this.title,
                res_model: this.modelName,
                views: [[false, 'list'], [false, 'form']],
                domain: ev.data.domain,
            });
        },
        _onAddButtonClick: function (ev) {
            this.do_action({
                type: 'ir.actions.act_window',
                name: this.title,
```

```
                        res_model: this.modelName,
                        views: [[false, 'form']],
                        target: 'new'
                });
        },


        });


        return M2mGroupController;

});
```

6. Add a new file called /static/src/js/m2m_group_renderer.js, and add the following content to it:

```
odoo.define('m2m_group.Renderer', function (require) {
    'use strict';

    var AbstractRenderer = require('web.AbstractRenderer');
    var core = require('web.core');

    var qweb = core.qweb;

    var M2mGroupRenderer = AbstractRenderer.extend({
        events: _.extend({},
AbstractRenderer.prototype.events, {
            'click .o_primay_button': '_onClickButton',
        }),
        _render: function () {
            var self = this;
            this.$el.empty();
            this.$el.append(qweb.render('ViewM2mGroup', {
                'groups': this.state,
            }));
            return this._super.apply(this, arguments);
        },
        _onClickButton: function (ev) {
            ev.preventDefault();
            var target = $(ev.currentTarget);
            var group_id = target.data('group');
            var children_ids =
_.map(this.state[group_id].children, function (group_id) {
                return group_id.id;
            });
            this.trigger_up('btn_clicked', {
                'domain': [['id', 'in', children_ids]]
            });
```

```
        }
    });

    return M2mGroupRenderer;

});
```

7. Add a new file called /static/src/js/m2m_group_view.js, and add
   the following content to it:

```
odoo.define('m2m_group.View', function (require) {
    'use strict';

    var AbstractView = require('web.AbstractView');
    var view_registry = require('web.view_registry');
    var M2mGroupController = require('m2m_group.Controller');
    var M2mGroupModel = require('m2m_group.Model');
    var M2mGroupRenderer = require('m2m_group.Renderer');


    var M2mGroupView = AbstractView.extend({
        display_name: 'Author',
        icon: 'fa-id-card-o',
        config: {
            Model: M2mGroupModel,
            Controller: M2mGroupController,
            Renderer: M2mGroupRenderer,
        },
        viewType: 'm2m_group',
        groupable: false,
        init: function (viewInfo, params) {
            this._super.apply(this, arguments);
            var attrs = this.arch.attrs;

            if (!attrs.m2m_field) {
                throw new Error('M2m view has not defined
    "m2m_field" attribute.');
            }

            // Model Parameters
            this.loadParams.m2m_field = attrs.m2m_field;
        },
    });

    view_registry.add('m2m_group', M2mGroupView);

    return M2mGroupView;
```

```
});
```

8. Add the QWeb template for the view to the
   `/static/src/xml/qweb_template.xml` file:

```xml
<t t-name="ViewM2mGroup">
    <div class="row ml16 mr16">
        <div t-foreach="groups" t-as="group" class="col-3">
            <t t-set="group_data" t-value="groups[group]" />
            <div class="card mt16">
                <img class="card-img-top" t-attf-
src="/web/image/#{group_data.model}/#{group}/image"/>
                <div class="card-body">
                    <h5 class="card-title mt8"><t t-
esc="group_data['name']"/></h5>
                </div>
                <ul class="list-group list-group-flush">
                    <t t-foreach="group_data['children']" t-
as="child">
                        <li class="list-group-item"><i
class="fa fa-book"/> <t t-esc="child.name"/></li>
                    </t>
                </ul>
                <div class="card-body">
                    <a href="#" class="btn btn-sm btn-primary
o_primay_button" t-att-data-group="group">View books</a>
                </div>
            </div>
        </div>
    </div>
</t>

<div t-name="ViewM2mGroup.buttons">
    <button type="button" class="btn btn-primary">
        Add Record
    </button>
</div>
```

9. Add all of the JavaScript files to the backend assets:

```xml
...
<script type="text/javascript"
src="/my_library/static/src/js/m2m_group_view.js" />
<script type="text/javascript"
src="/my_library/static/src/js/m2m_group_model.js" />
<script type="text/javascript"
src="/my_library/static/src/js/m2m_group_controller.js" />
<script type="text/javascript"
```

```
src="/my_library/static/src/js/m2m_group_renderer.js" />
...
```

10. Finally, add our new view for the `library.book` model:

```
<record id="library_book_view_author" model="ir.ui.view">
    <field name="name">Library Book Author</field>
    <field name="model">library.book</field>
    <field name="arch" type="xml">
        <m2m_group m2m_field="author_ids"
color_field="color">
        </m2m_group>
    </field>
</record>
```

11. Add `m2m_group` in the book action:

```
...
<field name="view_mode">tree,m2m_group,form</field>
...
```

Update the `my_library` module to open the book view, and then, from the view switcher, open the new view that we just added. This will look as follows:

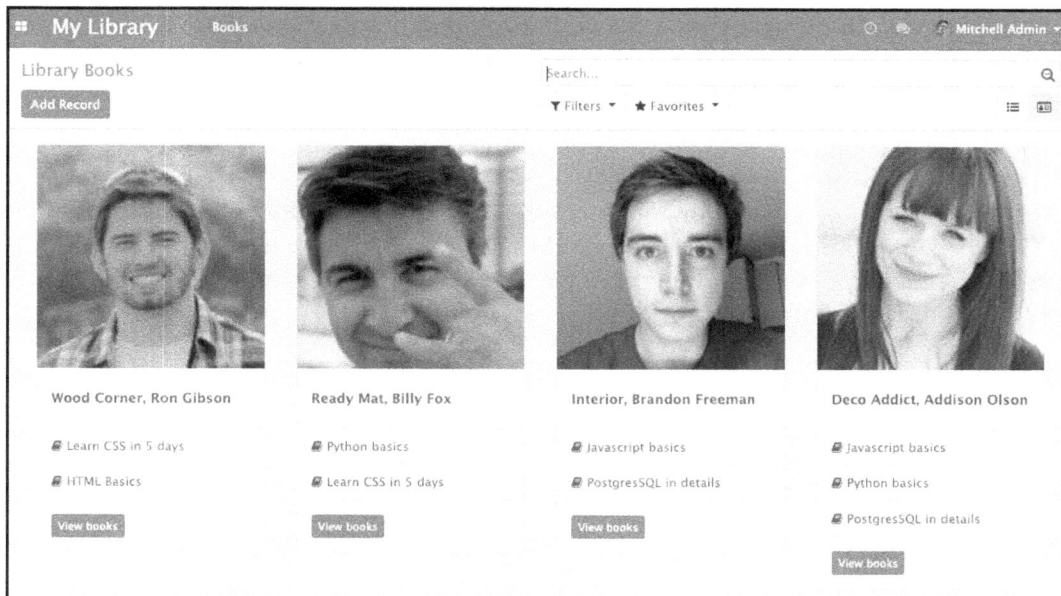

Odoo views are very easy to use and are very flexible. However, it is often the case that easy and flexible things have complex implementations under the hood. This is the same case with the Odoo JavaScript views: they are easy to use, but complex to implement. It consists of lots of components, like the model, renderer, controller, view, QWeb template, and so on. In the next section, we have added all of the required components for the views and have also used a new view for the `library.book` model. If you don't want to add everything manually, grab a module from the example file in this book's GitHub repository.

How it works...

In steps 1 and 2, we registered a new type of view, called `m2m_group`, in `ir.ui.view` and `ir.actions.act_window.view`.

In step 3, we added the `get_m2m_group_data` method in the base. Adding this method in the base will make that method available in every model. This method will be called via an RPC call from the JavaScript view. The view will pass two parameters—the domain and `m2m_field`. In the domain argument, the value of the domain will be the domain generated with a combination of the search view domain and the action domain. The `m2m_field` is the field name by which we want to group the record. This field will be set on the view definition.

In the next few steps, we added the JavaScript files that are required to form the view. An Odoo JavaScript view consists of the view, model, renderer, and controller. The word *view* has historical meaning in the Odoo codebase, so **model, view, controller (MVC)** becomes **model, renderer, controller (MRC)** in Odoo. In general, the view sets up the model, renderer, and controller, and sets the MVC hierarchy so that it looks similar to the following:

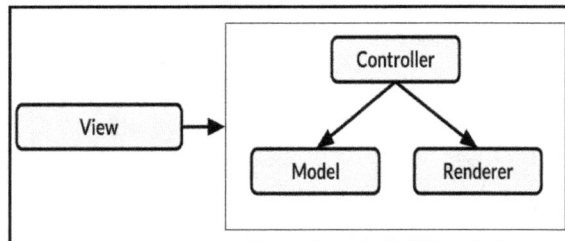

Let's look at the roles of **Model**, **Renderer**, **Controller**, and **View**. Abstract versions of the **Model**, **Renderer**, **Controller**, and **View** have all the basic things that are needed to form a view. Consequently, in our example, we have created the model, renderer, controller, and view by inheriting them.

Here is an in-depth explanation of the different parts that are used to create a view:

- `Model`: The role of the **Model** is to hold the state of the view. It sends an RPC request to the server for the data, and then passes the data to the controller and renderer. We then override the `load` and `reload` methods. When the view is being initialized, it calls the `load()` method to fetch the data, and when the search conditions are changed and the view needs a new state, then the `reload()` method is called. In our case, we have created the common `_fetchData()` method to make an RPC call for data. Note that we used the `get_m2m_group_data` method that we added in step 3. The `get()` method will be called from the controller to get the state of the model.

- `Controller`: The role of the **Controller** is to manage coordination between the **Model** and the **Renderer**. When an action occurs in the **Renderer**, it passes that information to the controller and performs the action accordingly. Sometimes, it also calls some methods in the **Model**. In addition to this, it manages the buttons in the control panel. In our example, we added a button to add new records. To do so, we had to override the `renderButtons()` method of `AbstractController`. We also registered `custom_events` so that when a button in the author card is clicked, the renderer will trigger the event to the controller to make it perform the action.

- `Renderer`: The role of the **Renderer** is to manage the DOM elements for the view. Every view can render data in a different way. In the renderer, you can get the state of the model in a state variable. It calls the `render()` method for the rendering. In our example, we rendered the `ViewM2mGroup` QWeb template with its current state to display our view. We also mapped the JavaScript events to take user actions. In this recipe we have bind the click event for the buttons of the card. Upon clicking the author card button, it will trigger the `btn_clicked` event to the controller, and it will open the list of books for that author.

Note that events and custom_events are different. Events are normal JavaScript events, while custom_events events are from the Odoo JavaScript framework. Custom events can be invoked via the trigger_up method.

- View: The role of the **Renderer** is to get all the basic things that are required to build views, like a set of fields, a context, a view arch, and some other parameters. After that, the view will initialize the controller, renderer, and model triplet. It will set them in the MVC hierarchy. Usually, it sets up the parameters that are required in the model, view, and controller. In our example, we want the m2m_field name to get proper grouped data in the **Model**, so we have set the model parameter in it. In the same way, this.controllerParams and this.rendererParams can be used to set the parameters in the controller and renderer.

In step 8, we added a QWeb template for the views and control panel buttons. To learn more about the QWeb template, refer to the *Using client-side QWeb templates* recipe in this chapter.

Odoo views have tons of methods for different purposes; we looked at the most important one in this section. If you want to learn more about views, you can explore them further by going to the /addons/web/static/src/js/views/ directory. This directory also includes code for the abstract model, controller, renderer, and view.

In step 9, we added JavaScript files in the assets.

Finally, in the last two steps, we added a view definition for the book.library model. In step 10, we used the <m2m_group> tag for the view, and we also passed the m2m_field attribute as the option. This will be passed to the model to fetch the data from the server.

There's more...

If you don't want to introduce the new view type and you just want to modify a few things in the view instead, you can use `js_class` on the view. For example, if we want a view similar to the kanban one that we created, then we can extend it as follows:

```
var CustomRenderer = KanbanRenderer.extend({
    ...
});

var CustomRendererModel = KanbanModel.extend({
    ...
});

var CustomRendererController = KanbanController.extend({
    ...
});

var CustomDashboardView = KanbanView.extend({
    config: _.extend({}, KanbanView.prototype.config, {
        Model: CustomDashboardModel,
        Renderer: CustomDashboardRenderer,
        Controller: CustomDashboardController,
    }),
});

var viewRegistry = require('web.view_registry');
viewRegistry.add('my_custom_view', CustomDashboardView);
```

We can then use the kanban view with `js_class` (note that the server still thinks of this as a kanban view):

```
...
<field name="arch" type="xml">
    <kanban js_class="my_custom_view">
        ...
    </kanban>
</field>
...
```

Debugging your client-side code

For debugging server-side code, this book contains a whole chapter, that is, `Chapter 8`, *Debugging*. For the client-side part, you'll get a kick-start in this recipe.

Getting ready

This recipe doesn't really rely on specific code, but if you want to be able to reproduce exactly what's going on, grab the previous recipe's code.

How to do it...

What makes debugging client-side script difficult is that the web client heavily relies on jQuery's asynchronous events. Given that break points halt execution, there is a high chance that a bug caused by timing issues will not occur when debugging. We'll discuss some strategies for this later:

1. For the client side debugging, you will need to activate debug mode with the assets. If you don't know how to activate debug mode with the assets rede the *Activating the Odoo developer tools* recipe from `Chapter 1`, *Installing the Odoo Development Environment*.

2. In the JavaScript function you're interested in, call the `debugger`:

   ```
   debugger;
   ```

3. If you have timing problems, log in to the console through a JavaScript function:

   ```
   console.log("I'm in function X currently");
   ```

4. If you want to debug during template rendering, call the debugger from QWeb:

   ```
   <t t-debug="" />
   ```

5. You can also have QWeb log in to the console, as follows:

   ```
   <t t-log="myvalue" />
   ```

All of this relies on your browser offering the appropriate functionality for debugging. While all major browsers do that, we'll only look at Chromium here, for demonstration purposes. To be able to use the debug tools, open them by clicking on the top-right menu button and selecting **More tools⏐Developer tools**:

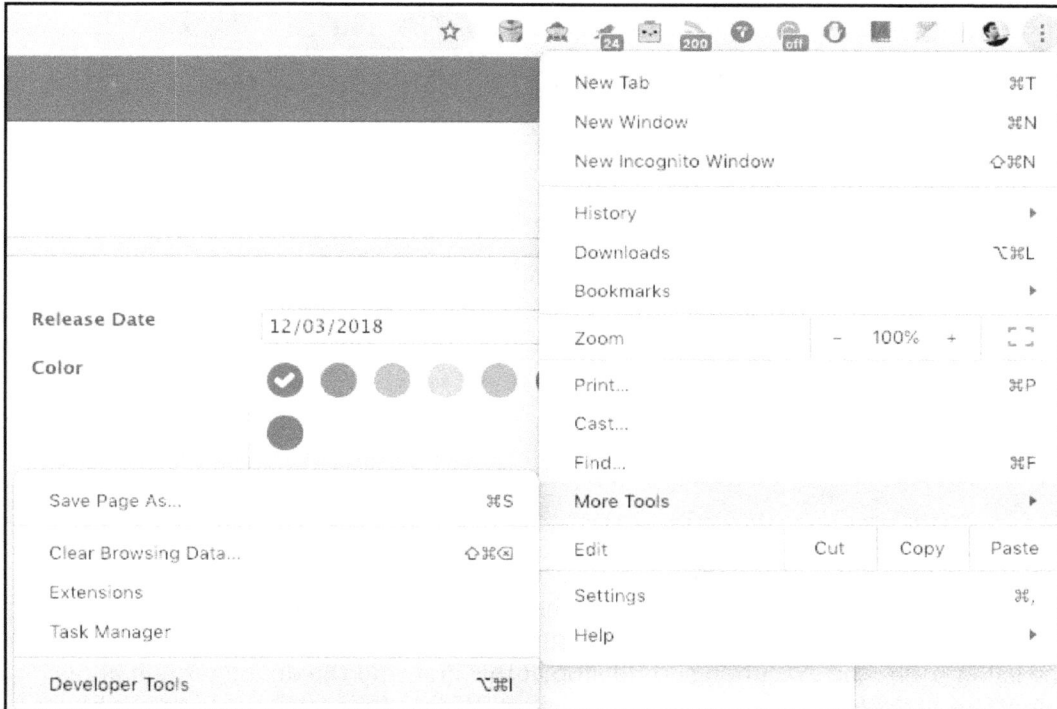

How it works...

When the debugger is open, you should see something similar to the following screenshot:

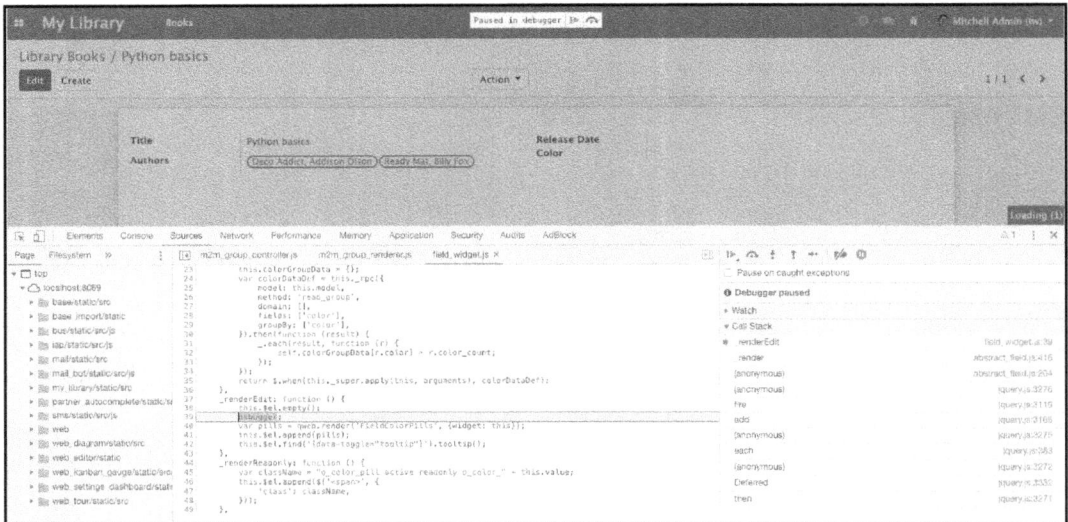

Here, you have access to a lot of different tools in the separate tabs. The currently active tab in the preceding screenshot is the JavaScript debugger, where we set a break point in line **31** by clicking on the line number. Every time our widget fetches the list of users, the execution should stop at this line, and the debugger will allow you to inspect variables or change their values. Within the watch list to the right, you can also call functions to try out their effects without having to continuously save your script file and reload the page.

The debugger statements we described earlier will behave the same as soon as you have the developer tools open. The execution will then stop and the browser will switch to the **Sources** tab, with the file in question opened and the line with the debugger statement highlighted.

The two logging possibilities from earlier will end up in the **Console** tab. This is the first tab you should inspect in case of problems, anyway, because if some JavaScript code doesn't load at all because of syntax errors or similar fundamental problems, you'll see an error message there explaining what's going on.

There's more...

Use the **Elements** tab to inspect the DOM representation of the page the browser currently displays. This will prove helpful when it comes to familiarizing yourself with the HTML code the existing widgets produce, and it will also allow you to play with classes and CSS attributes, in general. This is a great resource for testing layout changes.

The **Network** tab gives you an overview of which requests the current page made and how long it took. This is helpful when it comes to debugging slow page loads, as in the **Network** tab, you will usually find the details of the requests. If you select a request, you can inspect the payload that was passed to the server and the result returned, which helps you to figure out the reason for unexpected behavior on the client side. You'll also see the status codes of requests made—for example, **404**—in case a resource can't be found because you misspelled a filename, for instance.

Improving onboarding with tour

After developing a large application, it is crucial to explain software flows to the end users. The Odoo framework includes a built-in tour manager. With this tour manager, you can guide an end user through learning specific flows. In this recipe, we will create a tour so that we can create a book in the library.

Getting ready

We will be using the `my_library` module from the previous recipe. Tours are only displayed in the database without demo data, so if you are using a database with demo data, create a new database without demo data for this recipe.

How to do it...

To add a tour to a library, follow these steps:

1. Add a new `/static/src/js/my_library_tour.js` file with the following code:

```
odoo.define('my_library.tour', function (require) {
    "use strict";
```

```
            var core = require('web.core');
            var tour = require('web_tour.tour');

            var _t = core._t;

            tour.register('library_tour', {
                url: "/web",
            }, [tour.STEPS.SHOW_APPS_MENU_ITEM, {
                    trigger: '.o_app[data-menu-
xmlid="my_library.library_base_menu"]',
                    content: _t('Manage books and authors in<b>Library
app</b>.'),
                    position: 'right'
            }, {
                trigger: '.o_list_button_add',
                content: _t("Let's create new book."),
                position: 'bottom'
            }, {
                trigger: 'input[name="name"]',
                extra_trigger: '.o_form_editable',
                content: _t('Set the book title'),
                position: 'right',
            }, {
                trigger: '.o_form_button_save',
                content: _t('Save this book record'),
                position: 'bottom',
            }
]);

});
```

2. Add the tour JavaScript file in the backend assets:

```
...
<script type="text/javascript"
src="/my_library/static/src/js/my_library_tour.js" />
...
```

Update the module and open the Odoo backend. At this point, you will see the tour, as shown in the following screenshot:

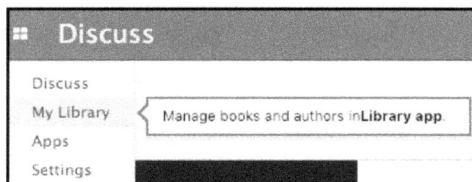

How it works...

The tour manager is available under the `web_tour.tour` namespace.

In the first step, we imported `web_tour.tour`. We can then add a new tour with the `register()` function. We registered our tour with the `library_tour` name and passed the URL on which this tour should run.

The next parameter is a list of these tour steps. A tour step requires three values. The trigger is used to select the element on which the tour should be displayed. This is a JavaScript selector. We used the XML ID of the out menu, because it is available in the DOM.

The first step, `tour.STEPS.SHOW_APPS_MENU_ITEM`, is the predefined step from the tour for the main menu. The next key is the content, and this is displayed when the user hovers over the tour drop. We used the `_t()` function because we want to translate the string, while the position key is used to decide on the position of the tour drop. Possible values include top, right, left, or bottom.

> The tours improve the onboarding experience of the user, as well as managing the integration tests. When you run Odoo with test mode internally, it also runs the tours and causes the test case to fail if a tour has not finished.

Mobile app JavaScript

Odoo v10 introduced the Odoo mobile application. It provides a few small utilities to perform mobile actions, like vibrate phone, show toast message, scan QR code, and so on.

Getting ready

We will be using the `my_library` module from the previous library. We will show you the toast when we change the value of the **color** field from the mobile app.

> **Warning:** The Odoo mobile app only supports Enterprise edition, so if you don't have Enterprise edition, then you cannot test it.

How to do it...

Follow these steps to show toast in the Odoo mobile app:

1. Import `web_mobile.rpc` in `field_widget.js`:

```
var mobile = require('web_mobile.rpc');
```

2. Modify the `clickPill` method to display toast when user changes color from mobile device:

```
clickPill: function (ev) {
    var $target = $(ev.currentTarget);
    var data = $target.data();
    if (mobile.methods.showToast) {
        mobile.methods.showToast({ 'message': 'Color
changed' });
    }
    this._setValue(data.val.toString());
}
```

Update the module and open the form view of the `library.book` model in the mobile app. When you change the color, you will see toast, as shown in the following screenshot:

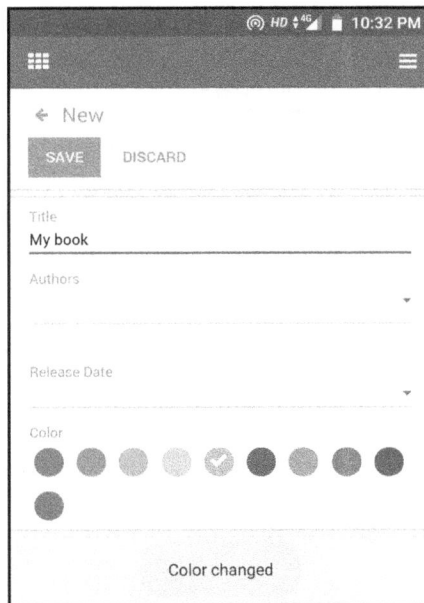

How to works...

`web_mobile.rpc` provides the bridge between a mobile device and Odoo JavaScript. It exposes a few basic mobile utilities. In our example, we used the `showToast` method to display toast in the mobile app. We also need to check the availability of the function. The reason behind this is that some mobile phones might not support a few features for example, if devices don't have a camera, then you can't use the `scanBarcode()` method. In such cases, to avoid tracebacks, we need to wrap them with the `if` condition.

There's more...

The mobile utilities that are in Odoo are as follows:

- `showToast()`: To display toast
- `vibrate()`: To make a phone vibrate
- `showSnackBar()`: To display a snack bar with a button
- `showNotification()`: To display a mobile notification
- `addContact()`: To add a new contact in the phonebook
- `scanBarcode()`: To scan QR codes
- `switchAccount()`: To open the account switcher in Android

To learn more about mobile JavaScript, refer to `https://www.odoo.com/documentation/12.0/reference/mobile.html`.

In-App Purchasing with Odoo 17

In this chapter, we will cover the following recipes:

- **In-app purchase (IAP)** concepts
- Registering an IAP service in Odoo
- Creating an IAP service module
- Authorizing and charging IAP credits
- Creating an IAP client module
- Displaying offers when accounts lack credits

Introduction

Odoo introduced IAPs in version 11. The IAP is used to provide recurring services without any complex configurations. Usually, apps purchased from the app store only require a one-time payment from the customer, because they are normal modules and their use won't cost the developer anything. In contrast to this, IAP apps are used to provide services to users, and therefore, they have an operational cost to provide a continuous service. In such cases, it is not possible to provide a service with just the single initial purchase. The service provider needs something that charges the user in a recurring manner, based on usage. Odoo IAP fixes these issues and provides a way to charge based on usage. In this chapter, we will create a small service to provide full book information based on ISBN numbers.

Technical requirements

The technical requirements for this chapter include the online Odoo platform.

All the code used in this chapter can be downloaded from the GitHub repository, at `https://github.com/PacktPublishing/Odoo-12-Development-Cookbook-Third-Edition/tree/master/Chapter17`.

Check out the following video to see the Code in Action:

`http://bit.ly/2ULQAc0`

In-app purchase concepts

In this recipe, we will explore the different entities that are a part of the IAP process. We will also look at the role of each entity and how they combine to complete the IAP process cycle.

How it works...

There are three main entities in the IAP process: the customer, the service provider, and Odoo itself. These are described as follows:

- The **customer** is the end user that wants to use the service. In order to use the service, the customer needs to install the application provided by the service provider. The client then needs to purchase a service plan according to their usage requirements. With that, the client can start to use the service straight away. This prevents difficulties for the customer, as it is not necessary to carry out complex configurations. Instead, they just pay for the service and start to use it.
- The **service provider** is the developer that wants to sell the service (probably you). The client will ask the provider for the service, at which point the service provider will check whether there is enough credit in the client account. If the client has enough credit, the service provider will deduct the credit and serve the service to the customer.

- **Odoo** is a kind of broker in this. It provides the medium for handling payments, credits, plans, and so on. Customers purchase the service credit from Odoo, and the service provider draws this credit when serving the service. Odoo then fills the gap between the customer and the service provider, so the customer has no need to do complex configurations and the service provider has no need to set up a payment gateway, customer account management, and so on. In return, Odoo takes commission from the sale. At the time of writing this book, Odoo takes 25% commission from the packs.

There is also an optional entity in the process, which is the **external service**. In some cases, service providers use some external services. However, we will ignore external services here, as they are the secondary service provider. An example of this could be an SMS service. If you are providing an SMS IAP service to Odoo users, then you (the service provider) will use an SMS service internally.

The IAP service flow

Now, we will look at how all IAP entities work together to provide the service. The following diagram illustrates the IAP process:

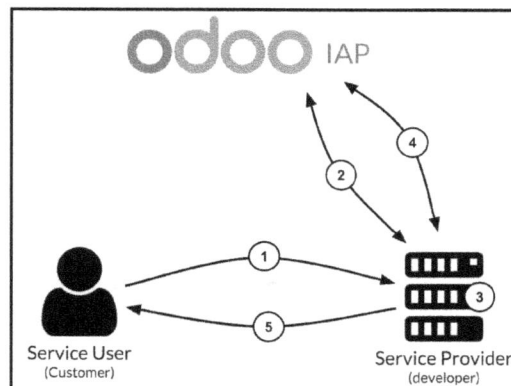

Here is an explanation of every step of the IAP service flow:

1. A **Customer** will make a request to the **Service Provider** for a service. With this request, the **Customer** will pass the account token, which will be used by the **Service Provider** to identify the user. (Note that the customers will have your module installed in their server.)
2. After receiving a request from the **Customer**, the **Service Provider** will ask the **Odoo IAP** whether the **Customer** has enough credit in this account. If the **Customer** has enough credit, then it will create the transaction to reserve that credit before providing the service.
3. After reserving the credit, the **Service Provider** will perform the service. In some cases, the **Service Provider** will call an external service to perform the requested service.
4. After performing the service requested by the **Customer**, the **Service Provider** goes back to the **Odoo API** to capture the credit reserved in step 2. If the requested service cannot be served due to an error, the **Service Provider** will ask **Odoo** to release the reserved credit.
5. Finally, the **Service Provider** will get back to the **Customer** to notify them that the requested service has been served. Some services might return the resulting information; here, you will get the result of the service. This resulting information is used by the **Customer** based on his/her specifications (depending on the service).

There's more...

If the customer does not have enough credit, the service flow is as follows:

1. The customer requests the service (just like in the previous flow).
2. A service provider gets the request and asks Odoo whether the user has enough credit. Suppose that the customer does not have enough credit.
3. The service provider returns to the customer and informs them that there is not enough credit in the account, showing information (an Odoo service packs link) on where the user can purchase the service.
4. The customer is redirected to Odoo and purchases the credit for the service.

Registering an IAP service in Odoo

In order to draw credits from the customer account, the service providers need to register their services on Odoo. You also define plans for the services. The user will purchase your plans through this registered service. In this recipe, we will register our service on Odoo and define plans for our service.

Getting ready

To sell the services from the IAP platform, the service provider needs to register services and plans to Odoo. We are going to register our service on `https://iap-sandbox.odoo.com/`. This IAP endpoint is used for testing purposes. You can purchase a service pack for free. For production, you need to register a service at `https://iap.odoo.com`. For this recipe, we will use the sandbox IAP endpoint.

How to do it...

Follow these steps to create an IAP service on Odoo:

1. Open `https://iap-sandbox.odoo.com/` and log in (sign up if you don't have an account).
2. Click on the **Manage my service** button on the home page.
3. Click on the **Create** button to create a new service.

4. This will open a form like the following screenshot. Here, fill in information including the **Service Logo**, **Technical Name** (must be unique), **Unit Name**, **Private Policy**, and so on:

5. Saving a service will show a **Service key**, like in the following screenshot. Note the **Service key** at this point, as it will not be displayed again:

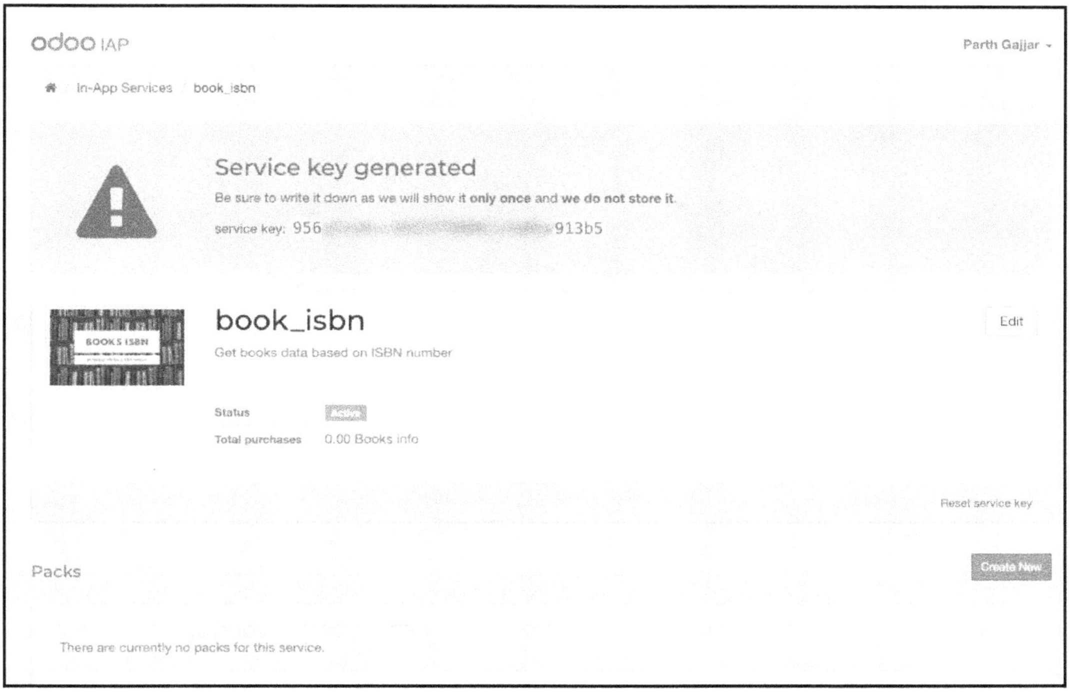

6. Create a few packs (plans) for the service by clicking on the **Create new** button in the **Packs** section. For example, `Get 50 books info in 10 Euro`. The following screenshot shows the page to create a new pack:

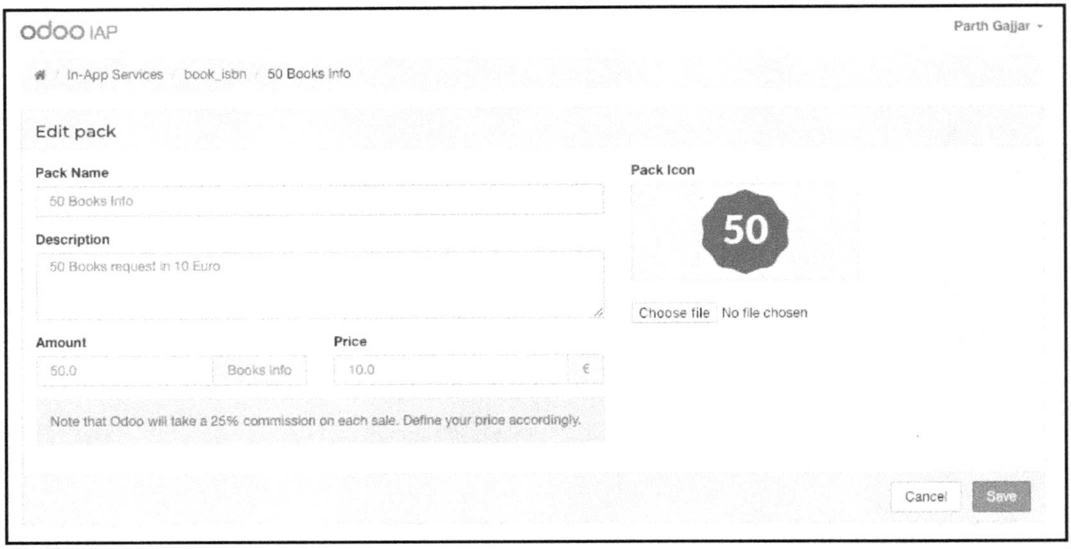

After the configuration is complete, your service page will look like this:

odoo IAP   Parth Gajjar ▾

🏠 / In-App Services / book_isbn

book_isbn   Edit
Get books data based on ISBN number

Status   `Active`

Total purchases   0.00 Books info

Reset service key

Packs   Create New

Name	Amount	Price	
50 50 Books Info	50.00 Books info	10.00 €	Edit
100 100 Books Info	100.00 Books info	18.00 €	Edit

How it works...

We have created an IAP service on `https://iap-sandbox.odoo.com/`, as we want to test the IAP service before moving the service into the production. Let's explore the use of the fields that we filled in while creating the service:

- The **Technical name** is used to identify your service, and it must be a unique name. We have added the `book_isbn` technical name here. (It is not possible to change this later.)
- The **Label, Description,** and **Service Logo** are used for informational purposes. This information will be displayed on the web page when the user is purchasing the service.

- The **Unit Name** is the unit by which your service is sold. For example, in an SMS service, your **Unit Name** will be SMS (for example, 100 SMS in $5). In our case, we have used the Books info **Unit Name**.
- The **Trial Credit** is the free credit provided to a customer for testing. This is only provided once per customer.
- The **Privacy Policy** is the URL of the privacy policy for your service.

After submitting these details, your service will be created and it will display the service key. Refer to the image shown in step 5 of this recipe for more information. Store this key securely, because it won't be displayed again, although it is possible to generate a new key from the same page. The service key will be used to capture customer credit during a service request.

We still need to create plans for our service. You need to provide the plan name, description, logo, amount, and price. The amount field is used for the number of service units for that plan. The price field is used for defining the amount that a user needs to pay to get this plan. In step 6 of this recipe, we created a plan for **50 Books Info** in **10 Euro**. Here, **Book Info** is the unit type that we submitted during the creation of the service. This means that if a user purchases this plan, he will be able to get the information for 50 books.

> Odoo takes 25% commission from this price, so define your service plan price accordingly.

Now, we will create an IAP service and an IAP client module in the following sections.

Creating an IAP service module

In this recipe, we will create a service module to be used by the service provider. This module will accept the IAP request from the customer and return the service result in the response.

Getting ready

We will create the `iap_isbn_service` module. This service module will handle customer IAP requests. Customers will send the book info requests with the ISBN numbers. The service module will capture the credit from the customer account and return information like the name, author, and cover image.

To provide easy understanding, we will develop a service module by splitting it into two recipes. In this recipe, we will create a basic module that creates a table for the book's information. Upon a customer request, the service provider will return the book information by searching in this table. In the next recipe, we will add the second part of the service module; in that module, we will add the code to capture the credits.

How to do it...

Follow these steps to generate a basic service module:

1. Create a new `iap_isbn_service` module and add `__init__.py`:

```
from . import models
from . import controllers
```

2. Add `__manifest__.py`, with the following content:

```
{
    'name': "IAP ISBN service",
    'summary': "Get books information by ISBN number",
    'website': "http://www.example.com",
    'category': 'Uncategorized',
    'version': '12.0.1',
    'depends': ['iap', 'web', 'base_setup'],
    'data': [
        'security/ir.model.access.csv',
        'views/book_info_views.xml',
        'data/books_data.xml',
    ]
}
```

3. Add a `book.info` model at `models/book_info.py`, with a method to fetch the book data:

```python
from odoo import models, fields, api

class BookInfo(models.Model):
    _name = 'book.info'

    name = fields.Char('Books Name', required=True)
    isbn = fields.Char('ISBN', required=True)
    date_release = fields.Date('Release Date')
    cover_image = fields.Binary('BooksCover')
    author_ids = fields.Many2many('res.partner',
string='Authors')

    @api.model
    def _books_data_by_isbn(self, isbn):
        book = self.search([('isbn', '=', isbn)], limit=1)
        if book:
            return {
                'status': 'found',
                'data': {
                    'name': book.name,
                    'isbn': book.isbn,
                    'date_release': book.date_release,
                    'cover_image': book.cover_image,
                    'authors': [a.name for a in
book.author_ids]
                }
            }
        else:
            return {
                'status': 'not found',
            }
```

4. Add an `http` controller in the `controller/main.py` file (don't forget to add the `controllers/__init__.py` file):

```python
from odoo import http
from odoo.http import request

class Main(http.Controller):
    @http.route('/get_book_data', type='json', auth="public")
    def get_book_data(self):
        # We will capture credit here
        return {
            'test': 'data'
        }
```

5. Add access rules to `security/ir.model.access.csv`:

```
id,name,model_id:id,group_id:id,perm_read,perm_write,perm_crea
te,perm_unlink
acl_book_backend_user,book_info,model_book_info,base.group_use
r,1,1,1,1
```

6. Add views, menus, and actions to `views/book_info_views.xml`:

```xml
<?xml version="1.0" encoding="utf-8"?>
<odoo>
    <!-- Form View -->
    <record id="book_info_view_form" model="ir.ui.view">
        <field name="name">Book Info Form</field>
        <field name="model">book.info</field>
        <field name="arch" type="xml">
            <form>
                <sheet>
                    <field name="cover_image" widget='image'
class="oe_avatar"/>
                    <div class="oe_title">
                        <label for="name"
class="oe_edit_only"/>
                        <h1>
                            <field name="name"
class="oe_inline"/>
                        </h1>
                    </div>
                    <group>
                        <group>
                            <field name="isbn"/>
                            <field name="author_ids"
widget="many2many_tags"/>
                        </group>
                        <group>
                            <field name="date_release"/>
                        </group>
                    </group>
                </sheet>
            </form>
        </field>
    </record>

    <!-- Tree(list) View -->
    <record id="books_info_view_tree" model="ir.ui.view">
        <field name="name">Book Info List</field>
        <field name="model">book.info</field>
        <field name="arch" type="xml">
```

```xml
            <tree>
                <field name="name"/>
                <field name="date_release"/>
            </tree>
        </field>
    </record>

    <!-- action and menus -->
    <record id='book_info_action'
model='ir.actions.act_window'>
        <field name="name">Book info</field>
        <field name="res_model">book.info</field>
        <field name="view_type">form</field>
        <field name="view_mode">tree,form</field>
    </record>
    <menuitem name="Books Data" id="books_info_base_menu" />
    <menuitem name="Books" id="book_info_menu"
parent="books_info_base_menu" action="book_info_action"/>
</odoo>
```

7. Add some sample book data to `data/books_data.xml` (don't forget to add cover images to the given directory):

```xml
<?xml version="1.0" encoding="utf-8"?>
<odoo noupdate="1">
    <record id="book_info_data_1" model="book.info">
        <field name="name">Learning PostgreSQL 10</field>
        <field name="isbn">1788392019</field>
        <field name="author_ids" eval="[(0, 0, {'name':
'Salahaldin Juba'}), (0, 0, {'name': 'Andrey Volkov'})]"/>
        <field name="date_release">2017/12/01</field>
        <field name="cover_image" type="base64"
file="iap_isbn_service/static/img/postgres.jpg"/>
    </record>

    <record id="book_info_data_2" model="book.info">
        <field name="name">Odoo 10 Development
Essentials</field>
        <field name="isbn">9781785884887</field>
        <field name="author_ids" eval="[(0, 0, {'name':
'Daniel Reis'})]"/>
        <field name="date_release">2016/09/25</field>
        <field name="cover_image" type="base64"
file="iap_isbn_service/static/img/odoo.jpg"/>
    </record>

</odoo>
```

After installing the module, you will see a new menu with book data, like the following:

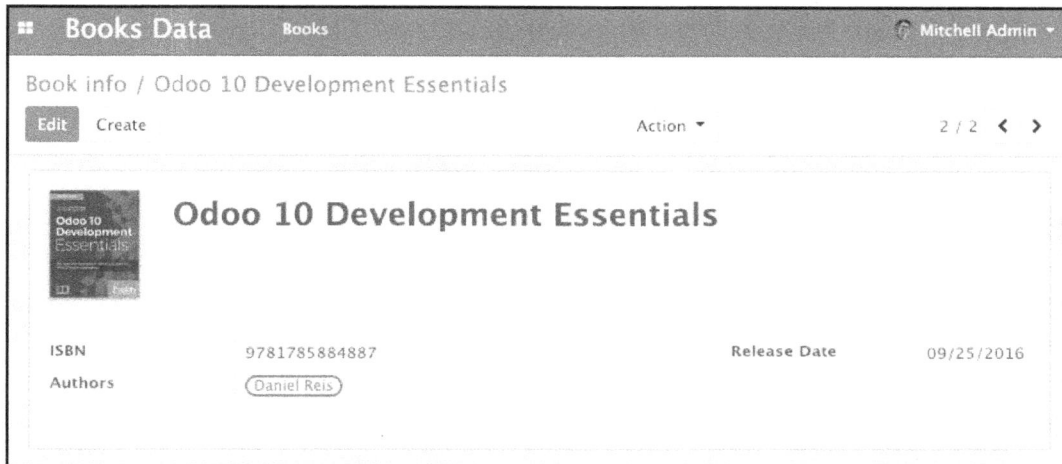

How it works...

We have now created the `iap_isbn_service` module. We have created a new `book.info` table. Consider this table the main table, where we will store data for all of the books. When the customer requests book data, we will search in this table. If the requested data is found, we will charge credits in exchange for book data.

> If you want to create this service for commercial purposes, you will need to have information about every book in the world. In the real world, you will need to have an external service as the book's information source. For our exercise, assume that we have the data of all of the books in the `book.info` table, and we will give book data from this table only.

In the model, we have also created the `_books_data_by_isbn()` method. This method will find a book from an ISBN number and generate the proper data so that it can be sent back to the customer. The `status` key in the result will be used to indicate whether the book data is found. It will be used to release reserved credit when the book data is not found.

We have also added `/get_book_data route`. The IAP customer will make a request on this URL to get the book details. We still need to add the code for capturing IAP credit for the service, which will be done in the next recipe. However, for testing purposes, you can make a test request through `curl`, like this:

```
curl --header "Content-Type: application/json" \
     --request POST \
     --data "{}" \
     http://localhost:8069/get_book_data
```

This will return something like this: `{"jsonrpc": "2.0", "id": null, "result": {"test": "data"}}`.

The rest of the steps in this recipe are from previous recipes, and don't need a detailed explanation. In the next recipe, we will update our module to capture the customer's credit and return the book data to them.

Authorizing and charging IAP credits

In this recipe, we will complete the IAP service module. We will use the IAP platform to authorize and capture credit from the customer account. We will also add an optional configuration to save the service key generated in the *Registering an IAP service in Odoo* recipe of this chapter.

Getting ready

For this recipe, we will be using the `iap_isbn_service` module.

As we are using the IAP sandbox service, we need a set IAP endpoint in the system parameter. To set the IAP sandbox endpoint, follow these steps:

1. Activate developer mode.
2. Open the menu at **Technical | Parameters | System Parameters**.
3. Create a new record and add a **Key** and **Value**, as follows:

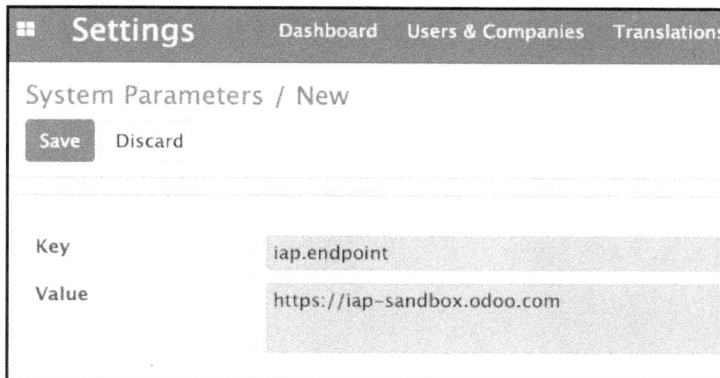

How to do it...

In order to complete the service module, we will add a configuration option to the store service key. Follow these steps to add a new field to set the isbn_service_key in the general settings:

1. Add an isbn_service_key field in res.config.settings:

```
from odoo import models, fields

class ConfigSettings(models.TransientModel):
    _inherit = 'res.config.settings'

    isbn_service_key = fields.Char("ISBN service key",
config_parameter='iap.isbn_service_key')
```

2. Add an isbn_service_key field in the general settings view:

```
<?xml version="1.0" encoding="utf-8"?>
<odoo>
    <record id="view_general_config_isbn_service"
model="ir.ui.view">
        <field name="name">Configuration: IAP service
ksy</field>
        <field name="model">res.config.settings</field>
        <field name="inherit_id"
ref="base_setup.res_config_settings_view_form" />
        <field name="arch" type="xml">
            <div id="business_documents" position="before">
                <h2>IAP Books ISBN service</h2>
                <div class="row mt16 o_settings_container">
```

```
                            <div class="col-12 col-lg-6
o_setting_box">
                                <div class="o_setting_right_pane">
                                    <span class="o_form_label">IAP
service key</span>
                                    <div class="text-muted">
                                    Generate service in odoo IAP and
add service key here
                                    </div>
                                    <div class="content-group">
                                        <div class="mt16 row">
                                            <label
for="isbn_service_key"
                                                 class="col-3 col-
lg-3 o_light_label"/>
                                            <field
name="isbn_service_key"
                                                 class="oe_inline"
required="1"/>
                                        </div>
                                    </div>
                                </div>
                            </div>
                        </div>
                    </div>
                </field>
            </record>
</odoo>
```

This will add a field in the **General Settings** to store a service key, as shown in the
following screenshot. If you remember, we generated the service key in the
Registering an IAP service in Odoo recipe of this chapter. Add the generated service key
in this field. See the following screenshot for more information:

Now, we will update the `/get_book_data` controller to capture the customer credit. Update the `main.py` file, as follows:

```python
from odoo import http
from odoo.http import request
from odoo.addons.iap.models import iap

class Main(http.Controller):
    @http.route('/get_book_data', type='json', auth="public")
    def get_book_data(self, account_token, isbn_number):
        service_key = request.env['ir.config_parameter'].sudo()
                        .get_param('iap.isbn_service_key', False)
        if not service_key:
            return {
                'status': 'service is not active'
            }
        credits_to_reserve = 1
        data = {}
        with iap.charge(request.env, service_key,
                        account_token, credits_to_reserve):
            data =
request.env['book.info'].sudo()._books_data_by_isbn(isbn_number)
            if data['status'] == 'not found':
                raise Exception('Book not found')
        return data
```

Update the module to apply these changes.

How it works...

In order to draw credit from the customer's account, we will need a service key generated from the IAP platform. In the *Registering an IAP service in Odoo* recipe of this chapter, we generated a service key. (It's no problem if you have lost the service key; it can be regenerated from the service page). We have added an `isbn_service_key` field in the general settings so that we can store a service key in Odoo. You may have noticed that we used the `config_parameter` attribute in the file definition.

The use of this attribute in the field will store the value in the `ir.config_parameter` model, also known as the **System Parameters.** After saving it, you can check its value in the **Technical | Parameters | System Parameters** menu, in developer mode. While capturing IAP credits, we will retrieve the service key from the **System Parameters**. To retrieve the values from the **System Parameters**, you can use `get_param()`. For example, you can fetch a service key like this:

```
self.env['ir.config_parameter'].sudo().get_param('iap.isbn_service_key
', False)
```

Here, the first argument is the key of the parameter that has a value you want to access, and the second argument is a default value. If the requested key is not present in the database, then the default value will be returned.

Next, we updated the `/get_book_data` route. Now, it is accepting two arguments:

- The `account_token`, which is the customer token used to identify the user. The credit purchased by the customer for the service will be linked to this `account_token` in the IAP platform. Service providers will send this token while capturing credit.
- The `isbn_number` is the ISBN number of the book whose information the customer wants in exchange for credit.

> These arguments are not fixed here. Our example service needs an `isbn_number`, so we have passed it. However, you can pass any number of arguments that you want. Just make sure that you have passed the `account_token`, because without it, you cannot capture credit from the customer account.

The IAP provides the `iap.charge()` helper method, which handles the process of capturing credit from the customer account. The `charge()` method accepts four parameters: the environment, the provider service key, the customer account token, and the amount of credit to capture. The `charge()` method manages the following things:

- Creating the transaction object and reserving the specified number of credits. If a customer account doesn't have enough credit, then it will raise `InsufficientCreditError`.
- If enough credit is found in a customer account, it will run code in the `with` block.

- If the code in the `with` block runs successfully, it captures the received credit.
- If the code in the `with` block generates an exception, it will release the reserved credit, as the service request cannot be completed.

In the previous example, we used the same `iap.charge()` method to capture credit for a book request. We used our service key and customer account token to reserve the `1` credit for the book info. Then, inside the `with` block, we used the `_books_data_by_isbn()` method to get book data based on the ISBN number. If the book data is found, then it will execute the `with` block without any errors and one reserved credit will be deducted from the customer account. Later, we will return this data to the customer. If the book data is not found, then we raise the `Exception` so that the reserved credit is released.

There's more...

In our example, we are handling the request of only one book's data, and capturing the single credit is simple; but things get complicated with multiple credits. A complex pricing structure can introduce a few corner cases. Let's look at this issue through the following example. Suppose that we want to handle multiple book requests. In this case, a customer has requested the data of 10 books, but we only have the data of five books. Here, if we complete the `with` block without encountering any errors, the `charge()` will capture 10 credits, which is incorrect, because we only have the data for a certain amount of books. Furthermore, if we raise the exception, then it will release all 10 credits and show the customer that the book info is not found. To fix this issue, Odoo provides the object of the transaction in the `with` block. In some cases, the services can not fully served. Example for, the user asked for data of 10 books but you only have data for 5 books. In such cases, you can change the actual credit amount on the go and capture partial credits. See the following example for a further explanation:

```
...
isbn_list = [<assume list of 10 isbn number>]
credits_to_reserve = len(isbn_list)
data_found = []
with iap.charge(request.env, service_key, account_token,
credits_to_reserve) as transection:
    for isbn in isbn_list:
        data = request.env['books.info']._books_data_by_isbn(isbn)
        if data['status'] == 'found':
            data_found.appned(data)
    transection.credit = len(data_found)
```

```
return data_found
```

In the preceding code block, we have updated the value of the credit to capture on the fly, according to `transection.credit`; this is how we can only charge credit for the book data that is found.

See also

- IAP is not limited to the Odoo framework. You can develop a service provider module in any other platform or framework. Just make sure that it can handle JSON-RPC2 (`https://www.jsonrpc.org/specification`) requests.
- If you develop a service provider in any other platform, you will also need to manage a transaction manually by using IAP endpoints. You will need to authorize and capture credit by requesting IAP endpoints. You can get endpoint information at `https://www.odoo.com/documentation/12.0/webservices/iap.html#json-rpc2-transaction-api`.

Creating an IAP client module

In the previous recipe, we created the IAP service module. Now, we will create an IAP client module to complete the IAP service flow.

Getting ready

We will need the `my_library` module from Chapter 4, *Creating Odoo Add-On Modules*. We will add a new button in the book's form view, and clicking that button will create a request to an IAP service and fetch the book data.

As per the IAP service flow, the customer makes the request to the service provider. Here, to make a customer's request, we need to run the separate server for the IAP service. If you want to test this on the same machine, you can run the service instance on a different port and different database, like this:

```
./odoo-bin -c server-config -d service_db --db-filter=^service_db$ --http-port=8070
```

This will run the Odoo server on port `8070`. Make sure that you have installed the service module in this DB and have added the IAP service key. Note that this recipe is written assuming that you have an IAP service running on the `http://localhost:8070` URL.

How to do it...

We will create a new `iap_isbn_client` module. This module will inherit the `my_library` module and add a button in the book's form view. Clicking on a button will send a request to our IAP service running on the `8090` port. The IAP service will capture the credit and return the information of the requested book. We will write this information in the book's record. Follow these steps to complete the IAP client module:

1. Create a new `iap_isbn_client` module and add __init__.py:

```
from . import models
```

2. Add __manifest__.py, with the given content:

```
{
    'name': "Books ISBN",
    'summary': "Get Books Data based on ISBN",
    'website': "http://www.example.com",
    'category': 'Uncategorized',
    'version': '12.0.1',
    'depends': ['iap', 'my_library'],
    'data': [
        'views/library_books_views.xml',
    ]
}
```

3. Add `models/library_book.py` and add a few fields by inheriting the `library.book` model:

```
from odoo import models, fields, api
from odoo.exceptions import UserError
from odoo.addons.iap import jsonrpc


class LibraryBook(models.Model):
    _inherit = 'library.book'

    cover_image = fields.Binary('Books Cover')
```

```
isbn = fields.Char('ISBN')
```

4. Add the `fetch_book_data()` method in the same model. This will be called upon a button click:

```python
def fetch_book_data(self):
    self.ensure_one()
    if not self.isbn:
        raise UserError("Please add ISBN number")

    user_token = self.env['iap.account'].get('book_isbn')
    params = {
        'account_token': user_token.account_token,
        'isbn_number': self.isbn
    }
    service_endpoint = 'http://localhost:8070'
    result = jsonrpc(service_endpoint + '/get_book_data',
params=params)
    if result.get('status') == 'found':
        self.write(self.process_result(result['data']))
    return True
```

5. Add the `process_result()` method process IAP service response:

```python
@api.model
def process_result(self, result):
    authors = []
    existing_author_ids = []
    for author_name in result['authors']:
        author =
self.env['res.partner'].search([('name','=',author_name)],
limit=1)
        if author:
            existing_author_ids.append(author.id)
        else:
            authors.append((0, 0, {'name': author_name}))
    if existing_author_ids:
        authors.append((6, 0, existing_author_ids))
    return {
        'author_ids': authors,
        'name': result.get('name'),
        'isbn': result.get('isbn'),
        'cover_image': result.get('cover_image'),
        'date_release': result.get('date_release'),
    }
```

6. Add `views/library_books_views.xml`, and add a button and fields by inheriting the book's form view:

```xml
<?xml version="1.0" encoding="utf-8"?>
<odoo>

    <record id="library_book_view_form_inh"
model="ir.ui.view">
        <field name="name">Library Book Form</field>
        <field name="model">library.book</field>
        <field name="inherit_id"
ref="my_library.library_book_view_form"/>
        <field name="arch" type="xml">
            <xpath expr="//group" position="before">
                <header>
                    <button name="fetch_book_data"
string="Fetch Book Data" type="object"/>
                </header>
            </xpath>
            <field name="date_release" position="after">
                <field name="isbn"/>
                <field name="cover_image" widget="image"
class="oe_avatar"/>
            </field>
        </field>
    </record>

</odoo>
```

Install the `iap_isbn_client` module. This will add a **Fetch Book Data** button to the book form. After doing this, add a valid **ISBN** number (for example, **1788392019**) and click on the button. This will make a request and fetch the data from the service. If you are making the IAP service call for the first time, then your Odoo instance won't have information about the linked account, so Odoo will raise a popup to buy the credits, as follows:

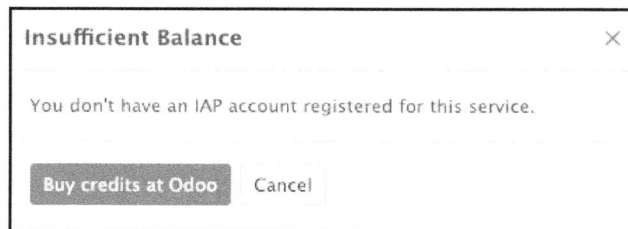

Upon clicking on the **Buy credits at Odoo** button, you will be redirected to the IAP service page, where you will see the information about the available packs to purchase. For our recipe, you will see the packs that we defined while registering our service in the *Registering an IAP service in Odoo* recipe of this chapter. Take a look at the following screenshot; it is a list of packs to purchase:

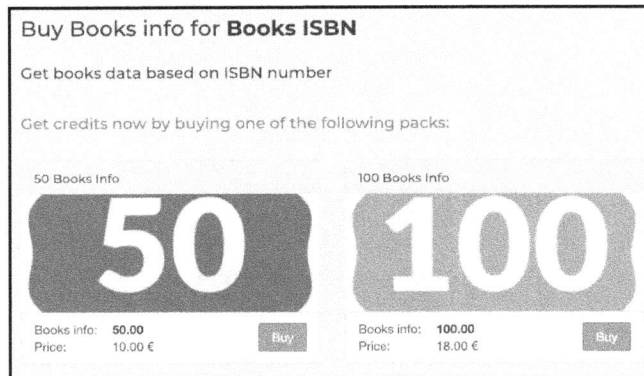

As we are using the sandbox endpoint, you can buy any pack without any payment. After that, you can request the book information from the book's form view.

How it works...

We have created a `/get_book_data` route in the service module. This route is used to handle a customer's IAP requests. So, from this client module, we will make a JSON-RPC request to that route. This IAP request will capture the credit and fetch the book's data. Luckily, the IAP module provides a wrapper for a `jsonrpc` request, so we will use it.

The `library.book` model of the `my_library` module doesn't have the ISBN and `cover_image` field, so we have extra fields in the `library.book` model by inheritance. Refer to the *Adding features to a Model using inheritance* recipe from `chapter 5` *Application Models*. We have added fields through inheritance because we don't want to use these fields when the `iap_isbn_client` module is not installed.

In order to initiate a request, we have added a button to the book's form view through inheritance. A button click will trigger the `fetch_book_data()` method, and in that method, we have made the `jsonrpc` request to the service endpoint. With the request, we have passed two parameters: the customer account tokens and the ISBN number for the book data.

You can get a customer account token from the `get()` method of the `iap.account` model. The token generation is automatic. You just need to call the `get()` method with the name of the service. In our case, the service name is `book_isbn`. This will return the record set of the customer IAP account, and you can grab the customer token `account_token` field.

We have made a `jsonrpc` request to fetch the book info. If the customer doesn't have enough credit, the service module will generate `InsufficientCreditError`. The `jsonrpc` will handle this exception automatically, and it will display a popup to the customer to purchase the credit. The popup will have a link to the page where the customer can purchase the service plans. As we are using the sandbox, you can get any pack without payment. However, in production, the customer needs to make a payment for the service.

Upon a button click, if everything goes well, the customer has enough credit, and our database has data for the requested ISBN, the credit will be deducted from the customer account and `jsonrpc` will return the book's data. Then, we simply pass the result to the `process_result()` method and write data to the book's record.

There's more...

If you want to find out the remaining credit for the services, you can see it at the link provided on the dashboard:

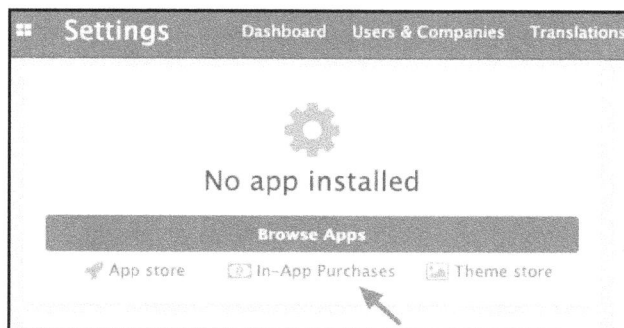

Displaying offers when an account lacks credits

If you make an IAP service request after all of the purchased credits are consumed, then the service module will generate an `InsufficientCreditError`, and the client-side module will handle this error automatically and display a popup. Whenever all of your IAP account credit is consumed, Odoo will display a popup like the following screenshot to purchase more credit:

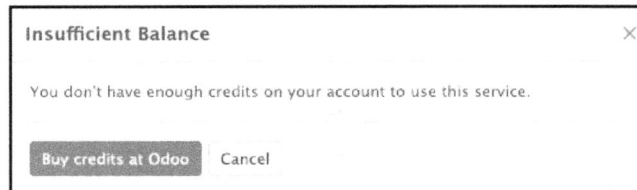

Insufficient Balance	×
You don't have enough credits on your account to use this service.	
Buy credits at Odoo Cancel	

The default popup is too simple and does not provide enough information. In this recipe, we will look at how you can change the content of this popup with an attractive template.

Getting ready

We will be using the `iap_isbn_service` module for this recipe. The offer template is created on the IAP service provider module, so it can be changed at any time without updating the client module.

How to do it...

Follow these steps to add a custom credit template:

1. Add a template with service information at `views/templates.xml`:

```
<odoo>
<template id="no_credit_info" name="No credit info">
    <section class="jumbotron text-center bg-primary">
        <div class="container pb32 pt32">
            <h1 class="jumbotron-heading">Library ISBN</h1>
            <p class="lead text-muted">
                Get full book information with cover image
just by the ISBN number.
```

```
            </p>
            <span class="badge badge-warning" style="font-
size: 30px;">
                20% Off
            </span>
        </div>
    </section>
    <div class="container">
        <div class="row">
            <div class="col">
                <div class="card mb-3">
                    <div class="card-header">
                        <i class="fa fa-database"/> Large
books database
                    </div>
                    <div class="card-body">
                        <p class="card-text">
                            We have largest book databse. It
contains more
                            then 2500000+ books.
                        </p>
                    </div>
                </div>
            </div>
            <div class="col">
                <div class="card mb-3">
                    <div class="card-header">
                        <i class="fa fa-image"/>
                        With cover image
                    </div>
                    <div class="card-body">
                        <p class="card-text">
                            More then 95% of our books having
high quality
                            book cover images.
                        </p>
                    </div>
                </div>
            </div>
        </div>
    </div>
</template>
</odoo>
```

2. Add a template to __manifest__.py:

```
    ...
    'data': [
            'security/ir.model.access.csv',
            'views/book_info_views.xml',
            'data/books_data.xml',
            'views/res_config_settings.xml',
            'views/templates.xml'
    ]
    ...
```

3. Add a template reference to iap.charge at controllers/main.py:

```
    ...
with iap.charge(request.env, service_key, account_token,
credits_to_reserve,
credit_template='iap_isbn_service.no_credit_info'):
    data =
request.env['book.info'].sudo()._books_data_by_isbn(isbn_numbe
r)
    if data['status'] == 'not found':
        raise Exception('Book not found')
```

Update the module to apply the changes. After the update, you will see a credit popup if all of the customer's credit is consumed:

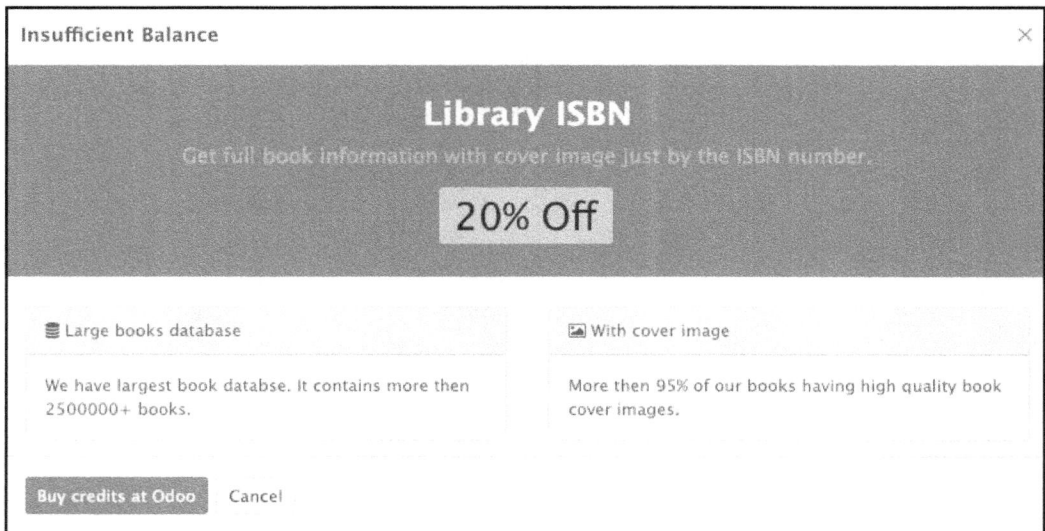

How it works...

In order to display an attractive popup on the client side, we need to create a QWeb template. In step 1, we created the QWeb template `no_credit_info`. This is made with simple bootstrap contents. Note that it just contains static HTML content. In the next step, we added the template file to the app manifest.

After designing the template, you need to pass the template XML reference to the `iap.charge()` method. This can be passed through the optional `credit_template` parameter. In step 3, we passed a template reference to the `charge` method. After passing the template, if the `InsufficientCreditError` is raised, then the template will be passed along with the error message to the customer. On the client side, if an error message is received with the template body, then this custom template will be displayed in a popup instead of the default popup.

There's more...

We don't have an image in the template, but if you want to use an image in the template, you need to be extra careful. The reason is that here, you cannot use an absolute image URL like you normally would. Because the service module is running on a separate server, the popup will not display the image. To fix this issue, you need to pass a full image URL with the domain, as this template is going to be displayed on the client screen. For example, if your service domain is `http://localhost:8070`, then you need to use an image like the following:

```
<image src="http://localhost:8070/module_name/static/img/image.png "/>
```

18
Automated Test Cases

In this chapter, we will cover the following recipes:

- Python test cases
- Running tagged Python test cases
- Setting up Headless Chrome for client-side test cases
- Client-side QUnit test cases
- Adding tour test cases
- Running client-side test cases from the UI
- Debugging client-side test cases
- Generating videos/screenshots for failed test cases

Introduction

When it comes to developing large applications, automated test cases are a good practice for improving the reliability of your module. This makes your module more robust. Every year, Odoo releases a new version of its software, and automated test cases are very helpful in detecting regression in your application, which may have been generated due to a version upgrade. Luckily, an Odoo framework comes with different automated testing utilities. Odoo includes the following three main types of tests:

- **Python test case**: Used to test Python business logic
- **JavaScript QUnit test**: Used to test JavaScript implementation in Odoo
- **Tours**: Integration test to check that Python and JavaScript work with each other properly

In this chapter, we will look at all of these test cases in detail. In order to cover all of test cases in the same module, we have created a small module. Its Python definition is as follows:

```
class LibraryBook(models.Model):
    _name = 'library.book'
    name = fields.Char('Title', required=True)
    date_release = fields.Date('Release Date')
    author_ids = fields.Many2many('res.partner', string='Authors')
    state = fields.Selection(
        [('draft', 'Not Available'),
         ('available', 'Available'),
         ('lost', 'Lost')],
        'State', default="draft")
    color = fields.Integer()

    def make_available(self):
        self.write({'state': 'available'})

    def make_lost(self):
        self.write({'state': 'lost'})
```

This Python code will help us to write test cases for Python business cases. For JavaScript-side test cases, we have added the `int_color` widget from the *Creating custom widgets* recipe in `Chapter 16`, *Web Client Development*.

You can grab this initial module from the GitHub repository of this book, at the following link: `https://github.com/PacktPublishing/Odoo-12-Development-Cookbook-Third-Edition/tree/master/Chapter18/r0_initial_module`

Technical requirements

The technical requirements for this chapter include the online Odoo platform.

All the code used in this chapter can be downloaded from the GitHub repository, at `https://github.com/PacktPublishing/Odoo-12-Development-Cookbook-Third-Edition/tree/master/Chapter18`.

Check out the following video to see the Code in Action:

Place holder link

Python test cases

Python test cases are used to check the correctness of the business logic. In `Chapter 6`, *Basic Server-Side Development,* you saw how you can modify the business logic of the existing app. This makes it even more important, as customization might break the app's functionality. In this chapter, we will write a test case to validate the business logic to change the book's state.

Getting ready

We will be using the `my_library` module from the `Chapter18/r0_initial_module` directory of the GitHub repository.

How to do it...

Follow these steps to add Python test cases in the `my_library` module:

1. Add a new file, `tests/__init__.py`, as follows:

   ```
   from . import test_book_state
   ```

2. Add a `tests/test_book_state.py` file, and add the test case, as follows:

   ```
   from odoo.tests.common import TransactionCase

   class TestBookState(TransactionCase):

       def setUp(self, *args, **kwargs):
           super(TestBookState, self).setUp(*args, **kwargs)
           self.test_book =
   self.env['library.book'].create({'name': 'Book 1'})

       def test_button_available(self):
           """Make available button"""
           self.test_book.make_available()
           self.assertEqual(self.test_book.state, 'available',
                   'Book state should changed to available')

       def test_button_lost(self):
           """Make lost button"""
           self.test_book.make_lost()
           self.assertEqual(self.test_book.state, 'lost',
                   'Book state should changed to lost')
   ```

In order to run the test cases, start the Odoo server with the following option:

```
./odoo-bin -c server.conf -i my_library --test-enable
```

Now, check the server log. You will find the following logs if our test cases ran successfully:

```
... INFO test odoo.modules.module:
odoo.addons.my_library.tests.test_book_state running tests.
... INFO test odoo.addons.my_library.tests.test_book_state:
test_button_available
(odoo.addons.my_library.tests.test_book_state.TestWizard)
... INFO test odoo.addons.my_library.tests.test_book_state: ` Make
available button
... INFO test odoo.addons.my_library.tests.test_book_state:
test_button_lost
(odoo.addons.my_library.tests.test_book_state.TestWizard)
... INFO test odoo.addons.my_library.tests.test_book_state: ` Make
lost button
... INFO test odoo.addons.my_library.tests.test_book_state: Ran 2 test
```

How it works...

In Odoo, Python test cases are added in the tests/ directory of the module. Odoo will automatically identify this directory and run the test under the folder.

Odoo uses Python unittest https://docs.python.org/3.5/library/unittest.html for Python test cases. It also provides some helper classes, wrapped over unittest. These classes simplify the process of developing test cases. In our case, we have used TransactionCase. The TransactionCase runs each test case method in a different transaction. Once a test case method runs successfully, a transaction is automatically rolled back.

The class method starts from test_ and is considered a test case. In our example, we have added two test cases. This checks the methods that change the book's state. The self.assertEqual method is used to check whether the test case runs successfully. We have checked the book state after performing operations on the book's record. So, if the developer made a mistake and the method is not changing states as expected, the test case will be failed.

Note that the setUp() method will automatically call for every test case we run, so in this recipe, we have added two test cases, so that setUp() will call twice. As per the code in this recipe, there will only be one record of the book present during testing, because with TransactionCase, the transaction is rolled back with every test case.

The docstrings on the methods will be printed in the logger. This will be very helpful for checking the status of the particular test case.

There's more...

The test suite provides the following additional test utility classes:

- SingleTransactionCase: Test cases generated through this class will run all cases into a single transaction, so changes made from one test case will be available in the second test case. In this, the transaction is begun with the first test method and it is only rolled back at the end of the last test case.
- SavepointCase: This is the same as SingleTransactionCase, but in this case, test methods run inside a rolled-back savepoint, instead of having all test methods in a single transaction. This is used for creating large test cases to make them faster by generating test data only once. Here, we use the setUpClass() method to generate the initial test data.

Running tagged Python test cases

When you run the Odoo server with the --test-enabled module, the test cases run immediately after the module is installed. If you want to run a test case after the installation of all the modules, or if you just want to run a test case for only one module, a tagged() decorator is the answer. In this recipe, we will illustrate how to use this decorator to mold test cases.

Getting ready

For this recipe, we will be using the my_library module from the last recipe. We will modify the sequence of the test case.

How to do it...

Add a `tagged()` decorator (like the following) on the test class to run it after the installation of all modules:

```
from odoo.tests.common import TransactionCase, tagged

@tagged('-at_install', 'post_install')
class TestBookState(TransactionCase):
    ...
```

After that, run the test case as follows, just like before:

```
./odoo-bin -c server.conf -i my_library --test-enable
```

Now check the server log. This time, you will see our test case log after the following logs, meaning that our test cases are run after all of the modules are installed, as follows:

```
... INFO test odoo.modules.loading: 10 modules loaded in 21.43s, 346
queries
... INFO test odoo.modules.loading: Modules loaded.
... INFO test odoo.service.server: Starting post tests
```

In these logs, the first line shows that 10 modules are loaded. The second line shows that all requested modules and their dependencies were installed successfully, and the third line shows that it will start running the test cases that are tagged as `post_install`.

How it works...

By default, all of the test cases are tagged with `standard`, `at_install` and the current module's technical name (in our case, the technical name is `my_library`). Consequently, if you are not using a `tagged()` decorator, your test case will have these three tags.

In our case, we want to run the test case after installing all of the modules. To do so, we have added a `tagged()` decorator on the `TestBookState` class. By default, the test case has the `at_install` tag. Because of this tag, your test case will run immediately after the module is installed; it will not wait for other modules to be installed. We don't want this, so to remove the `at_install` tag, we have added –`at_install` in the tagged function. The tags that are prefixed by – will remove that tag.

By adding `-at_install` in the `tagged()` function, we stopped the test case execution after the module installation. As we haven't specified any other tag in this, the test case won't run.

So, we have added a `post_install` tag. This tag specifies that the test case needs to be run after the installation of all modules is completed.

> Before Odoo version 12, the `common.at_install()` and `common.post_install()` decorators were used for changing the execution sequence of the test case. In version 12, these decorators were deprecated and replaced by the `at_install` and `post_install` tags.

As you have seen, all test cases are tagged with the `standard` tag, by default. Odoo will run all of the test cases tagged with the `standard` tag, in case you don't want to run the specific test case all of the time and you only want to run the test case when it is requested. To do so, you need to remove the `standard` tag by adding `-standard` in the `tagged()` decorator, and you need to add a custom tag like this:

```
@tagged('-standard', 'my_custom_tag')
class TestClass(TransactionCase):
    ...
```

All of the non-standard test cases will not run with the `--test-enable` option. To run the preceding test case, you need to use the `--test-tags` option, as follows. (Note that here, we do not need to pass the `--test-enable` option explicitly):

```
./odoo-bin -c server.conf -i my_library --test-tags=my_custom_tag
```

There's more...

During the development of the test case, it is important to run the test case for just one module. By default, the technical name of the module is added as a tag, so you can use the module's technical name with the `--test-tags` option. For example, if you want to run test cases for the `my_library` module, then you can run the server like this:

```
./odoo-bin -c server.conf -i my_library --test-tags=my_library
```

Setting up Headless Chrome for client-side test cases

Odoo v12 uses Headless Chrome for performing JavaScript test cases and tour test cases. In this recipe, we will install Headless Chrome and other packages, in order to run JavaScript test cases.

How to do it...

You will need to install a Chrome browser to enable a JavaScript test case. For the development of the modules, we mostly use the desktop OS. Consequently, if you have a Chrome browser installed in your system, then there is no need to install it separately. You can run client-side test cases with desktop Chrome itself. Make sure that you have a Chrome version higher than Chrome 59. Odoo also supports the Chromium browser.

> Note that with Headless Chrome, client-side test cases work fine with macOS and Linux, but Odoo does not support Headless Chrome test cases on the Windows system.

Things change slightly when you want to run test cases in the production server or in Server OS. Server OS does not have GUI, so you need to install a Chrome browser differently. If you are using a Debian-based server OS, you can install a Chromium browser with the following command:

```
apt-get install chromium-browser
```

> Ubuntu 18.04 Server Edition has not enabled the universe repository by default. So it's possible that installing the chromium-browser will show an installation candidate error. To fix this error, enable the universe repository with the following command: sudo add-apt-repository universe.

Odoo also uses WebSockets for JavaScript test cases. For that, Odoo uses the websocket-client Python library. To install it, use the following command:

```
pip3 install websocket-client
```

How it works...

Odoo uses Headless Chrome for JavaScript test cases. The reason behind this is that it runs the test cases in the background, so it can be run in the server OS, too. Headless Chrome prefers to run the Chrome browser in the background, without opening a GUI browser. Odoo opens the Chrome tab in the background and starts running the test cases in it. It also uses **JQuery QUnit** for JavaScript test cases. In the next few recipes, we will create a **QUnit** test case for our custom JavaScript widgets.

> Headless Chrome was introduced in Odoo version 12. In the older version of Odoo, `phantomjs` is used for the client-side test cases. Odoo moved to Headless Chrome because it provides more features, and because the `phantomjs` project is no longer being maintained.

For test cases, Odoo opens Headless Chrome in a separate process, so to find out the status of the test case running in that process, the Odoo server uses WebSockets. The `websocket-client` Python library is used to manage WebSockets to communicate with Chrome from the Odoo server.

Client-side QUnit test cases

Building new fields or views is very simple in Odoo. In just a few lines of XML, you can define a new view. However, under the hood, it uses JavaScript in large amounts. Modifying/adding new features on the client side is complex, and it might break a few things. Most of the client-side issues go unnoticed, as most errors are only displayed in the console. So, QUnit test cases are used in Odoo to check the correctness of different JavaScript components.

Getting ready

For this recipe, we will continue using the `my_library` module from the previous recipe. We will add a QUnit test case for the `int_color` widget.

How to do it...

Follow these steps to add JavaScript test cases for the int_color widget:

1. Add /static/tests/colorpicker_tests.js with the following code:

```
odoo.define('colorpicker_tests', function (require) {
"use strict";

var FormView = require('web.FormView');
var testUtils = require('web.test_utils');

QUnit.module('Color Picker Tests', {
    beforeEach: function () {
        this.data = {
            book: {
                fields: {
                    name: { string: "Name", type: "char" },
                    color: { string: "color", type:
"integer"},
                },
                records: [{
                    id: 1,
                    name: "Book 1",
                    color: 1
                }, {
                    id: 2,
                    name: "Book 2",
                    color: 3
                }]
            }
        };
    }
}, function () {

    QUnit.test('int_color field test cases', function
(assert) {
        assert.expect(2);

        var form = testUtils.createView({
            View: FormView,
            model: 'book',
            data: this.data,
            arch: '<form string="Books">' +
                '<group>' +
                    '<field name="name"/>' +
                    '<field name="color" widget="int_color"/>'
+
```

```
                '</group>' +
                '</form>',
            res_id: 1,
            viewOptions: {
                mode: 'edit',
            },
        });
        assert.strictEqual(
            form.$('.o_int_colorpicker
.o_color_pill').length, 10,
            "colorpicker should have 10 pills");

        form.$('.o_int_colorpicker
.o_color_pill:eq(5)').click();
        assert.strictEqual(
            form.$('.o_int_colorpicker
.o_color_5').hasClass('active'), true,
            "click on pill should make pill active");

        form.destroy();
    });
});
});
```

2. Add the following code in `/views/template.xml` to register it in the test suite:

```
...
<template id="qunit_suite" name="colorpicker test"
inherit_id="web.qunit_suite">
    <xpath expr="." position="inside">
        <script type="text/javascript"
src="/my_library/static/tests/colorpicker_tests.js" />
    </xpath>
</template>
...
```

To run this test case, start your server with the following command in the Terminal:

```
./odoo-bin -c server.conf -i my_library,web --test-enable
```

To check that the tests have run successfully, search for the following log:

```
... INFO test odoo.addons.web.tests.test_js.WebSuite: console log:
"Color Picker Tests" passed 2 tests.
```

How it works...

In Odoo, JavaScript test cases are added in the `/static/tests/` directory. In step 1, we have added a `colorpicker_tests.js` file for the test case. In that file, we have imported the form view and test utils reference. The `web.FormView` is imported because, we have created an `int_color` widget for the form view, so to test the widget, we will need the form view. The `web.test_utils` will provide us with the test utilities we require to build the JavaScript test cases. If you don't know how JavaScript import works, refer to the *Extending CSS and JavaScript for the website* recipe in `Chapter 15`, *CMS Website Development*.

Odoo client-side test cases are built with the **QUnit** framework, which is the JQuery framework for the JavaScript unit test case. Refer to `https://qunitjs.com/` to learn more about this. The `beforeEach` function is called before running the test cases, and this helps to initialize the test data. The reference of the `beforeEach` function is provided from the **QUnit** framework itself.

We have initialized some data in the `beforeEach` function. Let's see how that data is being used in the test case. The client-side test case runs in an isolated (mock) environment, and it doesn't make a connection to the database, so for these test cases, we need to create test data. Internally, Odoo creates the mock server to mimic the **Remote Procedure Call (RPC)** calls and uses the `this.data` property as the database. Consequently, in `beforeEach`, we have initialized our test data in the `this.data` property. The keys in the `this.data` property are considered a table, and the values contain the information about the fields and the table rows. The `fields` key is used for defining table fields and the records key is used for the table rows. In our example, we have added a `book` table with two fields: `name(char)` and `color(integer)`. Note that here, you can use any Odoo fields, even relational fields; for example, `{string: "M2o FIeld", type: "many2one", relation: 'partner'}`. We have also added two book records with the `records` key.

Next, we have added the test cases with the `QUnit.test` function. The first argument in the function is a `string` to describe the test case. The second argument is the function in which you need to add code for the test cases. This function is called from the QUnit framework, and it passes the assert utilities as the argument. In our example, we have passed the number of the expected test cases in the `assert.expect` function. We are adding two test cases, so we have passed 2.

We want to add to the test case `int_color` widget in the editable form view, so we have created the editable form view with `testUtils.createView`. The `createView` function accepts different arguments, as follows:

- `View` is the reference of the view you want to create. You can create any type of view for the test case; you just need to pass the view reference here.
- `model` is the name of the model for which the given view is created. All of the models are listed in the `this.data` property. We want to create a view for the book model, so in our example, we have used `book` as a model.
- `data` is the record that we are going to use in the view.
- `arch` is the definition of the view you want to create. Because we want to test the `int_color` widget, we have passed the view definition with the widget. Note that you can only use the fields that are defined in the model.
- `res_id` is the record ID whose record is being displayed. This option is only used for form views. In our case, the form view will be displayed with the data of the `book  1` record, as we padded 1 as `res_id`.
- The `viewOptions` are the parameters passed in the view. Here, you can pass all the valid view parameters, like the domain, context, mode, and so on.

After creating the form view with the `int_color` widget, we added two test cases. The first one is used to check the number of color pills on the UI, and the second test case is used to check that the pill is activated correctly after the click. We have the `strictEqual` function from the asserted utility of the QUnit framework. The `strictEqual` function passes the test case if the first two arguments are matched. If it is not matched, it will fail the test case.

> There are a few more assert functions available for QUnit test cases, like `assert.deepEqual`, `assert.ok`, and `assert.notOk`. To learn more about QUnit, refer to its documentation at `https://qunitjs.com/`.

There's more...

Odoo provides more utilities for advanced cases. One of them is `createAsyncView`, which is used to create a view asynchronously. To learn more about it, explore the JavaScript files in the `/addons/web/static/tests/helpers/` directory.

Adding tour test cases

You have now seen Python and JavaScript test cases. Both of these work in an isolated environment, and they don't interact with each other. To test integration between JavaScript and Python code, tour test cases are used.

Getting ready

For this recipe, we will continue using the `my_library` module from the previous recipe. We will add a tour test case to check the flow of the book model.

How to do it...

Follow these steps to add a tour test case for `books`:

1. Add a `/static/src/js/my_library_tour.js` file, and add a tour like this:

```
odoo.define('my_library.tour', function (require) {
"use strict";

var core = require('web.core');
var tour = require('web_tour.tour');

var _t = core._t;

tour.register('library_tour', {
    url: "/web",
}, [tour.STEPS.SHOW_APPS_MENU_ITEM, {
        trigger: '.o_app[data-menu-
xmlid="my_library.library_base_menu"]',
        content: _t('Manage books and authors in<b>Library
app</b>.'),
        position: 'right'
    }, {
        trigger: '.o_list_button_add',
        content: _t("Let's create new book."),
        position: 'bottom'
    }, {
        trigger: 'input[name="name"]',
        extra_trigger: '.o_form_editable',
        content: _t('Set the book title'),
        position: 'right',
```

```
            run: function (actions) {
                actions.text('Test Book');
            },
        }, {
            trigger: '.o_int_colorpicker',
            extra_trigger: '.o_form_editable',
            content: _t('Set the book color'),
            position: 'right',
            run: function () {
                this.$anchor.find('.o_color_3').click();
            }
        }, {
            trigger: '.o_form_button_save',
            content: _t('Save this book record'),
            position: 'bottom',
        }
    ]);

    });
```

2. Add a `/tests/test_tour.py` file, and run the tour through `HttpCase`, as follows:

```
from odoo.tests.common import import HttpCase, tagged

class TestBookUI(HttpCase):

    @tagged('post_install', '-at_install')
    def test_01_book_tour(self):
        """Books UI tour test case"""
        self.browser_js("/web",
"odoo.__DEBUG__.services['web_tour.tour'].run('library_tour')"
,
"odoo.__DEBUG__.services['web_tour.tour'].tours.library_tour.r
eady",
                login="admin")
```

In order to run test cases, start the Odoo server with the following option:

```
./odoo-bin -c server.conf -i my_library --test-enable
```

Now, check the server log. Here, you will find the following logs if our test cases ran successfully:

```
...INFO test odoo.addons.my_library.tests.test_tour.TestBookUI:
console log: Tour library_tour succeeded
...INFO test odoo.addons.my_library.tests.test_tour.TestBookUI:
console log: ok
```

How it works...

In order to create tour test cases, you need to create the UI tour first. If you want to learn more about UI tours, refer to the *Improve onboarding with tours* recipe in `Chapter 16`, *Web Client Development*.

In step 1, we registered a new tour with the name `library_tour`. This tour is exactly like the tour we created in the recipe *Improve onboarding with tours* in `Chapter 16`, *Web Client Development*.

Here, we have one extra property: `run`. In the `run` function, you have to write the logic to perform the operation that is normally done by the user. For example, in the fourth step of the tour, we ask the user to enter the book title.

To automate this step, we have added a run function to set the value in the `title` field. The `run` function passes the action utility as the parameter. This provides some shortcuts to perform basic actions. The most important ones are mentioned as follows:

- `actions.click(element)` is used to click on the given element.
- `actions.dblclick(element)` is used to double-click on the given element.
- `actions.tripleclick(element)` is used to triple-click on the given element.
- `actions.text(string)` is used to set the input values.
- `action.drag_and_drop(to, element)` is used to drag and drop the element.
- `action.keydown(keyCodes, element)` is used to trigger particular keyboard events on the element.

- `action.auto()` is the default action. When you don't pass the run function in the tour step, `action.auto()` is performed. Auto action will mostly click on the trigger element of the tour step. The only exception here is an input element. If the trigger element is `input`, the tour will set the default value `Test` in the input. That is why we don't need to add run functions to all of the steps.

Alternatively, you can perform whole actions manually, in case default actions are not enough. In the next tour step, we want to set a value for the color picker. Note that we have used the manual action, because default values won't help here. Consequently, we have added the `run` method with the basic JQuery code to click on the third pill of the color picker. Here, you will find the trigger element with the `this.$anchor` property.

By default, registered tours are displayed to the end user to improve the onboarding experience. In order to run them as a test case, you need to run them in Headless Chrome. To do so, you need to use the `HttpCase` Python test case. This provides the `browser_js` method, which opens the URL and executes the command passed as the second parameter. You can run the tour manually, like this:

```
odoo.__DEBUG__.services['web_tour.tour'].run('library_tour')
```

In our example, we have passed the name of the `tour` as the argument in the `browser_js` method. The next parameter is used to wait for a given object to be ready before performing the first command. The last parameter in the `browser_js()` method is the name of the user. This username will be used to create a new test environment, and all of the test actions will be performed on behalf of this user.

Running client-side test cases from the UI

Odoo provides a way to run client-side test cases from the UI. This helps you to see the status of each test case from the user interface.

How to do it...

You can run both the QUnit test case and the tours test case from the UI. It is not possible to run Python test cases from the UI. In order to see the options to run test cases from the UI, you need to enable developer mode.

Running QUnit test cases

Click on the bug icon to open the drop-down menu, as shown in the following image. Click on the **Run JS Tests** option:

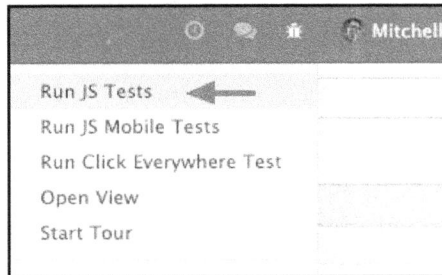

This will open the QUnit suite and it will start running the test cases one by one, as shown this screenshot. By default, it will only show failed test cases. To show all the passed test cases, uncheck the **Hide passed tests** checkbox, as shown in the following screenshot:

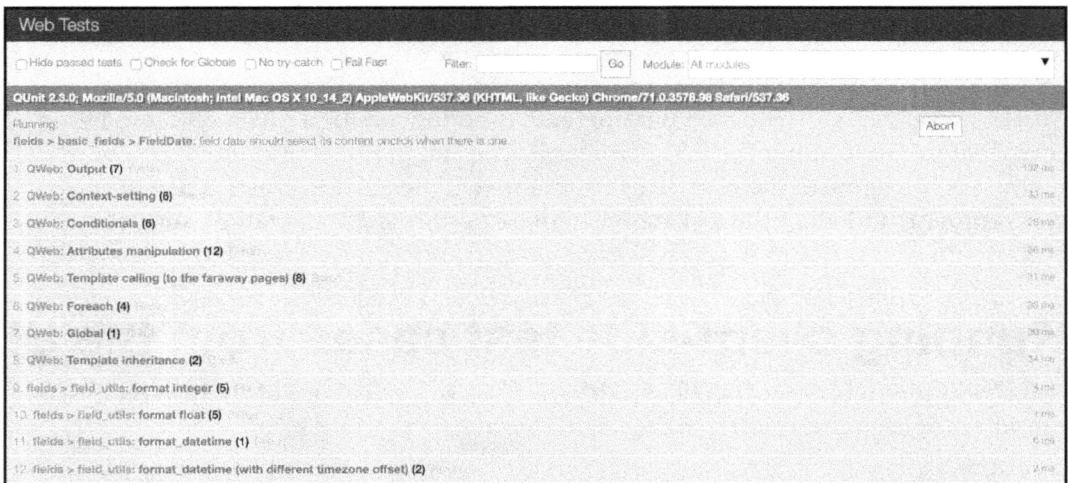

Running tours from the UI

Click on the bug icon to open the drop-down menu, as shown in the following screenshot, and then click on **Start Tour:**

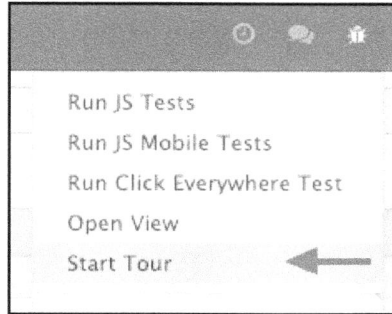

This will open the dialog with a list of registered tours, as you can see in the following screenshot. Click on the play button on the side to run the tour:

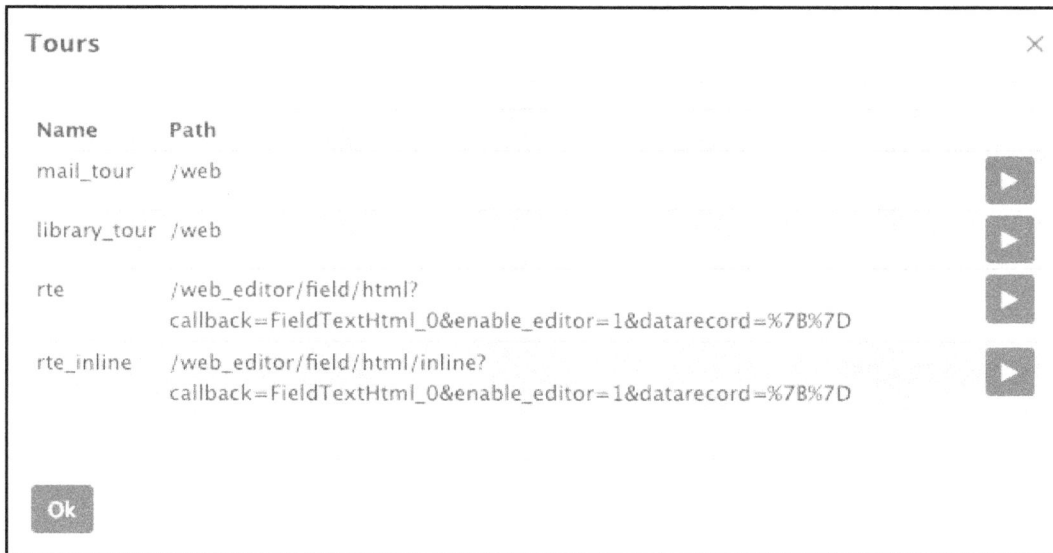

How it works...

The UI for QUnit is provided by the QUnit framework itself. Here, you can filter the test cases for the modules. You can even run the test case for just one module. Here, you can see the progress of each test case, and you can drill down to each step of the test case. Internally, Odoo just opens the same URL in Headless Chrome.

Clicking on the **Run tours** option will display the list of available tours. By clicking on the play button on the list, you can run the tour. Note that when the tour runs via the command-line options, it runs in the rolled-back transaction, so changes made through the tour are rolled back after the tour is successful. However, when the tour runs from the UI, changes made from the tour are not rolled back and stay there, so use this option carefully.

Debugging client-side test cases

Developing complex client-side test cases can be a headache. In this recipe, you will learn how you can debug the client-side test cases in Odoo. Instead of running all of the test cases, we will just run the single one. Additionally, we will display the UI of the test case.

Getting ready

For this recipe, we will continue using the `my_library` module from the previous recipe.

How to do it...

Follow these steps to run the test case in debug mode:

1. Open the file `/static/tests/colorpicker_tests.js`, and update the test `QUnit.test` with `QUnit.only`, like this:

   ```
   ...
   QUnit.only('int_color field test cases', function (assert) {
   ...
   ```

2. Add the debug parameter in the `createView` function, as follows:

```
var form = testUtils.createView({
    View: FormView,
    model: 'book',
    data: this.data,
    arch: '<form string="Books">' +
        '<group>' +
            '<field name="name"/>' +
            '<field name="color" widget="int_color"/>' +
        '</group>' +
        '</form>',
    res_id: 1,
    viewOptions: {
        mode: 'edit',
    },
    debug:1
});
```

Open the developer mode and open the drop-down menu by clicking on the bug icon on the top menu, then click on **Run JS tests**. This will open the QUnit suit.

How it works...

In the first step, we have replaced `QUnit.test` with `QUnit.only`. This will run this test case only. During the development of the test case, this can be time-saving. Note that using `QUnit.only` will stop the test case from running via the command-line options. This can only be used for debugging or testing, and it can only work when you open the test case from the UI, so don't forget to replace it with `QUnit.test` after the development.

In our example of the QUnit test case, we have created the form view to test the `int_color` widget. If you run the QUnit test cases from the UI, you will learn that you are not able to see the created form views in the UI. From the UI of the QUnit suite, you are only able to see the logs. This makes developing a QUnit test case very difficult. To solve this issue, the debug parameter is used in the `createView` function. In the second step, we have added `debug: true` in the `createView` function. This will display the test form view in the browser. Here, you will be able to locate Document Object Model (DOM) elements via the browser debugger.

Warning: At the end of the test case, we destroy the view through the destroy() method. If you have destroyed the view, then you won't be able to see the form view in the UI, so in order to see it in the browser, remove that line during development.

Generating videos/screenshots for failed test cases

Odoo version 11 uses PhantomJS to run the test cases on the server side, but Odoo 12 uses Headless Chrome. This opens new possibilities. With Odoo 12, you can record videos of the failed test cases, or you can take screenshots of the failed test cases.

How to do it...

Recording a video for the test case requires an ffmpeg package. To install this, you need to execute the following command in the Terminal (note that this command only works on a Debian-based OS):

```
apt-get install ffmpeg
```

Generating a video or screenshot requires the directory location of the log file, so if you are not saving the log in a separate log file, then do it through the --logfile option in the command line, like this:

```
./odoo-bin -c server.conf -i my_library --test-enable --log-file=/var/log/odoo.log
```

How it works...

In order to generate screenshots for the failed test cases, you need to run the server with the path of the log files. When you run the test cases along with the name of the log file, Odoo will save the screenshot of the failed test cases in the same directory. If you are not saving the log in a separate log file, then you can do it through the --logfile option in the command line.

To generate the video of the test case, Odoo uses the `ffmpeg` package. If you haven't installed this package in the server, then it will only save the screenshot of the failed test case. After installing the package, you will be able to see the `mp4` file of the failed test case. Note that screenshots and videos are only generated for the failed test cases, so if you want to test them, you need to write a test case that fails.

> Generating videos for test cases can consume more space on disks, so use this option with caution, and only use it when it is really necessary.

19
Managing, Deploying, and Testing with Odoo.sh

In this chapter, we will cover the following recipes:

- Exploring some basic concepts of Odoo.sh
- Creating an Odoo.sh account
- Adding and installing custom modules
- Managing branches
- Accessing debugging options
- Getting a backup of your instance
- Checking the status of your builds
- All Odoo.sh options

Introduction

In 2017, Odoo released Odoo.sh, a new cloud service. Odoo.sh is a platform that makes the process of testing, deploying, and monitoring the Odoo instances as easy as possible. In this chapter, we will look at how Odoo.sh works, when you should use it over other deployment options, and its features.

This chapter is written under the assumption that you have Odoo.sh access. It is a paid service and you will need a subscription code to access the platform. If you are an Odoo partner, you will get a free Odoo.sh subscription code. Otherwise, you will need to purchase it from `https://www.odoo.sh/pricing`.

You can still go through this chapter even if you don't have a subscription code. It contains enough screenshots to help you understand the platform.

Technical requirements

The technical requirements for this chapter include the online Odoo platform.

All the code used in this chapter can be downloaded from the GitHub repository, at `https://github.com/PacktPublishing/Odoo-12-Development-Cookbook-Third-Edition/tree/master/Chapter19`.

Check out the following video to see the Code in Action:

Place holder link

Exploring some basic concepts of Odoo.sh

In this recipe, we will look at some of the features of the Odoo.sh platform. We will answer some basic questions, such as when you should use it, and why.

What is Odoo.sh?

Odoo.sh is a cloud service that provides the platform with the ability to host Odoo instances with custom modules. Put simply, it is Odoo's **platform as a service** (**PaaS**) cloud solution. It is fully integrated with GitHub; any GitHub repository with valid Odoo modules can be launched on Odoo.sh within minutes. You can examine the ongoing development by testing multiple branches in parallel. Once you have moved your instance to production, you can test some new features with the copy of the production database; this helps to avoid regression. It also takes daily backups. Put simply, with Odoo.sh, you can deploy Odoo instances efficiently, even if you don't have sound knowledge of DevOps. It automatically sets up an Odoo instance with top-notch configurations. Note that Odoo.sh the Enterprise edition of Odoo. You cannot use the Odoo Community edition here.

Why was Odoo.sh introduced?

Before Odoo.sh was introduced, there were two ways to host Odoo instances. The first was to use Odoo online, which is a **Software as a Service** (**SaaS**) cloud service. The second method was the on-premises option, in which you needed to host an Odoo instance and configure it on your server by yourself. Now, both of these options have pros and cons. In the Odoo online option, you don't need to carry out any configuration or deployment, as it is an SaaS service. However, you cannot use custom modules on this platform. On the other hand, with the on-premises option, you can use custom modules, but you need to do everything by yourself. You need to purchase the server, you need to configure Nginx, and you need to set up the mail server, daily backups, and security.

For this reason, there was a need for a new option that provided the simplicity of Odoo online and the flexibility of the on-premises option. Odoo.sh lets you can use custom modules without complex configuration. It also provides additional features, such as testing branches, staging branches, and automated tests.

> It is not completely true that customization is not possible on Odoo online. With Odoo Studio and other techniques, you can carry out customization. The scope of this customization, however, is very narrow.

When should you use Odoo.sh?

If you don't need customization or you only have a small amount of customization that is possible in Odoo online, you should go for Odoo online. This will save both time and money. If you want a significant amount of customization and you have teamed up with expert DevOps engineers, you can choose the on-premises option. Odoo.sh is suitable for when you have good knowledge of Odoo customization but you do not have any expertise in DevOps. With Odoo.sh, there's no need to carry out complex configurations; you can start using it straight away, along with your customization. It even configures the mailing server.

Odoo.sh is very useful when you are developing a large project with agile methodology. This is because on Odoo.sh, you can test multiple development branches in parallel and deploy the stable development in production in minutes. You can even share the test development with the end customer.

What are the features of Odoo.sh?

Odoo has invested a lot of time in the development of the Odoo.sh platform, and it is packed with features as a result. Let's have look at the features of Odoo.sh. Note that Odoo adds new features from time to time. In this section, I have mentioned the features that are available at the time of writing this book, but you might find some further features, as well:

- **GitHub integration:** This platform is fully integrated with GitHub. You can test every branch, pull, or commit here. For every new commit, a new branch will be pulled automatically. It will also run the automated test for the new commits. You can even create/merge branches from the Odoo.sh UI itself.
- **Web shell:** Odoo.sh provides the web shell in the browser for the current build (or production server). Here, you can see all the modules and logs.
- **Web code editor:** Just like the web shell, Odoo.sh provides the code editor in the browser. Here, you can access all of the source code and also get the Odoo interactive shell for the current build.
- **External dependencies:** You can install any Python packages. To do this, you just need to add `requirement.txt` in the root of your GitHub repository. Right now, you can only install the Python packages. It is not possible to install system packages (apt packages).
- **Server logs:** You can access the server log for each build from this browser. These logs are in real time and you can also filter the logs from here.

- **Automated tests:** Odoo.sh provides your own runbot, which you can use to perform a series of automated tests for your development. Whenever you add a new commit or a new development branch, Odoo.sh will automatically run all of the test cases and show the status of the test. You can access the full test log, which will help you find issues if a test case fails.

- **Staging and development branches:** Odoo.sh provides two types of branches: the development branch and the staging branch. In the development branch, you can test ongoing development with demonstration data. The staging branch is used when the development is finished and you want to test the feature before merging it into production. The staging branch does not load the demonstration data; instead, it uses a copy of the production server.

- **Mail server:** Odoo.sh automatically sets up a mail server for the production server. Just like Odoo online, Odoo.sh does not need any extra configuration for email, although it is possible to use your own mail server.

- **Mail catcher:** The staging branch uses a copy of your production database, so it has information about your real customers. Testing on such a database can make it possible to send emails to real customers. To avoid this issue, the email feature is only activated on production branches. Staging and development branches do not send real emails, but instead, they use a mail catcher so that you can test and see emails in the staging and development branch.

- **Share the build:** With Odoo.sh, you can share the development branches with your customer so they can test them before merging the feature into production.

- **Faster deployment:** As Odoo.sh is fully integrated with GitHub, you can merge and deploy the development branches directly from the browser with a simple drag and drop procedure.

- **Backup and recovery:** Odoo.sh keeps full backups for the production instance. You can download or restore any of these backups in just a few clicks. Refer to the *Getting a backup of your instance* recipe to learn more about backups.

- **Community modules:** You can test install any community module in a few simple clicks. You can also test free modules directly from the app store.

Creating an Odoo.sh account

In this recipe, we will create an Odoo.sh account and an empty repository for the custom add-ons.

Getting ready

For this recipe, you will need a GitHub account on which you can add custom modules. You will also need an Odoo.sh subscription code. If you are an Odoo partner, you will get a free Odoo.sh subscription code. Otherwise, you will need to purchase it from `https://www.odoo.sh/pricing`.

How to do it...

Follow these steps to create an Odoo.sh account:

1. Open `https://www.odoo.sh` and click on **Sign in** in the top menu. This will redirect you to the GitHub page:

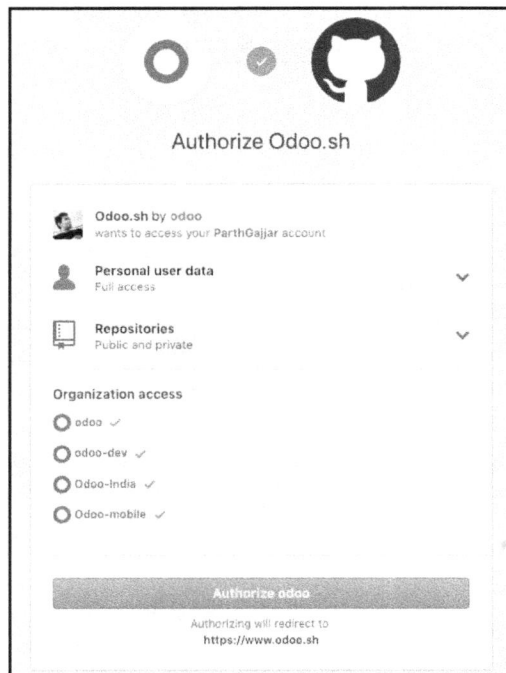

2. Give authorization to your repositories, which will redirect you back to
    Odoo.sh. Fill in the form to deploy the instance:

3. This will deploy the instance and you will be redirected to the Odoo.sh control panel. Wait for the build status to be successful; then, you can connect to your instance with the **CONNECT** button displayed in the following screenshot:

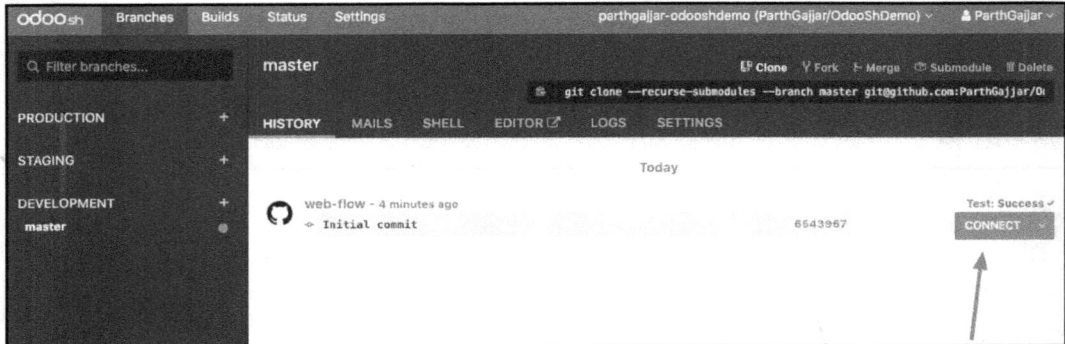

How it works...

The Odoo.sh platform is integrated with GitHub. You need to give full authorization to Odoo.sh, so that it can have access to your repositories. Odoo.sh will also create the webhooks. GitHub webhooks notify the Odoo.sh platform when a new commit or branch has been added to your repository. When you sign in for the first time, Odoo.sh will redirect you to GitHub. GitHub will show a page similar to the screenshot in step 1, in which you will need to provide access to all of your private and public repositories. If you are not the owner of the repository, you will see the button to make an access request to the owner for the rights.

After you grant repository access to Odoo.sh, you will be redirected back to Odoo.sh, where you will see the form to deploy the Odoo instance. To create a new instance, you will need to add the following information:

- **Github repository**: Here, you will need to set the GitHub repository with your custom modules. The modules in this repository will be available to the Odoo instance. You will see a list of all your existing repositories. You can select one of them or create a new one.
- **Odoo version**: Choose the Odoo version you want to deploy. You can select from the currently-supported Odoo LTS versions. Make sure you select the version that is compatible with the modules in the GitHub repository. For our example, we will select version 12.0.

- **Subscription code**: This is the code to activate the instance. You will receive the code via email after purchasing an Odoo.sh plan; if you are an official Odoo partner, you can ask for this code from Odoo.
- **Hosting location**: Here, you need to choose a server location based on your geographic location. The server that is nearest will give the best performance. Note that if you are creating an instance for your customer and the customer is in another country, you will need to select a server location that is near the customer location.

Once you submit this form, your Odoo instances will be deployed and you will be redirected to the Odoo.sh control panel. Here, you will see your first build. It will take a few minutes, and then you will be able to connect to your Odoo instance. If you check the left panel, you will see that there are no branches in the production and staging sections and that only one branch is in the development section. In the next few recipes, we will see how you can create staging and production branches.

There's more...

Right now, Odoo.sh only works with GitHub. Other version-control systems, such as GitLab and bitbucket, are not supported right now. If you want to use a system other than GitHub, you can use the intermediate GitHub repository that is linked to your actual repository via the submodule. In the future, Odoo will add support for GitLab and bitbucket, but this is not the priority at the moment, according to the Odoo officials. The method suggested here is just a workaround if you want to use GitLab or bitbucket.

Adding and installing custom modules

As we described earlier, in the *Exploring some basic concepts of Odoo.sh* recipe, in the Odoo.sh platform, you can add custom Odoo modules. The platform is integrated with GitHub, so adding a new commit in the registered repository will create a new build in the respective branch. In this recipe, we will add a custom module in our repository and access that module in Odoo.sh.

Getting ready

For our example, we will choose the `my_library` module from chapter 18, *Automated Test Cases*. You can add any valid Odoo module in this recipe, but we will use the module with test cases here, as the Odoo.sh platform will perform all the test cases automatically. For simplicity, we have added this module in the GitHub repository of this book, at `Chapter19/r0_initial_module/my_library`.

How to do it...

Follow these steps to add your custom modules to Odoo.sh:

1. Get your `git` repository in your local machine, add the `my_library` module in it, and then execute the following command to push the module in the GitHub repository:

```
git add .
git commit -am"Added my_library module"
git push origin master
```

2. Open your project in Odoo.sh. Here, you will find a new build for this commit. It will start running test cases and you will see the following screen:

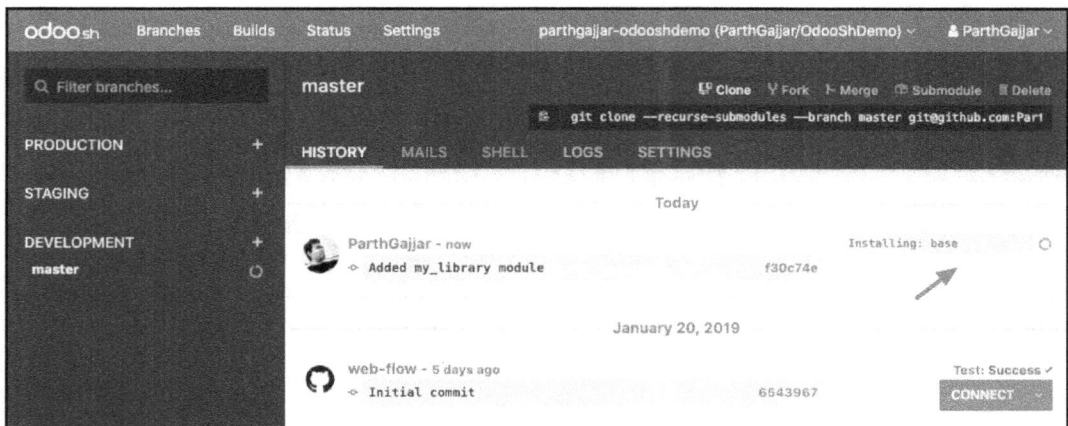

3. After a new commit is pulled in your Odoo.sh project, you will see the installation progress on the right side. Wait for the installation to be complete then access your instance by clicking on the green **CONNECT** button. It will open the Odoo instance with the `my_library` module:

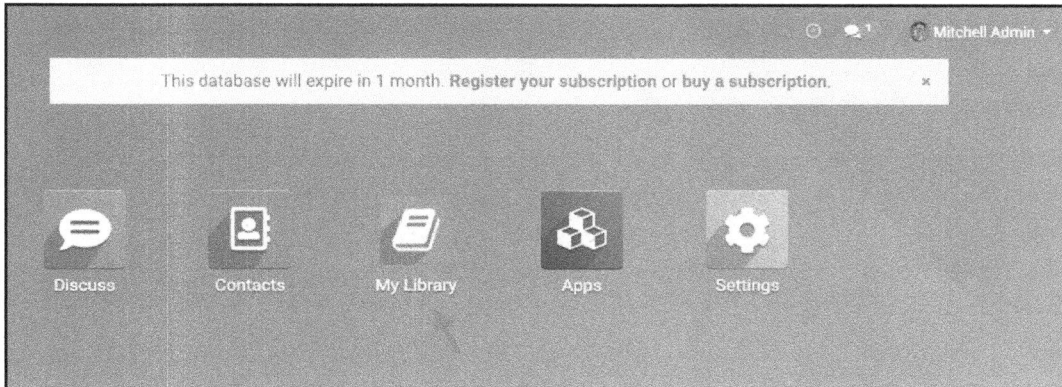

Explore and test the `my_library` module. Note that this is not a production build, so you can test it however you like.

How it works...

In step 1, we uploaded the `my_library` module on the GitHub repository. Odoo.sh will be notified about these changes instantly, through webhook. Then, Odoo.sh will start building a new instance. It will install all your custom modules and their dependencies. A new build will automatically perform the test cases for the installed modules.

> By default, Odoo.sh will only install your custom modules and their dependencies. If you want to change this behavior, you can do it from the module installation section of the global settings. We will look at these settings in detail in the next few recipes.

In the **HISTORY** tab, you will be able to see the full history of the branch. Here, you can find some basic information about the build. It will display the commit message, the author information, and the GitHub link of the commit. On the right side, you will get the live progress of the build. Note that the builds in the development section will install the modules with demonstration data. In the next few recipes, you will see the difference between the production, development, and staging branches, in detail.

After a successful build, you will see a button to connect the instance. By default, you will be connected with the admin user. Using **CONNECT** as a drop-down menu, you can log in as a demo and portal user, instead.

There's more...

Odoo.sh will create a new build for every new commit. You can change this behavior from the **SETTINGS** tab of the branch:

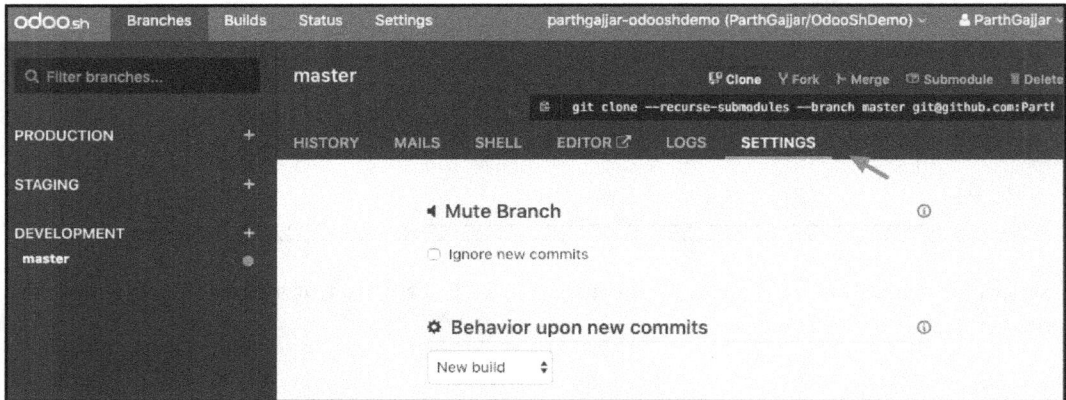

Here, you can mute the branch. If you click on the **Ignore new commits** checkbox, Odoo.sh will stop listening to the new commits and it will not generate any more new builds. The other option is **Behavior upon new commits.** Changing this option will update the existing build instead of creating a new build for a new commit.

Managing branches

In Odoo.sh, you can create multiple development and staging branches along with the production branch. In this recipe, we will create different types of branches and see the differences between them. You will see the full workflow of how you can develop, test, and deploy the new features.

Getting ready

Visit `https://www.odoo.sh/project` and open the project we created in the *Creating an Odoo.sh account* recipe. We will create a development branch for the new feature and then test it in the staging branch. Finally, we will merge the feature in the production branch.

How to do it...

In this recipe, we will create all types of branches in Odoo.sh. At the moment, we don't have any branches in production, so we will start by creating a production branch.

Creating the production branch

Right now, we only have one **master** branch in the development section. The last build of the **master** branch shows a green label that reads **Test: success**, meaning that all of the automated test cases have run successfully. We can move this branch into the **PRODUCTION** branch, as the test case status shows that everything is fine. In order to move your **master** branch into the **PRODUCTION** branch, you just need to drag the **master** branch from the development section and drop it in the production section, as shown in the following screenshot:

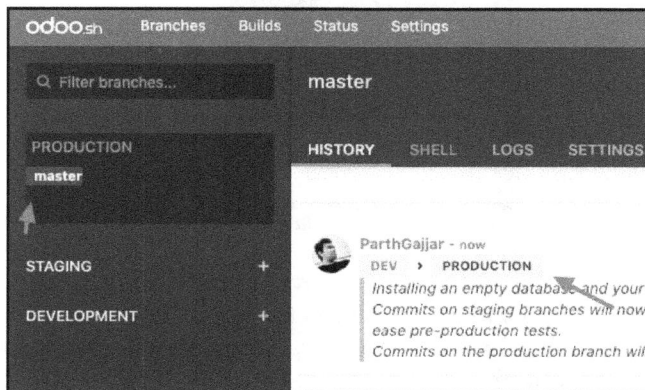

This will create your **PRODUCTION** branch. You can access the production branch with the **connect** button on the right side. Once you open the production instance, you will notice that there are no applications installed in the production database. This is because the production instance requires you or your end customer to install and configure the operation according to the requirements. Note that this is a production instance, so in order to keep the instance running, you need to enter your Enterprise subscription code.

Creating a development branch

You can create development branches directly from the browser. Click on the plus (+) button next to the development section. This will show two types of input. One is the branch to fork, and the other is the name of the development branch. After filling in the input, hit the *Enter* key.

This will create a new branch by forking the given branch, as shown in the following screenshot:

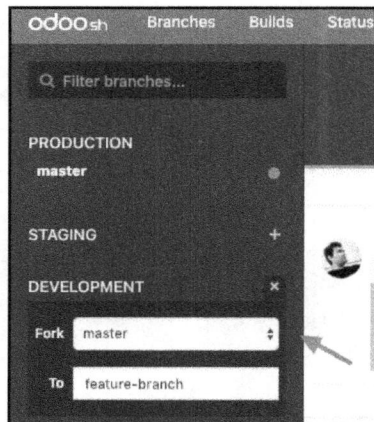

> **TIP**
>
> If you don't want to create a development branch from the user interface, you can create it directly from GitHub. If you add a new branch in the GitHub repository, Odoo.sh will create a new development branch automatically.

Branches in development are usually new feature branches. As an example, we will add a new field in the `library.book` model. Follow these steps to add a new HTML field in the books model:

1. Increase the module version in the manifest file:

   ```
   . . .
   'version': '12.0.2',
   . . .
   ```

2. Add a new field in the `library.book` model:

   ```
   . . .
   color = fields.Integer()
   description = fields.Html()

   def make_available(self):
   . . .
   ```

3. Add a `description` field in the book's form view:

   ```
   . . .
       </group>
       <notebook>
           <page string="Description">
               <field name="description"/>
           </page>
       </notebook>
   </sheet>
   . . .
   ```

4. Push the changes in the feature branch by executing the following command in the Terminal:

   ```
   git commit -am"Added book description"
   git push origin feature-branch
   ```

This will create a new build on Odoo.sh. After a successful build, you can test this new feature by accessing the instance. You will be able to see a new HTML field in the book's form view. Note that this branch is the development branch, so the new feature is only available to this branch. Your production branch is not changed.

Creating a staging branch

Once you complete the development branch and the test cases are successful, you can move the branch to the **STAGING** section. This is the pre-production section. Here, the new feature will be tested with a copy of the production database. This will help us to find any issues that might be generated in the production database. To move from the development branch to the **STAGING** branch, just drag and drop the branch into the **STAGING** section:

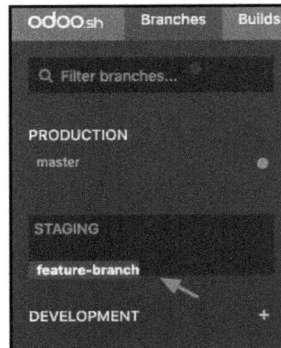

Once you move the **DEVELOPMENT** branch to the **STAGING** section, you can test your new development with production data. Just like any other build, you can access the **STAGING** branch with the **CONNECT** button on the right. The only difference is that you will be able to see the data of the production database, in this case. Here, your development module is only upgraded automatically if you have increased the module version from the manifest. If you haven't changed the module version, you will need to upgrade the modules manually to see the new features in action.

> The staging branch will use a copy of the production database, so the staging instance will have real customers and their emails. For this reason, in the staging branch, real emails are disabled so that you don't send any by accident when testing a new feature in the staging branch.

Merging new features in the production branch

After you test the new development with the production database (in the staging branch), you can deploy the new development into the **PRODUCTION** branch. Like before, you just need to drag and drop the **STAGING** branch into the **PRODUCTION** branch. This will merge the new feature branch into the **master** branch. Like the **STAGING** branch, your development module is only upgraded automatically if you have increased the module version from the manifest. After this, the new module is available for the end customer:

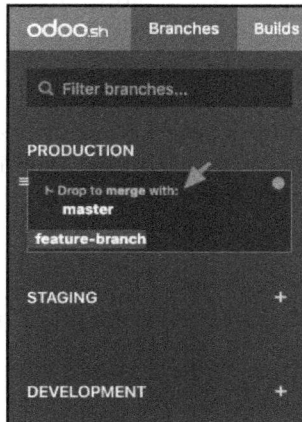

How it works...

In the previous example, we performed a full workflow to deploy a new feature into production. The following list explains the purposes of the different types of branches in Odoo.sh:

- **Production branch:** This is the actual instance that is used by the end customer. There is only one production branch, and the new features are intended to merge with this branch. In this branch, the mailing service is active, so your end customer can send and receive emails. Daily backup is also active for this branch.

- **Development branches:** This type of branch shows all the active development. You can create unlimited development branches, and every new commit in the branch will trigger a new build. The database in this branch is loaded with the demonstration data. After the development is complete, this branch will be moved to the staging branch. The mailing service is not active in these branches.
- **Staging branches:** This is the intermediate stage in the workflow. A stable development will be moved to the staging branch to be tested with a copy of the production branch. This is a very important step in the development life cycle; it might happen that a feature that works fine in the development branch does not work as expected with the production database. The staging branches give you an opportunity to test the feature with the production database before deploying it in production. If you find any issues with the development in this branch, you can move the branch back to development. The number of the staging branches is based on your Odoo.sh plan. By default, you only have one staging branch, but you can purchase more if you want to.

This is the complete workflow of how new features should be merged into production. In the next recipe, you will see some other options that we can use with these branches.

Accessing debugging options

Odoo.sh provides different features for analysis and debugging purposes. In this recipe, we will explore all of these features and options.

How to do it...

We will be using the same Odoo.sh project for this recipe. Each option will be shown in a different section, with a screenshot.

Branch history

You have already have seen this feature in previous recipes. The **HISTORY** tab shows the full history of the branch. You can connect to the builds from here:

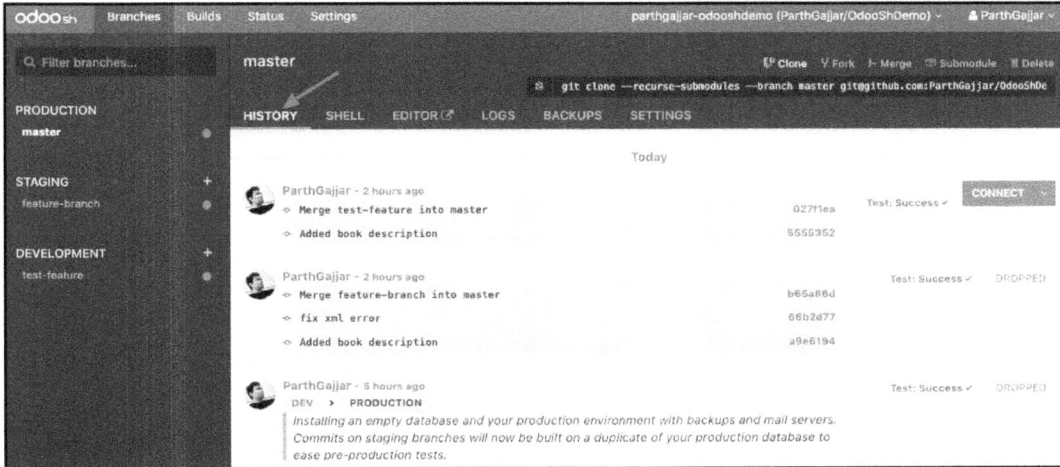

Mail catcher

The staging branch uses a copy of your production database, so it has information about your customers. Testing the staging branch can send emails to real customers. This is why emails are only activated on production branches. The staging and development branches do not send real emails. If you want to test the email system before deploying any feature into production, you can use the mail catcher where you can see the list of all outgoing emails. The mail catcher will be available in the staging and development branches.

The mail catcher will display an email with the source and any attachments, as shown in the following screenshot:

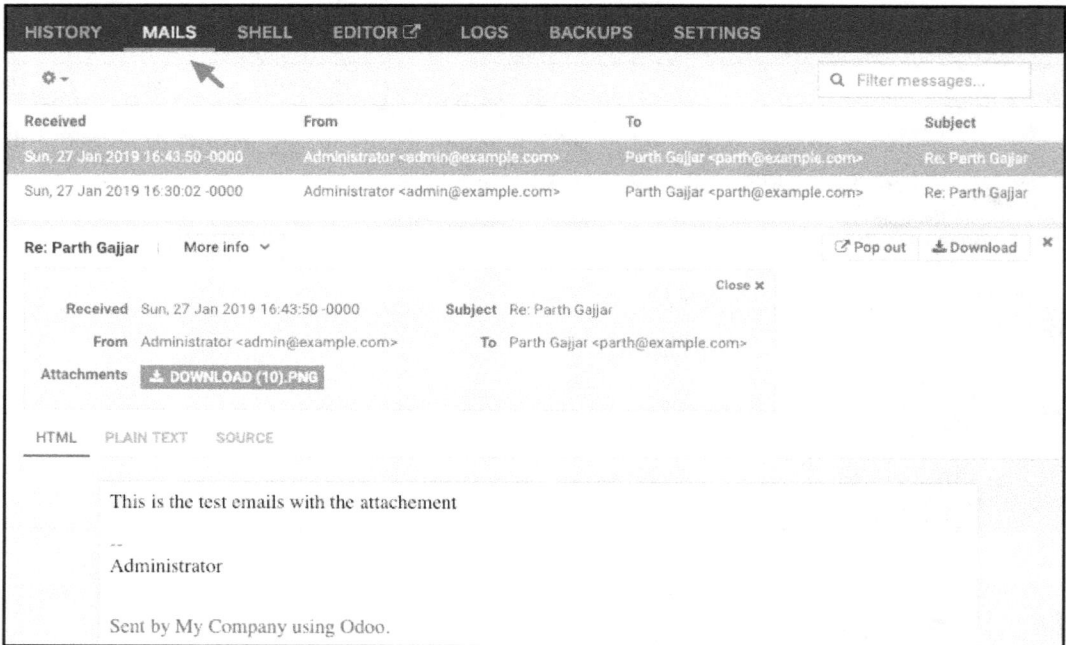

Web shell

From the **SHELL** tab, you can access the web shell. Here, you can access the source code, the logs, the file store, and so on. It provides all of the shell features with editors such as nano and Vim. You can install the Python package with `pip` and maintain multiple tabs.

Take a look at the following screenshot; you can access the web shell from the **SHELL** tab:

Here is the directory structure from the root directory:

```
.
├──── data
│    ├──── addons
│    ├──── filestore
│    └──── sessions
├──── logs
│    ├──── install.log
│    ├──── install.log.1
│    ├──── odoo.log
│    └──── pip.log
├──── Maildir
│    ├──── cur
│    ├──── new
│    └──── tmp
├──── repositories
│    └──── git_github.com_ParthGajjar_OdooShDemo.git
├──── src
│    ├──── enterprise
│    ├──── odoo
│    ├──── themes
│    └──── user
└──── tmp
```

Code editor

If you are not comfortable with shell access, Odoo.sh provides a full-feature editor. Here, you can access the Python shell, the Odoo shell, and the Terminal. You can also edit the source code from here, as you can see in the given image. After modifying the source code, you can restart the server from the **Odoo** menu at the top:

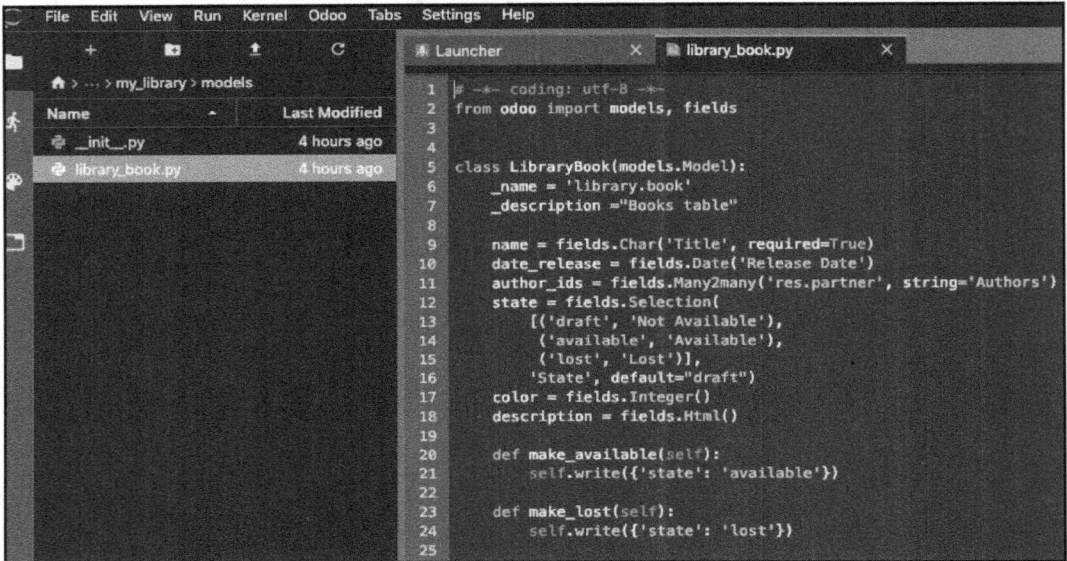

Logs

From the **LOGS** tab, you can access all of the logs for your instance. You can see the live logs without reloading the pages. You can filter the logs from here. This allows you to find issues from the production server. Here is a list of the different log files you can find in the **LOGS** tab:

- `install.log`: This is for the logs that are generated when installing the modules. The logs of all the automated test cases will be located here.
- `pip.log`: You can add Python packages with the `requirement.txt` file. In this log file, you will find the installation log of these Python packages.
- `odoo.log`: This is the normal access log of Odoo. You will find the full-access log here. You should look in this log to check production errors.

- `update.log`: When you upload a new module with a different manifest version, your module gets updated automatically. This file contains the logs of these automatic updates.

Take a look at the following screenshot. This shows the live logs for the production branch:

There's more...

Some commonly used `git` commands are available on the top of the module, as shown in the following screenshot. You can run these by using the **Run** button on the left. These commands can't be edited, but if you want to run a modified command, you can copy it from here and then run it from the shell:

Getting a backup of your instance

Backups are essential for the production server. Odoo.sh provides a built-in backup facility. In this recipe, we will illustrate how you can download and restore backups from Odoo.sh.

How to do it...

In the production branch, you can access the full information about the backups from the backup tab at the top. This will display a list of backups:

From the buttons at the top, you can carry out backup operations, such as downloading the dump, performing a manual backup, or restoring from a backup.

How it works...

Odoo automatically takes a backup of your production instance daily. Odoo also takes an automatic backup whenever you merge a new development branch and update the module. You can also perform a manual backup from the button at the top.

Odoo.sh keeps a total of 14 full backups for the Odoo production instance for up to three months—one per day for seven days, one per week for four weeks, and one per month for three months. From the backup tab, you can access one month of backups (seven daily and four weekly backups). If you want to get older backups, you can ask for help from Odoo.com (https://www.odoo.com/).

If you are moving to Odoo.sh from the on-premise or online option, you can import your database with the **Import Database** button. If you import your database directly in the production, it might cause issues. To avoid this, you should import the database in the staging branch first.

Checking the status of your builds

Whenever you make a new commit, Odoo.sh creates the new commit. It also performs the automated test cases. To manage all of this, Odoo.sh has its own runbot. In this recipe, we will check the statuses of all the builds from the runbot.

How to do it...

Click on the **Builds** menu at the top to open the runbot. Here, you can see a full overview of all of the branches and their commits:

By clicking on the **Connect** buttons, you can connect to the instance. You can see the status of the build by the background color of the branch.

How it works...

On the runbot screen, you will get extra control over the builds. You can connect to the previous builds from here. Different colors show the status of the build. Green means that everything is fine; yellow indicates a warning, which can be ignored, but it is recommended that you fix it. Red means there is a critical issue that you have to fix before merging the development branch into the production. Red and yellow branches show the exclamation icon, (!), near the connect button. When you click on this, you will get a popup with the error and warning log. Usually, you need to search the installation log files to find the error or warning logs, but this popup will filter out the other logs and only display the error and warning logs. This means that whenever a build goes red or yellow, you should come here and fix the errors and warnings before merging them into the production.

Inactive development branches are destroyed after some time. Normally, a new build will be created when you add a new **Commit** button. If you want to reactivate the build without a new commit, however, you can use the rebuild button on the right side. The builds for the staging branches are also destroyed after some time, apart from the last one, which will remain active.

There's more...

From the **Status** menu in the bar at the top, you can see the overall statistics of your instance. The servers of the platform are continuously monitored. On the **Status** screen, you will see the statistics of the server's availability, which will be computed automatically from the platform's monitoring system. It will show data, including the server uptimeThe **Status** page will and the input and output data from the server. The status page will display the following information:

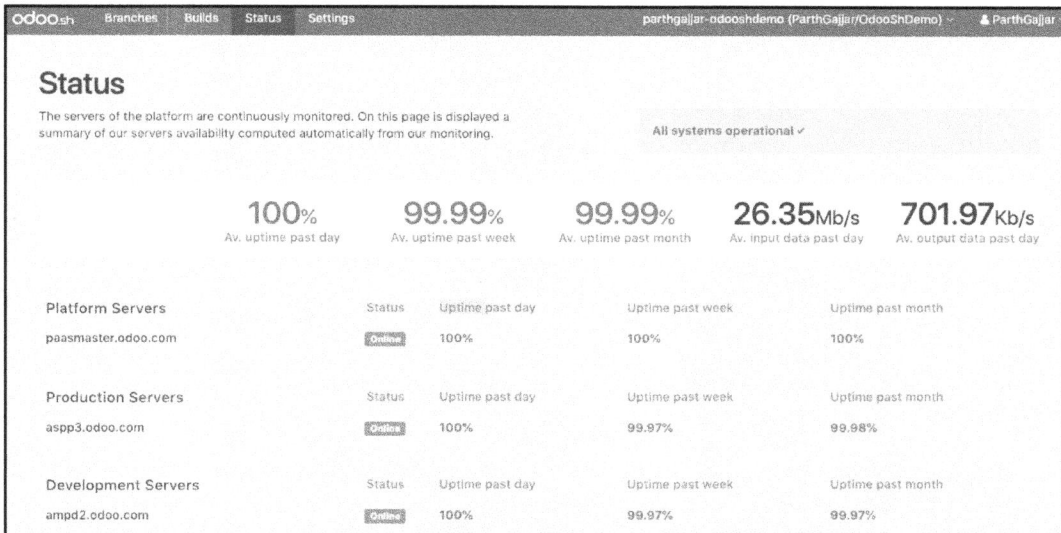

All Odoo.sh options

Odoo.sh provides a few further options under the settings menu. In this recipe, you will see all of the important options used to modify the default behavior of certain things on the platform.

Getting ready

We will be using the same Odoo.sh project that we used in previous recipes. You can access all the Odoo.sh settings from the settings menu in the top bar. If you are not able to see this menu, that means you are accessing a shared project and you don't have admin access.

How to do it...

Open the settings page from the settings menu in the top bar. We'll take a look at the different options in the following sections.

Project name

You can change the name of the Odoo.sh project from this option. The **Project Name** in the input will be used to generate your production URL. Development builds also use this project name as a prefix. In this case, the URL of our feature branch will be something like `https://parthgajjar-odooshdemo-feature-branch-260887.dev.odoo.com:`

	Project Name	
https://	parthgajjar-odooshdemo	.odoo.com

This will change URLs for all future builds and for the production build.

> **TIP**
>
> This option will change the production URL, but you cannot get rid of `*.odoo.com`. If you want to run a production branch on a custom domain, you can add your custom domain in the settings tab of the production branch. You will also need to add a CNAME entry in your DNS manager.

Collaborators

You can share the project by adding collaborators. Here, you can search and add a new collaborator by their GitHub ID. A collaborator can have either **Admin** or **User** access rights. A collaborator with admin access rights will have full access (to the settings, as well). A collaborator with user access rights, on the other hand, will have restricted access rights. They will be able to see all builds, but they will not be able to access the backups, logs, shells, or emails of the production or staging branches, though they will have full access for the development branches:

Collaborators		
Github username		Add
ParthGajjar (ParthGajjar)	Admin	✕
kig-odoo (kig-odoo)	User	✕
pga-odoo (pga-odoo)	User	✕

You will need to give access to the GitHub repository to these users, too; otherwise, they won't be able to create a new repository from the browser.

Public access

Using this option, you can share builds with your end customer. This can be used for demonstration or testing purposes. To do so, you need to enable the **Allow public access** checkbox:

🔒 Public Access   ⓘ

☐ Allow public access

Note that the staging branch will have the same password as your production branch. However, in the development branch, you will have the username and password shown in this table:

Username	Password
admin	admin
demo	demo
portal	portal

Module installation

This will change the method of **Module installation** for the development branches. It provides three options, as shown in the following screenshot:

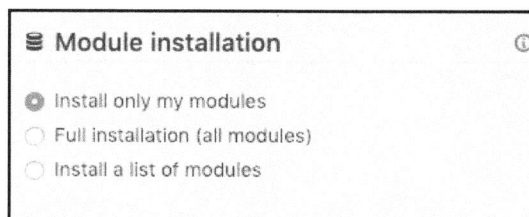

⊜ Module installation   ⓘ

◉ Install only my modules
○ Full installation (all modules)
○ Install a list of modules

By default, it is set to **Install only my modules**. This option will install all of your custom modules and their dependent modules in the new development branches. Only automated test cases are performed for these modules. The second option is **Full installation**. This option will install all of the modules and perform automated test cases for all of those modules. The final option is to **Install a list of modules**. In this option, you will need to pass a list of comma-separated modules, such as sales, purchases, and `my_library`. This option will install the given modules and their dependencies.

This setting only applies to development builds. Staging builds duplicate the production build, so they will have the same modules that are installed in the production branch and perform test cases for modules that have an updated version manifest.

Submodules

The submodules option is used when you are using private modules as submodules. This setting is only needed for private submodules; public submodules will work fine, without any issues. It is not possible to download private repositories publicly, so you need to give repository access to Odoo.sh. Follow these steps to add access to the private submodules:

1. Copy the SSH URL of your private submodule repository in the input and click on **Add**.
2. Copy the displayed **Public Key**.
3. Add this public key as a deploy key in your private repository settings in GitHub (similar settings are also available on bitbucket and GitLab):

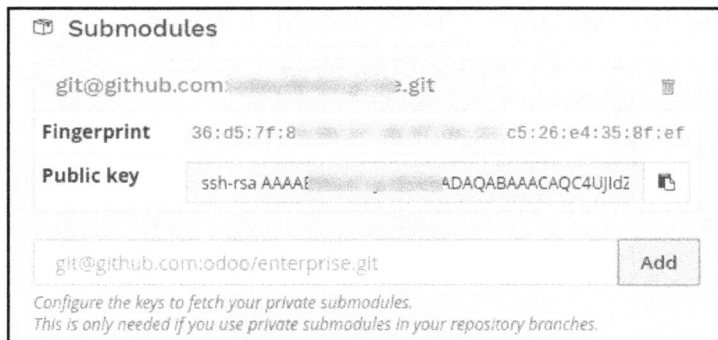

Database workers

You can increase the number of workers for the production build. This is useful when you have more users; usually, a single worker can handle 25 backend users or 25,000 daily website visitors. This formula is not perfect; it can vary based on usage. This option is not free, and increasing the number of workers will increase the price of your Odoo.sh subscription:

⊘ **Database Workers**   ⓘ

As a rule of thumb, you could count about 1 worker per 25 users or 25000 daily visitors. It can vary much depending on the database usage and its website.

Database Workers   1   Worker(s)

These **Database Workers** are multithreaded, and each one is able to handle 15 concurrent requests. It is necessary to have enough workers to serve all incoming requests as they arrive, but an increasing number of workers does not increase the speed of the requests' processing time. It is only used to handle a large number of concurrent users.

Staging branches

Staging branches are used to test a new development with the production database. By default, Odoo.sh gives you one staging branch. If you are working on large projects with lots of developers, this might be a bottleneck in the development process, so you can increase the number of **Staging Branches** at an extra cost:

⟜ **Staging Branches**

Staging branches allow you to test and validate features with production data.

Staging Branches   2   Staging Branch(es)

There's more...

Along with the configuration options, the settings menu will also display some statistics related to the platform.

Database size

This section will display the size of your production database. The Odoo.sh platform charges the database at *$1 /GB/month*. This option helps you keep track of your database. The displayed database size is only for the production database; it does not include the databases of the staging and development branches:

🛢 Production Database Size

This project's production database has a size of **35.5 MB**. It consists of its PSQL Database of **24.5 MB** and its container filestore of **10.9 MB**.

The price per GB is fixed at **$1** per month. Only the number of GB used by your production database is billed. All backups, replication and other builds are included at no extra cost. The disk space used will be automatically synchronized with your subscription.

show details ⌄

Odoo source code revisions

This section will display the GitHub revision number of Odoo's project. It will display the revision hash for the community, enterprise, and theme projects that are currently being used in the platform. This source code will automatically be updated every week. This option will help you get the exact same versions in your local machine. You can also check this from the web shell, through the `git` command in the repository.

20
Remote Procedure Calls in Odoo

The Odoo server supports **Remote procedure calls** (**RPC**), which means that you can connect Odoo instances from external applications. With the Odoo RPC API, you can perform any CRUD operations on a database. Odoo RPC is not limited to CRUD operations; you can also invoke public methods of any model. Of course, you will need to have proper access to rights to perform these operations because RPC respects all of the access rights and record rules you have defined in your database. Consequently, it is very safe to use. Odoo RPC is not platform-dependant, so you can use it on any platform, including Odoo.sh, online, or self-hosted platforms. Odoo RPC can be used with any programming language so you can integrate Odoo with any external application.

Odoo provides two types of RPC API—XML-RPC and JSON-RPC. In this recipe, we will learn how to use these RPCs from an external program. Finally, you will learn how to use Odoo RPC through OCA's `odoorpc` library.

In this chapter, we will cover the following recipes:

- Logging into/connecting Odoo with XML-RPC
- Searching/reading records through XML-RPC
- Creating/updating/deleting records through XML-RPC
- Calling methods through XML-RPC
- Logging in/connecting Odoo with JSON-RPC
- Fetching/searching records through JSON-RPC
- Create/Update/Delete records through JSON-RPC
- Calling methods through JSON-RPC
- The OCA odoorpc library

Technical requirements

In this chapter, we will be using the `my_library` module, which we created in Chapter 19, *Managing, Deploying, and Testing with Odoo.sh*. You can find the same initial `my_library` module on the GitHub repository: `https://github.com/PacktPublishing/Odoo-12-Development-Cookbook-Third-Edition/tree/master/Chapter20/r0_initial_module`.

Here, we will not introduce a new language as the reader might not be familiar with it. We will continue using Python to access the RPC API. You can use another language if you want to, as the same procedure can be applied in any language to access the RPC.

To connect Odoo through the RPC, you will need a running Odoo instance to connect with. Throughout this chapter, we will assume that you have the Odoo server running on `http://localhost:8069` and called `test-12` database and that you have installed the `my_library` module in it. Note that you can connect any valid IP or domain through the RPC.

Logging in/connecting Odoo with XML-RPC

In this recipe, we will carry out user authentication through RPC to check whether the supplies credentials are valid.

Getting ready

To connect an Odoo instance through RPC, you will need a running Odoo instance to connect with. We will assume that you have the Odoo server running on `http://localhost:8069` and you have installed the `my_library` module.

How to do it...

Perform the following steps to carry out user authentication through RPC:

1. Add the `odoo_authenticate.py` file. You can place this file anywhere you want because the RPC program will work independently.

2. Add the following code to the file:

```
from xmlrpc import client

server_url = 'http://localhost:8069'
db_name = 'test-12'
username = 'admin'
password = 'admin'

common = client.ServerProxy('%s/xmlrpc/2/common' % server_url)
user_id = common.authenticate(db_name, username, password, {})

if user_id:
 print("Success: User id is", user_id)
else:
 print("Failed: wrong credentials")
```

3. Run the following Python script from the Terminal with the following command:

```
python3 odoo_authenticate.py
```

This will print a success message with the user ID if you have provided a valid login name and password.

How it works...

In this recipe, we used the Python `xmlrpc` library to access Odoo instances through XML-RPC. This is a standard Python library and you do not have to install anything else in order to use it.

For authentication, Odoo provides XML-RPC on the `/xmlrpc/2/common` endpoint. This endpoint is used for meta methods, which do not require authentication. The `authentication()` method itself is a public method, so it can be called publicly. The Authentication method accepts four arguments—database name, username, password, and user agent environment. The user agent environment is a compulsory argument, but if you do not want to pass the user agent parameter, at least pass the empty dictionary.

When you execute the `authenticate()` method with all valid arguments, it will make a call to the Odoo server and perform authentication. It will then return the user ID, if the given login ID and password are correct. It will return `False` if the user is not present or if the password is wrong.

You need to use the authenticate method before accessing any data through RPC. This is because accessing data with the wrong credentials will generate an error. Additionally, the methods used to access data require a user ID instead of a username, so the authenticate method is needed in order to get the ID of the user.

> Odoo's online instances (`*.odoo.com`) use OAuth authentication and so the local password is not set on the instance. To use XML-RPC on these instances, you will need to set the user's password manually from the **Settings** | **Users** | **Users** menu of your instance.

There's more...

The `/xmlrpc/2/common` endpoint provides one more method: `version()`. You can call this method without credentials. It will return version information of the Odoo instance. The following is an example of the `version()` method usage:

```
from xmlrpc import client

server_url = 'http://localhost:8069'
common = client.ServerProxy('%s/xmlrpc/2/common' % server_url)
version_info = common.version()

print(version_info)
```

The preceding program will give the following output:

```
$ python3 version_info.py
{'server_version': '12.0', 'server_version_info': [12, 0, 0, 'final', 0, ''], 'server_serie': '12.0',
'protocol_version': 1}
```

Searching/reading records through XML-RPC

In this recipe, we will see how you can fetch the data from an Odoo instance through RPC. The user can access most data, except data that is restricted by the security-access control and record rules. RPC can be used in many situations, such as collecting data for analysis, manipulating a lot of data at once, or fetching data for display in another software/system. There are endless possibilities and you can use RPCs whenever necessary.

Getting ready

We will create a Python program to fetch the book data from the `library.book` model. Make sure you have installed the `my_library` module and that the server is running on `http://localhost:8069`.

How to do it...

Perform the following steps to fetch a book's information through RPC:

1. Add the `books_data.py` file. You can place this file anywhere you want to because the RPC program will work independently.
2. Add the following code to the file:

```
from xmlrpc import client

server_url = 'http://localhost:8069'
db_name = 'test-12'
username = 'admin'
password = 'admin'

common = client.ServerProxy('%s/xmlrpc/2/common' % server_url)
user_id = common.authenticate(db_name, username, password, {})

models = client.ServerProxy('%s/xmlrpc/2/object' % server_url)

if user_id:
    search_domain = ['|', ['name', 'ilike', 'odoo'], ['name',
'ilike', 'sql']]
    books_ids = models.execute_kw(db_name, user_id, password,
        'library.book', 'search',
```

```
            [search_domain],
            {'limit': 5})
        print('Books ids found:', books_ids)

        books_data = models.execute_kw(db_name, user_id, password,
            'library.book', 'read',
            [books_ids, ['name', 'date_release']])
        print("Books data:", books_data)
    else:
        print('Wrong credentials')
```

3. Run the Python script form the Terminal with the following command:

python3 books_data.py

The preceding program will fetch the book data and give you the following output (the output may be different based on your data):

```
$ python3 books_data.py
Books ids: [1, 3, 4, 7, 8]
Books data: [{'id': 1, 'name': 'Odoo 12 Development Cookbook', 'date_release': '2019-02-13'}, {'id': 3,
'name': 'PostgresSQL basics', 'date_release': '2018-02-15'}, {'id': 4, 'name': 'MySQL basics',
'date_release': '2018-02-15'}, {'id': 7, 'name': 'Odoo basics', 'date_release': '2018-02-15'}, {'id':
8, 'name': 'Odoo 11 Development Cookbook', 'date_release': '2018-02-15'}]
```

How it works...

In order to access the book data, first you have to carry out authentication. At the beginning of the program, we did the authentication in the same way as we did in the *Logging in/connecting Odoo with XML-RPC* recipe earlier. If you provided valid credentials, the authentication method will return the id of the user's record. We will use this user ID to fetch the book data.

The /xmlrpc/2/object endpoint is used for database operation. In our recipe, we used the object endpoint to fetch the book data. In contrast to the /xmlrpc/2/common endpoint, this endpoint does not work without credentials. With this endpoint, you can access the public method of any model through the execute_kw() method. execute_kw takes the following arguments:

- Database name
- User ID (we get this from the authenticate method)
- Password

- Model name, for example, `res.partner`, `library.book`
- Method name, for example, `search`, `read`, `create`
- An array of positional arguments
- A dictionary for keyword arguments (optional)

In our example, we want to fetch the book's information. This can be done through a combination of `search()` and `read()`. Book information is stored in the `library.book` model so in `execute_kw()`, we use `library.book` as the model name and `search` as the method name. This will call the ORM's search method and returns record IDs. The only difference here is that ORM's search method returns a recordset while this search method returns a list of IDs.

In `execute_kw()`, you can pass arguments and keyword arguments for the provided method. The `search()` method accepts a domain as a positional argument so we passed a domain to filter books. The search method has other optional keyword arguments, such as `limit`, `offset`, `count`, and `order`, from which we have used the `limit` parameter to fetch only five records. This will return the list of book IDs whose names contain the `odoo` or `SQL` strings. Still, we need to fetch book data from the database. We will use the `read` method to do this. The `read` method accepts a list of IDs and fields to complete the task. At the end of *step 3*, we used the list of book IDs that we received from the `search` method then used the book IDs to fetch the `name` and `release_date` of the books. This will return the list of the dictionary with the book's information.

> Note that the arguments and keyword arguments passed in `execute_kw()` are based on the passed method. You can use any public ORM method via `execute_kw()`. You just need to give the method name, the valid arguments, and the keyword arguments. These arguments are going to be passed in the method in the ORM.

There's more...

The data fetched through a combination of the `search()` and `read()` methods is slightly time-consuming because it will make two calls. `search_read` is an alternative method for fetching data. You can search and fetch the data in a single call. Here is the alternative way to fetch a book's data with `search_read()`.

It will return the same output as the previous example:

```python
from xmlrpc import client

server_url = 'http://localhost:8069'
db_name = 'test-12'
username = 'admin'
password = 'admin'

common = client.ServerProxy('%s/xmlrpc/2/common' % server_url)
user_id = common.authenticate(db_name, username, password, {})

models = client.ServerProxy('%s/xmlrpc/2/object' % server_url)

if user_id:
    search_domain = ['|', ['name', 'ilike', 'odoo'], ['name', 'ilike',
'sql']]
    books_ids = models.execute_kw(db_name, user_id, password,
        'library.book', 'search_read',
        [search_domain, ['name', 'date_release']],
        {'limit': 5})
    print('Books data:', books_ids)

else:
    print('Wrong credentials')
```

> The read and search_read methods will return id fields even if the id field is not requested. Furthermore, for the many2one field, you will get an array made up of the id and display name. For example, the create_uid many2one field will return data like this: [12, 'Parth Gajjar'].

Creating/updating/deleting records through XML-RPC

In the previous recipe, we saw how to search and read data through RPC. In this recipe, we will perform the remaining CRUD operations through RPC, which are Create, Update (write), and Delete (unlink).

Getting ready

We will create the Python program to `create`, `write`, and `unlink` data on the `library.book` model. Make sure you have installed the `my_library` module and that the server is running on `http://localhost:8069`.

How to do it...

Perform the following steps to create, write, and update a book's information through RPC:

1. Add the `books_operation.py` file. You can place this file anywhere you want because the RPC program will work independently.
2. Add the following code to the file:

```python
from xmlrpc import client

server_url = 'http://localhost:8069'
db_name = 'test-12'
username = 'admin'
password = 'admin'

common = client.ServerProxy('%s/xmlrpc/2/common' % server_url)
user_id = common.authenticate(db_name, username, password, {})

models = client.ServerProxy('%s/xmlrpc/2/object' % server_url)

if user_id:
    # create new books
    create_data = [
        {'name': 'Book 1', 'release_date': '2019-01-26'},
        {'name': 'Book 3', 'release_date': '2019-02-12'},
        {'name': 'Book 3', 'release_date': '2019-05-08'},
        {'name': 'Book 7', 'release_date': '2019-05-14'}
    ]
    books_ids = models.execute_kw(db_name, user_id, password,
        'library.book', 'create',
        [create_data])
    print("Books created:", books_ids)

    # Write in existing book record
    book_to_write = books_ids[1] # We will use ids of recently
created books
    write_data = {'name': 'Books 2'}
    written = models.execute_kw(db_name, user_id, password,
```

```
            'library.book', 'write',
            [book_to_write, write_data])
        print("Books written:", written)

        # Delete the book record
        books_to_delete = books_ids[2:] # We will use ids of
    recently created books
        deleted = models.execute_kw(db_name, user_id, password,
            'library.book', 'unlink',
            [books_to_delete])
        print('Books unlinked:', deleted)

    else:
        print('Wrong credentials')
```

3. Run the Python script form the Terminal with the given command:

python3 books_operation.py

The preceding program will create four records of the books. Updating the data in the book records and later deleting two records gives you the following output (the IDs created may be different based on your database):

```
$ python3 books_operation.py
Books created: [18, 19, 20, 21]
Books written: True
Books unlinked: True
```

How it works...

In this recipe, we performed create, write, and delete operations through XML-RPC. This operation also uses the /xmlrpc/2/object endpoint and the execute_kw method.

From Odoo v12, the create() method supports the creation of multiple records in a single call. In *step 2*, we first created a dictionary with the book's information. Then we used the book's dictionary to create new records of the books through XML-RPC. The XML-RPC call needs two parameters to create new records—the create method name and the book data. This will create the four book records in the library.book model. In ORM, when you create the record, it returns a recordset of created records, but if you create the records RPC, it will return a list of IDs.

The `write` method works in a similar way to the `create` method. In the `write` method, you will need to pass a list of record IDs, and the field values, to be written. In our example, we updated the name of the book created in the first section. This will update the name of the second book from `Book 3` to `Book 2`. Here, we passed only one `id` of the book, but you can pass a list of IDs if you want to update multiple records in a single call.

In the third section of the program, we deleted two books that we'd created in the first section. You can delete records with the `unlink` method and list of record IDs.

After the program is executed successfully, you will find two book records in the database.

There's more...

When you are performing a CRUD operation through RPC, it might generate an error if you don't have permission to do that operation. With the `check_access_rights` method, you can check whether the user has the proper access rights to do a certain operation. The `check_access_rights` method returns `True` or `False` values based on the access rights of the user. Here is an example showing whether a user has the rights to create a books record:

```
from xmlrpc import client

server_url = 'http://localhost:8069'
db_name = 'test-12'
username = 'admin'
password = 'admin'

common = client.ServerProxy('%s/xmlrpc/2/common' % server_url)
user_id = common.authenticate(db_name, username, password, {})

models = client.ServerProxy('%s/xmlrpc/2/object' % server_url)

if user_id:
    has_access = models.execute_kw(db_name, user_id, password,
        'library.book', 'check_access_rights',
        ['create'], {'raise_exception': False})
    print('Has create access on book:', has_access )
else:
    print('Wrong credentials')

# Output: Has create access on book: True
```

Calling methods through XML-RPC

With Odoo, the RPC API is not limited to CRUD operations; you can also invoke business methods. In this recipe, we will call the `make_available` method to change the book's state.

Getting ready

We will create the Python program to call `make_available` on the `library.book` model. Make sure you have installed the `my_library` module and the server is running on `http://localhost:8069`.

How to do it...

Perform the following steps to create, write, and update a book's information through RPC:

1. Add the `books_method.py` file. You can place this file anywhere you want because the RPC program will work independently.
2. Add the following code to the file:

```python
from xmlrpc import client

server_url = 'http://localhost:8069'
db_name = 'test-12'
username = 'admin'
password = 'admin'

common = client.ServerProxy('%s/xmlrpc/2/common' % server_url)
user_id = common.authenticate(db_name, username, password, {})

models = client.ServerProxy('%s/xmlrpc/2/object' % server_url)

if user_id:
    # Create book with state draft
    book_id = models.execute_kw(db_name, user_id, password,
        'library.book', 'create',
        [{'name': 'New Book', 'date_release': '2019-01-26',
'state': 'draft'}])

    # Call make_available method on new book
    models.execute_kw(db_name, user_id, password,
```

```
        'library.book', 'make_available',
        [[book_id]])

    # check book status after method call
    book_data = models.execute_kw(db_name, user_id, password,
        'library.book', 'read',
        [[book_id], ['name', 'state']])
    print('Book state after method call:',
book_data[0]['state'])
else:
    print('Wrong credentials')
```

3. Run the Python script from the terminal with the following command:

python3 books_method.py

The preceding program will create one book with draft and then we will change book state by calling the make_available method. After that, we will fetch the book data to check the book's status, which will give the following output:

```
$ python3 books_method.py
Book state after method call: available
```

How it works...

You can call any modal method from RPC. This helps you to perform business logic without encountering any side-effects. For example, you created the sales order from RPC and then called the action_confirm method of the sale.order method. This is equivalent to clicking on the **Confirm** button on a sales order form.

You can call any public method of the model, but you cannot call a private method from RPC. A method name that starts with _ is called a private method, such as _get_share_url() and _get_data().

It is safe to use these methods, as they go through the ORM and follow all security rules. If the method is accessing unauthorized records, it will generate errors.

In our example, we created a book with the state draft. Then we made one more RPC call to invoke the `make_available` method, which will change the book state to `available`. Finally, we made one more RPC call to check the state of the book. This will show that the book's state is changed to `available`.

> Methods that do not return anything internally return `None` by default. Such methods cannot be used from RPC. Consequently, if you want to use your method from RPC, at least add the return True statement.

There's more...

If an exception is generated from a method, all of the operations performed in the transaction will be automatically rolled back to the initial state. This is only applicable to a single transaction (a single RPC call). For example, imagine you are making two RPC calls to the server and there is an exception generated in the second call. This will roll back the operation that is carried out in the second RPC call. The operation performed through the first RPC call won't be rolled back. Consequently, you want to perform a complex operation through RPC. It is recommended to perform this in a single RPC call by creating a method in the model.

Logging in/connecting Odoo with JSON-RPC

Odoo provides one more type of RPC API: JSON-RPC. As its name suggests, the JSON-RPC works in the JSON format and uses the `jsonrpc 2.0` specification. In this recipe, we will see how you can log in with JSON-RPC. The Odoo web client itself uses JSON-RPC to fetch data from the server.

Getting ready

In this recipe, we will perform user authentication through JSON-RPC to check whether the given credentials are valid. Make sure you have installed the `my_library` module and the server is running on `http://localhost:8069`.

How to do it...

Perform the following steps to perform user authentication through RPC:

1. Add the `jsonrpc_authenticate.py` file. You can place this file anywhere you want because the RPC program will work independently.
2. Add the following code to the file:

```python
import json
import random
import requests


server_url = 'http://localhost:8069'
db_name = 'test-12'
username = 'admin'
password = 'admin'

json_endpoint = "%s/jsonrpc" % server_url
headers = {"Content-Type": "application/json"}

def get_json_payload(service, method, *args):
    return json.dumps({
        "jsonrpc": "2.0",
        "method": 'call',
        "params": {
            "service": service,
            "method": method,
            "args": args
        },
        "id": random.randint(0, 100000000),
    })

payload = get_json_payload("common", "login", db_name,
username, password)
response = requests.post(json_endpoint, data=payload,
headers=headers)
user_id = response.json()['result']

if user_id:
    print("Success: User id is", user_id)
else:
    print("Failed: wrong credentials")
```

3. Run the Python script from the Terminal with the following command:

```
python3 jsonrpc_authenticate.py
```

When you run the preceding program and you have passed a valid login name and password, the program will print a success message with **id** of the user, as follows:

```
python3 jsonrpc_authenticate.py
Success: User id is 2
```

How it works...

The JSON-RPC is using the JSON format to communicate with the server. It uses the /jsonrpc endpoint to communicate with the server. In our example, we used the Python requests package to make POST requests, but if you want to you can use other packages, such as urllib.

The JSON-RPC only accepts a payload formatted in the **JSON-RPC 2.0** specification, refer to; this link to learn more about the JSON-RPC format https://www.jsonrpc.org/specification. In our example, we created the get_json_payload() method. This method will prepare the payload in the valid JSON-RPC 2.0 format. This method accepts the service name and the method to call and the remaining arguments will be placed in *args. We will be using this method in all subsequent recipes. The JSON-RPC accepts requests in JSON format and these requests are only accepted if the request contains a {"Content-Type": "application/json"} header. The result of the requests will be in the JSON format.

Like XML-RPC, all public methods, including login, come under the common service. For this reason, we passed common as a service and login as a method to prepare the JSON payload. The login method required some extra arguments, so we passed database name, username, and password. Then we made the POST request to the JSON endpoint with the payload and headers. If you passed the correct username and password, the method returns the user id. The response will be in the JSON format and you will get the result in the result key.

> Note that the get_json_payload() method created in this recipe is used to remove repetitive code from the example. It is not compulsory to use it, so feel free to apply your own adaptations.

There's more...

Like XML-RPC, the version method is also available in the JSON-RPC. This version method comes under the common service and is accessible publicly. You can get version information without login information. See the following example showing how to fetch the version info of the Odoo server:

```
import json
import random
import requests


server_url = 'http://localhost:8069'
json_endpoint = "%s/jsonrpc" % server_url
headers = {"Content-Type": "application/json"}

def get_json_payload(service, method, *args):
    ... # see full function definition in last section

payload = get_json_payload("common", "version")
response = requests.post(json_endpoint, data=payload, headers=headers)

print(response.json())
```

This program will display the following output:

```
$ python3 jsonrpc_version.py
{'jsonrpc': '2.0', 'id': 686620048, 'result': {'server_version': '12.0', 'server_version_info': [12, 0,
0, 'final', 0, ''], 'server_serie': '12.0', 'protocol_version': 1}}
```

Fetching/searching records through JSON-RPC

In the previous recipe, we saw how you can do authentication through JSON-RPC. In this recipe, we will see how you can fetch the data from the Odoo instance with the JSON-RPC.

Getting ready

In this recipe, we will fetch book information with the JSON-RPC. Make sure you have installed the `my_library` module and the server is running on `http://localhost:8069`.

How to do it...

Perform the following steps to fetch book data from the `library.book` model:

1. Add the `jsonrpc_fetch_data.py` file. You can place this file anywhere you want because the RPC program will work independently.
2. Add the following code to the file:

```
# place authentication and get_json_payload methods (see first
jsonrpc recipe)

if user_id:
    # search for the books ids
    search_domain = ['|', ['name', 'ilike', 'odoo'], ['name',
'ilike', 'sql']]
    payload = get_json_payload("object", "execute_kw",
        db_name, user_id, password,
        'library.book', 'search', [search_domain], {'limit':
5})
    res = requests.post(json_endpoint, data=payload,
headers=headers).json()
    print('Search Result:', res) # ids will be in result keys

    # read data for books ids
    payload = get_json_payload("object", "execute_kw",
        db_name, user_id, password,
        'library.book', 'read', [res['result'], ['name',
'date_release']])
    res = requests.post(json_endpoint, data=payload,
headers=headers).json()
    print('Books data:', res)
else:
    print("Failed: wrong credentials")
```

3. Run the Python script from the Terminal with the following command:

```
python3 jsonrpc_fetch_data.py
```

The preceding program will give you the following output. The first RPC call will print the book's `id` and the second one will print the information for the book's `id`:

```
$ python3 jsonrpc_fetch_data.py
Search Reasult: {'jsonrpc': '2.0', 'id': 924727329, 'result': [1, 3, 4, 7, 8]}
Books Data: {'jsonrpc': '2.0', 'id': 855811251, 'result': [{'id': 1, 'name': 'Odoo 12 Development
Cookbook', 'date_release': '2019-02-13'}, {'id': 3, 'name': 'PostgresSQL basics', 'date_release':
'2018-02-15'}, {'id': 4, 'name': 'MySQL basics', 'date_release': '2018-02-15'}, {'id': 7, 'name': 'Odoo
basics', 'date_release': '2018-02-15'}, {'id': 8, 'name': 'Odoo 11 Development Cookbook',
'date_release': '2018-02-15'}]}
```

How it works...

In the *Logging in/connecting Odoo with JSON-RPC* recipe, we saw that you can validate `username` and `password`. If the login details are correct, the RPC call will return `user_id`. You can then use this `user_id` to fetch the model's data. Like XML-RPC, we need to use the `search` and `read` combination to fetch the data from the model. To fetch the data, we use `object` as a service and `execute_kw` as the method. `execute_kw` is the same method that we used in XML-RPC for data, so it accepts the same argument, as follows:

- Database name
- User ID (we get this from the authenticate method)
- Password
- Model name, for example, `res.partner`, `library.book`
- Method name, for example, `search`, `read`, `create`
- An array of positional arguments (`args`)
- A dictionary for keyword arguments (`optional`) (`kwargs`)

In our example, we called the `search` method first. The `execute_kw` method usually takes mandatory arguments as positional arguments, and optional arguments as keyword arguments. In the search method, `domain` is a mandatory argument so we passed it in the list and passed the `optional` argument limit as the `keyword` argument (dictionary). You will get a response in the JSON format, and in this recipe the response of the `search()` method RPC will have the book's IDs in the `result` key.

In *step 2*, we made an RPC call with the read method. To read the book's information, we passed two positional arguments—the list of book IDs and the list of fields to fetch. This RPC call will return the book information in JSON format and you can access it in the result key.

> Instead of execute_kw, you can use execute as the method. This does not support keyword arguments, so you need to pass all of the intermediate arguments if you want to pass some optional arguments.

There's more...

Similar to XML-RPC, you can use the search_read() method instead of the search() and read() method combination as it is slightly time-consuming. The following is an alternative way to fetch book data with search_read(). It will return the same output as in the previous example:

```
# place authentication and get_json_payload methods (see first jsonrpc
recipe)

if user_id:
    # search and read for the books ids
    search_domain = ['|', ['name', 'ilike', 'odoo'], ['name', 'ilike',
'sql']]
    payload = get_json_payload("object", "execute_kw",
        db_name, user_id, password,
        'library.book', 'search_read', [search_domain, ['name',
'date_release']],
        {'limit': 5})
    res = requests.post(json_endpoint, data=payload,
headers=headers).json()
    print('Books data:', res)
else:
    print("Failed: wrong credentials")
```

Create/update/delete records through JSON-RPC

In the previous recipe, we looked at how to search and read data through JSON-RPC. In this recipe, we will perform the remaining CRUD operations through RPC—Create, Update (write), and Delete (unlink).

Getting ready

We will create a Python program to `create`, `write`, and `unlink` data on the `library.book` model. Make sure you have installed the `my_library` module and the server is running on `http://localhost:8069`.

How to do it...

Perform the following steps to create, write, and unlink a book's information through RPC:

1. Add the `jsonrpc_operation.py` file. You can place this file anywhere you want because the RPC program will work independently.
2. Add the following code to the file:

```
# place authentication and get_json_payload method (see last
recipe for more)

if user_id:
    # creates the books records
    create_data = [
        {'name': 'Book 1', 'date_release': '2019-01-26'},
        {'name': 'Book 3', 'date_release': '2019-02-12'},
        {'name': 'Book 5', 'date_release': '2019-05-08'},
        {'name': 'Book 7', 'date_release': '2019-05-14'}
    ]
    payload = get_json_payload("object", "execute_kw",
db_name, user_id, password, 'library.book', 'create',
[create_data])
    res = requests.post(json_endpoint, data=payload,
headers=headers).json()
    print("Books created:", res)
    books_ids = res['result']

    # Write in existing book record
    book_to_write = books_ids[1] # We will use ids of recently
created books
    write_data = {'name': 'Book 2'}
    payload = get_json_payload("object", "execute_kw",
db_name, user_id, password, 'library.book', 'write',
[book_to_write, write_data])
    res = requests.post(json_endpoint, data=payload,
headers=headers).json()
    print("Books written:", res)
```

```
    # Delete in existing book record
    book_to_unlink = books_ids[2:] # We will use ids of
recently created books
    payload = get_json_payload("object", "execute_kw",
db_name, user_id, password, 'library.book', 'unlink',
[book_to_unlink])
    res = requests.post(json_endpoint, data=payload,
headers=headers).json()
    print("Books deleted:", res)

else:
    print("Failed: wrong credentials")
```

3. Run the Python script from the Terminal with the following command:

python3 jsonrpc_operation.py

The preceding program will create four books. Writing one book and deleting two books gives you the following output (the IDs created may be different based on on your database):

```
$ python3 jsonrpc_operation.py
Books created: {'jsonrpc': '2.0', 'id': 21804281, 'result': [80, 81, 82, 83]}
Books written: {'jsonrpc': '2.0', 'id': 81603666, 'result': True}
Books deleted: {'jsonrpc': '2.0', 'id': 767449164, 'result': True}
```

How it works...

execute_kw is used for the create, update, and delete operations. From Odoo version 12, the create method supports creating of multiple records. So we prepared the dictionary with information from the four books. Then we made the JSON-RPC call with library.book as the model name and create as the method name. This will create four book records in the database and return a JSON response with the IDs of these newly-created books. In the next RPC calls, we want to use these IDs to make an RPC call for update and delete operations, so we assign it to the books_ids variable.

> Both JSON-RPC and XML-RPC generate an error when you try to create the record without providing values for the required field, so make sure you have added all the required fields in the create values.

In the next RPC call, we used the `write` method to update the existing records. The `write` method accepts two positional arguments; the records to update and the values to write. In our example, we have updated the name of the book by using the ID of the second book from a created book's IDs. This will change the name of the second book from `Book 3` to `Book 2`.

Then we made the last RPC call to delete two book records. To do so, we used the `unlink` method. The `unlink` method accepts only one argument, which is the ID of the records you want to delete. This RPC call will delete the last two books.

There's more...

Like XML-RPC, you can use the `check_access_rights` method in JSON-RPC to check whether you have access rights to perform the operation. This method requires two parameters—model name and the operation name. In the following example, we check access rights for the `create` operation on the `library.book` model:

```
# place authentication and get_json_payload method (see last recipe
for more)
if user_id:
    payload = get_json_payload("object", "execute_kw",
        db_name, user_id, password,
        'library.book', 'check_access_rights', ['create'])
    res = requests.post(json_endpoint, data=payload,
headers=headers).json()
    print("Has create access:", res['result'])

else:
    print("Failed: wrong credentials")
```

This program will give the following output:

```
python3 jsonrpc_access_rights.py
Has create access: True
```

Calling methods through JSON-RPC

In this recipe, we will learn how to invoke a custom method of the model through JSON-RPC. We will change the status of the book by calling the `make_available()` method.

Getting ready

We will create the Python program to call `make_available` on the `library.book` model. Make sure you have installed the `my_library` module and the server is running on `http://localhost:8069`.

How to do it...

Perform the following steps to create, write, and update a book's information through RPC:

1. Add the `jsonrpc_method.py` file. You can place this file anywhere you want because the RPC program will work independently.

2. Add the following code to the file:

```
# place authentication and get_json_payload method (see last
recipe for more)
if user_id:
    # Create the book in draft state
    payload = get_json_payload("object", "execute_kw",
        db_name, user_id, password,
        'library.book', 'create', [{'name': 'Book 1', 'state':
'draft'}])
    res = requests.post(json_endpoint, data=payload,
headers=headers).json()
    print("Has create access:", res['result'])
    book_id = res['result']

    # Change the book state by calling make_available method
    payload = get_json_payload("object", "execute_kw",
        db_name, user_id, password,
        'library.book', 'make_available', [book_id])
    res = requests.post(json_endpoint, data=payload,
headers=headers).json()

    # Check the book status after method call
```

```
    payload = get_json_payload("object", "execute_kw",
        db_name, user_id, password,
        'library.book', 'read', [book_id, ['name', 'state']])
    res = requests.post(json_endpoint, data=payload,
headers=headers).json()
    print("Book state after the method call:", res['result'])

else:
    print("Failed: wrong credentials")
```

3. Run the Python script from the terminal with the following command:

    python3 jsonrpc_method.py

The preceding command will create one book using `draft` and then we will change the book state by calling the `make_available` method. After that, we will fetch book data to check the book status, which will give the following output:

```
$ python3 jsonrpc_method.py
Book created with id: 86
Book state after the method call: [{'id': 86, 'name': 'Book 1', 'state': 'available'}]
```

How it works...

`execute_kw` is capable of calling any public method of the model. As we saw in the *Calling methods through XML-RPC* recipe, public methods are those whose name is not stated with _ (underscore). Methods that start with _ are private and you cannot invoke them from the JSON-RPC.

In our example, we created a book with the state draft. Then we made one more RPC call to invoke the `make_available` method, which will change the book state to `available`. Finally, we made one more RPC call to check the state of the book. This will show that the book's state is changed to available.

> Note that methods that do not return anything internally return None by default. Such methods cannot be used by RPC. If you want to use your method from RPC, at least add the return True statement.

The OCA odoorpc library

The **Odoo Community Association** (**OCA**) provides a Python library called odoorpc. This is available at https://github.com/OCA/odoorpc. The odoorpc library provides a user-friendly syntax from which to access Odoo data through RPC. It provides a similar syntax to the server. In this recipe, we will see how you can use the odoorpc library to perform operations through RPC.

Getting ready

The odoorpc library is registered on the Python package (PyPi) index. In order to use the library, you need to install it with the following command. You can use this in a separate virtual environment if you want:

```
pip install OdooRPC
```

In this recipe, we will do some basic operations using the odoorpc library. We will use the library.book model to perform these operations. Make sure you have installed the my_library module and the server is running on http://localhost:8069.

How to do it...

Perform the following steps to create, write, and update a book's information through RPC:

1. Add the odoorpc_library.py file. You can place this file anywhere you want because the RPC program will work independently.

2. Add the following code to the file:

```
import odoorpc

db_name = 'test-12'
user_name = 'admin'
password = 'admin'

# Prepare the connection to the server
odoo = odoorpc.ODOO('localhost', port=8069)
odoo.login(db_name, user_name, password) # login

# User information
user = odoo.env.user
print(user.name) # name of the user connected
print(user.company_id.name) # the name of user's company
print(user.email) # the email of usser

BookModel = odoo.env['library.book']
search_domain = ['|', ['name', 'ilike', 'odoo'], ['name',
'ilike', 'sql']]
books_ids = BookModel.search(search_domain, limit=5)
for book in BookModel.browse(books_ids):
    print(book.name, book.date_release)

# create the book and update the state
book_id = BookModel.create({'name': 'Test book', 'state':
'draft'})
print("Book state before make_available:", book.state)
book = BookModel.browse(book_id)
book.make_available()
book = BookModel.browse(book_id)
print("Book state before make_available:", book.state)
```

3. Run the Python script from the Terminal with the following command:

```
python3 odoorpc_library.py
```

The program will do the authentication, print user information, and perform an operation in the `library.book` model. It will generate the following output:

```
$ python3 odoorpc_library.py
Mitchell Admin
YourCompany
admin@yourcompany.example.com
Odoo 12 Development Cookbook 2019-02-13
PostgresSQL basics 2018-02-15
MySQL basics 2018-02-15
Odoo basics 2018-02-15
Odoo 11 Development Cookbook 2018-02-15
Book state before make_available: draft
Book state before make_available: available
```

How it works...

After installing the `odoorpc` library, you can start using it straightaway. To do so, you will need to import the `odoorpc` package and then we will create the object of the `ODOO` class by passing the server URL and port. This will make the `/version_info` call to the server to check the connection. To log in, you need to use the `login()` method of the object. Here, you need to pass the `database name`, `username`, and `password`.

Upon successful login, you can access the user information at `odoo.env.user`. `odoorpc` provides a user-friendly version of RPC so you can use this user object exactly like the recordset in the server. In our example, we accessed the name, email, and company name from this user object.

If you want to access the model registry, you can use the `odoo.env` object. You can call any model method on the model. Under the hood, the `odoorpc` library uses `jsonrpc` so you can't invoke any private model method name that starts with an _. In our example, we accessed the `library.book` model from the registry. After that, we called the `search` method with the `domain` and `limit` parameters. This will return the IDs of the books. By passing the book IDs to the `browse()` method, you can generate a recordset for the `library.book` model. At the end of the program, we created a new book and changed the book state by calling the `make_available()` method. If you look closely at the syntax of the program, you will see it uses the same syntax as the server.

There's more...

Though it provides a user-friendly syntax like the server, you can use the library just like the normal RPC syntax. To do so, you need to use the `odoo.execute` method with the model name, method name, and arguments. Here is an example of reading book information in the raw RPC syntax:

```
import odoorpc

db_name = 'test-12'
user_name = 'admin'
password = 'admin'

# Prepare the connection to the server
odoo = odoorpc.ODOO('localhost', port=8069)
odoo.login(db_name, user_name, password) # login

books_info = odoo.execute('library.book', 'search_read',
    [['name', 'ilike', 'odoo']], ['name', 'date_release'])
print(books_info)
```

See also

There are several other implementations of RPC libraries for Odoo; the following:

- https://github.com/akretion/ooor
- https://github.com/OCA/odoorpc
- https://github.com/odoo/openerp-client-lib
- http://pythonhosted.org/OdooRPC
- https://github.com/abhishek-jaiswal/php-openerp-lib

21
Performance Optimization

With the help of the Odoo framework, you can develop large and complex applications. Good performance is key to the success of any project. In this recipe, we will explore patterns and tools you need to optimize performance. The recipes included in this chapter are for improving performance at the ORM level, not for performance optimizations on the client side or the deployment side.

In this chapter, we will cover the following recipes:

- The prefetching pattern for the recordsets
- The in-memory cache – ormcache
- Generating image thumbnails
- Accessing grouped data
- Creating or writing multiple records
- Accessing records through database queries
- Profiling Python code

The prefetching pattern for the recordsets

When you access data from a recordset, it makes a query in the database. With the prefetching pattern, you can reduce the number of queries made by fetching the data in batches.

How to do it...

When you are working with multiple recordsets, prefetching helps reduce the number of SQL queries. It does this by fetching all of the data at once. Usually, prefetching works automatically in Odoo, but you lose this feature in certain circumstances. In this recipe, we will explore how you can use prefetching efficiently.

The following example is a normal compute method. In this method, `self` is the recordset of multiple records. In this kind of pattern, prefetching works perfectly. Take a look at the first paragraph of the *How it works* section to find out more:

```
# Correct prefetching
def compute_method(self):
    for rec in self:
        print(rec.name)
```

In some cases, prefetching becomes more complex, such as when fetching data with the `browse` method. In the following example, we browse records one by one in the `for` loop. This will not use prefetching efficiently and it will execute more queries than usual:

```
# Incorrect prefetching
def some_action(self):
    record_ids = []
    self.env.cr.execute("some query to fetch record id")
    for rec in self.env.cr.fetchall():
        record = self.env['res.partner'].browse(rec[0])
        print(record.name)
```

By passing a list of IDs to the `browse` method, you can create a recordset of multiple records. If you perform operations on this recordset, prefetching works perfectly fine:

```
# Correct prefetching
def some_action(self):
    record_ids = []
    self.env.cr.execute("some query to fetch record id")
    record_ids = [ rec[0] for rec in self.env.cr.fetchall() ]
    recordset = self.env['res.partner'].browse(record_ids)
    for record_id in recordset:
        print(record.name)
```

How it works...

Prefetching significantly improves the performance of ORM. Let's explore how prefetching works under the hood.

When you iterate on a recordset through a `for` loop and access the value of a field in the first iteration, the prefetching process starts its magic. Instead of fetching data for the current record in the iteration, prefetching will fetch the data for all of the records. The logic behind this is that if you are accessing a field in the `for` loop, you are likely to fetch that data for the next record in the iteration as well. In the first iteration of the `for` loop, prefetching will fetch the data for all of the recordset and keep it in the cache. In the next iteration of the `for` loop, data will be served from this cache, instead of making a new SQL query. This will reduce the query count from `O(n)` to `O(1)`.

Let's suppose the recordset has 10 records. When you are in the first loop and access the `name` field of the record, it will fetch the data for all 10 records. This is not only the case for the `name` field; it will also fetch all the fields for those 10 records. In the subsequent `for` loop iterations, the data will be served from the cache. This will reduce the number of queries from `10` to `1`:

```
for record in recordset: # recordset with 10 records
    record.name # It will prefetch data of all 10 records in the first
loop
    record.email # data of email will be served from the cache.
```

Note that the prefetching will fetch the value of all of the fields (except the `*2many` fields) even if those fields are not used in the body of the `for` loop. This is because the extra columns only make a minor impact on performance compared to the extra queries for each column. Sometimes, prefetched fields reduce performance. In these cases, you can control the fields that are being prefetched by passing a list of fields to prefetch in the context. To do this, you need to pass `prefetch_fields` in the context as follows:

```
recordset.with_context(prefetch_fields=[list of the fields to
prefetch])
```

If you want to disable prefetching, you can pass `False` into the `prefetch_fields` context, as shown:

```
recordset.with_context(prefetch_fields=False)
```

> If you want to know what the prefetch context in the current recordset is, you can use the `recordset._prefetch` attribute. It will contain the dictionary, the model name as a key, and a list of the record IDs as a value.

There's more...

If you split recordsets, the ORM will generate a new recordset with a new prefetch context. Making operations on such recordsets will only prefetch the data for their 'respective records. If you want to prefetch all the records after the `prefetch`, you can do this by passing the `prefetch` dictionary in the `with_prefetch()` method. In the given example, we spilt the recordset into two parts. Here, we passed a common prefetch context in both recordsets, so when you fetch the data from one of them, ORM will fetch the data for the other and put the data in the cache for future use:

```
recordset = ... # assume recordset has 10 records
prefetch = self.env['base']._prefetch.
recordset1 = a[:5].with_prefetch(prefetch)
recordset2 = a[5:].with_prefetch(prefetch)
```

> **TIP**
>
> The prefetch context is not limited to splitting recordsets. You can also use the `with_prefetch()` method to have a common prefetch context between multiple recordsets. This means that when you fetch data from one record, it will fetch data for all other recordsets too.

The in-memory cache – ormcache

The Odoo framework provides the `ormcache` decorator to manage the in-memory cache. In this recipe, we will explore how you can manage the cache for your functions.

How to do it...

The classes of this ORM cache are available at `/odoo/tools/cache.py`. In order to use these in any file, you will need to import them as follows:

```
from odoo import tools
```

After importing the classes, you can use the ORM cache decorators. Odoo provides different types of in-memory cache decorator. We'll take a look at each of these in the following sections.

ormcache

This one is the simplest and most-used cache decorators. You need to pass the parameter name on which the method's output depends. The following is an example method with the ormcache decorator:

```
@tools.ormcache('mode')
def fetch_mode_data(self, mode):
    # some calculations
    return result
```

When you call this method for the first time, it will be executed and the result will be returned. ormcache will store this result based on the value of the mode parameter. When you call the method again with the same mode value, the result will be served from the cache without executing the actual method.

Sometimes, your method's result depends on the environment attributes. In these cases, you can declare the method as follows:

```
@tools.ormcache('self.env.uid', 'mode')
def fetch_data(self, mode):
    # some calculations
    return result
```

The method given in this example will store the cache based on the environment user and the value of the mode parameter.

ormcache_context

This cache works similarly to ormcache, except that it depends on the parameters plus the value in the context. In this cache's decorator, you need to pass the parameter name and a list of context keys. For example, if your method's output depends on the lang and website_id keys in the context, you can use ormcache_context:

```
@tools.ormcache_context('mode', keys=('website_id','lang'))
def fetch_data(self, mode):
    # some calculations
    return result
```

ormcache_multi

Some methods carry out an operation on multiple records or IDs. If you want to add a cache on these kinds of method, you can use the `ormcache_multi` decorator. You need to pass the `multi` parameter and during the method call, ORM will generate the cache keys by iterating on this parameter. In this method, you will need to return the result in dictionary format with an element of the `multi` parameter as a key. Take a look at the following example:

```
@tools.ormcache_multi('mode', multi='ids')
def fetch_data(self, mode, ids):
    result = {}
    for i in ids:
        data = ... # some calculation based on ids
        result[i] = data
    return result
```

Suppose we called the preceding method with `[1,2,3]` as the IDs. The method will return a result in the `{1:... , 2:..., 3:... }` format. The ORM will cache the result based on these keys. If you make another call with `[1,2,3,4,5]` as the IDs, your method will receive `[4, 5]` in the ID parameter, so the method will carry out the operations for the `4,5` IDs and the rest of the result will be served from the cache.

How it works...

The ORM cache keeps the cache in dictionary format (the cache lookup). The keys of this cache will be generated based on the signature of the decorated method and the values will be the result. Put simply, when you call the method with the `x, y` parameters and the result of the method is `x+y`, the cache lookup will be `{ (x, y) : x+y }`. This means that the next time you call this method with the same parameters, the result will be served directly from this cache. This saves computation time and makes the response faster.

The ORM cache is an in-memory cache, so it is stored in the RAM and occupies memory. Do not use the `ormcache` to serve large data, such as images or files.

> Methods using this decorator should never return a recordset. If you do this, they will generate a `psycopg2.OperationalError` because the underlying cursor of the recordset is closed.

You should use the ORM cache on pure functions. A pure function is a method that always returns the same result for the same arguments. The output of these methods only depends on the arguments and so they return the same result. If this is not the case, you need to manually clear the cache when you perform operations that make the cache's state invalid. To clear the cache, call the `clear_caches()` method:

```
self.env[model_name].clear_caches()
```

There's more...

The ORM cache is the **Least-Recently Used** (**LRU**) cache, meaning that if a key in the cache is not used frequently, it will be removed. If you don't use the ORM cache properly, it might do more harm than good. If you want to learn how your cache is performing, you can pass the `SIGUSR1` signal to the Odoo process:

```
kill -SIGUSR1 2697
```

Here, `2697` is the process ID. After executing the command, you will explore the status of the ORM cache in the logs:

```
> 2019-02-16 12:01:20,493 2697 INFO test-12 odoo.tools.cache: 1
entries, 39 hit, 5 miss, 0 err, 88.6% ratio, for
res.users._compute_session_token
> 2019-02-16 12:01:20,493 2697 INFO test-12 odoo.tools.cache: 7
entries, 64 hit, 24 miss, 0 err, 72.7% ratio, for res.users._has_group
> 2019-02-16 12:01:20,493 2697 INFO test-12 odoo.tools.cache: 1
entries, 3 hit, 2 miss, 0 err, 60.0% ratio, for res.users.context_get
```

If the cache's hit-and-miss ratio is too low, you should remove the ORM cache from the method.

Generating image thumbnails

Large images can be a difficult issue for website. They increase the size of the web page and make them slower as a result. This leads to bad SEO rankings and visitor abandonment. In this recipe, we will explore how you can create images of different sizes.

How to do it...

In Odoo, all image utilities are placed in the `odoo/tools/image.py` file. You need to add an `import` statement to use these image utilities:

```
from odoo import tools
```

The `image_resize_images()` method of the image utility helps you manage three different image sizes. To do this, you need to add three binary fields to store the different-sized images:

```
image = fields.Binary(attachment=True) # 1024x1024px
image_medium = fields.Binary(attachment=True) # 128x128px
image_small = fields.Binary(attachment=True) #64x64px
```

When a user uploads an image from the form view, it is uploaded to full-size. We need to override the `create` and `write` methods to convert the image into three different sizes:

```
@api.model
def create(self, vals):
    tools.image_resize_images(vals)
    return super().create(vals)

@api.multi
def write(self, vals):
    tools.image_resize_images(vals)
    return super().write(vals)
```

This will resize uploaded images and save them in the `image`, `image_medium`, and `image_small` fields.

How it works...

Odoo uses the PIL library for image processing. By default, the `image_resize_images()` method resizes the actual image to sizes of `1024 x 1024` `px`, `128 x 128 px`, and `64 x 64 px`. These are then stored in the `image`, `image_medium`, and `image_small` fields, respectively. This behavior, however, can be customized. Take a look at the `image_resize_images()` method signature:

```
def image_resize_images(vals, big_name='image',
medium_name='image_medium', small_name='image_small', sizes={}):
    ...
```

In the given method signature, `vals` is the values dictionary sent from the `write` or `create` method. This dictionary will contain the actual image. The `big_name`, `medium_name`, and `small_name` parameters are used to define the field names in which the resized images will be returned. The `sizes` parameter is used to change the default image sizes. Let's say you want to save images into the `image_lg`, `image_md`, and `image_sm` fields with custom sizes. To do this, you can call the following methods:

```
sizes = {'image_lg': (1000, 1000),'image_md': (500x500),'image_sm':
(50x50)}

tools.image_resize_images(vals, big_name='image_lg',
medium_name='image_md', small_name='image_sm', sizes=sizes)
```

This will save the images into different fields and with different sizes.

There's more...

There are few more methods available as the image utilities. The following is a list of methods and how they are used:

- `image_resize_image()`: This method is used to resize images from `base64` sources.
- `image_resize_and_sharpen()`: Creating thumbnails sometimes makes images blurry. In these cases, you can use this function to make better-looking images by sharpening them.
- `image_save_for_web()`: This function is used to optimize image sizes for a website. This will reduce the image size without compromising their quality.
- `crop_image()`: This method is used to crop images to different sizes.
- `image_colorize()`: This method is used to colorize the transparent part of an image.

If you want to learn more about these methods, take look at `odoo/tools/image.py`.

Accessing grouped data

When you want data for statistics, you often need it in a grouped form, such as a monthly sales report, or a report that shows sales per customer. It is time-consuming to search records and group them manually. In this recipe, we will explore how you can use the read_group() method to access grouped data.

How to do it...

The read_group() method is widely used for statistics and smart stat buttons. Let's assume you want to show the number of sales orders on the partner form. This can be done by searching sales orders for a customer and then counting the length:

```
# in res.partner model
so_count = fields.Integer(compute='_compute_so_count', string='Sale
order count')

def _compute_so_count(self):
    sale_orders = self.env['sale.order'].search(domain=[('partner_id',
'in', self.ids)])
    for partner in self:
        partner.so_count = len(sale_orders.filtered(lambda so:
so.partner_id.id == partner.id))
```

This example will work, but it is not optimized. When you display the so_count field on the tree view, it will fetch and filter sales orders for all the partners in a list. With this small amount of data, the read_group() method won't make much difference, but as the amount of data grows, it could be a problem. To fix this issue, you can use the read_group method. The following example will do the same as the preceding one, but it only consumes one SQL query, even for large datasets:

```
# in res.partner model
so_count = fields.Integer(compute='_compute_so_count', string='Sale
order count')

def _compute_so_count(self):
    sale_data = self.env['sale.order'].read_group(
        domain=[('partner_id', 'in', self.ids)],
        fields=['partner_id'], groupby=['partner_id'])
    mapped_data = dict([(m['partner_id'][0], m['partner_id_count'])
for m in sale_data])
    for partner in self:
        partner.so_count = mapped_data[partner.id]
```

How it works...

The `read_group()` method internally uses the GROUP BY feature of SQL. This makes the `read_group` method faster, even if you have large datasets. Internally, the Odoo web client uses this method in the charts and the grouped tree view. You can tweak the behavior of the `read_group` method by using different arguments.

Let's explore the signature of the `read_group` method:

```
def read_group(self, domain, fields, groupby, offset=0, limit=None,
orderby=False, lazy=True):
```

The different parameters available for the `read_group` method are as follows:

- `domain`: The `domain` is used to filter the records. This will be the search criteria for the `read_group` method.
- `fields`: This is a list of the fields to fetch with the grouping. Note that the fields you have mentioned here should be in the `groupby` parameter, unless you use some aggregate functions. From Odoo version v12, the `read_group` method supports the SQL aggregate functions. Let's say you want to get the average order amount per customer. In this case, you can use `read_group` as follows:

```
self.env['sale.order'].read_group([], ['partner_id',
'amount_total:avg'], ['partner_id'])
```

- If you want to access the same field twice but with a different aggregate function, the syntax is a little different. You need to pass the field name as `alias:agg(field_name)`. This example will give you the total and average number of orders per customer:

```
self.env['sale.order'].read_group([], ['partner_id',
'total:sum(amount_total)', 'avg_total:avg(amount_total)'],
['partner_id'])
```

> Refer to the documentation if you want to learn more about PostgreSQL aggregate functions: https://www.postgresql.org/docs/current/functions-aggregate.html.

The following is a list of the parameters supported by the `read_group` method:

- `groupby`: This parameter will be a list of fields by which the records are grouped. It lets you group records based on multiple fields. To do this, you will need to pass a list of fields. For example, if you want to group the sales orders by customer and order state, you can pass `['partner_id ', 'state']` in this parameter.
- `offset`: This parameter is used for pagination. If you want to skip a few records, you can use this parameter.
- `limit`: This parameter is used for pagination; it indicates the maximum number of records to fetch.
- `lazy`: This parameter accepts Boolean values. By default, its value is `True`. If this parameter is `True`, the results are grouped only by the first field in the `groupby` parameter. You will get the remaining `groupby` parameters and the domain in the __context and __domain keys in the result. If the value of this parameter is set to `False`, it will group the data by all fields in the `groupby` parameter.

There's more...

Grouping on `date` fields can be complicated because it is possible to group records based on days, weeks, quarters, months, or years. You can change the grouping behavior of the `date` field by passing the `groupby_function` after : in the `groupby` parameter. If you want to group the monthly total of the sales orders, you can use the `read_group` method:

```
self.env['sale.order'].read_group([], ['total:sum(amount_total)'],
['order_date:month'])
```

Creating or writing multiple records

If you are new to Odoo development, you might execute multiple queries to write or create multiple records. In this recipe, we will look at how to create and write records in batches.

How to do it...

Odoo v12 added support for creating records in batches. If you are creating a single record, simply pass a dictionary with the field values. To create records in a batch, you just need to pass a list of these dictionaries instead of a single dictionary. The following example creates three book records in a single create call:

```
vals = [{
    'name': "Book1",
    'date_release': '2018/12/12',
}, {
    'name': "Book2",
    'date_release': '2018/12/12',
}, {
    'name': "Book3",
    'date_release': '2018/12/12',
}]

self.env['library.book'].create(vals)
```

Write operations are carried out on the recordset. You should avoid using write operations in the `for` loop if you are writing the same data on multiple recordsets:

```
# not good
data = {...}
for record in recordset:
    record.write(data)

# good
data = {...}
recordset.write(data)
```

If you are writing a single value, it is possible to write data by assigning values such as `self.name = 'Admin'`. Check the following example to explore the correct usage of the write operation:

```
# not good
recordset.name= 'Admin'
recordset.email= 'admin@example.com'

# good
recordset.write({'name': 'Admin', 'email'= 'admin@example.com'})
```

How it works...

In order to create multiple records in a batch, you need to pass value dictionaries in the form of a list to create new records. This will automatically manage batch-creating the records. When you create records in a batch, internally doing so will insert a query for each record. This means that creating records in a batch is not done in a single query. This doesn't mean, however, that creating records in a batch does not improve performance. The performance gain is achieved through batch-calculating computing fields.

Things work differently for the `write` method. When you perform a write on multiple records, this is done in a single query. In the `create` method, it is possible to pass different values for records, but in the `write` method, you can only use batch writing if you want to write the same values in all records.

There's more...

If you want to duplicate an existing record, you can use the `copy()` method as follows. Internally, this method will fetch the data and then call the `create` method. This method will return a new recordset with duplicate values:

```
new_record = old_record.copy()
```

Accessing records through database queries

Odoo ORM has limited methods and sometimes it is difficult to fetch certain data from the ORM. In these cases, you can fetch data in the desired format and you need to perform an operation on the data to get a certain result. Due to this, it becomes slower. To handle these special cases, you can execute SQL queries in the database. In this recipe, we will explore how you can run SQL queries from Odoo.

How to do it...

You can perform database queries through the `self._cr.execute` method:

```
self._cr.execute("SELECT id, name, date_release FROM library_book
WHERE name ilike %s", ('%odoo%',))
data = self._cr.fetchall()
print(data)
```

Output:
```
[(7, 'Odoo basics', datetime.date(2018, 2, 15)), (8, 'Odoo 11
Development Cookbook', datetime.date(2018, 2, 15)), (1, 'Odoo 12
Development Cookbook', datetime.date(2019, 2, 13))]
```

The result of the query will be in the format of a list of tuples. The data in the tuples will be in the same sequence as the fields in the query. If you want to fetch data in dictionary format, you can use the `dictfetchall()` method. Take a look at the following example:

```
self._cr.execute("SELECT id, name, date_release FROM library_book
WHERE name ilike %s", ('%odoo%',))
data = self._cr.dictfetchall()
print(data)
```

Output:
```
[{'id': 7, 'name': 'Odoo basics', 'date_release': datetime.date(2018,
2, 15)}, {'id': 8, 'name': 'Odoo 11 Development Cookbook',
'date_release': datetime.date(2018, 2, 15)}, {'id': 1, 'name': 'Odoo
12 Development Cookbook', 'date_release': datetime.date(2019, 2, 13)}]
```

If you want to fetch only a single record, you can use the `fetchone()` and `dictfetchone()` methods. These methods work like `fetchall()` and `dictfetchall()`, but they only return a single record and you need to call them multiple times if you want to fetch multiple records.

How it works...

There are two ways to access the database cursor from the recordset: one is from the recordset itself, for example `self._cr`, and the other is from the environment, for example `self.env.cr`. This cursor is used to execute database queries. In the preceding example, we saw how you can fetch data through raw queries. The table name is the name of the model after replacing . with _, so the `library.book` model becomes `library_book`.

You need to consider a few things before you execute raw queries. Only use raw queries when you have no other choice. By executing raw queries, you are bypassing the ORM layers. You are therefore also bypassing security rules and ORM performance advantages. Sometimes, wrongly-built queries can introduce SQL injection vulnerabilities. Consider the following example, in which queries can allow an attacker to perform SQL injection:

```
# very bad, SQL injection possible
self.env.cr.execute('SELECT id, name FROM library_book WHERE name
ilike + search_keyword + ';')

# good
self.env.cr.execute('SELECT id, name FROM library_book WHERE name
ilike %s ';', (search_keyword,))
```

Don't use the string format function either; it will also allow an attacker to perform SQL injection. Using SQL queries makes your code harder to read and understand for other developers, so avoid using them where possible.

> Some Odoo developers believe that executing SQL queries makes operations faster as it bypasses the ORM layer. This is not completely true, however; it depends on the case. In some operations, ORM performs better than RAW queries and faster, because data is served from the recordset cache.

There's more...

Operations done in one transaction are only committed at the end of the transaction. If an error occurs in the ORM, the transaction is rolled back. If you have made an INSERT or UPDATE query and you want to make it permanent, you can use self._cr.commit() to commit the changes.

> Note that using commit() can be dangerous because it can put records in an inconsistent state. An error in the ORM can cause incomplete rollbacks, so only use commit() if you are completely sure.

Profiling Python code

Sometimes, you are unable to pinpoint the cause of an issue. This is especially true for performance issues. Odoo provides some built-in profiling tools that help you find the real cause of an issue.

How to do it...

Odoo's profiler is available at `odoo/tools/profiler.py`. In order to use the profiler in your code, import it into the file:

```
from odoo.tools.profiler import profile
```

After importing it, you can use the `profile` decorator on the methods. To profile a particular method, you need to add the `profile` decorator on it. Take a look at the following example. We put the `profile` decorator on the `make_available` method:

```
@profile
def make_available(self):
    if self.state != 'lost':
        self.write({'state': 'available'})
    return True
```

So, when this method is called, it will print the full statistics in the logs:

```
calls     queries   ms
library.book ----------------------
/Users/pga/odoo/test/my_library/models/library_book.py, 24

1         0         0.01      @profile
                             def make_available(self):
1         3         12.81        if self.state != 'lost':
1         7         20.55            self.write({'state':
'available'})
1         0         0.01         return True

Total:
1         10        33.39
```

How it works...

After adding the `profile` decorator on your method, when you call that method, Odoo will print the full statistics in the log, as shown in the previous example. It will print the statistics in three columns. The first column will contain the number of calls or how many times a line is executed. (This number will increase when the line is inside a `for` loop or the method is recursive). The second column represents the number of queries fired with the given line. The last column is the time taken by the given line in milliseconds. Note that the time displayed in this column is relative; it is faster when the profiler is off.

The `profiler` decorator accepts some optional arguments, which help you to get detailed statistics of the method. The following is the signature of the `profile` decorator:

```
def profile(method=None, whitelist=None, blacklist=(None,),
files=None,
 minimum_time=0, minimum_queries=0):
```

The following is a list of parameters supported by the `profile()` method:

- `whitelist`: This parameter will accept a list of model names to display in the log.
- `files`: This parameter will accept a list of filenames to display.
- `blacklist`: This parameter will accept a list of model names that you do not want to display in the log.
- `minimum_time`: This will accept an integer value (in milliseconds). It will hide logs whose total time is less than the given amount.
- `minimum_queries`: This will accept an integer value of the number of queries. It will hide the logs whose total number of queries is less than the given amount.

There's more...

One further type of profiler that is available in Odoo generates a graph for the executed method. This profiler is available in the `misc` package, so you need to import it from there. It will generate a file with statistics data that will generate a graph file. To use this profiler, you need to pass the path of the file path as an argument. When this function is called, it will generate a file on the given location. Take a look at the following example, which generates the `make_available.prof` file on the desktop:

```
from odoo.tools.misc import profile
...
@profile('/Users/parth/Desktop/make_available.profile')
def make_available(self):
    if self.state != 'lost':
        self.write({'state': 'available'})
        self.env['res.partner'].create({'name': 'test', 'email':
'test@ada.asd'})
    return True
```

When the `make_available` method is called, it will generate a file on the desktop. To convert this data into graph data, you will need to install the `gprof2dot` tool and then execute the given command to generate the graph:

```
gprof2dot -f pstats -o /Users/parth/Desktop/prof.xdot
/Users/parth/Desktop/make_available.prof
```

This command will generate the `prof.xdot` file on the desktop. Then, you can display the graph with `xdot` with the given command:

```
xdot /Users/parth/Desktop/prof.xdot
```

The preceding `xdot` command will generate the graph shown in the following screenshot:

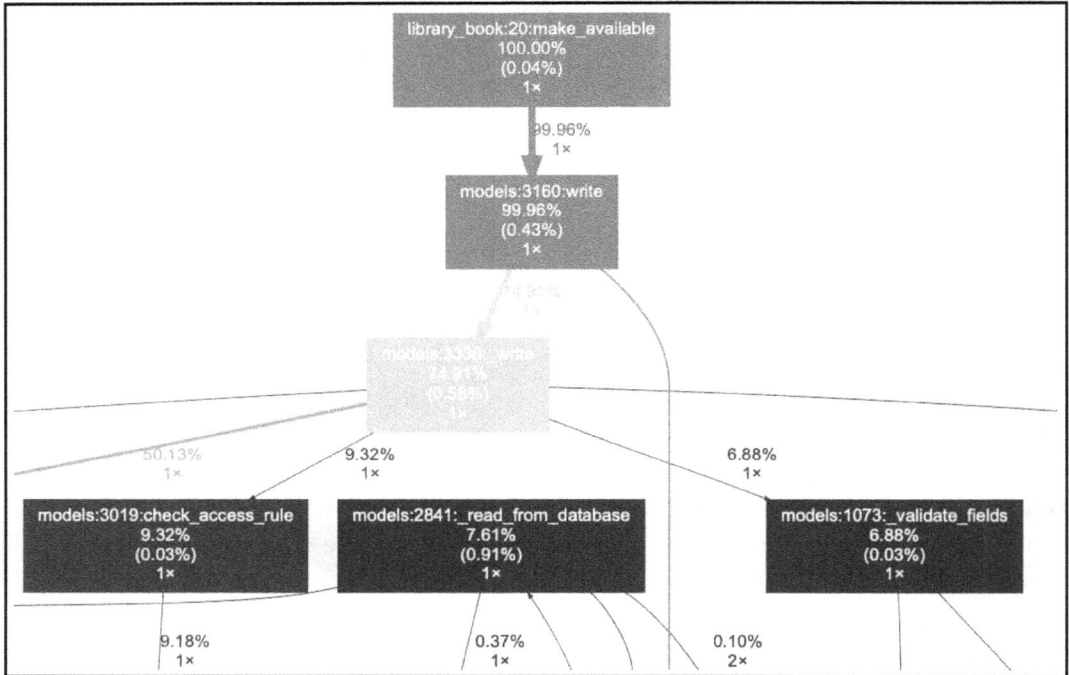

Here, you can zoom in, check the call stack, and look at details of execution times for the methods.

22
Point of Sale

In this chapter, we will cover the following recipes:

- Adding custom JavaScript/SCSS files
- Adding an action button on the keyboard
- Making RPC calls
- Modifying the POS screen UI
- Modifying existing business logic
- Modifying customer receipts

Introduction

So far in this book, we have explored two different code bases. The first one is the backend code base that is used to create views, actions, menus, wizards, and so on. The second one is the backend code base that is used to create webpages, controllers, snippets, and so on. Now, in this chapter, we will explore the third code base, which is used for the Point of Sale. You might wonder why the Point of Sale needs a different code base. This is because it uses a different architecture, so it can work offline. In this chapter, we will see how to modify the Point of Sale.

> The Point of Sale application is mostly written in JavaScript. This chapter is written assuming that you have a basic knowledge of JavaScript and jQuery. This chapter also uses client-side QWeb templates and widgets, so if you are unaware of these terms, check out `Chapter 16`, *Web Client Development*.

Throughout this chapter, we will be using an addon module called `pos_demo`. This `pos_demo` module will have a dependency on `point_of_sale` as we are going to do customization in the Point of Sale application. To get started with this recipe quickly, we have prepared an initial `pos_demo` module and you can grab it from the `Chapter22/r0_initial_module/pos_demo` directory in the GitHub repository of this book.

Technical requirements

The technical requirements for this chapter include the online Odoo platform.

All the code used in this chapter can be downloaded from the following GitHub repository `https://github.com/PacktPublishing/Odoo-12-Development-Cookbook-Third-Edition/tree/master/Chapter22`.

Check out the following video to see the Code in Action:

`http://bit.ly/2UH0WJV`

Adding custom JavaScript/SCSS files

The Point of Sale app uses different asset bundles for managing JavaScript and style sheet files. In this recipe, we will learn how to add **SCSS** and **JavaScript** files to the Point of Sale asset bundle.

Getting ready

In this recipe, we will load an SCSS style sheet and a JavaScript file into the Point of Sale application.

How to do it...

To load assets in the Point of Sale application, follow these steps:

1. Add a new SCSS file at `/pos_demo/static/src/scss/pos_demo.scss` and insert the following code:

```
.pos .pos-content {
    .price-tag {
        background: #00abcd;
        width: 100%;
        right: 0;
        left: 0;
        top:0;
    }
}
```

2. Add a JavaScript file at `/pos_demo/static/src/js/pos_demo.js` and add the following:

```
console.log('Point of Sale JavaScript loaded');
```

3. Register these JavaScript and SCSS files into the `point_of_sale` assets:

```
<?xml version="1.0" encoding="utf-8"?>
<odoo>
    <data>
        <template id="assets"
inherit_id="point_of_sale.assets">
            <xpath expr="." position="inside">
                <script type="text/JavaScript"
src="/pos_demo/static/src/js/pos_demo.js"/>
                <link rel="stylesheet"
href="/pos_demo/static/src/scss/pos_demo.scss"/>
            </xpath>
        </template>
    </data>
</odoo>
```

Install the `pos_demo` module. To see your changes in action, open the `point-of-sale` session from the **Point of Sale|Dashboard** menu.

How it works...

In this recipe, we loaded one JavaScript file and one SCSS file into the Point of Sale application. In step 1, we changed the background color and the border radius of the pricing label of the product card. After installing the `pos_demo` module, you will be able to see changes to pricing labels:

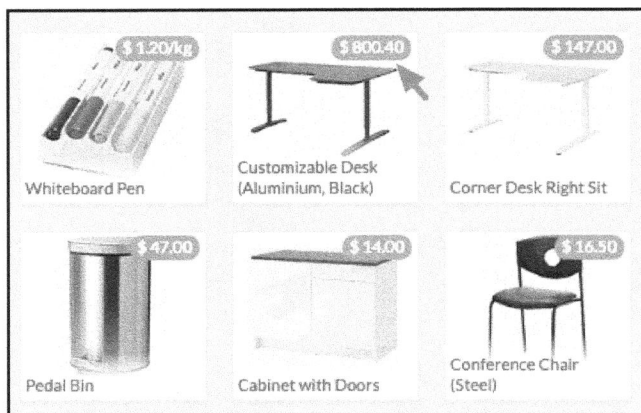

In step 2, we added the JavaScript file. In it, we added the log into the console. In order to see the message, you will need to open the browser's Developer tools. In the **Console** tab, you will see the following log. This shows that your JavaScript file is loaded successfully. Right now, we have only added the log into the JavaScript file, but in upcoming recipes, we will add more to it:

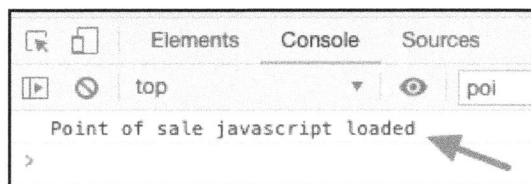

In step 3, we added the JavaScript file and the SCSS file into the Point of Sale assets. The external ID of the Point of Sale assets is `point_of_sale.assets`. Here, only the external ID is different; everything else works like regular assets. If you don't know how assets work in Odoo, refer to the *Static-assets management* recipe in `Chapter 15`, *CMS Website Development*.

There's more...

Odoo also has an add-on module for the Point of Sale solution for restaurants. Note that this Point of Sale restaurant module is just an extension of the Point of Sale application. If you want to do customization in the restaurant module, you will need add your JavaScript and SCSS files in the same `point_of_sale.assets` assets bundle.

Adding an action button on the keyboard

As we discussed in the previous recipe, the Point of Sale application is designed in such a way that it works offline. Thanks to this, the code structure of the Point of Sale application is different from the remaining Odoo applications. The code base of the Point of Sale is largely written with JavaScript and provides different utilities for customization. In this recipe, we will use one such utility and create an action button on top of the keyboard panel.

Getting ready

In this recipe, we will be using the `pos_demo` module created in the *Adding custom JavaScript/SCSS files* recipe. We will add a button on top of the keyboard panel. This button will be a shortcut to applying the discount on the order lines.

How to do it...

Follow these steps to add the 5% discount action button on the keyboard panel of the Point of Sale application:

1. Add the following code to the `/static/src/js/pos_demo.js` file, which will define the action button:

```
odoo.define('pos_demo.custom', function (require) {
  "use strict";

var screens = require('point_of_sale.screens');
var discount_button = screens.ActionButtonWidget.extend({
    template: 'BtnDiscount',
    button_click: function () {
        var order = this.pos.get_order();
        if (order.selected_orderline) {
```

```
                    order.selected_orderline.set_discount(5);
            }
        }
    });

    screens.define_action_button({
        'name': 'discount_btn',
        'widget': discount_button
    });

    });
```

2. Add the QWeb template for the button in the `/static/src/xml/pos_demo.xml` file:

```xml
<?xml version="1.0" encoding="UTF-8"?>
<templates id="template" xml:space="preserve">

    <t t-name="BtnDiscount">
        <div class='control-button'>
            <i class='fa fa-gift' /> 5% discount
        </div>
    </t>

</templates>
```

3. Register the QWeb template in the manifest file as follows:

```
'qweb': [
        'static/src/xml/pos_demo.xml'
    ]
```

Update the `pos_demo` module to apply the changes. After that, you will be able to see a **5% discount** button above the keyboard:

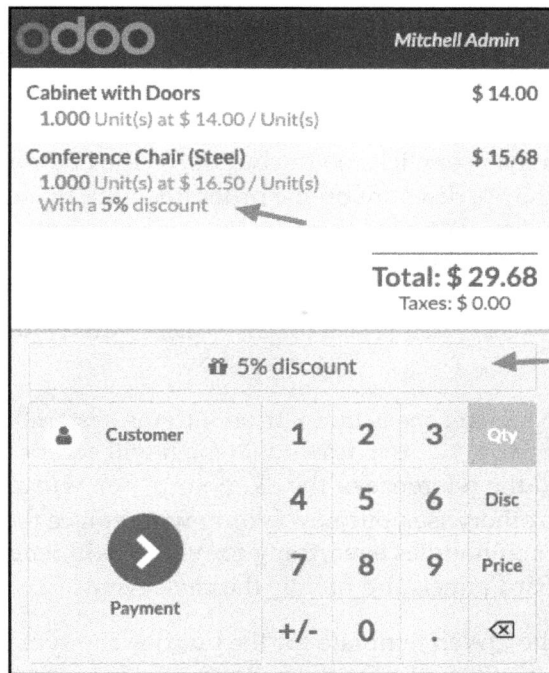

After clicking this, the discount will be applied on the selected order line.

How it works...

To create the action button in the Point of Sale application, you will need to extend `ActionButtonWidget`. `ActionButtonWidget` is defined in `point_of_sale.screens` and so, to use it in your code, you will need to import it. In step 1, we imported screens with `require('point_of_sale.screens')` and created `discount_button` by extending `ActionButtonWidget`. If you want to learn how the `require` mechanism works in Odoo JavaScript, refer to the *Extending CSS and JavaScript for the website* recipe in `Chapter 15`, *CMS Website Development*.

In `ActionButtonWidget`, you will need to pass the name of the template and the click event-handler function. Check the code in step 1; we added the event-handler function with the `button_click` key. The name of the click-event handler function must be `button_click`. This will automatically bind button-click events for you and call the function when the user clicks on the button. In the body of the `button_click` function, we applied the 5% discount on the order line with the help of the `set_discount()` function. We used the `set_discount()` function to apply the discount. There are several other methods, such as `set_discount()`, available in the Point of Sale application. Explore the `/point_of_sale/static/src/js/models.js` file if you want to learn more about other methods.

Next, you will need to register the action button into the system. You can do so by calling the `define_action_button` function, which will accept two parameters: the `name` of the button and the reference of the `discount_btn` widget. Note that the name must be unique, otherwise your new button will replace the existing button. `define_action_button` handles everything for you: it will render the button, append it to the keyboard panel, and handle the click events.

In step 2, we created the QWeb template for the button. The syntax is simple: you just need to create the `<div>` element with the `control-button` class. In step 3, we registered the template file in the module manifest.

There's more...

The `define_action_button` method supports one more optional parameter condition. This parameter is used to hide/show the button based on some condition. The value of this parameter is the function that returns the `boolean`. Based on the returned value, the Point of Sale system will hide or show the button. Take the look at the following example for more information:

```
screens.define_action_button({
    'name': 'reprint',
    'widget': ReprintButton,
    'condition': function(){
        return this.pos.config.print_via_proxy;
    }
});
```

Making RPC calls

Though the Point of Sale application works offline, it is still possible to make RPC calls to the server. The RPC call can be used for any operation; you can use it for CRUD operations, or to perform an action on the server. In this recipe, we will make an RPC call to fetch information about a customer's last five orders.

Getting ready

In this recipe, we will be using the `pos_demo` module created in the *Adding an action button on the keyboard* recipe. We will define the action button. When the user clicks on the action button, we will make an RPC call to fetch the order information and display it on the popup.

How to do it...

Follow these steps to display the last five orders for the selected customer:

1. Import the RPC utility in the `/static/src/js/pos_demo.js` file by adding the following code

    ```
    var rpc = require('web.rpc');
    ```

2. Add the following code to the `/static/src/js/pos_demo.js` file; this will add a new action button to fetch and display the information about the last five orders when a user clicks on the button:

    ```
    var lastOrders = screens.ActionButtonWidget.extend({
        template: 'LastOrders',
        // Add step 3 and 4 here
    });

    screens.define_action_button({
        'name': 'last_orders',
        'widget': lastOrders
    });
    ```

3. Add the `button_click` function in the `lastOrders` widget to manage button clicks:

```
button_click: function () {
    var self = this;
    var order = this.pos.get_order();
    if (order.attributes.client) {
        var domain = [['partner_id', '=',
order.attributes.client.id]];
        rpc.query({
            model: 'pos.order',
            method: 'search_read',
            args: [domain, ['name', 'amount_total', 'cu']],
            kwargs: { limit: 5 },
        }).then(function (orders) {
            if(orders.length > 0){
                var order_list = _.map(orders, function (o) {
                    return { 'label': _.str.sprintf("%s -
TOTAL: %s", o.name, o.amount_total) };
                });
                self.show_order_list(order_list);
            } else {
                self.show_error('No previous order found for
the customer');
            }
        });
    } else {
        this.show_error('Please select the customer');
    }
},
```

4. Add methods to show the order list and errors:

```
show_order_list: function(list) {
    this.gui.show_popup('selection', {
        'title': 'Please select a reward',
        'list': list,
        'confirm': function (reward) {
            order.apply_reward(reward);
        },
    });
},
show_error: function (message){
    this.gui.show_popup('error', {
        title: "Warning",
        body: message,
    });
}
```

5. Add the QWeb template for the button in the `/static/src/xml/pos_demo.xml` file:

```
<t t-name="LastOrders">
 <div class='control-button'>
 <i class='fa fa-shopping-cart' /> Last orders
 </div>
 </t>
```

Update the `pos_demo` module to apply the changes. After that, you will be able to see the **Last Orders** button above the keyboard panel. When this button is clicked, a popup will be displayed with the order information:

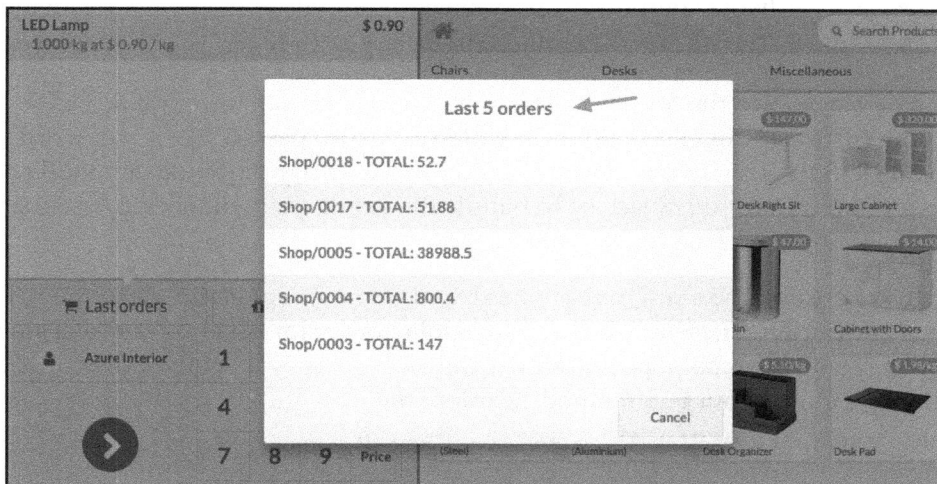

How it works...

The RPC utility is available at the `web.rpc` namespace. In step 1, we imported the RPC utility through `require('web.rpc')`.

In step 2, we defined an action button to fetch and display order information for the selected customer. Before going into the technical details, let's understand what we wanted to accomplish with this action button. Once clicked, we want to display information for the last five orders for the selected customer. There are a few cases where the customer is not selected or customers have no previous orders. In such cases, we want to show a popup with an appropriate message.

Let's get back to the technical details for step 2. Here, we created and registered the action button. If you want to learn more about the action button, refer to the *Adding an action button on the keyboard* recipe. In the step 3, we added the click-handler function. On clicking the action button, the click-handler function will be called. This function will make the RPC call the server to fetch the order information. We used the `rpc.query()` method to make RPC calls. The following is a list of the parameters you can pass in the `rpc.query()` method:

- `model`: The name of the model on which you want to perform the operation
- `method`: The name of the method you want to invoke
- `args`: A list of compulsory positional arguments accepted by the method
- `kwargs`: The dictionary of the optional arguments accepted by the method

In this recipe, we used the `search_read` method to fetch data through RPC. We passed the customer domain to filter the orders. We also passed `limit` keyword arguments to fetch only five orders. `rpc.query()` is an asynchronous method and returns a JQuery Deferred object, so to handle the result, you will need to use the `then()` method.

In step 4, we created the `show_order_list` and `show_error` methods in the `lastOrders` button. These will be used to display order information and warnings in the popup. To display the popup, we used the `show_popup()` method of `gui`. If you want to learn more about `gui` methods, explore the `addons/point_of_sale/static/src/js/gui.js` file.

In step 5, we added the QWeb template for the action button. The Point of Sale application will render this template to display action button.

The RPC call does not work in offline mode. If you have a good internet connection and you do not use offline mode frequently, you can use the RPCs. Though the Odoo Point of Sale application works offline, a few operations, such as creating or updating a customer, need an internet connection, as those features are use RPC to call internally.

Modifying the POS screen UI

The user interface of the Point of Sale application is written with the QWeb template. These templates are the client-side QWeb templates and, because of that, you cannot use XPath to modify the elements. The client-side template uses another method to modify existing UI elements. In this recipe, we will learn how you can modify UI elements in the Point of Sale application.

Getting ready

In this recipe, we will be using the pos_demo module created in the *Making RPC calls* recipe. We will modify the UI of the product card and display the profit margin per product.

How to do it...

Follow these steps to display the profit margin on the product card:

1. Add the following code to the /static/src/js/pos_demo.js file to fetch the extra field for the product's actual price:

```
var pos_model = require('point_of_sale.models');
    pos_model.load_fields("product.product",
"standard_price");
```

2. Add the following code to /static/src/xml/pos_demo.xml in order to display a profit margin product card:

```
<t t-extend="Product">
<t t-jquery=".price-tag" t-operation="after">
<span t-if="product.standard_price" class="sale_margin">
<t t-set="margin"
t-value="product.list_price - product.standard_price"/>
<t t-esc="widget.format_currency(margin)"/>
</span>
</t>
</t>
```

3. Add the following style sheet to style the margin text:

```
.sale_margin {
        top: 21px;
        line-height: 15px;
        right: 2px;
        background: #CDDC39;
        position: absolute;
        border-radius: 10px;
        padding: 0px 5px;
}
```

Update the `pos_demo` module to apply the changes. After that, you will be able to see the profit margin on the product card:

How it works...

In this recipe, we want to use the `standard_price` field as the purchase cost of the product. This field is not loaded by default in Point of Sale applications. In step 1, we added the `standard_price` field for the `product.product` model. After this, product data will have one more field: `standard_price`.

In step 2, we extended the default product card template. You will need to use the `t-extend` attribute to extend the existing QWeb template. Then you need to use the `t-jquery` attribute to select the element on which you want to perform the operation. It is exactly like XPath, but instead of XPath this uses JQuery selectors. This selector must match the element in the initial template. In our case, we used `t-jquery=".price-tag"`. To cross-verify, you can check the element with `class="price-tag"` in the initial product template. This initial product template is placed in the `point_of_sale/static/src/xml/pos.xml` file.

With the JQuery selector, you will also need to pass the operation you want to perform with the parameter. In our case, we used `t-operation="after"`, which means your customization will be added after the selected elements. Here is a list of possible operations:

- `append`: Add the customization as the last child of the selected element
- `prepend`: Add the customization as the first child of the selected element
- `before`: Add the customization before the selected element
- `after`: Add the customization after the selected element
- `replace`: Replace the selected element with the customization
- `inner`: Replace the inner content's selected element with the customization
- `attribute`: Modify the attribute of the selected element

In step 3, we added the style sheet to modify the position of the margin element. This will add the background color to the margin element and place it under the price pill.

Modifying existing business logic

In the previous recipes, we saw how to fetch data through an RPC and how to modify the UI of the Point of Sale application. In this recipe, we will see how you can modify or extend the existing business logic.

Getting ready

In this recipe, we will be using the pos_demo module created in the *Modifying the UI of the POS screens* recipe, which is where we fetched the purchase price of a product and displayed the product margin. Now, in this recipe, we will show a warning to the user if they sell the product below the product margin.

How to do it...

Most of the business logic of the Point of Sale application is written in JavaScript, so we just need to make changes to it to achieve the goal of this recipe. Add the following code to /static/src/js/pos_demo.js to show a warning when the user sells the product below the purchase price:

```
var screens = require('point_of_sale.screens');

screens.OrderWidget.include({
    set_value: function (val) {
        this._super(val);
        var orderline = this.pos.get_order().get_selected_orderline();
        var standard_price = orderline.product.standard_price;
        if (orderline && standard_price) {
            var line_price = orderline.get_base_price();
            if (line_price < orderline.quantity * standard_price) {
                this.gui.show_popup('alert', {
                    title: "Warning",
                    body: "Product price is set below product actual
cost",
                });
            }
        }
    }
});
```

Update the pos_demo module to apply the changes. After the update, add the discount on the order line in such a way that the product price becomes less than the purchase price. A popup will appear with the following warning:

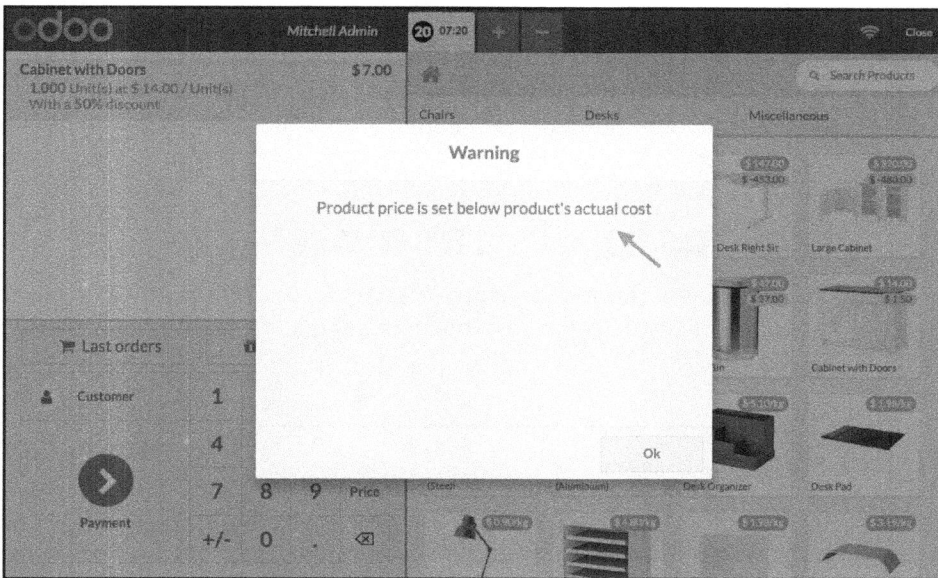

How it works...

In order to modify the existing business, we need to use the `include()` function. This function will internally do the monkey patching and replace the original object properties with the new ones. If you want to access the initial method, you can use the `this._super` attribute.

The `set_value()` function of the OrderWidget is used to update the product price from the keyboard. The same function is used to apply the discount. So, in our recipe, we replaced the `set_value()` method with our own implementation. We do not want to change the default implementation, so we called `_super()` first, which will call the default `set_value()` method. After the super call, we placed our logic to display a warning if the user sets a lower price than the purchase price of the product. To display the popup, we used the `show_popup()` method of the `gui`.

We placed our business logic after the default implementation (`_super`) is called. If you want to write business logic before the default implementation, you can do it by moving the `_super` call to the end of the function.

Using `include()` can break things if not used carefully. If the method is inherited from several files, you must call the super method, otherwise it will skip the logic in the subsequent inheritance. This sometimes leads to a broken internal data state.

Modifying customer receipts

When you are customizing a Point of Sale application, a common request you get from customers is to modify customer receipts. In this recipe, you will learn how to modify customer receipts.

Getting ready

In this recipe, we will be using the `pos_demo` module created in the *Modifying existing business logic* recipe. We will add one line in the Point of Sale receipt to show how much money the customer saved in the order.

How to do it...

Follow these steps to modify a customer receipt in the Point of Sale:

1. Add the following code in the `/static/src/js/pos_demo.js` file. This will add extra data in the receipt environment:

```
var screens = require('point_of_sale.screens');

screens.ReceiptScreenWidget.include({
    get_receipt_render_env: function () {
        var receipt_env = this._super();
        var order = this.pos.get_order();
        var saved = 0;
        _.each(order.orderlines.models, function (line) {
            saved += ((line.product.list_price -
line.get_base_price()) * line.quantity);
        });
        receipt_env['saved_amount'] = saved;
        return receipt_env;
    }
});
```

2. Add the following code in `/static/src/xml/pos_demo.xml`. This will extend the default receipt template and add our customization:

```
<t t-extend="PosTicket">
<t t-jquery=".receipt-change" t-operation="after">
<t t-if="saved_amount">
<br/>
<div class="pos-center-align">
<t t-esc="widget.format_currency(saved_amount)"/>
you saved in this order
</div>
</t>
</t>
</t>
```

Update the `pos_demo` module to apply the changes. After that, add a product with the discount and check the receipt; you will see one extra line in the receipt:

How it works...

There is nothing new in this recipe. We just updated the receipt by using previous recipes. In step 1, we overrode the `get_receipt_render_env()` function to send more data to the receipt environment. We compared the product's base price with the product price in the receipt to calculate how much money the customer saved. We sent this data into the receipt environment via the `saved_amount` key. If you want to learn more about method overriding, refer to the *Modifying existing business logic* recipe.

In step 2, we modified the default QWeb template of the receipt. The template name of the actual receipt is `PosTicket`, so we used it as a value in the `t-extend` attribute. In step 1, we'd already sent the information needed to modify a receipt. In the QWeb template, we get the saved amount in the `saved_amount` key so we just added one more `<div>` element in the recipe at the end. This will print the saved amount in the receipt. If you want to learn more about overriding, refer to the *Modifying the UI of the POS screens* recipe.

There's more...

The technique demonstrated in this recipe will update the receipt that is printed from the Point of Sale receipt screen. If you are using POS Box or IOT Box, this technique will not update the receipt printed from it. It used the XML format to print a receipt to ESC/POS-compatible receipt printers. To modify the receipt, you will need to extend the `XmlReceipt` template instead of `PosTicket`. See the following example; this will update the receipt printed from the POS Box or IOT Box:

```
<t t-extend="XmlReceipt">
    <t t-jquery='.after-footer' t-operation='after'>
        <div>
            <t t-esc="saved_amount"/>
            you saved in this order
        </div>
    </t>
</t>
```

Odoo uses the XML-ESC/POS Python library to generate receipts. Refer to https://github.com/fvdsn/py-xml-escpos to learn about the supported XML structure.

Manage Emails in Odoo

23

Email integration is the most prominent feature of Odoo. You can send and receive emails directly from the Odoo user interface. You can even manage email threads on business documents, such as leads, sales orders, and projects. In this chapter, we will explore a few important ways to deal with emails in Odoo. Here, we'll cover the following topics:

- Configuring incoming and outgoing mail servers
- Managing chatter on documents
- Managing activities on documents
- Sending mail using the Jinja template
- Sending mail using the QWeb template
- Managing the mail alias
- Logging user changes in chatter

Technical requirements

The technical requirements for this chapter include the online Odoo platform.

All the code used in this chapter can be downloaded from the following GitHub repository https://github.com/PacktPublishing/Odoo-12-Development-Cookbook-Third-Edition/tree/master/Chapter23.

Check out the following video to see the Code in Action:

http://bit.ly/2UCfxq1

Configuring incoming and outgoing mail servers

Before you start sending and receiving emails in Odoo, you will need to configure the incoming and outgoing mail servers. In this recipe, you will learn how to configure email servers in Odoo.

Getting ready

There is no development needed for this recipe, but you will require mail server information, such as the server URL, port, server type, user name, and password. We will use this information to configure the mail servers.

> If you are using **Odoo Online** or **Odoo.sh**, you do not need to configure the mail servers. You can send and receive emails without any complex configurations on those platforms. This recipe is for on-premise Odoo instances.

How to do it...

Configuring incoming and outgoing mail servers contains a few common steps and a few separate steps. So first, we will see common configuration steps, and then we will configure the incoming and outgoing mail servers individually. The following are the common steps that are required for both incoming and outgoing mail servers:

1. Open the **General Settings** form menu, **Settings | General Settings.**
2. Go to the **Discuss** section and enable **External Email Servers**. This will display the following options:

3. In the **Alias Domain** field, enter the domain name on which your mail server is running. Then save the configuration.

Configuring the incoming mail server

Perform the following steps to configure the incoming mail server:

1. Open **General Settings** and click on the **Incoming Email Servers** link. This will redirect you to a list view of incoming mail servers.
2. Click on the **Create** button, which will open the following form view. Enter the details of your incoming mail server (see the *How it works* section for an explanation of each field):

3. Click on the **Test & Confirm** button to verify your configuration. It will show an error message if you have wrongly configured the incoming mail server.

Configuring the outgoing mail server

Follow these steps to configure the outgoing mail server:

1. Open **General Settings** and click on the **Outgoing Email Servers** link. This will redirect you to the list view of outgoing mail servers.

2. Click on **Create**, which will open the following form view. Enter the details of your outgoing mail server (see the *How it works* section for explanation of each fields):

3. Click on **Test connection** at the bottom of the screen to verify your configuration. It will show an error message if you have wrongly configured the outgoing mail server.

> The outgoing mail server will display the error dialog even if you have configured it properly. Look for the **Connection Test Succeeded! Everything seems properly set up!** message in the error dialog body. It means your outgoing server is configured correctly.

How it works...

The steps given in this recipe are self-explanatory and do not require further explanation. But the outgoing mail and incoming mail records have several fields, so let's see their purpose.

Here is the list of fields used to configure the incoming mail server:

- `Name`: The name of the server, which helps you identify a specific incoming mail server when you have configured multiple incoming mail servers.
- `Server Type`: Here you need to choose from three options: POP, IMAP, and Local. The value of this field will be based on your mail service provider.
- `Server Name`: The domain of the server on which the service is running.
- `Port`: The port number on which the server is running.
- `SSL/TLS`: Check this field if you are using SSL/TLS encryption.
- `Username`: The email address for which you are fetching emails.
- `Password`: The password for the email address provided.

The following is the list of fields used for configuring the outgoing mail server:

- `Description`: The description of the server, which helps you identify a specific incoming mail server when you have configured multiple incoming mail servers.
- `Priority`: This field is used to define the priority of the outgoing mail server. The lower number gets a higher priority so mail servers with a lower priority will be used most.
- `SMTP server`: The domain of the server on which the service is running.
- `SMTP port`: The port number on which the server is running.
- `Connection security`: The type of security used to send the mail.
- `Username`: The email account used for sending the emails.
- `Password`: The password for the email account provided.

There's more...

By default, incoming emails are fetched every five minutes. If you want to change this interval, follow these steps:

1. Activate the developer mode
2. Open the list of **Scheduled Actions** at **Settings | Technical | Automation | Scheduled Actions**
3. Search and open the **Scheduled Action** named **Mail: Fetchmail**
4. Change the interval using the field labeled **Execute Every**

Managing chatter on documents

In this recipe, you will learn how to manage chatter on your documents, and add a communication thread to the record.

Getting ready

For this recipe, we will reuse the `my_library` module from Chapter 9, *Advanced Server-side Development Techniques*. You can grab a copy of the module from the `Chapter09/r1_user_performing_actions` directory of the GitHub repository for this book. In this recipe, we will add chatter on the `library.book.rent` model.

How to do it...

Follow these steps to add chatter on the records of the `library.book.rent` model:

1. Add the `mail` module dependency in the `__manifest__.py` file:

```
...
'depends': ['base', 'mail'],
...
```

2. Inherit `mail.thread` in the Python definition of the `library.book.rent` model:

```
class LibraryBookRent(models.Model):
    _name = 'library.book.rent'
    _inherit = ['mail.thread']
...
```

3. Add chatter widgets on the form view of the `library.book.rent` model:

```
...
</sheet>
<div class="oe_chatter">
    <field name="message_follower_ids"
widget="mail_followers"/>
    <field name="message_ids" widget="mail_thread"/>
</div>
</form>
...
```

Install the `my_library` module to see the changes in action:

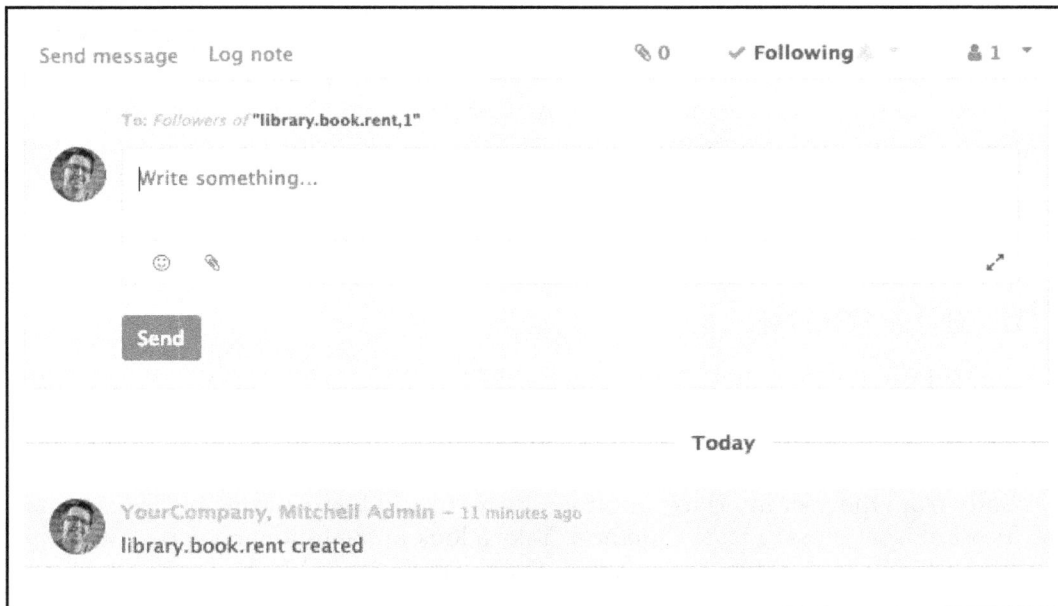

As shown in the preceding screenshot, after installing the module you will be able to see chatter in the form view.

How it works...

In order to enable chatter on any model, you will need to install the `mail` module first. This is because all the code required to enable chatter or mailing capabilities is part of the `mail` module. That's why in step 1 we added the `mail` module dependency in the manifest file of the `my_library` module. This will automatically install the `mail` module whenever you install the `my_library` module.

The fields and methods required to operate chatter are part of the `mail.thread` model. The `mail.thread` model is an abstract model and is just used for inheritance purposes. In step 2, we inherited the `mail.thread` model in the `library.book.rent` model. This will add all the necessary fields and methods required for chatter in the `library.book.rent` model. If you don't know how model inheritance works, refer to the *Using abstract models for reusable model features* recipe in `Chapter 5`, *Application Models*.

In the first two steps, we added all the fields and methods required for chatter. The only remaining thing for chatter is adding a user interface in the form view. In step 3, we added a message thread and follower widget. You might be wondering about the `message_follower_ids` and `message_ids` fields. These fields are not added in the `library.book.rent` model definition but they are added from the `mail.thread` model through inheritance.

There is more...

When you post messages in chatter, mail will be sent to the follower. If you notice in the example of this recipe, the borrower of the book is not the follower of the records, so they will not receive the messages. If you want to send the mail notification to the borrower, you will need to add it to the borrower list. You can add the follower manually from the user interface, but if you want to add them automatically, you can use the `message_subscribe()` method. Take a look at the following code—when we place a book on rent, the given code will automatically add borrowers to the list of followers:

```
@api.model
def create(self, vals):
    res = super(LibraryBookRent, self).create(vals)
```

```
res.message_subscribe(partner_ids=[res.borrower_id.id])
return res
```

Similarly if you want to remove followers from the list, you can use the `message_unsubscribe()` method.

Managing activities on documents

When using chatter, you can also add activities. These are used to plan your actions on the record. It is kind of a To-Do-List for each record. In this recipe, you will learn how to enable activities on any model.

Getting ready

For this recipe, we will be using the `my_library` module from the previous recipe *Managing chatter on documents*. We will add activities on the `library.book.rent` model.

How to do it...

Follow these steps to add activities on the `library.book.rent` model:

1. Inherit `mail.activity.mixin` in the Python definition of the `library.book.rent` model:

   ```
   class LibraryBookRent(models.Model):
       _name = 'library.book.rent'
       _inherit = ['mail.thread', 'mail.activity.mixin']
       ...
   ```

2. Add `mail_activity` widgets in the chatter of the `library.book.rent` model:

   ```
   ...
   <div class="oe_chatter">
       <field name="message_follower_ids"
   widget="mail_followers"/>
       <field name="activity_ids" widget="mail_activity"/>
       <field name="message_ids" widget="mail_thread"/>
   </div>
   ...
   ```

Update the `my_library` module to apply the changes. This will display chatter activities:

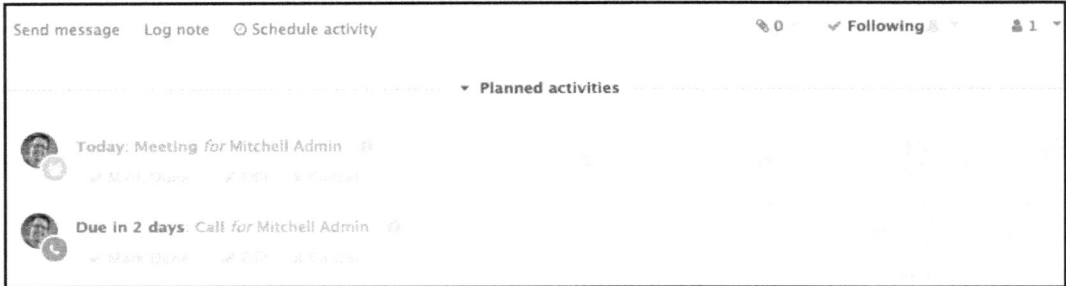

This is how the user will be able to manage different chatter activities. Note that an activity scheduled by one user is visible to all other users too.

How it works...

Activities are part of the `mail` module and you can optionally enable them in chatter. In order to enable activities on records, you need to inherit `mail.activity.mixin`. Similar to the `mail. thread` model, `mail.activity.mixin` is also an abstract model. Inheriting `mail.activity.mixin` will add all the necessary fields and methods in the module. These methods and fields are used to manage activities on records. In step 1, we added `mail.activity.mixin` into the `library.book.rent` model. Because of this, the inheritance of `library.book.rent` will get all the methods and fields required to manage activities.

In step 2, we added the `mail_activity` widget in the form view. This will display the UI for managing activities. The `activity_ids` field is added in the `library.book.rent` model through inheritance.

Activities can be of different types. By default, you can create activities with types such as Email, Call, Meeting, and To-Do. If you want to add your own activity type, you can do it by going to **Settings | Technical | Email | Activity Types** in developer mode.

There's more...

If you want to schedule an activity automatically, you can use the
`activity_schedule()` method of the `mail.activity.mixin` model. This will
create the activity on a given due date. You can schedule the activity manually with
the `activity_schedule()` method, as follows:

```
@api.model
def create(self, vals):
    res = super(LibraryBookRent, self).create(vals)
    if res.return_date:
        res.activity_schedule('mail.mail_activity_data_call',
                              date_deadline=res.return_date)
    return res
```

This example will schedule call activity for the librarian whenever someone borrows
a book. The deadline of the activity will be set as the return date of the book, so the
librarian can make a call to the borrower on that date.

Sending mail using the Jinja template

Odoo supports creating dynamic emails through Jinja templates. In this recipe, we
will create a Jinja mail template and then send mail with its help.

Getting ready

For this recipe, we will be using the `my_library` module from the previous recipe
Managing activities on documents. We will add the Jinja template to send an email to
the borrower to tell him/her the book is overdue.

How to do it...

Follow these steps to send a reminder email to the borrower:

1. Create a new file called `my_library/data/mail_template.xml` and add
   the mail template:

   ```xml
   <?xml version="1.0" encoding="utf-8"?>
   <odoo noupdate="1">
       <record id="book_return_reminder" model="mail.template">
           <field name="name">Book Return Reminder</field>
   ```

```
        <field
name="email_from">${object.book_id.create_uid.email}</field>
        <field
name="email_to">${object.borrower_id.email}</field>
        <field name="subject">Reminder for book return</field>
        <field name="model_id"
ref="my_library.model_library_book_rent"/>
        <field name="body_html">
            <![CDATA[
                <p>Dear ${object.borrower_id.name},</p>
                <p>You had rented the
                    <b>${object.book_id.name}</b> book on
${format_date(object.rent_date)}
                <br/>
                The due date of book is <b
style="color:red;">${format_date(object.return_date)}.</b>
                </p>
                <br/>

                <p>Best regards,
                <br/> Librarian</p>
            ]]>
        </field>
    </record>
</odoo>
```

2. Register the template file in the manifest file:

```
...
'data': [
    'security/groups.xml',
    'security/ir.model.access.csv',
    'views/library_book.xml',
    'views/library_book_categ.xml',
    'views/library_book_rent.xml',
    'data/mail_template.xml'
],
...
```

3. Add a **Send reminder** button in the form view of the `library.book.rent` model to send the email:

```
...
<header>
    <button name="book_return" string="Return the Book"
states="ongoing" type="object"/>
    <button name="book_return_reminder" string="Send reminder"
states="ongoing" type="object"/>
    <field name="state" widget="statusbar"/>
</header>
...
```

4. Add the `book_return_reminder()` method in the `library.book.rent` model:

```
...
def book_return_reminder(self):
    template_id =
self.env.ref('my_library.book_return_reminder')
    self.message_post_with_template(template_id.id)
```

Update the `my_library` module to apply the changes. This will add a **Send reminder** button in the form view of the `library.book.rent` model. When they click on the button, followers will get the following message:

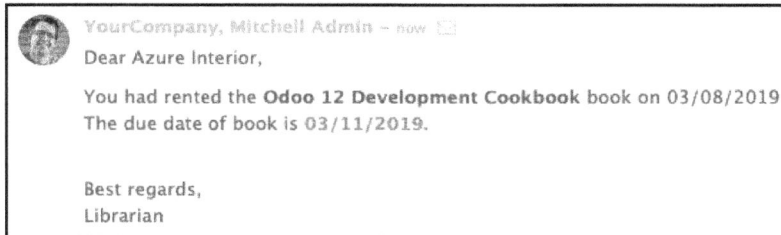

YourCompany, Mitchell Admin – now
Dear Azure Interior,

You had rented the **Odoo 12 Development Cookbook** book on 03/08/2019
The due date of book is 03/11/2019.

Best regards,
Librarian

The procedure shown in this recipe is useful when you want to send updates to your customer through emails. Because of the Jinja template, you can send emails dynamically based on individual records.

How it works...

In step 1, we created a mail template using Jinja. Jinja templates help us generate a dynamic email based on record data. The mail template is stored in the `mail.template` model. Let's see the list of fields you will need to pass in order to create a Jinja mail template:

- `name`: The name of the template that is used to identify a specific template.
- `email_form`: The value of this field will be the email address from which this email is sent.
- `email_to`: The value of this field will be the email address of the recipient.
- `subject`: This field contains the subject of the email.
- `model_id`: This field contains the reference of the model. The mail template will be rendered with the data of this model.
- `body_html`: This field will contain the body of the email template. It is a Jinja template so you can use variables, loops, conditions, and so on. If you want to learn more about Jinja templates, go to http://jinja.pocoo.org/docs/2.10/. Usually we wrap the content in the CDATA tag so the content in the body is considered as character data and not as a markup.
- `auto_delete`: This is the Boolean field that deletes the email once the email is sent. The default value of this field is `False`.
- `lang`: This field is used to translate the mail template into another language.

> **TIP**
>
> You can use `${}` in the `email_form`, `email_to`, `subject`, and `lang` fields. This helps you to set values dynamically. Take a look at *step 1* in our recipe—we used `${object.borrower_id.email}` to set the `email_to` field dynamically.

If you look closely at the content of the `body_html` field, you will notice we used `${object.borrower_id.name}`. Here, the object is the record set of the `library.book.rent` model. During the rendering, `${object.borrower_id.name}` will be replaced with the borrower's name. Like `object`, some other helper functions and variables are passed in the rendering context. Here is the list of helpers passed to the renderer context:

- `object`: This variable will contain the recordset of the model, which is set in the template by the `model_id` field
- `format_date`: It is a reference to the method used to format date-time objects

- `format_tz`: It is a reference to the method used to convert UTC date time into the time zone based date time
- `format_amount`: It is a reference to the method used to convert `float` into `string` with the currency symbol
- `user`: This will be the record set of the current user
- `ctx`: It will contain the dictionary of the environment context

In step 2, we registered the template file in the manifest file.

In step 3, we added a button in form view to invoke the `book_return_reminder()` method, which will send the email to the followers.

In step 4, we added the `book_return_reminder()` method, which will be invoked by clicking the button. The `message_post_with_template()` method is used to send the email. The `message_post_with_template()` method is inherited in the model through `mail.thread` inheritance. To send the email, you just need to pass the template ID as the parameter.

> If you want to see the list of templates, activate developer mode and open the **Settings | Technical | Email | Templates** menu. The form view of the template also provides a button to preview the rendered template.

There's more...

The `message_post_with_template()` method is used to send mail with the Jinja template. If you just want to send an email with plain text, you can use the `message_post()` method:

```
self.message_post(body="Please return your book on time")
```

The preceding code will add the **Please return your book on time** message in the chatter. All of the followers will be notified with this message. If you just want to log the message, call the method with the `subtype_id` parameter.

Sending mail using the QWeb template

In the previous recipe, we learned how to send mail using the Jinja template. In this recipe, we will see another way to send dynamic mail. We will send email with the help of the QWeb template.

Getting ready

For this recipe, we will use the `my_library` module from the previous recipe *Sending mail using the Jinja template*. We will use the QWeb template to send an email to the borrower to tell him/her the book is overdue.

How to do it...

Follow these steps to send a reminder email to the borrower:

1. Add the QWeb template into the `my_library/data/mail_template.xml` file:

```xml
<template id="book_return_reminder_qweb">
    <p>Dear <span t-field="object.borrower_id.name"/>,</p>
    <p>You had rented the
        <b>
            <span t-field="object.book_id.name"/>
        </b> book on <span t-field="object.rent_date"/>
        <br/>
            The due date of book is
            <b style="color:red;">
                <span t-field="object.return_date"/>
            </b>
    </p>
    <br/>

    <p>Best regards,
    <br/>
    Librarian
    </p>
</template>
```

2. Add a `Send reminder (QWeb)` button in the form view of the `library.book.rent` model to send the email:

```xml
...
<header>
    <button name="book_return" string="Return the Book"
states="ongoing" type="object"/>
    <button name="book_return_reminder" string="Send reminder"
states="ongoing" type="object"/>
    <button name="book_return_reminder_qweb" string="Send
reminder(QWeb)" states="ongoing" type="object"/>
    <field name="state" widget="statusbar"/>
```

```
</header>
. . .
```

3. Add the `book_return_reminder_qweb()` method in the `library.book.rent` model:

```
. . .
def book_return_reminder_qweb(self):
self.message_post_with_view('my_library.book_return_reminder_q
web')
```

Update the `my_library` module to apply the changes. This will add a **Send reminder (QWeb)** button in the form view of the `library.book.rent` model. When the button is clicked, followers will get a message like this:

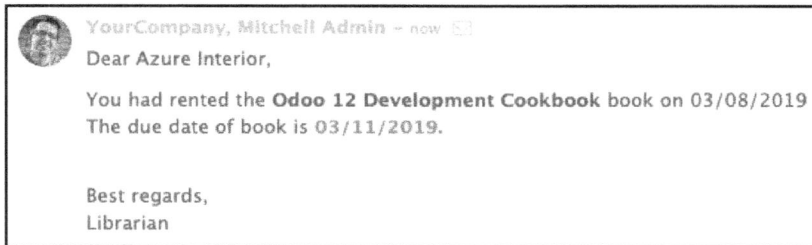

The procedure shown in this recipe works exactly like the previous recipe *Sending mail using the Jinja template*. The only difference is the template type, as this recipe uses QWeb templates.

How it works...

In *step 1*, we created a QWeb template with the `book_return_reminder_qweb` ID. If you check in the template, we are not using the `format_date()` data field method anymore. This is because the QWeb rendering engine handles this automatically and displays the date based on the user's language. For the same reason, you are not required to use the `format_amount()` method to display the currency symbols. The QWeb rendering engine will manage this automatically. If you want to learn more about QWeb templates, refer to the *Creating or modifying templates – QWeb* recipe from Chapter 15, *CMS Website Development*.

In step 2, we added a button in the form view to invoke the
`book_return_reminder_qweb()` method, which sends email to the followers.

In step 3, we added the `book_return_reminder_qweb()` method, which will be
invoked by a button click. The `message_post_with_view()` method is used to send
email. The `message_post_with_view()` method is inherited in the model through
`mail.thread` inheritance. To send the email, you just need to pass the web
template's XML ID as the parameter.

Sending mail with the QWeb template works exactly the same as the previous recipe,
but there are some subtle differences between the QWeb mail template and the Jinja
mail template. Here is a quick comparison between both templates:

- There is no simple way to send extra parameters in the email templates.
  You have to use a recordset in the object variable to fetch dynamic data. On
  the other hand, with QWeb mail templates you can pass extra values in the
  renderer context through the `values` parameter:

```
self.message_post_with_view(
    'my_library.book_return_reminder_qweb',
    values={'extra_data': 'test'}
)
```

- To manage the date format, time zone, and amount with currency symbols,
  in the Jinja template you have to use the `format_date`, `format_tz`, and
  `format_amount` functions, while in QWeb templates it is managed
  automatically.
- It is not possible to modify an existing template for other modules in Jinja,
  whereas in QWeb templates you can modify the mail template through
  inheritance. If you want to learn more about QWeb inheritance, refer to the
  Creating or modifying templates – QWeb recipe in `Chapter 15`, *CMS Website
  Development*.
- You can select and use a Jinja template directly from the message
  composer. In the following screenshot, the drop-down menu in the bottom-
  right corner is used to select a Jinja template:

Odoo   ×

Recipients   Followers of the document and

(Azure Interior ×) Add contacts to notify... ▾

Subject   Reminder for book return

✏ ▾ B *I* U ✐ 16 ▾ A ✒ ☰ ☰ ☰ ▾ ▦ ▾ % ▣ ↺ C

Dear Azure Interior,

You had rented the **Odoo 12 Development Cookbook** book on 03/08/2019
The due date of book is 03/11/2019.

Best regards,
Librarian

📎 Attach a file   **Use template**   Book Return Reminder ▾ ⬈

Send   Cancel   💾 Save as new template

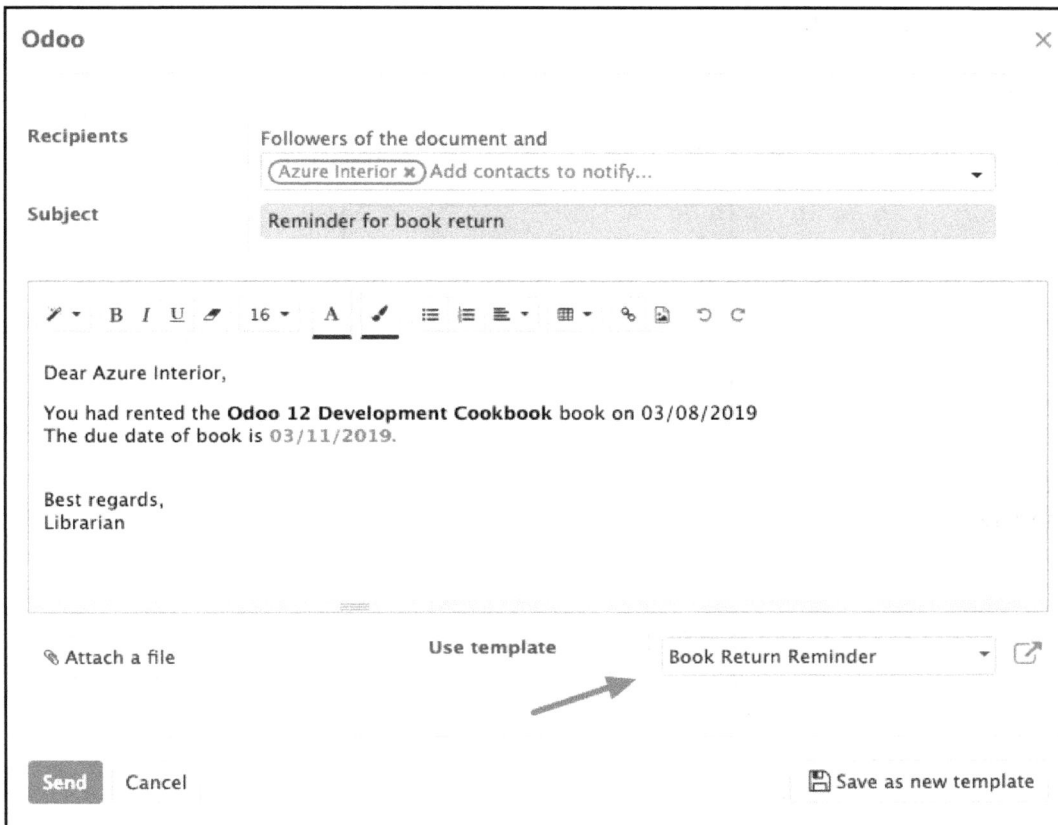

- Using QWeb, selecting a template directly from the message composer is not an option.

There's more...

All methods (`message_post`, `message_post_with_template`, and `message_post_with_view`) respect the user's preference. If the user changes the notification-management option from the user preference, the user will not receive emails; instead they will receive notifications in Odoo's UI. This is the same for customers; if a customer opts out of emails, they will not receive any updates through email.

Additionally, the Odoo message thread follows a concept called **subtypes**. Subtypes are used to receive emails only for information you are interested in. You can pass an extra parameter, subtype_id, in message_post_* methods to send emails based on the subtype. Usually, the user will manage their subtypes from the dropdown of the **Follow** button. Let's suppose the user has set their subtypes as follows:

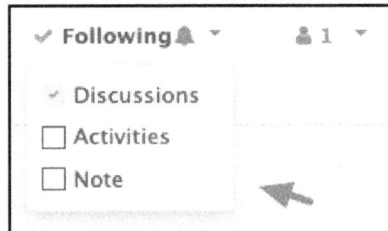

Based on the user's preference, the user will only get emails for Discussions messages.

Managing the mail alias

Email aliasing is the feature in Odoo that is used to create a record through incoming mail. The simplest example of a mail alias is sales teams. You just need to send an email to sale@yourdomain.com and Odoo will create a new record for the crm.lead in the sales team. In this recipe, we will create one mail alias to create a book's borrowing record.

Getting ready

For this recipe, we will be using the my_library module from the previous recipe *Sending mail using the QWeb template*. We will create our mail alias with the rent@yourdomain.com email address. If you send an email to this email address with the book's name in the subject, a record is created in the library.book.rent model.

How to do it...

Follow these steps to add a mail alias for the `library.book.rent` model:

1. Add mail alias data in the `my_library/data/mail_template.xml` file:

```xml
<record id="mail_alias_rent" model="mail.alias">
    <field name="alias_name">rent</field>
    <field name="alias_model_id"
ref="model_library_book_rent"/>
    <field name="alias_user_id" ref="base.user_admin"/>
    <field name="alias_contact">partners</field>
</record>
```

2. Add the following imports in the `my_library/models/library_book_rent.py` file:

```python
import re
from odoo.tools import email_split, email_escape_char
```

3. Override the `message_new()` method in the `library.book.rent` model:

```python
@api.model
def message_new(self, msg_dict, custom_values=None):
    self = self.with_context(default_user_id=False)
    if custom_values is None:
        custom_values = {}
    regex = re.compile("^\[(.*)\]")
    match = regex.match(msg_dict.get('subject')).group(1)
    book_id = self.env['library.book'].search([
        ('name', '=', match),
        ('state', '=', 'available')], limit=1)
    custom_values['book_id'] = book_id.id
    email_from =
email_escape_char(email_split(msg_dict.get('from'))[0])
    custom_values['borrower_id'] =
self._search_on_partner(email_from)
    return super(LibraryBookRent, self).message_new(msg_dict,
custom_values)
```

Update the `my_library` module to apply the changes. Then send an email to `rent@yourdomain.com`. Make sure you have included the book's name in the email subject, for example, *[Odoo 12 Development Cookbook] Request to borrow this book* . This will create the new `library.book.rent` record and it will be displayed as follows:

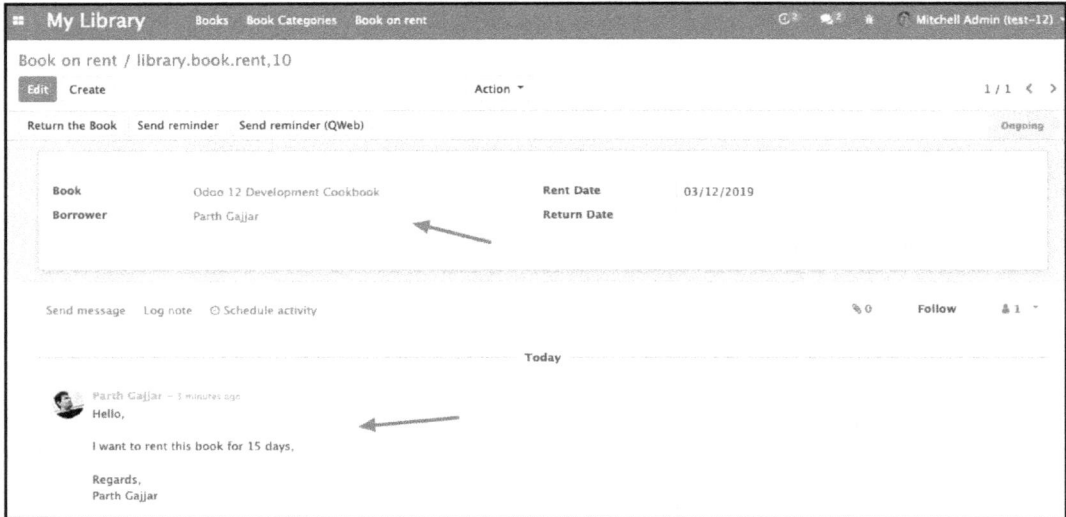

Whenever you send an email to `rent@yourdomain.com` with the book's name in the email subject, Odoo will generate a new borrowing record. Note that this will work only if the book is available in the library.

How it works...

In step 1, we created the `mail.alias` record. This alias will handle the `rent@yourdomain.com` email address. When you send the mail to this address, Odoo will create a new record in the `library.book.rent` model. If you want to see the list of active aliases in the system, open **Setting | Technical | Email | Aliases**. Here is the list of fields available to configure the alias:

- `alias_name`: This field holds the local part of the email address, for example, the `rent` in the `rent@yourdomain.com` is the local part of the email address.

- `alias_model_id`: The model reference on which the record should be created on incoming mail.
- `alias_user_id`: When incoming mail is received, records are created with the environment of the user in this field.
- `alias_contact`: This field holds the security preferences for the alias. Possible options are `everyone`, `partners`, `followers`, and `employees`.
- `alias_defaults`: When incoming mail is received, its record is created in the model specified on the alias. If you want to set default values in the record, give the values in the form of a dictionary in this field.

In step 2, we added the necessary imports.

In step 3, we overrode the `message_new()` method. This method is invoked automatically when a new email is received on the alias email address. This method will take two parameters:

- `msg_dict`: This parameter will be the dictionary that contains information about the received email. It contains email information such as the sender's email address, the receiver's email address, email subject, and email body.
- `custom_values`: This is a custom value used to create a new record. This is the same value you set on the alias record using the `alias_defaults` field.

In our recipe, we overrode the `message_new()` method and fetched the book's title from the mail subject through a regular expression. Then we fetched the email address of the sender with the help of the tools we imported in step 2. We used the sender email address to find the borrower's record. Then we updated `custom_values` with these two values: `books_id` and `borrower_id`. We pass this updated `custom_values` data to the `super()` method, which will create a new `library.book.rent` record with the given `books_id` and `borrower_id`. This is how the record is created when you send an email to the alias.

Note that this recipe generates an error when you don't send the proper email subject, such as `[book name]` `remaining subject`. You can update the program according to your business logic to avoid errors.

There's more...

Some business models have a requirement where you need a separate alias per record. For example, the sales team model has separate aliases for each team, such as `sale-in@example.com` for Team India and `sale-be@example.com` for Team Belgium. If you want to manage such aliases in your model, you can use `mail.alias.mixin`. In order to use it in your model, you will need to inherit the mixin:

```
class Team(models.Model):
    _name = 'crm.team'
    _inherit = ['mail.alias.mixin', 'mail.thread']
```

After inheriting the mixin, you will need to add the `alias_name` field into the form view so the end users can add aliases by themselves.

Logging user changes in chatter

The Odoo framework provides a built-in facility to log field changes in chatter. In this recipe, we will enable logging on some of the fields, so when changes are made in them, Odoo will add logs in the chatter.

Getting ready

For this recipe, we will be using the `my_library` module from the previous recipe *Managing the mail alias*. In this recipe, we will log changes from a few fields in the `library.book` model.

How to do it...

Modify the definitions of the fields, to enable logs for the fields when you change them. This is shown in the following code snippet:

```
class LibraryBookRent(models.Model):
    _name = 'library.book.rent'
    _inherit = ['mail.thread', 'mail.activity.mixin']

    book_id = fields.Many2one('library.book', 'Book', required=True)
    borrower_id = fields.Many2one('res.partner', 'Borrower',
required=True)
```

```
        state = fields.Selection([('ongoing', 'Ongoing'), ('returned',
'Returned')],
                                 'State', default='ongoing',
required=True,
                                 track_visibility='always')
        rent_date = fields.Date(default=fields.Date.today,
    track_visibility='onchange')
        return_date = fields.Date(track_visibility='onchange')
```

Update the my_library module to apply the changes. Create a new record in the library.book.rent model, make some changes in the fields, and then return the book. If you check the chatter, you will see the following logs:

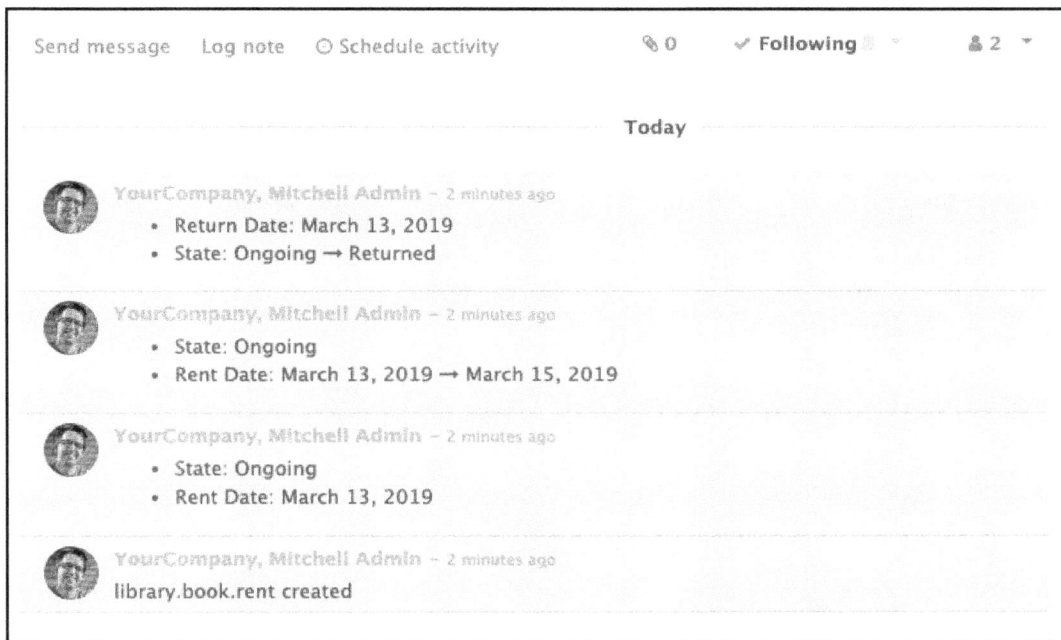

Whenever you make changes to state, rent_date, or return_date, you will see a new log in the chatter. This will help you to see the full history of the record.

How it works...

By adding the `track_visibility` attribute on the field, you can enable logging for that field. It has two possible values—`onchange` and `always`. When you set the `track_visibility="onchage"` attribute, Odoo will add a log that changes in the chatter whenever you update the field value. When you set the `track_visibility="always"` attribute, Odoo will always display the field value in the log even if its value is not changed. This is used to make the log more informative. Of course, fields with the `track_visibility="always"` attribute will add logs when the value of the field is changed.

In our recipe, we added `track_visibility='always'` on the `state` field and `track_visibility='onchange'` on the `rent_date` and `return_date` fields. This means Odoo will log the changes when you update the values of the `rent_date`, `return_date`, or `state` fields. But because the `state` field is set to `track_visibility='always'`, its value will be logged even if its value is not changed. Take a look at the screenshot in the *How to do it* section; we have only changed the `rent_date` field, and set the log to display **State: Ongoing**.

Note that the `track_visibility` feature only works if your model inherits the `mail.thread` model because the code-related chatter and logs are part of the `mail.thread` model.

24
IoT Box

With version 12, Odoo has added support for the **Internet of Things (IoT)**. Odoo uses hardware called the **IoT Box**, which is used to connect devices such as the printer, caliper, and foot switch. In this chapter, you will learn how to set up and configure the IoT Box. Here, we'll cover the following topics:

- Flashing the IoT Box image for Raspberry Pi
- Connecting the IoT Box with the network
- Adding the IoT Box to Odoo
- Loading drivers and listing connected devices
- Taking input from devices
- Accessing the IoT Box through SSH
- Configuring a point of sale

The IoT Box is a Raspberry Pi-based device. The recipes in this chapter are based on the Raspberry Pi 3 Model B+, available at `https://www.raspberrypi.org/products/raspberry-pi-3-model-b-plus/`. The IoT is the part of Enterprise edition, so you will need to use Enterprise edition to follow recipes in this chapter. Note that the goal of this chapter is to install and configure the IoT Box. Developing hardware drivers is outside the scope of this book. If you want to learn about the IoT Box in depth, explore the `iot` module in the Enterprise edition.

Technical requirements

The technical requirements for this chapter include the online Odoo platform.

All the code used in this chapter can be downloaded from the following GitHub repository, at: `https://github.com/PacktPublishing/Odoo-12-Development-Cookbook-Third-Edition/tree/master/Chapter24/r5_take_device_inputs/my_library`.

Check out the following video to see the Code in Action:

Place holder link

Flashing the IoT Box image for Raspberry Pi

In this recipe, you will learn how to flash a microSD card with an image of the IoT Box. Note that this recipe is only for those who have purchased the blank Raspberry Pi. If you have purchased the official IoT Box from Odoo, you can skip this recipe as it is preloaded with the IoT Box image.

Getting ready

Raspberry Pi 3 Model B+ uses a microSD card, so we have used a microSD for this recipe. You will need to connect a microSD card to your computer.

How to do it...

Perform the following steps to install an IoT Box image onto your SD card:

1. Insert a microSD card into your computer (use an adapter if your computer doesn't have a dedicated slot).
2. Download the IoT Box image from Odoo's nightly builds. The image is available at `https://nightly.odoo.com/master/iotbox/`.
3. Download and install **Balena Etcher** on your computer. You can download this from `https://www.balena.io/etcher/`.

4. Open Balena Etcher, select the IoT Box image, and choose to flash your microSD card. You'll see the following screen:

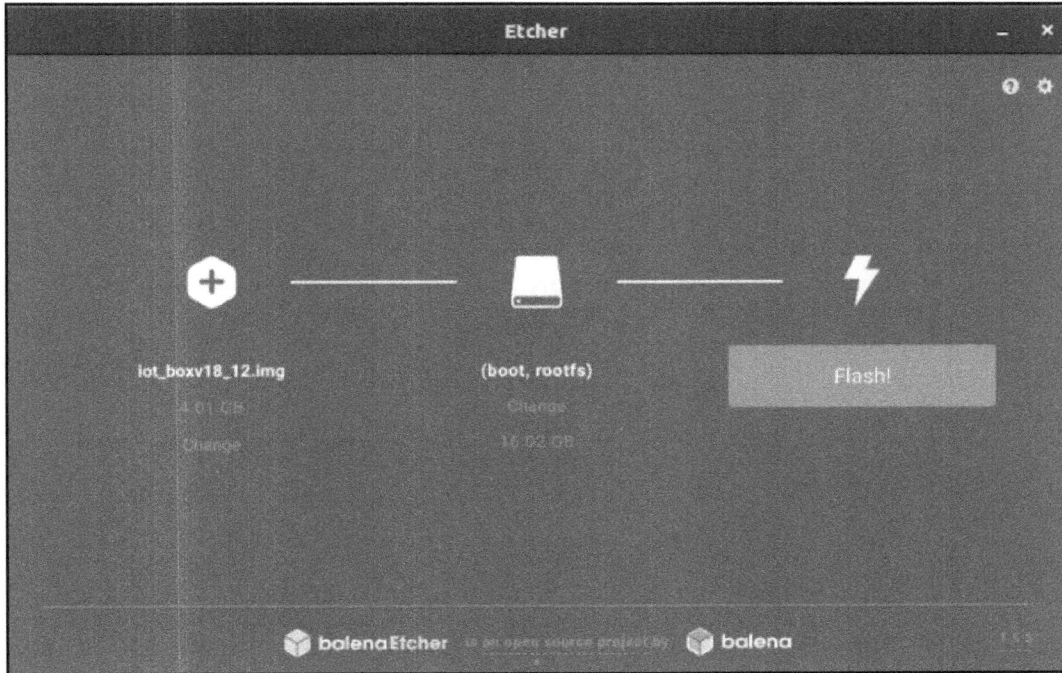

5. Click on the **Flash!** button and wait until the process completes.
6. Remove the microSD card and place it in Raspberry Pi.

After the given steps, your microSD card is loaded with the IoT Box image and is ready to be used in the IoT Box.

How it works...

In this recipe, we have installed the IoT Box image on the microSD card. In the second step, we downloaded the IoT Box image from the Odoo nightly builds. On the nightly page, you can find different images for the IoT Box. You need to choose the latest image from the Odoo nightly builds. When writing this book, we used the latest image, which was iotboxv18_12.zip. The Odoo IoT Box image is based on the Raspbian Stretch Lite OS and the image is loaded with the libraries and modules required to integrate the IoT Box with the Odoo instance.

In step 3, we downloaded the Balena Etcher utility tool used to flash the microSD card. In this recipe, we used Balena Etcher to flash the microSD card, but you can use any other tools to flash the microSD card.

In step 4, we flashed the microSD card with the IoT Box image. Note that this process can take several minutes. After the completion of the process, the microSD card will be ready to be used.

Perform the following steps if you want to verify whether the image is flashed successfully:

1. Mount the microSD card into the Raspberry Pi.
2. Connect it with the power supply and attach the external display through a HDMI cable (in practical usage, an external display is not compulsory; we have used it here just for verification purposes).
3. The OS will boot up and show the following page:

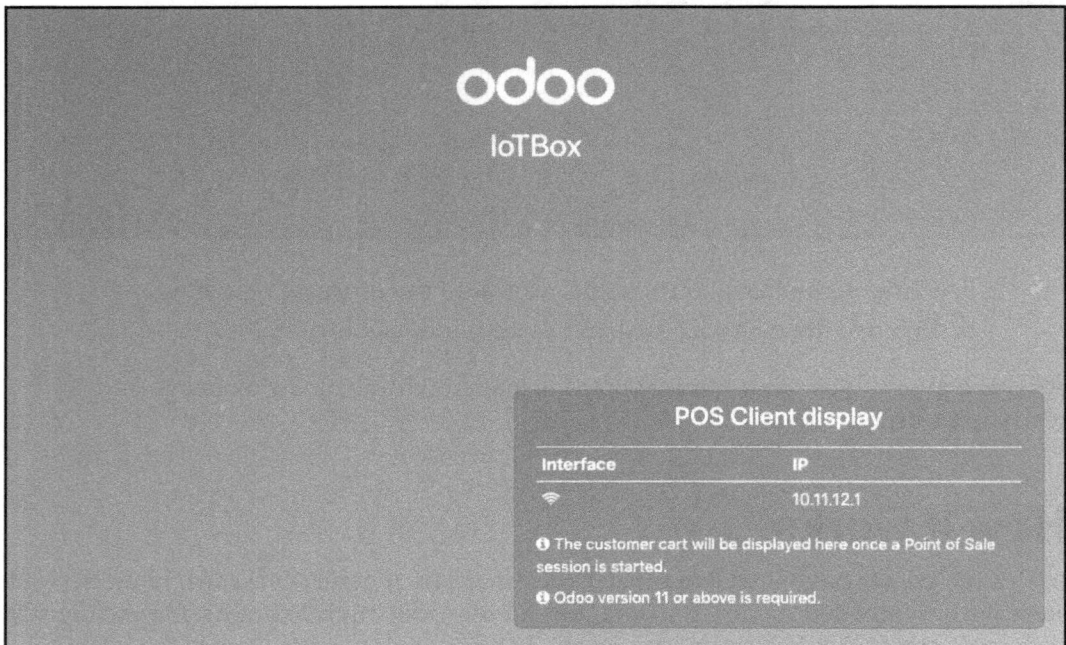

There's more...

In previous versions of Odoo, PosBox was used in Point of sale applications. The IoT Box supports all the features of the PosBox, so if you are using the Community edition of Odoo and you want to integrate devices, you can use the same IoT Box image to connect Odoo instances with different devices. See the *Configuring a point of sale* recipe for more information.

Connecting the IoT Box with the network

The IoT Box communicates with the Odoo instance through the network. Connecting the IoT Box is a very crucial step and if you make a mistake here, you might encounter errors when connecting the IoT Box with Odoo.

Getting ready

Mount the microSD card with the IoT Box image into the Raspberry Pi and then connect the Raspberry Pi with the power supply.

How to do it...

Raspberry Pi 3 Model B+ supports two types of network connection—through ethernet and through WiFi. Connecting the IoT Box through ethernet is simple; you just need to connect your the IoT Box with the RJ45 Ethernet cable, and the IoT Box is then ready to be used. Connecting the IoT Box through WiFi is complicated as you might not have a display attached to it. Perform the following steps to connect the IoT Box through WiFi:

1. Connect the IoT Box with the power supply (if the ethernet cable is plugged in to the IoT Box, remove it and restart the IoT Box).

2. Open your computer and connect to the WiFi network, named **IoTBox**, as shown in the following screenshot (no password is needed):

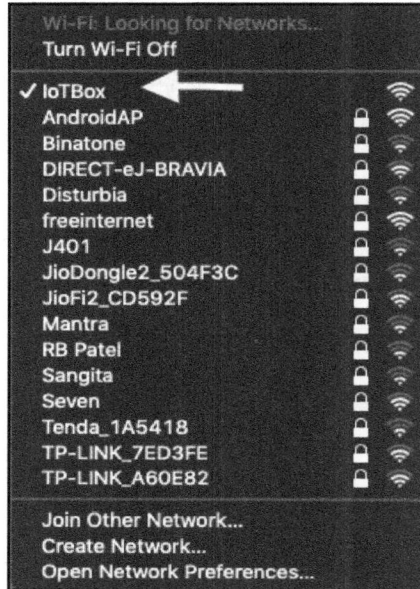

3. After connecting to the WiFi, you'll see a popup with the IoT Box home page like the following screenshot (if this does not work, open the IP address of the box in the browser):

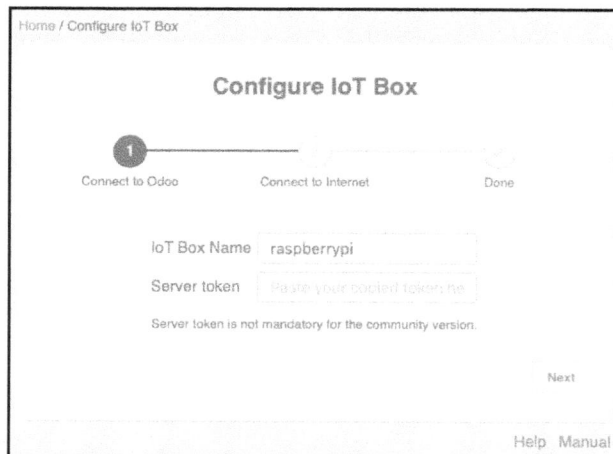

4. Set the **IoT Box Name** and keep the **Server token** empty, then click on **Next**. This will redirect you to a page where you can see a list of WiFi networks:

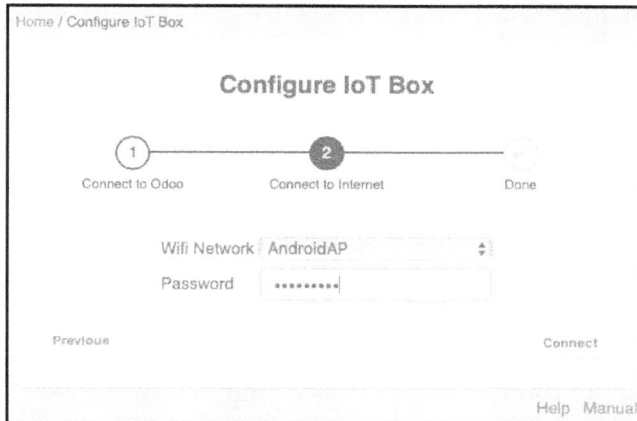

5. Select the **WiFi Network** you want to connect to and fill in the **Password**. After doing this, click on the **Connect** button. If you entered the correct information, you will be redirected to the final page:

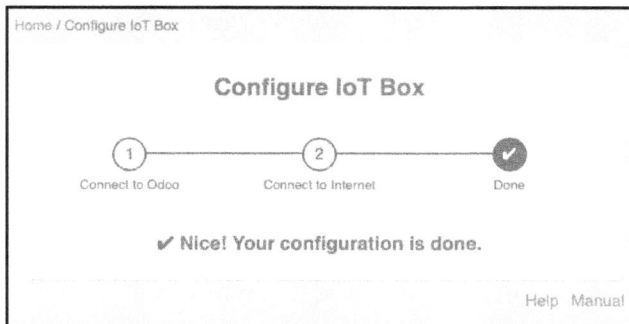

After performing these steps, your IoT Box is connected to the network and ready to be integrated with the Odoo instance.

How it works...

Connecting the Odoo instance to the IoT Box through ethernet is simple; just connect your IoT Box with the RJ45 Ethernet cable and the IoT Box is ready to be used. It's different when you want to connect the IoT Box with WiFi; this is difficult because the IoT Box doesn't have any display or GUI. You do not have any interface to enter your WiFi network password. Consequently, the solution to this problem is to disconnect your IoT Box from the ethernet cable (if it is connected) and restart it. In such cases, the IoT Box will create its own WiFi hotspot, named **IoT Box**, as shown in step 2. You need to connect the wifi with the name **IoT Box**; luckily it does not require a password. Once you connect to the **IoT Box** WiFi, you'll get a popup, as shown in step 3. Here, you can name your IoT Box something like *Assembly-line IoT Box*. Keep the server token empty for now; we will learn more about it in the *Adding IoT Box to Odoo* recipe. Then click on the **Next** button.

Upon clicking the **Next** button, you will be shown a list of WiFi networks, as shown in step 4. Here, you can connect the IoT Box to your WiFi network. Make sure you choose the right network. You need to connect the IoT Box with the same WiFi network as the computer on which the Odoo instance is going to be used. The IoT Box and the Odoo instance communicate within a **local area network** (**LAN**). This means that if both are connected in different networks, they cannot communicate and so IoT will not work.

After choosing the right WiFi network, click on **Connect**. Then the IoT Box will turn off its hotspot and reconnect to your configured WiFi network. That's it, the IoT Box is ready to be used.

Adding the IoT Box to Odoo

Our IoT Box is connected to the local network and ready to be used with Odoo. In this recipe, we will connect the IoT Box with the Odoo instance.

Getting ready

Make sure the IoT Box is on and you have connected the IoT Box to the same WiFi network as the computer with the Odoo instance is connected to.

There are a few things you need to take care of otherwise the IoT Box will not be added to Odoo:

- If you are testing the IoT Box in a local instance, you will need to use `http://192.168.1.*:8069` (your local IP) instead of `http://localhost:8069`. If you use localhost, the IoT Box will not be added in your Odoo instance.

- You need to connect the IoT Box with the same WiFi/ethernet network as the computer on which the Odoo instance is being used. Otherwise, the IoT Box will not be added in your Odoo instance.

- If your Odoo instance is running with multiple databases, IoT Box will not auto-connect with the Odoo instance. Use the `--db-filter` option to avoid these issues.

How to do it...

In order to connect the IoT Box with Odoo, first you will need to install the `iot` module in your Odoo instance. To do so, go to the **Apps** menu and search for the **Internet of Things** module. The module will look like the following screenshot. Install the module and we are good to go:

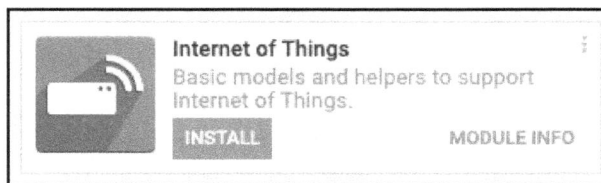

After installing the `iot` module, you can connect your instance with the IoT Box. There are two ways to do this: through **Auto connect** or **Manual connect**. Let's start with auto connect.

Connecting the IoT Box automatically

Perform the following steps to automatically connect your IoT Box with the Odoo instance:

1. Open the **IoT** menu.
2. Click on the **Connect** button on the control panel. This will show the following popup. Click on the **SCAN** button:

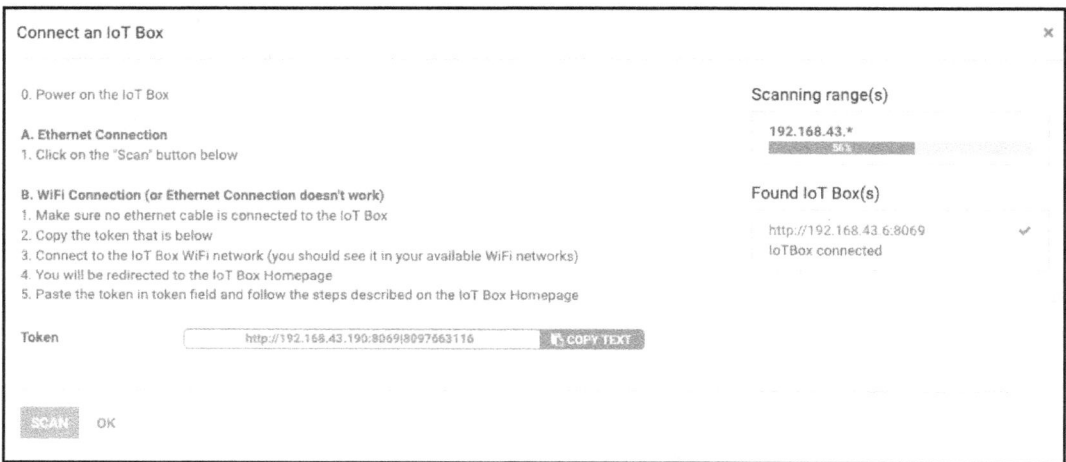

3. This will automatically scan all local IPs to find the IoT Box. If Odoo find the IoT Box, it will be displayed on the right-hand side; see the previous screenshot.
4. Close the popup. You will now see that the IoT Box has been added to the list:

Connecting the IoT Box manually

Perform the following steps to connect your the IoT Box manually with the Odoo instance:

1. Open the **IoT** menu.
2. Click on the **Connect** button on the control panel. This will show the following popup. Copy the **Token**:

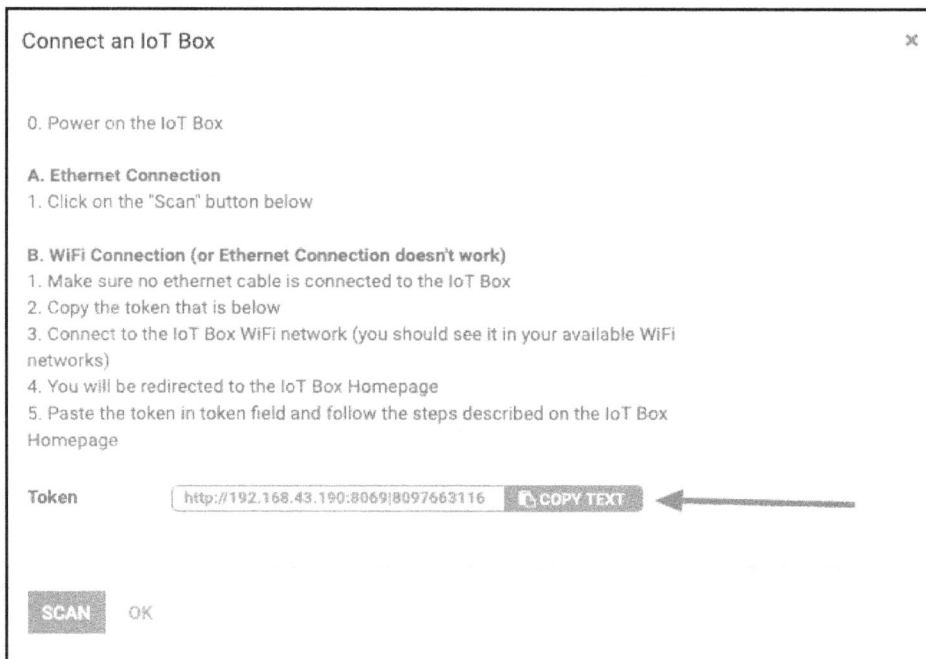

3. Open the IP of the IoT Box with port 8069. This will display the home page of the IoT Box. Click on the **Configure** button in the name section:

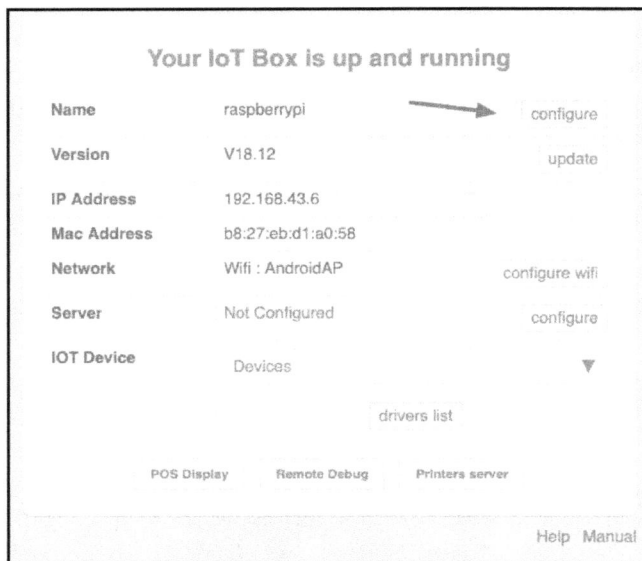

4. Set the IoT Box name and paste the server token. Then click on the **Connect** button. This will start configuring the IoT Box. Wait for the process to be completed:

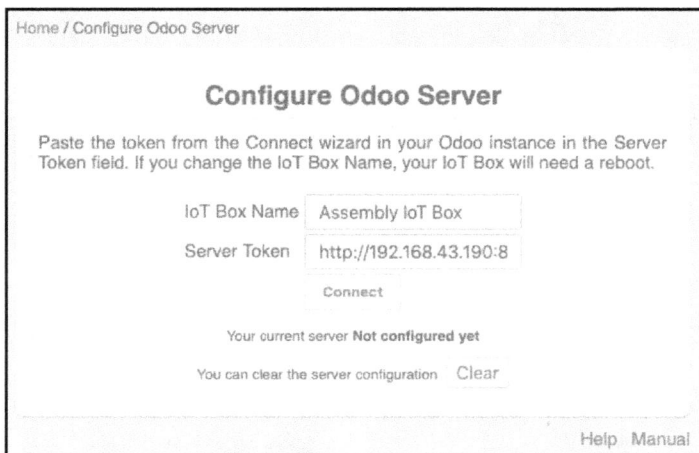

5. Check the **IoT** menu in your Odoo instance. You will find a new IoT Box:

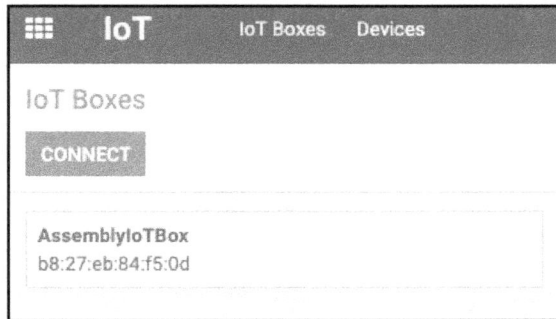

How it works...

After installing the Internet of Things module, a new IoT menu will be displayed whereby you can connect your IoT Box with Odoo. In our recipe, we first used the automatic method to connect the IoT Box. This method will scan your local IP range to find a possible IoT Box. If any IoT Box is found, Odoo will add its entry as an IoT Box. Note that if you have multiple IoT Boxes in the network, this method will add all of them. If the IoT Box is already connected, Odoo will not add the IoT Box again.

The second method is the manual one. This method is useful when you have multiple IoT Boxes in the network and you just want to add some of them. In this method, you have to grab a token from the IoT Box popup. Then you need to open the IoT Box IP and add the token into the configuration. This will add the IoT Box into your Odoo instance.

If you want to add the IoT Box in Odoo instances during WiFi configuration, this is possible. In the *Connecting the IoT Box with the network* recipe, we kept the **Server token** field empty. You just need to add the server token in this step:

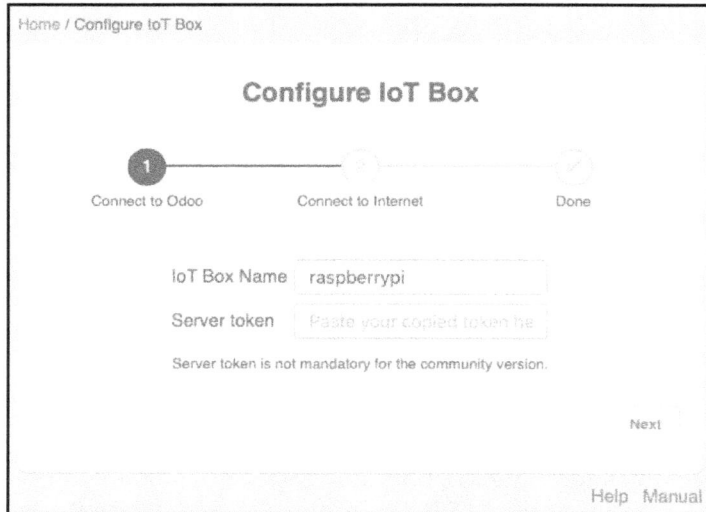

Home / Configure IoT Box

Configure IoT Box

1 ────────────── ────────────

Connect to Odoo   Connect to Internet   Done

IoT Box Name   raspberrypi

Server token   Paste your copied token he

Server token is not mandatory for the community version.

Next

Help Manual

Avoid using the DHCP network when using the IoT Box. This is because the IoT Box network configuration is added based on the IP address. If you use the DHCP network, then the IP address is assigned dynamically. So there is a chance that your IoT Box will stop responding due to the new IP address. To avoid this issue, you can map the MAC address of the IoT Box to the fixed IP address.

There's more...

Once you connect to the IoT Box with the Odoo instance, you cannot use that IoT Box with other Odoo instances. If you try to scan for the IoT Box and it is already configured, a warning icon will be displayed:

```
Scanning range(s)

192.168.43.*
    28%

Found IoT Box(s)

http://192.168.43.6:8069        ⚠
This IoTBox has already been connected
```

If you want to connect an existing IoT Box with any other Odoo instance, you will need to clear the configuration. You can clear the IoT Box configuration with the **Clear** button in the Odoo server configuration page of the IoT Box:

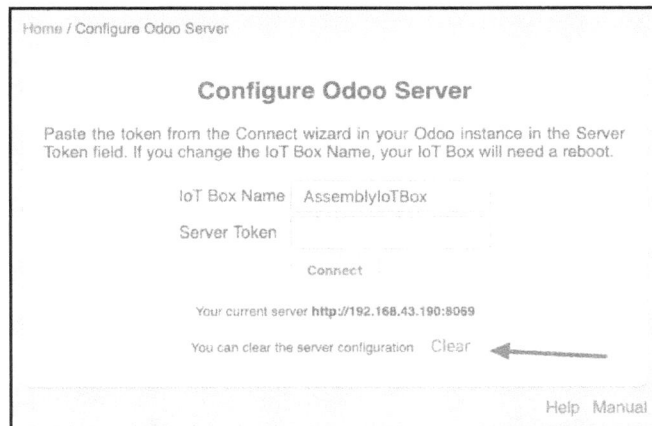

```
Home / Configure Odoo Server

               Configure Odoo Server

    Paste the token from the Connect wizard in your Odoo instance in the Server
    Token field. If you change the IoT Box Name, your IoT Box will need a reboot.

            IoT Box Name   AssemblyIoTBox
            Server Token

                       Connect

            Your current server http://192.168.43.190:8069

    You can clear the server configuration   Clear   ⬅

                                              Help  Manual
```

Loading drivers and listing connected devices

The IoT Box needs to load device drivers in order to communicate with hardware devices. In this recipe, we will see how you can load drivers and get a list of connected devices.

Getting ready

Make sure the IoT Box is on and you have connected it with the same WiFi network as the computer with the Odoo instance is connected to.

How to do it...

Perform the following steps to load device drivers into the IoT Box:

1. Open the IoT Box home page and click on the **drivers list** button at the bottom:

Your IoT Box is up and running

Name	AssemblyIoTBox	configure
Version	V18.12	update
IP Address	192.168.43.6	
Mac Address	b8:27:eb:d1:a0:58	
Network	Wifi : AndroidAP	configure wifi
Server	http://192.168.43.191:8069	configure
IOT Device	Devices	▼

drivers list ◀──────

POS Display   Remote Debug   Printers server

Help   Manual

2. The **drivers list** button will redirect you to the **Drivers list** page, where you will find the **Load drivers** button. Click on the button to load drivers:

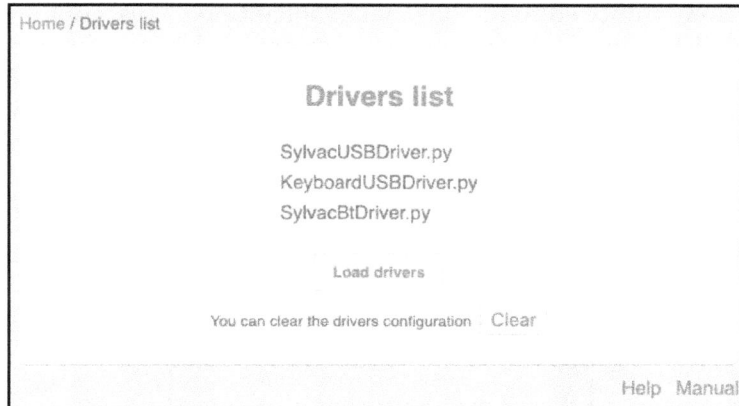

3. Go back to the IoT Box home page. Here, you will see a list of connected devices:

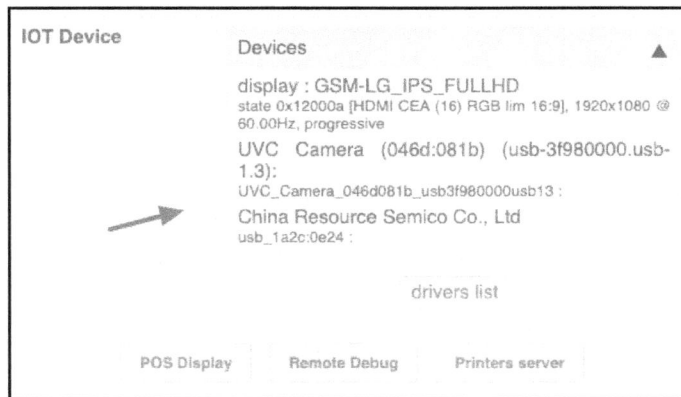

After performing these steps, the IoT Box will be ready with the devices you specified and you can start using devices in your applications.

How it works...

The IoT Box is not just limited to the Community edition. You can use it like the PoSBox in the Community edition. The device's integration is part of the Enterprise edition, so the IoT Box image does not come with device drivers; you need to load them manually. You can load the drivers from the home page of the IoT Box. You can do this from the **Load drivers** button at the bottom. Note that this will only work if your IoT Box is connected with the Odoo instance via the Enterprise edition. After loading the drivers, you will be able to see a list of devices in the IoT Box home page. You can also see a list of connected devices in the Odoo instance through the **IoT | Devices** menu. In this menu, you will see a list of connected devices for each IoT Box:

Right now, the IoT Box supports limited hardware devices, such as cameras, foot switches, printers, and calipers. The following is a list of devices that are recommended by Odoo: `https://www.odoo.com/page/iot-hardware`. If your device is not support, you can pay for driver development.

Taking input from devices

The IoT Box only supports limited devices. Right now these hardware devices are integrated with the manufacturing application. But if you want, you can integrated supportable devices in your module. In this recipe, we will capture a picture from a camera through the IoT Box.

Getting ready

We will be using the `my_library` module from the *Logging user changes in chatter* recipe in `Chapter 23`, *Manage Emails in Odoo*. In this recipe, we will add a new field to capture and store images when a borrower returns a book. Make sure the IoT Box is on and you have connected a supportable camera device with it.

How to do it...

Perform the following steps to capture a picture from a camera through the IoT Box:

1. Add a dependency in the manifest file:

```
...
'depends': ['base', 'mail', 'quality_mrp_iot'],
...
```

2. Add new fields in the `library.book.rent` model:

```
...
device_id = fields.Many2one('iot.device', string='IoT Device',
  domain="[('type', '=', 'camera')]")
ip = fields.Char(related="device_id.iot_id.ip")
identifier = fields.Char(related='device_id.identifier')
picture = fields.Binary()
...
```

3. Add these fields into the form view of the `library.book.rent` model:

```
<group>
    <field name="book_id" domain="[('state', '=',
'available')]"/>
    <field name="borrower_id"/>
    <field name="ip" invisible="1"/>
    <field name="identifier" invisible="1"/>
    <field name="device_id" required="1"/>
    <field name="picture" widget="iot_picture"
            options="{'ip_field': 'ip', 'identifier':
'identifier'}"/>
</group>
```

Update the `my_library` module to apply the changes. After the update, you will have a button to capture pictures:

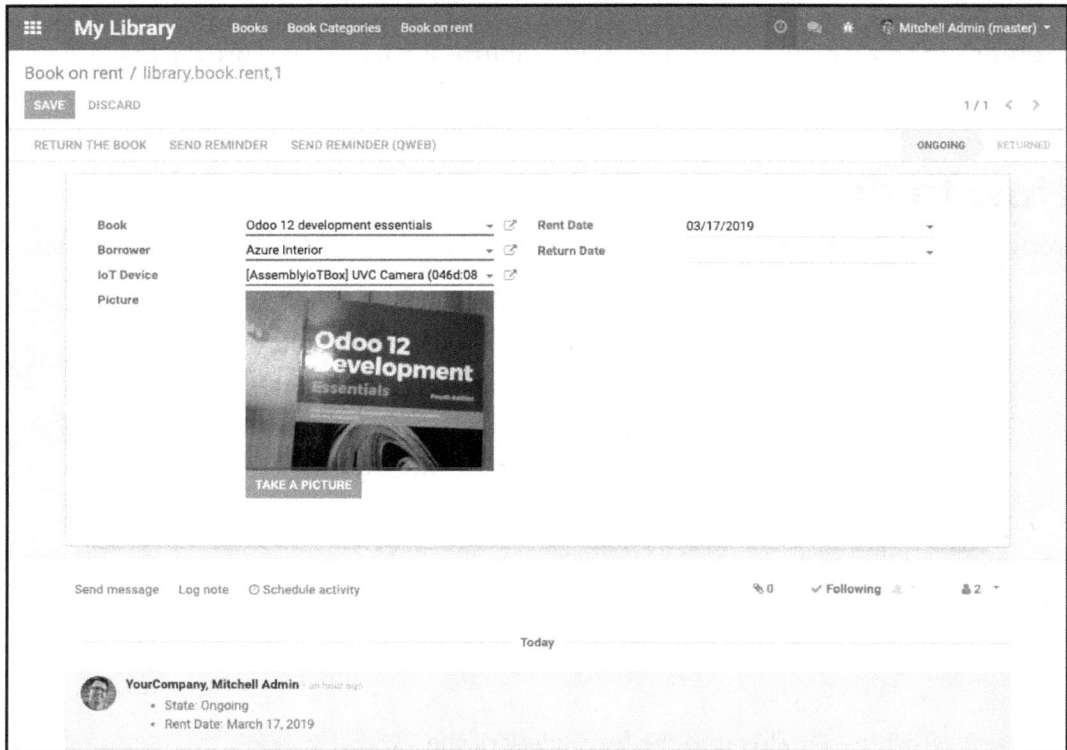

How it works...

In step 1, we added a dependency to the `quality_mrp_iot` module in the manifest file. The `quality_mrp_iot` module is part of the Enterprise edition and contains a widget that allows you to request an image from a camera through the IoT Box. This will install the `mrp` modules, but for the sake of simplicity, we will use `quality_mrp_iot` as a dependency. If you do not want to use this dependency, you can create your own field widget. Refer to the *Creating custom widgets* recipe in `Chapter 16`, *Web Client Development*, to learn more about widgets.

In step 2, we added the fields required to capture an image from the camera. To capture the image, we need two things: the device identifier and the IP address of the IoT Box. We want to give the user the option to select the camera, so we added a `device_id` field. The user will choose a camera to capture the image, and based on the selected camera device, we extracted IP and device identifier information through related fields. Based on these fields, Odoo will know where to capture the image, if you have multiple IoT Boxes. We have also added a binary field, `picture`, to save the image.

In step 3, we added fields in the form view. Note that we used the `iot_picture` widget on the `picture` field. We added the `ip` and `identifier` fields as invisible fields because we do not want to show them to the user; rather, we want to use them in the `picture` field options. This widget will add the button in the form view; on clicking the button, **Odoo** will make a request to the IoT Box to capture the image. The IoT Box will return image data as the response. This response will be saved in the `picture` binary field.

There is more...

Odoo IoT Box supports the Bluetooth caliper. If you want to take measurements in your module, you can use the `iot_take_measure_button` widget to fetch them in Odoo. To do so, you will have to use the `<widget>` tag, as shown in the following code. Note that like `iot_picture`, here you will also need to add the `ip` and `identifier` invisible fields in the form view:

```
<widget name="iot_take_measure_button"
        options="{'ip_field': 'ip',
                  'identifier_field': 'identifier',
                  'measure_field': 'measure'}"/>
```

Accessing the IoT Box through SSH

The IoT Box is running on Raspbian OS and it is possible to access the IoT Box through SSH. In this recipe, we will learn how to connect the IoT Box through SSH.

Getting ready

Make sure the IoT Box is on and you have connected the IoT Box with the same WiFi network as the computer with the Odoo instance is connected to.

How it works...

In order to connect the IoT Box through SSH, you will need the IP address of the IoT Box. You can see this IP address in its form view. As an example, in this recipe we will use 192.168.43.6 as the IoT Box IP address, so replace this with your IP address. Perform the following steps to access the IoT Box through SSH:

1. Open the Terminal and execute the following command:

```
$ ssh pi@192.168.43.6
pi@192.168.43.6's password:
```

2. The Terminal will ask you for a password; enter raspberry as the password.

3. If you added the right password, you can access the shell. Execute the following command to see the directory:

```
pi@AssemblyIoTBox:~ $ ls -l
total 260
-rw-r--r-- 1 root root 244271 Jan 16 14:17
init_posbox_image.log
drwxr-xr-x 5 pi pi 4096 Jan 16 12:57 odoo
-rw-r--r-- 1 pi pi 27 Jan 16 14:20 odoo-remote-server.conf
-rw-r--r-- 1 pi pi 11 Jan 16 14:20 token
-rw-r--r-- 1 pi pi 20 Jan 16 14:26 wifi_network.txt
```

How to do it...

We used the Pi user with password *raspberry* to access the IoT Box through SSH. The SSH connection is used when you want to debug a problem in the IoT Box. SSH doesn't need any explanation, but let's see how Odoo works in the IoT Box.

Here is some information that might help you debug the issue:

- The IoT Box is internally running some Odoo modules. The name of these modules usually starts with `hw_` and are available in the Community edition. You can find all the modules in the `/home/pi/odoo/addon` directory.
- If you want to see the Odoo server log, you can access it from the `/var/log/odoo/odoo-server.log` file.
- Odoo is running through a service named `odoo`, you can use the following command to `start`, `stop`, or `restart` the `service`:

  sudo service odoo start/restart/stop

- Customers mostly turn the IoT Box off by disconnecting the power. This means that the IoT Box OS does not shut down properly in such cases. To avoid corruption of the system, the IoT Box filesystem is read-only.

There's more...

Note that the IoT Box is only connected with the local machine. Consequently, you cannot access the shell directly from a remote location (through the internet). If you want to access the IoT Box remotely, you can paste the `ngrok` authentication Token key in the IoT Box's remote debug page as show in the following screenshot. This will enable the TCP tunnel from the IoT Box so you can connect the IoT Box through SSH from anywhere. Learn more about `ngrok` at `https://ngrok.com/`:

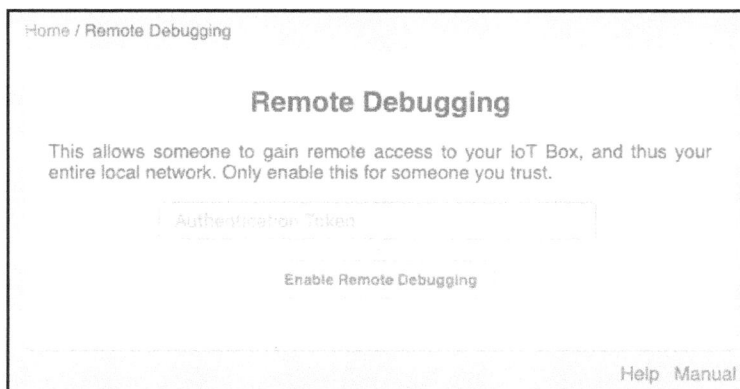

Configuring a point of sale

In Odoo 12, the IoT Box works with MRP and the point of sale application. In this recipe, we will learn how to configure the IoT Box for the point of sale application.

Getting ready

Make sure the IoT Box is on and you have connected IoT Box with the same WiFi network as the computer with the Odoo instance is connected to. Also install the point of sale application if it is not already installed.

How to do it...

Perform the following steps to configure the IoT Box for the point-of-sale application:

1. Open the point of sale application, and open **Settings** from the POS session dropdown:

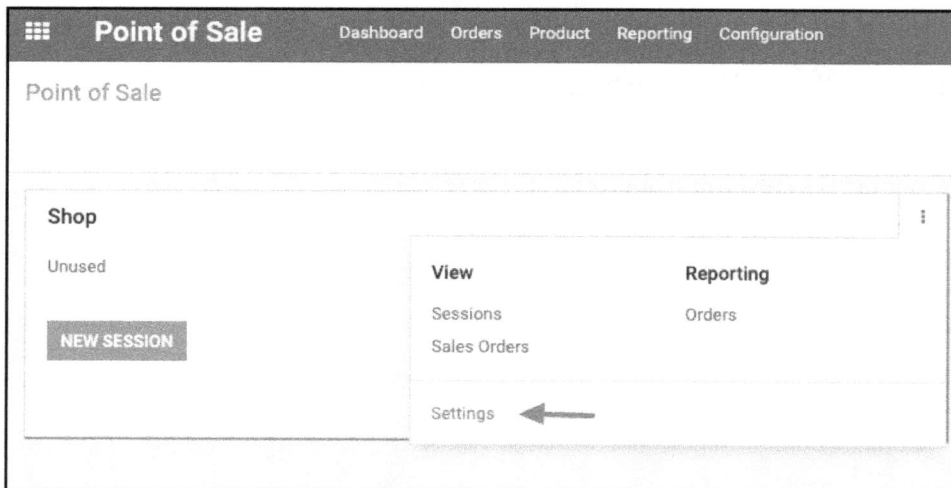

2. Click on the **Settings** button. You will be redirected to the **Settings** page. Search for the **IotBox / Hardware Proxy** section and click on the **PosBox** checkbox. This will enable more options:

IotBox / Hardware Proxy

☑ **PosBox**
Use an integrated hardware setup like IoT Box

IoT Box ▼

Barcode ☐
Scanner

Electronic Scale ☐

Cashdrawer ☐

Receipt Printer ☐

Customer ☐
Display

3. Select the **IoT Box** that you want to used in a point of sale session. If you are going to use hardware, barcode scanner, select the respective checkbox.
4. Save the changes by clicking the **Save** button in the control panel.

After the configuration, you will be able to use the IoT Box in the point-of-sale application.

How it works...

In the previous version of Odoo, the PosBox was used to integrate hardware with the point-of-sale application. In version 12, the IoT Box was introduced and this can be used with a point of sale application like the PosBox. In order to use the IoT Box in a point of sale application, you have to connect the IoT Box with the Odoo instance. If you don't know how to connect the IoT Box, follow the *Adding the IoT Box to Odoo* recipe. Once you have connected the IoT Box with Odoo, you will be able to select the IoT Box in the point of sale application, as shown in step 2.

Here, you can select the hardware you want to use in the point of sale session. After saving the change, if you open the point of sale session, you will be able to use the enabled hardware in the point of sale. If you enabled specific hardware from the settings but the hardware is not connected to the IoT Box, you will see the following warning in the top bar:

There's more...

The point of sale application is part of the Community edition. If you are using the Community edition, instead of the **IoT Box** selection you will see the **IP Address** field in the point of sale settings:

If you want to integrate hardware in the Community edition, you will need to use the IP address of the **IoT Box** in the field.

Other Book You May Enjoy

If you enjoyed this book, you may be interested in these other books by Packt:

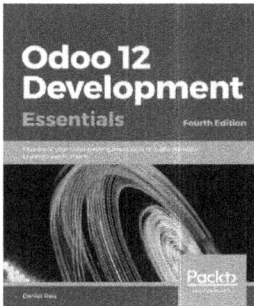

Odoo 12 Development Essentials - Fourth Edition
Daniel Reis

ISBN: 9781789532470

- Manage Odoo server instances
- Create a new Odoo application from scratch using the most frequently used elements
- Develop new models and use inheritance to extend existing models
- Use ORM methods in the Odoo server and from external clients
- Create Kanban views using QWeb effectively
- Build custom web and website CMS pages
- Use external APIs to integrate Odoo with external applications
- Add automated tests and techniques to debug module business logic

Leave a review - let other readers know what you think

Please share your thoughts on this book with others by leaving a review on the site that you bought it from. If you purchased the book from Amazon, please leave us an honest review on this book's Amazon page. This is vital so that other potential readers can see and use your unbiased opinion to make purchasing decisions, we can understand what our customers think about our products, and our authors can see your feedback on the title that they have worked with Packt to create. It will only take a few minutes of your time, but is valuable to other potential customers, our authors, and Packt. Thank you!

Index

-

--dev options 227, 228
-side test cases
  Headless Chrome, setting up for 556, 557

A

abstract models
  using, for reusable Model features 161, 163
access security
  adding 122, 123, 124
Access-Control Lists (ACLs) 346
access
  restricting, to web accessible paths 427, 428,
  429
act window 214
action 329
action button
  adding, on keyboard 659, 660, 661, 662
actions
  parameters, passing to 301, 302, 303, 304
active 187
activities
  managing, on documents 683, 684, 685
add-on module file structure
  organizing 111, 112, 113
add-on module manifest
  completing 108, 109, 110
add-on module
  creating 105, 106
  installing 105, 106
  updating 218, 220, 221
add-on modules list
  updating 47, 48
add-on modules
  creating 107
  installing 53, 58, 60, 107

installing, from command line 57
installing, from GitHub 60, 61, 62
installing, from web interface 54, 55, 57
updating 59
upgrading 53, 60
add-on
  modification, applying to 62, 63
  Odoo image, running with 91
add-ons path
  configuring 44, 45, 46
Affero General Public License version 3
  (AGPLv3) 10
API decorators
  using 170, 171, 172, 173
asset bundles
  using, in Odoo 438
attachments
  displaying, on side of form view 324, 325,
  326
attrs
  used, for dynamic form elements 322
auto-reload 227, 228
automated actions
  using, on event conditions 413, 414, 416
  using, on time conditions 408, 409, 410, 412

B

backup
  obtaining, of instance 596, 597
backups 74
base language 370
bootstrap
  reference 456
bottom 311
branch
  history 591
branches in Odoo.sh, types

development branches 590
production branch 589
staging branches 590
branches
managing 584
builds
status, checking of 597, 598
business logic
extending, in model 194, 196
modifying 669, 670, 671
buttons
adding, to forms 300, 301

C

calendar view 331, 332
campaigns
tracking, of visitors 476, 478
CDN at Odoo
configuring 98, 99, 100
CDN Base URL 101
CDN provider
configuring 96
certbot program
reference 85
Certification Authority (CA) 87, 88
chatter
managing, on documents 680, 682
user changes, logging in 698, 699
check_access_rights method
using, in JSON-RPC 627
classical inheritance 159
client-side code
debugging 508, 509, 510, 511
client-side QUnit test case 557, 559, 560, 561
client-side QWeb templates
using 490, 491, 492, 493
client-side test cases
debugging 568, 569
running, form UI 565
running, from UI 568
Cloudflare
content delivery networks (CDN), configuring
with 101
code editor 594
code

checking, Flake8 used 247
checking, Pylint used 246, 247
cohort view 336, 337
columns
kanban cards, displaying in 329, 330
command-line interface 232
computed fields
adding, to model 152, 153, 154, 155
concepts
exploring, of Odoo.sh 574
configurable precision
float field, using with 138, 139, 140
configuration file
adapting, for production 75, 76, 77, 78
Odoo image, running with 91
connected devices
listing 715, 717, 718
considerations, for deployment of instance
backups 74
PostgreSQL tuning 71, 73
server dimensioning 71
source code version 73
constraint validations
adding, to model 149, 150, 151
content delivery networks (CDN)
configuring, with Cloudflare 101
managing, for website 95
content
adding, to form view 294, 295
context 266, 301, 302, 303, 304
converters 431
copy() method
using 648
create()
extending 198, 199, 200
Cross-Site Request Forgery (CSRF) attack 469
CSS
extending, for website 443, 445, 447
CSV files
used, for loading data 216, 217, 218
currency 140
custom assets 440, 441
custom modules
adding 581, 583, 584
installing 581, 583, 584

custom settings options
  adding 278, 279, 280, 281
customer receipts
  modifying 672, 673, 674
Customer Relationship Management (CRM) 10

D

dashboard view 338, 339
data fields
  adding, to model 131, 132, 133, 134, 136
data
  fetching, in groups with read_group() 204,
    205, 206
  loading, CSV files used 216, 217, 218
  loading, XML files used 211, 212, 213, 214
  migrating 218, 220, 221
database queries
  records, accessing through 648, 649, 650
debug methods
  server logs, producing to help 229, 230, 231,
    232
debug mode options 248, 249, 250, 251, 252
debugging options
  accessing 590
Decimal Precision Configuration module 138
decorators 172
default values 181
delegation inheritance
  used, for copying features to model 164,
    165, 167
dependencies 17
deprecated 174
developer mode 38
development branch
  creating 586, 587
devices
  input, obtaining from 718, 719, 721
Docker image
  creating 91
  setting up 94
docker-compose
  Odoo, running through 92, 93
Docker
  about 89
  used, for running Odoo 89, 90

document-style forms 320, 321
documents
  activities, managing on 683, 684, 685
  chatter, managing on 680, 682
domain
  about 305, 306
  operators 307
  used, for pitfalls of searching 308
drivers
  loading 715, 717, 718
duplicity
  reference 74
dynamic form elements
  using, attrs 322
dynamic record stages
  managing 386, 387, 389
dynamic relations
  adding, Reference fields used 157, 158
dynamic routes
  managing 456, 458, 459

E

emacs (po-mode)
  reference 380
embedded views 323, 324
empty recordset
  obtaining, for model 176, 178
Enterprise resource planning (ERP) 10
environment 256
errors
  reporting, to user 174, 175, 176
event conditions
  automated actions, using on 413, 414, 416
external IDs
  using 208, 209
Extra Rights 345

F

failed test cases
  video/screenshot, generating for 570, 571
features
  activating, security group used 356, 357,
    358, 361
  activating, security groups used 360, 362
  merging, in production branch 589

fields
  access, limiting in models 350, 351, 352
file
  instance configuration, storing in 34, 35, 37
  translation strings, exporting to 376, 377, 378
filters
  defining, on record lists 305, 306
Flake8
  reference 247
  used, for checking code 247
float field
  using, with configurable precision 138, 139, 140
forcecreate flag
  using 214, 215
form view
  attachments, displaying on side of 324, 325, 326
  content, adding to 294, 295
  widgets, adding to 294, 295
forms
  buttons, adding to 300, 301
  parameters, passing to 301, 302, 303, 304
functions
  invoking, from XML files 223, 224, 225

G

gantt views 331, 332, 333
gettext tools
  used, for easing translations 380, 381
git commands
  using 595
Git repositories 11
git submodule
  reference 74
Git
  configuration 20
GitHub
  add-on modules, installing from 60, 61, 62
Global Interpreter Locks (GIL) 78
Global record rules 356
GNU gettext documentation
  reference 382
GNU/Linux environment 13

graph view 335
graph views 334, 336
group by 314
group tag
  used, for grouping filters 314
grouped data
  accessing 644, 645, 646
groups
  menus, hiding based on 365, 366
  view elements, hiding based on 365, 366
Gtranslator
  reference 380

H

handler
  modifying 432, 433, 434, 435
  parameters passed, consuming 430, 431, 432
Headless Chrome
  setting up, for -side test cases 556, 557
hierarchies 146
hierarchy
  adding, to model 146, 147, 148, 149
HTTP status 175

I

IAP client module
  creating 538, 539, 541, 542, 543
IAP credits
  authorizing 532, 533, 534, 535, 537, 538
  charging 532, 533, 534, 536, 537, 538
IAP service flow 519, 520
IAP service module
  creating 526, 528, 529, 530, 531
IAP service
  reference 521
  registering, in Odoo 521, 523, 524, 526
ID 277
image thumbnails
  generating 641, 642
image utilities
  methods 643
in-app purchase (IAP) concepts 518
in-memory cache
  managing, with ormcache 638, 640

incoming mail server
  configuring 677, 679
  fields 679
incoming mail servers
  configuring 676, 677
inheritance
  used, for adding features to model 159, 160, 161
init hooks
  implementing 282, 283
input
  obtaining, from devices 718, 719, 721
  obtaining, from users 466, 467, 468, 469
inside 317
instance configuration
  storing, in file 34, 35, 37
instance directory layout
  standardizing 49, 50, 51, 52
instance
  backup, obtaining 596, 597
  starting 21
Integer column 277
interactive kanban cards
  creating 396, 399
Internet of Things (IoT) 701
IoT Box image
  flashing, for Raspberry Pi 702, 703, 704, 705
IoT Box
  about 701
  accessing, through SSH 721, 722, 723
  adding, to Odoo 708, 709, 713, 714
  automatically, connecting with Odoo 710
  connecting, with network 705, 706, 707, 708
  manually, connecting with Odoo 711, 712
ipdb
  reference 240
ir.actions.act_window.view 293

J

JavaScript files
  adding 656, 657, 658
JavaScript
  extending, for website 443, 445, 446
Jinja template

used, for sending mail 685, 686, 687, 688, 689
JQuery QUnit
  using 557
JQuery
  reference 496
JSON-RPC2
  reference 538
JSON-RPC
  methods, calling through 628, 629
  Odoo, connecting with 618, 620
  Odoo, logging in with 618, 620
  records, creating through 624, 626, 627
  records, deleting through 624, 626, 627
  records, fetching through 621, 623
  records, searching through 621, 623
  records, updating through 624, 626, 627
  reference 620

K

kanban board
  features 393
kanban card
  displaying, in columns 329, 330
  quick create form, adding in 394, 395
kanban stages
  managing 391, 392, 393
kanban views
  about 327, 328, 329
  progress bar, adding in 400, 401
keyboard
  action button, adding on 659, 660, 662

L

language-related settings
  configuring 371, 372, 373
language
  installing 367, 368, 369, 370, 371
Latest books 463
Least-recently Used (LRU) 641
LESS
  reference 446
Lesser General Public License v3.0 (LGPLv3)
  license 10
Let's Encrypt

reference 81
reverse proxy, configuring with 81, 82, 83, 84, 85, 86
SLL, configuring with 85
SSL, configuring with 81, 82, 83, 84, 86
Linux Containers (LXC) 89
list views 309, 310, 311
local area network (LAN) 708
log handler 232
logging level 232
logs 594
Lokalize
 reference 380
Long Term Support (LTS) 11

M

Mac OS X 13
mail alias
 managing 694, 696, 697, 698
mail catcher 591
mail
 sending, Jinja template used 685, 686, 687, 688, 689
 sending, QWeb template used 689, 690, 691, 693
Many2one fields 145, 146
Many2one widget
 using 203
mapped() method
 using 192
menu item
 about 214
 adding 286, 287, 289, 290
menu items
 adding 116, 117, 119, 120, 122
 attributes 121
menus
 hiding, based on groups 365, 366
message_post_with_template() method
 used, for sending mail with Jinja template 689
method execution
 tracing, Python debugger used 235, 236, 237, 238
methods

calling, Odoo shell used 232, 233, 234
calling, through JSON-RPC 628, 629
calling, through XML-RPC 616, 617, 618
calling, with modified context 258, 259
implementation, extending 197
Microsoft Windows 13
mobile app JavaScript 513, 514, 515
model methods
 defining 170, 171, 172, 173
model representation
 defining 128, 129, 130, 131
model, renderer, controller (MRC) 504
model, view, controller (MVC) 504
model
 about 128
 adding 114, 115, 116
 business logic, extending in 194, 196
 computed fields, adding to 152, 154
 constraint validations, adding to 149
 data fields, adding to 131, 132
 defining, based on SQL view 275, 276, 277
 empty recordset, obtaining for 176
 features, adding inheritance used 159, 160, 161
 features, copying delegation inheritance used 164
 fields, access limiting in 350, 351, 352
 hierarchy, adding to 146, 147
 monetary field, adding to 140, 141
 related fields, exposing 155, 156
 relational fields, adding to 142, 144
 security access, adding to 346, 347, 348, 349, 350
modified context
 method, calling with 258, 259
module
 computed fields, adding to 153, 155
 constraint validations, adding to 150, 151
 creating, scaffold command used 124, 126
 data fields, adding to 133, 134, 136
 empty recordset, obtaining for 178
 features, copying delegation inheritance used 165, 167
 hierarchy, adding to 148, 149
 relational fields, adding to 142

monetary 140
monetary field
  adding, to Model 6
  adding, to model 140, 141
multi-company Odoo 187
multiple Odoo instances
  running 91
multiple records
  creating 646, 647
  writing 646, 647

N

n-app purchase (IAP) concepts
  about 520
  entities 518
namespaces
  using 208, 209
Nested set model
  reference 146
network
  IoT Box, connecting with 705, 706, 707, 708
  path access, making from 422, 423, 426
nginx configuration options
  reference 88
nginx
  reference 81
  reverse proxy, configuring with 81, 82, 83, 84, 85, 86
  SSL, configuring with 81, 82, 83, 84, 85, 86
noupdate flag
  using 214, 215

O

object 301, 329
OCA odoorpc library 630, 631
Odoo add-on module
  about 104, 105
  types 112
Odoo app store
  about 12
  reference 12
Odoo Community Association (OCA) 60, 240
Odoo community association (OCA) 13, 630
Odoo Community Association maintainer quality tools

using 240, 242, 243, 244, 245, 246
Odoo developer tools
  activating 38, 39, 40
Odoo ecosystem 10
Odoo editions 10
Odoo environments
  managing, start command used 22, 23
Odoo help forum 13
Odoo image
  running, with add-ons 91
  running, with configuration file 91
Odoo Online 676
Odoo server databases
  backing up 29, 30
  backup, restoring 30, 31
  creating 26, 27
  database management interface, accessing 24
  duplicating 28
  managing 23, 31, 33
  master password, modifying 24, 25
  master password, setting 24, 25
  removing 28
Odoo shell
  used, for interactively calling methods 232, 233, 234
Odoo source code
  downloading 20
Odoo's treatment
  return values 424, 425
odoo.http.request 425
odoo.http.route 424
Odoo.sh 676
odoo.sh account
  creating 578, 579, 580, 581
Odoo.sh options 599
odoo.sh project
  creating, reference 585
Odoo.sh project
  database size 604
  database workers 603
  module installation 601
  Project Name 600
  source code revisions 604
  staging branches 603

submodules 602
Odoo.sh, features
  automated tests 577
  backup 577
  community modules 577
  development branches 577
  external dependencies 576
  faster deployment 577
  GitHub integration 576
  mail catcher 577
  mail server 577
  recovery 577
  server logs 576
  share the build 577
  staging branches 577
  web code editor 576
  web shell 576
Odoo.sh
  about 575
  concepts, exploring of 574
  features 576
  need for 575
odoo.sh
  reference 578
Odoo.sh
  using 576
Odoo
  accessing, as superuser 119, 120
  connecting, with JSON-RPC 618, 620
  connecting, with XML-RPC 606, 607
  IAP service, registering in 521, 523, 524,
    526
  installing, for production use 67, 68, 70
  installing, from source 13, 14, 16, 17
  IoT Box, adding to 708, 709, 713, 714
  logging in, with JSON-RPC 618, 620
  logging in, with XML-RPC 606, 607
  reference 521
  running, Docker used 89, 90
  running, through docker-compose 92, 93
  setting up, as system service 80, 81
  translation files, importing into 382, 384
  updating, from source 40, 41, 42
offers
  displaying, when account lacks credits 544,

546, 547
on-boarding
  improving, with tour 511, 512, 513
onchange methods
  calling, on server side 272, 273, 274
  defining 268, 269, 270, 271
order
  defining 128, 129, 130, 131
ormcache
  about 639
  used, for managing in-memory cache 638,
    640
ormcache_context 639
ormcache_multi 640
outgoing mail server
  configuring 678, 679
  fields 679
outgoing mail servers
  configuring 676, 677

P

parameters
  passing, to actions 301, 302, 303, 304
  passing, to forms 301, 302, 303, 304
path access
  making, from network 422, 423, 426
pdb.set_trace() statement
  inserting, into pdb for debugging 239
pdb
  reference 240
pivot view 334, 335, 336
platform as a service (PaaS) 575
poedit
  reference 380
point of sale
  configuring 724, 725, 726
POS screens
  UI, modifying of 667, 668, 669
PostgreSQL aggregate functions
  reference 645
PostgreSQL tuning 71, 73
  reference 72
PostgreSQL
  configuration 19
prefetching pattern

for recordset 635, 636, 638
production branch
  creating 585
  features, merging in 589
production usage
  Odoo, installing for 67, 68, 70
production
  configuration file, adapting for 75, 76, 77, 78
profile() method
  parameters 652
progress bar
  adding, in kanban views 400, 401
Project Name
  collaborators 600
  public access 601
proposed pull requests
  applying 64, 65, 66
  trying 64, 65, 66
prototype inheritance 161
pudb
  reference 240
Pull Request (PR) 64
Pull Requests (PR) 11
Pylint
  reference 246
  used, for checking code 246, 247
Python code server actions
  using 405, 407, 408
Python code
  evaluating, in restricted context 405
  profiling 651, 652, 653
Python debugger (PDB) 229
Python debugger
  used, for tracing method execution 235, 236,
  237, 238
Python test cases 551, 552, 553
Python unittest
  reference 552

Q

quick create form
  adding, in kanban card 394, 395
QUnit framework 560
QUnit test case
  creating 557

QUnit test cases
  running, from UI 566
QUnit
  reference 561
QWeb template
  conditionals 454
  creating 447, 448, 450, 456
  dynamic attributes 452
  fields 453
  inline editing 455
  loops 450, 451
  modifying 447, 448, 450, 456
  subtemplates 454
  used, for sending mail 689, 690, 691, 693
  variables, setting 454
QWeb-based PDF reports
  creating 417, 418, 419, 420

R

Raspberry Pi
  IoT Box image, flashing for 702, 703, 704,
  705
raw SQL queries
  executing 260, 261, 262, 263
read_group()
  data, fetching in groups with 204, 205, 206
record access
  limiting, record rules used 353, 354, 355
record lists
  filters, defining on 305, 306
record rules
  about 187
  used, for limiting record access 353, 354,
  355
records
  accessing, through database queries 648,
  649, 650
  creating 178, 179, 180
  creating, through JSON-RPC 624, 626, 627
  creating, through XML-RPC 612, 614, 615
  deleting, from XML files 222, 223
  deleting, through JSON-RPC 624, 626, 627
  deleting, through XML-RPC 612, 614, 615
  fetching, through JSON-RPC 621, 623
  reading, through XML-RPC 609, 610, 611

searching 185, 186
searching, customization 201, 202, 203
searching, through JSON-RPC 621, 623
searching, through XML-RPC 609, 610, 611
updating, through JSON-RPC 624, 626, 627
updating, through XML-RPC 612, 614, 615
recordset records
    values, updating of 182, 183, 184
recordset relations
    traversing 191, 192
recordsets
    accessing, as superuser 362, 363, 364
    combining 188, 189
    filtering 189, 190
    prefetching pattern for 635, 636, 638
    sorting 193, 194
Reference fields
    used, for adding dynamic relations 157, 158
registry 177
related fields
    exposing, stored in module 155, 156
relational fields
    adding, to model 142, 144
Remote procedure calls (RPC) 605
replace
    using 318
RequireJS
    reference 446
Resource Calendar 412
ReStructuredText (RST) format 109
Return on Investment (ROI) 476
reusable Model features
    abstract models, using for 161, 163
reverse proxy
    about 79
    configuring, with Let's Encrypt 81, 82, 83, 84,
        85, 86
    configuring, with nginx 81, 82, 83, 84, 85, 86
RPC calls
    making 663, 664, 665, 666
    making, to server 493, 495
rpc.query() method
    parameters 666
runbot
    about 11

reference 12

S

scaffold command
    used, for creating modules 124, 126
SCSS files
    adding 656, 657, 658
SCSS
    reference 446
search views 311, 313, 314
search() method 187
search_read() method
    using 624
security access
    adding, to models 346, 347, 348, 349, 350
security groups
    assigning, to users 342, 344
    creating 342, 344
    used, for activating features 356, 357, 358,
        360, 361, 362
selection field 136, 137
SEO options
    managing, for webpages 470, 471, 472
server actions
    creating 402, 403, 404, 407
server dimensioning 71
server logs
    producing, to help debug methods 229, 230,
        231, 232
server side
    onchange methods, calling on 272, 273, 274
server
    RPC calls, making to 493, 495
sitemaps
    managing, for website 472, 473
SLL certificate
    configuring, with Let's Encrypt 86
    configuring, with nginx 86
snippets
    offering, to user 460, 461, 462, 463, 464,
        465
Software as a service (SaaS) 575
sorted() method
    using 194
source

Odoo, installing from 13, 14, 16, 17
Odoo, updating from 40, 41, 42
SQL view
  model, defining based on 275, 276, 277
SSH
  IoT Box, accessing through 721, 722, 723
SSL certificate
  about 85
  configuring, with Let's Encrypt 81, 82, 83, 84, 85
  configuring, with nginx 81, 82, 83, 84
staging branch
  creating 588
start command
  used, for managing Odoo environments 22, 23
state field
  using 390
static assets
  managing 438, 441
static code checkers 246
status
  checking, of builds 597, 598
sudo()
  using 257, 364
superuser
  about 256
  recordsets, accessing as 362, 363, 364
System Parameters 536
system service
  Odoo, setting up as 80, 81

T

tagged Python test cases
  running 553, 554, 555
tags 298
tags, elements
  button 296
  field 297
  form 295, 296
  general attributes 298
  group 296
  header 296
  notebook 297
  page 297

template 214
texts
  translating, through web client user interface 373, 374, 375
time conditions
  automated actions, using on 408, 409, 410, 412
top 311
tour test case
  adding 562, 563, 564
tour
  on-boarding, improving with 511, 512, 513
  running, from UI 567
traditional inheritance 159
translation files
  importing, into Odoo 382, 383
translation strings
  exporting, to file 376, 377, 378
translations
  easing, gettext tools used 380, 381

U

Ubuntu 14
UI
  client-side test cases, running from 565, 568
  modifying, of POS screens 667, 668, 669
  QUnit test cases, running from 566
  tours, running from 567
Urchin Tracking Module (UTM) 476
user preferences
  configuring 367, 368, 369, 370, 371
user
  actions, modifying 256
  errors, reporting to 174, 175, 176
  inputs, obtaining from 466, 467, 468, 469
  modifying, that performs action 254, 255, 256
  security groups, assigning to 342
  security groups,assigning to 344
  snippets, offering to 460, 461, 462, 463, 464, 465

V

values
  updating, of recordset records 182, 183, 184

video/screenshot
  generating, for failed test cases 570, 571
view elements
  hiding, based on groups 365, 366
view inheritance
  about 315, 316, 317
  order of evaluation 318
  tricks 319
views
  adding 116, 117, 119, 120, 122
  attributes 121
  creating 496, 497, 499, 501, 502, 504, 505, 506, 507
  modifying 315, 316, 317
virtual environments 17
visitor's country information
  obtaining 474, 475, 476
visitors
  campaigns, tracking of 476, 478
voice over Internet Protocol (VoIP) 10

W

web accessible paths
  access, restricting to 427, 428, 429
web client user interface
  texts, translating through 373, 374, 375
web interface
  used, for installing add-on modules 54, 55, 57
web shell 592
webpages
  SEO options, managing for 470, 471, 472
website
  content delivery networks(CND), managing for 95
  CSS, extending for 443, 445, 446
  JavaScript, extending for 443, 445, 447

  managing 479, 480, 481
  sitemaps, managing for 472, 473
werkzeug
  used, for handling HTTP requests 459
widgets
  adding, to form view 294, 295
  creating 484, 485, 488, 489, 490
window action
  adding 286, 287, 289, 290
  specific view, opening 291, 292
wizard enhancement
  code, reusing 267
  context, used for computing default values 266
  user redirection 268
wizard
  writing, for user guidance 263, 264, 265, 266
workers
  about 78
  issues 79
write()
  extending 198, 199, 200

X

XML files
  functions, invoking from 223, 224, 225
  records, deleting from 222, 223
  used, for loading data 211, 212, 213, 214
XML-RPC
  methods, calling through 616, 617, 618
  Odoo, connecting with 606, 607
  Odoo, logging in with 606, 607
  records, creating through 612, 614, 615
  records, deleting through 612, 614, 615
  records, reading through 609, 610, 611
  records, searching through 609, 610, 611
  records, updating through 612, 614, 615

www.ingramcontent.com/pod-product-compliance
Lightning Source LLC
Chambersburg PA
CBHW081208220326
41598CB00037B/6711